TEXAS GOLF

The Best of the Lone Star State

By Kevin Newberry

Foreword by Jim Nantz

TEXAS GOLF

The Best of the Lone Star State

By Kevin Newberry

Foreword by Jim Nantz

Publisher/President – Rick McMillen
Vice President/Chief Financial Officer
  – Marna McMillen
Vice President/Director of Publishing Operations
  – Sir McMillen

Executive Editor – Jim Carley
Research Editor – Jim Walden
Research Assistants – Laura Friedman,
  Jennifer Condi, Amber Mayne

Creative Director – Jeff Wolf
Design/Graphics – Cheryl Leary, David Medina
Production – Aaron Brittain
Photography – David Lineman, Harmon Newberry,
  Tom Payne, Bob Rowley, Richard Stockton,
  Rick Turner, SkyCam Photography
Cover Photo – Eighth hole on the Miller Course
  at Bentwater Country Club in Willis

Circulation Manager – Bambi McMillen
Data Processing – Danette Daniel, Erin Folks,
  Adrian Jackson, Kudirat Muhammed,
  Jessica Ortega, Diane Thorne

Business Manager – Bobbye Jean Smith
Executive Assistant – Stormy Waters

Advertising Director – Al Allen
Corporate Sales Director – Harvey Hooker
Advertising Coordinator – Tiffany McMillen
  http://www.mcmillencomm.com

©1998 Gulf Publishing Company
3301 Allen Parkway, Houston, TX 77019
P.O. Box 2608, Houston, TX 77252
http://www.gulfpub.com/books.html

ISBN# 0-88415-891-8
Gulf Publishing Company

Library of Congress
Catalog Card Number: 98-073063

One of the greatest things about golf is not just the game itself or the golf courses on which it is played, but the people who play it, the people who work to promote the game and make it better, and the people who work to preserve its rich history.

Golf in Texas turns 100 years old in 1998, so it is only appropriate that we commemorate the centennial anniversary with this "bible for Texas golf," the most complete book ever published on golf in the Lone Star State.

Texas Golf is not only a celebration of the more than 800 golf courses in the state, but is also a tribute to the people behind the scenes who make it all possible — from the golf course architects to the golf professionals of the PGA of America to volunteer organizations. All of these people and groups have been extremely valuable in making golf in Texas great.

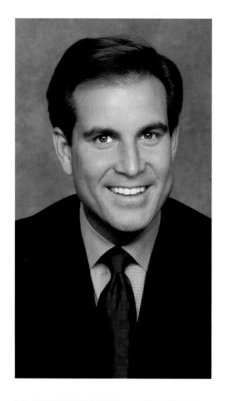

Golf in Texas: Where par and pride meet

I t really is special to me to be a part of this book, *Texas Golf: The Best of the Lone Star State*. To begin with, there are so many legends this state has produced in golf, truly world-wide figures who have left an indelible Texas-size mark on the sport

We're talking about guys like Jimmy Demaret and Ben Hogan and Byron Nelson. It's just an endless list. I've hosted the Texas Golf Hall of Fame banquet and it's amazing when you start to look down the list of golfers whom we can claim as Texans.

There's even a golfing astronaut in Alan Shepard (who hit the first golf drive on the moon). He was our honoree one year at the Three Amigos Tournament I co-host along with Fred Couples and Blaine McCallister. President Bush, who is in the Texas Golf Hall of Fame, was another honoree at our tournament.

Then there are the great college golfers and coaches from Texas like the man I played for, Dave Williams, at the University of Houston. He turned UH into the UCLA of golf for many years winning 16 national championships. He was the John Wooden of college golf. And there are many others like Harvey Penick who had a magnificent group of golfers at the University of Texas.

Texas also has been the site of many of the game's biggest tournaments, classics like the 1941 U.S. Open at Colonial and the 1963 PGA Championship and the 1991 U.S. Women's Open just to name a few.

The state of Texas has some of the top courses as well. Colonial in Dallas always gets rated highly. Personally, I'm always pulling for the Houston courses because I think they get slighted. Like River Oaks — it's a great course and it never gets the credit it deserves. And especially Houston Country Club which played host to the historic Ben Hogan-Sam Snead match in 1964. I think people get ideas in their head that it's too hot, but we have a lot of months down in Houston where the weather is perfect.

And there are so many other beautiful courses all across the state of Texas because we've got such a great variety of landscapes — from the hills of Austin to the mountain layouts in El Paso to the lushness you get at courses in Houston and Dallas.

It goes on and on forever. Texas golf even goes into the area of world known golf writers like

Dan Jenkins. Texas has it all.

Texas golf is even more special for us now at CBS because with the new television contract we just signed, we get the whole Texas swing of PGA golf tournaments. I don't think any network has ever had that. Obviously, that's especially pleasing for me for selfish reasons.

I trace my roots in Texas golf back to my college days when I played on the golf team and roomed with Blaine McCallister and Fred Couples at UH. Houston also was where I started out in broadcasting, doing a Saturday morning radio show on KTRH called "Gulf Coast Golf" when I was a junior in college in 1979–80. We were fortunate enough to have such people as Dave Marr and Jimmy Demaret on as guests. I didn't really interview Jimmy Demaret. He just told golf stories for us and it was wonderful. I still have cassette tapes of those shows.

That's also the time I got to know Dave Williams as not only a coach but a great person. He had such a positive influence on every person he ever knew. He's one of the most genuine, kind-hearted people you'd ever meet and he stood for so many great virtues, such as how to treat people and how to conduct yourself.

All of us who were lucky enough to play on his golf teams learned lessons of life that will prove far more valuable than what he did for us in golf. I love the man. We have two awards at our Three Amigos Tournament — one is the George Bush Inspiration Award and the other is the Dave Williams Contribution to Golf Award.

I feel a book on Texas golf is a perfect combination because the state and the game are very similar. Texas has more pride than most places. I like it here because of that. Intense pride is part of the deal if you're a Texan.

Golfers in general are the same way. They are proud of their sport. You never hear of baseball or football players saying they are doing something just for the good of the game, but you always hear golfers saying that. They never want the game to be compromised. Golf has its own pulse and golfers are very passionate about their sport.

In a very similar way, people talk about the state of Texas. They speak of their state with that same pride and passion. So it's fitting that the two are linked with each other. I'm proud of my connections to Texas golf and glad to be even a small part of a book on this special subject.

Jim Nantz is one of the foremost sports broadcasters in America. He has been with CBS-TV for 14 years and is known as the Voice of CBS Sports. He has broadcast numerous golf tournaments during that time, including 14 Masters Tournaments, and has also announced such diverse events as the 1998 Winter Olympics, 14 NCAA Final Fours, the U.S. Open Tennis Championships and countless other sports. Along with Fred Couples and Blaine McCallister, Nantz, who played on the golf team at the University of Houston from 1978–81, also co-hosts the Dr Pepper Three Amigos Celebrity Golf Classic every year at Pine Forest Country Club in Houston.

Contents

TEXAS GOLF

The Best of the Lone Star State

Texas Legends Render Legendary Deeds

Legends are the stuff Texas is made of. From 10 gallon hats to the Dallas Cowboys. From Black Gold to the Alamo. From the Red River to the Rio Grande.

Everything about Texas is larger than life.

The same holds true with its golfers.

The wide variety of Texas courses, from the tall pines of East Texas to the rugged Texas Hill Country to the desert courses of El Paso, has been the proving ground for some of the greatest players in the history of the game.

You can't get any more legendary than the likes of Ben Hogan, Byron Nelson, Harvey Penick, Babe Zaharias, Kathy Whitworth, Jimmy Demaret, Tommy Bolt, Jackie Burke, Carol Mann, Tom Kite or Ben Crenshaw. The list goes on and on. These are men and women whose accomplishments and contributions to the game will survive long after they are gone.

These are the men and women who put the Lone Star State on the golf map.

And these are their stories.

Texas Legends

Ben HOGAN

Few golfers ever played the game with more intensity, determination and skill than the legendary Ben Hogan.

The swing.
The stare.
The Five Fundamentals.
The results.

Take your pick on how you remember Ben Hogan. They all tell the same story, and they all speak more loudly than Hogan ever did himself.

Ben Hogan was a man of action who never strayed from the game he loved by pursuing outside interests. He simply wanted to be the best, and took the necessary steps to make it happen.

Simply put: practice, practice, practice.

Hogan figured no amount of words would help him toward that goal. In the same way, words seem inadequate to describe his accomplishments in the game of golf. He won a total of 62 PGA Tour events between 1938 and 1953, including victories in every major championship. In 1946, Hogan had his best year with 13 victories, including the PGA Championship, his first major.

Hogan did few indepth interviews. Most of the writings about him are essays which attempt to put his accomplishments down on paper. His only writings — The Five Fundamentals — is required reading for every golfer.

Like Byron Nelson, his rival from childhood to adulthood, Hogan got his start in the caddyshack at Fort Worth's Glen Garden Country Club.

The Ben Hogan Story is one of the few golf-oriented films that have ever been made, and what a story it was. It told the tale of Hogan's miraculous comeback from a near-fatal car accident on Feb. 2, 1949, to winning the 1950 U.S. Open.

Hogan's right leg was shattered in the accident, threatening to end his career at its very peak. Up to that point, he had already won the 1948 U.S. Open, the 1946 and '48 PGA Championship and the 1953 British Open and won the Vardon Trophy in 1940, '41 and '48.

But through rehabilitation and determination, Hogan came all the way back to pick up where he left off. It was the stuff Hollywood was made of, and he appropriately completed his return at the 1950 U.S. Open at Merion.

Only 16 months after the accident, Hogan survived a 36-hole final round and a three-way playoff with George Fazio and Lloyd Mangrum to win the second of what would be four U.S. Open victories. (He won 1948, '50, '51 and '53 having missed the 1949 Open due to his injury.)

When the week began, Hogan told reporters his still shaky legs "would be nip and tuck." When rain forced a 36-hole finale, his chances were dimmed because he had not played 36 in one day since the accident.

The largest crowd in golf history at the time — 12,500 — watched the final round as Hogan's story unfolded before them. They watched Hogan hold the lead going into the last four holes, until his legs buckled on the 69th and 71st holes. He staggered and almost fell after his drive on the 12th hole.

Hogan needed to shoot only three-over par on the last four holes to clinch the victory, but shot four-over and had to run down a five-foot putt on the 72nd hole to salvage a tie.

"Let's not say anything more about it," Hogan said of his injured legs. "I think the people are a little tired of reading about my injuries."

In the 18-hole playoff on the following day, Hogan returned to his usual form and shot a machine-like 69 to post a four-stroke victory, including sinking a dramatic 50-foot birdie putt on the 17th hole.

A rushing crowd of 10,000 cheered his triumph.

Texas Legends

Hogan's Career Highlights

- *Nine Major Championships:*
  Masters: 1951, '53
  U.S. Open: 1948, '50, '51 and '53
  British Open: 1953
  PGA Championship: 1946, '48
- *54 Regular Tour Victories*
  (not including majors)
- *Leading Money Winner: 1940, '41,*
  '42, '46 and '48
- *Vardon Trophy Winner: 1940,*
  '41 and '48
- *Player of the Year: 1948, '50,*
  '51 and '53
- *Led Tour in Victories: 1941, '42,*
  '46, '47, '48 and '53
- *Second All-Time Vardon Trophy*
  Average: 69.30 in 1948
- *Ryder Cup Captain: 1947, '49*
  and '67

Texas Legends

Byron
NELSON

Byron Nelson's string of 11 consecutive victories in 1945 will never be duplicated. For that matter, neither will he.

Few players in the history of sports have ever been as universally loved and respected by their fans and peers as Byron Nelson. Never had they seen a man more dedicated to the game. There was absolutely nothing to dislike about sports' ultimate role model.

"I think I'm one man who has a better reputation than I actually deserve," Nelson said humbly, "but I work very hard at it."

Nelson was a perfectionist who sought to play golf as simply and consistently as possible. He worked religiously throughout his early years to produce a swing that would enable him to flight and place the ball exactly as he chose.

Along with the superlative records, the near perfect swing is considered the model for present day technique. This is why the mechanical testing machines used by golf club manufacturers have been called "the Iron Byron."

In 1945, America stormed the shores of Normandy and, for 11 consecutive tournaments, every Sunday was V-day for Byron Nelson. Perhaps it was his unprecedented combination of all of the above that enabled him to win 11 consecutive tournaments — a feat that will never be accom-

plished again in golf.

The Byron Nelson story sounds more like a bedtime fantasy that golfers tell their sons before they go to bed at night. Indeed, if the newspaper accounts and PGA records didn't validate the story, you might think Nelson was just another superhero from Greek mythology.

But it's all true, and these are some of the miraculous details:

Nelson won 18 of 30 tournaments in 1945. He had a single-season scoring average of 68.33, including a 67.68 mark in final rounds. He had 19 consecutive rounds under 70. He collected total prize money of $13,085, plus another $48,689 in war bonds that were worth 75

percent of face value. He earned 14.5 percent of the year's total purses, which in 1995 terms translated to $8.32 million.

While you might be wondering what Nelson was doing playing golf in 1945 instead of fighting a war, he had been kept out of military service by a medical condition that kept his blood from clotting quickly enough. Instead, he began doing countless exhibitions and clinics to raise money for U.S. troops.

But as the war came to a close in 1945, Nelson had only one thing on his mind. After travelling the world playing golf most of his life, he was ready to settle down with his wife Louise. He set his sights on a piece of land outside of Dallas. It was a 741-acre spread with a three-bedroom house that he eventually bought in 1946 for $55,000 and named Fairway Ranch.

But first, he had to come up with the money. And that's where the story of his 1945 season began. After playing poorly in 1944, he worked on his short game in the offseason and came back in 1945 ready to make the most of his ability.

"I wouldn't do anything that would detract from my ability," he said. "I worked so hard and gave so much, and only one year did I make enough to shake a stick at."

His streak began in early March, when Nelson and Jug McSpaden won the the two-man International Four-Ball in Miami.

Nelson's streak almost never got started the following week in Charlotte, N.C. He trailed Sam Snead by one stroke with two holes to play, but Snead three-putted the final green to force a playoff. The two men remained tied after an 18-hole playoff on the following day, and then Nelson won a second 18-hole playoff by four shots.

"At the time, it didn't feel special," Nelson said. "When I was doing it, one thing that really helped me was that I never said, 'Well, I won four, maybe I can win another one.' I could never tell you how many straight I had won unless someone told me.

"I learned from my amateur days to play one hole, one shot, one tournament at a time. If you don't, you end up focusing on the wrong thing. And your focus in golf had better be right. That's important if you want to win."

He ran his string to eight before he ran into trouble again. At the PGA Championship, Nelson was two down with four to play in his Match-Play final against Mike Turnesa. But Nelson tied the match with birdies at Nos. 16 and 17, then eagled the 18th for his ninth victory.

"I was 7-under and still lost," Turnesa said after the match. "How the hell are you supposed to beat this man."

Nelson went on to win two more events and Nelson was named athlete of the year in 1944 and '45. He cashed his war bonds and his earnings the following year and bought his ranch. He retired soon afterward.

"Some say my career wasn't long enough. But I won 54 tournaments, including five majors. So what if I had won a few more?

"I wanted to go out a winner. I wanted to do other things. I was tired of playing, tired of competing. I wanted to improve the ranch. And I realized that if I lost my focus, lost my drive, I would not compete as well, anyway."

Before retiring, Nelson won 54, placing him fifth on the all-time list. His five major championships included the 1937 and '42 Masters; the 1940 and '45 PGA; and the 1939 U.S. Open. He was inducted into the World Golf Hall of Fame in 1974.

Texas Legends

Byron Nelson's 11 Straight Victories in 1945			
Date	Tournament	Score	Money
March 8-11	Miami Four Ball	8 & 6	$1,500
March 16-19	Charlotte Open	272	$2,000
March 23-26	Greensboro Open	271	$1,000
March 30-April 1	Durham Open	276	$1,000
April 5-8	Atlanta Open	263	$2,000
June 7-10	Montreal Open	268	$2,000
June 14-17	Philadelphia Invitational	269	$3,000
June 29-July 1	Chicago Open	275	$2,000
July 9-15	PGA Championship	4 & 3	$3,750
July 26-29	Tam O'Shanter Open	269	$10,000
August 2-4	Canadian Open	280	$2,000

Harvey PENICK

Harvey Penick will be remembered as one of golf's greatest teachers, and his down-home wisdom will live forever.

The year 1913 was an historic one at Austin Country Club. Harvey Penick, one of the five local Penick boys, was hired as a caddie where he started out making 20 cents a day.

Little did anyone know that this gentle 9-year-old would grow up from such humble beginnings to become one of the best teachers of the world's most difficult game. His love for golf and the people who play it was unsurpassed, and he made the game fun by keeping his teachings of golf — and life — simple.

In a game in which success is measured by dollars earned, Penick had a perfect love of the game unmarred by monetary aspirations. His only goal was that his pupils improved and enjoyed the game, and his only requirement of them was that they practice hard and try their best.

Penick never lost sight that living a good life was more important than playing good golf, but if you could do both it was a perfect combination. That was a concept not lost on the likes of such great golfers as Tom Kite, one of the PGA Tour's all-time money leaders, two-time Masters champion Ben Crenshaw and Davis Love III. They hung on his every word,

hoping to extract another bit of wisdom from each story or parable that Penick would tell.

Constrained to a wheelchair and a golf cart in his latter years, Penick taught the game he loved almost up to April 2, 1995, the day he died, at the age of 90.

"I never considered myself a genius, but a teacher and a learner," Penick said a year before his death. "Just a grown caddy."

"I've lived golf and nothing else, but I've met people who

have always been good to me. Why would anyone want to do anything else?"

While his presence on the practice tee at Austin Country Club will be missed, Mr. Penick can rest in peace knowing that his teachings will live on forever, and his disciples will no doubt continue to prosper.

Almost everyone who has anything to do with the game of golf has heard his name, read his books or seen his videos, but not many people know much about Harvey Penick.

Penick had the rare opportunity to go straight from high school to become the head pro at Austin Country Club. Later, Penick also doubled as the head coach at the University of Texas, where he coached such standout golfers as Kite, Crenshaw, Davis Love Jr., Kathy Whitworth and Betsy Rawls.

But it was Penick the teacher, who started his career playing and teaching with golfers like Byron Nelson and Jimmy Demaret, that earned him the respect of the golf world. The best players in the game would come to Austin whenever their games fell on hard times. Always, Penick would have a simple answer.

Penick was an equal opportunity teacher. He would share his knowledge with anyone who was willing to learn, and was actually flattered by anyone who thought enough of him to ask his advice. He would give daily lessons to club members and anyone else who came to the club.

"Harvey's simple philosophies about golf and life will stay with us for as long as the game is played," Crenshaw said. "He was a major influence on my life. Anyone who had the chance to know him was truly blessed."

Ironically, it was not until the final few years of his life that Penick became a household name around the world and his teachings in *The Little Red Book* became the best-selling sports hardback of all time with more than 1.3 million copies sold.

The success of his instructional books led to a wide range of Penick tapes, calendars, newsletters, videos and clubs. Harvey Penick signature irons and woods were produced by Austin-based Golfsmith International in 1994.

"He led a fantastic life and was a fantastic person," said Carl Paul, co-founder of Golfsmith. "I count it one of the highlights of my life to have known him."

"For all the pain and suffering he endured, Mr. Penick was the most content man I ever met," says Tom Wishon, Golfsmith's chief technical officer who worked with Penick to design three lines of Penick signature clubs for the company.

"Nothing was ever as complicated as it seemed with Mr. Penick. As I would sit there and talk with him, I came to understand it was not Harvey Penick the golf legend that I admired, but Harvey Penick the man."

Crenshaw wasn't quite a teenager when he first began to realize how special Harvey Penick was. Crenshaw, like most boys who grow up with a rag-tag set of clubs and big-time dreams, had the good fortune of being in the right place at the right time.

"I kept seeing all these incredible players coming to him for lessons," Crenshaw said, listing names such as Mickey Wright, Don January and George Knudson. The latter list, of course, would include Crenshaw, Kite, Love and even Michael Jordan.

Crenshaw's first two clubs were a five-iron and a blade putter that Penick cut down to size and put a little leather grip on them. They were enough to teach him lessons that would last a lifetime.

"He taught me the grip," Crenshaw said. "He put my hands on the club for the first time and I don't think I've ever changed it. I'm thinking of him always, all day. We've lost somebody we owe our lives to. Whatever I accomplish in my career, I owe to Harvey."

The weeks following Penick's death were emotional for Crenshaw, but just days later Crenshaw drew on everything Penick had taught him to win his second Masters title. It was Crenshaw's ultimate tribute.

"I believe in fate. It was like someone put their hand on my shoulder this week and guided me through. I don't know where I grew such confidence over a few practice days. I don't think I ever had a quicker transformation, but I just played my heart out. I had a good feel for a lot of things. But I had a 15th club in my bag this week, and it was Harvey Penick."

Penick's influence on the golf world was so strong and the lives he touched so numerous, that he can rest in peace knowing that his teachings will live on in his books, videos, and former pupils who will pass his knowledge down the line.

Virtually everyone who ever took a lesson from Penick will surely remember his simple principles, and pass them along to anyone that is willing to listen, willing to learn.

Mark Steinbauer may not be as famous as Kite or Crenshaw or Love, but is one of the best teachers that Penick left behind. Once a Penick student, Steinbauer came full circle when he won the Harvey Penick Award as Teacher of the Year in the Southern Texas PGA.

"Harvey didn't say much, but when he did, everyone listened," Steinbauer says. "He really loved golf, and he loved to help other people, too. No one will ever compare to Harvey. He will always be in his own category."

Texas Legends

"What a beautiful place a golf course is. From the meanest country pasture to the Pebble Beaches and St. Andrews of the world, a golf course is to me holy ground. I feel God in the trees and grass and flowers, in the rabbits and the birds and the squirrels, in the sky and the water. I feel that I am home."

— Harvey Penick

Lee
TREVINO

From caddy to international superstar,
'The Merry Mex' is golf's greatest rags-to-riches story.

It would take a book this size to tell the complete Lee Trevino story but, briefly enough, he already has left his mark as one of the great players and personalities in the history of golf.

Everybody loves a rags-to-riches story, and there are few better than Trevino's. He learned to play on the public links of Dallas and picked up extra money by hustling the regulars while playing with only a family-sized soda bottle.

"I wrapped the bottle with adhesive tape and made a good hitting surface," Trevino explained. "I got to a point that I could drive a ball 150 yards with the bottle and could hit a tree from that distance every time. And I won most of my bets."

Trevino turned pro in 1960, and catapulted himself from obscurity to international fame during one infamous week in 1968. At the time, he was a $30-a-week assistant pro at Horizon Hills Country Club outside El Paso, struggling to make a living on the pro tour.

He finished 54th in the 1966 U.S. Open and fifth in 1967. In 1968, Horizon Hills head pro Don Whittington financed Trevino's trip back to the Open, and he completed his climb to the top by

beating Jack Nicklaus for the 1968 Open title.

Trevino fired four consecutive rounds in the 60s at Oak Hill, including a final-round 69, to beat Jack Nicklaus by four shots and earn the $30,000 first prize.

"I'm going to buy the Alamo," Trevino said with a smile, "and give it back to Mexico."

It was his sense of humor that made him known around the world as the "Merry Mex." From 1968–81, Trevino won 26 events, winning at least once every year. He won the Open again in 1971, a year in which he was named Athlete of the Year by virtually every publication, the 1974 PGA Championship and the 1971 and '72 British Opens.

He was the Vardon Trophy winner from 1970–72, '74 and a record fifth time in 1980. The year of 1971 was his banner year, when he won the U.S. and British opens and was named *The Sporting News* Man of the Year, *Sports Illustrated's* Sportsman of the Year and Associated Press' Male Athlete of the Year.

Trevino's zest for life was magnified in 1975, when he and three other players were struck by lightning during a rain delay in the second round of the Western Open in Chicago. Trevino was leaning on his bag underneath an umbrella behind the 13th green when a bolt of lightning bounced off a nearby lake and through Trevino's bag and shoulder.

"It's fantastic that the three men were struck and are all living," said Dr. Paul Frederickson, the attending physician at nearby Hinsdale Hospital. "I believe Lee was hit harder than any of them. He was quite shaken up. He had an exit mark on his back and muscle rigidity for some time in the upper back. I think they are all fortunate to be here."

Trevino won only a few more times after that incident. A divorce and a pair of back operations had him thinking about retirement, and he began an alternate career as a TV commentator for NBC. But at the age of 44 he made a major comeback in 1984 by winning his second PGA title and his sixth major.

"When you're young, you think it is inevitable that you're going to win," Trevino said. "When you're old, the inevitable is over with. You never know if you're going to win again."

Six years later, Trevino discovered the fountain of youth when he turned 50 and joined the Senior PGA Tour, where he has continued to dominate the competition with 28 more victories.

Texas Legends

Lee Trevino's Career Highlights
- *27 Career Victories*
- *10 Career Senior PGA Victories*
- *Ryder Cup Team Member: 1969,*
  '71, '73, '75, '79 and '81
- *Ryder Cup Captain: 1985*
- *Major Championships:*
  1968 U.S. Open
  1971 U.S. Open
  1971 British Open
  1972 British Open
  1974 PGA Championship
  1984 PGA Championship
- *1971 PGA Player of the Year*
- *Inducted into the World Golf*
  Hall of Fame, 1981
- *Vardon Trophy winner 1970,*
  '71, '72, '74 and '80

Texas Legends

Jimmy
DEMARET

Jimmy Demaret started out in the caddie yard and grew up to become one of golf's biggest ambassadors.

Jimmy Demaret became Houston's first native son to make it big in the golf world. A carpenter's son who grew up near the railroad tracks on Center Street, he learned the game as a caddie at Houston's Hermann Park.

He played in only one match as an amateur for Northside High School before he began receiving pay for his services as an assistant pro at the age of 14.

From such humble beginnings came one of golf's greatest ambassadors. A man who became known as the Father of the Senior PGA Tour and was an innovator in golf television.

From the caddie yard at Hermann Park, Demaret went on to hold several club pro jobs before concentrating on the life of a touring pro. After honing his skills while working with teaching pro Jack Burke Sr., he found himself among golf immortals like Gene Sarazen and Ben Hogan.

Demaret was the 27-year-old flashy-dressing head pro at Houston's BraeBurn Country Club and part-time touring pro when he qualified for his first Masters as one of the leading money winners in 1939.

He had won the National Match-Play Open in 1938 and the

Los Angeles Open in 1939, but the Masters was a dream come true and moved him into the ranks of golf's elite.

"I had the feeling of what I — as a kid and a caddie — had

thought was the epitome of golf," he later recalled. "The Masters and Bobby Jones. This was the end."

Demaret was a flashy dresser who played in 13 events in 1940 and won six of them, including his first of three Masters titles. But his banner year was 1947, when he was both the Vardon Trophy winner with a 69.90 scoring average and leading money winner ($27,936).

He became the first three-time Masters champ with victories in 1940, '47 and '50. His 31 career victories earned him a place in the World Golf Hall of Fame in 1983.

He was named to four Ryder Cup teams, including the 1941 team that did not compete against the British because of World War II.

Demaret was a companion of movie stars, royalty, heads of state and astronauts, was a pioneer in TV golf and co-hosted Shell's Wonderful World of Golf Series, which helped golf gain popularity around the world.

For Demaret, golf was as much a social experience as it was a sport and a golf course just turned out to be the perfect place to entertain his many friends.

After his playing days were over, Demaret also owned and developed Onion Creek Golf Club in Austin and teamed with longtime friend and business partner Jack Burke Jr. to build Champions Golf Club in Houston in 1957.

He also developed the concept for the Legends of Golf in 1978, by teaming with Fred Raphael to lure some of the game's greatest players out of retirement into a unique team event. The event was so successful, and the players and fans alike had such a good time, that it became the forerunner of the modern Senior PGA Tour.

Texas Legends

Jimmy Demaret's Career Highlights

- *31 Career victories*
- *Became the first player to win three Masters championships in 1940, '47 and '50*
- *Inducted into the World Golf Hall of Fame in 1983*
- *Was named to four Ryder Cup teams.*
- *Won the Vardon Trophy in 1947 with a 69.90 scoring average*
- *Won the money title in 1947 with $27,936*
- *Created Legends of Golf in 1978 and became Father of the Senior PGA Tour*
- *Co-Hosted Shell's Wonderful World of Golf TV Series from 1961–1970*
- *Co-Founded Champions Golf Club in 1957. Co-Founded Onion Creek Golf Club in 1974*
- *Won six of 13 events in 1940*

John BREDEMUS

Texas was just a distant outpost on the golf frontier until John Bredemus came along to become "The Father of Texas Golf."

John Bredemus had it all. He was intelligent, an all-around athlete and handsome. He attended Dartmouth and Princeton, where he received his degree in civil engineering in 1912.

He competed against Jim Thorpe in the Stockholm Olympics that year, finishing second in the decathlon only to watch Thorpe later be stripped of his gold medal for violating amateur status rules.

A native of the northeast, Bredemus moved to San Antonio in 1919 to become a math teacher and found Texas severely lacking in golf courses — both in number and in quality.

Up until the time Bredemus became Texas' first resident golf course architect, the designers of the state's layouts came, put down holes, and left the problems of new and growing courses to whomever happend to be around.

Needless to say, some layouts thrived and many did not. Course design and construction moved at a snail's pace and, consequently, golf as a business and pastime poked along as well.

By 1922, there was a marked change. Pro tournaments were staged in every metro area, clubs began to have year-round pros

tend to the needs of amateurs, course building and maintenance merged as professions.

Strange though it may seem, Bredemus had a hand in all three.

Bredemus assumed the role of pro golfer in 1916 because of an interest in architecture rather than a talent for playing. He competed, though not very well and worked as a club pro and teacher until

1926, when he turned exclusively to course design and the promotion of golf in Texas and Mexico.

Bredemus co-founded the Texas Professional Golfers Association in 1922 and the first Texas Open in 1923 and was largely responsible for bringing the Southwest's first major championship, the 1927 PGA Championship, to Dallas.

The Bredemus legacy also includes being the patriarch of the initial pro tournaments in Dallas, Houston, Corpus Christi and Beaumont.

With golf course architecture, Bredemus was able to combine his engineering background with his love for golf.

He began building courses around the state, thus becoming the "Father of Texas Golf" by accounting for 80 percent of the state's earliest courses. In 1928, Bredemus established the first bentgrass greens in Texas at San Angelo Country Club.

It was true that he once took his shoes off before entering a client's office, but it was not true that he preferred to play barefoot.

He did once consider viewing a potential golf course site from atop some small trees on the site, but he was not so eccentric as to design every course from a treetop.

In the late 1930s, Bredemus moved to Mexico, reportedly following a dispute with the U.S. government over income taxes. He designed over a half-dozen fine Mexican layouts, but returned to Texas to complete one last course.

His golf courses were his most lasting legacy. They include Colonial Country Club in 1936, which still ranks as the state's No. 1 course.

In 1991, he was post-humously inducted into the Texas Golf Hall of Fame.

BURKE JR.

Jack Burke Jr. turned pro at 17 and retired at 34, but that's all the time he needed to earn a place in the record books.

One of the most refreshing characters in golf is Jack Burke Jr., a man who never hesitates to share his opinion whether or not he is in the popular majority.

Burke was the son of one of the game's greatest teachers who moved to Houston from Philadelphia in 1924 to become the pro at River Oaks. Burke Sr., however, died of a heart attack in 1943 and Burke Jr. has been fulfilling his father's legacy ever since.

Burke Jr. turned pro at the age of 17 and became good friends with Jimmy Demaret, one of his father's pupils. Before and after a stint in World War II — where Burke was a judo instructor — they traveled the tour together, with Burke winning 16 tournaments and played in five Ryder Cup matches and was twice a captainbefore retiring at the early age of 34. He still holds the modern-day record for his four consecutive victories in 1952, the longest streak since Byron Nelson's incomparable streak of 11 in 1945. He was inducted into the PGA Hall of Fame in 1976.

During the course of his career, he earned the reputation as one of the wisest men in golf and always had the game to back up his opinions.

Never was that more evident than in 1952, when he won four consecutive tournaments, including the Houston Open as the second tournament in the string.

Playing under the pressure of winning in his hometown, Burke led from the second round and entered the final day with a five-shot lead at Memorial Park.

"I remember I had a good round in the rain at Memorial Park and went way ahead and stayed ahead the rest of the way," Burke recalls. "When you win in your hometown, it's not easy. My friends were betting on me. All the caddies were betting on me.

My mother was in the gallery."

Burke went on to win at Baton Rouge, La., and St. Petersburg, Fla., before his string ended at the Masters, where he finished second, two shots behind Sam Snead.

"When I was on the hot streak, my clubs didn't know I was winning everything," Burke later said. "The ball didn't know it. The course didn't know it. Listen, I

didn't start playing well until I figured out that I was responsible for my own actions. Blaming it on other factors doesn't help.

"You can't start looking for excuses. You can't say I've won two in a row. I'm not destined to win a third. Athletes are the biggest bunch of complainers. They're looking for alibis and when they've reached a certain level they find them. After winning one tournament, I went to the next stop ready and confident. I didn't look back and ponder whether I was destined to win.

"The only one who puts pressure on a golfer is himself. The gallery doesn't put it on you. They want you to win. If you make four putts in a row and don't think you can make the fifth, the putter and ball don't know you made the last four.

"A man can talk himself out of almost anything. There's a lot of poor thinking in today's golf, but I had supreme confidence."

In 1956, his last year on tour, Burke won both the Masters and the PGA Championship, won the Vardon Trophy with a stroke average of 70.54 and was named Player of the Year. He then retired to build Champions Golf Club, which he still owns.

Ben
CRENSHAW

*Austin's Gentle Ben is a living reminder of
what the game of golf is all about.*

Ben Crenshaw is one of the most revered names in golf. Long known as "Gentle Ben," Crenshaw is enamored with golf history, and lives the type of quiet unassuming lifestyle with which golf's forefathers and his teacher would be proud.

Crenshaw's first two clubs were a five-iron and a blade putter that teacher Harvey Penick cut down to size and put a little leather grip on them. They remained his only clubs for a long time, but they were enough to teach him lessons that would last a lifetime.

Crenshaw wasn't quite a teenager when he first began to realize how special Harvey Penick was. Crenshaw, like most boys who grow up with a rag-tag set of clubs and big-time dreams, had the good fortune of being in the right place at the right time.

"I kept seeing all these incredible players coming to him for lessons," Crenshaw said, listing names such as Mickey Wright, Don January and George Knudson. The latter list, of course, would include Crenshaw, Kite, Love and even Michael Jordan.

"He taught me the grip," Crenshaw said. "He put my hands on the club for the first time and I

don't think I've ever changed it. I'm thinking of him always, all day. We've lost somebody we owe our lives to. Whatever I have accomplished in my career, I owe to Harvey."

Crenshaw has 19 tour victories to his credit, including two Masters championships in 1984 and 1995, the last coming just days after the death of his longtime friend and mentor Harvey Penick.

"I believe in fate. It was like someone put their hand on my shoulder this week and guided me through. I don't know where I grew such confidence over a few practice days. I don't think I ever had a quicker transformation, but I just played my heart out. I had a good feel for a lot of things. But I had a 15th club in my bag this week, and it was Harvey Penick."

Crenshaw grew up on the practice tee with longtime friend Tom Kite, creating a competitive rivalry that propelled them both to successful pro careers. Together, they led the University of Texas to national championships in 1971 and '72. Crenshaw won three consecutive individual NCAA titles from 1971–73, sharing the honor with Kite in '72.

Crenshaw turned pro in 1973 and won the PGA Qualifying tournament by a then-record 12 strokes, earning him the reputation as "the next Jack Nicklaus." He then proceeded to win his first professional golf tournament at the 1973 Texas Open.

In the middle of his career, Crenshaw battled with the effects of Graves disease, but he has never gone more than three years without a victory. He has played on four Ryder Cup teams in 1981, '83, '87 and 1995.

In the latter part of his career, Crenshaw also got into the golf course design business. Long a student of the game's great architects, Crenshaw teamed with architect Bill Coore to produce top courses such as the Plantation Course at Kapalua on the island of Maui.

Greatness is one of those nebulous terms that has no specific qualifications. There are no predetermined entrance requirements, per se, to join the club. It just happens.

Which brings us to the subject of Tom Kite, an Austin native who has been an enigma most of his career. His career statistics are an example of how hard it is to determine greatness.

On one hand, he is considered one of the most consistent performers of golf's modern era. With 19 victories, he became the PGA Tour's all-time money leader in the early 1990s with more than $9 million in career earnings. While Kite only led the tour in earnings twice — 1981 and '89 — it was his consistent performance that moved him to the top of the money pile. Between 1974 and 1994, his worst finish on the money list was No. 39. In 10 of those years, he was in the top 10. His consistency helped him earn berths on seven Ryder Cup teams.

But through it all, Kite was tagged as "the best player to never win a major," a label that haunted him until his victory at the 1992 U.S. Open at Pebble Beach.

Kite grew up on the same practice tee at Austin Country Club as longtime friend and rival Ben Crenshaw under the tutelage of legendary instructor Harvey Penick. They led the Texas Longhorns to national titles in 1971–72, with Kite and Crenshaw tying for individual honors in 1972. As individuals, Crenshaw won 18 college tournaments and Kite won 8.

While Crenshaw came out of college with the highest expectations, it was Kite who pulled down rookie of the year honors by making the cut in 31 of 34 events and producing 15 top 25 finishes.

Tom

KITE

Austin native Tom Kite used his consistency over three decades to become one of golf's all-time leading money winners.

Carol MANN

Carol Mann was always a woman with a mission, and has always stood out in a crowd wherever she goes.

Wherever she goes, LPGA Hall of Famer Carol Mann always stands out in a crowd.

Carol Mann never had to worry about standing out in a crowd. If it wasn't her 6-foot-3 frame or her golf game that grabbed your attention, it was her outgoing personality and innovative thinking.

Mann was one of the pioneers of the LPGA and in 1977 she became the ninth player to be inducted into the LPGA Hall of Fame, which to this day ranks as one of the most difficult achievements in sport.

She ranks eighth on the all-time victory list with 38 and her victory in the 1965 U.S. Open started a streak of five consecutive years with two or more victories.

Although she grew up in Buffalo, N.Y., and played golf at North Carolina-Greensboro, she moved to Houston in the 1970s and still lives in The Woodlands. She recently completed her first book and wrote a regular column for *The Houston Post* before the newspaper closed.

Mann was instrumental in the formation of the modern LPGA and in getting the LPGA to move its national headquarters to Houston between 1982–89.

She also is a trustee of the Women's Sports Foundation and a national leader for women's rights in sports.

Mann started playing golf at the age of nine, and went on to win 38 times on the LPGA tour and earn a place in both the LPGA and Texas Golf halls of fame and has been selected as one of *Golf Magazine's* 100 Heroes of American golf.

She was a multiple winner in eight of her 21 active years on tour. In 1968, she claimed 10 titles and the Vare Trophy, establishing a season-scoring average record of 72.04 that stood for 10 years until Nancy Lopez broke it in 1978. That year she had 23 rounds in the 60s, a mark not broken until Amy Alcott had 25 in 1980. She was inducted into the Women's Sports Hall of Fame in 1982 and LPGA Hall of Fame in 1977.

Dave Marr had modest aspirations as a youngster who grew up as the son of a golf pro in Houston. Marr dreamed merely of following in his father's footsteps.

Little did he know that swinging a golf club at a little white ball would transport him out of the boondocks to international fame and to a star-gazed life that had him telling stories and bellying up to the bar with the greatest golfers of all time.

Marr died in his sleep in October 1997 at M.D. Anderson Cancer Center, where he spent so many of his final years undergoing chemotherapy treatments for the cancer in the lining of his stomach. He was 63.

A sparkling conversationalist and storyteller, Marr made friends with writers and broadcasters during his days and nights in New York, where Dan Jenkins dubbed him "The Pro from 52nd Street."

Marr dined out longer on one transcendent victory than any golfer in history. His 1965 PGA Championship, where he held off a charge by Jack Nicklaus, made him a star and propelled him onto the Ryder Cup team.

"For a player like me, it all had to come together," Marr said. "I thought I was a good player, not a great player. If I played my best and Jack played his best, he still would have beat me."

Marr soon gravitated toward the TV booth, doing part-time work for ABC. By 1975, Marr's Texas-flavored, New York-seasoned wit and on-air chemistry with Jim McKay made him a natural to supplant Byron Nelson as ABC's main analyst. Marr stayed with ABC until an ill-considered housecleaning swept him out in 1991. He was rescued by the BBC and later NBC in 1994.

Marr's career highlight, however, came from serving as non-playing captain of the 1981 U.S.

Dave

MARR

The life of Dave Marr was a classic example of the "local boy does good" story. And nobody deserved it more.

Ryder Cup team, a squad stacked with stars at the top of their games such as Jack Nicklaus, Tom Watson and Lee Trevino, that trounced Europe on British soil.

Marr was an Irish-American — the original family name was O'Meara — but it was changed to Marr at Ellis Island. Marr was only 14 when his father died of a heart attack in 1948, so Memorial Park pro Robie Williams became a surrogate father and gave Marr guidance and odd jobs to help the family pay the bills.

From his father, Marr inherited a love for the game, a sense of

honor and faithfulness to friends, as well as a bad temper that may have prevented him from reaching his potential. "I don't think I ever finished a round of golf with my father," Marr said. "He had a bad temper, and mine was worse."

But it was several surrogate fathers — including Williams, second-cousin Jack Burke Jr. and legendary golf teacher Claude Harmon — who shaped Marr's career.

Williams was instrumental in giving Marr odd jobs and spending money and golf clubs that he and his mother could never afford.

When Marr began cutting classes at Rice and University of Houston to play golf, Williams warned: "You can't do that to your mother. You don't want to hang around here and become a bum."

So Marr left college at 19 and became an assistant pro at the famed Winged Foot Golf Club, where he worked under the tutelage of Harmon. After seven years, Harmon told Marr he had enough talent to make about $15,000 a year on tour.

"To a guy who was making $150 a week as a club pro," Marr said, "that sounded like winning the lottery."

Texas Legends

Doug SANDERS

Golf was Doug Sanders' first-class ticket from the cotton fields to hob-nob with politicians, entertainers and movie stars.

Doug Sanders grew up picking cotton in Cedartown, Ga., but during all those days in the fields as a youth he dreamed of one day doing something big. After all, the more humble the beginnings, the bigger the dreams.

While picking cotton as a youth, Sanders learned he could make more money working as a caddie at nearby Cherokee Country Club. That's where he taught himself how to play and developed his telephone-booth swing that earned him a ticket to the big time.

Sanders turned pro and became an instant international playboy who played the 19th hole with consistency, had a weakness for pretty women and hob-nobbed with the rich and famous. His operating philosophy became, "If I can't go first class, then to hell with going at all."

In 1955, Houston developer Frank Sharp brought Sanders to Houston to be the tour representative for Sharpstown Country Club in hopes of attracting the young, upwardly mobile segment of the golf community. He later was named the first golf director at The Woodlands Country Club when it opened in 1974 to become Houston's new golf mecca.

Sanders went on to win 20 tournaments, and he remained in Houston to become the only active tour player to have a tournament with his name on it — the Doug Sanders Celebrity Classic. On several occasions, Sanders used his influence to attract former President George Bush to play in the tournament. In 1990, Bush became the first sitting president to play in a tour event.

Sanders was inducted into the Georgia and Florida Sports Halls of Fame in the early 1970s. He was among the tour's top 60 moneywinners 13 times from 1958–1972. He never won a major championship, but was a two-time runner up in the British Open, finishing second to Jack Nicklaus in 1966 at Muirfield and again in 1970 at St. Andrews. In the latter, he lost an 18-hole playoff by a single shot. He also finished second in two other major championships behind Bob Rosburg at the 1959 PGA and behind Gene Littler at the 1961 U.S. Open.

Sanders has sponsored the Doug Sanders International junior tournaments in North America, Europe and Australia since the early 1980s, offering scholarships to top juniors around the world.

One of those players to earn a scholarship was Steve Elkington, who used the scholarship to attend the University of Houston and is now one of the rising stars on the PGA Tour.

LPGA Hall of Famer Kathy Whitworth has won more professional tour victories than any other golfer in the United States. She boasts 88 career victories and was the first female player to break the $1 million barrier.

She was born in Monahans, Texas, grew up in New Mexico, and now lives in Roanoke, Texas, near Texas golf legend Byron Nelson. She began playing at the age of 15, but learned the game quickly and captured the New Mexico State Women's Amateur in 1957 and 1958. She also is a member of the World Golf, Texas

Kathy

Texas Legends

WHITWORTH

Kathy Whitworth grew up in Monahans, Texas, and went on to become the winningest golfer in history — male or female.

Sports and Women's Sports Halls of Fame.

She was the LPGA's leading money winner eight times and the Player of the Year seven times.

Whitworth's last LPGA victory came in 1985 at the United Virginia Bank Classic. That win brought to 88 her total number of career victories, an all-time record for both the men's and women's U.S. tours. Whitworth is the most decorated player in LPGA history. She was the leading money winner eight times (1965–68, and 70–73) and the Player of the Year seven times (1968–69 and 71–73). In 1983, she tied Sam Snead's then record of 84 official professional victories in 1983 by winning the Lady Michelob. 1983 was also her most successful financial season, as she won $190,000.

She was tutored by Harvey Penick and Hardy Loudermilk. She was Associated Press Athlete of the Year in 1965 and '67. She was named Golfer of the Decade by *Golf Magazine* for the years 1968–77. She is in the Texas and World Golf Halls of Fame, as well as the New Mexico Hall of Fame, the Texas Sports Hall of Fame and the Women's Sports Foundation Hall of Fame.

Dave
WILLIAMS

When it came to coaching college golf, nobody did it better than he did at the University of Houston.

In 1952, Dave Williams was a chemical engineering professor at the University of Houston who didn't know a mashie from a niblick. He had only played half a dozen rounds in his lifetime when athletic director Harry Fouke approached him with the offer of coaching the Cougar golf team.

Williams accepted, starting one of the most unlikely and incredible stories that saw him over the next three decades lead Houston to 16 national championships, produce more than 70 professionals and become the Father of College Golf by inventing team scoring and bringing television and corporate sponsorship to the college level.

Williams produced more tour professionals than any other coach in America — among them current PGA stars Fred Couples, Steve Elkington, Fuzzy Zoeller, John Mahaffey, Bruce Lietzke and Billy Ray Brown.

While he didn't know that much about the game and was never a great player himself, Williams knew people. From the onset, the phone was the best club in his bag.

"My philosophy is to sign good players and make them want to be great players," Williams said.

"If you have the desire, you'll find a way to play the game.

"Love and belief in yourself are two of the strongest virtues. I've been working with young people for 44 years. If you love them, you have a chance to help them. I think I was made to be a coach. I loved to teach kids how to win."

From 1952 to 1985, Williams produced more NCAA titles than any other coach in any other sport. The Cougars won their first title in 1956 and proceeded to win the next five and 10 of the next 13.

Williams started the All-America Invitational Tournament, which he billed as the "Masters of College Golf," with only the top teams in the nation invited each year. He also brought the idea of corporate sponsorship to college golf with that tournament.

Williams wrote his own book, "How to Coach and Play Championship Golf," which was ghost written by former sportswriter Art Casper. He even started his own Hall of Fame, which honored the supporters of his All-America Invitational Tournament.

Williams also started the Dave Williams Cystic Fibrosis Tournament to raise money for the Cystic Fibrosis Foundation. To date, the tournament has raised more than $2 million in the fight against the dreaded children's disease.

The winningest coaches in college sports history — the University of Houston's Dave Williams and UCLA's John Wooden.

It was at the suggestion of legendary sportswriter Grantland Rice that Mildred Didriksen started playing golf in 1935, three years after her remarkable performance at the Los Angeles Olympic Games, where she won two gold medals and a silver, breaking world records in the javelin throw and the 80-meter hurdles.

Mildred, nicknamed Babe after Babe Ruth by playmates when she hit five home runs in one game, won the 1935 River Crest Invitational in Fort Worth. Subsequently, she was declared a professional due to her baseball and basketball earnings.

Married to professional wrestler George Zaharias in 1938, Babe became America's greatest woman athlete, excelling in tennis, swimming, diving, rollerskating,

Babe

ZAHARIAS

Mildred "Babe" Zaharias was not the greatest woman golfer of all time — she was one of the greatest athletes in history.

bowling and softball.

In 1946 and '47, she won 17 amateur tournaments in a row including the 1946 U.S. Women's Amateur and the 1947 British Amateur. In winning the latter, she was the first American to capture the British title since it was first played in 1893.

She turned pro for real in 1947 and in 1950 helped found the LPGA. During her golf career, she won 31 tournaments and earned a place in the LPGA Hall of Fame.

She led the Tour in earnings from 1948–51 and captured the Vare Trophy in 1954. She claimed three U.S. Women's Open titles (1948, '50 and '54), three Women's Titleholder tournaments (1947, '50 and '52) and four Western Open victories (1940, '44, '45 and '50) to account for her 10 major championships. Her 1954 U.S. Women's Open triumph came just months after her first cancer operation. In all, she won 31 of the 128 LPGA events scheduled during her eight-year career.

She was voted Woman Athlete of the First Half of the 20th Century by AP and Woman Athlete of the Year by AP in 1931, 1945, '46, '47, '50 and 1954.

In track and field, she either held or tied for the world record in four events including the javelin, 80-meter hurdles, high jump and long jump.

She was named Golfer of the Decade by *Golf Magazine* for the years 1948–57.

In 1953 Babe was stricken with breast cancer and underwent surgery. She recovered enough by 1954 to win again. She eventually died of cancer at the age of 42 and was buried in Beaumont, where the Babe Didriksen Zaharias Museum is open daily to the public.

Tommy

BOLT

Terrible Tommy could throw a club almost as far as he hit a golf ball.

If Tommy Bolt could sink putts as well as he could throw a three-iron, he might have gone on to become one of the greatest players who ever lived.

Bolt was a carpenter from Pasadena who was nicknamed everything from Thunder-Bolt to Tempestuous Tommy to Terrible-Tempered Tommy from his days growing up at Memorial Park to his days on the pro tour.

Golf writer Jack Agness once wrote: "Bolt could fling a club 20 yards farther than any living man. He'd stomp out after it like an angry bull, pick it up and thrust it into his bag as if he were harpooning a shark . . . sometimes he would get a running start and let 'er fly like a javelin thrower."

Here's how Bolt, winner of the 1958 U.S. Open and 14 other pro events, described himself in his book, *The Hole Truth.*

"As for my temper, I'll admit that it's equipped with a trigger fuse and, by nature, I have a low boiling point. But I haven't broken as many clubs as I've been accused of. I've thrown a lot just to keep the gallery happy."

Charles

COODY

Winning the 1971 Masters and gaining a berth on the Ryder Cup Team had to be the highlight of Charles Coody's career. However, the tall Texan continued his winning ways on the Senior PGA Tour. In fact, he more than doubled his career earnings since joining the over-50 set in 1987.

Coody was always a solid player even back in his early days as an amateur at Texas Christian University. The same year he won the Masters he also captured the World Series of Golf.

He also won twice in Great Britain in 1973, the Willis Open in England and the John Player Classic in Scotland.

Texans are well aware of Coody's exploits as an amateur, since he reached the semifinals in the U.S. Amateur in 1962 and won his first spot in the Masters.

On the Senior Tour, Coody won the 1989 General Tire Las Vegas Classic and the Vantage Championship in 1990.

For years, Coody had 100 percent attendance in the tournaments on the Texas circuit. He was honored for his loyalty by the Houston Golf Association in 1976.

Ralph

GULDAHL

"Ralph Guldahl might've been the greatest golfer ever, for a short period of time," the late Jimmy Demaret frequently noted.

Guldahl, the handsome, 6-foot-2, Dallas native won the Western Open when the Western Open was considered a major, in 1936, 1937 and 1938. He was runner-up to fellow Texan Byron Nelson in the 1937 Masters, finished second to Henry Picard in 1938 and then edged Sam Snead for the coveted championship in 1939. Guldahl won his first U.S. Open at Oakland Hills in 1937 and repeated a year later.

For a time Guldahl was magic. Then, just as quickly as it had come, the magic vanished. He retired in 1942 after winning 14 events and being selected for the 1937 and '39 Ryder Cup Teams.

His career began after he won the Dallas City Championship. It was the summer of 1929, two years after Dallas hosted the 1927 PGA Championship. Riding a wave of confidence, Guldahl traveled to San Antonio the following winter and declared himself a pro while he was tied for fourth place going into the final round. He ultimately finished 10th.

Sandra

HAYNIE

Don

JANUARY

Bruce

LIETZKE

LPGA Hall of Famer Sandra Haynie played her way into the record books by winning three major championships in a career that spanned 30 years. A native of Fort Worth, Haynie was an early disciple of A.G. Mitchell of River Crest Country Club.

As a teenager, she won the 1957 and '58 Texas State Public Links tournaments plus the 1958 and '59 Women's Texas Golf Association titles.

As a professional, Haynie actually had two careers; one from 1961–76 and following a layoff due to injuries and arthritis, began again in 1980.

Between the years of 1961 and 1973, Haynie was one of the LPGA's hottest players, racking up a total of 39 victories. During that time she won the Player of the Year Award (1970) and was the tour's second-leading money winner four times.

In 1974, she became only the second woman to win the LPGA Championship and the U.S. Women's Open in the same season. She was inducted into the LPGA Hall of Fame in 1977 and the Texas Golf Hall of Fame in 1984.

As a member of the PGA Tour from 1956 until 1976, Don January won 10 events. He later added 22 Senior PGA Tour triumphs to that total and has a place in the record books as the first player to surpass the $1 million mark in Senior Tour earnings in 1985. January had already gained notice as a collegian, who along with teammates Billy Maxwell and Joe Conrad, played on three consecutive NCAA Championship teams at North Texas State.

As a professional, January won the 1967 PGA Championship and won the Vardon Trophy for the tour's lowest scoring average in 1976 at the age of 46.

January earned spots on the 1966 and 1977 Ryder Cup Teams.

Between his stints on the PGA and Senior PGA tours, January dabbled in golf course architecture and teamed with longtime friend and business partner Billy Martindale to design more than 20 courses throughout the state.

Among his best works were Royal Oaks Country Club, Oakmont Country Club, Los Rios Country Club and Plano Golf Course.

Although Bruce Lietzke goes quietly amid the hoopla of the PGA Tour, he is a force to be reckoned with. Dangerous when aroused is the best way to describe Lietzke, who gained a Tour card in 1975 and has been making an exceptional living ever since. Bruce, who began playing golf at age five with a set of cut-down clubs provided by brother Duane (an assistant pro), grew up in Beaumont. He attended the University of Houston and played alongside the likes of Texans John Mahaffey and Bill Rogers.

During the 1972–73 collegiate year, Lietzke won the Inwood Forest tournament and was a member of the UH team that won the Southwest Conference match play tourney.

In 1973, after leaving UH, Lietzke put his clubs in the closet for a time. Having played non-stop for almost 15 years, he was tired of it. Six months later, he turned pro and earned his tour card in 1975. Since that time, Lietzke has never finished worse than 74th on the money list. In 1977 he was fifth, in 1979 he was eighth; in 1981 he was fourth and in 1984 he was sixth again. He played on the 1991 U.S. Ryder Cup.

Lloyd
MANGRUM

Sandra
PALMER

Betsy
RAWLS

Darkly handsome Lloyd Mangrum is best described as a cool customer on the course and one who made magic inside 20 yards of the green. Observers said that in his prime, Mangrum went for weeks at a time without three-putting.

Mangrum got his initial exposure to golf by parking cars at the old Cliff Dale Country Club in Dallas, which no longer exists. His boss was his brother Ray.

Even though he was around the game from a young age, amazingly Mangrum never played as an amateur but instead turned pro at the age of 15.

Mangrum hit the big time when he won the U.S. Open in 1946. He also won big in 1948 by claiming $22,000 out of a $48,000 purse at George S. May's World Championship while playing at his home course at Tam O'Shanter in Chicago.

Mangrum, a Vardon Trophy winner in 1951 and 1953, played in four Ryder Cup matches (1947, '49, '51 and '53), as well as serving as honorary captain in 1955. He was also selected in 1939 but those matches were not played due to WWII.

Tiny Sandra Palmer grew up as one of a host of fine female golfers who called Fort Worth's River Crest Country Club home.

And with a name like Palmer, she was destined for greatness.

As a youngster, Sandra was tutored by the late professional A.G. Mitchell, the man behind many other successful Texas touring pros. Other professionals who influenced her career in a later time were Harvey Penick, Ernie Vossler and Johnny Revolta.

As an amateur, Palmer won the West Texas championship four times and the Texas State Amateur in 1963.

Prior to that, while a student at North Texas State, she was runner-up in the NCAA championships in 1961. She was also a cheerleader at North Texas.

After turning pro in 1964, Palmer struggled through seven lean years. From then on, however, she won no less than two events per season for the next seven years.

Palmer became the LPGA's 13th millionaire in 1986 and was inducted into the National Collegiate Hall of Fame in 1988.

Betsy Rawls grew up in Arlington and did not take up golf until she was in her late teens. As a University of Texas student, Rawls sought out Austin teacher Harvey Penick.

Rawls, a physics and math major who graduated Phi Beta Kappa, learned quickly from Penick. Four years after taking up golf, she won the Texas Amateur and the Women's Trans National. In 1950, she won the Texas Amateur again.

Rawls turned pro shortly thereafter and went on to capture 55 LPGA victories and is fourth on the list of the Tour's leading money winners. She won eight majors and led the tour in victories in 1952, '57 and '59.

Her 20-year career was highlighted in 1959 when she won 10 titles and broke the earnings record with nearly $27,000.

She was inducted into the World Golf Hall of Fame in 1987 and was one of *Golf Magazine's* 100 Heroes in 1988.

An LPGA Hall of Famer since 1960, Rawls also won eight majors championships and was inducted into the Texas Golf Hall of Fame in 1983.

The Best of the Best in the Lone Star State

The phrase "top golf course," is nebulous enough to leave something to the imagination and personal preference. Golf is an individual sport with individual tastes, where one man's dream course is another's nightmare.

As the saying goes, there are "different strokes for different folks."

Yet the Texas Top 100 is the tie that binds them all together and represents everything that is good about the game of golf, in general, and in Texas, in particular.

These courses are the common denominator for all golfers because they are superior in all facets of what makes a golf course great — from the strategy of the design to the characteristics of the site to the daily course maintenance. Not to forget beauty and difficulty.

Simply put, the Texas Top 100 is the best of the best.

Texas Top 100

1. Colonial Country Club

I t all started with a blade of grass. A bent blade, at that. After getting the opportunity to putt on the superior putting surfaces of bentgrass greens while on a vacation in the 1930s, Fort Worth businessman Marvin Leonard returned home an enlightened man. No longer satisfied with the slow and bumpy Bermuda greens found in Texas, Leonard began pounding the pavement to get some of the existing courses to make a change.

Despite his clout as owner of the Leonard Brothers Department Stores, Leonard was rebuffed at every turn. Bentgrass greens won't work in Texas, they told him. If he wanted bentgrass greens so badly, they told him, why didn't he build a course all his own?

The rest, as they say, is history. In 1936, Leonard took them up on the idea. He bought some rich land in the Trinity River bottom and began sowing the seed for what has been Texas' best golf course for the past 60 years. Colonial is consistently rated in the top 50 in the world and the top 30 in the U.S.

It was the first course south of the Mason-Dixon Line to host the U.S. Open in 1941. It also hosted the 1975 Players Championship, the 1991 U.S. Women's Open and has been home of the PGA Tour's Colonial Invitation since 1946.

Designed by John Bredemus with later assists from Ralph Plummer and Press Maxwell, Colonial is a monument to the golden age of American golf architecture.

It is a testament to perseverance, as it survived the Fort Worth Flood of 1949; those bentgrass greens have withstood relentless Texas summers; and 15 of the holes survived a 1968 Flood Control Project in which the Trinity River was rerouted.

The clubhouse has survived three fires. Only Big Annie, a giant oak that used to stand guard at the elbow of the 17th fairway, is missing after having been struck by lightning.

Nine holes were changed during the 1968–69 flood control project. The seventh, eighth and 13th holes were all drastically changed. The eighth is probably missed the most. It was a long par 3 over a curve in the Trinity to a tiny green on the other side.

"It was," Byron Nelson remembers, "one of the hardest holes in golf. You had to hit the shot down the river to this itty-bitty green."

Colonial's Horrible Horseshoe — the backbreaking combination of holes 3–5 — survived in a place known as Hogan's Alley because no man ever dominated a major tournament like Ben Hogan did the Colonial. He was a five-time winner here and at one time or another held every record. It was also the site of his last career victory in 1959.

COLONIAL COUNTRY CLUB

Colonial Country Club

3735 Country Club Circle
Fort Worth 76109
817-927-4243
Pro: Dow Finsterwald Jr.
A private club that annually hosts the PGA Tour's Colonial Invitation. From downtown Fort Worth, take I-30 West to University, then south to Country Club. Turn right to club entrance.

• • •

USGA rating: 73.7
Slope rating: 132
Sand traps: 65
Water holes: 11
Doglegs: 4 left/7 right
Type greens: Bentgrass
Record: 62
Designer: John Bredemus
Year opened: 1935

• • •

Hole	Par	Yards	Hole	Par	Yards
1	5	572	10	4	416
2	4	401	11	5	609
3	4	470	12	4	435
4	3	226	13	3	172
5	4	466	14	4	431
6	4	415	15	4	436
7	4	453	16	3	176
8	3	192	17	4	387
9	4	405	18	4	434
Out	35	3600	In	35	3496

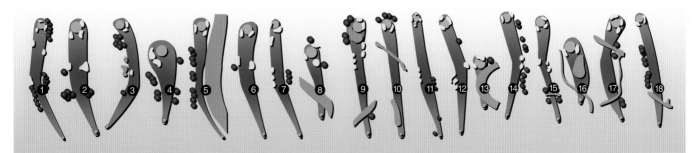

2. Crown Colony Country Club

Tradition is an important element of golf. In the case of Crown Colony, a lack of tradition may be the only thing keeping it from being recognized as the best course in Texas.

While Crown Colony is fewer than two decades old, it is more of a traditional layout like Colonial, which opened in 1936.

Crown Colony, carved out of an East Texas forest in the outskirts of Lufkin, is a product of architect Robert von Hagge, with an assist from former PGA Tour regular Bruce Devlin.

As top players have toured it, the Crown jewel has grown steadily in stature. In 1994, Crown Colony loosened Colonial's grip as the No. 1 course in the state by the *Dallas Morning News*. While Colonial still held down the top spot, Crown Colony became the first course to gain more votes than Colonial in a single year.

"It's scenic, fair and tough. "It has everything a golfer can ask for in a course," says longtime Texas club pro Steve Wheelis. "If you can't enjoy golf at Crown Colony, there's something wrong with you."

Says Waco pro Joe Barger: "This course is more beautiful than Augusta National. If you put all the flowers of Augusta on this course and move it to Dallas, a membership would go for a minimum of $100,000."

Adds pro Scott Erwin: "If it had Northern California weather,

the initiation fee would be $150,000 and they'd be standing in line to join."

It doesn't take long for Crown Colony to capture a player. Crown Colony begins revealing its greatness on the first hole, a 540-yard par 5. A golfer who finds the tree-lined fairway off the tee faces a second shot through a deep depression before reaching the elevated green.

The par-5 third is one of the state's true beauties. At 583 yards, it is an elegantly tough hole guarded by pines and water from tee to green. It doglegs out of the pines, turns left alongside a lake, then presents the view of an undulating putting surface nestled along the water's edge.

Make no mistake. It can also quickly destroy a good score. The two finishing holes, a fierce par-3 17th and a treacherous par-5 18th, can tear away the score of any player.

Crown Colony opened on April 14, 1979, after being developed by Sabine Investments for a paltry $750,000. That sum wouldn't even be enough to get a golf course off the ground in the modern era.

Von Hagge, who moved his offices from Florida to Texas during construction, said he and Devlin did not make much money on the project, but their handiwork has enabled von Hagge to build many of his more than 200 courses around the world. They still use it to show clients what they can do.

Crown Colony Country Club
900 Crown Colony Drive
Lufkin 75901
409-637-8800
Pro: Bob Diamond
From Houston, take Highway 59 going north, enter Crown Colony just off Champions Drive and look for the clubhouse.

• • •

USGA rating: 73.9
Slope rating: 137
Sand traps: 73
Water holes: 14
Doglegs: 6
Type greens: Bentgrass
Record: 64
Designers: Robert von Hagge and Bruce Devlin
Year opened: 1975

• • •

Hole	Par	Yards	Hole	Par	Yards
1	5	540	10	4	437
2	4	385	11	4	379
3	5	583	12	3	195
4	3	183	13	5	503
5	4	381	14	3	185
6	4	388	15	4	380
7	3	138	16	5	481
8	4	359	17	3	203
9	4	390	18	5	582
Out	36	3,347	In	36	3,445

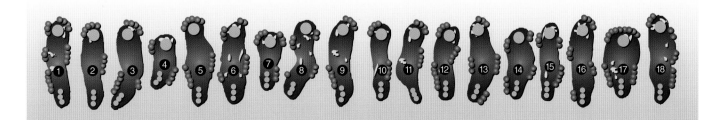

Texas Top 100

3. Barton Creek Resort and Country Club — Fazio Course

BARTON CREEK
COUNTRY CLUB

While opened less than a decade, the Barton Creek Resort and Country Club has already gained its place as one of the top resorts in the United States.

The development, owned by Club Resorts Inc., features three separate and highly acclaimed courses designed by some of the best players or architects in the game. The best of the bunch is the Barton Creek Country Club, a private resort course that has won dozens of awards for its stunning Hill Country beauty.

Designed by Tom Fazio, it was the site for the Legends of Golf from 1990–94, hosting the tournament that helped launch the Senior PGA Tour. It was an appropriate gathering place for all of the men who pioneered the game, and still is for anyone who wants to get away from it all or challenge one of the best courses in the state.

The second Barton Creek course was designed by Ben Crenshaw and Bill Coore and is played by tourists and many of the conventioneers who frequent the lavish property. The Lakeside course was designed by Arnold Palmer and Ed Seay and is open to member and guest play.

But the Fazio course captured the attention of most golfers when it opened in 1986. Fazio has gained international acclaim by building courses in all kinds of natural environments, but this test in west Austin proved his mastery over extremely challenging terrain. Fazio took full advantage of elevation changes of more than 100 feet.

The front nine is flatter and more rolling than the back side, but there is more than enough trouble to challenge even the best golfers.

No. 5 is a monstrous 661-yard dogleg left par 5 that requires three well-played shots to reach the green. On the final approach, golfers must clear a bunker that protects the front of the green, which is also guarded by three small bunkers in back.

No. 7 is the most difficult hole. It is a 442-yard par 4 that usually plays into a prevailing wind.

No. 9 is a 175-yard par 3 with an elevated tee that features a waterfall to the left and a large grass slope to the right. The 10th kicks off a beautiful back nine with a tee situated at least 100 feet above the fairway.

The par-5 15th usually plays into the wind with Barton Creek and a steep drop over the left side of the green. The par-4 16th has been recognized as one of the most scenic in Texas with a waterfall in front of the green. The par-3 17th is a stern challenge.

The par-5 18th is a fine finishing hole with more unique Hill Country touches. A huge cave and cascading waterfall guard any attempt to go for the green in two strokes. After the first 200 yards, the hole is uphill all the way to a tiered green.

Barton Creek Resort and Country Club Fazio Course

8212 Barton Club Drive
Austin 78735
800-336-6158
Director of Golf: Brent Buckman
One of three 18-hole courses.
Take I-35 South to Highway 71, west to
Bee Caves Road, south to Barton Creek
Boulevard, turn left to Barton Club Drive.

• • •

USGA rating: 74.0
Slope rating: 135
Sand traps: 37
Water holes: 6
Doglegs: 1 left/0 right
Type greens: Bentgrass
Record: 63
Designer: Tom Fazio
Year opened: 1986

• • •

Hole	Par	Yards	Hole	Par	Yards
1	4	460	10	4	418
2	4	377	11	4	415
3	3	153	12	4	270
4	4	410	13	4	477
5	5	611	14	3	170
6	4	388	15	5	527
7	4	442	16	4	420
8	5	494	17	3	203
9	3	175	18	5	546
Out	36	3510	In	36	3446

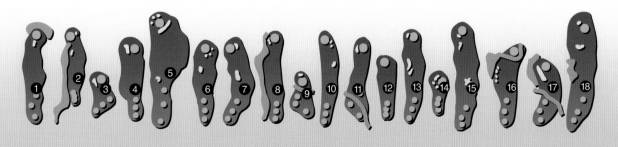

Texas Top 100

4. *The Hills of Lakeway*

Put perhaps the prettiest hole in the state with one of the most scenic locations and a design by golf great Jack Nicklaus, and you should expect a special golf experience.

That's certainly the case with the Hills of Lakeway just west of Austin. The private course has annually been ranked as one of the top five in the state since it opened in 1981, and for good reason.

The par 72 layout ambles up and down the Lakeway area and alongside Hurst Creek. The views are stunning, the holes are tough and the par-3 seventh is unforgettable to those who have played it.

When Nicklaus first examined the property in the late 1970s while interviewing for the job, he proclaimed, "This is one of the finest pieces of natural land on which to build a golf course that I've ever seen."

As one of the first Nicklaus courses in Texas, The Hills showcases the design characteristics of Nicklaus and associate Bob Cupp, especially their use of broad landscaping and disdain for blind shots.

The Golden Bear must have been pleased with the results, because he purchased a home on the course as did former Dallas Cowboys coach Tom Landry.

"The multiple tees allow golf to be fun for high handicappers, men and women alike, and yet the course affords a demanding and thoughtful shot strategy for better players," Nicklaus said.

The Hills was recently sold as part of the massive auction by the Resolution Trust Corporation and course matters are waiting on the new owners, Cobblestone Golf Group and Ross Perot Jr., to emerge from the morass of legal work. In the meantime, the course has suffered little. In fact, the Hills hosted Austin's only USGA national championship in 1989 with the U.S. Women's Mid-Amateur Championship.

Pro Myron Klement, who has been at the course since it opened in 1981, said the key to a good score on the course is a good short game. Nicklaus was always an excellent long iron player and, like many of his layouts, The Hills demands no less from its players.

"The course is very demanding from the fairways to the greens with more than 50 bunkers," Klement says, noting Hurst Creek comes into play on 13 holes. "There are several narrow openings to the green, making a good short game vital."

The par-3 seventh doesn't have a creek, but an entire waterfall guarding the green. There is a 15-foot natural fall directly below the green. The hole ranges from 95 to 165 yards and requires a long carry over the water.

The par-4, 418-yard 18th has a bit of everything: water and out-of-bounds on the left with sand, trees and homes on the right.

The Hills of Lakeway

26 Club Estates Parkway
Austin 78738
512-261-7272
Pro: Myron Klement
This 6,813 yard private course is home to the nationally renowned Academy of Golf Dynamics. From downtown Austin, take Highway 71 West to RR 620 North. The club is on the right.

• • •

USGA rating: 73
Slope rating: 130
Sand traps: 57
Water holes: 3
Doglegs: 4 left/ 3 right
Type greens: Bentgrass
Record: 62
Designer: Jack Nicklaus
Year opened: 1981

• • •

Hole	Par	Yards	Hole	Par	Yards
1	5	400	10	4	424
2	3	116	11	5	518
3	4	463	12	3	185
4	4	418	13	4	356
5	4	424	14	3	178
6	4	402	15	4	368
7	3	165	16	4	375
8	4	405	17	5	505
9	5	495	18	4	418
Out	36	3486	In	36	3327

5. Horseshoe Bay Resort — Ram Rock Course

Horseshoe Bay Resort and Country Club, located 50 miles west of Austin, is like the song: it was a top southwest golf resort, when a golf resort wasn't cool.

Long before the Barton Creeks and Hyatts of the Austin-San Antonio golf world appeared, Horseshoe Bay was making its mark as one of the top resorts in the world. Things haven't changed much in 20 years.

The resort boasts three courses all designed by legendary architect Robert Trent Jones Sr., who produced some of the greatest and prettiest layouts in the world.

All three courses are considered among the top 10 in Hill Country. The Ram Rock course is ranked No. 3 in the state by the *Dallas Morning News* and garnered six first-place votes.

Horseshoe Bay's Apple Rock course is No. 8 and Slick Rock is No. 9, but both also received first-place votes. Last year, almost 100,000 rounds were played on this trio of courses.

Most of the credit goes to developer Norman Hurd and his cousin Wayne, who teamed up in the early 1970s to buy a 2,500-acre cattle ranch on the lake.

"With a build-it-and-they-will-come" mentality, Hurd put up $550,000 to build the first facilities and had the foresight to hire Jones to give golfers a reason to come and a feeling that it was worth the trip when they leave.

Slick Rock came first in 1974, followed by Ram Rock in 1979 and Applerock in 1986. San Antonio master professional Bob Putt was the first pro at Horseshoe Bay. The courses are open to the club's 1,700 members and resort guests, offering something for every level of golfer.

The course most cussed and discussed is the Ram Rock layout. Annually, it has been cited in statewide surveys as the toughest course in Texas. The par-4, 488-yard second hole is also one of the toughest in the Austin-San Antonio area.

At 6,956 yards from the back tees, the par-71 layout has caused more than one golfer to threaten to find another sport if they had to play Ram Rock every day. It is rated 73.9 by the USGA with a 137 slope, one of the highest in the area.

The idea for Ram Rock apparently was born after the first Texas State Open was played at Slick Rock. Several of the pros said the layout wasn't challenging enough. Their wish was Hurd's command.

So with Ram Rock, Jones used all the weapons at his disposal to create a feisty foe. The fairways are narrow with natural streams, waterfalls, rock gardens and granite outcroppings.

Add blind tee shots, all manner of trees and wildflowers, and golfers have more than their hands and eyes full.

Horseshoe Bay Resort Ram Rock Course

PO Box 7766
Horseshoe Bay 78654
800-292-1545
Director of Golf: Scott McDonough
This is one of three 18-hole courses at this exclusive resort, all three of which are in the Texas Top 100. From Austin, take Highway 71 West to Highway 281, north to FM 2147, left to Horseshoe Bay.

• • •

USGA rating: 73.9
Slope rating: 137
Sand traps: 61
Water holes: 10
Doglegs: 7 left/2 right
Type greens: Bentgrass
Record: 66
Designer: Robert Trent Jones Sr.
Year opened: 1979

Hole	Par	Yards	Hole	Par	Yards
1	4	414	10	4	344
2	4	488	11	4	399
3	4	442	12	3	169
4	3	191	13	4	438
5	4	430	14	5	541
6	4	468	15	4	420
7	5	533	16	4	417
8	3	220	17	3	214
9	5	540	18	4	378
Out	36	3626	In	35	3320

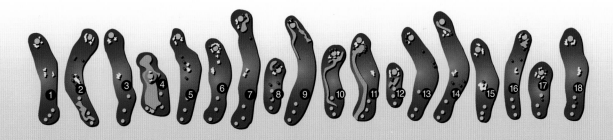

Texas Top 100

6. La Cantera Golf Club

I t has been a good ride for Tom Weiskopf and Jay Morrish. In a decade of partnership, they have produced some of the best golf courses in America. Weiskopf brought to the table all of his experience as a 15-time winner on the PGA Tour, while Morrish used his experience in engineering and landscape architecture.

In 1995, the two men decided to go their separate ways when Morrish teamed up with his son Carter, but not before they went out with one more masterstroke called La Cantera Golf Club.

La Cantera is part of a $100 million, 1,600-acre project being developed by USAA, the San Antonio-based financial services and insurance giant. In addition to the FIESTA, Texas theme park adjacent to the course, the project will eventually include major hotels and retail centers and another 18-hole course designed by Tom Fazio.

Carved out of the Hill Country limestone and an old cement quarry, La Cantera takes golfers on a roller-coaster ride unlike any other. It is set on an extremely hilly site above the music-amusement park with clear views to downtown.

It is built out of the same kind of rugged Hill Country terrain that produced The Quarry and Austin's Barton Creek Resort, where the Tom Fazio course is ranked among the best in the state.

"Perhaps once in a decade, an architect might find that a golf course surpasses expectations," Morrish says. "Everything came together just right on this project.

"The result is an unforgettable golf course — one that will test the mettle of the world's greatest golfers and yet provide just as rewarding an experience for those of us who are mere mortals."

It didn't take long for La Cantera to also earn status as one of the best courses in the state, and in 1995 it became the host site for the best players in the world during the PGA Tour's La Cantera Texas Open.

The course has already been ranked as one of the best in the state by *Golf* and *Golfweek* magazines. Take the 315-yard, par-4 seventh hole. Golfers tee off from the top of an 80-foot quarry wall, with a rattlesnake bunker on the left-hand side of the fairway and the FIESTA, Texas roller coaster in the background carrying thousands of screaming passengers each day.

Some of the golfers at La Cantera may be screaming on their way down from the top of quarry on the No. 7 tee. Some players try to drive the green here, but do so at the risk of finding the lake that runs down the right side.

The course features more than 70 bunkers with Babcock Creek coming into play on four holes.

The 414-yard 12th, however, might become known as one of the foremost par 4s in Texas. The hole requires the player to overcome visual intimidation.

La Cantera Golf Club

16401 La Cantera Parkway
San Antonio 78257
800-4-GOLFUS
Director of Golf: Buddy Cook
A daily-fee course that opened in 1994.
From downtown San Antonio, take I-10
West to La Cantera Parkway. Turn left
on La Cantera for 1.2 miles to entrance.

• • •

USGA rating: 72.0
Slope rating: 132
Sand traps: 65
Water holes: 9
Doglegs: 5 left/5 right
Type greens: Bermuda
Record: 68
Designers: Tom Weiskopf
and Jay Morrish
Year opened:1994

• • •

Hole	Par	Yards	Hole	Par	Yards
1	5	665	10	5	558
2	4	470	11	4	467
3	3	215	12	4	414
4	4	438	13	3	144
5	5	535	14	5	537
6	3	183	15	4	466
7	4	315	16	4	353
8	4	348	17	3	190
9	4	405	18	4	442
Out	36	3574	In	36	3571

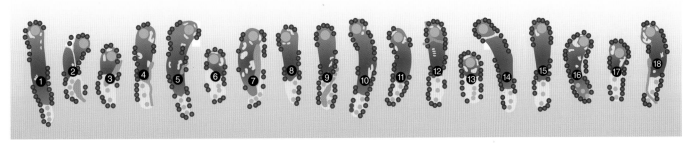

Texas Top 100

7. Brook Hollow Golf Club

By definition, a course designed by A.W. Tillinghast is fantastic, beautiful, difficult and elusive. That holds true whether you are talking about such legendary courses as Winged Foot and Baltusrol, or Texas courses like Cedar Crest and Brook Hollow.

Tillinghast never got caught up in the egotistical, quantity–vs.–quality syndrome. While many of his peers put their names on courses they actually set foot on only a handful of times during construction, Tillinghast was a hands-on architect who built only 60 courses in his lifetime — all of them high quality.

A single-digit handicapper himself, Tillinghast tired of some of the unimaginative designs and went into business for himself. The members at Brook Hollow golf club will be forever thankful.

While Tillinghast did most of his work in the northeast, he ventured to Texas in 1915 to build the state's first public course at San Antonio's Brackenridge Park. He built Cedar Crest in 1919, before being asked to design Brook Hollow out of 129 acres near where the Elm Fork then emptied into the main part of the Trinity River, about six miles from downtown.

"This is a thinking man's course," says Pat Puell, a Brook Hollow member responsible for bringing the 1978 Trans-Miss Championship here. "You have to be cautious and hit the ball straight. If they don't, they can get 9s and 10s very easily. You can get in jail."

Take, for instance, the 578-yard, par-5 fifth or the 449-yard, par-4 seventh. They are just two of nine holes at Brook Hollow nominated among the toughest in DFW.

Probably the most notorious, however, is the 363-yard, par-4 13th. It is long and tight with trees down both sides and a tiny green. It is a slight dogleg left with a forced carry over cross bunkers.

The course was closed temporarily in 1993 while it was renovated by the team of Ben Crenshaw and Bill Coore, who worship Golden-era architects like Tillinghast and try to achieve the same natural style in their own designs.

In 1946, Brook Hollow hosted the PGA Tour's Dallas Open, which started only the previous year at Lakewood. Ben Hogan held on for a two-stroke victory over Paul Runyan and Herman Keiser with a total of 284 that made him the only man in history to win at Dallas and Fort Worth the same year.

That was the last year the Dallas Open was held until 1956, when it resumed with two tournaments in consecutive months at Brook Hollow.

The next week Arnold Palmer made his Dallas debut, but didn't finish in the top 10. Instead, Australian Peter Thomson became the first foreigner to win in Dallas.

BROOK HOLLOW GOLF CLUB

Brook Hollow Golf Club

8301 Harry Hines Boulevard
Dallas 75235
214-637-1914
Pro: Robert Hoyt
A private par-71, 6,743-yard course.
From downtown Dallas, take I-35E North to Regal Row, East on Regal Row to Harry Hines Boulevard, South approximately two blocks to the club.

• • •

USGA rating: 72.7
Slope rating: 133
Sand traps: N/A
Water holes: 2
Doglegs: 4 left/5 right
Type greens: Bentgrass
Record: 63
Designer: A.W. Tillinghast
Year opened: 1920

• • •

Hole	Par	Yards	Hole	Par	Yards
1	5	483	10	3	167
2	4	368	11	4	446
3	4	399	12	4	440
4	3	152	13	4	363
5	5	578	14	4	348
6	4	427	15	5	519
7	4	449	16	4	385
8	3	186	17	4	420
9	4	378	18	4	395
Out	36	3420	In	35	3483

8. Champions Golf Club — Cypress Creek Course

T he name says it all. Indeed, Champions Golf Club has enjoyed a storied history since it was founded by Houston golf legends Jack Burke and Jimmy Demaret in 1957.

Since then, it has been the home of Houston's best golfers and has helped bring the world's best golfers and biggest golf events to Houston.

In 1967, Champions celebrated its 10-year anniversary by playing host to the Ryder Cup.

In 1969, Champions was the site of Orville Moody's victory over Deane Beman and Al Geiberger in the U.S. Open. Champions also hosted the PGA Tour's Houston Open from 1966 to 1971. Arnold Palmer, Frank Beard, Roberto De Vicenzo, Gibby Gilbert and Hubert Green all walked away winners.

In 1971, it also was the scene of Ben Hogan's last competitive tournament. Hogan was injured while climbing down the bank of Cypress Creek to hit a ball on the par-3 fourth hole, where he made a nine that day. Hogan re-injured a knee that was damaged in a car accident earlier in his career.

Champions dropped out of the national spotlight for nearly two decades before PGA Tour Commissioner Deane Beman was instrumental in bringing the Nabisco Championships to Houston in 1990. The club underwent a $1 million facelift. In the

tournament, Jodie Mudd rallied with three birdies on the last five holes to force a playoff in which he beat Bill Mayfair for golf's richest championship.

Despite the number of pro events Champions has hosted, Burke and Demaret believed amateur golf is the backbone of the game and the Champions Cup Invitational they started in the 1960s continues to be one of the most prestigious amateur events in the nation. In 1993, Champions looked better than ever as it played host to the 93rd U.S. Amateur Championship, and has tossed its cap in the ring to hold another U.S. Open in the future.

"This is what golf is all about," says Burke, an ambassador for golf since retiring in his prime at the age of 34. "We want to keep Houston in the spotlight and give our people a chance to see the best players in the world. I may not be around when the Open comes back here, but we at least want to get on the dance card."

Both the Cypress Creek and Jackrabbit courses are exceptionally long. Cypress is a course that can bogey you to death.

"The quality of both courses is just impeccable," said USGA executive director David Fay. "It was created by two of the game's great players who realized that amateurs are the backbone of the game and they have always treated them accordingly. We couldn't ask for anything more."

Champions Golf Club Cypress Creek Course

13722 Champions Drive
Houston 77069
281-444-6449
Pro: Tad Weeks
A prestigious 36-hole private club.
Take I-45 North to FM 1960, then left to Champions Drive. Turn right to entrance.

• • •

USGA rating: 73.8
Slope rating: 131
Sand traps: 46
Water holes: 12
Doglegs: 4 left/5 right
Type greens: Bermuda
Record: 63
Designer: Ralph Plummer
Year opened: 1957

• • •

Hole	Par	Yards	Hole	Par	Yards
1	5	449	10	5	464
2	4	253	11	4	247
3	3	183	12	4	252
4	3	236	13	4	223
5	3	149	14	3	174
6	5	488	15	5	461
7	3	191	16	3	149
8	4	300	17	4	315
9	4	388	18	4	399
Out	35	2637	In	36	2684

Texas Top 100

9. Preston Trail Golf Club

I t can be scary to be a forward thinker. There is the possibility of winding up at a dead end if you drive an uncharted avenue.

In real estate, to be too far ahead of your time could result in financial ruin. But that's the kind of gamble that separates the haves from the have-nots. And in 1962, some of Dallas' most promising businessmen and some of its legendary golfers decided to put their money and their reputations on the line.

Stuart Hunt owned some scenic property out on a bumpy, two-lane road 17 miles north of downtown Dallas.

Hunt convinced others like Pollard Simon, Jim Chambers and John Murchison that Dallas would eventually grow in that direction, and they called on Byron Nelson and Ralph Plummer to build a golf course for an all men's club.

"In 1962, I was asked to help build a golf course in North Dallas at a place the owners had decided to call Preston Trail," Nelson remembers in his autobiography, *How I played the Game.*

"At the time, Preston Trail was so far from the heart of Dallas — 17 miles, actually — that everyone thought we were crazy. But we felt the natural direction for Dallas to grow was northward and time proved us right.

"But because of the distance, selling memberships wasn't so easy.

The first 50 were the toughest to get. After that, people figured it was safe and began signing up."

The result was one of Dallas' most prestigious golf clubs. It is one of only two all-male clubs in Texas and one of fewer than 20 in the nation.

After a somewhat vagabond existence that took it from six different clubs over the first 20 years, the Dallas Open was renamed the Byron Nelson Classic in 1968 and moved to Preston Trail, where it enjoyed increased attendance and became one of the strongest events on the PGA Tour. It remained there until 1983, when the tournament moved to the Las Colinas Sports Club.

An all-star cast showed up, including Arnold Palmer, who finished sixth, Jack Nicklaus (10th), Gary Player (fourth) and Billy Casper (17th). But it was Miller Barber who became the first winner with a 10-under 270.

By far the most dominant player at Preston Trail, however, was Tom Watson. Watson, a long-time protégé of Nelson, won the tournament for the first time in 1975 and then won it three consecutive years from 1978–80. If Colonial was Hogan's Alley, then Preston Trail was Tom's Turf.

As you might imagine, one of Texas' greatest players and one of its greatest architects conspired to put together a strong collection of holes that put a premium on shot placement.

Preston Trail Golf Club

17201 Preston Trail Drive
Dallas 75248
972-248-8448
Pro: Gordon Johnson
One of only two all-male clubs in Texas.
From downtown Dallas, take I-635 to Preston Road, then go north to Campbell. Turn left one block to Preston Trail, then left to entrance.

• • •

USGA rating: 73.4
Slope rating: 133
Sand traps: 73
Water holes: 9
Doglegs: 4 left/3 right
Type greens: Bentgrass
Record: 61
Designer: Ralph Plummer
Year opened: 1965

• • •

Hole	Par	Yards	Hole	Par	Yards
1	4	428	10	5	527
2	4	398	11	3	180
3	5	591	12	4	406
4	3	194	13	3	158
5	4	431	14	4	445
6	5	498	15	4	568
7	4	422	16	5	428
8	3	227	17	4	355
9	4	413	18	4	422
Out	36	3602	In	36	3489

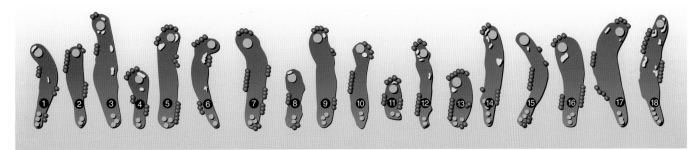

Texas Top 100

10. Walden on Lake Conroe

Naturally beautiful terrain is a rare commodity in Houston, where most of the land is flat, open prairie that requires a great deal of imagination and money to be turned into a golf course. Walden on Lake Conroe is one rare exception where man and nature teamed to create the No. 1 course in the Houston area.

If ever there was a can't-miss opportunity for a golf course architect, this was it. Developers Conrad Weil and Jerry Deutser hired Robert von Hagge and Bruce Devlin to do the job, and they accepted the challenge so readily they moved their corporate offices from Florida to Houston a year later.

At Walden, they were provided with rolling terrain and a dense covering of hardwoods along the southwest shore of Lake Conroe. The challenge was not to mess up what nature took centuries to create.

Before they started, however, they drastically changed the original land plan. Deutser and Weil, like most developers, believed using lakefront property for the golf course instead of home sites was a "waste" of prime real estate. But they reluctantly gave the architects the authority to change the plan to accommodate what turned out to be some of the most unique holes in the state.

While nature provided most of the scenery, the architects moved 300,000 cubic yards of dirt to connect part of the shoreline to a marshy island and actually extend the lakefront property. That area became home of the 589-yard, par-5 No. 11, ranked among the state's best holes in difficulty, beauty and design.

"We didn't want to build just another golf course," Weil says. "We wanted to build a golf course that was special. We gave the architects quite a bit of leeway, more than we originally wanted, but it paid off. We got more than we ever imagined."

Walden is ranked as one of the top courses in the Houston area because of its combination of natural beauty, shot values and maintenance. Like the name Walden indicates, it is a great place for self-examination introspection, not to mention golf. It also is among the most difficult courses to play. All of the holes are memorable with a rare stretch of three consecutive par 5s on Nos. 9, 10 and 11.

Most players will never forget — for better or worse — No. 11. It is a double-dogleg where opportunities for mistakes abound as players must conquer distance, wind, water, sand, trees, and above all, their own nerves.

"Golfers have ample opportunity to hit many types of shots," pro Ron Coville says, "but the premium lies in accurate shots, sound strategy and patience. Disaster is apt to strike on any hole at any time."

Walden on Lake Conroe

13101 Walden Road
Montgomery 77356
409-448-6441
Pro: Ron Coville
A par-72, 6,765-yard private club.
Take I-45 North to Highway 105 in Conroe. Then go west for 12 miles to Walden Road. Turn right to entrance.

• • •

USGA rating: 73.1
Slope rating: 143
Sand traps: 95
Water holes: 11
Doglegs: 4 left/4 right
Type greens: Bermuda
Record: 66
Designers: Robert von Hagge and Bruce Devlin
Year opened: 1976

• • •

Hole	Par	Yards	Hole	Par	Yards
1	4	426	10	5	536
2	5	516	11	5	589
3	4	350	12	3	152
4	3	199	13	4	408
5	4	377	14	3	176
6	3	191	15	4	403
7	4	408	16	5	519
8	4	402	17	3	159
9	5	518	18	4	436
Out	36	3387	In	36	3378

Texas Top 100

11. Deerwood Club

After playing a round of golf at the hallowed Augusta National, late Friendswood Development president John Turner returned to Houston to build the Deerwood Club based on that design.

Turner wanted to build an exclusive club, like Champions Golf Club did some 30 years earlier, for top golfers but without the frills of a normal club.

Turner hired golf legend Byron Nelson and architect Joe Finger to build a course out of the boggy swampland along the shore of Lake Houston with shot values only the best of golfers could appreciate. It was a course that, given today's strict environmental restrictions, might never have been built.

"It was a joy to work with Byron," said Finger, who lives near Nelson at the Riverhill Club in Kerrville. "When we were building Deerwood, he saw things from a perspective that only he could see. Who was I to say he was wrong?"

Nelson was one of the greatest players in the history of the game, with a swing so fluid and so solid that the machine now used to test all golf clubs is named "Iron Byron."

It was with that same repeating swing that Nelson, in 1945, accomplished one of the most remarkable achievements in the history of sports with 11 consecutive victories, a record that will likely persevere. Deerwood, which opened in 1982, ranks at the top of Houston-area golf courses.

Like Champions, Deerwood has one of the best playing memberships in Houston. Among its members are Senior PGA Tour pros Charlie Sifford and Don Massengale, PGA Tour pros John Dowdall and Brad Lardon, Texas State Amateur champ Randy Sonnier and PGA Tour rules official Vaughn Moise.

If nothing else, they stand as a testament to the quality of the course at Deerwood.

Nelson and Finger took unrestrained advantage of the natural environment to present golfers with long, tight fairways that demand accuracy and length off the tee in addition to some of the most undulating putting surfaces in Houston.

Five holes, with the 453-yard, par-4 No. 4 leading the way, are among the most difficult in the Houston area. One pro says No. 4 "borders on the impossible," requiring a long drive and carry over water to a green that's difficult to hit on the approach.

The green on No. 16 was loosely patterned after the No. 8 green at Augusta National Golf Club, home of The Masters.

"This is one of my favorite courses on the tour," says Mike Hill, who won the Sanders in 1991 and '92. "It's a great driving course because the tee shots set up the whole course. If you're not driving well, you're in for some trouble."

Deerwood Club

1717 Forest Garden
Kingwood 77345
281-360-1060
Director of Golf: Scott Curiel
A private, par-72, 7,108-yard club.
From downtown Houston, take U.S. 59
North to Kingwood Drive, then east 5
miles. Right on Forest Garden to club.

• • •

USGA rating: 74.0
Slope rating: 139
Sand traps: 65
Water holes: 15
Doglegs: 4 left/4 right
Type greens: Bermuda
Record: 64
Designers: Joe Finger
    and Byron Nelson
Year opened: 1982

• • •

Hole	Par	Yards	Hole	Par	Yards
1	5	590	10	4	390
2	4	419	11	4	468
3	3	172	12	4	397
4	4	453	13	3	170
5	4	420	14	5	565
6	4	371	15	4	381
7	5	513	16	5	511
8	3	191	17	3	196
9	4	442	18	4	459
Out	36	3571	In	36	3537

Texas Top 100

12. The Quarry Golf Club

This is the era of environmental sensitivity in which Americans are learning to make the most of our natural resources by turning something useless into something useful.

Jack Parker used to grimace every time he drove by the old Alamo Cement plant in San Antonio. The old smokestacks were a San Antonio landmark.

The plant had long been closed and left an 86-acre black hole and 82 acres of unsightly scrub clay for all passers-by to see. It was not the kind of image the Alamo City wanted to project in its drive toward becoming a top tourist destination.

In 1991, Parker and partner Jay Eddy got the opportunity to develop the property. They proceeded to perform the golf course equivalency of pulling a rabbit out of a hat by turning the old rock quarry into one of the most unique courses in America.

The Quarry opened in 1993 and immediately became one of the most unique and one of the best golf courses in Texas.

"Golf courses provide a beautiful, useful greenbelt that might otherwise become a concrete jungle," says Parker, who drew on his 40 years in the golf business to envision a golf course at the site.

"In order to continue productive development, we must convince politicians that golf courses are friendly to the environment. A perfect example is The Quarry, which has transformed a black hole into a beautiful tourist attraction."

The course was designed by Arthur Hills president Keith Foster, who rose to the occasion to produce his first and best solo layout. While the treeless front nine holds its own with a links-type layout that features tall native grasses and mounding, the back nine is built in the bottom of the old cement quarry and is encircled by 130-foot vertical drop quarry walls.

Many golfers have nicknamed the 18 links-style holes as the "Crescendo Course." Golfers start with the friendly first hole and excitement and enthusiasm builds to a crescendo right through the 18th hole. On Nos. 12 and 13, golfers must traverse a 10-acre lake spanned by a 90-foot suspension bridge. The 15th green, at the end of a 528-yard par 5 named "The Wall," lies at the face of a huge stone wall.

Each hole has a name that relates to its particular character traits. They include Alcatraz, Escape from Alcatraz, Gibraltar and, simply, Reload.

No. 17, nicknamed "Reload," is the most dramatic. A 50-foot waterfall greets golfers off the tee with another long dogleg left over a quarry wall.

Says two-time PGA champion Paul Runyan, "This is already one of the 50 best courses in the world."

The Quarry Golf Club

444 E. Basse Road
San Antonio 78209
210-824-4500
Pro: Courtney Connell
A par-71, 6,489-yard daily fee course
From San Antonio, take Highway 37
North, exit Basse Road, go east
to club on right.

• • •

USGA rating: 71.8
Slope rating: 122
Sand traps: 38
Water holes: 7
Doglegs: 3 left/1 right
Type greens: Bermuda
Record: 68
Designer: Keith Foster
Year opened: 1993

• • •

Hole	Par	Yards	Hole	Par	Yards
1	4	388	10	4	474
2	4	453	11	4	370
3	3	168	12	3	205
4	4	325	13	4	362
5	5	544	14	4	442
6	4	383	15	5	528
7	4	399	16	3	242
8	3	158	17	4	386
9	4	349	18	5	564
Out	35	3167	In	36	3573

Texas Top 100

13. TPC at The Woodlands

Originally called The Woodlands East, it was designed as a member and resort course by Robert von Hagge and Bruce Devlin in 1978. The only stipulation was that one week a year it must be challenging enough to be the home of the Houston Open.

There was no consideration of the course becoming one of the PGA Tour's Tournament Players Course collection.

In fact, the TPC formula did not even exist at the time. But after it was built, PGA Tour Commissioner Deane Beman and von Hagge toured the course in 1983 and decided to make it the first course to be converted to a TPC layout. Beman wanted the tournament moved from the West Course, which was never designed with a pro tournament in mind.

"The East Course is pretty doggone good for spectators and we wouldn't accept it if we didn't think it was an incredible golf course or if it wouldn't increase the enjoyment for the spectators," Beman said.

"This course is more difficult — a better test of golf — and it won't even be close on spectator appeal. We are well satisfied with the improvements for this course. We think it will help local sponsors and at the same time help people enjoy the tournament."

The TPC opened in 1985 after a few revisions that included spec-tator mounding to accommodate tournament crowds and 25,000 cubic yards of dirt that was used to raise the fairways on Nos. 9 and 11. Since it opened, it has been one of the favorites in the TPC collection.

"It was an immediate success from the players' standpoint," von Hagge says. "That is especially gratifying since it was not specifi-cally designed in the TPC format and did not benefit the big con-struction budgets of the other TPC facilities."

The idea wasn't to create another of Pete Dye's monsters like the TPC at Sawgrass, site of The Players Championship. Nevertheless, it was ranked by *Golf Digest* as one of the nation's top 25 resort courses.

Players appreciate its good shot values and risk-reward fac-tors. There is opportunity for play-ers with nothing to lose to free-wheel it and post a low score, but there always is an accompanying risk of a big score.

Indeed, the TPC features two of Houston's finest closing holes. The par-4 17th and 18th both require approach shots over water and have been the scene of some spectacular finishes in the Houston Open.

"We're pretty proud of that layout," says Devlin. "We never could understand why the tour never asked us to build any of the TPC layouts that followed. I guess we didn't play politics."

The Woodlands

TPC at The Woodlands

1730 South Millbend
The Woodlands 77380
281-367-7285
Pro: Garry Rippy
A par-72, 7,045-yard public course.
Take I-45 North to Woodlands Parkway,
then west to Grogan's Mill Road. Turn
left to South Millbend, left to entrance.

• • •

USGA rating: 73.6
Slope rating: 135
Sand traps: 64
Water holes: 10
Doglegs: 3 left/5 right
Type greens: Bermuda
Record: 62
Designers: Robert von Hagge
   and Bruce Devlin
Year opened: 1978

• • •

Hole	Par	Yards	Hole	Par	Yards
1	5	515	10	4	430
2	4	364	11	4	421
3	3	165	12	4	393
4	4	418	13	5	530
5	4	460	14	3	195
6	5	577	15	5	525
7	4	413	16	3	177
8	3	222	17	4	376
9	4	427	18	4	437
Out	36	3561	In	36	3484

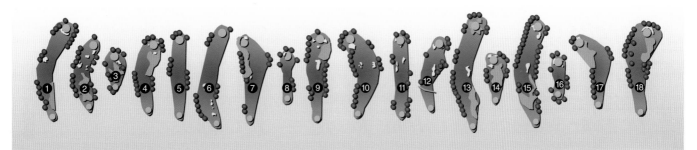

14. Four Seasons Las Colinas Resort — TPC Course

So many factors go into building a golf course, it is difficult to get them right from the start. From obtaining the financing to obtaining the land to obtaining the right architect to the right concept, the path from start to completion is doused with opportunity for failure.

Donald Ross constantly tinkered with Pinehurst No. 2. Augusta National has been tweaked more than Dr. Alister Mackenzie would like to know.

If following in those footsteps is any indication, then the evolutionary process of the Las Colinas Sports Club could also one day lead to greatness.

Over a period of 10 years, Robert Trent Jones Jr. and Jay Morrish have had their say. So have Byron Nelson, Ben Crenshaw and Tom Watson. Contrary to the "too many cooks spoil the soup" adage, this is one that keeps getting better with additional input.

It all started in 1985, when Jones was hired to build a TPC stadium course to become the new home for the PGA Tour's Byron Nelson Classic, which draws annual crowds of 200,000.

That course, with a first green shaped like Texas and a bunker shaped like Oklahoma, was used as the tournament site until 1987, when Morrish built 18 new holes to blend in with the original 18 Jones built.

Holes 1 and 11–18 remain from Jones' original design. Morrish added Nos. 2–10 to arrive at the new TPC layout. The other 18 holes were joined and are known as Cottonwood Valley.

It was ranked in 1992 as among the top three TPC courses and featured the best playing conditions of any course on tour. The par 70 course measures 6,850 yards from the championship tees and is considered an "intelligent course" with rolling, narrow fairways and extensive bunkering.

Grassy mounds stair-step around the majority of greens to provide viewing in this Stadium Golf concept. The emphasis was on shot-play ability and requiring players to work the ball.

Morrish was called again in late 1992 to begin an extensive update of the TPC which once again dramatically changed the way the course looks and plays.

More than $1 million worth of landscape and design enhancements were completed in April, 1993. Throughout the course, 10 new bunkers and eight new tees were added. A scenic lake on No. 17 created a beautiful, if not intimidating, view from the tee.

"The players term the course as very fair," Crenshaw says. "The wind is such a big factor here, we tried to adjust for it by opening up the entrances to the greens."

One of the highlights at the Four Seasons Las Colinas is a nine-foot tall bronze statue of Byron Nelson, which was erected in 1992 to celebrate Nelson's 80th birthday.

Four Seasons Resort and Club DALLAS AT LAS COLINAS

TPC Las Colinas

Four Seasons Las Colinas Resort TPC Course

4200 N. MacArthur Boulevard
Irving 75038
214-717-2520
Director: Michael Abbott
This is a 36-hole resort and country club. From Dallas, take I-35 to Highway 183, west to MacArthur Boulevard, 3 miles north to resort entrance.

• • •

USGA rating: 73.5
Slope rating: 135
Sand traps: 56
Water holes: 7
Doglegs: 3 left/3 right
Type greens: Bentgrass
Record: 61
Designers: Robert Trent Jones Jr. and Jay Morrish
Year opened: 1986

Hole	Par	Yards	Hole	Par	Yards
1	4	385	10	4	447
2	3	176	11	4	331
3	4	474	12	4	426
4	4	423	13	3	183
5	3	174	14	4	390
6	4	396	15	4	445
7	5	533	16	5	554
8	4	451	17	3	217
9	4	406	18	4	415
Out	35	3418	In	35	3408

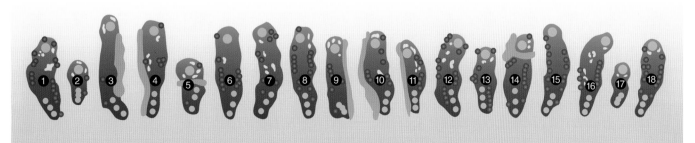

15. Gleneagles Country Club — King's Course

Just when it appeared the market for upscale country clubs had run dry and the golf market began turning to daily-fee courses instead, former Dallas mayor Robert Folsom and world-renowned architect Robert von Hagge decided there was room for one more exclusive private club.

It would be exclusive. The homes would be of the luxury variety. The golf course(s) would be awesome. And it would be called Gleneagles Country Club.

The master plan in Plano originally called for only one spectacular golf course, but initial real-estate sales were so brisk that Folsom eventually asked von Hagge and partner Bruce Devlin to squeeze in an additional 36 holes for more home sites.

Blessed with one of their biggest construction budgets to date, von Hagge and Devlin produced two links-style layouts that continually rank among Dallas' best and toughest layouts.

"Bob gave us the freedom to do whatever we wanted with the land," von Hagge said. "He just said, 'Don't do anything nuts.' There was much debate over one or two courses — the first concept was better," von Hagge said. "The first 18 began but the lots were selling so good that they eventually decided to build 27 holes and finally 36. There wasn't quite enough land for that, and we had to squeeze some holes in."

Von Hagge and Devlin decided on a links course with moguls used to define the fairways. All holes feature excellent shot values.

Longtime Dallas-area pro Eldridge Miles later wrote von Hagge: "I have played many of your courses and have always liked your work; however, I believe the Gleneagles course represents some of the most creative, interesting and challenging work that you have ever produced."

There were a lot of architects toward the end, von Hagge said, and he and Devlin eventually sold their half of the interest to Folsom over a disagreement in the size of the clubhouse. Von Hagge and Devlin believed a monstrous clubhouse would become a financial liability to a young club, and that eventually proved true when Folsom later declared bankruptcy and the club became the flagship of Club Corporation of America.

The Kings Course is the favorite of club members. It is a lot like the Queens Course in many ways, but has more trees and water comes into play. It also has deep sand and grass bunkers with Scottish-looking trees. It's the favorite of members.

The Queens is open with few trees. It's Scottish-looking with deep sand and grass bunkers and rolling Hills and is very difficult with any kind of wind. Nos. 17 and 18 are two of the toughest holes in the state.

Gleneagles

Gleneagles Country Club King's Course

5401 W. Park Boulevard
Plano 75093
214-867-6666
Pro: Eldridge Miles
A private 36-hole club. From Dallas take North Dallas Tollway to West Park Boulevard. Go right on West Park 1.5 miles to entrance on the left.

• • •

USGA rating: 74
Slope rating: 136
Sand traps: 75
Water holes: 17
Doglegs: 3 left/6 right
Type greens: Bentgrass
Record: 63
Designers: Robert von Hagge
          and Bruce Devlin
Year opened: 1985

Hole	Par	Yards	Hole	Par	Yards
1	4	417	10	5	484
2	4	439	11	3	218
3	4	383	12	5	496
4	3	178	13	4	329
5	5	579	14	4	462
6	4	377	15	3	163
7	3	200	16	5	532
8	5	539	17	3	197
9	4	377	18	4	436
Out	36	3489	In	36	3317

16. Lochinvar Golf Club

Lochinvar is synonymous with exclusivity. It is one of only two all-male clubs in Texas and one of fewer than 20 in the United States.

It is one of only two Jack Nicklaus-designed courses in the state and one of only four in the area with bentgrass greens. It has a membership of only 250 and an initiation fee of $50,000.

Houston businessman Curtis Hankamer got the idea for a stag club in the late 1960s after playing Dallas' Preston Trail Golf Club, the state's only other all-male club. Over the next 10 years, Hankamer pieced together seven parcels of land for a total of 200 acres loaded with tall pines near Intercontinental Airport.

In keeping with the all-male theme, he named it after Lochinvar, the original male chauvinist and hero of the Sir Walter Scott poem "Marmion."

Among the members are past or present touring pros Jay Hebert, Bruce Devlin, Blaine McCallister and Dave Marr.

"Men do all of the voting for officers and club policy, and all of the memberships are listed under men's names," said Hankamer, who eventually had a major falling out with the members and sold the club.

"We want to tee up without fear of women's groups ahead of us. Generally, they create slow play. We want to play in uncrowded conditions on any given day or week. If the women object, let them build their own course. They control all of the money, don't they?"

Nicklaus helped opened the course on Nov. 3, 1980, when he played a round with some of the club founders, among them former Houston Oiler quarterback Jacky Lee.

"Lochinvar is one of the finest golf facilities I've seen," Nicklaus said. "It represents the efforts of a group of successful businessmen who love golf and demanded the best in course design, maintenance and practice facilities."

The course has some Scottish-links style features with its grass bunkers and "valley of sin" undulations. It hosted the 1989 U.S. Senior Amateur and is ranked among the top courses in the state.

Legendary teaching pro Claude Harmon, who won the Masters in 1948, was the senior pro at Lochinvar the first several years and one of his sons, Claude "Butch" Harmon Jr., followed in his footsteps and was golf director until 1997. Harmon's students — including Tiger Woods and Greg Norman — were frequent attendees of the Lochinvar practice tee.

The 393-yard, par-4 12th is Lochinvar's signature hole. It requires a perfectly placed drive to reach the green in two. The green is protected by a stream and a rock wall in the front and by a bunker in the rear.

Lochinvar

Lochinvar Golf Club

200 Farrell Road
Houston 77073
281-821-0220
Pro: Brian Smith

An exclusive all-male club in north Houston. From Houston, take I-45 to Rankin Road, right on Rankin to Hardy Toll Road, left on Hardy to Farrell Road, then right to club.

• • •

USGA rating: 72
Slope rating: 126
Sand traps: 58
Water holes: 8
Doglegs: 5 left/2 right
Type greens: Bentgrass
Record: 60
Designer: Jack Nicklaus
Year opened: 1980

• • •

Hole	Par	Yards	Hole	Par	Yards
1	4	392	10	4	437
2	3	192	11	3	172
3	4	412	12	4	393
4	5	511	13	4	446
5	4	366	14	3	184
6	4	420	15	5	500
7	3	175	16	4	449
8	4	403	17	4	388
9	5	520	18	5	519
Out	36	3391	In	36	3488

17. Dallas Athletic Club — Blue Course

Every golf course has its heyday, but Dallas Athletic Club has had the good fortune of having more than its share.

DAC started out as a popular downtown club more for tennis and social purposes. For those members who liked to play golf, the club had an arrangement for its members to play on the now defunct Glen Lakes Country Club.

By 1952, however, the club totaled 3,500 members and Glen Lakes was busting at the seams. So on Nov. 25, 1952, members voted to build a country club on a 350-acre site in northeast Dallas.

The land, formerly part of the Chapman Ranch, was sold for $400 an acre for a total of $140,000. The club financed the golf courses with a mere $48 increase in monthly dues from $150 to $198 annually. The club was originally known as Dallas Athletic Club Country Club.

The club celebrated its 10-year anniversary in August 1963, when it played host to the PGA Championship and drew national attention. Crowds endured record temperatures ranging up to 113 degrees — still the hottest week on record in Texas — to get a glimpse of Jack Nicklaus and Arnold Palmer vying for one of golf's four major championships.

Nicklaus, at the age of 23, was the winner joining Ben Hogan, Byron Nelson and Gene Sarazen as the only men in golf history to win the PGA, U.S. Open and the Masters. Nicklaus outdueled little-known pro Dave Ragan for a 2-shot victory with rounds of 69-73-69-68.

In 1985, DAC began its second heyday when Nicklaus the architect returned to renovate Ralph Plummer's original layouts to bring the club once again to the top of the charts in Dallas golf.

Plummer originally built the Blue Course in 1954 and the Gold Course in 1962, but his layouts were relatively flat, the trees still young and the greens relatively unimaginative.

But thanks to Nicklaus, the courses now feature bentgrass greens, waterfalls around the fifth and 11th greens, mounding and grass bunkers that make the course much more challenging.

"You could hold a major tournament on either the Gold or the Blue Course here," Nicklaus said at the unveiling of the new and improved Gold Course. There used to be a big disparity between the Blue and Gold courses. The Gold was considered much easier, and most of the club's better players preferred to play the Blue.

But Nicklaus returned in 1989 to redesign the Gold, which now stretches more than 7,000 yards. It features eight lakes and many mature trees, combined with modern design techniques to provide golfers a variety of interesting golf shots on every hole.

DALLAS ATHLETIC CLUB

Dallas Athletic Club Blue Course

4111 La Prada Drive
Dallas 75228
214-279-3671
Pro: Dennis Ewing
A 36-hole private club. From downtown Dallas, take I-75 North to I-635, then go east on I-635 to La Prada Drive. Turn right on La Prada to club entrance on the right.

• • •

USGA rating: 73.4
Slope rating: 133
Sand traps: 36
Water holes: 9
Doglegs: 5 left/3 right
Type greens: Bentgrass
Record: 65
Designer: Ralph Plummer
Year opened: 1954

• • •

Hole	Par	Yards	Hole	Par	Yards
1	5	496	10	5	487
2	4	390	11	4	344
3	5	531	12	4	324
4	3	179	13	5	513
5	4	360	14	3	157
6	4	364	15	4	370
7	3	166	16	3	175
8	4	280	17	4	398
9	4	377	18	4	382
Out	36	3143	In	36	3150

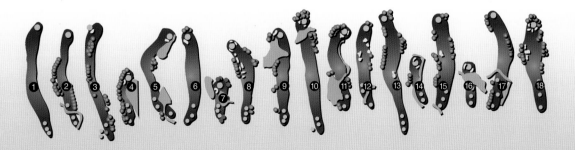

18. Barton Creek Resort & Country Club — Crenshaw Course

To many golf purists, Ben Crenshaw is a hero.

Crenshaw is a devout historian who longs to protect the game's tradition, and the Austin native eschews many of the modern methods associated with the game in the 1990s.

Crenshaw, the pro golfer, isn't likely to be seen using a graphite driver or an extra–long putter. And you can be sure when it comes to golf course design that Crenshaw, the architect, avoids the use of island greens, double railroad ties and target golf concepts that require players to hit a certain type of shot into a green or off the tee.

Crenshaw learned the game from one of its greatest teachers, Harvey Penick. As a youth growing up in Austin, he had the rare opportunity to be around Penick on a daily basis, which helped him form the foundation of a pro career that earned him 20 victories on the PGA Tour.

When it comes to golf course design, Crenshaw simply learned from history. His appreciation of history and its importance to the game are evident in every course he builds. While everything in the golf world keeps hurtling forward with new advancements, Crenshaw keeps trying to take the game backwards to its roots.

That's what makes the Crenshaw Course at Barton Creek such a delight to fans of traditional golfing venues. Just across the street from its flashier sibling designed by Tom Fazio, the Crenshaw course is a monument to tradition and the way golf was meant to be played.

The course measures 6,678 yards from the back tees with a par of 71. The fairways and greens are large enough to land a small plane on, but there is plenty of Hill Country trouble to get in your way.

"We're committed to the philosophy that what makes it fun for the average golfer can make it difficult for the better player," says Bill Coore, Crenshaw's golf course design partner.

Such is the case on this layout. The greens are large enough that many golfers can brag about hitting all 18 in regulation, but once they arrive at their ball they may find a putt of 100 feet or more and a potential three-putt may be in store.

"This is one course where you can hit most greens," Crenshaw said "and still shoot a high score."

Crenshaw has long been recognized as one of the top putters in golf, and it should come as no surprise that the golf courses he designs demand no less of its players. There are plenty of challenging putts on these large, undulating Bermuda greens.

The par-3 17th is just 125 yards, but requires a shot over a large ravine with the green sloping toward the drop-off.

As far as the beautiful Hill Country views, Crenshaw doesn't take any credit for those.

BARTON CREEK
COUNTRY CLUB

Barton Creek Resort and Country Club Crenshaw Course

8212 Barton Club Drive
Austin 78735
800-336-6158
Director of Golf: Brent Buckman
One of three 18-hole courses. Take I-35 South to Ben White Boulevard, go west to Bee Caves Road, go south 1.1 miles to Barton Creek Boulevard, go left 1.8 miles turn left on Barton Club Drive.

• • •

USGA Rating: 71
Slope rating: 124
Sand traps: 33
Water holes: 0
Doglegs: 5 left/5 right
Type greens: Bermuda
Record: 63
Designer: Ben Crenshaw
Year opened: 1986

Hole	Par	Yards	Hole	Par	Yards
1	4	354	10	4	455
2	5	470	11	3	185
3	4	370	12	5	535
4	4	424	13	3	160
5	3	210	14	4	410
6	4	464	15	5	590
7	4	345	16	5	575
8	3	169	17	3	125
9	4	444	18	4	393
Out	35	3250	In	36	3428

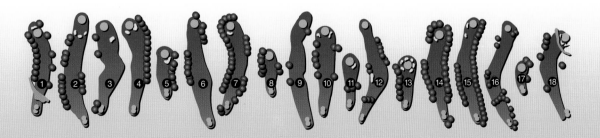

19. Kingwood Country Club — Forest Course

FOREST COURSE

Before the first shot had been officially fired on the Forest Course at Kingwood Country Club, it already had received national recognition as host site of the Kevin Costner movie, "Tin Cup."

The movie was a rags–to–riches love story in which Costner, a West Texas driving range pro, qualified for the U.S. Open and held the lead going into the final day when he decided to "go for broke" on the final hole.

His approach to the final green required a heroic 230-yard carry over water to the green but, instead of letting common sense prevail and laying up, he ended up using every ball in his bag and they all found a watery grave short of their target.

It was with that same "go for broke" mentality that architect Ken Dye designed the Forest Course. Unlike Costner, Dye pulled it off. Dye faced a difficult challenge to build a course that was uniquely different from the first three and could also withstand occasional flooding inherent to its location amidst the swampy backwaters of Lake Houston.

In fact, much of Dye's early work on the Forest Course was washed away when a 1994 flood completely covered the course and washed away much of the sod and irrigation network and forced construction crews to start over.

While most Houston-area golf courses have been built below normal ground level with convex fairways to repel rainfall, Dye built his course underground — between six–to–eight feet below the surrounding property.

As you walk down the fairways, tree trunks on the surrounding property are at eye level. By building the golf course to receive rainfall and get rid of it through an underground drainage system, enabled Dye to use extensive mounding, use deep, gaping bunkers and collection areas. There are few level lies to be found.

"If the land has no redeeming qualities, you have to create them," Dye says.

The course measures 7,092 yards and has a slope rating of 138 from the back tees. There is little rest for the weary anywhere, but it has a great closing stretch of holes starting with the 473-yard par-4 15th. In addition to its near par-5 length, the 15th requires a long-iron or fairway wood on the approach to a green protected by water on the front and left sides and by a series of four bunkers on the right.

"I don't think there is a doubt that this is the best course we've done in Houston," Dye said. "In terms of the creativeness that went into the design, it may be the best we've ever done anywhere. We're really happy with how it turned out."

Kingwood Country Club Forest Course

1700 Lake Kingwood Trail
Kingwood 77339
281-358-2171
Pro: David Preisler
This is a 72-hole private club.
From downtown Houston, take U.S. 59
North to Kingwood Drive, then right
six miles on Lake Kingwood Trail
to entrance.

• • •

USGA rating: 74.6
Slope rating: 138
Sand traps: 60
Water holes: 13
Doglegs: 5 left/2 right
Type greens: Bermuda
Record: 66
Designer: Ken Dye
Year opened: 1996

Hole	Par	Yards	Hole	Par	Yards
1	4	371	10	5	510
2	4	425	11	3	210
3	5	556	12	4	343
4	3	202	13	4	369
5	5	530	14	3	178
6	3	158	15	4	473
7	4	478	16	4	392
8	4	414	17	5	602
9	4	426	18	4	455
Out	36	3475	In	36	3532

20. Northwood Club

The war was over. Since the last golf course had been built in Dallas, two world wars and a Great Depression had passed. It was time to play.

Postwar shortages of labor and materials had eased. Shorter working hours and larger pay envelopes once again made the country-club lifestyle affordable.

So on Sept. 4, 1946, a group of Dallas businessmen met at Highland Park Village and formed the charter membership of the Northwood Club. Within three months, they had purchased 160 acres of wooded, rolling land that once was owned by oilman E.E. Buddy Fogelson for $165,000.

The land was bordered by White Rock Creek and its tributaries on the northern fringe of Dallas. Within three months, workmen began hacking out underbrush and Indianapolis-based architect Bill Diddel designed a layout of more than 7,000 yards, the longest in Dallas at the time. The construction took 18 months and cost $100,000.

While some non-golfers contend the game is not a sport because it requires no contact, the game's call for mental discipline and physical coordination was not lost on Diddel.

Diddel was an all-around athlete who lettered in baseball, basketball, football and track at Wabash College in Indiana. He led Wabash to a national basketball title and later coached for one season at his alma mater.

He would have played golf in college, too, but the school didn't have a team. Still, he achieved success by winning the Indiana Amateur in 1905, '06, '07, '10 and '12. Perhaps his most remarkable accomplishment is that he retained his golfing skills throughout his life and shot his age more times (over 1,000 rounds in all) than any golfer in history before he died in 1985 at the age of 101.

While Northwood was the only Texas golf course Diddel built, it is perhaps one of his best. To be sure, it is the only one good enough to host the U.S. Open. Only five years after he finished designing the Northwood layout, the best players in the world came to Dallas to play it for the 1952 U.S. Open won by Julius Boros.

While the memories of the '52 Open have faded, Diddel left behind a strong collection of holes that were updated in 1990 by Tom Weiskopf and Jay Morrish. Eight different holes were nominated as among the toughest in Dallas-Fort Worth.

Among them are the 213-yard, par-3 16th, the 453-yard, par-4 eighth and the 455-yard, par-4 11th. All require strong long-iron play to reach the green in regulation. On the 16th, players must tee off through a chute of trees to a green protected by bunkers front, right and left with water all the way down on the far left.

Northwood Club

6524 Alpha Road
Dallas 75240
214-239-1366
Pro: Bob Elliott
A par-71, 6,835-yard private club that hosted the 1952 U.S. Open. From downtown Dallas, take Dallas North Tollway to Alpha Road, then turn east on Alpha to course entrance.

• • •

USGA rating: 73
Slope rating: 130
Sand traps: 50
Water holes: 6
Doglegs: 4 left/ 2 right
Type greens: Bentgrass
Record: N/A
Designer: Bill Diddel
Year opened: 1947

• • •

Hole	Par	Yards	Hole	Par	Yards
1	4	354	10	4	380
2	5	564	11	4	455
3	4	454	12	3	186
4	4	446	13	4	367
5	3	161	14	5	500
6	5	468	15	4	404
7	4	418	16	3	213
8	4	453	17	4	394
9	3	210	18	4	408
Out	36	3528	In	35	3307

21. Club at Sonterra — Sunburst Course

obert von Hagge and Bruce Devlin have built golf courses all over the world. Innovative and sometimes controversial, their courses rarely fail to grab your attention. Rarely is that more evident than with the Club at Sonterra, where in 1985 they conspired with gas station moguls Tom Turner Sr. and son to build their dream course to entertain their friends.

What evolved was nothing short of a masterpiece now known as Sunburst. It is a 7,070-yard layout that ranks among the best courses in the Hill Country and has three of its toughest holes. Needless to say, it is one of von Hagge's favorites.

The club gained instant popularity and grew so quickly that the Turners, instead of building another course, annexed the old Canyon Creek Country Club layout, now known as Deer Canyon, to form the only 36-hole country club complex within the San Antonio city limits.

What makes Sunburst so outstanding is the variety of shots required and the combination of challenge and natural beauty. It is the southernmost course in Texas to have bentgrass greens. Like all von Hagge-Devlin layouts, the course is a target layout with plenty of water, natural areas, elevated greens and elevation changes from tee to green.

There are very few trees in play, but 66 bunkers give golfers incentive to keep the ball in the fairway.

Take for example, the par-5 first hole. From the back tees, it measures 571 yards and doglegs right. The green is elevated and fronted by large sand traps. The pine tree on the front left makes it difficult for anyone to get close.

The second hole features a double fairway with trees in the middle. The 532-yard par-5 fifth hole is another killer which requires golfers to hit a blind tee shot over a ridge to a fairway that slopes toward an out-of-bounds area.

While the first and fifth are beasts, No. 6 is certainly a beauty. At 165 yards, it is acknowledged as one of the prettiest in the state with a tee shot over a waterfall and large lake to a small green. The hole leaves little margin for error, making proper judgment of wind conditions and club selection vital.

Turner sold Sonterra to investor Kiyonori Higa in April 1990, making it one of the first Japanese-owned courses in Texas. Deer Canyon, located on the opposite side of Loop 1604, first opened in 1964 and served as a private 18-hole club for 20 years. The club was purchased by Turner in 1984 and underwent a renovation by von Hagge and Devlin. Unlike the North, it has no water and Bermuda greens and plays through acre upon acre of large oak trees.

Club at Sonterra Sunburst Course

901 Sonterra
San Antonio 78258
210-496-1500
Pro: Gary Bailey
A 36-hole private club. From San Antonio, take Highway 281 North to Loop 1604, take access road left to Stone Oak Parkway, left to Sonterra, club is on left.

• • •

USGA rating: 74.7
Slope rating: 137
Sand traps: 66
Water holes: 9
Doglegs: 5 left/6 right
Type greens: Bentgrass
Record: 69
Designers: Robert von Hagge
and Bruce Devlin
Year opened: 1985

• • •

Hole	Par	Yards	Hole	Par	Yards
1	5	571	10	3	173
2	4	467	11	4	414
3	3	169	12	4	391
4	4	410	13	5	513
5	5	532	14	3	192
6	3	165	15	5	577
7	4	433	16	4	372
8	4	422	17	4	427
9	4	426	18	4	416
Out	36	3595	In	36	3595

22. *Stonebriar Country Club*

Throughout his career Joe Finger took pride in building low-budget golf courses that were easy to maintain but strong enough to challenge the best players in the game.

Finger and Byron Nelson had only a small percentage of input on this modern layout designed by Houston-based architect Ken Dye, but it was only appropriate that his last course before retirement was his most expensive.

Stonebriar was built at a cost of about $5 million and has all the modern features of waterfalls, intricate stone work, heavy contouring and sharp shadow lines.

You might say they got their money's worth, since it was nominated as one of *Golf Digest's* Best New Private Courses in America in 1989. Stonebriar hosted the Senior PGA Tour's Muratec Seniors Reunion from 1989–1993 and featured two of the most difficult holes on the senior circuit and also has hosted the LPGA Skins Game.

"Stonebriar is an outstanding, modern golf course," Finger says. "It has some spectacular landscaping and waterfall holes and it has dramatic shadow lines that make it a pleasure to look at and play."

The course plays 7,064 yards with a rating of 74.9 and a 140 slope rating. It features six long par 4s over 420 yards, and two par 3s of 215 yards.

Many of the greens are tucked into the corner of one of four interconnecting lakes that come into play on 13 holes, requiring accuracy on play from the fairways.

No. 9 was the hardest hole on the Senior PGA Tour each of the last two years. In 1992, the senior pros had an average score of 4.675. There were only nine birdies the entire week.

Three different bodies of water converge to leave virtually no landing area off the tee beyond 225 yards.

Two ponds on the right side run all the way to the green, and a creek runs from the landing area to the green on the left to tighten the landing area even more. That means players still face a long iron approach to a kidney-shaped green that is protected by water on the right.

No. 15 is a 423-yard par 4 that ranked as the eighth most difficult on the senior tour in 1992. A creek runs all the way down the right side from tee to green, then players must hit their approach to a double-green shared with the seventh hole.

In 1991, Stonebriar was bought by developer Ross Perot Jr.'s Hillwood Investment Corp. and Club Corporation of America for an estimated $25 million.

Hillwood now runs the real estate operation and CCA, which owns and operates 16 clubs in the DFW area, manages the golf operations.

Stonebriar Country Club

5050 Country Club Drive
Frisco 75034
214-625-5050
Pro: Bill Andre
A par-72, 7,064-yard private club.
From Dallas, take the Dallas North Tollway to Route 121. Go left one mile to club entrance on the right.

• • •

USGA rating: 74.9
Slope rating: 140
Sand traps: 59
Water holes: 10
Doglegs: 3 left/2 right
Type greens: Bentgrass
Record: 64
Designers: Ken Dye, Joe Finger
*   and Byron Nelson*
Year opened: 1988

• • •

Hole	Par	Yards	Hole	Par	Yards
1	4	382	10	4	366
2	3	215	11	4	442
3	5	568	12	4	363
4	4	465	13	4	436
5	4	443	14	3	218
6	3	148	15	4	423
7	4	327	16	3	509
8	5	577	17	4	188
9	4	438	18	5	556
Out	36	3563	In	36	3501

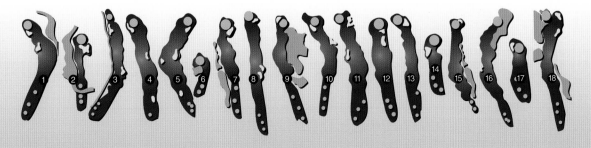

23. Clubs at Stonebridge — Dye Course

If you want to build a golf course that will bring pro golfers to their knees, who ya, gonna call?

If you want to build a golf course that will stand out from the crowd, who ya, gonna call?

First, call Pete Dye.

Then call 911.

Since leaving the insurance business to design golf courses in the 1960s, Dye has become well-known for building the toughest golf courses in America. It has become his calling card and, to be sure, he is called quite frequently.

So when developers of Stonebridge Country Club wanted to host a Senior PGA Tour event in Dallas, Dye was the man they called. And he delivered in classic Dye fashion, producing a golf course that is the most difficult in the state with a rating of 76.3 from the back tees.

To wit: No. 18 is a 477-yard par 4 that curves left around a lake that runs from tee to green. It requires a pinpoint long iron or fairway wood to a green that is poised perilously close to the water's edge.

Nos. 6 (470 yards) and No. 9 (461 yards) are very similar but curve to the right around the water's edge. Dye gives golfers the opportunity to decide how much of the water they feel lucky enough to carry. Anything to the right is wet.

No. 6 requires a definite carry of about 180 yards off the tee, but you'll need to hit it much longer to have any hopes of getting home in two.

On the approach on both holes, you'll still have a long iron in your hand as you try to hit a narrow green protected by water on the right side. Anything right is wet.

The vast 6,687-acre golf/real estate complex was developed by Dallasite Richard Strauss but fell into the hands of the RTC before Mobil Land Development purchased it from federal regulators in 1991 for $34 million — only 20 percent of what it cost to originally build it.

The community features two 18-hole golf courses, a beach and tennis club, 13 lakes and more than five miles of pedestrian trails.

"We probably couldn't have afforded to build what's there," Mr. Midtbo said. "There are not many opportunities like Stonebridge Ranch."

"When they first started out, they were trying to build a golf course for a championship," says Dye, who believes Stonebridge is tougher than his famed PGA West course in Palm Springs.

"Right now, Stonebridge is the best conditioned golf course in Dallas. We have bentgrass on the greens and they've done very well out there. And we went to Texas A&M and we got a hybrid fescue growing in the rough, so it's not all Bermuda. It gives a massive contrast."

STONEBRIDGE
COUNTRY CLUB

Clubs at Stonebridge Dye Course

7003 Beacon Hill Road
McKinney 75070
Main: 214-540-1000
Pro: Stuart Pierce
A private, 36-hole club.
From Dallas, take I-75 North to Virginia Parkway. Go west 8 miles to Stonebridge Drive, then south 1/4 mile to Beacon Hill. Turn right to entrance.

• • •

USGA rating: 76.3
Slope rating: 141
Sand traps: 69
Water holes: 9
Doglegs: 3 left/2 right
Type greens: Bentgrass
Record: 68
Designer: Pete Dye
Year opened: 1988

• • •

Hole	Par	Yards	Hole	Par	Yards
1	4	415	10	4	406
2	4	342	11	4	418
3	5	514	12	3	205
4	4	432	13	5	544
5	3	209	14	4	396
6	4	470	15	4	464
7	5	540	16	5	616
8	3	179	17	3	224
9	4	461	18	4	477
Out	36	3562	In	36	3750

Texas Top 100

24. Horseshoe Bay Resort — Slick Rock Course

When Wayne and Norman Hurd first began the planning stages for Horseshoe Bay Resort, they had a couple of options. They wanted golf to be the center of attention for this upscale resort, and they wanted the golf experience to be like no other.

So who better to call than Robert Trent Jones Sr.? As the most prolific and influential golf course architect in the 20th century, Jones arrived on the scene in 1974 and took full advantage of all the elements that nature had to offer when he built the first of three courses.

The land sits on a pristine hillside overlooking the waters of Lake LBJ and the surrounding Hill Country.

"I know of no area, including those known for several courses, that has a more interesting variety of golf than Horseshoe Bay," Jones says. "I rank this among the best in the world."

Slick Rock was the original course at Horseshoe Bay and embodies the Jones philosophy of "hard par, easy bogey." The course is characterized by Jones' hallmark — five sets of tees — enabling the course to be continually changing from day to day and challenging but fun for players of all levels.

Slick Rock plays just 6,834 yards to a par of 72 and a slope rating of 125. The course has been rated among the best in the nation, and the *Dallas Morning News* ranks it as the No. 2 resort course in Texas.

Slick Rock showcases many of Jones' design character traits. The front nine winds through many different kinds of trees, flowers and granite outcroppings. The back nine is more open and features the trademark hole at Horseshoe Bay.

The 14th has a $1–million waterfall that continually pumps 8,000 gallons of water near the green with a cart path going right through the middle of the fall.

"It's a true resort course that's Texas friendly," one pro says. "The waterfall is spectacular with a colorful mixture of trees and wildflowers."

The finishing three holes at Slick Rock are tough enough with water on two and the 18th green situated on an elevated spot with another panoramic view.

The course features bentgrass greens, which offer a faster, truer putting surface but are sometimes difficult to maintain during the hot, steamy Texas summers. Rotating fans on several holes cool the greens and the golfers who may be overheated by these challenges.

No. 17 is a 219-yard par 3 that requires a carry over water. No. 12 is a 530-yard par 5 with a lake protecting the green on three sides. No. 7 is the longest par 4 at 421 yards, where golfers must work their drives around a bunker in the center of the fairway.

Horseshoe Bay Resort Slick Rock Course

PO Box 7766
Horseshoe Bay 78654
800-292-1545
Director of Golf: Scott McDonough
This is one of three 18-hole courses at this exclusive resort. From downtown Austin, take Highway 71 West to Highway 281, go north to FM 2147, left to Horseshoe Bay.

• • •

USGA rating: 72.6
Slope rating: 125
Sand traps: 72
Water holes: 12
Doglegs: 3 left/4 right
Type greens: Bentgrass
Record: 62
Designer: Robert Trent Jones Sr.
Year opened: 1974

• • •

Hole	Par	Yards	Hole	Par	Yards
1	4	389	10	5	580
2	3	162	11	4	344
3	5	575	12	5	530
4	4	394	13	3	188
5	5	503	14	4	361
6	4	385	15	4	383
7	4	421	16	4	419
8	3	190	17	3	219
9	4	371	18	4	420
Out	36	3,390	In	36	3,444

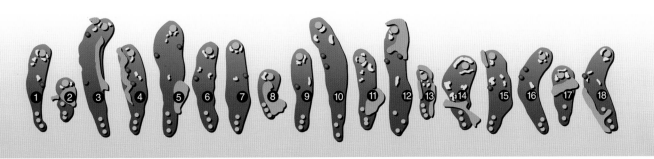

Texas Top 100

25. Bear Creek Golf Club — West Course

For the first 70 years of golf in Dallas/Fort Worth, to find a golf course you could play and be sure the layout was challenging, the grass was green and the greens rolled true, you had to join a country club. No ifs, ands or buts about it.

But 1980 was a turning point in D/FW golf. With golf courses becoming too expensive for most municipalities, private investors and major corporations got involved in the golf business.

They could spend more money to build and maintain better golf courses. And golfers would be willing to pay for it.

These "country clubs for the day" offered public links players the best of both worlds. They got a well-manicured, championship layout and a country-club atmosphere without a hefty initiation fee or monthly dues.

At the front of this trend was Bear Creek Golf Club, where internationally acclaimed architect Ted Robinson designed two courses in the shadow of D/FW Airport to serve residents and business travelers looking for a golf course that was a cut above the usual "municipal" fare.

Woodbine Development sold the golf course operations to Dallas-based Club Corp. in 1994. Then, and now, Bear Creek has done exactly what it set out to do.

"Our program out here has always been to maintain two courses in the best condition in the Southwest," said Bear Creek pro Larry Box. "Club Corp recognizes that and wants to maintain that level. The staff remains intact, so I see nothing but positives in all areas."

The layouts themselves have maintained their status as among the most challenging public courses in the area. Both courses have been ranked on *Golf Digest's* list of Top 25 Non-Private Courses.

"I think a lot of people would be surprised what they would find right here in the shadow of the airport," head pro Larry Box says. "The golf courses are challenging and beautifully landscaped."

Robinson, who has built many resort layouts in California and Hawaii, made his first venture to Texas to build two layouts that are very similar in looks and equally challenging.

The average player seems to prefer the West Course mainly because after the first seven holes, the course becomes a fairly wide open track.

On the West, the signature hole is the 175-yard, par-3 17th, which plays over and alongside a small lake.

The 380-yard, par-4 No. 7 is the most demanding hole on the West, playing over water and into the wind.

No. 6 is a 525-yard par 5 where players hit over a hill to a blind fairway, then across a creek to reach the green.

Bear Creek Golf Club West Course

3500 W Airfield Drive
Dallas 75261
(972) 615-6800
Director of Golf: Larry Box
A 36-hole daily fee facility at D/FW Airport. From Highway 183, go north on Highway 360 for 3 miles, take MidCities exit east, club is on the right.

• • •

USGA rating: 72.7
Slope rating: 125
Sand traps: 56
Water holes: 11
Doglegs: 3 left/2 right
Type greens: Bentgrass
Record: 62
Designer: Ted Robinson
Year opened: 1980

• • •

Hole	Par	Yards	Hole	Par	Yards
1	4	370	10	5	526
2	4	385	11	4	420
3	4	430	12	4	377
4	5	505	13	4	372
5	3	187	14	3	181
6	5	525	15	5	503
7	4	380	16	4	358
8	3	185	17	3	175
9	4	388	18	4	403
Out	36	3355	In	36	3315

Texas Top 100

26. Austin Country Club

Harvey Penick is gone, but his life and lessons will live forever.

This is where it all started for Penick, who in 1913 became a caddie for 20 cents a day, became head pro at Austin Country Club upon graduation from high school and eventually became one of the greatest teachers the game has known.

While Penick died April 2, 1995, at the age of 90, his legacy lives on. Penick's son, Tinsley, succeeded him as the head pro in 1971. And standing near the ninth green is a bronze monument of Penick showing him dispensing some of his wisdom to Tom Kite, one of the PGA Tour's all-time money leaders.

The current Austin Country Club layout, on the shores of Lake Austin by the Colorado River, is the third site for the club originally chartered in 1898.

Many members of this famed club, one of the two oldest in the state, claim the newest version designed by Pete Dye in 1984 is the hardest and most scenic of the three and ranks among the best in the state.

The original nine-hole, sand-green course near downtown was walked off by a committee of members, led by Lewis Hancock. Penick's first bit of advice to the members at ACC came in 1924 when he convinced them to change from sand to grass greens.

To achieve the changeover,

the club hired John Bredemus, the state's original professional golf course architect.

When ACC made its first move to Riverside Drive in 1950, where Kite and Crenshaw honed their skills before going on to the PGA Tour, it was Perry Maxwell who designed the course. Maxwell, known most for his Southern Hills Country Club in Tulsa, advanced the club again with the installation of bentgrass greens.

In 1984, the club moved to its current location and chose none other than Pete Dye, one of the world's preeminent architects, to design it. Known for his famously tough courses such as TPC at Sawgrass and PGA West, Dye lived up to expectations by creating one of the toughest layouts in the Austin-San Antonio area.

It is rated at 73.4 from the back tees. The first five holes, surrounding Lake Austin, take on a links-type design.

The last 13 holes are of the traditional Hill Country nature with dramatic elevation changes including canyons, creeks and ravines. It features some of the most spectacular views anywhere in the area.

The signature hole at Austin Country Club is the 446-yard par 4 11th. It doglegs slightly left to give the appearance of an approach shot over canyon. There is a hill on the right side of the fairway along with traps and a gully in front of the green.

Austin Country Club

4408 Long Champ Drive
Austin 78746
512-328-0090
Pro: Tinsley Penick
A par-72, 6,848-yard private club. From downtown Austin, take Mopac to Bee Caves Road, go west to Loop 360, then north to Westlake Drive, then right to Long Champ, and left to club entrance.

• • •

USGA rating: 73.4
Slope rating: 135
Sand traps: 54
Water holes: 8
Doglegs: 4 left/3 right
Type greens: Bentgrass
Record: 64
Designer : Pete Dye
Year opened: 1984

• • •

Hole	Par	Yards	Hole	Par	Yards
1	4	393	10	4	393
2	3	192	11	4	446
3	5	521	12	4	432
4	4	314	13	3	150
5	4	464	14	4	370
6	4	440	15	5	552
7	5	519	16	3	202
8	3	144	17	5	477
9	4	363	18	4	476
Out	36	3350	In	36	3498

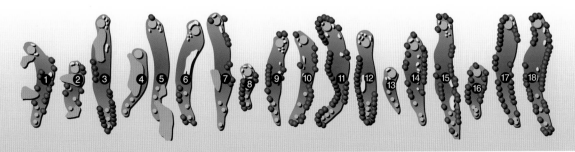

Texas Top 100

27. Buffalo Creek Golf Club

If history and experience are any indication, then good things are in store for Buffalo Creek Golf Club.

A successful golf course, like a football team or a Fortune 500 company, starts at the top. And when you're talking about Buffalo Creek, the man at the top is Charles Perry, an internationally recognized authority in golf course development.

Next in line are golfing great Tom Weiskopf and architect Jay Morrish, who have produced some of the best golf courses in the United States.

Put that team together with a piece of hilly, wooded terrain on the eastern shore of Lake Ray Hubbard and you've got a winner. In 1994, it became the youngest golf course in the six-year history of *The Dallas Morning News'* poll of Top 10 public courses in Texas.

From 1976–1985, Perry was president and CEO of Golden Bear International and business partner with golf legend Jack Nicklaus.

In that role, Perry was involved with more than 100 major golf course projects around the world. Some of the most well-known include Muirfield Village, Desert Highlands, Castle Pines, Grand Cypress, Kiawah Island and Hills of Lakeway.

Buffalo Creek was supposed to be a private golf course community, but the project was stalled in the late 1980s.

Perry resurrected the project and decided to make it a top-of-the-line, daily-fee course.

When Weiskopf and Morrish returned to finish the project, Perry issued explicit instructions not to compromise their design just because it was going to be open to the public and part of a master-planned community.

"It truly provides the avid golfer with an alternative to the private club," Perry says. "The overall design strategy of the course was designed to make every golfer use every club in his or her bag.

"They completed their mission of creating a great golfing facility with absolute professionalism."

The layout blends into the land in complete harmony. The entire golf course looks as if the trees, creeks, lakes and hills were placed there just for a world-class golf course.

Weiskopf was a four-time runner-up at the Masters and player of the year in 1973. Morrish started designing courses in 1964 with Robert Trent Jones Sr. and two years later with the Fazios, but has earned a national reputation on his own merit.

Among the top holes are the 572-yard, par-5 third, the 478-yard, par-4 sixth — which for most golfers plays like a par 5 — and the 551-yard, par-5 16th. At No. 3 players must negotiate a double-dogleg to a green protected by two bunkers and a pond.

Buffalo Creek Golf Club

624 Country Club Drive
Rockwall 75087
214-771-4003
Pro: Rick DeLoach
A par 72, 7,028-yard daily-fee course
From downtown, take I-30 East to Ridge Road, go south 1.6 miles to club entrance on the left.

• • •

USGA rating: 73.8
Slope rating: 133
Sand traps: 76
Water holes: 11
Doglegs: 4 left/4 right
Type greens: Bentgrass
Record: 66
Designers: Tom Weiskopf and Jay Morrish
Year opened: 1992

• • •

Hole	Par	Yards	Hole	Par	Yards
1	4	408	10	4	430
2	4	435	11	4	378
3	5	572	12	3	196
4	3	227	13	4	352
5	4	347	14	5	523
6	4	478	15	4	466
7	4	397	16	5	551
8	3	156	17	3	171
9	4	450	18	4	481
Out	36	3470	In	36	3548

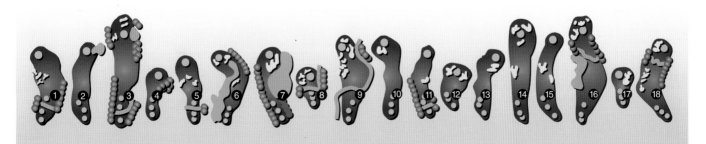

Texas Top 100

28. Hyatt Hill Country Resort

Accented by the beauty of the Texas Hill Country, golf course architect Arthur Hill's design is a spectacular layout. The Hyatt Hill Country Resort is a monument to Hills' understated style.

Across the highway from Sea World on a 170-acre tract in far Northwest San Antonio, the property opened in 1993. Visitors headed to see the whales and dolphins would never guess a championship golf course is just a few hundred feet away.

Covered with wildflowers in the spring, surrounded by plenty of cactus, brush and barbed wire, golfers will not believe they are in a booming metropolis. However, you might feel fenced in by the tight fairways.

"What we tried to do," Hills said when the course opened, "was design a course that would fit into the scenic backdrop here."

The resort has a colorful history. It was once Wiseman Ranch, where cattle roamed the land golf balls now assault.

After the success of Sea World, Hyatt decided to build the first destination resort inside the San Antonio city limits. It turned out to be the first of many resorts that focus on turning millions of Alamo City tourists into golfers.

Hills and associate Keith Foster used the rolling hills to form a course that is a challenge to all levels of golfers. It has four tee areas on every hole, and the greens can be extremely fast.

The No. 1 handicap hole is the par-4 fifth. It slopes downward and right to a large pond, which has consumed many second shots.

The eighth and ninth holes can also be killers. No. 8 is a 563-yard par 5 where golfers must cross water and creek beds not once but twice on their way to the green. The green is positioned far to the right with water and sand on the right edge of the green and a huge mound on the left.

No. 9 hole is another long 554-yard downhill par 5 with a huge lake in front of the double green. A stone wall circles the lake. Large trees block anything but a perfect drive from trying to go for the green in two shots.

No. 16 is one of several long par 4s on the course at 458 yards. No. 2 is 446 and No. 5 is 452.

The 18th is surrounded by sand on the right and water on the left. The four par 3s feature a carry over water, sand or cactus. While the name resort is applied to the course, a golfer who hits the ball off the fairway will find it anything but relaxing.

The course has earned much acclaim in its short history. It has been named by *Golf Magazine* as one of the Top 10 You Can Play.

In 1993, it was named the best public course in San Antonio in the annual *San Antonio Express-News survey,* and that same year it was the site of the first Alamo Bowl golf tournament.

HILL COUNTRY GOLF CLUB

Hyatt Hill Country Resort

9800 Hyatt Resort Drive
San Antonio 78251
210-647-1234
Director of Golf: Paul Earnest
A par-72, 6,913-yard resort course. From downtown San Antonio, take I-35 South to Highway 90, then west to Sea World exit, go west past Loop 410, then 3.5 miles to Hyatt Resort, then right to club.

• • •

USGA rating: 73.9
Slope rating: 136
Sand traps: 33
Water holes: 4
Doglegs: 8 left/3 right
Type greens: Bermuda
Record: 68
Designer: Art Hills
Year opened: 1993

• • •

Hole	Par	Yards	Hole	Par	Yards
1	4	421	10	4	369
2	4	446	11	4	407
3	4	328	12	4	328
4	3	159	13	4	420
5	4	452	14	3	172
6	3	216	15	5	540
7	4	336	16	4	458
8	5	563	17	3	195
9	5	554	18	5	549
Out	36	3475	In	36	3438

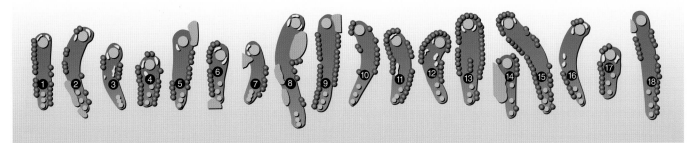

Texas Top 100

29. The Woodlands Country Club — Palmer Course

When George Mitchell dreams, the dreams usually come true. Already the father of Galveston Island's resort-type atmosphere, Mitchell dreamed about a country-living atmosphere in a heavily wooded site 27 miles north of Houston.

If anybody can tame the wilderness and turn it into civilization, it is George Mitchell. He was a man with a vision that was so far ahead of its time that not even his most loyal employees were sure what he had in mind.

But more than 25 years later, vision has become reality for The Woodlands is a 25,000-acre incorporated city that has become a recreational Mecca for Houston.

The Woodlands Corporation has spent $25 million on its four golf courses and clubhouse facilities and has been home of the PGA Tour's Houston Open since it opened in 1975. All of the fairways are carved out of the thick forest pines and hardwoods.

Nearly 15 years after The Woodlands opened, golf legend Arnold Palmer was hired to build The Woodlands' newest — and possibly best — course.

The course opened in 1990 after spending years on the drawing boards. Ground originally was broken in late 1983, but was put on hold because of Houston's lagging economy at the time. The par 72, 7,180-yard course features the same tree-lined fairways as the other courses, but Palmer created more rolling terrain, moguls, grass bunkers and undulations.

As expected on a Palmer-designed course, driving is at a premium with both distance and accuracy required to be in position to reach many of the long par 4s in two strokes. The tree-lined fairways are generous, but there is usually one optimal position from which to approach the green.

Water comes into play on 15 holes, but is never more ominous than on the 13th and 14th holes.

The 13th is a 509-yard par 5 where golfers must thread their tee shot to the left of a lake that protects the right side of the fairway and either short of or between a bunker placed squarely in the middle of the fairway. On the approach, players then must contend with another pond that protects the left side of the green.

The 14th hole is a 403-yard par 4 where water comes into play off the tee and on the approach. Water protects the left side of the fairway and surrounds the green on three sides, leaving little margin for error on the approach.

The 17th is a 574-yard par 5 slight dogleg left that tempts long hitters to go for the green in two by carrying a lake that cuts across the fairway in front of the green.

Palmer challenged players who dare to play the back tees, especially on the par 4s, which have lengths of 426, 420, 445, 423, 449, 426 and 423 yards.

The Woodlands Country Club Palmer Course

2301 North Millbend
The Woodlands 77380
281-367-1100
Pro: Richard Cromwell
A 72-hole resort and country club. From downtown Houston, take I-45 North to Woodlands Parkway, turn left and follow signs to club entrance.

• • •

USGA rating: 74.2
Slope rating: 130
Sand traps: 49
Water holes: 10
Doglegs: 6 left/5 right
Type greens: Bermuda
Record: 63
Designers: Arnold Palmer and Ed Seay
Year opened: 1990

• • •

Hole	Par	Yards	Hole	Par	Yards
1	4	426	10	4	449
2	3	178	11	3	191
3	5	564	12	4	402
4	4	420	13	5	509
5	4	445	14	4	403
6	3	202	15	3	201
7	5	549	16	4	426
8	4	423	17	5	574
9	4	394	18	4	423
Out	36	3602	In	36	3578

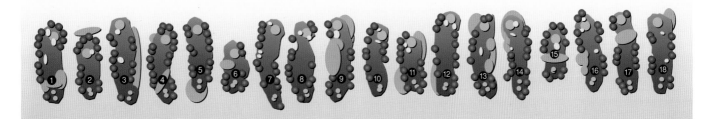

30. Barton Creek Resort & Country Club — Lakeside Course

BARTON CREEK
COUNTRY CLUB

Build it and they don't always come. Even if Arnold Palmer built it.

You'd think a golf course designed by Palmer would have been an instant success. Palmer brought golf into the national and international spotlight. Four decades later, he's still making millions in endorsements.

Palmer also has earned a reputation as a solid golf course architect, although not as big a name as former playing rival Jack Nicklaus.

While Nicklaus has built his reputation as an architect by building difficult, high-end courses, Palmer has excelled in building user-friendly courses for the masses of the golf population.

When Palmer and partner Ed Seay first set foot on this beautiful piece of Texas Hill Country, the golf course was named Hidden Hills Country Club with its own private membership.

But the year was 1986 and the Texas economy went into the dumps and the club struggled until it was acquired several years later by Barton Creek Resort just down the street.

It was not until this golf course was taken over by Barton Creek Resort that the Lakeside course began receiving the credit it was due. Water comes into play on only five holes, but half of the holes feature doglegs through the trees and rugged hillsides.

While it is the lesser known of the three Barton Creek layouts, some members claim it is the best of the three layouts with holes that wind around Lake Travis.

The centerpieces are the par-4 13th with a graveyard along the right side and the par-3 11th and 14th holes.

No. 13 is a 485-yard par 4 that ranks one of the longest par 4s in Texas since most holes over 475 yards are usually rated as a par 5.

The 11th is surrounded by waterfalls while the 14th is the shortest on the course.

No. 12 is a 578-yard par 5 with a horseshoe-shaped fairway that requires golfers to negotiate two left doglegs to reach the green protected by two bunkers.

No. 2 is a relative short par 5 at only 496-yards, but a pond in front of the greens adds risk to players who try to go for the green in two. It requires a carry over a canyon, usually with a strong wind blowing, with a brilliant view of Lake Travis from the green.

"The worst thing is to build a golf course that you get bored on," Palmer says. "One day, I'd like to build a golf course for myself.

"I take pride in not patterning myself after anyone in building golf courses, but there are things at Pinehurst No. 2 and Augusta that I would have to incorporate in my golf course."

Barton Creek Resort and Country Club Lakeside Course

1800 Clubhouse Drive
Spicewood 78735
800-888-2257
Director of Golf: Brent Buckman
One of three 18-hole courses. Take I-35 South to Ben White Boulevard, go west to Bee Caves Road, go south 1.1 miles to Barton Creek Boulevard, go left and turn left on Barton Club Drive.

• • •

USGA rating: 71.0
Slope rating: 124
Sand traps: 51
Water holes: 5
Doglegs: 6 left/3 right
Type greens: Bentgrass
Record: 60
Designer: Arnold Palmer
Year opened: 1986

Hole	Par	Yards	Hole	Par	Yards
1	4	400	10	4	371
2	5	496	11	3	201
3	3	162	12	5	578
4	4	418	13	4	485
5	4	395	14	3	126
6	3	565	15	5	519
7	5	403	16	4	405
8	3	201	17	3	163
9	4	381	18	4	388
Out	36	3421	In	35	3236

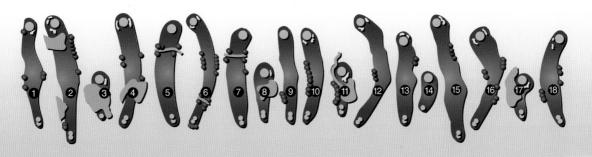

31. Houston Country Club

At the turn of the century, golf was riding a giant tidal wave. The surge was nationwide. However, Houstonians of that era had a problem. Today there are approximately 130 golf courses in the Greater Houston Area. At that time there were none.

Lionel Hohenthal changed that. In 1903, Hohenthal lived his dream. He set out to build a golf course and did so by finding 100 men to pay $25 each. The birth of golf in Houston started for the same price of a green today at many courses.

It still took some time to work up a membership, but they eventually leased 45 acres from Rice Institute off old San Felipe Road (now East Dallas). They laid out a nine-hole golf links between West Dallas and Buffalo Bayou and built a clubhouse near the site of old Jefferson Davis Hospital in 1905.

By 1908, the membership had grown to 500, the links were overcrowded and the English-style clubhouse was too small.

So the new Houston Country Club was organized with William Marsh Rice, Jr. serving as its first president. Original members included philanthropist Jesse H. Jones, W.L. Clayton and Col. Joseph W. Evans.

They moved the club to 175 acres well outside the city limits toward the ship channel and member A.W. Pollard designed the new 18 holes. HCC set the standard for opulence and pageantry, and memberships were a must for Houston's rich and famous.

From 1914 to 1951, it hosted one of the best amateur tournaments west of the Mississippi with the Houston Invitational.

In the 1950s, HCC again began to feel the pinch of Houston's industrial growth. As business and industry began to creep ever closer, members began looking for a new home and found 165 acres with Buffalo Bayou running through it.

They purchased the land in 1955 and hired legendary architect Robert Trent Jones, who had built more than 450 courses around the world, to design his first Houston course.

American General president Gus Wortham bought the old property and later sold it to the city for $3.6 million and it is now one of the city's six public courses. It is now called Gus Wortham Golf Course.

HCC celebrated its grand re-opening on Jan. 18, 1957. Three decades later, in 1987–88, Ben Crenshaw and architect Bill Coore were hired to do a major reconstruction of the greens, bunkers and tees as well as replanting new grasses throughout while leaving the original design unchanged.

The layout starts with a bang with two long par 4s of 435 and 457 yards, and features two long par 3s of 224 yards and 228 yards at Nos. 9 and 14, respectively.

Houston Country Club

One Potomac Drive
Houston 77057
713-465-8381
Pro: Paul Marchand
An ultra-exclusive club that was Houston's first. Take Loop 610 West to Woodway, then go west on Woodway to Potomac. Right on Potomac to entrance.

• • •

USGA rating: 72.9
Slope rating: 125
Sand traps: N/A
Water holes: N/A
Doglegs: N/A
Type greens: Bermuda
Record: N/A
Designers: Robert Trent Jones Sr.
*   and Ben Crenshaw ('87)*
Year opened: 1957

• • •

Hole	Par	Yards	Hole	Par	Yards
1	4	435	10	4	423
2	4	457	11	4	402
3	5	511	12	5	564
4	3	182	13	4	448
5	4	405	14	3	228
6	4	357	15	4	415
7	4	302	16	3	190
8	5	511	17	5	561
9	3	224	18	4	408
Out	36	0	In	36	3,639

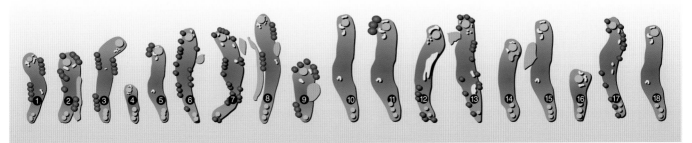

32. Gleneagles Country Club — Queen's Course

T

rue golfers who yearn to learn more about the game's history don't need a travel agent, a passport or an expensive plane ticket to Scotland to learn more about what the game's first courses looked like.

They can just drive to Plano.

It is here in this former small-town farming community just outside of Dallas that architects Robert von Hagge and Bruce Devlin brought golf's tradition and history to Texas.

Gleneagles carries on the prestigious tradition of its world-renowned namesake in Scotland. And the Texas version has not one but two championship golf courses that feature all the characteristics of golf's earliest layouts.

The club also features one of the top clubhouses in the state, measuring 80,000 square feet with marble and mahogany floors and 10-foot doorways. And then there's the pro shop, which also has been rated among the best in the state.

Gleneagles also features an indoor teaching facility, consisting of four indoor teaching bays with state-of-the art audio-video equipment. There is also a 300-yard driving range, an enormous grass and sand bunker practice area and two large putting greens. One putting green is actually one acre.

Gleneagles, if you can't already tell, stands for excellence.

Gleneagles has been described as a golfer's paradise with its two courses known as the King's and Queen's courses, both of which are ranked among the best in the state with their combination links-style, target-golf design. Of the 36 holes, only eight are not enhanced with numerous man-made lakes to complement White Rock Creek.

Gleneagles features two 18-hole golf courses, both ranked in the top 32 in the state. von Hagge and Devlin took advantage of the tree-lined White Rock Creek and moved just enough dirt to create the rolling terrain reminiscent of golf's motherland.

Given a blank canvas with which to work, von Hagge and Devlin decided on a link's style course with moguls used to define the fairways. All holes feature excellent shot values, and several holes on each course rank among the toughest in the Dallas-Fort Worth area.

Do not confuse the name "Queen's Course" as being the easier of the two target-style golf courses. With a rating of 74.0 and a slope rating of 136, the Queen's Course is one stroke more difficult than its sibling at 6,901 yards from the back tees. The Queen's is open with few trees. It features deep sand and grass bunkers and rolling hills and is very difficult with any kind of wind. Nos. 17 and 18 are two of the toughest holes in the state.

Gleneagles

Gleneagles Country Club Queen's Course

5401 W. Park Boulevard
Plano 75093
214-867-6666
Pro: Eldridge Miles
A private 36-hole club. From Dallas take North Dallas Tollway to West Park Boulevard. Go right on West Park 1.5 miles to entrance on the left.

• • •

USGA rating: 74
Slope rating: 136
Sand traps: 75
Water holes: 17
Doglegs: 3 left/ 6 right
Type greens: Bentgrass
Record: 63
Designers: Robert von Hagge and Bruce Devlin
Year opened: 1985

Hole	Par	Yards	Hole	Par	Yards
1	4	388	10	5	492
2	3	186	11	3	155
3	5	571	12	4	451
4	3	193	13	4	414
5	4	464	14	4	403
6	4	467	15	3	215
7	4	427	16	5	562
8	5	490	17	3	190
9	4	411	18	4	422
Out	36	3597	In	35	3304

Texas Top 100

33. River Oaks Country Club

While Houston Country Club gets the credit for being the first club in Houston, River Oaks is responsible for starting Houston on the road to becoming the golfing metropolis it is today.

The club was founded in 1923, two decades after HCC, and opened on July 4, 1925. Even though golf was starting to sweep the Northeast, Houston was still a distant outpost on the American golf frontier and most people had yet to learn the game.

Houston's first real pioneer was Jack Burke Sr., a native of Philadelphia who was regarded as one of the best teachers in the nation when he became the first pro at River Oaks.

It wasn't long before Craig Wood, Sam Snead, Ben Hogan and others began coming to Houston for regular lessons and gave rise to a new generation of players like Jimmy Demaret.

Later, Claude Harmon Sr., another one of the game's best teachers, replaced Burke when he died in 1943.

"My daddy always told me he should've been wearing a coonskin cap when he gave lessons," Jack Burke Jr. recalls. "He was pioneering the game."

Since then, the name River Oaks speaks for itself and has been the address of choice for Houston's rich and famous since it was developed by the family of Will and Ima Hogg and Varner Realty. The timeless layout designed by legendary architect Donald Ross lives up to the high standards.

There has been a waiting list for three decades to get in and only a handful of memberships become available each year.

Former pro Jackson Bradley calls it a "freak property" by Houston standards. It is stately and elegant, Houston's best version of Alister MacKenzie's Augusta National Golf Club.

Ross, who built the famous No. 2 course at Pinehurst Country Club in Pinehurst, N.C., had a different challenge at River Oaks.

Pinehurst is a course that favors long hitters, but at River Oaks he had to cram an 18-hole course into a relatively small amount of high-priced real-estate covered with pines and moss-draped oaks along the banks of Buffalo Bayou.

Even though the club was built by oil-rich wildcatters, Ross didn't have the luxury of a big construction budget or modern machinery and still managed to build some of the city's best short holes that accentuate accuracy instead of length.

In 1967, the club spent $275,000 to hire Joe Finger to renovate the course. He retooled all of the greens and tees and rerouted some of the holes. He built four new lakes that brought water into play on five holes.

River Oaks Country Club

1600 River Oaks Boulevard
Houston 77019
713-529-4321
Pro: Dick Harmon
An exclusive par-72, 6,868-yard club.
From Houston, take Loop 610 West to San Felipe, then east on San Felipe to River Oaks Boulevard.
Turn left to entrance.

• • •

USGA rating: 73.5
Slope rating: 126
Sand traps: 92
Water holes: 5
Doglegs: N/A
Type greens: Bermuda
Record: 64
Designer: Donald Ross
Year opened: 1923

• • •

Hole	Par	Yards	Hole	Par	Yards
1	4	361	10	5	540
2	4	398	11	3	225
3	3	191	12	4	410
4	5	549	13	4	414
5	4	356	14	5	521
6	3	173	15	3	182
7	4	398	16	4	444
8	5	523	17	4	376
9	4	380	18	4	425
Out	36	3329	In	36	3539

Texas Top 100

34. Bentwater Country Club — Miller Course

Scott Miller understands the great responsibility with which golf course architects are charged — to take land God created and reshape it in a way that even the Almighty would be proud.

Unlike some architects who cut up the land and then try to put it back together again, Miller took what Mother Nature took centuries to build, cut a few cups and stuck 18 pins in the ground.

The business of building a golf course is obviously a little more complicated than that, but it is that "keep it simple, stupid" mentality that has helped Miller produce what has become one of the best courses in the state.

At Bentwater, hard on the northwest shore of Lake Conroe, Miller was given the opportunity to build work on a gorgeous piece of lakefront property that is covered with trees, rolling hills and beautiful vistas of the 10,000-acre Lake Conroe.

"This is absolutely the finest piece of land I've ever been able to work on," Miller says. "Mother Nature worked a long time to put this here. Who am I to come in and mess it up?"

Miller has seen the best and worst of what Houston landscape has to offer and each time he has risen to the occasion to turn them into some of the area's best golf courses. While working as the senior designer under Jack Nicklaus from 1978–88, Miller designed the layout at Lochinvar Golf Club on an undistinguished 200-acre tract of land that featured only a two-foot change in elevation. He still produced a golf course that ranks No. 16 in the state by the *Dallas Morning News*.

At Bentwater, on the other hand, the land is ideal for golf with its densely wooded terrain and rolling hills not found inside Houston's city limits. It is bounded by 158,000 acres of national forest and 12.5 miles of shoreline on the other.

Given more of Mother Nature's tools to work with, Miller produced a park-land type golf course that features virtually no rough, pine needles scattered throughout the trees.

In addition to the 74 bunkers on the course, Miller also used heavily-sculptured swales around the green that put a premium on a soft-touch short game.

Pressed to label his style, he calls it "classical/natural." He likes to keep it simple. Even the flagsticks are a simple green and white. Unlike courses built in the 1980s, when architects deviated from tradition by forcing players to hit certain shots, Miller gives his players an option. He is a 10–12 handicapper, doesn't believe in building masochistic courses.

"The way I look at it," he said, "I'm only going to play the course a few times, so I have to remember the people who are going to be playing it long after I'm gone."

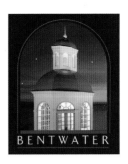

Bentwater Country Club Miller Course

800 Bentwater Drive
Montgomery 77356
Pro: Brett Lossin
281-353-1912
An exclusive 36-hole private club on Lake Conroe. Go north on I-45 to the Bentwater exit, then west for 7.5 miles to entrance on the left.

• • •

USGA rating: 71.4
Slope rating: 125
Sand traps: 74
Water holes: 6
Doglegs: 6
Type greens: Bentgrass
Record: 65
Designer: Scott Miller
Year opened: 1994

• • •

Hole	Par	Yards	Hole	Par	Yards
1	4	410	10	4	410
2	5	543	11	5	536
3	3	204	12	4	427
4	4	344	13	4	310
5	4	327	14	3	200
6	4	470	15	5	529
7	5	550	16	4	418
8	3	207	17	3	180
9	4	411	18	4	423
Out	36	3,466	In	36	3,441

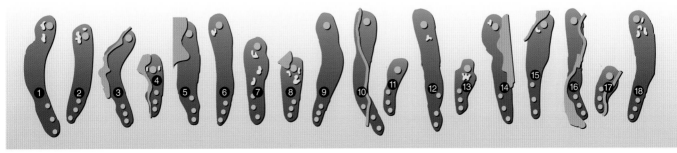

Texas Top 100

35. Texas Star Golf Course

Keith Foster probably deserves his own section in this book. As the creator of three Texas Top 100 courses in the past year, he is making as big an impact on Texas golf as Tiger Woods is on the PGA.

So who better to design a golf course named Texas Star?

That's the name of one of the Dallas-Fort Worth area's new courses. And, as always, Foster rose to the challenge of building a golf course that looks as if it has always been there amidst the century-old oak trees, rolling hills, exciting vistas and Texas Hill Country-type terrain.

"This dynamic golf course is nestled in native woodlands, allowing golfers to enjoy a golf experience rather than just a golf game," Foster says. "All 18 holes on the course will be considered signature holes."

Spread over 210 acres and built along the banks of Hurricane Creek, which meanders throughout the layout, the course measures 6,936 yards. Foster incorporated beautiful landscape design with stacked rock ponds, waterfalls, elevating and descending regions and cascading tees.

It is a links-like course which demands accuracy. Dense growth directly off the generous fairways make it hard to find stray shots. There are no home sites bordering the fairways.

Each hole even has its own name, including No. 1 Reveille, No. 7 Tombstone, No. 9 Devil's Point, No. 11 Double Barrel and No. 15 Battle Cry.

Texas Star was built by the city of Euless and is just five minutes away from D/FW Airport. In conjunction with the golf course, the city has built a state of the art conference center.

As Jim Witt, editor of the *Fort Worth Star-Telegram*, stated, "I've played virtually every course worth playing in Tarrant and Dallas counties, and I can tell you this course is truly going to be the "star" of golf around here."

The hardest hole at Texas Star is the 457-yard par 4 No. 12. It is a dogleg right with three fairway bunkers protecting the inside corner of the fairway. The sheer length of the hole will prevent many players from reaching the green in two shots.

No. 15 measures only 370 yards, but offers golfers plenty of options off the tee. With a lake cutting the fairway in half and protecting the front of the green, golfers can lay up and clear the water on their second shot. Bigger hitters can go for a second fairway to the right, but must carry the ball about 220 yards in the air to clear the lake.

Nos. 10 and 18 are both long par 5s with a creek running down the left side of the fairway and crossing in front of the green to make golfers think twice about going for the green in two.

TEXAS STAR

Texas Star Golf Course

1400 Texas Star Parkway
Euless 76040
1-888-TEXSTAR
Pro: Duff Cunningham
A par-71, 6,963-yard public course.
From Dallas, take Highway 183, exit Highway 157, go south to Highway 10. Turn right to course entrance on left.

• • •

USGA rating: 73.6
Slope rating: 135
Sand traps: 49
Water holes: 9
Doglegs: 4 left/3 right
Type greens: Bentgrass
Record: 65
Designer: Keith Foster
Year opened: 1997

• • •

Hole	Par	Yards	Hole	Par	Yards
1	4	425	10	5	539
2	4	382	11	4	337
3	3	147	12	4	457
4	4	420	13	4	431
5	4	454	14	3	245
6	4	389	15	4	370
7	5	516	16	3	179
8	3	217	17	4	471
9	4	422	18	5	535
Out	35	3,372	In	71	3,564

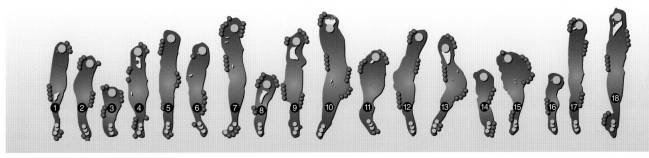

Texas Top 100

36. Dominion Country Club

Country clubs have an important place in American society. Some are playgrounds for the rich and famous, a place for opulence and extravagance for people who like the finer things in life and have the money to get them.

That idea was not lost on the developers of The Dominion.

Stunning, unique, outstanding and unmatched are just a few of the words used to describe this club since it opened in 1984. Country music star George Strait lives on the back nine. A few doors up on the hill, NBA superstar David Robinson resides.

The course was designed by former Texas Open champion Bill Johnston and the clubhouse by San Antonio's Ralph Bender. Both have drawn rave reviews from members, visitors and Senior PGA Tour pros.

Since a year after it opened, The Dominion has been host of the Senior PGA Tour's SBC Seniors at The Dominion. The tournament has drawn record crowds and fields the last several years, producing winners such as Lee Trevino, Chi Chi Rodriguez, J.C. Snead and Jim Albus.

While pros praise the lush conditions and overall challenge of the course, it is actually the clubhouse that is the main drawing card for the top players.

The idea behind the clubhouse was simply to build the best, regardless of cost. Quite simply,

Bender didn't disappoint. With a big idea and deep pockets, Bender produced a $17 million clubhouse that is unmatched anywhere in the state, if not the country. Members and guests are greeted by a facility that includes hand-carved stone, golden domes and glittering chandeliers put into place. It is perennially ranked as the top clubhouse in the state.

The course offers plenty of its own uniqueness and charm. The 18 holes are set on 160 acres, surrounded by some of the nicest and largest homes any golfer will ever see. Owners Ernest and Kane Hui have considered the construction of another 18 holes on land adjacent to the existing course.

Johnston built only six courses during his brief career as an architect after 15 years as a touring pro. As an architect, he had the wisdom to design Dominion so that no golfer would ever have to hit a shot directly into the rising or setting sun.

The par 4 second hole offers the big hitter or gambler the chance to hit over Leon Creek with a 300-yard shot. Most golfers will play a safe 180-yard lay-up, then have a second shot over the creek and fountain to the left.

The creek comes back into play on the par-5 seventh, with the fairway sloping toward the water off the tee. The par-5 ninth has a drainage ditch to the left with a green-side pond and another fountain.

Dominion Country Club

One Dominion Drive
San Antonio 78257
210-698-3364
Pro: Marc DeWall
A par-72, 6,927-yard private club that is home of the SBC Seniors Senior PGA Tour event. From San Antonio, take I-10 West to Camp Bullis exit, stay on access road, course is on right.

• • •

USGA rating: 72.2
Slope rating: 126
Sand traps: 65
Water holes: 9
Doglegs: 3 left/4 right
Type greens: Bermuda
Record: 64
Designer: Bill Johnston
Year opened: 1984

• • •

Hole	Par	Yards	Hole	Par	Yards
1	4	413	10	4	438
2	4	363	11	5	522
3	4	385	12	4	406
4	4	421	13	4	381
5	3	214	14	4	438
6	4	391	15	3	185
7	5	538	16	4	457
8	3	189	17	3	153
9	5	488	18	5	545
Out	36	3402	In	36	3525

37. The Falls Resort & Club

Jay Riviere has spent his career making something out of nothing. Of the more than 20 courses he has designed in Houston, almost all of them have been built on rice fields or the open prairie.

As a Houston native, he knew that was about all he would ever have to work with. And he became quite good at it over the years, designing such courses as the Masters course at Bear Creek and South Shore Harbour.

Finally in 1985, Riviere and Dave Marr got the chance of a lifetime when they were asked to build a championship course on the rolling, wooded countryside 90 miles west of Houston.

Deer are so abundant on the property that it is rare to play an entire 18-hole round without having to take a momentary pause to appreciate their gracefulness.

"It's nice to have creeks, tall trees and some roll to the land, but so often that's not what you get," Marr says.

"We waited a long time to find a course with so much contour and terrain. We wore our feet to a nub out there. We walked and walked and walked. Jay would see things in his mind that I could never have imagined."

Riviere and Marr both interned at the famed Winged Foot Golf Club in Mamaroneck, N.Y., where they both were influenced by the traditional approach to golf course design.

The setting at The Falls is spectacular. A series of clear-water lakes follow the descending natural terrain after the series of eight cascading waterfalls.

The Falls was one of only a handful of courses in Houston with bentgrass greens until it recently converted to bermuda.

It was designed to attract golfers from all over the country, but the timing was all wrong. The Falls opened during Houston's economic downturn of the mid-80s and never completely took off, even though it changed ownership several times.

As for the course, the 209-yard No. 3 is one of the area's toughest par 3s when the pin is in the front finger of the green, protected by water and sand.

The par-4, 407-yard No. 6 also can be a nightmare. Accuracy off the tee is imperative because water protects the right side and a long bunker guards the left. The approach is a scary sight to an elevated green that slopes drastically left and toward the water. Short of the green are tiered sand traps that leave a blind sand shot to the green.

The 448-yard, par-4 No. 17 is a different kind of challenge. Off the tee, the fairway pushes everything toward the water and woods to the right if you're too long. The smart drive to the left side leaves a long-iron approach to an green protected by a meandering creek.

The Falls Resort and Club

1001 North Falls Drive
New Ulm 78950
281-578-5550
Pro: Todd Coover
A semi-private resort and club.
Take I-10 West from Houston to Highway 36. Turn north to FM 1094. Go left 22 miles to FM 109, then left on FM 109 for 3.5 miles to entrance.

• • •

USGA rating: 72.5
Slope rating: 135
Sand traps: 59
Water holes: 11
Doglegs: 3 left/6 right
Type greens: Bentgrass
Record: 65
Designer: Jay Riviere and Dave Marr
Year opened: 1985

• • •

Hole	Par	Yards	Hole	Par	Yards
1	5	515	10	5	535
2	4	373	11	4	428
3	3	209	12	3	188
4	3	424	13	4	407
5	4	522	14	3	198
6	4	407	15	5	520
7	4	420	16	3	149
8	3	186	17	4	448
9	4	430	18	4	440
Out	36	3500	In	36	3313

Texas Top 100

38. Mira Vista Golf Club

MIRA VISTA

To look out of the clubhouse at Mira Vista is to see a meeting of the past and present.

The best of the golden age of golf course architecture, the best of modern technology and the best of what Mother Nature has to offer. Not to mention, the best of Tom Weiskopf and Jay Morrish.

Built by two of golf's premier architects in 1987, Mira Vista is a perfect blend of modern golf course architecture with golf's grandest traditions. Native grasses and a panorama of wildflowers provide an extraordinary park-like environment.

Three lakes enhance the course layout as it meanders through scenic hills and valleys and features elevation changes of up to 150 feet, offering spectacular views along the way. The picturesque variations in the terrain are emphasized by well-placed street arrangements to preserve the native trees and sloping hillsides.

"Our goal with Mira Vista was to get away from common course design and put some strategy back in golf," Weiskopf said.

"It will always be demanding but fair, offering a pleasurable experience for golfers of every skill level," Morrish said.

Mira Vista is a favorite playground of local PGA pros when they get a rare day off because of its strong collection of holes. Among the many strong holes at Mira Vista

are the 647-yard, par-5 sixth hole and the 453-yard, par-4 13th.

No. 6, nicknamed "Longcliff," doglegs to the left along an intimidating rock cliff that runs down the right side of the fairway and out of bounds down the left.

Add a thick row of trees down both sides and that doesn't leave much room for error. The narrow green is protected by two bunkers in back and a fairway bunker about 80 yards in front of the green.

Perhaps the most interesting hole is the 343-yard, par-4 18th, which features two different fairways bisected lengthwise by a creek. One fairway makes the hole a dogleg right; one makes it a dogleg left. It is called Jay's Revenge.

If you play left, you will never have to cross the creek but it will always be haunting you down the right side of the fairway. The left side of the left fairway is also lined with a long series of bunkers and row of trees, leaving an approach to a long, narrow green that is 45 yards deep.

If you play right, you have to cross the creek just in front of the tee box and again on the short approach to the green. This appears to be the easiest route, if you don't mind clearing the creek and a bunker in front of the green with a finesse approach.

Mira Vista boasts three par 4s over 450 yards — including No. 2 (451 yards), No. 10 (451) and No. 13 (453.)

Mira Vista Golf Club

6600 Mira Vista Boulevard
Fort Worth 76132
817-294-6600
Pro: Lindy Miller
A par-71, 6,844-yard private club.
From Fort Worth, take I-35W South to Loop 820. Go west to Bryant Irvin Boulevard, then south five miles to Mira Vista Boulevard. Turn right to entrance.

• • •

USGA rating: 73.2
Slope rating: 135
Sand traps: 115
Water holes: 13
Doglegs: 4 left/4 right
Type greens: Bentgrass
Record: 63
Designers: Tom Weiskopf
 and Jay Morrish
Year opened: 1987

Hole	Par	Yards	Hole	Par	Yards
1	4	437	10	4	451
2	4	451	11	5	540
3	3	188	12	3	170
4	4	416	13	4	453
5	4	431	14	4	388
6	5	647	15	3	223
7	3	150	16	4	310
8	4	346	17	5	542
9	4	389	18	4	343
Out	35	3455	In	36	3389

Texas Top 100

39. Bear Creek Golf Club — East Course

One of the first things you are greeted by when you fly into Dallas/Fort Worth International Airport is not a flight attendant or a gate agent or a sky cab or a taxi driver.

It's two 18-hole golf courses known as the Hyatt Bear Creek Golf Club.

Welcome to Dallas.

With over 335 acres set among gently rolling Texas hills, internationally acclaimed architect Ted Robinson combined the rolling North Texas terrain, stands of mature live oaks and meandering Bear Creek to create a stunning visual landscape.

For the first 70 years of golf in Dallas/Fort Worth, to find a golf course you could play and be sure the layout was challenging, the grass was green and the greens rolled true, you had to join a country club.

No ifs, ands or buts about it.

But 1980 was a turning point in D/FW golf. With golf courses becoming too expensive for most municipalities, private investors and major corporations got involved in the golf business.

They could spend more money to build and maintain better golf courses. And golfers would be willing to pay for it.

Named one of the "The top 50 Resort courses" in America by *Golf Digest*, Bear Creek gives you a choice of two 18-hole layouts that have hosted PGA qualifiers

in 1985 and the Texas State Open in 1984.

Golfers can be assured not only of convenience, but the most impeccably maintained daily-fee course you'll find, and a great view of 747s as they take off for parts unknown.

The East Course measures 6,670 yards and plays to par of 72. It features tighter fairway landing areas and smaller greens than the West and is also rolling and well-wooded and more of a target-oriented design that caters to lower-handicap players.

The West Course is 6,609 yards and also plays to par of 72. It is very hilly and well-wooded and is beautifully landscaped. Once you get past the first seven holes, it is quite forgiving.

The signature hole on the East is the 385-yard, par-4 fifth hole. The hole doglegs slightly to the left and requires an approach over water.

The most difficult hole is the 423-yard, par-4 15th, which requires a blind second shot.

Also watch out for No. 8, a 418-yard par 4 with water cutting across the fairway in the landing area and running all the way down the right side.

Fourteen of the holes dogleg through the trees and many also feature substantial elevation changes to make club selection difficult. All of the par 5s are over 500 yards, so there are no gimme birdies here.

Bear Creek Golf Club East Course

3500 W Airfield Drive
Dallas 75261
972-615-6800
Director of Golf: Larry Box
A 36-hole daily fee facility at D/FW Airport. From Highway 183, go north on Highway 360 for three miles, take MidCities exit east for one-fourth mile. Resort entrance is on the right.

• • •

USGA rating: 72.5
Slope rating: 127
Sand traps: 60
Water holes: 7
Doglegs: 7 right/7 left
Type greens: Bentgrass
Record: 62
Designer: Ted Robinson
Year opened: 1980

• • •

Hole	Par	Yards	Hole	Par	Yards
1	5	528	10	5	510
2	4	416	11	4	365
3	3	175	12	4	344
4	5	520	13	4	384
5	4	385	14	3	189
6	4	372	15	4	423
7	3	166	16	5	515
8	4	418	17	3	175
9	4	402	18	4	383
Out	36	3382	In	36	3288

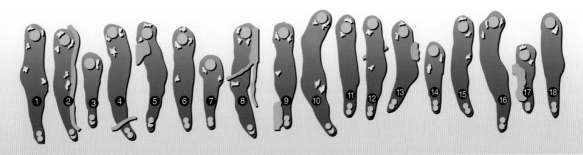

40. Cypresswood Golf Club — Tradition Course

Golf course architects are a lot like novelists and movie directors. Once you've built your reputation, people will buy your next book or buy a ticket to your next movie sight unseen.

That's becoming more and more the case for Keith Foster. Whenever he builds a new golf course — whether it's in Texas or Arizona — it is sure to pop up on somebody's Top List.

And, once again, that's the case with The Tradition at Cypresswood.

Although the newest golf course at this sprawling 54-hole golf facility in Houston has only been open since the spring of 1998, it has drawn rave reviews.

And Foster even impressed himself on this traditional, Pinehurst-style layout that meanders its way through the dense woods in a way in which Donald Ross would have been proud.

"I've built a lot of courses in Texas the last few years," Foster says. "All of them were on different types of land, but I believe The Tradition is the best of all."

The course is a wonderful piece of property with towering tree cover, dramatic topography, no homes and no out of bounds.

Constructed over 350 acres, you have the opportunity to return to what the game should be — fun, exciting and a chance to get away from it all.

Foster carefully blended and sculpted the layout with the landscape as though it has always been there. It takes on traditional design with gentle, rolling fairways and links-style bunkers.

The Tradition Course is your classic golf course. If you can hit a long and straight tee shot, you should be able to easily score like the pros. Accurate mid-to-short irons to the greens are a must.

With the greens being large and rolling, the pin placement can be tucked in some very nasty spots. Although the golf course is built in low-lying land, Foster moved lots of dirt to create a soft roll and gentle undulations to the fairways and greens.

The 18th is a 546-yard par 5. It is a long and straight hole that requires a tee shot favoring the right side that avoids the pine straw area and the bunkers. Your second shot needs to avoid the creek that crosses the fairway 145 yards from the green and a fairway bunker strategically placed right where you want to hit your lay-up shot. A lake runs the entire length of the left side of the green with bunkers left and right. All this trouble surrounding the green makes your approach shot all the more difficult.

The No. 1 handicap hole is the 448-yard, par-4 No. 4 called Stone Pond. A good tee shot will get you over the crest of the hill. This will set you up for a downhill second shot to a large green with bunkers left and water right. Par is like a birdie on this hole.

Cypresswood Golf Club Tradition Course

21602 Cypresswood Drive
Spring 77373
281-821-6300
Dir: Kelly Walker
A 54-hole daily-fee facility.
Take I-45 North to FM 1960, then east 6 miles to Cypresswood Drive. Go left, course entrance is on the right.

• • •

USGA rating: 74.4
Slope rating: 134
Sand traps: 100
Water holes: 11
Doglegs: 6 left/4 right
Type greens: Bermuda
Record: 66
Designers: Keith Foster
Year opened: 1998

• • •

Hole	Par	Yards	Hole	Par	Yards
1	4	463	10	4	405
2	4	384	11	3	236
3	3	203	12	5	543
4	4	448	13	4	464
5	5	606	14	3	185
6	4	376	15	4	394
7	5	528	16	4	472
8	3	196	17	4	318
9	4	453	18	5	546
Out	36	365	In	36	3563

Texas Top 100

41. Horseshoe Bay Resort — Applerock Course

obert Trent Jones Sr. certainly left his mark on this earth.

Jones has been the most prolific and most influential golf course architect of the 20th century, having either designed or redesigned 26 of *Golf Digest's* Top 100 Courses and 10 host courses for the U.S. Open.

It is here in the heart of Texas Hill Country that Jones left his biggest mark by designing not one or two championship golf courses, but three.

All of which, as you would expect from Jones, have been ranked among the best in the nation and are still among the best in the state. Building 54 holes at one site is something that Jones, in all his years, has never done before or since.

This is Horseshoe Bay, where a good walk is never spoiled. Here, the air is clean. The sky is clear. Near perfect year-round weather and the water from rivers, creeks and natural springs combine to nourish the land that is lush with vegetation and wildlife.

"I know of no area, including those known for several courses, that has a more interesting variety of golf than Horseshoe Bay," Jones says. "I rank this among the best in the world."

Of the three courses — the others are known as Ram Rock and Slick Rock — Applerock is the most breathtaking of the three and was selected in 1986 as the nation's "Best Resort Course" by *Golf Digest*. It currently ranks as the third best resort course in Texas in the annual rankings by the *Dallas Morning News*.

Applerock plays 6,999 yards from the back tees with a par 72. Its length, along with 56 sand traps and six water hazards and the shores of Lake LBJ, earned it a USGA rating of 74.0 and a slope of one hundred thirty four.

Applerock begins at the highest point on the Horseshoe Bay property and offers panoramic views of the rolling hills with Lake LBJ in the background.

Perhaps the most dramatic holes are the back-to-back par five 10th (567 yards) and 11th holes (509 yards), which dive from the top of the Caprock down to the shores of Lake LBJ.

The signature hole on Applerock is the 179-yard par 3 12th, where golfers have to hit over a stretch of Lake LBJ to reach the green.

Applerock was taken from some of the highest and most scenic land on the entire Horseshoe Bay property. Jones used the natural ebb and flow of the landscape to serve up stunning views of the entire area.

"The course has many beautiful vistas of the Texas Hill Country and Lake LBJ," one pro says. "It has remained a picturesque course since it opened with elevated greens and native oak and elm trees."

Horseshoe Bay Resort Applerock Course

PO Box 7766
Horseshoe Bay 78657
Dir.: Scott McDonough
830-598-2511
This is one of three 18-hole courses at this exclusive resort. From downtown Austin, take Highway 71 West to Highway 281, go north to FM 2147, left to Horseshoe Bay.

• • •

USGA rating: 74
Slope rating: 134
Sand traps: 56
Water holes: 8
Doglegs: 2 left/ 6 right
Type greens: Bentgrass
Record: 68
Designer: Robert T. Jones Sr.
Year opened: 1986

• • •

Hole	Par	Yards	Hole	Par	Yards
1	4	431	10	5	567
2	4	463	11	5	509
3	3	212	12	3	179
4	5	564	13	4	461
5	4	396	14	4	357
6	4	451	15	4	380
7	5	505	16	4	379
8	3	187	17	3	196
9	4	403	18	4	359
Out	36	3,612	In	36	3,387

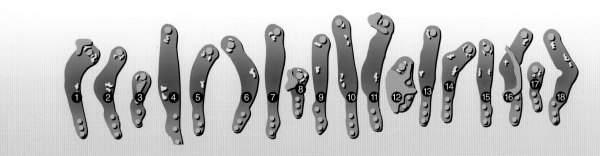

42. Waterwood National Country Club

For better or worse, Pete Dye is one of the most recognizable names in golf. As a golf course architect who has built some of the most difficult golf courses in the world, he is either loved or hated, usually depending on your handicap.

Dye made his money early in his career as a successful life insurance salesman and then he went into a business that makes golfers want to buy insurance by bringing them to their knees. If only you could purchase double-bogey protection at the first tee.

While most resort courses are built with the intention of allowing the guests to relax and have a good time, it should come as no surprise that Dye designed a course at Waterwood that might require you to take another vacation just to recuperate.

As one Huntsville resident says, you might love Waterwood or you might hate it, but surely won't forget it.

Waterwood is the toughest course in the Greater Houston area with a slope rating of 142 and a USGA rating of 73.7 (2.7 strokes over par). That ranks it among the 20 most difficult in the nation.

The high degree of difficulty is one of the reasons it hosted the finals of the PGA Tour Qualifying School three times. Graduating from Q-School is one of the most difficult feats in golf and

Waterwood is an appropriate place to play host to such a grueling test. It also ranks No. 10 in the *Shell Golf Guide* Top twenty five.

"It is a hell of a property," states Dye, who designed the course with his brother Roy before philosophical differences between the brothers and the developers led to their departure in the pre-construction stages. Bill Coore was called in to finish the job.

Long before Dye even dreamed of building PGA West, one of the most diabolical layouts in America, Waterwood National set the standard for cruel and unusual punishment when it opened in 1975.

The layout featured not only the characteristic railroad ties and bulk-headed water hazards for which Dye is known, but tight, tree-lined fairways and long carries over water, small greens and abundance of water and sand. Waterwood is relentless from the first tee to the 18th green.

As one pro says, "It's my personal favorite for self-abuse."

All of the holes have nicknames, but the most notable is the 225-yard, par-3 No. 14, which is nicknamed "The Cliffs" and is ranked among the toughest in the nation by *Golf Digest*.

The Waterwood layout was the brainchild of Roy Dye, who decided to put a tee box on one bluff overlooking Lake Livingston and the green on another, with little bailout area in between.

Waterwood National Country Club

1 Waterwood Parkway
Huntsville 77346
800-441-5211
Pro: Eddie Dey
A par-71, 6,871-yard, semi-private resort.
From Houston, take I-45 north to Highway 190, then east 18 miles to Waterwood Parkway. Turn left to entrance.

• • •

USGA rating: 73.7
Slope rating: 142
Sand traps: 66
Water holes: 10
Doglegs: 6 left/2 right
Type greens: Bermuda
Record: 63
Designers: Pete Dye and Roy Dye
Bill Coore (1982)
Year opened: 1975

• • •

Hole	Par	Yards	Hole	Par	Yards
1	4	442	10	5	547
2	3	225	11	3	198
3	4	413	12	4	398
4	4	450	13	4	428
5	4	425	14	3	225
6	4	443	15	4	385
7	3	151	16	4	352
8	5	491	17	4	377
9	4	401	18	5	536
Out	35	3445	In	36	3426

Texas Top 100

43. Bent Tree Country Club

The son of a Scottish golfer, Desmond Muirhead has been called a rebel, radical and a visionary. Muirhead was a landscape planner by trade who held a somewhat irreverent attitude about the game that originated in his homeland. He didn't get interested in golf course design until he emigrated to the United States in the 1950s and began working on retirement communities in Arizona.

With his interest in the game heightened, Muirhead returned to his homeland to make a whirlwind tour of the world's greatest courses. He came back to the United States in 1962 convinced he could do better and went on to become one of the most controversial architects in golf history.

"I owe very little allegiance to St. Andrews," Muirhead once said. "These courses have no mystique whatsoever."

Muirhead became one of the most prolific architects of the 1960s, but shortly after he built Bent Tree he suffered from burnout and exiled himself for 10 years to Australia when he resurfaced in Florida he designed more radical layouts and shaped sand traps like mermaids or alligators.

Before Muirhead went off the deep end, Dallas real estate developers Robert Folsom and John Murchison brought him to Dallas in 1974 to design Bent Tree Country Club to be the center-piece for a 700-acre, $250 million project adjacent to the ultra-exclusive Preston Trail Golf Club.

The golf course was built at an expense of $4.5 million and covers 190 acres of former cotton fields. The club got its name from the way the wind bent the trees. New trees, in fact, were actually planted with bands to make them bend.

The course was the home of the LPGA's annual tour stop in Dallas from 1979–1982 and later hosted the Senior PGA Tour's Reunion Pro-Am from 1985 through 1988. Nancy Lopez (1979), Jerilyn Britz (1980), Jan Stephenson (1981), and Sandra Spuzich (1982) were the LPGA winners. Peter Thomson (1985), Don January (1986), Chi Chi Rodriguez (1987), Orville Moody (1988) were the senior winners.

Muirhead's original design has remained intact, but Chicago-based architect Dick Nugget and former PGA of America President Joe Black added excitement to the course in 1990.

"The big thing was that the senior tour pros thought the back nine was a good golf course but the front nine was kind of blah," Nugent says. "The holes are exactly the same, but we redid the greens, did some things to make big greens play small, bunkering and mounds and some plantings to strengthen the shot-making requirements and did some things to bring water into play that wasn't there before."

Bent Tree Country Club

Bent Tree Country Club

5201 Westgrove
Dallas 75248
214-931-7326
Pro: David Price
A par-72, 7,113-yard private club.
From Dallas, take Dallas North Tollway to Westgrove, then turn east on Westgrove to club entrance.

• • •

USGA rating: 74.9
Slope rating: 139
Sand traps: 73
Water holes: 12
Doglegs: 6
Type Greens: Bentgrass
Record: 64
Designer: Desmond Muirhead
Year opened: 1974

• • •

Hole	Par	Yards	Hole	Par	Yards
1	4	418	10	4	383
2	4	445	11	4	438
3	5	578	12	4	398
4	4	422	13	5	555
5	3	209	14	3	191
6	5	530	15	4	405
7	4	439	16	5	570
8	3	191	17	3	180
9	4	374	18	4	387
Out	36	3606	In	36	3507

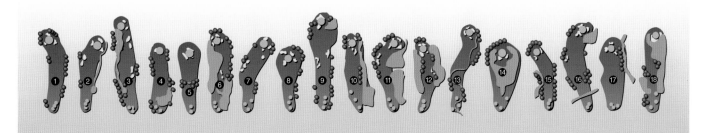

Texas Top 100

44. The Cliffs on Possum Kingdom

THE CLIFFS

The law of the land in real estate is location, location and location.

Location is also tantamount in the golf business. You have to have a good piece of land that is suitable for an interesting golf course. At the same time, you also have to be conveniently located to the masses.

At The Cliffs at Possum Kingdom, architect Robert von Hagge was blessed with more of the former and less of the latter. He designed one of the state's most interesting golf courses on this rolling, rocky terrain above Possum Kingdom Lake. The only problem is, many Dallas-Fort Worth golfers have never made the 1–2 hour trip to play it.

G. Robert Johnson, President of Hilton Head Island-based Landwest, Inc., was the original developer along with von Hagge. The developers experienced a financing delay during construction, and von Hagge said The Cliffs had the chance to be one of his best-ever designs before he had to cut back on his construction budget.

Nonetheless, with elevation changes of up to 100 feet on some holes, this golf course features as many as 13 different signature holes.

"I want to congratulate you on a spectacular golf course design," Johnson said after the course opened. "Normally if a course has one or two signature holes the developer is grateful, but in the case of The Cliffs we are indeed fortunate to have a golf course with 10, or in the opinion of some, as many as 12 or 13."

Von Hagge's objective is to "create beautiful golf courses without ever repeating himself. To that end, he must evaluate potential course site carefully.

"You've got to look at the property and determine the affirmatives and the negatives. If you have negatives like smokestacks, you've got to plan away from them. If you have beauty, you bring it into the shot picture. You plan your routing around the best things the land offers."

The 162-yard, par-3 15th hole at The Cliffs is a prime example.

"Exhilarating. Scary. Beautiful. Fun. Not another like it in Texas," says longtime golf writer Harless Wade of *The Dallas Morning News*. "You need an elevator to play it."

Seven tee boxes, from 97 to 162 yards, on the edge of a cliff, looking down 100 feet to a slender green, guarded by water right, stone wall left, sand in front and a levee rear."

Not long after the course opened, however, the savings and loan that financed the project went belly-up and the course was operated on a survival budget by the FDIC for several months before it was bought by Dallas-based Double Diamond, Inc.

The Cliffs on Possum Kingdom

Star Route Box 19
Graford 78449
940-549-7721
Pro: Glenn Sockwell
This course is located on Star Route in the City of Graford, 75 miles northwest of Fort Worth near Highway 16.

• • •

USGA rating: 73.8
Slope rating: 139
Sand traps: 54
Water holes: 2
Doglegs: 4 left/2 right
Type greens: Bentgrass
Record: 65
Designer: Robert von Hagge and Bruce Devlin
Year opened: 1989

• • •

Hole	Par	Yards	Hole	Par	Yards
1	5	538	10	4	388
2	4	445	11	4	400
3	3	196	12	3	175
4	5	548	13	4	388
5	4	368	14	4	416
6	3	166	15	3	162
7	4	425	16	5	555
8	5	555	17	4	431
9	3	195	18	4	457
Out	36	3,436	In	35	3,372

45. Dallas Athletic Club — Gold Course

Every golf course has its heyday, but Dallas Athletic Club has had the good fortune of having more than its share.

DAC started out as a popular downtown club more for tennis and social purposes. For those members who liked to play golf, the club had an arrangement for its members to play on the now defunct Glen Lakes Country Club.

By 1952, however, the club totaled 3,500 members and Glen Lakes was busting at the seams. So on Nov. 25, 1952, members voted to build a country club on a 350-acre site in northeast Dallas.

The land, formerly part of the Chapman Ranch, was sold for $400 an acre for a total of $140,000. It was financed by a $48 increase in monthly dues from $150 to $198 annually. The club was originally known as Dallas Athletic Club Country Club.

The club celebrated its 10-year anniversary in August 1963, when played host to the PGA Championship and drew national attention. Crowds endured record temperatures ranging up to 113 degrees — still the hottest week on record in Texas — to get a glimpse of Jack Nicklaus and Arnold Palmer vying for one of golf's four major championships.

Little-known Dick Hart was the first-round leader with an opening round 66 and had a three-shot lead over Nicklaus, Shelley Mayfield, Julius Boros, Bob Charles and Mason Rudolph. He maintained that lead through 36 holes with a 72 on Friday that gave him a 138 total, still three shots ahead of Mayfield and Boros and four ahead of Nicklaus.

But in the third round, always noted as moving day, scores plummeted. Eleven players broke 70, led by Bruce Crampton's low round of the tournament of 65 that gave him a three-shot lead over little-known Dave Ragan.

Crampton faltered over the last few holes and Nicklaus, at the age of 23, joined Ben Hogan, Byron Nelson and Gene Sarazen as the only men in golf history to win the PGA, U.S. Open and the Masters.

In 1985, DAC began its second heyday when Nicklaus the architect returned to renovate Ralph Plummer's original layouts to bring the club once again to the top of the charts in Dallas golf.

Plummer originally built the Blue Course in 1954 and the Gold Course in 1962, but his layouts were relatively flat, the trees still young and the greens unimaginative. But, thanks to Nicklaus' renovation, the courses now feature bentgrass greens, waterfalls around the fifth and 11th greens, mounding and grass bunkers that make the course much more challenging.

"You could hold a major tournament on either the Gold or the Blue Course here," Nicklaus said at the unveiling of the new Gold Course.

Dallas Athletic Club Gold Course

4111 La Prada Drive
Dallas 75228
972-279-3671
Pro: Dennis Ewing
A 36-hole private club.
From Dallas, take I-75 North to I-635, then go east to La Prada Drive. Turn right on La Prada to club entrance on the right.

• • •

USGA rating: 73.4
Slope rating: 133
Sand traps: 36
Water holes: 9
Doglegs: 5 left/3 right
Type greens: Bentgrass
Record: 65
Designer: Ralph Plummer
Year opened: 1954

• • •

Hole	Par	Yards	Hole	Par	Yards
1	5	496	10	5	487
2	4	390	11	4	344
3	5	531	12	4	324
4	3	179	13	5	513
5	4	360	14	3	157
6	4	364	15	4	370
7	3	166	16	3	175
8	4	280	17	4	398
9	4	377	18	4	382
Out	36	3143	In	36	3150

46. Shady Oaks Country Club

A young girl was outside the clubhouse working on her swing, using her reflection in the window to double-check her motion through the hitting zone. She repeated time and again, checking her weight shift, hand position, shoulder turn.

Suddenly an image appeared from the other side of the window. Ben Hogan smiled, and offered her a few pointers.

Perhaps the only thing you need to know about Shady Oaks Country Club is that it was the home of the late Ben Hogan. One of golf's greatest legends, who grew up in Fort Worth. Hogan passed away in July 1997.

Both Colonial and Shady Oaks were the brainchild of Fort Worth developer Marvin Leonard. Just over two decades after his dream came true at Colonial, Leonard decided to build another club that was perhaps even more exclusive.

Leonard spent $3.52 million — an incredibly large sum of money for any club in 1958 — to build a club that was "different and beautiful" that rivaled any in America for luxury and attention to detail. Above the fireplace, workers went to painstaking detail to build a shady oak Mosaic of semiprecious stones.

The original memberships went on sale for $6,500 with $35 monthly dues. Now, the pricetag is $20,000 to join and $284 a month. The maximum membership was set at 650.

"I didn't build this course for the championship golfer," Leonard said. "It is for the average golfer. The fellow who can hit a tee shot 190 yards and keep his other shots straight — can par this course. I think a woman has just as much right to enjoy a golf course as her husband."

Says Hogan, who shot his age for the first time here on June 6, 1967, when he carded a 64: "You won't find anything like this — course, clubhouse, everything — any place else in the world."

Shady Oaks was torn from a 1,200-acre tract Leonard bought in 1955 from the Amon Carter Foundation. It was known in Fort Worth as the "Lone Oak Tract" and, legend has it, that the first swings ever taken at Shady Oaks were those of five horse thieves swinging from the lone oak that inspired the course's name.

Leonard hired legendary architect Robert Trent Jones to lay out a course on 200 acres to fit the terrain of the land and the tree-flecked fairways. All greens averaged 180 feet from fringe to fringe, and Jones used a strain of bentgrass developed at Colonial in Leonard's personal nursery.

The layout measures 6,975 yards with three par-5s, including two back to back. The course is very hilly and, despite the large greens, accurate iron shots are required to get in birdie range.

Shady Oaks Country Club

320 Roaring Springs Road
Fort Worth 76114
817-732-3333
Pro: Mike Wright
A par-71, 6,975-yard private club.
From Fort Worth, take I-30 West to Roaring Springs Road, then go north on Roaring Springs to club entrance on the left.

• • •

USGA rating: 70
Slope rating:
Sand traps: 48
Water holes: 3
Doglegs: 4 left/3 right
Type Greens: Bentgrass
Record: N/A
Designer: Robert Trent Jones Sr.
Year opened: 1958

• • •

Hole	Par	Yards	Hole	Par	Yards
1	4	334	10	4	401
2	4	447	11	4	423
3	4	401	12	3	225
4	4	384	13	4	435
5	3	234	14	5	568
6	4	422	15	5	531
7	3	184	16	3	159
8	5	618	17	4	397
9	4	381	18	4	431
Out	35	3405	In	36	3570

Texas Top 100

47. Royal Oaks Country Club

Golf course architects have the best of all worlds. First, they get to play with other people's money. Second, they get paid to design a golf course and leave their fingerprints in the earth.

Thirdly, if the course turns out good, they revel in the spotlight; if it doesn't, they wipe their hands and move on to the next project. Don January and Billy Martindale were PGA tour pros who designed many courses for other people. But they were always limited by the developer. The developer would take the best pieces of land for home sites and leave the rest for the golf course.

When it came to Royal Oaks, January and Martindale found a promising piece of land into which they could sink both their teeth and their money. Since their own money was at stake, it should come as no surprise that Royal Oaks was by far their best effort.

They teamed with developer Dale Mann to purchase a heavily wooded area near Central Expressway and Greenville Avenue in a flood plain bisected by White Rock Creek. They built a golf course that originally was going to be a men's-only club, but before it was finished they decided to make it open to everyone. The developers leased the club to the members on a 20-year lease basis, with the option to buy the land from the three developers at a predetermined price.

The course opened in September 1969, with former SMU football player Raleigh Blakley serving as the first president and a board of directors that included such notable figures as Tom Landry, Stuart Hunt, Bob Folsom, Graham Ross, Robert Strauss, Jim Chambers and Jim Lawson. Before the course was finished, more than 200 members had signed up for the $1,500 initiation fee.

The layout, which has been the stomping grounds of such players as U.S. Amateur champion and British Open Champion 1998 Justin Leonard, features some of the most demanding holes in D/FW. The layout was renovated in 1985 by Jay Morrish and bentgrass greens were added. Further renovation on the 13th hole and driving range was done in the 1990s. The best hole is the 467-yard, par-4 13th, which one pro says is "too long, has too many trees and requires too much carry." It is unquestionably one of the toughest holes in D/FW. Some par 5s are shorter.

The hole doglegs to the right along a curve in White Rock Creek. Players must cross water immediately off the tee, but it poses its biggest problem on the second shot since the creek crosses the fairway again in front of the green. Because of the length of the hole, most players will be forced to carry the ball about 220 yards or more to clear the creek and reach the angled green.

Royal Oaks Country Club

7915 Greenville Avenue
Dallas 75231
214-691-6091
Pro: Randy Smith
A par-71, 6,949-yard private club.
From Dallas, take I-35 North to North Central Expressway, north to Royal Lane, east to Greenville Avenue, south one-half mile to entrance.

• • •

USGA rating: 74.3
Slope rating:141
Sand traps: 55
Water holes: 11
Doglegs: 5 left/4 right
Type greens: Bentgrass
Record: 63
Designers: Billy Martindale
Year opened: 1969

• • •

Hole	Par	Yards	Hole	Par	Yards
1	4	440	10	4	415
2	4	391	11	4	428
3	4	439	12	3	199
4	3	191	13	4	467
5	5	555	14	5	547
6	4	412	15	4	346
7	4	456	16	3	218
8	3	171	17	4	396
9	4	368	18	5	510
Out	35	3423	In	36	3526

48. San Antonio Country Club

San Antonio Country Club was designed by some of golf's greatest architects and is the oldest and one of the finest private courses in the area.

Located near downtown in the fashionable Alamo Heights area, the course opened in 1907 after being designed by architect Alex Findlay, one of America's true golf pioneers. Findlay opened what is now the back nine and followed with the front nine in 1913. He laid out a short, compact course lined by the upscale neighborhood homes and the still fairly new Fort Sam Houston. The fort served as the main army base for the South Texas area soldiers who were just returning from the Spanish-American War.

At the time, apartments were available for rent inside the clubhouse for the members and guests. Tragedy struck in 1916 as a huge fire raged through the clubhouse, killing three sleeping guests.

The first renovation came from noted architect A.W. Tillinghast. His work at SACC came in the late 1920s, when he designed nearby Oak Hills Country Club and did some work at Fort Sam Houston. Despite being a great architect in his own right, Tillinghast made no major changes in Findlay's classic, old-style design. There is nothing tricky about the layout, only long graceful holes along the rolling hills.

It was during this time that the club sold some land to the government to accommodate Fort Sam Houston expansion. It was a move now reflected upon with sadness by members who complain of cramped course conditions. Fort Sam also gave birth to a popular club legend that almost all putts break toward the nearby water tower.

Among the changes longtime head pro Tod Menefee has witnessed is the changing of the nines. The front nine is now started by a 165-yard par 3 on what used to be grazing land for dairy cattle.

During World War II, Menefee opened one of the first private club driving ranges in the nation.

"We lost all our caddies during the war and couldn't buy any new golf balls," Menefee says. "I collected the balls from the shag bags, let the members hit them, then hired a boy to wash the balls so they could hit them again."

In 1946, SACC became one of the first clubs in Texas to use motorized carts. The club hosted the Texas Seniors tournament for 21 years and the carts were known as senior specials.

Kerrville architect Joe Finger remodeled 15 greens in 1957 and Jay Morrish reworked a few more holes in 1986. The course annually hosts the national AJGA San Antonio Shootout, hosting some of the best young players in the nation.

Former British Open champion Bill Rogers became golf director in 1990.

San Antonio Country Club

San Antonio Country Club

4100 New Braunfels Avenue
San Antonio 78209
210-824-8861
Director of Golf: Bill Rogers
A par 72, 6,759-yard private club.
From the San Antonio Airport, take Highway 281 south, turn left on Hildebrand to clubhouse.

• • •

USGA rating: 72.1
Slope rating: 122
Bunkers: 67
Water holes: 6
Doglegs: 5 left/2 right
Type greens: Bermuda
Record: 63
Designer: Alex Findlay
Year opened: 1907

• • •

Hole	Par	Yards	Hole	Par	Yards
1	3	165	10	4	351
2	4	379	11	3	195
3	3	162	12	5	484
4	4	463	13	4	381
5	5	508	14	4	39
6	4	431	15	3	168
7	4	429	16	5	505
8	4	320	17	4	436
9	5	597	18	4	424
Out	36	3454	In	36	3336

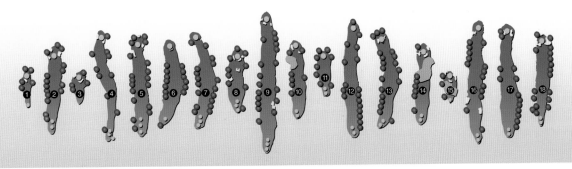

Texas Top 100

49. Oak Hills Country Club

As an architect, Albert Warren Tillinghast was a true original, a man who always preferred quality over quantity. His golf courses have become enduring classics. Just listen. Winged Foot in New York. Baltusrol in New Jersey. San Francisco Golf Club.

Not to forget Oak Hills Country Club in San Antonio.

Designed by Tillinghast during a South Texas trip in the 1920s, the course has drawn praise for its tree-lined fairways, deep bunkers and tricky greens and is one of the state's most historic courses since it was opened in 1922.

It was originally known as Alamo Country Club, but closed during the Depression and later reopened as Oak Hills in 1946.

Oak Hills hosted the PGA Tour's Texas Open from 1977 to 1994. It has finished first in the *San Antonio-Express News'* private club survey each of the last two years. Ben Crenshaw won the Vantage Championship here in 1986 and Tom Watson won his last American tournament here in 1987 at the Nabisco Championships.

"If they had another 500 yards out here," says Austin native and PGA Tour star Tom Kite, "this would be one of the finest courses in the country."

The space problem is brought on by something Tillinghast likely never imagined seven decades ago. The large and ever-growing

South Texas Medical Center sits along the right side of the driving range and front nine.

From the front gate to the first tee, the golfer gets an idea of the Tillinghast touch.

"This is a wonderful blend of holes that requires finesse and power, strategy and skill," pro Warren Chancellor says.

The course used to be even tighter before a tornado in the mid-80s took out many of the trees on the back side. But where it lacked in length, Tillinghast made up for it with doglegs that sometimes take the driver out of your game and instead put emphasis on placement.

A prime example is the par-4 No. 8. At 309 yards from the back tee, it is driveable for many big hitters but the fairway winds to the left with several huge bunkers protecting the front of the green.

Both nines end with a par 3. The 198-yard 18th is a gambler's delight. There is a fountain in front of the green with sand and grass traps all around.

Several finishes to the Texas Open have been decided on this short piece of property. Jay Morrish did some renovations in 1984, but didn't change Tillinghast's basic design.

"Oak Hills requires you to hit every shot in your bag," says Nick Milanovich, executive director of the San Antonio Golf Association. "If you get off-line, you can't just walk out there and find your ball."

OAK HILLS
Country Club

Oak Hills Country Club
5403 Fredericksburg Road
San Antonio 78229
210-349-5151
Pro: Warren Chancellor
A par-71, 6,650-yard private club.
Take I-10 West, take Callahan Road to Fredericksburg Road, turn right and go to signal light, then left to club.

• • •

USGA rating: 71.8
Slope rating: 128
Sand traps: 54
Water holes: 4
Doglegs: 3 left/3 right
Type greens: Bermuda
Record: 61
Designers: A.W. Tillinghast and Jay Morrish (1984)
Year opened: 1922.

• • •

Hole	Par	Yards	Hole	Par	Yards
1	4	349	10	5	506
2	3	175	11	4	426
3	4	456	12	4	44
4	4	389	13	3	220
5	5	604	14	4	328
6	4	352	15	5	527
7	4	460	16	4	385
8	4	309	17	4	367
9	3	155	18	3	198
Out	35	3249	In	36	3401

Texas Top 100

50. Timarron Country Club

Nobody knew exactly what kind of impact D/FW International Airport would have on the local economy when it was built in the 1970s.

At the time it seemed too far from both downtown Dallas and Fort Worth to benefit anyone other than cab drivers and shuttle bus services escorting passengers on their long voyage home.

It has taken almost two decades in fact for the big picture to materialize. With the addition of Fort Worth Alliance Airport in 1988, the fight is now on for real estate between the two airports to build homes and communities to meet a new surge in growth in population.

Small towns like Colleyville, Keller and Southlake were once unknown to most D/FW residents, but now are on the verge of a growth explostion. This is the land of opportunity. The new North Dallas, if you will.

Among the players in this high-stakes game are Mobil Land Development, IBM and Ross Perot. The winners will be Dallas residents looking for easy access to the airport and new places to play golf. Perot owns 20,000 acres in north Tarrant County, and donated the land on which the Alliance airport was built.

Mobil Land, which owns thousands of acres in the area and also owns Stonebridge Ranch in McKinney and Highland Shores in Lewisville, produced the area's first major subdivision with its 1,100-acre Timarron in northern Colleyville and southeast Southlake.

"We think we are well-positioned for some time to come," said Larry T. Midtbo, president of Mobil Land's Southwestern division. "Part of our strategy has been to build a little synergism. There is no one in Dallas that has as many master-planned communities." Wanting to be associated with nothing less than first-class facilities, Mobil hired architect Baxter Spann to work with Byron Nelson for the construction of the Timarron Golf Course, which opened in 1994 and was rated as the seventh "Best New Public Course" by *Golf Digest* in 1995. Sandra Haynie, an LPGA Hall of Famer and Dallas native, was hired as the director of golf.

"I'm thrilled to be associated with such a prestigious new course," said Haynie, winner of 42 LPGA Tour events. "Especially one in which Mr. Nelson has been such an active force."

This rolling course has mounded fairways and the course winds back and forth over Old Bear Creek. There are several trees guarding the fairways and the bentgrass greens are large, undulating, and fast.

The signature hole is No.18, a 535-yard, par 5, which is open on the left side from the tee, then drops downhill over the creek to an island green that has bunkers on the left and right.

TIMARRON COUNTRY CLUB

Timarron Country Club

1400 Byron Nelson Parkway
Southlake 76092
817-481-7529

A par-72, 7,000-yard semi-private club. From Highway 114, exit White Chapel Boulevard, go south to Continental Boulevard, left to Byron Nelson Parkway. Turn right to course entrance..

• • •

USGA rating: 74.2
Slope rating: 137
Sand traps: 23
Water holes: 7
Doglegs: 3 left/ 2 right
Type Greens: Bentgrass
Record: 64
Designers: Byron Nelson and Ken Dye
Year opened: 1995

• • •

Hole	Par	Yards	Hole	Par	Yards
1	5	540	10	4	395
2	4	370	11	4	440
3	3	185	12	4	455
4	4	410	13	5	550
5	3	160	14	3	195
6	5	520	15	4	350
7	4	430	16	4	420
8	4	445	17	3	215
9	4	385	18	5	535
Out	36	3445	In	36	3555

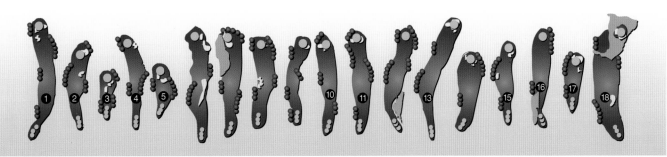

51. Hollytree Country Club

For more than a decade in the mid-70s and 80s, the architectural team of Robert von Hagge and Bruce Devlin designed the most golf courses in Texas — more than any other architect. Many of those are also among the best in Texas.

On the Texas Top 100 list, for instance, they designed No. 2 Crown Colony, No. 10 Walden on Lake Conroe, No. 13 TPC at The Woodlands, No. 15 Gleneagles Kings Course, No. 21 Club at Sonterra, No. 32 Gleneagles Queen's Course, No. 44 Cliffs on Possum Kingdom, No. 56 Chase Oaks' Blackjack Course and No. 69 Club at Falcon Point. And, not to forget, No. 51 Hollytree.

Von Hagge and Devlin had somewhat of a Jekyl and Hyde approach to golf design. Devlin, as a former PGA and Senior PGA Tour player, was the kinder-gentler partner. Von Hagge, on the other hand, might have been considered diabolical, if not genius.

Their target-golf designs put a premium on risk-reward ratios. The higher the risk, the greater the reward. And since most golfers love to gamble, a von Hagge-Devlin course is a good place to get their fix.

Hollytree is certainly no exception. Carved out of the East Texas pines, oaks, dogwoods and azaleas, it is both challenging and beautiful, and hosts the annual Azalea Invitational for the state's top amateurs every march. It also hosts the NCAA Southland Conference championship in April.

The total yardage is only 6,663 yards from the back tees with five par 3s and five par 5s, but it still measures out to a demanding 136 slope rating.

Where it lacks in lengths, Devlin and von Hagge more than made up for it with a wide variety of natural water hazards (streams, creeks, ponds and five lakes) on 14 holes and narrow, tree-lined fairways. Nine holes require a carry over water off the tee.

The signature hole is the par-4 15th, which has water off the tee and down the left side of the fairway and in front of the heavily bunkered, two-tiered green. After a well-placed drive, it still takes a second shot with a mid or long iron to reach the green.

No. 14 is a 554-yard par 5 that doglegs right with water protecting the left side of the fairway all the way to the green, out of bounds down the right side and a small stream crossing in front of the green.

Nos. 7 and 9 share the same tee box and both require a carry of 150 yards over water to reach their respective fairway.

No. 3 has creeks all over the place. It measures only 387 yards, but creeks run down both sides of the fairway and in front of the green. A row of five bunkers divides the fairway in half, leaving little margin for error off the tee.

HOLLYTREE

Hollytree Country Club
6700 Hollytree Drive
Tyler 75703
903-581-7723
A par 72, 6,663-yard private club.
From Dallas take I-20 to Tyler/Lindale exit, at Loop 323, turn right to South Broadway, right at Grande Street and right at Hollytree Drive then left to club entrance.

• • •

USGA rating: 73.3
Slope rating: 136
Sand traps:
Water holes: 13
Doglegs:
Type greens: Bermuda
Record: N/A
Designers: Robert von Hagge
*   and Bruce Devlin*
Year opened: 1983

Hole	Par	Yards	Hole	Par	Yards
1	5	512	10	4	363
2	4	413	11	3	161
3	4	387	12	4	394
4	3	176	13	3	169
5	5	513	14	5	554
6	3	164	15	4	433
7	4	362	16	5	479
8	3	221	17	4	395
9	5	552	18	4	442
Out	36	3,300	In	36	3,390

Texas Top 100

52. Kingwood Country Club — Island Course

Joe Finger is one of the more interesting characters in the golf architecture business, having gotten into the business quite by accident at a time when golf course architecture was not really considered big business.

Finger was the son of the architect who built Houston City Hall. He received his masters degree in engineering from MIT in 1941, and then went to work in the petroleum industry where he developed a number of patented products in the plastics industry.

But it was not until legendary Texas architect Ralph Plummer came to Westwood Country Club, where Finger was chairman of the greens committee, that Finger finally fell in love with golf architecture — since it enabled him to combined his creativity and engineering background with his love for golf.

Finger learned well from his master, and eventually became one of the most active Texas golf course designers over the next 40 years. Finger has had five golf courses in *Golf Digest's* Top 100 in America.

His engineering background came in handy in trying to build golf courses and solve the omnipresent drainage problems that go hand-in-hand with the flat Texas terrain. He more than met the challenge at Kingwood Country Club's Island Course,

which was built in 1974 and still ranks among his best works.

The Island Course at Kingwood forces golfers to think about their playing strategy on every shot — before they pull out their driver on the tee box.

In 1974, the 573-yard, par-5 No. 6 hole was selected as the Hole of the Year by the American Society of Golf Course Architects. But the most distinguished hole is the par-5 No. 18, which is ranked No. 4 in area's toughest 25 and is one of the toughest in the state with its double-fairway and island green. In '76, *Golf Digest* ranked it as the toughest finishing hole in golf.

It plays 576 yards with a lake that runs the length of the fairway on the left and then surrounds the green. The fairway splits about 300 yards from the green, but there are two more lakes — one in the middle of the fairway and another on the far right side. Players must choose their club and shot placement carefully, because the hole leaves little margin for error. As one pro says, "It spells disaster all the way."

"I love that hole," says Finger, who is now retired. "Off the tee, I don't think it's that difficult. I give you two choices — one to play it safe and one to gamble. There is plenty of room to land the ball, but from the tee box it doesn't look that way. The second shot is the one that gets me. You just can't miss a shot or it will grab you."

Kingwood Country Club Island Course

1700 Lake Kingwood Trail
Kingwood 77339
Pro: David Preisler
281-358-2171
This is a 72-hole private club.
From Houston, take U.S. 59 North to Kingwood Drive, then right 6 miles on Lake Kingwood Trail to entrance.

• • •

USGA rating: 74.8
Slope rating: 136
Sand traps: 67
Water holes: 11
Doglegs: 7 left/3 right
Type greens: Bermuda
Record: 65
Designer: Joe Finger
Year opened: 1974

• • •

Hole	Par	Yards	Hole	Par	Yards
1	5	514	10	4	444
2	4	412	11	5	587
3	3	168	12	3	189
4	4	411	13	4	426
5	4	407	14	4	420
6	5	573	15	4	462
7	4	428	16	4	415
8	3	194	17	3	228
9	4	453	18	5	576
Out	36	3560	In	36	3749

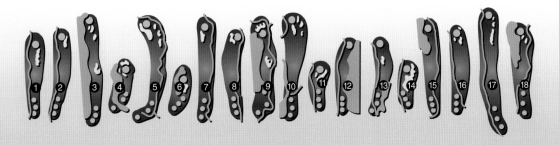

53. Bentwater Country Club — Weiskopf Course

Developer J.B. Belin has perfected the business of building master-planned communities with a golf course as the feature attraction. He has built many of them since the 1960s and each new one seems to get a little better.

The first key to success is location. The second is the topography of the land. And the third is a great design.

At Bentwater Country Club, on the northwest shore of Lake Conroe, all of the keys to success fell into place. The final masterstroke was hiring the architectural team of Tom Weiskopf and Jay Morrish to pick up where Mother Nature left off by designing a golf course that would make surrounding homeowners proud.

Built in 1992, Bentwater East was the first of two golf courses at the exclusive residential community, where members must buy property before they join. Both courses are ranked in the Texas Top 100.

In more than a decade of partnership, Weiskopf and Morrish have produced some of the best golf courses in America. Weiskopf brought to the table all of his experience as a 15-time winner on the PGA Tour, while Morrish used his experience in engineering and landscape architecture.

"For the most part, we have not built a bad course yet," Weiskopf says. "We built some excellent courses and some better than average."

While most of their best works have been desert-style courses in Arizona, they rose to the occasion again at Bentwater to take full advantage of the densely wooded terrain and rolling hills not found inside Houston's city limits.

The back nine might be the most scenic in the state. The par-4 12th features a double fairway with a green on the edge of Lake Conroe. A stand of trees divides the fairway in half, and on the tee golfers must choose to take the shorter, tighter route to the green or the longer, wider route. The approach is downhill to a green protected in front and on the left by Lake Conroe.

When players step on the tee at the par-3 14th, players are offered a beautiful view of Lake Conroe and its countless sailboats, jet skis and speedboats. And then they turn to face one of the scariest shots of the day, a 200-yard carry over the edge of the lake to the green.

No. 16 is another great hole. It is a 418-yard par 4 with Lake Conroe protecting the entire left side of the fairway and green. Off the tee, a fairway bunker also guards the right corner of the fairway. Just finding the fairway is the biggest factor here.

No. 6 is one of the hardest holes in the Houston area. It is a 470-yard par 4 that plays uphill and usually into the wind. Par here is reason to celebrate.

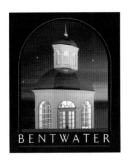

Bentwater
Country Club
Weiskopf Course
800 Bentwater Drive
Montgomery 77356
281-353-1912
Pro: Brett Lossin
An exclusive 36-hole private club. Go north on I-45 to Bentwater exit, then west for 7.5 miles to entrance on left.

• • •

USGA rating: 72.4
Slope rating: 124
Sand traps: 73
Water holes: 4
Doglegs: 3 left/6 right
Type greens: Bermuda
Record: N/A
Designers: Jay Morrish
*   and Tom Weiskopf*
Year opened: 1989

• • •

Hole	Par	Yards	Hole	Par	Yards
1	4	410	10	4	418
2	5	543	11	5	536
3	3	204	12	4	427
4	4	344	13	4	310
5	4	327	14	3	200
6	4	470	15	5	529
7	5	550	16	4	418
8	3	207	17	3	180
9	4	411	18	4	423
Out	36	3466	In	36	3441

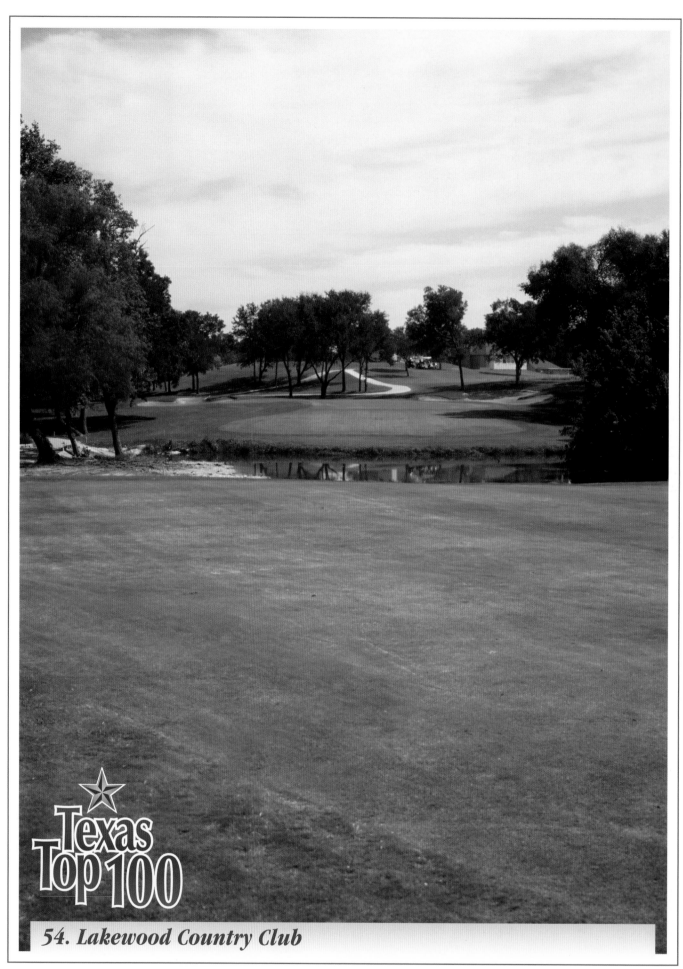

54. Lakewood Country Club

I t didn't take long for the game of golf to catch on in Dallas. After watching the great success of Dallas Country Club at the turn of the century, a group of Dallas' most outstanding civic leaders decided to tame another undeveloped area east of downtown.

In 1912, such notable Dallas figures as Herbert Marcus, Edward Titche, W.J. Lawther and the Linz Brothers — Albert, Ben and Simon — were among a small group of businessmen who assembled to incorporate with the purpose of "supporting and maintaining the ancient game of golf and other innocent sports."

The club was financed at $15,000, divided into 300 shares at $50 each. By 1917, shares were $250 each. Now it is $25,000 for a full golf membership and the members now number more than 1,100.

Eight decades later Lakewood Country Club is situated in one of the oldest and most beautiful residential sections of Dallas. While the club now offers tennis and swimming, it is still first and foremost a golf club with well-kept greens, verdant wooded fairways, winding creeks, lakes and natural hazards.

The original layout was designed by legendary architect Tom Bendelow, who built Dallas' first course at Dallas Country Club and later designed such famed layouts as the No. 2 course at Medinah. Bendelow built the first four courses in the Dallas/Fort Worth area.

As the surrounding community grew around it, however, the club sold some of its original land to developers and the layout was redesigned in 1947 by Ralph Plummer. In 1995, Ben Crenshaw and Bill Coore renovated the course and brought it back to its original design.

Lakewood was the site of the first Dallas Open, which is now known as the Byron Nelson Classic. The first tournament in 1944 was won by none other than Nelson.

In 1951, Lakewood hosted the Weathervane Women's Open, one of five tournaments sponsored that year by Weathervane.

While the first hole is a 330-yard par 4 that plays downhill off the tee and then back up to an elevated green and is almost reachable for big hitters, the layout hits you hard with a 2-3-4 punch that rank as three of the toughest holes on the course and can make or break your round early.
No. 2 is a 432-yard dogleg left with out of bounds all the way down the left side and behind a green that is guarded by three bunkers. No. 3 is a 454-yard, par 4 that doglegs slightly left with two bunkers on left and a creek running the length of the left side. On the approach, players will be using a long iron to a green protected by two bunkers left and right.

Lakewood Country Club

6430 Gaston Avenue
Dallas 75214
214-821-1491
Pro: Gilbert Freeman
A par-71, 6,657-yard private club.
From Dallas, take I-30 East to Munger, left on Munger to Columbia. Right on Columbia to entrance on the right.

• • •

USGA rating: 72.4
Slope rating: 132
Sand traps: 65
Water holes: 5
Doglegs: 3 left/2 right
Type greens: Bentgrass
Record: 63
Designers: Tom Bendelow
*   and Ralph Plummer*
*   and Ben Crenshaw*
Year opened: 1912

Hole	Par	Yards	Hole	Par	Yards
1	4	330	10	4	390
2	4	432	11	4	426
3	4	454	12	3	154
4	5	554	13	4	393
5	3	201	14	3	212
6	4	359	15	4	427
7	3	201	16	4	355
8	4	340	17	5	491
9	5	523	18	4	415
Out	36	3394	In	35	3263

Texas Top 100

55. *Las Colinas Country Club*

Before the skyscrapers, before the multi-million dollar homes, there was Ben Carpenter, a 5,000-acre ranch, a lot of cattle and a dream.

In this place, Carpenter envisioned a new downtown area with modern, glass buildings and a modern tram to get from one place to the next. There would also be modern new homes to house all the people that worked here and, of course, a place for them to play golf.

This was 1963. This would be Dallas' new frontier, and he called on architect Joe Finger to help tame it.

Finger will never forget the day when he was out on the property checking to make sure the greens at Las Colinas Country Club were smooth, when he looked over the hill and saw a herd of angry Brahma steer coming at him being chased by several of Carpenter's ranch hands.

"Carpenter wasn't a golfer, so his cattle came first," Finger said. "I'm just glad none of them got hurt while running over my golf course." Some three decades later, Carpenter's dream city is a reality and the cattle have been replaced by people who live, work and play here.

In 1968, it hosted the U.S. Women's Amateur, where Catherine Lacost defeated Shelley Hamlin in the 36 hole final, 3 and 2.

Finger took advantage of the undulating terrain to create a balanced combination of uphill, downhill and side-hill holes and produce a layout that measures 6,809 yards but plays to par of 71 and a rating of 72.6.

"We built Las Colinas in the style of that era," Finger says. "We didn't do all the mounding and contouring that we did 20 years later down the road at Hackberry Creek. But because of the terrain, we didn't really need to."

The two most difficult holes are a pair of long par 4s, the 437-yard fifth and the 423-yard 16th.

No. 5 is a slight dogleg right over a creek off the tee. The creek then runs down the right side of the fairway along with a row of trees to the green.

The 16th is another long dogleg right, with fairway bunkers pinching the landing area from both corners of the fairway. On the approach, players are required to hit a long iron through a chute of trees to the green.

No. 15 is a finesse par-4 401 yards, in which players must carry their approach over water to a peninsula green protected by water on three sides and sand on the other.

Water comes into play on all three shots into the 550-yard, par-5 18th. A creek runs in front of the tee, but then golfers must be wary of a lake that cuts into the landing area and protects the front and right sides of the green on the approach shot.

Las Colinas Country Club

4400 North O'Connor Road
Irving 75062
972-541-1141
Pro: Robert Singletary
A par-71, 6,809-yard private club.
From Dallas, take I-35E north to
Highway 183, then go west on 183 to
Highway 114. North on 114 to O'Connor,
then left to club entrance.

• • •

USGA rating: 72.6
Slope rating: 129
Sand traps: 57
Water holes: 6
Doglegs: 3 left/2 right
Type greens: Bentgrass
Record: 62
Designer: Joe Finger
Year opened: 1963

• • •

Hole	Par	Yards	Hole	Par	Yards
1	4	444	10	5	542
2	4	347	11	3	194
3	5	521	12	4	394
4	3	196	13	3	155
5	4	437	14	4	439
6	3	189	15	4	401
7	5	556	16	4	423
8	4	403	17	3	173
9	4	445	18	5	550
Out	36	3538	In	35	3271

56. The Bandit at Long Creek

Golf has Tiger Woods. Golf architecture has Keith Foster.

Foster is one of the rising young stars of the golf course design business. He has been putting his finger and footprints in the earth all over the place and in the past year has produced three new courses in the Texas Top 100.

Foster's first entry in Texas was The Quarry in San Antonio, which was built out of an old abandoned rock quarry. His most recent entries are Texas Star in Euless, the Tradition at Cypresswood and, of course, the Bandit at Long Creek in New Braunfels.

Foster has learned to take whatever the land has to offer — be it a rock quarry, desert terrain, flood plain or thick forest — and produce a golf course that fits perfectly in that setting.

At The Bandit, Foster took advantage of 100-foot elevation changes, native grasses, trees, creeks and varying terrain and turned them into a memorable golfing challenge.

"The Bandit has everything going for it," Foster says. "It is easily one of the best natural locations for a golf course I have ever seen. I didn't so much 'design' the holes as simply uncover them.

"Once people start playing The Bandit, I think it will quickly become one of the most celebrated golf courses in the Southwest."

New Braunfels is well known to many Texans as a great launching point for a raft ride down the Guadalupe River, but Foster's 6,928-yard layout takes landlubbers on a wild ride with its many twists and turns, cliffs, bluffs, draws, ridges and water hazards.

Each of the holes has its own special personality and its own special name. To name a few, No. 1 is Blind Date, No. 2 is Two Much Too Soon, No. 10 is R.I.P., No. 11 is Pecan Pie and No. 17 is Stonewall.

The hardest hole at The Bandit is the 403-yard par 4 No. 5. It is a slight dogleg with a row of trees and a creek down the left side and a hill on the right to a green protected by two bunkers on the left.

No. 2 is a 241-yard par 3 that is one of the longest par 3s in the state. Thus it's name, Two Much, Too Soon.

Likewise, No. 15 is a 624-yard par 5 that is one of the longest par 5s in the state. Out of bounds runs down the entire right side of the fairway and golfers must contend with a creek that crosses the fairway twice — once about 200 yards from the green and again in front of the green.

No. 9 is a 459-yard par 4 known as Pinnacle. Here, golfers tee off over a creek and play straight ahead uphill to a green positioned at the base of a hill.

No. 12 is a 468-yard par 4 with out of bounds right and a lake behind the green.

The Bandit at Long Creek

6019 FM 725
New Braunfels 78130
830-609-4665
Pro: Quint Alexander
A par-71, 6,928-yard public course.
From San Antonio take I-35 to New Braunfels exit 187. Go right on FM 725 for 5.5 miles to club entrance on left.

• • •

USGA rating: 73.1
Slope rating: 133
Sand traps: 70
Water holes: 12 out of 18
Doglegs: 6
Type greens: Bermuda
Record: 66
Designer: Keith Foster
Year opened: 1997

• • •

Hole	Par	Yards	Hole	Par	Yards
1	4	421	10	4	417
2	3	241	11	3	189
3	5	520	12	4	468
4	4	341	13	3	185
5	4	403	14	4	369
6	3	209	15	5	624
7	5	550	16	4	424
8	4	401	17	3	155
9	4	459	18	5	552
Out	36	3,545	In	35	3,383

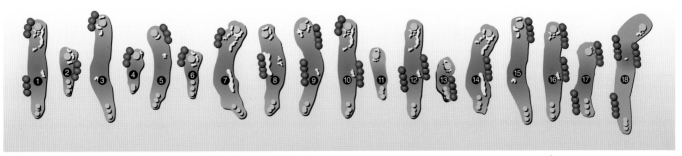

Texas Top 100

57. Twin Creeks Golf Club

Environmental concerns have become one of the biggest factors in American golf course construction over the past 10 years. For every 10 proposed courses that go on the drawing board, perhaps only one becomes a reality.

A great piece of real estate and developer do not necessarily make a good golf course. If the project would somehow be harmful to the environment or disturb an important natural area, it just won't fly.

Twin Creeks, a 2,700-acre master-planned community in northeast Allen, north of Dallas, is a prime example of how golf courses can work to preserve their surrounding environment.

Designed by golf legend Arnold Palmer, the Twin Creeks Golf Course is laid out along both sides of picturesque Rowlett Creek, home of many types of wildlife.

It is the centerpiece of this community that includes up to 3,000 homes and is one of the largest D/FW developments to be built in the last decade.

The land was owned by the Brittingham family of Dallas and was developed by Florida-based Arvida Corp., one of the nation's largest home builders.

Some residents expressed early concerns about Arvida's plan to use open space and natural landscape for the golf course.

That land had been set aside in the city's 1985 comprehensive plan for use as a pedestrian and bicycle trail.

As a compromise, Arvida agreed that the golf course would be accessible to all residents and that the hike and bike trails would meander through the golf course along Rowlett Creek.

"We want to keep this area the way it was, so we're only irrigating 80 acres of the course, just the part where golf is played," said Brett Johnston, manager of the Texas Division of Arvida.

Palmer's layout measures more than 7,000 yards, and his goal was to make the course challenging while not humiliating average golfers.

The 17th is a 409-yard par 4 that requires a long fairway guarded by water on the right. From the back tees, a drive of more than 250 yards is needed to carry the water for a second shot of 100 yards. But players can play to the left of the water's edge and have a 155 to 170 yard second shot to a large green with bunkers on the right and in the back.

"The worst thing is to build a golf course that you get bored on," Palmer says.

"One day, I'd like to build a golf course for myself. I take pride in not patterning myself after anyone in building golf courses, but there are things at Pinehurst No. 2 and Augusta that I would have to incorporate in my golf course."

Twin Creeks Golf Club

501 Twin Creeks Drive
Pro: Pete Witter
Allen 775013
972-390-8888

A par-72, 6,924-yard public course. Take I-75 north to the McDermott exit. Turn left on McDermott and go about 3 miles to Twin Creeks Drive. Turn right to clubhouse.

• • •

USGA rating: 72.2
Slope rating: 122
Sand traps: 36
Water holes: 5
Doglegs: 5
Type greens: Bentgrass
Record: 69
Designers: Arnold Palmer
Year opened: 1994

• • •

Hole	Par	Yards	Hole	Par	Yards
1	4	343	10	5	554
2	3	165	11	4	436
3	4	432	12	3	189
4	5	513	13	4	470
5	4	365	14	4	359
6	3	155	15	5	526
7	5	550	16	3	218
8	4	418	17	4	409
9	4	429	18	4	393
Out	36	3370	In	36	3554

Texas Top 100

58. Chase Oaks Golf Club

G olf courses are a lot like art. Everybody views them with a different pair of eyes and a different palette, and very seldom is there a consensus of opinion.

When it comes to golf courses, one of the exceptions to the rule has been Chase Oaks Golf Club. It is a 27-hole facility that features a difficult, championship 18-hole layout called Blackjack, and a nine-hole smart course called Sawtooth.

Not often has one golf course drawn such widespread support from the most discriminating golf customers.

That's high praise for a daily-fee facility that receives a lot of customers who could easily choose to play elsewhere. For that reason, Chase Oaks was ranked as the No. 1 public course in the state by *The Dallas Morning News* in 1991.

In September 1989, developers Charles Wilson and William D. Parsons sold the 260-acre club to the Japanese firm GGS Investment Inc., which was at the time one of the largest purchases by a Japanese company in the D/FW area.

"The positive reception for our golf course and facility by metroplex golfers has been excellent," former general manager Gary Dee said a year after the course opened.

"As the golf course continues to mature, the design features seem to get better and better."

No. 15 is a 372-yard, par-4 that doglegs right. Players must avoid the bunker in the corner of the dogleg, then hit their approach over a creek that runs across the fairway and protects a small green.

By modern-day standards, the 16th is not a long par 5, but the presence of a pond that cuts into the fairway near the front of the green and wraps around behind it will make players think twice about getting home in two.

Sawtooth is a nine-hole layout with two different sets of tees so players can play an 18-hole round. The layout measures 6,016 yards and plays to par of 72.

The golf course was designed by Houston-based architects Robert von Hagge and Bruce Devlin, who have designed some of the best courses in Texas. Counting their works at Crown Colony, TPC at The Woodlands, Gleneagles, Walden on Lake Conroe and The Cliffs of Possum Kingdom, von Hagge and Devlin created many of the top courses in Texas. Chase Oaks wasted no time making that list.

The golf course was built as the centerpiece of the 900-acre Chase Oaks residential and commercial development.

In addition to the Blackjack Course, Chase Oaks also features a nine-hole course called Sawtooth that, while shorter, is just as demanding.

Chase Oaks Golf Club

7201 Chase Oaks Boulevard
Plano 75025
972-517-7777
Pro: Ann Sowieja
A 27-hole, public course.
From Dallas, take I-75 north to Legacy Drive, then west on Legacy 3 miles to Chase Oaks Boulevard. Turn north on Chase Oaks to club entrance.

• • •

USGA rating: 74.4
Slope rating: 139
Sand traps: 43
Water holes: 10
Doglegs: 4 left/4 right
Type greens: Bentgrass
Record: 65
Designers: Robert von Hagge
    and Bruce Devlin
Year opened: 1986

Hole	Par	Yards	Hole	Par	Yards
1	5	521	10	3	151
2	4	446	11	5	501
3	4	407	12	4	383
4	3	180	13	4	388
5	4	399	14	3	165
6	4	450	15	4	372
7	3	188	16	5	517
8	5	510	17	4	420
9	4	354	18	4	410
Out	36	3455	In	36	3455

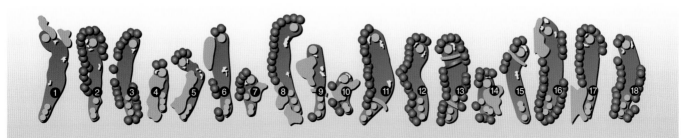

Texas Top 100

59. Greatwood Golf Club

Much of Houston's golfing population lives in the Southwest area of the city, but until 1990, there was a shortage of top-notch, daily–fee courses available in that area. American General recognized this crisis when it began to break ground on this 1,450-acre master-planned community.

Instead of building another country-club development, it decided to build a championship public course with a country-club atmosphere. The course would not only give public links golfers another place to play but also provide wider exposure for the surrounding real estate.

While the developers had a vested interest in selling residential lots, Houston golfers are now reaping the benefits. After opening in 1990, Greatwood is ranked among the top courses in the state.

The developers took great pride in the project and, unlike many developers who are in a hurry to hear the cash register ring after construction, allowed the Greatwood layout a year to mature before it opened.

"More public courses are needed all across the country," says Greatwood pro Michael Hoffman. "I think the developers here saw that need and realized they would get much more exposure to the real estate with a public course.

"We try to treat our players like country club members and so far it's working. The golfers like it because instead of paying a big initiation fee and monthly dues, they pay only for what they use," Hoffman says.

Houston-based architect Carlton Gipson used his uncanny ability to build courses challenging to all players by using a four tee-box system. Gipson had to move 500,000 cubic yards of dirt to create the required drainage and retention areas for storm waters, and he incorporated that into 80 acres of man-made lakes, gently rolling fairways and undulating greens. Carts are required because of the unusually long distances from one green to the next tee.

"It was a lot of fun because we had so much dirt to work with," says Gipson, sounding like a kid in a backyard sandbox. "In some cases, maybe too much. We created a lot of water."

In April 1994, two of the layout's more memorable holes were lost forever. The 622-yard, par-5 14th was the longest in the city before it was shortened to 520-yards and a lake was added in front of the green. The 217-yard par-3 15th was shortened to 153 yards over a ravine. No. 18 is a 576-yard challenge that dares you to go for the island green in two strokes.

"The par 4s are not back-breakers," Hoffman says. "There are a lot of birdie opportunities out there as long as you know where not to hit it."

GREATWOOD

Greatwood Golf Club

6767 Greatwood Parkway
Sugar Land 77479
281-343-9999
Pro: Mike Hoffman
A par-72, 6,829-yard public course.
From Houston, take U.S. 59 south to
Crabb River Road, left over freeway,
then U-turn on service road to entrance.

• • •

USGA rating: 72.6
Slope rating: 130
Sand traps: 77
Water holes: 12
Doglegs: 5 left/3 right
Type greens: Tiff
Record: 66
Designer: Carlton Gipson
Year opened: 1990

• • •

Hole	Par	Yards	Hole	Par	Yards
1	4	360	10	4	418
2	4	362	11	4	362
3	4	401	12	3	206
4	3	197	13	4	389
5	4	434	14	5	520
6	5	533	15	3	153
7	3	214	16	4	390
8	4	396	17	4	387
9	5	564	18	5	576
Out	36	3467	In	36	3368

60. Champions Golf Club — Jack Rabbit Course

Although it is better than 90 percent of the golf courses in Texas, the reputation of the Jack Rabbit Course at Champions has been overshadowed by its older brother, Cypress Creek.

For instance, while Cypress Creek has hosted the 1967 Ryder Cup, the 1969 U.S. Open and the 1993 U.S. Amateur as well as the 1990 and 1997 Tour Championship, the Jack Rabbit Course was simply used as a parking lot.

Champions also will host the 1999 Tour Championship, and owner and co-founder Jack Burke Jr. continues to lobby for another national championship.

But at any other club in Texas, members would be proud to call Jack Rabbit their home course.

Built in 1964, seven years after Ralph Plummer designed the Cypress Creek Course, architect George Fazio designed a layout that is equally long at 7,106 yards and in many ways is actually more difficult than Cypress Creek with a 131 slope rating compared to Cypress Creek's 130.

You have to play the Jack Rabbit course with the same kind of care and sensitivity with which you would treat a wounded animal. While Cypress Creek features broad fairways and big greens that can bogey you to death, Jack Rabbit can lash out at you at any moment with its smaller greens and out of bounds that comes into play on 14 holes.

Big numbers are only one misfire away.

You have to expect a little pent-up frustration from a golf course that has never gotten its fair share of respect.

Golf Digest ranked Jack Rabbit No. 15 in Texas in 1995–96 and No. 18 in 1997–98. It also ranked Jack Rabbit No. 68 in the nation in 1997 among America's 100 Best Modern Courses.

With more than 250 single-digit handicappers, Champions is home of one of the state's top-playing memberships — an important part of Champions' history.

Among the tougher holes are the 539-yard par-5 10th hole, which dog legs left off the tee. For those who are tempted to go for the green in two, the small green is protected by water on three sides. And it is the shortest of the par 5s, with the others measuring 541, 602 and 572 yards. Length is a factor on the par 3s and par 4s as well. The shortest par 3 is 193 yards, while the others are 194, 199 and 208.

"The quality of both courses is just impeccable," said USGA executive director David Fay, who helped bring the 1993 U.S. Amateur to Champions.

"This club was created by two of the game's great players who realized that amateurs are the backbone of the game and they have always treated them accordingly. We couldn't ask for anything more."

Champions Golf Club
Jack Rabbit Course

13722 Champions Drive
Houston 77069
281-444-6449
Pro: Tad Weeks
A 36-hole private club.
Take I-45 North to FM 1960, then left to Champions Drive. Turn right to entrance.

• • •

USGA rating: 72.4
Slope rating: 131
Sand traps: 27
Water holes: 7
Doglegs: 2 left/3 right
Type greens: Bermuda
Record: 64
Designer: George Fazio
Year opened: 1964

• • •

Hole	Par	Yards	Hole	Par	Yards
1	5	541	10	5	539
2	4	361	11	3	208
3	4	429	12	4	368
4	3	193	13	4	375
5	4	408	14	4	413
6	4	439	15	4	412
7	3	194	16	3	199
8	4	449	17	4	414
9	5	602	18	5	572
Out	36	3615	In	36	3500

Texas Top 100

61. Pecan Valley Golf Club

After having his right leg amputated, famed architect Perry Maxwell had to rely on his son Press to do much of the work for him in the latter part of his career.

Ten years after his father's death in 1952, Press did his father proud by designing a masterpiece known as Pecan Valley.

Press was known to fly his own Cessna from job to job on the Gulf Coast. He flew into San Antonio in early 1962 at the request of businessman E.J. Burke.

Burke was building a subdivision in southeast San Antonio called Highland Hills. The project was going well, but there was a 200-acre area around Salado Creek unsuitable for home building.

Burke asked his partners how they could utilize the land. They suggested a golf course, and Burke was smart enough to go after one of the best architects in the business.

When he called Maxwell in '62, Maxwell surveyed the site and told him that he could build a championship course. The following year, John Connally officially opened the site on Labor Day.

Maxwell produced a par-71, 7,116-yard layout that took advantage of the native trees and Salado Creek, which runs through the property. Golfers must cross it seven times during a round. Like his father, whose reputation for slick, undulating greens earned him the right to rebuild greens at Pine Valley and Augusta National, Press produced fast greens with multiple tiers.

By the time the course opened, Burke had taken up golf and began to lobby for golf's greatest players to play at Pecan Valley. He talked with officials of the PGA of America, including PGA president and Texas native Warren Cantrell, about bringing the PGA Championship to San Antonio in 1968. Pecan Valley also had the first fully-lighted nine-hole course in America.

In the PGA, only 18 rounds under par were shot during the record heat wave. Arnold Palmer appeared to have won his first PGA when he used a 3-wood to knock his second shot on the 72nd hole to within 12 feet of the cup. He two-putted for par, but saw his chance for victory dashed when Boros parred the final hole.

Such an auspicious debut for the young course, however, only set it up for a fall. After the glory of the PGA tournaments and several Texas Opens were long forgotten, the course fell into disrepair in the mid-1980s. That's when American Golf Corporation bought the course, restoring its grandeur and tradition.

Plaques have been placed along the scenic back nine along with memorabilia on display in the pro shop to preserve the history and footprints of champions.

Site of the 50th PGA Championship

Pecan Valley Golf Club

4200 Pecan Valley Drive
San Antonio 78223
800-336-3418
Pro: David Lugbauer
A par-71, 7,116-yard public course that hosted the 1968 PGA Championship. From San Antonio, take Highway 37 south, exit Southcross, go east to course entrance on left.

• • •

USGA rating: 74.5
Slope rating: 136
Sand traps: 40
Water holes: 7
Doglegs: 6 left/6 right
Type greens: Bermuda
Record: 65
Designer: Press Maxwell
Year opened: 1963

• • •

Hole	Par	Yards	Hole	Par	Yards
1	4	450	10	4	387
2	4	417	11	4	410
3	3	198	12	3	328
4	4	403	13	5	420
5	4	400	14	4	172
6	5	607	15	4	540
7	3	208	16	3	458
8	4	357	17	4	195
9	5	520	18	4	549
Out	36	3580	In	35	3438

Texas Top 100

62. Riverhill Country Club

RIVERHILL

J Joe Finger is one of the more interesting characters in the business of golf course architecture.

He earned a degree in engineering from Rice, played on the Owls' golf team for coach Jimmy Demaret, worked in the petroleum industry, patented a form of corrugated plastic and even owned his own dairy farm.

Come to think of it, there weren't too many things that Finger couldn't do well. That includes designing golf courses.

Finger went on to become one of America's most well-known architects in the 1950s and '60s, building courses from South Texas to New York. He could have lived on any of them, but he chose Riverhill Country Club in Kerrville.

The course first opened in 1952 as a nine-hole layout designed by Leon Howard. Golf legend Byron Nelson, who lived near Dallas, and Ralph Plummer had been asked by members of the Hunt family, Sherman and Stewart, to design an 18-hole championship course in Kerrville in the early 1970s.

Plummer became ill before the project got started and Nelson called Finger to ask if he would help design the new course. Housing lots had already been sold around the course in anticipation of a spectacular layout, and Finger and Nelson collaborated on a layout that didn't let anyone down.

"One of the most difficult things in golf is to build one really good challenge from the back tees," Finger says, "that's still enjoyable for the members. I'd rather have 15 members tell me they like the course than one pro.

"It's extremely difficult without one piece of flat ground, but the members really like it. As its name indicates, Riverhill has plenty of challenges with undulating greens, fairways and lots of brush and water."

Finger still plays the course every day he returns to town from one of his adventures into Mexico, a testament to the timeless challenge his layout presents.

The signature hole is the par-3 No. 11, which can play anywhere from 120 to 209 yards depending on the tee. Golfers face a testy tee shot over water to a very small green. Water also runs along the right side with trees on the left. The prevailing wind blows left to right, toward the water, and leaves little room to bail out.

"I'd say that's a pretty tough hole," Finger says. "I got under the trees one day and had to take an unplayable lie."

Riverhill has traditionally been ranked among the top courses in South Texas by the *San Antonio Express-News.*

"It's still a great course," Finger says. "It's very scenic with some tough holes."

Riverhill Country Club

100 Riverhill Club Lane
Kerrville 78028
830-792-1143
Pro: Mark Fuller
A par-72, 6,870-yard private club.
From San Antonio, take I-10
to Highway 16, go south 5 miles to Loop
173, left 2 miles to club on right.

• • •

USGA rating: 73.8
Slope rating: 130
Sand traps: 38
Water holes: 10
Doglegs: 4 left/2 right
Type greens: Bermuda
Record: 64
Course Designers: Byron Nelson
    and Joe Finger
Year opened: 1974

• • •

Hole	Par	Yards	Hole	Par	Yards
1	4	393	10	4	420
2	3	207	11	3	209
3	5	485	12	4	386
4	4	445	13	5	540
5	5	480	14	5	553
6	4	373	15	4	430
7	4	430	16	3	160
8	3	191	17	4	370
9	4	395	18	4	402
Out	36	3400	In	36	3470

63. Golf Club at Fossil Creek

Arnold Palmer has made a lasting impression on the game of golf.

It was Palmer who brought excitement to golf with his heroic charges, his aggressive swing and familiar hitch of his pants. It was that excitement that brought golf into the international spotlight. It was Palmer who, everywhere he played, was followed by thousands of loyal members of Arnie's Army.

They don't call him The King for nothing.

While Palmer will always be remembered for his accomplishments as a player — his nearly 90 victories around the world, including four Masters, two British Opens and a U.S. Open — he might be leaving a more lasting impression on the game with the golf courses he is building.

Palmer has turned into an equally great architect, and his layout at Fossil Creek is a testament to great shot values. It is his only project in the Dallas/Fort Worth area.

Built in 1987, Palmer and partner Ed Seay designed a course that winds through 1,150 acres of natural Texas terrain surrounded by rocky-ledge creeks, crystal lakes, gently contoured bluffs and towering trees.

In 1994, Woodbine Development sold the golf course operations to Dallas-based Club Corporation of America. While Marriott and Woodbine remain partners in the hotel, CCA added Fossil Creek to its growing list of D/FW area courses.

"We're going to try to keep up the high standards at both courses," said GolfCorp's Mike Ussery. "We'll see what we can do about improving certain things, but for the most part everything will continue just as it has."

No less than seven of these holes at Fossil Creek were nominated among the toughest in D/FW, depending on your perspective.

Foremost among them are the par-3 10th and 13th holes, both of which require lengthy carries over water from the back tees, and the 415-yard, par-4 15th.

No.10 measures 208 yards from the back tees and requires a long carry over the corner of a lake to a green that is protected by water on three sides. For the weaker of heart, there are six tee boxes that require shorter distance, but all of which require some type of carry to get to the green.

No. 13 is 194 yards from an elevated tee. Fossil Lake carves into the fairway in front of the tee, then swings around to protect the front right, right and back sides of the green. There is a small landing area in front of the green, which is open on the front left to receive roll-on shots.

All of the par 5s are well over 500 yards, ranging from the 523-yard third hole to the 555-yard finishing hole.

Golf Club at Fossil Creek

3401 Clubgate Drive
Fort Worth 76137
817-847-1900
Pro: Rob Larkin
A par-72, 6,861-yard public course.
From Fort Worth, take I-35W north to the Western Center exit. Immediately take the first possible right on Sand-Shell Drive.

• • •

USGA rating: 73.6
Slope rating: 131
Sand traps: 46
Water holes: 15
Doglegs: 4 left/3 right
Type greens: Bentgrass
Record: 64
Designer: Arnold Palmer
Year opened: 1987

• • •

Hole	Par	Yards	Hole	Par	Yards
1	4	402	10	3	208
2	3	157	11	5	547
3	5	523	12	4	372
4	4	339	13	3	194
5	3	209	14	4	387
6	4	377	15	4	394
7	4	430	16	4	379
8	5	537	17	4	456
9	4	399	18	5	555
Out	36	3373	In	36	3492

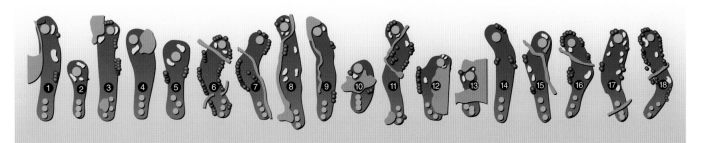

64. Hackberry Creek Country Club

Byron Nelson's career lasted so many years, he has seen a drastic evolution in golf course architecture.

From his days as a caddie at Glen Garden Country Club in Fort Worth to his days as a traveling tour star to his days as an architect, he has seen it all.

At Hackberry Creek, Nelson and architects Joe Finger and Ken Dye combined the best of what modern technology and their old-style values had to offer.

The result has been one of the most challenging layouts in the metroplex and is home of the best-playing memberships in the state — with a membership roster full of single-digit handicappers.

At Hackberry Creek, good golfers and a great golf course go hand in hand.

"That was a different period of construction," Finger says. "From 1945 to 1975, we didn't build courses to challenge the pros so much as the everyday members.

"But when more golf started to get on TV, more and more people wanted their golf courses to be more dramatic looking.

"Byron exerted his influence quite a bit on that project. Ken Dye was overcontouring the greens and Nelson did not like that — he wanted his greens to be subtle, so he had to sit on Ken pretty hard."

Hackberry Creek was originally a joint venture between Ben Carpenter, who developed the neighboring Las Colinas community 20 years earlier, and a Canadian firm that owned the land. It is now owned and operated by Club Corporation of America.

From the back tees, the layout features two par 3s longer than 225 yards and five par 4s longer than 425, putting a premium on long iron play.

Among the best holes are the 16th, a 445-yard par 4 with out of bounds down the right and a contoured fairway that slopes to the left toward a dry creek bed.

The contouring makes for a very challenging hole with a variety of uphill, side-hill and downhill lies, and makes it difficult to judge distance to the hole.

The 485-yard par-5 18th is guarded by Hackberry Creek all the way down the left side and then in front of the green.

Golfers have a choice on the second shot of laying up or cutting diagonally across the corner of the dogleg left, which turns sharply at about 400 yards and crosses the creek to a heavily-contoured green.

PGA Tour star Tom Watson once reached the green in two with a driver/three-iron combination. However, most mortals will choose to lay up in front of the green and take their chances with a wedge in their hand.

The par 3s offer no reprieve. No. 4 is 241 yards and No. 13 is 226 yards.

Hackberry Creek Country Club

1901 Royal Lane
Irving 75063
972-869-2631
Pro: Ben Burns
A par-72, 7,013-yard private club.
From downtown Dallas, take I-35E to Royal Lane, then left on Royal 6 miles to club entrance.

• • •

USGA rating: 73.9
Slope rating: 132
Sand traps: 16
Water holes: 16
Doglegs: 10
Type greens: Bentgrass
Record: 62
Designers: Byron Nelson
    and Joe Finger
Year opened: 1986

• • •

Hole	Par	Yards	Hole	Par	Yards
1	4	438	10	5	523
2	4	389	11	3	185
3	5	530	12	5	545
4	3	241	13	3	226
5	5	575	14	4	372
6	4	382	15	4	425
7	4	455	16	4	445
8	3	165	17	3	192
9	4	440	18	5	485
Out	36	3615	In	36	3398

Texas Top 100

65. Onion Creek Golf Club

ONION CREEK CLUB

Onion Creek Golf Club

2510 Onion Creek Parkway
Austin 78747
512-282-2162
Pro: Matt Jones
A par-70, 6,337-yard private club.
From downtown Austin, take I-35 south
to Onion Creek Parlway. Turn left
to club entrance.

• • •

USGA rating: 71.1
Slope rating: N/A
Sand traps: 60
Water holes: 12
Doglegs: 3 left/2 right
Type Greens: Bermuda
Record: 61
Designer: George Fazio
and Jimmy Demaret
Year opened: 1974

• • •

Few golfers were more colorful than Jimmy Demaret, who helped bring some character to the game with his colorful clothing, his affable personality and his sweet swing.

Demaret was one of the game's biggest ambassadors as he brought the best golfers and the best golf courses in the world home to television viewers in the 1960s as the commentator for the prime-time television series, Shell's Wonderful World of Golf.

As a golfer, Demaret was a three-time Masters champion, and a traditionalist at heart. So it should come as no surprise that Demaret, the architect, designed all of his attributes into the layout at Onion Creek Country Club.

Demaret never more than dabbled in golf course architecture, but many of the courses he collaborated on have become timeless classics.

He and longtime friend Jack Burke Jr., worked with Ralph Plummer and George Fazio in building Champions Golf Club in Houston, site of the 1967 Ryder Cup and the 1969 U.S. Open. He also combined with Joe Finger to build the Concord Golf Club in New York.

At Onion Creek, Demaret worked with Fazio again to build a course that helped launch the Senior PGA Tour. The Legends of Golf tournament, the forerunner to the senior tour, was held at Onion Creek for 12 years, bringing players like Demaret, Sam Snead and many other of the game's legends out of retirement to build a tour that now makes 43 stops a year.

At first sight, the senior pros were thrilled with the work of Demaret and Fazio on a course that measures only 6,337 yards but plays to a par of 70. It features 60 bunkers and 12 water holes along with plenty of Hill Country brush to present a stirring challenge.

"It's a very traditional style," former head pro Johnny Pilcher says. "Nothing tricky about it."

The front side has three par 3s and two par 5s. The back has one par 5 and two par 3s.

The final two holes are particularly interesting. The 17th is rated as the easiest hole on the course, a 146-yard par 3 with water on the left side.

The 18th is a 552-yard par 5 going uphill. The finish is right behind the clubhouse with several trees guarding the green.

Architect Jay Morrish was hired to renovate the course in 1985, but didn't change the basic design. The 890-acre complex, which includes The Demaret Grill, is run by a members' board of directors. The club is in the process of adding an additional nine holes and a new residential section.

The Legends of Golf has moved on, but what matters most is that the great golf course still remains.

Hole	Par	Yards	Hole	Par	Yards
1	5	519	10	4	377
2	3	129	11	3	158
3	4	367	12	4	345
4	4	417	13	4	375
5	4	422	14	4	433
6	3	166	15	4	413
7	5	612	16	4	358
8	3	206	17	3	146
9	4	372	18	5	552
Out	35	3210	In	35	3157

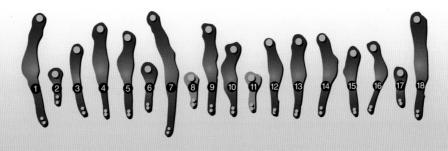

Texas Top 100

66. The Ranch Country Club

Two of America's premier golf course architects have left their considerable fingerprints on North Dallas.

They are called the Clubs at Stonebridge.

First, Pete Dye designed one of the most difficult golf courses in the state. And while he was doing his diabolical handiwork with railroad ties and pot bunkers across the way, nationally known architect Arthur Hills was building a kinder-gentler test of golf across the way.

Hills' layout is known as The Ranch Country Club, but combined they are known as the Clubs at Stonebridge. Either way, they are the centerpiece for a 7,000-acre master-planned golf and residential community.

The development was the brainchild of developer Richard Strauss, but it fell into the hands of the Resolution Trust Corporation and Mobil Land Development purchased it from federal regulators in 1991 for $34 million — only 20 percent of what it cost to originally build it.

"When they first started out, they were trying to build a golf course for a championship," says Dye, who believes Stonebridge is tougher than his highly acclaimed courses at PGA West.

"Right now, it's the best conditioned golf course in Dallas. We have bentgrass on the greens and they've done very well out there."

The Ranch measures 7,087 yards from the back tees but is more benevolent with a 130 slope, deep bunkers and slick greens.

Hills has been one of America's most prominent golf course architects in the 1980s and 1990s, and he is noted for producing golf courses that are an entire collection of strong holes.

Hills said he never liked to hang his hat on one signature hole, but likes them all to be signature holes.

At The Ranch, players who dare to play from the back tees will be greeted by five par 4s that measure anywhere from 429 to 464 yards and will provide a stiff test to the best shot-makers.

Every hole has four or five tee boxes and some holes — including the 156-yard par 3 11th, which requires a carry over water — have as many as eight.

The hardest hole on The Ranch is the 441-yard, par-4 No. 9. It requires a carry over water immediately off the tee, and a long iron to a green protected by two bunkers in front.

It is a good comeback hole from the par-3 No. 8, a 168-yard finesse hole where golfers have an all carry approach to a green protected by water on three sides.

No. 16 is a 549-yard par 5 with water running down the right side of the fairway all the way to the green and coming into play off the tee and on the approach.

No. 14 is the hardest hole. It is a 464-yard par 4.

THE RANCH
COUNTRY CLUB

AT STONEBRIDGE RANCH

The Ranch Country Club

5901 Glen Oaks Drive
McKinney 75070
972-529-5990
Pro: Bryan McMurray
A par-72, 7,087 private club.
From Dallas, take Highway 75 north to Highway 121, go north to Custer Road. Go north on Custer to Stonebridge Drive. Turn right to Glen Oaks Drive and right to entrance.

• • •

USGA rating: 73.8
Slope rating: 130
Sand traps: 47
Water holes: 8
Doglegs: 4 right/3 left
Type greens: Bentgrass
Record: 62
Designer: Arthur Hills
Year opened: 1988

Hole	Par	Yards	Hole	Par	Yards
1	4	410	10	4	390
2	3	211	11	3	156
3	5	510	12	4	385
4	4	429	13	5	582
5	4	451	14	4	464
6	4	388	15	3	198
7	5	570	16	5	549
8	3	168	17	4	328
9	4	441	18	4	457
Out	36	3578	In	36	3509

Texas Top 100

67. Dallas Country Club

M Money talks. People listen. Formed in 1896, Dallas Country Club is the oldest country club in Texas and one of the oldest in the nation.

Established on a 55-acre site just outside of downtown and originally known as Dallas Golf & Country Club, it was the original playground and address for Dallas' rich and famous.

But less than 10 years later, they got an offer they couldn't refuse. Developers Edgar Flippen and Hugh Prather were about to develop a new community called Highland Park a relatively distant four miles from downtown.

To lure potential home buyers "out into the country" on poor roads, Flippen and Prather came up with a plan to bring Dallas' wealthiest residents to the land on the banks of Turtle Creek.

They offered members 50 acres of Highland Park's original 1,350 acres at cost. They sweetened the deal with an offer of 65 adjoining acres at a very low price. They finally agreed on 150 acres for $30,000.

And it turned out to be a marriage made in heaven, or at least at the lobby of Flippen's First National Bank. Dallas' oldest club is still the most exclusive, and Highland Park is still the address for the wealthy.

Membership at the time was limited to 500 and the qualifications for membership were simply "integrity in business coupled with moral probity with a desire to participate in the ancient and royal game of golf. Each member paid $200. Before the golf course was built and even though cotton was still blooming on adjacent land, 172 of the 186 home lots had been sold.

First impressions are important. And when it came to introducing the game of golf to some of Dallas' first residents, the man in charge of all the handshakes was Tom Bendelow. Bendelow was much like a golfing missionary.

He went out into the highways and byways, preaching the word to pagans and heathens about the game of golf. He had 514 courses to his credit. At the time most of them were built, the going rate was $25 a course.

In 1908, he made his way to Dallas. As far as golf was concerned, this was like a third-world country hearing the gospel for the first time.

Bendelow said the land in Highland Park had "no superior in this country." Completion of the course, done by hand, took about two years. At the same time, a prairie style clubhouse was built, and later replaced in 1957 by a $1.5 million facility.

Bendelow is most known for his legendary layout at Chicago's Medinah CC. He organized America's first public golfers association and instituted the first system to reserve starting tee times.

Dallas Country Club

4110 Beverly Drive
Dallas 75205
214-521-3520
Pro: Billy Harris
A par-70, 6,250-yard private club.
From Dallas, take North Dallas Tollway to Mockingbird, then right one block past Preston Road to club entrance.

• • •

USGA rating: 70.3
Slope rating: 126
Sand traps: 51
Water holes: 4
Doglegs: 4 left/3 right
Type greens: Bentgrass
Record: N/A
Designer: Tom Bendelow
Year opened: 1896

• • •

Hole	Par	Yards	Hole	Par	Yards
1	4	337	10	4	413
2	4	344	11	5	451
3	4	352	12	4	406
4	5	515	13	4	436
5	4	379	14	4	363
6	3	189	15	3	161
7	4	350	16	3	176
8	4	439	17	4	362
9	3	212	18	4	281
Out	35	3117	In	35	3149

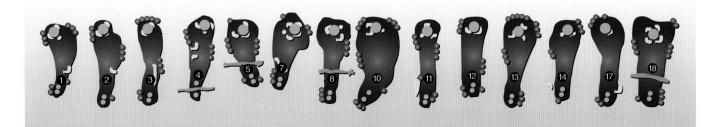

![Texas Top 100]

68. Club at Falcon Point

Golfers take no middle ground. They either love to play or love to hate the Club at Falcon Point.

This course, one of only a handful of area courses with bentgrass greens, offers even the best golfers a challenge, rating as one of the toughest courses in Houston.

Falcon Point has had its share of time in the red. The development came along at the wrong place at the wrong time. When Houston's economic downturn hit, the growth on Houston's western frontier came to a standstill. The project went bankrupt and developer H.C. Moore's dream was stranded on the 18th tee of purgatory.

For more than two years, the 570-acre site was tied up between the FDIC and the Resolution Trust Corporation. In 1993 a partnership assembled by Fort Worth financier Richard Rainwater purchased the club and surrounding real estate with an eye to the future and brighter days ahead.

"Every indication is that the growth in the home market in the west is as good as it has ever been," says Houston developer Sam Yeager, who was placed in charge of jump-starting the development.

Moore's original goal was based on the concept of a traditional golf club, instead of a lifestyle country club, with a strong course designed to challenge the more proficient players. Few question that architects Bob von Hagge and Bruce Devlin gave Moore what he wanted.

Even Devlin now admits that they may have made the course too difficult with too much water, too many long shots, too small greens and not enough consideration to the omnipresent wind that sweeps across the prairie.

Four holes at Falcon Point were nominated by area pros as among the toughest in Houston. The hardest of those is the 449-yard, par-4 No. 18. Water comes into play on every hole, thanks to the 10 interconnecting lakes built to provide flood control.

The 429-yard, par-4 No. 4 has water in play off the tee and the approach to an elevated green, and also plays into a prevailing wind. No. 17 is a 163-yard par 3 that requires an accurate shot because the green is protected by water on the left and bunkers on the right.

"It is very evident to us and all of those who have seen it that it is one of the premier courses in this part of the country," Moore wrote von Hagge after the opening. "We are thrilled with the way in which you have combined water, wind and turf to create a magnificent golfing experience."

THE CLUB AT FALCON POINT

Club at Falcon Point

24503 Falcon Point Drive
Katy 77494
281-392-7888
Pro: Dave Goldblum
A par-72, 6,771-yard private club.
From downtown Houston, take I-10
west to the Katy-Fort Bend Road exit,
then left 1 mile to clubhouse.

• • •

USGA rating: 73.6
Slope rating: 136
Sand traps: 79
Water holes: 17
Doglegs: 2 left/4 right
Type greens: Bentgrass
Record: 65
Designers: Robert von Hagge
    and Bruce Devlin
Year opened: 1985

• • •

Hole	Par	Yards	Hole	Par	Yards
1	4	389	10	4	382
2	3	148	11	4	373
3	4	422	12	5	518
4	4	429	13	3	151
5	5	475	14	4	424
6	4	385	15	4	441
7	3	222	16	5	495
8	4	404	17	3	163
9	5	501	18	4	449
Out	36	3375	In	36	3396

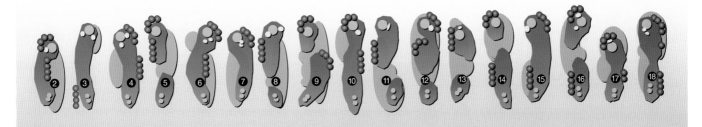

Texas Top 100

69. Bridlewood Golf Club

BRIDLEWOOD
GOLF CLUB

Most people know D.A. Weibring as an 18-year veteran of the PGA Tour.

Not a big name, by any means, but one of those steady players who make a comfortable living doing what they love to do.

Now, we introduce D.A. Weibring the architect.

Weibring's first venture into golf course architecture is known as Bridlewood Golf Club, a marvelous layout that challenges golfers with 25 acres of lakes and meandering Timber Creek, and is pleasing to the eye with its hills and thick stands of hardwoods.

"Every golf course designer relishes the opportunity to start with a site as beautiful as Bridlewood," says Weibring, who rose to the occasion by building a 7,000-yard layout that is as challenging as it is scenic.

"The gentle, rolling hills and thick forests of hardwood come together to make an outstanding setting for a unique golf course."

Water is in play on 14 holes, but is most evident on the back nine. The fairways and landing areas average a generous 40 yards wide, but are lined by grassy swales, mounds, hollows and bunkers, and force golfers to use every club in their bag.

"Because of the variety and balance of the holes, players will find a well-rounded golfing experience," Weibring says. "We have designed Bridlewood leaving a lot of decisions in the golfers' hands. With fairways surrounding each green, chipping will play a big role. Our goal was to accentuate the rolling terrain and forests without disturbing them."

Simply put, trees abound.

No. 6 is a 535-yard par 5 and the No. 1 handicap hole, requiring a medium iron shot uphill through a chute of trees on the approach to a hillside green. A double fairway on the second shot allows an alternate route.

A large oak guards the right edge of No. 9 green, a 463-yard par 4 that is one of the hardest on the course. No. 10 is a 392-yard par 4 that requires a drive through a chute of hardwoods.

No. 11 is a 429-yard par 4 that requires an accurate drive down a saddled fairway with water down the left side.

No. 13 is a 568-yard par 5 that is surrounded by trees from tee to green with a creek down the left side. A huge elm splits the fairway just before the creek crosses in front of the green.

A large, expansively branched Post Oak towers over the green at No. 15. Trees frame the gently contoured fairway of No. 16, large oaks frame the green on No. 17; trees, a lake and Timber Creek guard No. 18's fairway.

No. 17 is a 231-yard par 3 with Timber Creek down the left side. Swirling winds assist in putting a premium on accuracy. Few birdies are yielded here.

Bridlewood Golf Club

4000 West Windsor Drive
Flower Mound 75028
972-355-4800
A par-72, 7,046-yard public course.
From Longeville, take Highway 35E north to the Main Street exit, continue north for approx. 7.5 miles, course is on the north side of the road at Windsor Drive and Bridlewood Drive.

• • •

USGA rating: 73.6
Slope rating: 130
Sand traps: 30
Water holes: 7
Doglegs: 4 left/ 3 right
Type greens: Bentgreen
Record: 63
Designer: D.A. Weibring
Year opened: 1996

• • •

Hole	Par	Yards	Hole	Par	Yards
1	4	428	10	4	392
2	5	536	11	4	429
3	3	187	12	3	191
4	4	347	13	5	568
5	4	410	14	4	327
6	5	535	15	4	405
7	4	447	16	5	507
8	3	195	17	3	231
9	4	463	18	4	438
Out	36	3,548	In	36	3,488

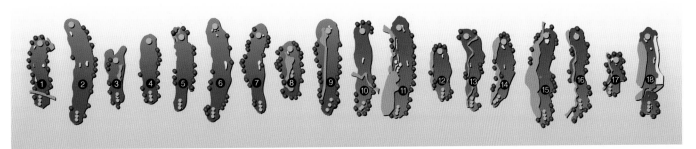

Texas Top 100

70. Garden Valley Golf Resort — Dogwood Course

Rarely has there been a golf course more appropriately named than Garden Valley.

With its maze of 100-foot pines, crape myrtle, Carolina jasmine, hollies, cedars and dogwoods, and 1,500 azaleas, rolling elevation changes and bentgrass greens, some consider Garden Valley to be Texas' most reasonable facsimile of the famed Augusta National Club.

This garden setting is home to two championship golf courses. The Dogwood Course, designed in 1992 by architect John Sanford, is the highest-rated and most demanding of the two.

Garden Valley was designed as a getaway resort for big-city golfers, luring them about an hour or so off the beaten path of the Dallas-Fort Worth area.

The only thing that keeps the courses from being rated even higher is that not enough golfers have made the trip.

The course features rolling terrain with elevation changes, elevated greens and tees and thickly tree-lined fairways.

The Dogwood Course was cut out of a forest and features narrow fairways. The course has 48 bunkers incorporated into its design, 30 of them positioned to protect the greens, so accuracy is at a premium throughout the course. Leave your driver at home and replace it with a camera.

The back nine is carved like a maze through a virtual nursery of trees and azaleas — the most beautiful part of the course.

Garden Valley is a testament that golf courses don't have to be over 7,000 yards to be demanding. It plays to a 132 slope rating, even though it has only two par 4s over 400 yards. Water, however, is in play on 12 holes

The 388-yard, par-4 No. 13 is the hardest hole on the course. Golfers start with a drive through a narrow tree-lined fairway. On the approach, A large lake protects the left side of the fairway and green.

No. 11 is similar, starting through the trees and opening up to an approach shot with a lake on the left and behind the green.

No. 9 is a 595-yard par 5 where three small lakes come into play all the way to the green. A pond dissects the fairway in the landing area off the tee, and another pond protects the left front edge of the green.

No. 12 is a 212-yard par 3 over the edge of the lake, with water also protecting the left side of the green and leaving little margin for error.

The course gets off to an easy start with two par 3s over water and two short par 4s before golfers reach the 526-yard par 5 No. 5.

No. 8 is a 456-yard par 4, where no water is in play but its length makes it difficult to par.

Garden Valley Golf Resort Dogwood Course

22049 FM 1995

Lindale 75771

903-882-6107

Pro: Mike Fish

A 36-hole resort.

From I-20, take Highway 110 to Exit 548 going south. Turn right at golf course sign to entrance.

• • •

USGA rating: 72.4

Slope rating: 132

Sand traps: 35

Water holes: 12

Doglegs: 4 left/3 right

Type greens: Bentgrass

Record: 63

Designer: John Sanford

Year opened: 1992

• • •

Hole	Par	Yards	Hole	Par	Yards
1	4	370	10	5	512
2	3	190	11	4	407
3	4	366	12	3	212
4	3	165	13	4	388
5	5	526	14	4	355
6	4	379	15	3	183
7	4	376	16	4	362
8	4	456	17	4	393
9	5	595	18	5	519
Out	36	3,423	In	36	3,331

71. Bay Oaks Country Club

Unlike many golf course architects, Art Hills is not on an ego trip. The former landscape architect has been building courses since 1966. He doesn't like to talk about them or himself.

Hills' simplistic approach is becoming the standard as the industry comes full circle from TPC-style, mad scientist type courses back to traditional, Donald Ross-inspired natural layouts.

"I think understated is a good word to describe my work," says Hills, even though the PGA Tour moved the Honda Classic from his TPC at Eagle Trace layout because it was too hard.

"I prefer subtleties. The membership loves the course, that's all I'm concerned about. What Greg Norman says isn't going to make me lose any sleep."

Hills' goal at Bay Oaks was to design a club suitable for players of all levels. However, the best golfers leave the 18th green shaking their heads. Bay Oaks is one of the most difficult in Houston.

Because of the flat terrain on the 167-acre site that straddles Horsepen Bayou, Hills moved more dirt than usual to create drainage with several man-made lakes.

The layout is a contrast of tree-lined fairways and wide-open holes, where the ever-present bay breeze can be the golfer's toughest enemy.

There are six long par 4s from 429 to 459 yards. The par 5s range from a tight and wooded 500 yards to a wide-open, let-it-all-hang-out 569 yards.

No. 5 is a 531 yard par 5 that curves to the right around a lake that comes into play all the way to the green and leaves a narrow landing area off the tee.

The signature hole is the par 4 No. 15. It is a 341-yard dogleg left carved out of the trees. The hole requires most players use a lay-up off the tee over a mound on the right side of the fairway to set up the approach to an elevated green guarded by a bunker, mound and deep hollows.

Nos. 17 and 18 are tough finishing holes. No. 17 is a 435-yard par 4 that doglegs to the right and requires a long and accurate approach. The green is guarded by water on the right.

The par-4 No. 18 plays 450 yards. The tee shot must carry a deep grassy swale on the right side. The approach shot needs to be accurate to avoid the water on the left.

No. 12 is a 184-yard par 3 that requires a carry over a lake that protects the front two-thirds of the green.

"The course can be a demanding championship test or a medium-length country club that can be enjoyed by a broader spectrum of players of varying skill levels," Hills says. "It has a broad appeal, it's pretty and those who have the opportunity to play it will always find it a fair and ample challenge."

Bay Oaks Country Club

14545 Bay Oaks Boulevard
Houston 77062
281-488-7888
Pro: Ken McDonald
A par-72, 7,011-yard private club.
Take I-45 South to Clear Lake City exit,
turn left to Highway 3, turn right on
Bay Oaks Boulevard to club entrance.

• • •

USGA rating: 72.9
Slope rating: 129
Sand traps: 32
Water holes: 9
Doglegs: 5 left/8 right
Type greens: Bermuda
Record: 64
Designer: Arthur Hills
Year opened: 1989

• • •

Hole	Par	Yards	Hole	Par	Yards
1	4	402	10	4	390
2	4	429	11	5	515
3	3	191	12	3	184
4	4	459	13	4	397
5	5	531	14	3	167
6	4	433	15	4	341
7	5	510	16	5	569
8	3	179	17	4	435
9	4	429	18	4	450
Out	36	3563	In	36	3448

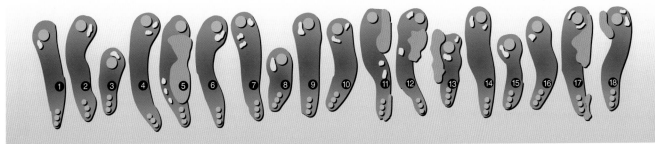

72. Tierra Santa Golf Club

When architect Jeff Brauer designed Tierra Santa Golf Club in 1997, it was the first upscale daily-fee golf course to be built in the Rio Grande Valley.

Brauer has built many such courses in major metropolitan areas throughout the United States, but he felt it was time to take championship golf out into the rural areas.

At Tierra Santa, Brauer teamed with PGA Tour star Steve Elkington, who drew on his many years of tour experience for his first golf course design project.

The final result is a 7,100-yard championship layout that incorporates 12 lakes that come into play on 16 of 18 holes.

Tierra Santa is the centerpiece of a master-planned residential community in the South Texas border town of Weslaco between Harlingen and McAllen.

The fairways are lush, wide, undulating and well-bunkered, but Brauer left lots of breathing room for high-handicap golfers with frequent bail-out areas.

The Bermuda greens are large, an average of 40 yards from front to back, undulating and fast. The greens are so large that hitting the green in regulation is only half the battle. The difference between a front pin placement and back pin placement could be a three-club difference on the approach.

The signature hole is No. 18, a 451-yard, par 4, with a fairway that is guarded on the left by water and bunkers on the right. The second shot is over a waterfall onto a green that is well guarded with bunkers and water.

Overall, the course is extremely challenging yet very fair and is one of the best public courses in the state. Since the course is subject to the wind, it might play a little shorter or longer than its actual length depending on the wind direction. The course plays to a 125 slope rating from the back tees.

Tierra Santa features five par 4s that are over 430 yards and will test even the best golfers.

No. 5 is the hardest hole on the course. It is a 443-yard par 5 that requires a carry of 200 yards to clear the edge of a lake off the tee, but water also runs down the left side of the fairway and guards the green on the approach.

No. 9 is a 460-yard par 4. There is no water on the hole, but players must negotiate their way between fairway bunkers on both sides off the tee and then hit a long approach to the green.

No. 1 is a 432-yard par 4 that starts the course with a bang with players forced to carry a lake from the back tees.

No. 3 is a 364-yard par 4 that offers a double fairway. Golfers who want to take a direct route to the green must negotiate a 200-yard carry over water. For the weak of heart, the optional fairway allows golfers to hit dry land.

Tierra Santa Golf Club

1901 Club DeAmistad
Weslaco 78596
956-973-1811
Pro: Carl Baker
A par-72, 7,100-yard public course. From Harlingen or McAllen, take Highway 83 to the Mile Six or Westgate exits, continue for 3.5 miles to the course entrance.

• • •

USGA rating: 74.1
Slope rating: 125
Sand traps: 30
Water holes: 16
Doglegs: 4 left/ 3 right
Type greens: Bermuda
Record: 68
Designer: Jeff Brauer
Year opened: 1997

• • •

Hole	Par	Yards	Hole	Par	Yards
1	4	432	10	4	415
2	5	572	11	5	524
3	4	364	12	4	398
4	3	201	13	3	185
5	4	443	14	5	610
6	4	359	15	4	444
7	5	547	16	4	367
8	3	168	17	3	161
9	4	460	18	4	451
Out	36	3,546	In	36	3,555

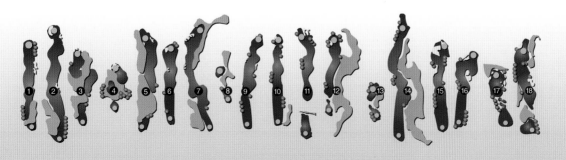

73. Amarillo Country Club

William McConnell doesn't show up anywhere in the annals of golf course architecture, but Bill Cantrell was a Texas native who had degrees in engineering and architecture. He started his own contracting business, and worked on such major projects as the roof for the Houston Astrodome in 1965.

Cantrell was a multi-talented man who was good at everything he did, including golf. So he eventually left his firm due to ill health, and instead turned pro.

Cantrell eventually left the firm because of ill health. A fine golfer, he turned pro and became a club pro in Lubbock, and eventually was elected president of the PGA of America from 1964–65 and served as golf coach at Texas Tech University from 1953–58.

All of his courses were in Texas and New Mexico.

At Amarillo Country Club, McConnell in 1919 produced a par-71, 6,501-yard layout with tree-lined fairways and only a handful of water hazards. It is still considered one of the best clubs in West Texas, and hosted the PGA Nike Tour's Amarillo Open in 1990, featuring John Daly.

Warren Cantrell redesigned and renovated the course in 1960, followed by architect Jay Morrish in 1983 to cover three generations in golf course architecture and design.

The layout measures only 6,501 yards from the back tees and plays to a par of 71, but when you combine the typical West Texas winds and not-so-typical tree-lined West Texas fairways, and out of bounds in play on several holes, you've got a demanding test of golf.

Amarillo plays to a 127 slope rating from the back tees.

The layout features a wide variety of short, medium and long holes to test all types of shot-making ability.

No. 3 is a 421-yard par 4 and No. 8 is a 430-yard, par-4. No. 14 measures 440. All three holes require two solid shots back to back to have a chance at a birdie.

At the same time, the course has many par 4s that range in length from 337 to 387 yards. These holes show a hole doesn't have to be long to be either great or difficult.

The signature hole, for instance, is No. 6. It is a 349-yard, par 4 that requires an approach shot over a lake to a well-bunkered green.

There are three par 5s at Amarillo. No. 9 is 539 yards and No. 13 is 529 yards and only big hitters will be able to reach the green in two shots.

No. 18, however, gives everybody a chance to go home happy. It is a 471-yard par 4 that is shorter than some par 4s and should give players the opportunity to finish their round with a birdie or even a rare eagle.

Amarillo Country Club

44800 Bushland Boulevard
Amarillo 79106
806-355-5021
Pro: Dell Wood
A par-71, 6,501-yard private club.
Take I-40 west to Western, go north on Western to Bushland, left on Bushland to club entrance.

• • •

USGA rating: 71.1
Slope Rating: 127
Water holes: 9
Sand traps: 52
Doglegs: 4 left/3 right
Type greens: Bentgrass
Designer: William A. McConnell
and Bill Cantrell (1960)
and Jay Morrish (1983)
Year opened: 1919

• • •

Hole	Par	Yards	Hole	Par	Yards
1	4	338	10	4	404
2	3	165	11	4	383
3	4	421	12	3	170
4	3	175	13	5	529
5	4	337	14	4	440
6	4	349	15	4	387
7	4	381	16	4	367
8	4	430	17	3	215
9	5	539	18	5	471
Out	35	3,135	In	36	3,366

Texas Top 100

74. Tour 18 Golf Course

In business, you go to Kinko's. In golf, you go to Tour 18.

For those of you who will never have the opportunity to travel across America to play the greatest golf courses, Dennis Wilkerson has given you the next best thing.

He has created your dream come true by re-creating 18 of the greatest holes in the nation. It's like a trip around the country, minus the airfare.

It's an idea that Wilkerson and some of his friends started in Houston in 1993 using revolutionary computer technology to turn aerial photography and photographs into reasonable facsimiles of holes that you see your favorite golfers play on TV.

It was a $5.5-million gamble that paid off with great success.

"This gives golfers a chance to see these holes on television on Sunday," says Tour 18 partner Barron Jacobson, "then come out and play them on Monday."

But if imitation is the sincerest form of flattery, then the Japanese owners at Pebble Beach would like their course to remain one of a kind, thank you.

On Pearl Harbor Day of 1993, the Japanese dropped a bomb on "America's Greatest 18" by filing a lawsuit over the reproduction of the par-5 14th hole at Pebble Beach.

The case received national attention on the network news, as pundits discussed the ethics of copying the design of a golf course. Tour 18 helped break new ground in the golf business.

"What this person has done is take famous holes from famous courses and tried to make money on it," Pebble Beach attorney Stephen Trattner said. "We don't want other people like him to get the impression they could copy our course."

Pinehurst and Sea Pines Plantation also joined in the lawsuit. The case concluded in U.S. federal court in Houston in 1995, and Tour 18 was forced to make only minor revisions.

Tour 18 first copied other great golf courses around the nation with its first course in Houston. The concept was so successful, now they are copying the Tour 18 concept itself in other markets like the D/FW area.

In Dallas, players have the opportunity to play versions of the famed Amen Corner at Augusta National, the 17th at Sawgrass, Doral's Blue Monster, the 18th at Harbour Town, the 17th at Muirfield Village and the 10th at Medinah.

"It's no secret that Japanese big business has been walking on Americans for decades," Jacobson said. "They may have bought Pebble Beach, but they didn't buy Americans' rights to their history, tradition and entrepreneurial spirit."

Tour 18 Golf Course

8718 Amen Corner
Flower Mound 75028
817-430-2000
Pro: Kevin Sheehan
An 18-hole public course that has recreated 18 of the greatest holes in the United States. From Dallas, take I-35 north to Main Street in Lewisville, then turn left 10 miles to course entrance on the right.

• • •

USGA rating: 74.3
Slope rating: 138
Sand traps: 89
Water holes: 9
Doglegs: 2 left/3 right
Type greens: Bentgrass
Record: N/A
Year opened: 1995

• • •

Hole	Par	Yards	Hole	Par	Yards
1	4	401	10	4	425
2	4	374	11	4	445
3	4	435	12	3	170
4	5	507	13	4	338
5	3	195	14	5	625
6	5	582	15	4	430
7	4	470	16	4	455
8	4	409	17	3	155
9	3	132	18	5	485
Out	36	3305	In	36	3528

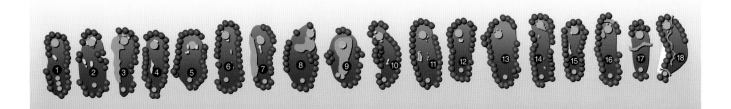

Texas Top 100

75. Silverhorn Golf Club

ood things come to those who wait. After a year of financial problems delayed the opening of San Antonio's newest daily-fee facility, Silverhorn Golf Club opened in early 1996.

From all indications, it was worth the wait.

Oklahoma City-based O-Sports Development began construction in 1994 on the 262-acre site in north San Antonio, but was halted a few months later. Construction began again in the spring of 1995, and the course was open for play in 1996.

The course was patterned after the highly-successful Silverhorn layout in Oklahoma City and follows the growing trend of "country club for the day" daily-fee facilities.

The par-72, 6,975-yard layout was designed by architect Randy Heckenkemper with input by PGA Tour pros Scott Verplank and Willie Wood.

"We want to work with good sites and have good people run them," O-Sports president Elby Beal said when construction began. "We feel like we've got both here in San Antonio."

This wooded course features narrow fairways and soft, undulating greens. The terrain is fairly flat, but some of the tees and greens are elevated. In addition, rock-bed creeks (generally dry) cross the fairways in front of the greens.

All the rock creeks come into play on the back nine. Watch out for them on holes No. 12, No. 15, No. 17, and No. 18. The back nine also is more heavily wooded, while the front nine is open.

Furthermore, four holes on the front nine have water hazards in play, so be sure to bring a good supply of balls. Unless you've played the course a few times before, the medium-sized greens can be hard to read because the subtle contours and breaks are difficult to perceive.

Locals proclaim hole No. 18 as a great finishing hole. From the back tee, this 505-yard par 5 requires a tee shot up a dogleg right fairway, then a well-positioned second shot so you can avoid the large oak tree growing on the right that can block your approach shot. Finally, it takes an approach shot over a depression in the fairway with a rock bed creek at its base to a green with a large sand bunker protecting its front.

No. 6 is a 542-yard dogleg left par 5 that curves from tee to green around a lake that comes into play on every shot. There are few trees here, but anything left is wet.

No. 7 continues along the water's edge, with golfers forced to skirt the lake on a 175-yard shot to the green.

Make sure to warm up before you hit the first tee, because No. 1 is a 578-yard par 5 that will require three long shots to reach the green. A row of trees lines the left side of the fairway from tee to green.

SILVERHORN

Silverhorn Golf Club

1100 Bitters Road
San Antonio 78216
210-545-5300
Pro: Tony Johnson
A par-72, 6,975-yard public course.
From San Antonio, take Highway 281 north to Bitters Road; then left on Bitters 2.1 miles to Partridge Trail. Turn left to course entrance.

• • •

USGA rating: 73.1
Slope rating: 129
Sand traps: 39
Water holes: 9
Doglegs: 6 left/2 right
Type greens: Bermuda
Record: N/A
Designer: Randy Heckenkemper
Year opened: 1996

• • •

Hole	Par	Yards	Hole	Par	Yards
1	5	578	10	5	550
2	4	408	11	4	412
3	4	400	12	4	383
4	4	432	13	3	183
5	3	233	14	4	333
6	5	542	15	4	451
7	3	175	16	3	173
8	4	342	17	4	439
9	4	436	18	5	505
Out	36	3546	In	36	3429

Texas Top 100

76. ColoVista Country Club

Les Appelt believed every man should have the opportunity to build his own golf course once he turns 75. So he did.

In a modern era in which most of America's golf courses are operated by corporate conglomerations and funded by numerous financial institutions and investors, Appelt built his golf course the old-fashioned way.

From scratch.

With his own hands.

With his own money.

ColoVista Country Club, then, is a tribute to the old school. Built on the high banks along the Colorado River in Bastrop, Appelt put nature in the driver's seat and just went along for the ride as he designed a championship layout that is one part links, one part traditional and one part Hill Country.

There are no eyesores here. You won't see massive stone monuments erected to hold water jugs. You won't see highways of concrete cutting across manicured fairways. What golfers see are mature trees, shimmering lakes, an abundance of wildlife and endless vistas of unadulterated countryside.

There is a continuum of wildlife and plant communities, a unique environment where prickly pear cactus and roadrunners intermingle with pine forest and giant woodpeckers, not to mention a few golfers and residents of the surrounding residential community.

The 18-hole championship course winds through an especially broad variety of terrain. The front nine is a links-style course, featuring long, open holes subject to windy conditions. The back nine is some 350 yards shorter, but probably more difficult, because it pinches down among the pines and calls for accuracy rather than length.

Appelt calls the 14th, 15th and 16th holes the "Hallelujah Triangle," because that's what you'll be saying if you escape those holes at even par.

The 191-yard par-3 15th is as breathtaking a hole as they come. It features a 120-foot drop from tee to green, while offering a panoramic view of the Colorado River Valley.

Another attraction to spectacular golf is the newly acquired golf collection of the late "King of Clubs" Matty Reed. Over the past 75 years Reed accumulated one of the finest collections of Hogan Clubs, and they were donated to put on display at ColoVista. In the creation of ColoVista, Appelt had a vision of community spirit.

"Our primary concern along with magnificent golf is how well people live here," he says.

"If we are successful, each resident and guest will feel a sense of pride and belonging that will make them wish to be a responsible and vital part of our day-to-day activities and act as stewards of the beautiful environment."

ColoVista Country Club

PO Box 608
Bastrop 78602
512-303-4045
Pro: Moore McDonough
A par-72, 6,966-yard public course.
From Austin, take Highway 71 east to
Bastrop. Course entrance is located just
before you reach the Colorado River.
Turn right to entrance.

• • •

USGA rating: 73.4
Slope rating: 123
Sand traps: 19
Water holes: 6
Doglegs: 4 left/4 right
Type greens: Bermuda
Record: N/A
Designer: Les Appelt
Year opened: 1996

• • •

Hole	Par	Yards	Hole	Par	Yards
1	4	468	10	4	411
2	4	423	11	5	529
3	3	158	12	4	391
4	5	501	13	3	170
5	3	240	14	4	383
6	4	415	15	3	191
7	5	607	16	4	370
8	4	466	17	5	486
9	4	383	18	4	374
Out	36	3661	In	36	3305

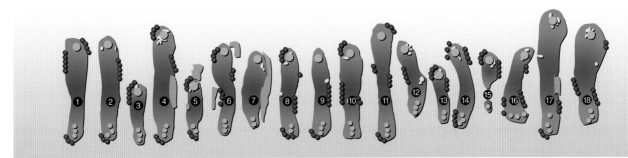

Texas Top 100

77. *TangleRidge Golf Club*

City government can still do something right. We present Exhibit A: TangleRidge Golf Club.

In the early 1990s, the City of Grand Prairie commissioned the construction of a $7-million public golf course. When it was done, they had more than a golf course. They had a new tourist attraction.

TangleRidge Golf Club has been ranked as high in the state as No. 8 by *Golf Digest*, as the 262-acre layout offers golfers the fill of Texas Hill Country within the shadows of the Dallas skyline.

Nestled between Joe Pool Lake and the Mountain Creek Escarpment, the par-72, 6,836-yard layout features dramatic elevation changes, panoramic views, gently rolling hills and bunkers guarding every hole.

Approximately 60 acres of tangled natural vegetation and wetlands remained untouched. With heavily forested areas of Mesquite, Hackberry, Cedar Elm, Easter Red Cedar, Pecan and Oak trees, players rarely see other holes while making their way through the layout.

"We wanted the golfer to have a feeling of seclusion while enjoying a peaceful round — getting away from urban stress," architect Jeff Brauer says.

TangleRidge is a strategic course requiring the player to use every club and shot in his arsenal. The fairways are generous but poorly hit shots may find the native areas.

The variety of grass and sand bunkers, creek crossings, dramatic mounding, berms, doglegs, and tree-lined roughs provide plenty of challenges. While the lake is visible for much of the course, water actually comes into play on only half of the 18 holes, with bunkers on almost every hole.

The first hole gives players an opportunity to size up some of the challenges they will face. It plays as a par 4, 469 yards from the back tees, and swings left off the tee. A creek crosses in front of the tee and bunkers line both sides of the fairway with out-of-bounds on the left side.

The par-5 No. 8 is the longest on the course at 575 yards and forces the golfer to confront a creek twice. Most golfers will lay up in front of the creek with their drive. Any try for the green in two will force the golfer to confront the creek again, where it angles just in front of the green.

The par-3 No. 9 is one of the most scenic. The hole measures just 152 yards, but golfers must hit over a brushy ravine that will grab any short shot. A pin placement to the far left of this multi-tiered green will force golfers to hit over a gathering of trees.

No. 18 is a 521-yard par 5 that features a double-fairway. The more direct route to the green requires a carry of about 200 yards to reach the fairway.

TangleRidge Golf Club

818 TangleRidge Drive
Grand Prairie 75052
972-299-6837
Pro: Mark Viskozki
A par-72, 6,836 public course.
From Dallas take Highway 360 south, exit Great Southwest Parkway, turn right, go 7 miles to Lake Ridge, turn right, go to Park Ridge and turn right to course entrance.

• • •

USGA Rating: 72.2
Slope Rating: 129
Sand Traps: 57
Water Holes: 9
Doglegs: 3 left/6 right
Type greens: Bentgrass
Record: 67
Designer: Jeff Brauer
Year opened: 1995

Hole	Par	Yards	Hole	Par	Yards
1	4	469	10	4	438
2	4	407	11	4	338
3	4	378	12	3	168
4	3	132	13	5	501
5	5	545	14	4	384
6	4	313	15	4	457
7	4	444	16	4	424
8	5	575	17	3	189
9	3	152	18	5	521
Out	36	3415	In	36	3420

78. Golf Club at Cinco Ranch

Carlton Gipson made a career out of making something from nothing. For years, he has turned rice fields and cow pastures into some of the Houston area's best golf courses.

He did it at The Woodlands. He did it at Greatwood. He did it at BraeBurn. He did it at Pecan Grove.

The way developers figured it, Gipson was the man to do it at Cinco Ranch, a 5,000-acre residential community in West Houston. Once upon a time, the prairie was home of some of Texas' earliest settlers.

It was owned by five different families, hence the name "Cinco" Ranch. Those pioneers wouldn't recognize the place now.

In 1991, American General created a man-made beach with a swimming lagoon and white sand. After the addition of greenbelts, a recreation center, lakes and parks, the only missing ingredient was a golf course.

That's where Gipson came in. In a span of 18 months, Gipson reshaped the prairie by moving 250,000 yards of dirt and planting 2,000 trees to create yet another championship course.

Gipson's work at BraeBurn, which is ranked No. 18 in Houston, prepared him for his most recent challenge. Gipson's 1990 renovation at BraeBurn effected what has been called "the greatest turnaround in Houston history."

At both BraeBurn and Cinco, Gipson incorporated flood control channels into the layout. They once were considered eyesores and necessary evils, but Gipson found a way to use them to his advantage.

The ravines remain dry 95 percent of the time and only fill up in the event of a heavy rain.

So Gipson received permission from the Harris County Flood Control District to make cuts into the sides of those channels to provide undulation in the fairways. If flash-flooding does occur, water could creep onto the course for a few hours but will drain quickly.

But the biggest adversary is the winds that sweep across the open prairie, which contribute to its lofty slope rating of 133 and USGA rating of 73.3.

Gipson says one of the best holes on the layout is the 557-yard par-5 fourth hole, which features a bunker 12 feet below the front of the green. The trap will keep balls from rolling into the creek below, "but it will take a helluva shot to get out of there."

"We moved a lot of dirt out there to create some rolling terrain on a very flat piece of property," says Gipson.

"There aren't a lot of hills in Houston and I've had the chance to use my imagination and by moving the dirt around."

No. 17 is a 468-yard par 4 that for most will play like a par 5. No. 13 measures 458 yards.

Golf Club at Cinco Ranch

25030 Cinco Ranch Boulevard
Katy 77494
281-395-4653
Golf Director: Paul K. Levy
A par-71, 6,922-yard, public course.
From Houston, take I-10 west to the Grand Parkway, then go south on Grand Parkway to Cinco Ranch Boulevard. Turn left to entrance.

• • •

USGA rating: 73.3
Slope rating: 133
Sand traps: 49
Water holes: 16
Doglegs: 3 left/2 right
Type greens: Bermuda
Record: 66
Designer: Carlton Gipson
Year opened: 1994

• • •

Hole	Par	Yards	Hole	Par	Yards
1	4	410	10	4	428
2	4	390	11	4	359
3	3	190	12	3	191
4	5	557	13	4	458
5	3	194	14	4	420
6	5	532	15	5	550
7	4	399	16	3	182
8	4	369	17	4	468
9	4	397	18	4	428
Out	36	3438	In	35	3484

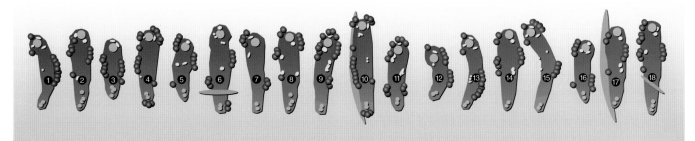

Texas Top 100

79. Pine Forest Country Club

In 1944, a group of citizens decided their community of Garden Oaks and Oak Forest-Heights deserved to have a golf course and country club.

Residents canvassed the neighborhood for 18 months selling charter memberships until they reached their goal of 350 members a year later.

H.B. Bettell, the group's first president, and his peers purchased 144 acres "loaded with timber" off North Shepherd Drive, just north of where Loop 610 stands today. It was located in the middle of Houston Heights.

Legendary architect John Bredemus built the course during World War II. It was a tight woodsy course that hosted the University of Houston's All-America Intercollegiate for 15 years and the 1949 Houston Open.

Pine Forest wasn't around long enough to age gracefully. Twenty-eight years after Bredemus did his handiwork, the club decided to move outward in 1974 to escape the city's growth. The move was a long time coming because most of Pine Forest's members began the move outward in the 1950s and '60s.

In 1967, a study of the club's mailing list showed that 75 percent of the members had moved west and were living in the Spring Branch area.

When it came time to refurbish the existing facility, many of the club's more aggressive members began to push for a new site west of town.

The club eventually accepted a $5.5-million offer from Food Fair to buy the land and they selected a 220-acre site west of Houston as the club's new location.

"We looked for a new location, by ground and by air, over God only knows how many feet of land," remembers then club president Roger Jeffery.

Leaving the nostalgia behind, the club then chose architect Jay Riviere to build a course that lived up to the club's tradition. Pine Forest features three nine-hole layouts. The Green/Gold combination plays to a 129 slope rating. A chain of lakes winds through the layout and brings water into play on all but six holes.

The 435-yard par-4 No. 6 on the Green Nine is the hardest hole on the course. It is a dogleg left around a row of trees to a green that is guarded on the front right by a pond.

No. 3 on the Gold Nine is a 420-yard par 4 with water in play off the tee and on the approach.

Pine Forest recently underwent a $1-million renovation. It also hosts the annual Three Amigos tournament hosted by Fred Couples, Blaine McCallister and CBS sportscaster Jim Nantz.

Charlie Epps, the self-proclaimed "Golf Doctor," and teacher of several PGA tour pros, is the director of golf.

Pine Forest COUNTRY CLUB

Pine Forest Country Club

18003 Clay Road
Houston 77084
281-463-0900
Pro: Charlie Epps
A 27-hole private club.
Take I-10 west to Highway 6, then right
5 miles to Clay Road. Turn left on
Clay to club entrance on left.

• • •

USGA rating: 73.0
Slope rating: 118
Sand traps: 96
Water holes: 21
Doglegs: 7 left/ 3 right
Type greens: Bermuda
Record: 64
Designer: Jay Riviere
Year opened: 1975

• • •

Hole	Par	Yards	Hole	Par	Yards
1	5	505	10	5	535
2	4	357	11	4	350
3	3	170	12	3	180
4	4	403	13	5	561
5	4	338	14	4	354
6	4	350	15	4	354
7	3	200	16	3	225
8	4	390	17	3	220
9	5	557	18	5	566
Out	36	3270	In	36	3345

80. Painted Dunes Golf Course

El Paso is halfway to Arizona for most Texans, and Painted Dunes Golf Course is the next best thing to being there. Of the more than 800 golf courses in the state, probably 90 percent of them look the same.

Painted Dunes falls in the other 10 percent, and it appears as if its roots lean more toward Arizona than Texas — if not Scotland.

Houston-based architect Ken Dye, who produced one of the state's best new courses at Kingwood's Forest Course in 1995, built Painted Dunes in 1991 and created a masterpiece out of the barren desert.

With its links design and desert terrain, it is a different atmosphere than you'll find anywhere in the state. Considering that Painted Dunes is a municipal course owned and funded by the city of El Paso, Painted Dunes is a modern-day marvel in the golf architecture business.

Using his background as both a golf course and landscape architect, Dye sculpted the sands beneath the Franklin Mountains into a beautiful desert-style course with many hour-glass fairways and multi-tiered bentgrass greens.

Golf Digest ranked it one of the best public courses in the state in 1997–98 and it has hosted PGA Tour qualifying tournaments.

The Dallas Morning News also ranked it as the No. 1 municipal course in the state in 1997–98.

Because of green fees of only $19 on weekdays and $23 on weekends, Painted Dunes represents probably the best golf value for your dollar in the state and is well-maintained despite being the busiest course in West Texas as it hosts more than 60,000 rounds a year.

Unless you live in El Paso, however, you'll spend the rest of your money just getting there. There isn't much water that comes into play and you don't have to hit the ball long to score well at Painted Dunes.

Accuracy, however, is a prerequisite. Painted Dunes is typical of the golf courses in Arizona where plush green fairways wind their way through the rocks and cactus on the desert floor. Once you get off the beaten path you might not be able to find your ball in the cactus, tall grasses and wildflowers. There are also ample bunkers throughout the course to collect stray shots.

Once on the multi-tiered greens, putting can be treacherous. Hitting your approach to the proper level of the green will help prevent a day of three-putts.

There are very few gimme birdies here. All of the par 5s are well over 500 yards, ranging from 542 to 577 yards, and two par 4s are over 430 yards. The hardest hole is the 446-yard par-4 No. 5. No. 9 is a 431 yard par 4 and No. 15 is 455 yards.

PAINTED DUNES
Desert Golf Course

Painted Dunes Golf Course
12000 McCombs Street
El Paso 79934
915-821-2122
Pro: Bill Barnard
A par-72, 6,925-yard public course.
From I-10 going north, take Highway 54 going east about 9 miles, follow the directional signs to the course.

• • •

USGA rating: 74.0
Slope rating: 137
Sand traps: 47
Water holes: 3
Doglegs: 7 left/4 right
Type greens: Bentgrass
Record: 60
Designer: Ken Dye
Year opened: 1991

• • •

Hole	Par	Yards	Hole	Par	Yards
1	4	383	10	5	564
2	3	192	11	3	173
3	5	542	12	4	414
4	4	359	13	4	401
5	4	446	14	4	351
6	4	365	15	4	455
7	5	577	16	3	208
8	3	149	17	4	363
9	4	431	18	5	552
Out	36	3444	In	36	3481

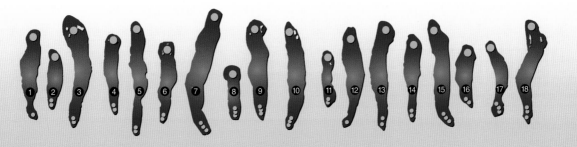

81. Longwood Golf Club

LONGWOOD

In the 1990s, virgin territory is hard to come by in Houston. Since settlers first set up shop along Buffalo Bayou over a century ago, almost every piece of prime real estate has been turned into either a skyscraper, apartment complex or a strip shopping center equipped with a Stop N' Go.

Somewhere along the way, a piece of land in Houston got lost in the shuffle. It's a virtual rain forest with oaks and pines more than 100 years old.

"When we went in there to do the clearing," Jack Montgomery says, "the underbrush was so thick you could walk in there 100 feet and couldn't get out without a compass."

Montgomery, Keith Fergus, Harry Yewens and the rest of the Golf Unlimited Group blazed a trail. In the fall of 1994, they paved the road that thousands of golfers have followed since they swung open the doors at Longwood Golf Club.

Montgomery and Fergus are both former touring professionals who have played on some of the best courses in the world.

And Montgomery and Fergus know what it is like to have a special piece of property since it was only in 1989 that they turned part of the Vivian Smith estate into a 27-hole facility in Richmond known as Old Orchard Golf Club. That still ranks among the best lay-outs in the city.

At Longwood, the golf course is part of a master-planned community. The land offers a wealth of riches, with plenty of trees to define the fairways and Little Cypress Creek running throughout the property.

Despite the promise of the land, Montgomery says he didn't decide to take the project until he was sure developers were committed to a championship course.

"It's going to be a really good golf course," he says. "It's going to look like it has been there for 30 years. One of our demands was that we didn't want houses on both sides of every fairway. We don't want players to be in Ms. Jones' kitchen while she's trying to cook supper."

The original course measures 7,000 yards from the back tees. While the fairways will be lined with trees, they will still be wide enough to allow players to work the ball. If you miss a fairway, you might be lucky to chip back to it. With a 139 slope rating, it is one of the most difficult daily-fee courses in the state.

The course was later expanded to 27 holes and is now owned by American Golf Corporation.

"The land has great definition," Montgomery says. "We've got some sophisticated golfers in our company and I think we appreciate a good golf course and a good site like this. You can be sure we'll make the most of it."

Longwood Golf Club

13300 Longwood Trace
Houston 77429
281-373-4100
Pro: David Findlay
A 27-hole, public course. From downtown Houston, take U.S. 290 west to Telge Road, then right on Telge. Course is at intersection of Telge and Huffmeister.

• • •

USGA rating: 73.6
Slope rating: 139
Sand traps: 35
Water holes: 7
Doglegs: 2 left/4 right
Type greens: Tiff Dwarf
Record: N/A
Designers: Keith Fergus and Harry Yewens
Year opened: 1995

Hole	Par	Yards	Hole	Par	Yards
1	5	493	10	4	426
2	3	214	11	4	449
3	5	530	12	3	169
4	3	183	13	5	511
5	4	464	14	4	419
6	4	339	15	4	443
7	5	566	16	3	173
8	3	172	17	5	488
9	4	446	18	4	440
Out	36	3,407	In	36	3,518

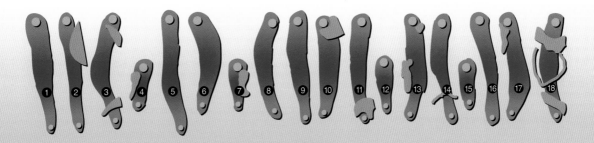

82. *Del Lago Resort*

T he name says it all. Del Lago means The Lake. And in Houston, when you say The Lake you're talking about beautiful Lake Conroe.

Nestled on the shore of one of the state's most beautiful lakes, Del Lago celebrated its 13th anniversary in 1998 as the southwest's most complete resort and conference center. That's a big statement, even for a Texas resort.

But Del Lago had the big picture in mind when they developed this project in 1985 to include a championship golf course, a 21-story hotel, a 300-slip full-service marina with a health spa and fitness center. It is close to Houston, but far removed from the metropolitan maze and haze.

If there is one word that describes Del Lago, it would be complete.

The year Del Lago opened, sports promoter George Liddy brought worldwide attention to Del Lago with the World Mixed Doubles Championship.

The first year featured tennis, but the second year Liddy added golf to the format and pitted Arnold Palmer and Nancy Lopez against Gary Player and Jan Stephenson. Lopez represented Del Lago on the LPGA tour the first few years.

The course designed by architect Jay Riviere and Texas golf legend Dave Marr features mostly tree-lined fairways and requires approach shots to well-trapped greens that overlook Lake Conroe.

They didn't forget that the idea of a resort concept is to provide a layout for a wide variety of players. They deviated from the trend at the time to try to create a name for the course by making it one of the toughest around.

"I think you can design a course so a guy can hit it 380 yards, but he'll have to hit it into a very narrow zone," says Riviere. "But we're trying to catch the big gun. The little guys have enough trouble already.

"We try to give the high handicapper, ladies or older players an entry to the green. Most architects today are putting trouble on both sides of every fairway. That's wrong."

The most difficult hole on the layout is the 464-yard, par-4 No. 9. It requires a long accurate tee shot to a fairway that slopes slightly from left to right. That will set you up for a mid- to long-iron approach to a long, narrow green protected by water in front and bunkers in back.

The back nine features the scenic 423-yard, par-4 No. 15 and 528-yard, par-5 No. 18. No. 15 requires a downhill tee shot, then goes back uphill to a generous green.

A long, well-placed tee shot on No. 18 can give you the chance to get home in two, but most players lay up short of the pond that protects the green.

Del Lago Resort

600 Del Lago Boulevard
Montgomery 77356
809-582-6100
Pro: Bobby Cleboski
A par-71, 6,638-yard semi-private resort. Take I-45 north to Highway 105, then turn west 12 miles to Walden Road. Turn right on Walden 2 miles to entrance on the right.

• • •

USGA rating: 71.4
Slope rating: 131
Sand traps: 55
Water holes: 11
Doglegs: 3 left/5 right
Type greens: Bermuda
Record: 63
Designers: Jay Riviere and Dave Marr
Year opened: 1983

• • •

Hole	Par	Yards	Hole	Par	Yards
1	5	513	10	4	440
2	3	160	11	3	178
3	4	417	12	4	410
4	5	520	13	4	426
5	4	452	14	3	165
6	3	196	15	4	423
7	4	447	16	5	506
8	4	584	17	3	197
9	4	464	18	5	528
Out	36	3366	In	35	3272

83. Columbia Lakes Resort

COLUMBIA LAKES

Columbia Lakes originally was developed by Tenneco as a meeting place where executives could devise new ways to expand the company resources.

For recreation, they would fish 300 acres of man-made lakes.

For economic reasons, the land was sliced up into a subdivision and architect Jack Miller was hired in 1973 to build a golf course from the surrounding thicket of majestic oaks.

West Columbia is an historical area and during construction, Miller uncovered a flintlock rifle, a cannonball and a sugar-cane crusher that were donated to the Varner-Hogg Plantation.

The land once was a sugar-cane plantation before Tenneco bought it from the Hogg family.

Although 55 miles southeast of Houston, it is a center of golf activity for Houston's regular golfers and conventioneers. In 1990 and 1991 Columbia Lakes was one of only four clubs across the nation to host the Jack Nicklaus–Jim Flick Golf School.

It also was home of the Columbia Lakes School of Golf, directed by Kathy Whitworth along with pros Mark Steinbauer and Betsy Cullen, and the Japanese-sponsored Super Lady Project that prepares young Japanese women for a pro career.

Miller and Tom Fazio, one of the nation's hottest architects who returned in the mid-80s to do some redesign work, turned the scenic property into one of the area's favorite courses. Seven different holes were nominated as among the most difficult in the Houston area.

"This project was a joy to work on," says Miller, who said the biggest problem was getting permission from Tenneco to remove certain trees.

"Tenneco furnished their jet helicopter for aerial views during construction. An aerial view of a green, fairway and teeing area helped evaluate the strategy of each hole."

The 533-yard, par-5 No. 5 is similar to No. 11 at Walden on Lake Conroe, the area's toughest hole. It's a dogleg to the right that curls around a lake that comes into play on all three shots.

Even with a good drive, players are left with a carry of approximately 250 yards over the water to the green and are forced to lay up to a small landing area and settle on a short approach.

The 408-yard, par-4 No. 18 requires a straight drive toward the right side of the fairway to leave a clear approach over the water and overhanging trees in front to a shallow green that is barely 15 yards deep.

In the early 80s, architect Tom Fazio conducted in a renovation and redesign of the course. It was his first design project in Texas before he built Barton Creek.

Columbia Lakes Resort

188 Freeman Boulevard
West Columbia 77486
800-231-1030
Pro: Gene Amman
A par-72, 6,967-yard semi-private resort. From downtown Houston, take Highway 288 south to Highway 35, then turn right to club entrance on the right.

• • •

USGA rating: 75.7
Slope rating: 131
Sand traps: 70
Water holes: 12
Doglegs: 2 left/3 right
Type greens: Bermuda
Record: 64
Designer: Jack Miller and Tom Fazio
Year opened: 1973

• • •

Hole	Par	Yards	Hole	Par	Yards
1	5	500	10	4	402
2	3	190	11	4	403
3	4	400	12	3	197
4	4	438	13	5	533
5	5	533	14	4	406
6	3	185	15	4	414
7	4	407	16	3	228
8	4	417	17	5	508
9	4	398	18	4	408
Out	36	3468	In	36	3499

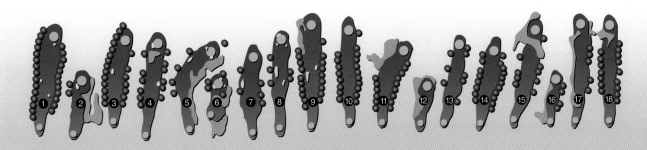

Texas Top 100

84. Old Orchard Golf Club

At one time, the property on which Old Orchard was built was known as the Lazy C Ranch. It was owned by rancher Ben Jack Cage and was famous around the United States as one of the finest horse farms in the world in the 1940s.

At one time, the ranch foreman and his top ranch hand divided one acre of land into 3,136,320 tracts of two square inches each and sold them throughout the country in airport terminals and in *The Wall Street Journal* as "ranchettes."

After that endeavor failed (only 168 were sold) the title to the land was purchased by R.E. "Bob" Smith in 1956. Smith later was one of the men behind the construction of the Astrodome and became one of the founders of the Houston Astros.

In 1987, a group of investors including former Astro catcher Alan Ashby, approached Smith's widow, Vivian, about the possibility of building a golf course on the land. An avid golfer — she had a 5-hole course built on land near her hunting lodge in Palacios — she embraced the idea but died before construction began.

She would be proud of what transpired in the next year. Architect Carlton Gipson teamed with former tour pros and co-owners Keith Fergus and Jack Montgomery to take advantage of the hundreds of mature pecans and naturally rolling terrain. Gipson added eight strategically placed lakes to create water hazards on 17 of the 27 holes. The course is a throwback to the early 20s, when architects had their pick of the best land available.

Gipson and Fergus, a noted environmentalist, often quibbled over the removal of any unnecessary trees. "He wants six-foot wide fairways," Gipson joked. "It just tears him up when we cut down a tree." Said Fergus: "It's amazing to see somebody take a load of dirt and turn it into a golf course. You can appreciate somebody with an imagination to make everything fit."

The developers took every precaution to preserve the land and the existing ambiance of the old Lazy C, even naming the three nine-hole layouts the Barn, Stables and Range. The Barn and Stables run through an old pecan orchard, while the Range is more open. The Lazy C's main ranch house is now the restaurant and the old foreman's house is the pro shop.

"Old Orchard was truly a design by committee," says Derrell Witt, a landscape architect who worked under Gipson at the time. "With several pro golfers as owners, I provided a routing plan, greens design, some grading plans and got out of the way. It is such a beautiful site, with rolling topography and huge native pecan trees, that it would have been hard to screw it up."

Old Orchard Golf Club

13134 FM 1464
Richmond 77469
281-277-3300
Dir.: Jack Montgomery
A 27-hole, public facility.
Take U.S. 59 south to Highway 6, go west to Highway 90. Turn right on FM 1464, then right to club entrance on the left.

• • •

USGA rating: 73.5
Slope rating: 130
Sand traps: 38
Water holes: 14
Doglegs: 6 left/3 right
Type greens: Bermuda
Record: 64
Designers: Carlton Gipson
*   and Keith Fergus*
Year opened: 1990

• • •

Hole	Par	Yards	Hole	Par	Yards
1	4	424	10	4	313
2	4	357	11	5	557
3	3	200	12	3	157
4	4	425	13	5	496
5	5	525	14	4	430
6	3	178	15	4	392
7	4	440	16	3	173
8	5	560	17	4	469
9	4	455	18	4	373
Out	36	3565	In	36	3363

Texas Top 100

85. Fair Oaks Ranch

From the time you step out of the car at Fair Oaks Ranch, you know you are about to step back into time.

This sprawling, 5,000-acre ranch used to be the personal residence for legendary Texas oilman Ralph Fair Sr. back in the 1930s. For decades, the land remained untamed, with Fair's home being the only dwelling.

When Fair died in 1970, his son Ralph Jr., decided to turn the acreage into a housing subdivision. It is located 30 minutes outside of San Antonio in the Hill Country community of Boerne, a perfect bedroom community for people who work in the city but want to live in the country.

Fair Oaks Ranch Golf and Country Club was built in 1973 to be the centerpiece for this new community, and Fair's old homestead was turned into a 20,000-square foot clubhouse.

The first of three nine-hole courses was built in 1973, and a fourth was finished in 1994 to give Fair Oaks two 18-hole championship courses.

Golf legend Gary Player had a hand in designing nine holes of both courses. The Blackjack Oak course was designed by Player and Dennis Griffiths and the Live Oak course was designed by Player and Ron Kirby.

Player was always an excellent iron player and his Blackjack layout demands no less of its players.

Whether it is a long par 5, a long par 4 or a long par 3, you'll be using plenty of long irons to negotiate your way around this course.

The course, built around a winding creek, measures 7,077 yards from the back tees and plays to a 131 slope rating.

Blackjack Oak begins with a 560-yard, downhill par 5 and ends with a par 4 that goes straight uphill. In between are plenty of scenic holes with water and sand coming into play.

The newest nine holes were incorporated into the existing layout (Nos. 6–14). They are more of a links-style design with more length required from the tee and more contour to the fairways and greens.

No. 3 is a stiff 239-yard par 3 with a green protected in front by two bunkers.

No. 4 is a 425-yard par 4 that doglegs to the right around a lake that protects the corner and cuts into the landing area.

Off the tee No. 6 is a 564-yard double dogleg par 5 with two sets of fairway bunkers protecting both corners and an approach that requires a carry over a creek to reach the green.

No. 9 is a brutal, straightaway 454-yard par 4 that just dares you to give it your best couple of shots to reach the green.

No. 15 is a 608-yard par 5 that has water down the right side of the landing area. It requires three great shots to get home.

FAIR OAKS RANCH
Golf & Country Club

Fair Oaks Ranch Blackjack Oak Course

7900 Fair Oaks Parkway
Boerne 78006
210-981-9600
Pro: Bill Keys
This is a 36-hole private club.
From San Antonio, take I-10 west to
Fair Oaks Parkway, go right 2 miles
and course is on the right.

• • •

USGA rating: 73.1
Slope rating: 131
Sand traps: 121
Water holes: 7
Doglegs: 7 left/7 right
Type greens: Bermuda
Record: N/A
Designers: Ron Kirby, Gary Player
        and Dennis Griffiths
Year opened: 1979

• • •

Hole	Par	Yards	Hole	Par	Yards
1	5	560	10	5	518
2	4	383	11	4	394
3	3	239	12	4	362
4	4	425	13	3	183
5	4	430	14	4	381
6	5	564	15	5	608
7	3	171	16	4	420
8	4	419	17	3	175
9	4	454	18	4	391
Out	36	3645	In	36	3432

Texas Top 100

86. Mill Creek Inn

A hundred summers or so ago, Texas damsels braved a dusty, bumpy stagecoach ride to Salado to dip in the town's clear, spring-fed waters.

Today's visitors come via a speedier form of transport to cool their toes in the cool stream and bask in the lingering aura of history colored by early Texas settlers in 1859. The tiny town north of Austin has numerous well-preserved 19th century buildings, 18 of which are listed in the National Registry of Historic Places.

This little slice of Texas history is the backdrop for the Mill Creek Inn golf resort, where architect Robert Trent Jones, Jr. designed a 6,486-yard layout with just enough trouble to make it interesting, enough roll and undulation to make it challenging and enough sand traps to test a golfer's ability with a wedge.

"The most beautiful golf course in Texas . . . if you can't relax and enjoy golf at Mill Creek, you can't do it anywhere," golf writer Pat Selig writes in his book *Great Texas Golf*. Built originally in 1981 as a private club, Mill Creek is now open to homeowners, members and guests.

Jones placed a heavy emphasis on accuracy and shot-making over brute strength.

"Mill Creek is one of my favorite courses because of the way the holes work together with the natural assets of the land,"

Jones said. "I think we created an intriguing and challenging course which makes golfers use every club in their bag . . . and it remains interesting each time it is played.

The main trouble a golfer will endure is common to most Jones courses. Plenty of undulating greens, sand and doglegs with a dash of water thrown in.

The signature hole featured in most of Mill Creek's advertising campaigns is the 340-yard, par-4 third hole. For anyone who doubted if Jones has a soft spot in his architect's heart, this is proof. The tee boxes are shaped like an arrow and point directly at the green. The fairway drops the final 80 yards with the final ledge giving you a good view of a heart-shaped green, surrounded by sand traps.

No. 4 is a 413-yard, par 4 that is the No. 1 handicap hole. It is a dogleg right with a huge tree that guards the inside corner of the fairway. The green is fronted by large limestone boulders and Salado Creek. The green doesn't provide a straight putt and there is a bunker on the back right side of it to catch any over-clubbed shot.

The rest of the course alternates between pretty views, ugly traps and tricky greens. The fairways rise and fall with the land.

Of the more than 200 courses Jones has designed, it shows him at his best. As Jones desired, Mill Creek is a course you can play frequently and not get bored.

Mill CreeK

THE HEART OF TEXAS

Mill Creek Inn

PO Box 67
Salado 76571
254-947-5698
Pro: Mike Cameron
A par-71, 6,486-yard resort course.
From Austin, take I-35 north to
Exit 285 and follow the signs.

• • •

USGA rating: 72.1
Slope rating: 128
Sand traps: 54
Water holes: 14
Doglegs: 10
Type greens: Bermuda
Record: 65
Designer: Robert Trent Jones, Jr.
Year opened: 1981

• • •

Hole	Par	Yards	Hole	Par	Yards
1	5	512	10	4	398
2	3	183	11	4	346
3	4	340	12	3	182
4	4	413	13	5	556
5	4	420	14	4	411
6	3	190	15	4	392
7	4	401	16	3	132
8	4	348	17	4	376
9	5	517	18	4	369
Out	36	3324	In	35	3162

87. Riverside Golf Club

Roger Packard won't soon forget his infrequent ventures to Texas.

A native of Chicago, where he and his father built many top courses, Packard came to Texas in the mid 1980s to build his first two Texas layouts.

Packard's first Texas assignment was in Houston in 1983, where he designed specifically for women to house the Ladies Professional Golf Association.

To maximize his time in Texas, Packard also won the contract to build Riverside Golf Course on the banks of the Trinity River in Grand Prairie. It turned out to be the bigger task.

"I'll never forget it," said Packard, who was honored by *Golf Digest's* Best New Resort Course in 1984 and Best New Public Course in 1990.

"It was so hot down there and the humidity was unbelievable. Sweat would just be rolling down our faces. We'd look at each other and think, 'When does the plane leave?'"

Packard would be pleased to know that the sweat of his brow is still reaping dividends long after he returned to cooler climates. His golf course is one of the most challenging public courses in the Dallas-Fort Worth area.

The course plays 7,025 yards from the back tees with a slope rating of 132. Water comes into play on 16 of 18 holes, so a com-

bination of length and accuracy is a must.

In fact, because of its close proximity to the Trinity, occasional flooding is unavoidable. But steps have been taken to minimize the damage when flooding does occur and to enable players to return to action as quickly as possible.

There's no better example of the layout's difficulty than the 438-yard, par-4 No. 18. A lake cuts into the landing area and surrounds the green, forces players to an approach of 200 yards to reach the green.

The 212-yard, par-3 No. 5 hole is another hole where the tee and green are nearly surrounded by water.

No. 6 is a 543-yard par 5 with water in play off the tee and on the approach. The hole doglegs left through the trees, with a creek protecting the left side. A lake protects the right front of the green on the approach.

No. 15 is a 421-yard dogleg right with trees down both sides of the fairway and water coming into play on the approach to the left and behind the green.

No. 4 is a 462-yard par 4 where golfers must hit a long approach to a green guarded on the left by a lake that wraps around the back of the green.

"I tried to make exciting golf here," Packard says. "I tried to make each hole individual, unique. The better the player, the more challenging."

RIVERSIDE
G O L F   C L U B

Riverside Golf Club

3000 Riverside Drive
Grand Prairie 75050
817-640-7801
Pro: Eric Kaspar
A par-72, 7,025-yard public course.
From Fort Worth, take I-30 east to Loop 360, then north to Riverside Parkway.
Left to club entrance.

• • •

USGA rating: 74.4
Slope rating: 132
Sand traps: 36
Water holes: 16
Doglegs: 5 left/ 3 right
Type greens: Bentgrass
Record: 63
Designer: Roger Packard
Year opened: 1984

• • •

Hole	Par	Yards	Hole	Par	Yards
1	4	411	10	4	402
2	5	504	11	5	544
3	4	377	12	4	355
4	4	462	13	3	181
5	3	212	14	5	545
6	5	543	15	4	421
7	4	434	16	3	179
8	3	198	17	4	366
9	4	453	18	4	438
Out	36	3594	In	36	3431

Texas Top 100

88. Tapatio Springs Resort

Jack Parker was one of those guys who started from the bottom rung on the ladder in the golf business. He was a dishwasher, cook, chef, assistant manager and manager before he ever learned to play golf.

There's something to be said for doing things the hard way. As the chairman of Parker Holdings/Club Consultants, Inc., which owns and operates two of San Antonio's favorite layouts, Parker has completed his climb to the top and is in a position to shape the game in the future.

Parker believes one of the growing problems in the game is a shortage of public facilities. So with that motive, he bought Tapatio Springs in 1993 from former partner Kiyonori Higa.

"Private clubs are unable to appeal to the amateur golfer, by far the largest segment of the golf market," Parker says. "The need to appeal to this amateur golf market is fueling the expansion of new public courses and will eventually create healthy and productive competition in the golf industry."

Original owner Clyde Smith selected some of the scenic land in this Hill Country region for his hideaway and built San Antonio's first destination resort in 1981. Until recently, the resort was connected with the local interstate only by a winding, two-lane dirt road. But once golfers arrive, they'll agree there are lots of advantages to playing golf off the beaten path.

Bill Johnston, the 1958 Texas Open champion who later designed the layout at Dominion, designed the golf course as the centerpiece for an entire project that totaled $30 million. That included a huge house where Smith still lives near the front gate. Smith's creation ran into financial difficulties in the late 1980s and he sold it to Parker and Higa in 1990.

Tapatio Springs winds through housing developments, native woods and features plenty of water and sand, with Fredericks Creek frequently coming into play.

No. 2 is a 382-yard par 4 with water down the left side. The third is a 120-yard par 3 that is one of the most scenic in the area. Water runs the length of the fairway down the left side against a 160-foot limestone cliff. On the par-4 No. 6, water cuts into the landing area and can be reached by big hitters using a driver off the tee.

The most difficult hole on the course is the 559-yard, par-5 No. 13. It bends left over water with trees and more huge cliffs along the left side. No. 17 is a short par 3 over a mini-waterfall with the finishing hole a 496-yard par 5 protected by a pond in front of the green.

Parker, who became the sole owner in 1993, still has 1,100 acres of undeveloped land and says plans call for an expanded hotel and another 18-hole course.

Tapatio Springs
RESORT &
COUNTRY CLUB

Tapatio Springs Resort

PO Box 550
Boerne 78006
800-999-3299
Pro: Jess Hawkins
A par-71, 6,472-yard resort.
From San Antonio, take I-10 west to Exit 539 (Johns Road). Go left 4 miles to club entrance.

• • •

USGA rating: 70.9
Slope rating: 122
Sand traps: 67
Water holes: 11
Doglegs: 2 left/2 right
Type greens: Bermuda
Record: 63
Designer: Bill Johnston
Year opened: 1981

• • •

Hole	Par	Yards	Hole	Par	Yards
1	5	486	10	4	490
2	4	382	11	4	158
3	3	120	12	4	293
4	4	335	13	5	559
5	4	371	14	3	408
6	4	396	15	5	426
7	3	196	16	4	387
8	4	431	17	3	159
9	4	379	18	5	496
Out	35	3096	In	36	3376

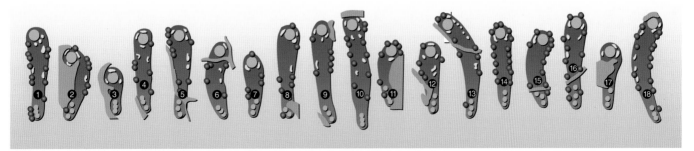

Texas Top 100

89. Memorial Park Golf Course

Memorial Park Golf Course celebrated its 60th birthday in 1996, but in many ways it is just like the new girl in town. She's so beautiful that every guy wants a date with her.

So many players.

So few tee times.

After being closed for just over a year, Houston's Grand Old Lady opened as good as new after a $4.25-million facelift that helped it regain its rightful place among the state's best golf courses. Like a classic car that has been stripped and restored piece by piece, Memorial park is a mean driving machine that everyone wants to take for a spin around the block.

Memorial Park was originally built in 1936 on land donated by Will and Ima Hogg, the developers of the River Oaks residential community, as a tribute to the soldiers who trained for World War I at Camp Logan.

Utilizing crews for the Civilian Conservation Corps, John Bredemus carved out what was considered one of the best courses in the country at the time. The layout helped produce such Houston golf legends as Jimmy Demaret, Dave Marr and Tommy Bolt. It's length, difficulty and design made it as good as Bredemus' work a few years later at Colonial Country Club, which still ranks as the state's No. 1 course.

Memorial hosted the Houston Open in 1947 and from 1951–63. Houston's Jack Burke Jr. was a hometown winner in 1952 and '59, and Arnold Palmer won in 1957 and Cary Middlecoff won in 1953. Memorial later hosted Doug Sanders' Senior PGA Tour celebrity tournament.

But time and mistreatment took their toll on one of the city's oldest courses and it eventually fell into disrepair. Tornadoes, hurricanes and disease depleted the original number of trees by 50 percent.

"It just hasn't been cared for properly," said Marr, who grew up working at Memorial. "The Old Grand Dame has a few wrinkles now and is in need of some plastic surgery. With tender loving care, she can be great again."

Burke agrees. "It would have been one of the premier clubs anywhere and it still can be," he said. "It's a very tender area and it should be dealt with that way. It needs people who have an interest in the restoration of the course and its history."

Those words rang true in the mid-90s when a joint effort by the city and private companies helped fund a $3-million project to restore, revitalize and reforest the golf course and once again make it the centerpiece for golf in Houston. Another $1.25 million was spent on the course to renovate and expand the clubhouse and to create a Memorial Park Hall of Fame to ensure its rich history is never lost again.

Memorial Park Golf Course

Memorial Park Loop
Houston 77007
713-862-4033
Pro: Ed Sehl
A par-72, 7,164-yard public course.
From Houston take Memorial Drive to Memorial Park Loop, right to course entrance.

• • •

USGA rating: 73.0
Slope rating: 122
Sand traps: 51
Water holes: 9
Doglegs: 6 left/4 right
Type greens: Bermuda
Record: 62
Designer: John Bredemus
Year opened: 1936

• • •

Hole	Par	Yards	Hole	Par	Yards
1	4	453	10	5	588
2	3	245	11	3	145
3	4	504	12	4	452
4	5	492	13	4	455
5	4	439	14	4	391
6	3	185	15	4	401
7	5	622	16	3	237
8	4	406	17	5	500
9	4	404	18	4	415
Out	36	3750	In	36	3583

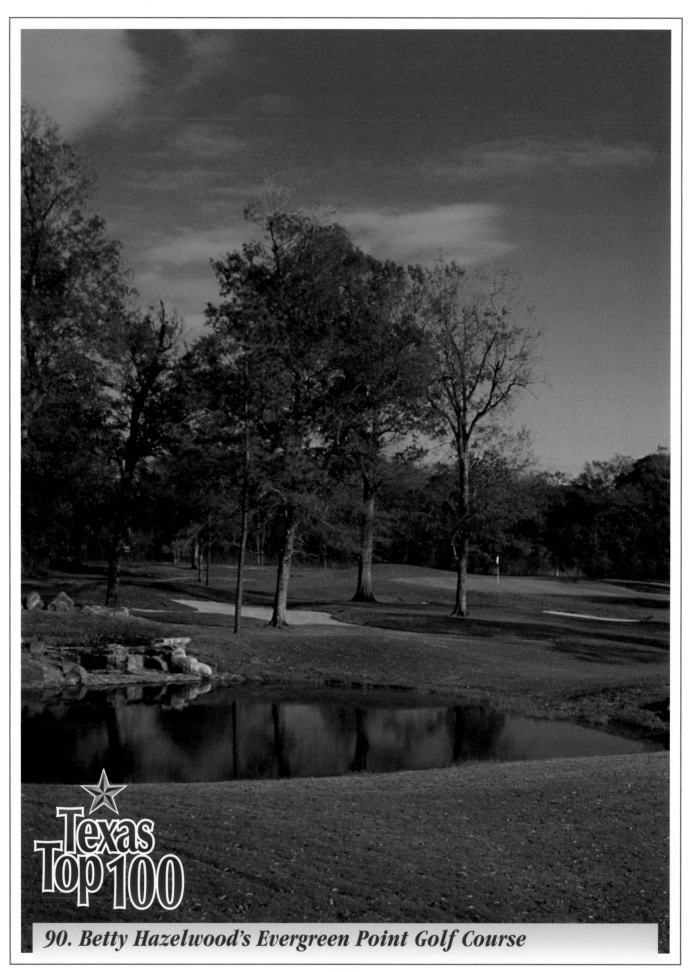

Texas Top 100

90. Betty Hazelwood's Evergreen Point Golf Course

Evergreen Point
Golf Course

Few men have ever made a little go further than Dave Marr.

Marr was the son of a club professional and is the second cousin of Jack Burke, Jr., one of the game's legendary players, so golf was in his blood. His father died at an early age and his mother was working as a waitress at a Howard Johnson's, so Marr helped pay the bills by working around the pro shop at Memorial Park.

Marr never lost the humility that he learned from such modest beginnings, but he took his talent and his personality and went on to become one of the golf's greatest ambassadors as a player and a popular color analyst on golf telecasts for ABC, NBC and the BBC.

If Tiger Woods is the face of golf in the 21st century, then Dave Marr was the voice of golf in the 1960s, '70s and '80s.

Marr was referred to by golf writer Dan Jenkins as "the Pro from 52nd Street," because of Marr's love of the Manhattan night life and his love for bellying up to the bar to share stories with the greatest golfers of all time.

"For a player like me, it all had to come together," Marr said of his victory over Jack Nicklaus at the 1965 PGA Championship, the last of his four pro victories.

"I thought I was a good player, not a great player. If I played my best and Jack played his best, he still would have beat me. I had to wait for him to stub his toe."

Marr died in 1997 after a long battle with cancer. One of the last marks he left on the game was the Betty Hazelwood's Evergreen Point Golf Club.

The club was named in honor of a Baytown humanitarian whose family built the course, but it also will be remembered for Marr's last work with longtime partner Jay Riviere.

Since Marr grew up on public courses and took the game to the public his whole life as a TV commentator, it's appropriate that this course is open to the public.

Riviere and Marr built numerous courses together in the Houston area, including The Falls Resort which is also in the Texas Top 100, and Evergreen Point. The latter was a unique project in that it offered a beautiful piece of property with rolling terrain, thick woods and natural creeks.

This well-manicured, gently rolling course has several lakes, and a stream that winds its way through the mature-treed course.

The bunkered greens are large-sized and undulating, while the contoured fairways are lined with oak, magnolias, pine and dogwood trees.

The signature hole is No. 3, a 462-yard, par 4, which is very difficult and requires a shot through tall Magnolia trees on both sides of the fairway to a slightly elevated green. Water hazards come into play on 15 holes and dogleg fairways on several others.

Betty Hazelwood's Evergreen Point Golf Course

1530 Evergreen Road
Baytown 77520
281-837-9000
A par-72, 7,046-yard public course.
From Houston take Highway 225 east to Highway 146, then go 2.5 miles to Spur 55. Turn right and take next right to course entrance.

• • •

USGA rating: 73.0
Slope rating: 129
Sand traps: 47
Water holes: 15
Doglegs: 2
Type greens: Bermuda
Record: 67
Designers: Jay Riviere and Dave Marr
Year opened: 1996

• • •

Hole	Par	Yards	Hole	Par	Yards
1	4	436	10	5	560
2	3	221	11	4	412
3	4	462	12	4	447
4	5	489	13	5	527
5	4	381	14	3	176
6	4	398	15	4	382
7	4	379	16	4	394
8	3	159	17	3	175
9	5	549	18	4	422
Out	36	3551	In	36	3495

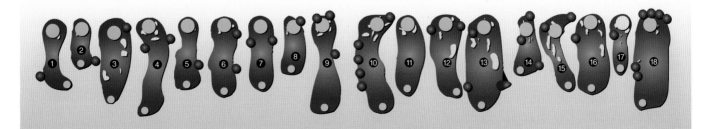

Texas Top 100

91. Rancho Viejo Resort & Country Club — Diablo Course

Located on the southernmost point of Texas, Rancho Viejo Resort enjoys the best of all worlds.

Rancho Viejo was founded as the first settlement of the Rio Grande Valley in 1771, and 200 years later the first golf course was built at Rancho Viejo.

Just 15 minutes from Mexico by car, it has developed into a great weekend getaway for golfers with two 18-hole championship layouts that offer the feel of a tropical paradise. For overnight guests, the resort also features golf villas, weekend getaway packages and other resort amenities.

The El Diablo Course is the most demanding of Rancho Viejo's two courses, playing 6,847 yards to a par of 70.

There is plenty of mischief awaiting golfers on the devil course. Well-manicured fairways with towering palms and tropical vegetation surround the challenge of strategically-placed fairway and greenside bunkers, undulating greens and innumerable resaca water hazards.

If you need more evidence to attest to the quality of Rancho Viejo, it was good enough to host a PGA Tour final stage qualifying tournament with PGA Tour stars such as Keith Fergus, Peter Jacobsen, Mike Reid and Jay Haas trying to conquer El Diablo to maintain their PGA Tour playing privileges.

The resort also is a host instructional site for the John Jacobs Golf School and has hosted a PGA Tour final stage qualifying tournament.

The layout plays to a 129 slope rating with water in play on only seven holes.

As the slogan says, "Tropical surroundings please the eye, but beware . . . the Diablo Course will steal a golfer's soul."

The El Diablo Course plays between houses in some places, so out of bounds is frequently in play. It also has large palm trees and tropical vegetation that can affect your shots, plus undulating greens. There are water hazards, known as resacas, that come into play on several holes. Both courses have large greens that are medium speed.

No. 3 is the No. 1 handicap hole. It is a 440-yard par-4 dogleg left with a lake in the landing area off the tee and on the approach. Even most big-hitters have to lay up short of the lake and leave a long approach over water.

No. 14 is a 546-yard par-5 double dogleg left around a lake. Water runs down the left side form tee to green, and an inlet cuts into the fairway in front of the green to catch those tempting to reach the green in two.

No. 8 doesn't need any water to be difficult. It is a 452-yard par 4 that plays straight to the green with threes on both sides of the fairway.

Rancho Viejo Resort and Country Club Diablo Course

1 Rancho Viejo Drive
Rancho Viejo 78575
800-531-7400
Pro: David Findlay
A 36-hole golf resort.
From Harlingen, take Highway 77 south toward Brownsville. Rancho Viejo is located on the west side of Highway 77 just outside of Brownsville.

• • •

USGA rating: 73.7
Slope rating: 129
Sand traps: 34
Water holes: 7
Type greens: Bermuda
Record: N/A
Designer: Dennis Arp
Year opened: 1971

• • •

Hole	Par	Yards	Hole	Par	Yards
1	4	397	10	4	403
2	4	429	11	4	444
3	4	440	12	3	192
4	3	201	13	4	401
5	5	533	14	5	546
6	3	229	15	4	405
7	4	368	16	3	218
8	4	452	17	4	363
9	4	403	18	4	423
Out	35	3452	In	35	3395

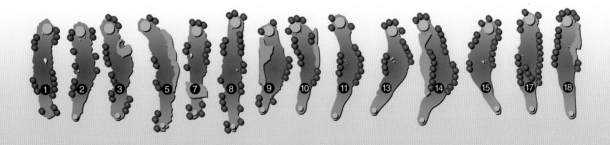

Texas Top 100

92. Southwyck Golf Club

Houston is about as far away as you can get from the grassy, rolling seaside terrain of Scotland, but architect Ken Kavanaugh re-created Houston's only true Scottish-links style course when he built Southwyck in 1988 on the open prairie southeast of downtown.

Southwyck originally was conceived as a private country club that would cater to accomplished golfers, but after Houston's oil bust in the '80s, developers decided to make it a public, daily-fee facility with the concept of a public course with a country club atmosphere.

While most golfers never get to make a pilgrimage to where the game started, Southwyck is the next best thing to being there.

It is both challenging and scenic, distinguished by its rolling hills, grassy knolls, Scottish mounds, pot bunkers and series of lakes.

Although you can't smell the ocean or feel the salt spray, it even comes equipped with omnipresent winds that average 15 mph and must be factored into every shot-making decision.

For those accustomed to playing on American park-land type courses with tree-lined fairways, Southwyck presents a small problem: Standing on the tee for the first time, it is not always obvious to golfers where they should be aiming their shots.

Depth perception is difficult and it takes local knowledge to know ideal shot placements.

Kavanaugh created an intriguing layout with as many as five tee locations per hole and various approaches to greens. Water comes into play on 13 holes and wind sweeps across the prairie just like it does in Scotland.

The course requires some target golf and there are not many level lies to be found because of the abundance of large mounds. There aren't many trees, either, but the fairways are lined by tall native grass that is virtually impossible to play from.

Southwyck was been one of the home courses for the University of Houston golf team, which has won an unprecedented 16 NCAA team titles.

It also was one of only a handful of golf facilities across the nation recognized with the Public Golf Achievement Award for promoting public golf.

The 467-yard par-4 No. 3 is one of the toughest in Houston. It is relatively straight, but fairway bunkers guard the right side and the hole plays directly into the prevailing wind.

And then there's the 250-yard par-3 No. 5, one of the longest par 3s in the state. And then the 212-yard par-3 No. 11 requires a long carry over a large ravine.

The signature hole is the par-3 No. 7, which has a waste area that runs the length of the fairway.

Southwyck Golf Club

2901 Clubhouse Drive
Pearland 77584
Pro: Louis Gantz
281-436-9999

A par-72, 7,015-yard public course. From downtown Houston, take U.S. 288 south to Highway 518, then go left 1 mile to first light, then right to club entrance.

• • •

USGA rating: 72.9
Slope rating: 123
Sand traps: 82
Water holes: 9
Doglegs: 3 left/1 right
Type greens: Bermuda
Record: 67
Designer: Ken Kavanaugh
Year opened: 1988

• • •

Hole	Par	Yards	Hole	Par	Yards
1	4	416	10	4	424
2	5	542	11	3	212
3	4	467	12	5	507
4	4	412	13	4	447
5	3	250	14	3	518
6	4	327	15	4	335
7	3	156	16	4	389
8	5	521	17	3	194
9	4	460	18	4	438
Out	36	3551	In	36	3464

Texas Top 100

93. South Padre Island Golf Club

Gerald Barton has never played golf, but he obviously knows how to create a good golf course.

Barton is the CEO of Landmark National, a company that has produced such prestigious golf resorts as PGA West in Palm Springs and Kiawah Island, site of the 1993 Ryder Cup Matches.

Now add South Padre Island Golf Club to the list.

While Landmark has built its reputation on the construction and management of some of the nation's most exclusive golf resorts, its new goal toward the 21st century is to now build more upscale daily fee courses that are within reach — both geographically and in price — of the average golfer.

South Padre Island Golf Club, which opened in 1997, was one of their first efforts in this direction, and it comes as no surprise that they produced another unique, championship layout.

Built on the mainland side of the Laguna Madre, the idea for the golf course was born when former Senator Lloyd Bentsen approached Barton and asked how to best utilize the waterfront property for the public good.

Barton told him a daily-fee golf course would raise surrounding property values and the wheels were set in motion.

Architects Chris Cole and Stephen Caplinger produced a links-style layout that is unique in many ways. It is the only course in Texas with five holes directly along Gulf waters. On some holes, it is bordered by wild native vegetation that is more than head high. On others, waste areas and deep rough in front of the tee require large carries to reach the undulating fairways. Four large man-made lakes come into play as do the natural flora of Mesquite trees, Spanish daggers, yuccas and more than 1,000 palm trees. Suffice it to say that stray shots likely never will be found.

Because of the obstacles and hazards, fairways were built wider to accommodate for the frequent windy conditions. The course measures 6,931 yards from the back tees, so it requires a total package of brains and brawn. At least the longer holes were designed to play downwind and the shorter holes play into the wind.

The course hosted the Texas State Senior Open in its first year, and Dallas pro Dwight Nevil won with a modest score of 1-over par.

Once you reach the landing areas in the fairways, the course does allow for hit-and-run shots into the greens except for No. 12, a 116-yard par 3 that is surrounded by wetlands.

The signature hole is No. 5, a 296-yard, par 4, featuring a dogleg left fairway that calls for a tee shot that must carry over the Laguna Madre Bay.

South Padre Island Golf Club

No. 1 Golf House Road
Laguna Vista 78578
(956) 943-5678
A par-72, 6,931-yard public course.
From South Padre, Highway 100 north to Laguna Vista, turn right on FM 520 continue for 2.5 miles to the course.

• • •

USGA rating: 73.0
Slope rating: 130
Sand traps: 35
Water holes: 6
Doglegs: 4 left/6 right
Type greens: Bermuda
Record: 66
Designers: Chris Cole
and Stephen Caplinger
Year opened: 1997

• • •

Hole	Par	Yards	Hole	Par	Yards
1	4	347	10	4	364
2	4	346	11	4	357
3	3	162	12	3	116
4	5	525	13	5	504
5	4	296	14	4	393
6	3	142	15	3	140
7	5	506	16	4	395
8	4	377	17	5	503
9	4	428	18	4	390
Out	36	3129	In	36	3162

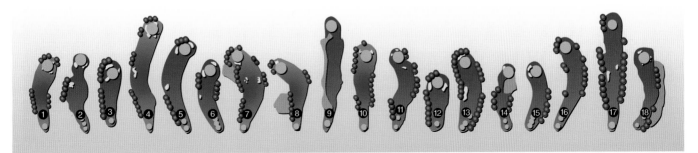

94. The Trophy Club — Ben Hogan Course

Ben Hogan is one of the most revered names in golf. His flawless swing, his fierce determination and his will to win were unlike anything the golf world had seen before or since.

After learning the game as a caddie along with Byron Nelson at Fort Worth's Glen Garden Country Club, Hogan grew up to become one of the greatest players of all time.

Hogan's resume reads like this: 63 career victories, including 13 in 1945, two Masters titles, four U.S. Opens, two PGA Championships, one British Open, four-time player of the year, three-time Vardon Trophy Winner and, of course, the golf hall of fame.

All that aside, it is a shame Hogan didn't leave a more lasting legacy than a trophy case filled to overflowing. Of all the knowledge he had about the golf swing and the way the game should be played, he kept most of it to himself.

The members at the Trophy Club, then, take great pride in the fact that this is the only course that Ben Hogan helped design.

Hogan was a perceptive golf course critic throughout his career. Hogan especially admired the works of Dick Wilson and shortly before the architect's death had talked about doing a course with him.

Ten years later, Hogan did collaborate with Wilson's chief assistant, Joe Lee, at the Trophy Club.

Typical of Hogan's intensity, he attacked each phase of the project with painstaking detail, even going so far as to personally hand-rake all the green contours.

The course, however, received only a lukewarm reception when it opened in 1976. An additional nine holes was built by Arthur Hills in 1984, and Hills later returned to complete the second 18 to create a 36-hole facility.

In the first year it opened, the LPGA's Civitan Open moved to the Trophy Club for one year and the purse was raised to $75,000. Silvia Bertolaccini defeated Kathy Whitworth with a 3-under 213.

It is kind of ironic that Hogan did his handiwork just a few miles down the road from the ranch of old rival Byron Nelson amidst the spectacular beauty of the rolling, tree-lined hills of Lake Grapevine.

The Hogan Course plays 6,953 yards from the back tees and features many tree-lined fairways that require shot-shaping off the tee and on the fairway.

Among the best holes is the 454-yard, par-4 18th. The hole doglegs left around a lake to a green protected by the lake on the left and two bunkers, requiring a steady and accurate long iron shot — the kind at which Hogan excelled at — to get home in two shots.

No. 6 is a 395-yard par 4 with trees down the right and a large bunker on the right. No. 7 is a 516-yard demanding par 5.

The Trophy Club
Ben Hogan Course
500 Trophy Club Drive
Roanoke 76262
817-430-0444
Pro: Jim Rose
A 36-hole private club.
Take Highway 114 west from Grapevine.
8 miles past Grapevine, turn right on Trophy Club Drive. Follow the signs and club is to your right.

• • •

USGA rating: 72.8
Slope rating: 123
Sand traps: 52
Water holes: 10
Doglegs: 4 left/3 right
Type greens: Bentgrass
Record: N/A
Designers: Ben Hogan and Joe Lee
Year opened: 1976

• • •

Hole	Par	Yards	Hole	Par	Yards
1	4	391	10	5	522
2	4	410	11	4	404
3	3	159	12	4	403
4	4	402	13	3	204
5	5	606	14	5	561
6	4	395	15	4	365
7	5	516	16	4	426
8	3	213	17	3	168
9	4	343	18	4	454
Out	36	3435	In	36	3507

95. Great Hills Country Club

You hear about a lot of golf courses with fancy names that conjure up images of greatness. Their advertising material shows pictures of deer and running streams and celestial waterfront views and fall just short of claiming that it was designed by God.

By now, most of you have probably discovered the hard way that you can't judge a golf course by its name. You got out of the car and unloaded your clubs only to find something much less than you expected, but a hefty green fee to help pay for all that advertising.

But if ever a golf course truly lived up to its name, it might be Great Hills. Right in the middle of the beautiful Hill Country, the course is played through hills, canyons and other areas typical of golf in South Texas.

The layout is short at 6,599 yards from the back tees, but has more challenges and beauty than most golfers can stand. The natural rolling terrain is conducive to good golf, as evidenced by the fact that Barton Creek Resort, Austin Country Club and the Hills of Lakeway are all in a 20-mile radius and all ranked among the best in the Hill Country.

"The back nine here is just spectacular," longtime pro Mark Coward says. "You go right around the hills and canyons."

Great Hills opened in 1973 after being designed by PGA Tour star and Texas native Don January and partner Billy Martindale.

Bill Cotton, who helped develop Balcones several years earlier, was the original developer of the project. January and Martindale, whose best work is Royal Oaks Country Club in Dallas, worked through a very unpopulated area at the time to produce another top-notch course.

The course underwent two changes in 1990 that lengthened the layout even more and raised the USGA rating to 71.2 and the slope to 123.

The members at Great Hills eventually bought the club from owner John Lloyd and turned it into an equity club that operates without debt. Most important to the golf layout was the switch of the last three holes.

Lloyd was interested in swapping a piece of land near the clubhouse for one where the final three holes were played. The members agreed and believe they got the best of the deal.

The par-4 No. 16 is just 378 yards from the middle tees, but is deceptively tough with hills and trees between tee and green.

The par-3 17th is a picturesque 183-yard gem with bite.

No. 18 is a 477-yard par 5 that may appear to be easy to reach on the scorecard, but is deceptively tough.

No. 4 (452 yards), No. 8 (448) and No. 13 (448) are challenging par 4s from the back tees.

GREAT HILLS

Great Hills Country Club

5914 Lost Horizon Drive
Austin 78759
512-345-6940
Pro: Mark Coward
A par-71, 6,599-yard private club.
From Austin, take Mopac to Spicewood Springs, west to Loop 360, north to Great Hills, left to Rain Creek, then left to Lost Horizon to club.

• • •

USGA rating: 71.2
Slope rating: 123
Sand traps: 21
Water holes: 6
Doglegs: 4 left/5 right
Type greens: Bermuda
Record: 64
Designers: Don January
    and Billy Martindale
Year opened: 1973

Hole	Par	Yards	Hole	Par	Yards
1	5	524	10	3	178
2	3	164	11	5	550
3	4	362	12	3	190
4	4	452	13	4	448
5	4	390	14	4	365
6	4	355	15	5	561
7	3	202	16	4	378
8	4	448	17	3	183
9	4	372	18	5	477
Out	35	3269	In	36	3330

Texas Top 100

96. Bear Creek Golf World — Masters Course

For three decades, Bear Creek Golf World was the largest public golf facility in the state with three 18-hole layouts. Bear Creek, in fact, ushered in the concept of daily-fee golf courses that were owned and operated by private entities, not city governments.

Bear Creek developer Dick Forester was a visionary. Even as the pro at the prestigious Houston Country Club, Forester saw the coming boom in demand for golf courses. At the time, there were 500,000 golfers in the city and only four municipal golf courses. And the city no longer had the money to build new courses to keep up with the demand.

"This is going to be the greatest thing that ever happened to public golf in Houston," said Houston golf legend Jackie Burke.

And he was right.

Bear Creek also was innovative from the standpoint that it was one of the first agreements between private and public entities for the public good. The Bear Creek developers leased a 397-acre tract of county land in the Addicks Reservoir, which was unused because it lay in a flood plain under the jurisdiction of the Federal Corps of Engineers.

Bear Creek was making history before the first golf shot was ever struck, but when the Masters Course, the second of the three courses, was built in 1975 it made history again. The course was rated among the Top 50 in the nation by *Golf Digest*, and hosted such prestigious events as the 1981 National Public Links Championship, 1984 NCAA Championship and the University of Houston's All-America Intercollegiate Invitational.

It was here that the University of Houston, in front of their hometown crowd, won the last of their record 16 NCAA Championships with the likes of Steve Elkington and Billy Ray Brown.

Riviere moved 200,000 yards of dirt to help build the course above flood level, but their worst fears came true in 1991.

After American Golf Corporation bought the course it spent nearly eight months under water in 1991 and forced a $1-million renovation in which all of the greens and tees were rebuilt.

The Masters is the most demanding of the three layouts, with a combination of length and tight fairways that demand accuracy off the tee. Both the 464-yard, par-4 No. 9 and 441-yard, par-4 No. 18 are great holes to finish back at the clubhouse and are among the toughest in Houston.

With a total of 54 holes, Bear Creek Golf World was the state's largest public golf facility for nearly three decades. The Presidents Course was the original course at Bear Creek and the Challenger Course is popular among beginning players.

Bear Creek Golf World Masters Course

16001 Clay Road
Houston 77084
281-859-8188
Pro: Ron Horton
A 54-hole public facility.
From Houston, take I-10 west to Highway 6, then turn right five miles to course entrance on the right.

• • •

USGA rating: 73.0
Slope rating: 131
Sand traps: 53
Water holes: 16
Doglegs: 2 left/2 right
Type greens: Bermuda
Record: 62
Designer: Jay Riviere
Year opened: 1975

• • •

Hole	Par	Yards	Hole	Par	Yards
1	5	502	10	4	420
2	4	408	11	4	431
3	4	408	12	3	184
4	3	151	13	4	412
5	4	454	14	5	509
6	5	557	15	5	528
7	4	423	16	4	392
8	3	182	17	3	182
9	4	464	18	4	441
Out	36	3549	In	36	3499

97. Quicksand Golf Course

Australia native Tom Crow made his name in the 1980s when he developed the Cobra Golf Company, which became one of the most innovative golf club manufacturers in the business.

Now his son, Jamie, is making a name for himself in the golf course business.

Quicksand Golf Club is Crow's first golf course venture and, like his father before him, his final product stands out in a crowd. In keeping with its treacherous name, Quicksand is one of the most difficult courses in Texas.

The name itself implies danger, and there is plenty. Architect Michael Hurdzan moved more than one million cubic yards of dirt to sculpt the flat terrain into a rolling, amusement park of a layout that will either frighten or entertain you with its 104 bunkers, undulating greens and natural surroundings.

The golf course is a mirage on the West Texas horizon, forcing golfers to blink once or twice to believe what they see.

Quicksand is majestically poised overlooking the scenic Concho River and is home to deer, turkey, quail, and all sorts of other wildlife.

As one of the preeminent speakers on building environmentally friendly golf courses, Hurdzan took special care to ensure harmony with the natural surroundings and wildlife and cre-

ated what he calls one of the most scenic combinations of desert and links-style architecture ever designed.

The golf course measures 7,100 yards from the back tees and plays to a 140 slope rating. Generous fairways were designed to allow for notorious West Texas winds of 30 mph or more, and they are lined by native grasses, mesquite trees and cactus.

No. 5 is only 357 yards from the tips to an elevated island green surrounded by a bunker. The hole requires an iron off the tee down a fairway guarded by 11 bunkers, and an uphill approach to a green that seems to slope back toward the bunker. Golfers landing in the front bunker will not be able to see the flag.

No. 7 is Quicksand's signature hole. It is a 621-yard, double dogleg par 5 with 23 bunkers. Those numbers speak for themselves.

The finishing holes are among the best in Texas.

No. 16 is a 367-yard par 4 that requires a layup off the tee and an approach over a pond to a postage stamp green protected by five bunkers.

No. 17 is a 208-yard par 3 with a full carry over water to a green protected by four bunkers.

And No. 18 is a 444-yard par 4 with water all the way down the left side and a large bear-claw bunker on the right. The approach requires a long iron to a green protected by water on three sides.

Quicksand Golf Course

2305 Pulliam
San Angelo 76905
915-482-8337
Pro: Don Bryant
A par-72, 7,171-yard public course.
From Midland go east on I-20, south on Highway 158, south on Highway 87 into San Angelo, east on Highway 67/277, take the 306 Loop exit to Smith Boulevard to entrance.

• • •

USGA rating: 75
Slope rating: 140
Sand traps: 104
Water holes: 5
Doglegs: 5
Type greens: Bermuda
Record: 70
Designer: Michael Hurdzan
Year opened: 1997

Hole	Par	Yards	Hole	Par	Yards
1	4	408	10	5	587
2	3	221	11	4	414
3	4	456	12	5	520
4	4	415	13	4	429
5	4	357	14	3	187
6	3	167	15	4	453
7	5	621	16	4	367
8	5	548	17	3	208
9	4	388	18	4	444
Out	36	3581	In	36	3590

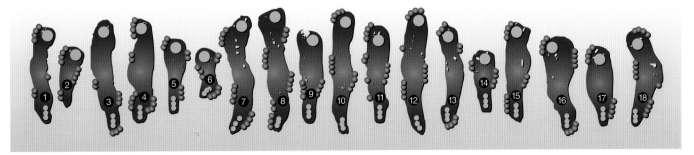

Texas Top 100

98. River Place Golf Course

You've heard the story about the best laid plans of mice and men.

This is a story about two men, a stubborn city council and a Texas golf legend. It's a long story, but it goes something like this:

In the mid-1970s, Hill Country developer Lawrence Clayton Smith purchased the 5,000-acre Wilding Ranch in Austin between Lake Austin Park and Ranch Road 620. Smith had a "build it and they will come" attitude, so he had architect Leon Howard begin construction on one of the 18-hole layouts with the belief that it would become the showcase to spur the sale of surrounding homesites.

The project eventually went bankrupt, and was purchased in the early 90s by Houston-based BSL Golf Corporation. It was closed for almost a year from November 1991 to November 1992 while PGA Tour star Tom Kite and architect Roy Bechtol and construction workers performed $3.2-million worth of magic.

All 18 greens were redone. Tee boxes were moved. Fairways were raised and filled with a total of 33 new bunkers. It reopened on November 7, 1992 with a new yardage of 6,611 yards and a slope rating of 128 from the back tees.

In addition to the Hill Country terrain, a creek meanders throughout the front nine and several small ponds come into play on the back nine. The back nine fairways are also more heavily wooded.

"Every hole," former pro Dale Morgan says, "has changed in some way for the better. What Tom did was bring the golf course credibility. He worked as a consultant for this course to make it fair.

"It's a beautiful course, but it can be hard. It's got a lot of up and downs to it, which is something people from Dallas or Houston aren't used to."

The first hole, a 402-yard par 4, slopes downhill while turning slightly to the left. A good drive will still leave golfers with a downhill lie on an approach that must carry a large ravine in front of the green. In fact, ravines come into play on seven of the first nine holes.

No. 7 is a 433-yard par 4 and is ranked as the hardest hole on the course. It is a dogleg right around a grove of trees, with a creek running down the right side of the fairway and behind the green.

No. 4 is a 561-yard par 5 with a creek running down the entire left side of the fairway, then crossing in front of the green. It is a small creek, but presents just enough danger to create problems on the approach to the green on the other side.

No. 12 is a demanding 141-yard par 3 where the green is protected by a small pond on the right.

No. 17 is the longest hole on the course. It is a 585-yard par 5 that plays straight through rows of trees on both sides of the fairway to the green.

River Place
On Lake Austin

River Place Golf Course

4207 River Place Boulevard
Austin 78730
512-346-6784
Pro: Bryan Cook
A par-71, 6,611-yard, public course.
From Austin, take Mopac north to 2222, west past Loop 360 for 4.5 miles to River Place Boulevard, then left to club.

• • •

USGA rating: 72
Slope rating: 128
Sand traps: 34
Water holes: 10
Doglegs: 7 left/1 right
Type greens: Bermuda
Record: N/A
Designers: Tom Kite and Roy Bechtol
Year opened: 1991

• • •

Hole	Par	Yards	Hole	Par	Yards
1	4	402	10	4	402
2	3	154	11	4	399
3	4	390	12	3	141
4	5	561	13	5	507
5	4	396	14	4	380
6	3	169	15	4	305
7	4	433	16	3	222
8	4	408	17	5	585
9	4	378	18	4	379
Out	35	3291	In	36	3320

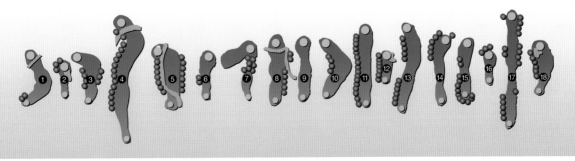

Texas Top 100

99. Ridglea Country Club — Men's Course

Alan Luther was a visionary. For every person who could not get into Fort Worth's ultra-exclusive Colonial Country Club, he wanted an alternative place to play golf and socialize. The needs of the many, after all, outweigh the needs of the few.

So when Luther was in the process of developing the community of Ridglea in the western part of the city, he developed a country club that would be the hub of all its activities.

Ridglea Country Club celebrated its 40th birthday in 1995 and remains true to its purpose. With two golf courses, a membership of 2,100 and 115,000 square feet of clubhouse, it is one of the largest clubs in Texas.

Luther was the leader of two groups that founded Ridglea in 1955. They built a modern clubhouse with stones from old Indian fences found in neighboring counties and bricks reclaimed from buildings in Tennessee.

The main entrance is reached by walking through a rain forest atrium where tropical plants and a rare collection of birds thrive.

To meet the needs of its large membership, Ridglea offers two different golf courses. The North Course was built in 1928 by John Bredemus and covers 122 acres with its own separate clubhouse.

The bentgrass greens and lush fairways have been legendary and are an example of classic design and playable beauty. The North Course is the easier of the two layouts.

The South Course measures 150 acres and was built in 1967 by Ralph Plummer. In 1988, architect Jay Morrish lent his skills and talents to rebuilding the greens, tees and natural streams while preserving the masterworks of yesteryear.

The South Course features several of the best holes in the Dallas-Fort Worth area, according to our survey of area professionals. It begins at No. 2, a 450-yard par 4 that is guarded down the left side by the Trinity River.

The 440-yard par-4 10th requires both a demanding drive and approach. A lake guards the right side of the landing area and runs all the way to the right side and behind the green, leaving no margin for error on the approach.

No. 12 is one of the most demanding driving holes you'll find anywhere. It is a 414-yard dogleg left par 4 where the Trinity weaves back and forth across the fairway three times. There is a very small landing area at the corner of the dogleg, making it difficult to get in position for the approach.

No. 14 is a 338-yard par 4 that is relatively short where the Trinity comes into play off the tee and in the landing area. The river crosses the fairway in front of the tee, then cuts back into the fairway at about 225 yards.

Ridglea Country Club Men's Course

3700 Bernie Anderson Drive
Fort Worth 76121
817-732-8111
Pro: Keith Davidson
A 36-hole private club.
From Fort Worth, take I-30 west to Ridglea, then go south on Ridglea two miles to club entrance.

• • •

USGA rating: 73.6
Slope rating: 131
Sand traps: N/A
Water holes: 12
Doglegs: 3 left/2 right
Type greens: Bentgrass
Record: N/A
Designer: Ralph Plummer
Year opened: 1951

• • •

Hole	Par	Yards	Hole	Par	Yards
1	4	405	10	4	440
2	4	450	11	4	415
3	3	175	12	4	414
4	5	562	13	3	172
5	4	430	14	4	338
6	4	401	15	4	387
7	3	205	16	4	425
8	5	545	17	4	411
9	4	415	18	5	535
Out	36	3588	In	36	3537

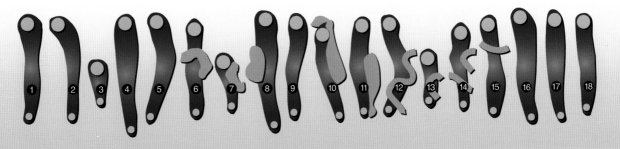

100. Firewheel Golf Park — Old Course

It's a long story that brought Dick Phelps to Texas but, if you're a public links player, it's a story with a very happy ending.

Phelps had built golf courses all over the world except Texas, until the city of Garland hired him in 1983 to build the first of three golf courses on land that was donated to the city 15 years earlier by Garland residents Austin N. and Margaret L. Stanton.

While Phelps had vast experience in golf course design, he had explicit instructions from the golf course steering committee:

Maintain the natural beauty of the land.

Design a golf course that would be economical to maintain. And design a golf course that would involve strategy, but at the same time accommodate players of all levels.

Those were the ingredients of what has become one of DFW's most successful municipal golf operations. Named after the red and yellow wildflower that blooms on the course from April to July, Firewheel Golf Park already has 36 holes and 18 more holes are on the drawing board.

The Old Course at Firewheel opened to rave reviews in 1981 and has long been one of the most popular public courses in Dallas.

It measures 7,054 yards with water in play on 16 holes. The only rude awakening Phelps experienced at his first golf project in Texas was dealing with the rugged limestone scattered throughout the property.

The signature hole on the Old Course is No. 9, a 552-yard par 5 that tumbles downhill toward the clubhouse. The first part of the fairway was carved out of a dense grove of trees, which creates for a demanding tee shot.

On the approach, players must make a decision to lay up or carry the creek that crosses the fairway about 150 yards from the green. On the final approach, Phelps left several strategically placed pecan trees to demand that force golfers to put themselves in the proper position for a clear shot to the green.

No. 18 is a 400-yard, par 4, requiring a tee shot and an approach shot over the same creek, which winds through the hole.

Besides hiring Phelps, the best decision the city forefathers made was to drop the name "municipal" from the name of the course.

Even though the golf course is owned and operated by the city, it is definitely not a typical "muni" course that many golfers are associated with. Every effort was made along the way to ensure it was a cut above.

"We're very proud of the Firewheel project, and the type of reception it has received," Phelps says. "We can't wait to come back and do it again."

Firewheel Golf Park Old Course

600 West Blackburn Road
Garland 75044
972-205-2795
Pro: Jerry Andrews
A 36-hole public course.
From Dallas, take Central Expressway north to Arapaho, go east 4 miles to North Garland exit, north 1.8 miles to Blackburn, east to club entrance.

• • •

USGA rating: 74.1
Slope rating: 129
Water holes: 16
Sand traps: 63
Doglegs: 3 left/2 right
Type greens: Bermuda
Designer: Dick Phelps
Year opened: 1981

• • •

Hole	Par	Yards	Hole	Par	Yards
1	4	425	10	4	425
2	4	391	11	4	457
3	5	566	12	3	180
4	3	180	13	5	517
5	4	420	14	4	383
6	4	414	15	4	404
7	4	372	16	5	567
8	3	234	17	3	167
9	5	552	18	4	400
Out	36	3554	In	36	3500

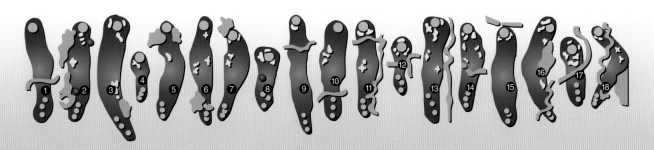

Texas Swing Popular Among Players and Fans

There were only a handful of golf courses in Texas when pro golf first came to the state in 1922. The birth of the Texas Open that year opened the floodgates for many more tournaments to follow in almost every major Texas city.

The Texas Open in San Antonio is the fifth oldest event on the PGA Tour and is one of four stops the game's best players make in Texas each year.

The following pages recap the history of the Texas Open, the Colonial, the Byron Nelson Classic and the Houston Open.

Byron Nelson Classic

A real classic:
Byron Nelson is the only player to have a tournament named in his honor, and it always lives up to his name.

Lord Byron. The name says it all. And few mortals have been more worthy of such distinction than Byron Nelson.

The Byron Nelson Classic, named in honor of the Fort Worth native and Texas golf legend, remains the only PGA Tour event named in honor of a golfer. And, in keeping with its namesake, the tournament is one of the best in the business. To name a tournament after Nelson is to set a high standard, indeed.

While the tournament was renamed for Nelson in 1968, its history dates back to 1944, when it was originally called the Dallas Open. While Sol Dreyfus had sponsored a pro tournament by the same name 20 years earlier at Cedar Crest, this was Dallas' first introduction to the modern pro tour as we now know it.

Lakewood was the site in 1944 of the first Dallas Open, won by none other than Byron Nelson in with a total of 276 for a 10-stroke victory. That year, Nelson was to win seven of the 22 tour events. Nelson went on to become the AP's Athlete of the Year, an award he earned again the following year with a record 11 consecutive victories.

In 1945, the war had ended a

month before Nelson returned to town. Sam Snead, who would go on to win three times in Dallas, claimed the first of his victories against a field of 22 golfers. It was one of only 12 of the scheduled 35 tournaments that year that Nelson didn't win. Snead posted rounds of 70-69-69-68 for a 12-under 276 total, five ahead of Nelson.

In 1946, Brook Hollow Golf Club hosted the Dallas Open, with Ben Hogan holding on for a two-stroke victory over Paul Runyan and Herman Keiser.

After a 10-year lapse, the tournament began a new chapter in 1959 when Oak Cliff Country Club, which provided the site and helped with the staging of Ling's tournament in 1958, took over

sponsorship of what is now the GTE Byron Nelson Classic and continued it on an annual basis through 1966.

Since the tournament started in 1946, six Dallas events had been held at five different locations, but the tournament seemed to get on its feet after moving to Oak Cliff. Snead won the first year and became the first back-to-back Dallas champion. Julius Boros came back to win in 1959 and Johnny Pott in 1960. In 1961, Dallas' own Earl Stewart Jr. became the PGA Tour's first hometown winner with a 278 total. In 1962, Jack Nicklaus made his first appearance and finished fifth, six shots behind Billy Maxwell.

There was no tournament in 1963, since the Salesmanship Club also sponsored the PGA Championship that year at Dallas Athletic Club. Charles Coody won the 1964 event, and there was no tournament again in 1965 while the tournament switched from a fall date to a spring date on the tour schedule.

In 1968, the Salesmanship Club gave the tournament a new look and name by calling it the Byron Nelson Golf Classic and moving it to Preston Trail. Nelson and architect Ralph Plummer had just finished the new layout at the ultra-exclusive, all-men's club in North Dallas. It proved to be a worthy challenge to the world's best players for the next 15 years.

In 1983, the tournament moved to Las Colinas Sports Club, where it has continued to grow into one of the best events on the PGA Tour, raising more than $3 million for charity each year. It has raised more than $26 million for charity since 1973. In each of the past five years, the Nelson has raised more than $3 million for the Salesmanship Club of Dallas and its programs to help troubled youth.

Byron Nelson Classic Past Champions					
1944	Byron Nelson	1961	Earl Stewart Jr.	1981	Bruce Lietzke
1945	Sam Snead	1962	Billy Maxwell	1982	Bob Gilder
1946	Ben Hogan	1963	No tournament	1983	Ben Crenshaw
1947	No tournament	1964	Charles Coody	1984	Craig Stadler
1948	No tournament	1965	No tournament	1985	Bob Eastwood
1949	No tournament	1966	Roberto De Vicenzo	1986	Andy Bean
1950	No tournament	1967	Bert Yancey	1987	Fred Couples
1951	No tournament	1968	Miller Barber	1988	Bruce Lietzke
1952	No tournament	1969	Bruce Devlin	1989	Jodie Mudd
1953	No tournament	1970	Jack Nicklaus	1990	Payne Stewart
1954	No tournament	1971	Jack Nicklaus	1991	Nick Price
1955	No tournament	1972	Chi Chi Rodriguez	1992	Billy Ray Brown
1956	Don January	1973	Lanny Wadkins	1993	Scott Simpson
1957	Sam Snead	1974	Brian Allin	1994	Neal Lancaster
1958	Sam Snead	1975	Tom Watson	1995	Ernie Els
1959	Julius Boros	1976	Mark Hayes	1996	Phil Mickelson
1960	Johnny Pott	1977	Raymond Floyd	1997	Tiger Woods
		1978	Tom Watson	1998	John Cook
		1979	Tom Watson		
		1980	Tom Watson		

Colonial National Invitation

*By invitation only:
Colonial is the only tournament that
has been played at the same site throughout its history.*

Marvin Leonard first conceived of the idea for the Colonial National Invitation in 1941 after his club had the rare opportunity to become the first club in Texas to host the coveted U.S. Open.

The Open was so well received by fans and players alike that Colonial officials resolved that the club should have an annual tournament. The birth of the Colonial event, however, was delayed five years due to World War II. In the meantime, members planned to emulate the very best golf tournament, the Masters, by adopting an invitation-only format.

While other tournaments on the PGA Tour are older, Colonial is the only tournament that has been played at the same site through its history. And it is the only tournament with the course's name in its event.

Appropriately Fort Worth native Ben Hogan won the first Colonial on May 19, 1946. He did it by firing a final round 33-32-65 to post a new course record and beat Harry Todd by one stroke for the $3,000 first prize. Hogan finished with a 279 total. Todd, a Dallas native and the third-round leader, finished with a 69 for a 280 total. Fred Haas Jr. was third at 281 and Sam Snead was three

back of Hogan at 282.

Colonial would eventually become known as Hogan's Alley — and probably always will. No one man ever dominated a tournament the way Hogan did the Colonial NIT. Five times Hogan won the NIT and at one time or another he held practically every record on the plush carpets of Colonial. It was also appropriate that Hogan's last PGA Tour victory was at Colonial in 1959.

Even after his golfing prime, Hogan was a consistent finisher in the Colonial top 10. After turning 50, Hogan competed in four consecutive NIT events (from 1964–67), carding finishes of fourth, 10th, fifth and third. At the time, only 13 sub-par totals over the full-route of 72 holes had

been recorded in Colonial history and Hogan owned four of them.

Furthermore, Hogan held the all-time Colonial money lead and four tournament records, including a 31 on the front nine and 65 for 18 holes.

Although Hogan was unable to compete in the 1968 and 69 tournaments, he returned at the age of 58 to shoot a first-round 69 before faltering to finish out of the money for the first time since 1954, when he had to withdraw due to illness after 36 holes.

The Hogan touch is evident in the Colonial layout itself, since he supervised the rebuilding of several greens in the early 1960s. Hogan's own designs were used in improving these greens to championship caliber. Hogan also was consulted during the rebuilding of nine holes on the course due to a 1968–69 flood control project on the Trinity River.

Colonial Country Club was built in 1936 by architect John Bredemus. Now in its second half-century of existence, it still ranks as the No. 1 course in the state and among the top 30 in the United States and top 50 in the world. It is a monument to the golden age of golf architecture.

Leonard decided to build Colonial after getting the opportunity to putt on the superior putting surface of bentgrass greens while on a vacation in the 1930s. He returned home an enlightened man. No longer satisfied with the slow and bumpy Bermuda greens found in Texas, he campaigned to get existing courses to change.

When Leonard met resistance at every turn, he decided to call on architect John Bredemus in 1936 to build his own course along the banks of the Trinity River, and it still ranks as the top course in the state 60 years later.

And Leonard finally got his bentgrass greens.

Colonial National Invitation
Past Champions

1946	Ben Hogan	1962	Arnold Palmer	1981	Fuzzy Zoeller
1947	Ben Hogan	1963	Julius Boros	1982	Jack Nicklaus
1948	Clayton Heafner	1964	Billy Casper	1983	Jim Colbert
1949	No tournament	1965	Bruce Crampton	1984	Peter Jacobsen
1950	Sam Snead	1966	Bruce Devlin	1985	Corey Pavin
1951	Cary Middlecoff	1967	Dave Stockton	1986	Dan Pohl
1952	Ben Hogan	1968	Billy Casper	1987	Keith Clearwater
1953	Ben Hogan	1969	Gardner Dickinson	1988	Lanny Wadkins
1954	Johnny Palmer	1970	Homero Blancas	1989	Ian Baker-Finch
1955	Chandler Harper	1971	Gene Littler	1990	Ben Crenshaw
1956	Mike Souchak	1972	Jerry Heard	1991	Tom Purtzer
1957	Roberto de Vicenzo	1973	Tom Weiskopf	1992	Bruce Lietzke
1958	Tommy Bolt	1974	Rod Curl	1993	Fulton Allem
1959	Ben Hogan	1975	No tournament	1994	Nick Price
1960	Julius Boros	1976	Lee Trevino	1995	Tom Lehman
1961	Doug Sanders	1977	Ben Crenshaw	1996	Corey Pavin
		1978	Lee Trevino	1997	David Frost
		1979	Al Geiberger	1998	Tom Watson
		1980	Bruce Lietzke		

Shell Houston Open

Opening the door:
Houstonians band together for top-flight golf.

Interest in golf and golf courses in Houston grew at a slow pace until a group of men formed the Houston Golf Association in 1945 with the intention of bringing an annual pro tournament to town instead of those "fly by night" affairs.

The year was 1945 and Lonnie Douglass, George Ross, George O'Leary, A.A. Gharrett, Bennie Strickland and Dr. Harry Coffman were on their way back to Houston from the Texas Open in San Antonio when they decided Houston deserved to have a tournament of its own.

Knowing it would take a tremendous effort to put on such a tournament, they formed the Houston Golf Association and held their first tournament in May of 1946.

Although other tournaments by the same name were held prior to that year, the first official Houston Open was played in 1946 at River Oaks Country Club. Sponsored by the HGA, it was called the Tournament of Champions and offered a $10,000 purse.

Lloyd Mangrum and Ben Hogan took the lead after the first round with a pair of 67s, and amateur Frank Stranahan grabbed

the 36-hole lead with a 68 on Friday that gave him a seven-under total of 137. But then came Nelson, who had won a record 11 consecutive tournaments the year before, charging into the lead with a 67 on Saturday. A crowd of 10,000 watched him shoot 68 on Sunday to post a two-shot victory over Hogan.

Attendance, however, had been disappointing and HGA member Dr. H.N. Coffman realized the gate receipts wouldn't cover the expenses, so he went to a banker and took out a loan to cover the prize money.

The Houston Open would continue to grow over the years, but never had a permanent home until 1975. After River Oaks, it was held at Memorial Park 14 of

the next 16 years, with brief stints at Pine Forest, BraeBurn, Sharpstown, Champions Golf Club, Quail Valley and Westwood.

It was not until the tournament moved to The Woodlands Conference Center and Resort that it began to grow in national prominence. Since 1975, the tournament has raised more than $20 million for charity. In 1997, the tournament ranked second only to the Byron Nelson Classic with $2 million raised for local youth-oriented charities.

The tournament is still conducted by the Houston Golf Association, a non-profit organization consisting of more than 200 members and countless volunteers who work to promote the game of golf.

Like many PGA Tour events, the Houston Open struggled for nearly a decade in the 1980s with several short-term sponsors and was even played a few years without a title sponsor. Shell Oil Company, which was instrumental in golf's international popularity with its prime-time television series *Shell's Wonderful World of Golf* in the 1960s, became the title sponsor in 1993 and has entered a long-term agreement with the HGA to continue to make the Houston Open one of the tour's premier events.

Since 1985, the Houston Open has been played on the TPC at The Woodlands, a challenging target-style golf course that annually creates some of the most exciting finishes of the year. With its high-risk reward ratios that make it difficult for players to hold a lead and easier for players in the back of the pack to shoot for the pins, more often than not the eventual winner starts the final round as many as seven shots behind the leader. The tournament also has been the site of frequent sudden-death playoffs.

Shell Houston Open Past Champions					
1946	Byron Nelson	1962	Bobby Nichols	1981	Ron Streck
1947	Bobby Locke	1963	Bob Charles	1982	Ed Sneed
1948	No tournament	1964	Mike Souchak	1983	David Graham
1949	Johnny Palmer	1965	Bobby Nichols	1984	Corey Pavin
1950	Cary Middlecoff	1966	Arnold Palmer	1985	Ray Floyd
1951	Marty Furgol	1967	Frank Beard	1986	Curtis Strange
1952	Jack Burke Jr.	1968	Roberto de Vicenzo	1987	Jay Haas
1953	Cary Middlecoff	1969	No tournament	1988	Curtis Strange
1954	Dave Douglas	1970	Gibby Gilbert	1989	Mike Sullivan
1955	Mike Souchak	1971	Hubert Green	1990	Tony Sills
1956	Ted Kroll	1972	Bruce Devlin	1991	Fulton Allem
1957	Arnold Palmer	1973	Bruce Crampton	1992	Fred Funk
1958	Ed Oliver	1974	Dave Hill	1993	Jim McGovern
1959	Jack Burke Jr	1975	Bruce Crampton	1994	Mike Heinen
1960	Bill Collins	1976	Lee Elder	1995	Payne Stewart
1961	Jay Hebert	1977	Gene Littler	1996	Mark Brooks
		1978	Gary Player	1997	Phil Blackmar
		1979	Wayne Levi	1998	David Duval
		1980	Curtis Strange		

LaCantera
TexasOpen

Texas Open

In the beginning:
The Texas Open was not only the first pro event
in Texas, but it helped launch the PGA Tour.

Up until the time John Bredemus became Texas' first resident golf course architect, the designers of the state's layouts came, put down holes, and left the problems of new and growing courses to whomever happened to be around. Needless to say, some tracks thrived and many did not. Course design and construction moved at a snail's pace and, consequently, golf as a business and pastime poked along as well.

By 1922, there was a marked change. Pro tournaments were staged in every metro area, clubs began to have year-round pros tend to the needs of amateurs, course building and maintenance merged as professions.

Strange though it may seem, Bredemus had a hand in all three.

Bredemus was a native of the northeast and an all-around athlete who defeated Jim Thorpe in the 1912 Olympics and also received engineering degrees from Dartmouth and Princeton.

He moved to San Antonio in 1916 to become a high school math teacher, and also worked as a club pro until 1926, when he turned exclusively to course design and the promotion of golf in Texas and Mexico.

Bredemus co-founded the

Texas Professional Golfers Association in 1922, the first Texas Open in 1922 and helped bring the Southwest's first major championship, the 1927 PGA, to Dallas. Bredemus legacy includes the first pro events in Dallas, Houston, Corpus Christi and Beaumont.

Bredemus teamed up with *San Antonio News* Sports Editor Jack O'Brien, who also had a special love for the game of golf, to set the stage for the first Texas Open at Brackenridge Park, the oldest public course in the state.

Pro tournaments those days were a rarity, with amateurs dominating the game of golf. In fact, there were only four major pro events: the U.S. and Canadian Opens, PGA Championship and

Western Open in Chicago, when O'Brien proposed the Texas Open in 1922.

In late 1921, the committee sent out telegrams to the leading pro golfers of the day inviting them to San Antonio in January of 1922 to compete in the first Texas Open. The prize money was then an unheard of $5,000, almost 10 times more than the U.S. Open was offering at that time. The mild weather and top money attracted a full field for the first event.

The course conditions were less than ideal by today's standards, but Scotsman Bob MacDonald won the first tournament with a 281 total. While more than 4,000 fans turned out for the first competition, O'Brien's financial estimates were a little overly optimistic and he passed the hat among spectators on the 18th green to help pay expenses.

The second event in 1923 helped cement the Texas Open's place in golf history. British Open champion Walter Hagen charged from six shots behind on the final day to capture the title, earning national headlines.

In the early years, players participated in pro-ams early in the week and played 36 holes on Saturday and Sunday to decide the tournament.

"Some people don't realize this was the tournament which helped launch the PGA Tour," said Harvey Penick, who played in 20 early Texas Opens.

In 1928, players' association president Tommy Armour helped draw up articles of incorporation in San Antonio for the Professional Touring Golfers Association, what is now known as the PGA Tour.

In 1997, the Texas Open celebrated its 75th anniversary, making it the fifth oldest stop on the PGA Tour.

Texas Open Past Champions

		1946	Ben Hogan	1972	Mike Hill
		1947	Ed Oliver	1973	Ben Crenshaw
1922	Bob MacDonald	1948	Sam Snead	1974	Terry Diehl
1923	Walter Hagen	1949	Dave Douglass	1975	Don January
1924	Joe Kirkwood	1950	Sam Snead	1976	Butch Baird
1925	Joe Turnesa	1951	Dutch Harrison	1977	Hale Irwin
1926	Mac Smith	1952	Jack Burke Jr.	1978	Ron Streck
1927	Bobby Cruickshank	1953	Tony Holguin	1979	Lou Graham
1928	Bill Mehlhorn	1954	Chandler Harper	1980	Lee Trevino
1929	Bill Mehlhorn	1955	Mike Souchak	1981	Bill Rogers
1930	Denny Shute	1956	Gene Littler	1982	Jay Haas
1931	Abe Espinosa	1957	Jay Hebert	1983	Jim Colbert
1932	Clarence Clark	1958	Bill Johnston	1984	Calvin Peete
1933	No tournament	1959	Wes Ellis	1985	John Mahaffe
1934	Wiffy Cox	1960	Arnold Palmer	1986	Ben Crenshaw
1935	No tournament	1961	Arnold Palmer	1987	No tournament
1936	No tournament	1962	Arnold Palmer	1988	Corey Pavin
1937	No tournament	1963	Phil Rodgers	1989	Donnie Hammond
1938	No tournament	1964	Bruce Crampton	1990	Mark O'Meara
1939	Dutch Harrison	1965	Frank Beard	1991	Blaine McCallister
1940	Byron Nelson	1966	Harold Henning	1992	Nick Price
1941	Lawson Little	1967	Chi Chi Rodriguez	1993	Jay Haas
1942	Chick Harbert	1968	No tournament	1994	Bob Estes
1943	No tournament	1969	Deane Beaman	1995	Duffy Waldorf
1944	Johnny Revolta	1970	Ron Cerrudo	1996	David Ogrin
1945	Sam Byrd	1971	No tournament	1997	Tim Herron

Eyes of Texas Have Seen Golf's Biggest Battles

Texas is not only home of some of golf's greatest players of the past and present, but over the past century it also has hosted the world's best players competing in some of golf's most coveted championships.

Golf was just getting started in the state back in 1927 when Dallas banker Sol Dreyfus helped lure the PGA Championship to town for the state's first major championship. The field included legendary players like Walter Hagen and Gene Sarazen, and thousands turned out to watch, including a young boy named Byron Nelson who decided he, too, wanted to grow up to be a pro golfer one day.

Over the years, Texas has hosted 11 major championships or events — including three PGA Championships, four U.S. Opens, three tour championships and the U.S. Amateur.

1927

PGA Championship

The best golfers in the world came to Dallas for the first time in 1927. Appropriately, the best golfer in the world – Walter Hagen – emerged victorious.

Seven years after opening his Cedar Crest Country Club, banker Sol Dreyfus brought DFW golf to the next level by bringing the best players in the world to Dallas. He personally bankrolled the first Dallas Open in 1926 and received such rave reviews from golfers that Dreyfus offered $12,000 to bring the PGA Championship to Dallas the following year.

It was here that Dallas golf fans got their first glimpse of the dapper PGA champion Walter Hagen, Tommy Armour, Gene Sarazen and local favorite Lighthorse Harry Cooper in the match-play competition. And it was here that a little boy who was nipping at Hagen's heels — there were no gallery ropes — was a kid named Byron Nelson, who decided that week that he, too, wanted to grow up to be a professional golfer.

"That was my first real thrill in golf," Nelson said. "I wanted to follow Walter Hagen. I stuck real close to him — there weren't any gallery ropes in those days — so I was right beside him the entire time."

Late in the day, Nelson even loaned the ever-dapper Hagen his schoolboy baseball cap to shade his eyes from the afternoon sun.

They were competing for the largest purse ever: $10,000 in money and expenses. The daily crowds were about 3,000, the largest ever.

In the first round, the match between Tommy Armour and Johnny Farrell had the most star appeal, as the U.S. Open and Canadian Open champion eliminated Farrell, 4 and 3. Former PGA champion Gene Sarazen was given a scare, as he was forced into extra holes before beating longshot J.G. Curley. Curley had a chance to win the match on the home green but missed the two-foot winning putt. Hagen, the defending PGA champion and medalist, won his match against Jack Farrell, 3 and 2, but the score didn't show the reality of the match. After shooting around 80 in the morning round, "The Haig" was 4-down and some in the gallery sensed an upset. But in the afternoon Hagen turned things around and played under par to pull out a victory.

In the second round, Hagen played a spotless round as he decimated Tony Manero, 11 and 10. Tommy Armour also played great in a 7 and 6 victory over Tom Harmon, which set up a quarterfinal match between Hagen and Armour. Huge crowds showed up for the second round, with most of them watching the match between local hero Harry Cooper and Al Espinosa.

Cooper's popularity didn't help a poor putting day and he was eliminated 5 and 4. The match of the day was played between Joe Turnesa and Willie Klein. After the first eight holes of play, Klein was 6-up and it took a furious rally by Turnesa to square the match on the 35th hole. Then, with a 20-foot putt on the final green, he pulled out a victory.

In the quarterfinals, Hagen found a hot putter but still had a hard-fought match against Armour in a 4 and 3 victory. Espinosa beat Martie Dutra, 1-up, but again the score was very misleading. With three holes left to play in the morning round, Espinosa was 6-up, but Dutra won the last three holes and in the afternoon took the first four holes to go 1-up. Espinosa, however, turned things around and led the match by one after 27. The match between Sarazen and Turnesa pitted two Americans of Italian descent with Turnesa handing Sarazen a 3 and 2 defeat.

In the two semifinal matches, Turnesa beat John Golden 7 and 6. In the other match between Espinosa and Hagen, it looked as if the defending PGA champion was going to be beaten. Espinosa won the 35th hole to go 1-up. On the second shots to the final green, Espinosa was 25 feet away with Hagen over the green. It seemed certain that Hagen was going to lose because he didn't have a chance to make a birdie. But he hit a great chip and Espinosa conceded a four-footer. Espinosa needed only two putts for the victory, but he left his first putt three feet short and missed the winning putt to send the match into sudden death. On the first extra hole, Espinosa again three-putted to give Hagen the victory.

"The Espinosa-Hagen match was a thriller all day," remembered Bobby Cruickshank, a club pro from Purchase, N.Y. "It is a fact, and golf record, that Espinosa really lost the match at the 35th hole when he was short on his putt. But it must be remembered that he was putting almost 40 feet from the pin, uphill into the bristle of the Bermuda grass, which will completely baffle any golfer at times."

In the finals, the gallery included players such as Armour and Sarazen, who had been defeated earlier in the week. Turnesa got off to a good start when he shot a 71 in the morning round to Hagen's 77. Despite the six-shot difference, Turnesa was only 2-up. Turnesa added another hole at the ninth, but the tide started to turn as he began to struggle with five-footers that were no problem in his earlier matches. Hagen made a birdie on the 29th hole to square the match, and a bogey by Turnesa at the 31st hole gave Hagen the lead. Turnesa missed several putts on the last six holes that would have tied the match, including a putt on the final hole that stopped on the lip of the cup.

"He was just too good for me, that's all." Turnesa said. "I did my best but it simply wasn't good enough to beat Walter Hagen."

Said Hagen of Turnesa: "He showed that he is a player of rare mettle and I hope when I relinquish my title Turnesa will be the man who receives my congratulations."

It was Hagen's fifth PGA title, a record fourth in a row. For his efforts, he earned $1,000 in cash, four diamond studded gold medals and exhibition engagements worth more than $100,000 the next year.

Hagen's Road to The Final:
    Def. Jack Farrell, 3 and 2
    Def. Tony Manera, 11 and 10
    Def. Tommy Armour, 4 and 3
    Def. Al Espinosa, 1-up 37 holes

Turnesa's Road to the Final:
    Def. Charles McKenna, 5 and 3
    Def. Willie Klein, 1-up
    Def. Gene Sarazen, 3 and 2
    Def. John Golden, 7 and 6

1941

U.S. Open

In Ben Hogan's back yard, the affable Craig Wood mastered the greens of Colonial to win the 1941 U.S. Open.

Like Sol Dreyfus did 15 years earlier at Cedar Crest, Fort Worth businessman Marvin Leonard was so proud of his new creation at Colonial Country Club that he began politicking to bring another national championship to the D/FW area. In 1941, five years after Colonial opened, his dream came true when it hosted the 45th U.S. Open.

It was the first time the Open was held south of the Mason-Dixon Line, and the success of the event gave birth to one of the most prestigious annual events on the PGA Tour – the Colonial National Invitation.

Colonial, designed by John Bredemus, received its first real test that year. To prepare for the best players in the world, Leonard hired architect Perry Maxwell to redesign the third, fourth and fifth holes at Colonial. This stretch soon became known as the "Horrible Horseshoe," because they comprised one of the layout's toughest stretches.

The Open field included such players as Ben Hogan, Gene Sarazen, Byron Nelson, Craig Wood, Sam Snead, Denny Shute, Paul Runyan, Tommy Armour, Johnny Farrell, Johnny Revolta, Henry Picard, Horton Smith, Vic Ghezzi, Lawson Little, Ralph Guldahl, Olin Dutra, Jimmy Demaret, Chick Harbert, Ed Dudley, Lloyd Mangrum and Billy

Burke. Some had already achieved fame, others were still relatively early in their careers.

The list of participants included winners of 19 U.S. Opens, 22 PGAs, four British Opens and 17 Masters tournaments, as well as 21 members of the PGA Hall of Fame. A total of 163 players, including three dozen amateurs, teed up on June 5, 1941, vying for the $6,000 purse and the national championship. The new-found golf lovers in the DFW area were enthusiastic in their support, producing the largest galleries in golf history.

Despite the quality of the field, Colonial proved a worthy challenger. Only two rounds – an opening 69 by former British Open and PGA champion Denny Shute and a 68 by Hogan – were under par. Those two measly sub-par scores were the fewest at the Open in 25 years. When all was said and done, however, Craig Wood stole the headlines. Wood, who had won his first major championship at the Masters a few months earlier, overcame severe back pain to outduel local favorite Ben Hogan.

The week before the tournament Wood, a perennial bridesmaid before winning the Masters, was a doubtful starter, laying strapped to a board. He had injured his back three weeks before when he dropped his razor and made a grab for it. He sneezed as he grabbed and in the process tore a ligament in his back and was laid up for nine days. He was so uncertain of his ability to play in the Open that he kept plane reservations for a couple of days during practice rounds until he decided to give it a try, wearing a corset around his waist for support.

There were some 10,000 people in the gallery when Wood sank a 30-foot birdie putt on the 18th hole to clinch the victory. The din was terrific and the man who had previously been golf's bridesmaid for nine years wearily smiled and walked right into the middle of the mob. His caddie was 16-year-old Danny Bodiford, who was one of the best caddies at Colonial. When the Open came to town, they drew numbers to pick their pro. Bodiford was No. 1, and he picked Wood.

"I figured a fine putter would win, and I didn't think there was any finer than Mr. Craig Wood," Bodiford said. "Now I know I was right."

Shute led off the tournament with a 69 on Thursday. It was the day's only sub-par round, good for a one-stroke lead over Vic Ghezzi and E.J. Harrison.

Friday's second round featured two rain delays, and all but two groups completed play. Shute was tied with Clayton Heafner, defending Open champ Lawson Little and Craig Wood at 144. Dick Metz and Paul Runyon were a stroke back. The cut was made at 156.

The golf course was little more than a hog's heaven of mud. It would take six-to-eight weeks to get the course back in perfect playing condition. Beautiful weather returned on Saturday for the 36-hole finale. At the 54-hole turn, Wood was two strokes ahead of Shute. Hogan, the year's leading money winner, was making a charge with a morning round of 68 that was the best of the tournament.

The 39-year-old Wood, who had lost playoffs in the British Open, Masters and U.S. Open, was a gallery favorite. He sank long birdie putts on holes 15 and 18 in the final afternoon to put away the competition with a 284 total (four-over par) and three-stroke victory over Shute and the $1,000 first prize. Hogan was five shots back.

1941 U.S. Open Leaderboard
At Colonial Country Club

Craig Wood		
73-71-70-70 — 284	$1,000
Denny Shute		
69-75-72-71 — 287	$800
Ben Hogan		
74-77-68-70 — 289	$650
Johnny Bulla		
75-71-72-71 — 289	$650
Herman Barron		
75-71-74-71 — 291	$412.50
Paul Runyan		
73-72-71-75 — 291	$216.66
Dutch Harrison		
70-82-71-71 — 294	$216.66
Gene Sarazen		
74-73-72-75 — 294	$216.66
Harold McSpadden		
71-75-74-74 — 294	$216.66
Ed Dudley		
74-74-74-73 — 295	$125
Lloyd Mangrum		
73-74-72-76 — 295	$125
Dick Metz		
71-74-76-74 — 295	$125
Sam Snead		
76-70-77-73 — 296	$100

1952

U.S. Open

Par and Julius Boros — The Moose — emerged victorious at the '52 U.S. Open.

The war was over and almost two decades had passed since the last golf course was built in Dallas before a group of Dallas businessmen met in 1946 at Highland Park Village and formed the charter membership of the Northwood Club.

Six years later, members had lured the U.S. Open back to Dallas. Despite its youth, the 7,000-yard layout, the longest in Dallas at the time, proved a more than adequate challenge.

Two-time Open champion Gene Sarazen predicted that a score of 284, four-over par, would win the tournament. A poll of 20 of the game's top players, however, tabbed Lloyd Mangrum as the pre-tournament favorite in a 162-player field that included Sarazen and Sam Snead, Byron Nelson and Ben Hogan.

After practice rounds, Sarazen said, "This has been child's play. When they go out on that course Thursday it will be as though they had never seen the layout before. The greens have been slow lately, but in the first two rounds Thursday and Friday they will begin to get slick. Then for those two rounds Saturday they will be lightning-fast.

"You may see a lot of par or sub-par rounds on the first day – maybe as many as 15 or 20 – but after that the scores will go up. So by Saturday if a player has under-par rounds it will be terrific."

Al Broach was the first-round leader with a two-under 68 – one of only eight sub-par rounds recorded all week and the lowest of the tournament – to take the lead over Hogan by a stroke.

While Broach skied to a 79 in Friday's second round, Hogan fired his second consecutive 69 to take a two-shot lead over George Fazio, who later became more famous for his golf course design. Hogan was trying for an unprecedented fourth consecutive Open title (He was unable to play in the 1949 Open after his car accident, but had won in 1948, '50 and '52). At the halfway mark, Hogan owned two of only four sub-par rounds in the tournament. Boros was four shots back at 142.

Saturday, was a different story. Hogan faltered to a 74, while Boros charged to the front with a 68, two shots ahead of Hogan and three ahead of Edward Oliver.

Sunday, nobody broke par but Boros shot his third 71 in four days while Oliver shot 72 and Hogan 74. Boros' one-over 281 total gave him a four-shot victory for the $4,000 top prize.

"Anybody who can go around this course in 281 strokes certainly must be a magician," Hogan said.

1952 U.S. Open Leaderboard
At Northwood Club

Julius Boros		
71-71-68-71 — 281	$4,000
Ed Oliver Jr.		
71-72-70-72 — 285	$2,500
Ben Hogan		
69-69-74-74 — 286	$1,000
Johnny Bulla		
73-68-73-73 — 287	$800
George Fazio		
71-69-75-75 — 290	$600
Dick Metz		
70-74-76-71 — 291	$500
Tommy Bolt		
72-76-71-73 — 292	$350
Ted Kroll		
71-75-76-70 — 292	$350
Lew Worsham		
71-75-74-75 — 292	$350
Lloyd Mangrum		
75-74-72-72 — 293	$200
Sam Snead		
70-75-76-72 — 293	$200
Earl Stewart		
76-75-70-72 — 293	$200
Clarence Doser		
71-73-73-77 — 294	$150
Harry Todd		
71-76-74-73 — 295	$150

1963

PGA Championship

At 23, Jack Nicklaus withstood a Texas heat wave to win the 1963 PGA Championship at Dallas Athletic Club.

Charlie Nicklaus almost predicted it. Walking the fairways of Dallas Athletic Club with son Jack during practice rounds for the 1963 PGA Championship, the elder Nicklaus boasted proudly of his son's game.

Although only 23, Nicklaus had already won the 1962 U.S. Open and the Masters earlier in the year. He was third on the money list behind Arnold Palmer and Julius Boros.

"He's in a wonderful frame of mind here," Nicklaus' father said. "He feels the course is very fair and superbly conditioned and he's been treated wonderfully by the people down here."

Nicklaus started the week by winning the PGA's annual long drive contest with a 341-yard drive for a $100 prize. And he continued to play well, despite a record heat wave that saw temperatures during Sunday's final round reach an all-time high of 103.

Little-known Dick Hart was the first-round leader with an opening round 66 and had a three-shot lead over Nicklaus, Shelley Mayfield, Julius Boros, Bob Charles and Mason Rudolph. He

At the age of 23, Jack Nicklaus won the 1963 PGA Championship to overtake Arnold Palmer as golf's No. 1 player.

maintained that lead through 36 holes with a 72 on Friday that gave him a 138 total, still three shots ahead of Mayfield and Boros and four ahead of Nicklaus.

The average score on Thursday was 76.2 and on Friday 75.6. The cut was made at nine-over 151, and only 10 players were under par.

But in the third round, always noted as moving day in pro tournaments, scores plummeted. Eleven players broke 70, led by Bruce Crampton's low round of the tournament of 65 that gave him a three-shot lead over little-known Dave Ragan.

On Sunday, however Crampton faltered over the last few holes and Nicklaus joined Ben Hogan, Byron Nelson and Gene Sarazen as the only men in golf history to win the PGA, U.S. Open and the Masters.

1963 PGA Championship
Leaderboard
At Dallas Athletic Club
Jack Nicklaus
    69-73-69-68 — 279 $13,000
Dave Ragan
    75-70-67-69 — 281 $7,000
Bruce Crampton
    70-73-65-74 — 282 $3,750
Dow Finsterwald
    72-72-66-72 — 282 $3,750
Al Geiberger
    72-72-66-72 — 284 $3,125
Billy Maxwell
    73-71-69-71 — 284 $3,125
Jim Ferrier
    73-73-70-69 — 285 $2,750
Gardner Dickinson
    72-74-74-66 — 286 $2,090
Tommy Jacobs
    74-72-70-70 — 286 $2,090
Bill Johnston
    71-72-72-71 — 286 $2,090
Gary Player
    74-75-67-70 — 286 $2,090

Art Wall
    73-76-66-71 — 286 $2,090
Julius Boros
    69-72-73-73 — 287 $1,550
Bob Charles
    69-76-66-71 — 286 $1,550
Tony Lema
    70-71-77-69 — 287 $1,550
Jack Sellman
    75-70-74-68 — 287 $1,550
Manuel de la Torre
    71-71-74-72 — 288 $1,075
Wes Ellis
    71-74-71-72 — 288 $1,075
Bob Goalby
    74-70-74-70 — 288 $1,075

1967

Ryder Cup

In 1967, Houston golf went big-time when it hosted the best players from America and Great Britain in the Ryder Cup.

Jack Burke and Jimmy Demaret began negotiating with the U.S. Golf Association and PGA in 1962 to host a national championship, and they were awarded a tournament by both organizations. The 1967 Ryder Cup and the 1969 U.S. Open.

These were the days before even many golfing households knew what the Ryder Cup was, because the Americans had dominated the competition since it started in 1927.

The British team was captained by Dal Rees and featured players such as Tony Jacklin and Christy O'Connor. The American team was captained by Ben Hogan, with members including Arnold Palmer, Billy Casper, Julius Boros, Gene Littler, Gay Brewer, Al Geiberger, Gardner Dickinson, Johnny Pott and local favorites Doug Sanders and Bobby Nichols.

The matches started at 8:30 a.m. on Friday, with the University of Houston band marching through the fog up the first fairway playing the national anthems. The only problem was the disappointing crowds. Rumors had spread that the limit of 15,000 tickets had sold out, and only 5,000 people showed up. The crowds grew to a generous estimate of 10,000 on Saturday before the televised college foot-

Jimmy Demaret (left) and Jack Burke Jr. get ready for the 1967 Ryder Cup.

ball shoot-out between Texas and Arkansas, the nation's No. 1 and No. 2 teams, caused the crowd to thin again in the afternoon.

The U.S. won five matches and tied one the first day to win 3.5 of 8 possible points. Jacklin and Dave Thomas provided two points for the British by beating Doug Sanders and Gay Brewer 4 and 3 in the morning and then beating Gene Littler and Al Geiberger 3 and 2 in the afternoon.

On the second day (four-ball play), the U.S. went undefeated and almost clinched the Cup by taking a 13-3 lead into the final day. The British team went into the last day needing to win 13 matches, but the Americans went 10-5-1 to close out a 23.5-8.5 victory, one of the biggest in Cup history.

"We have all of our media here and I know they'll write home and say we were routed," Rees said of the British effort. "But I suppose they have a right to. The points are up there on the board for everybody to see."

Burke and Demaret acknowledge it was a financial disaster but Burke said, "It was something that needed to be done for golf in the Houston community."

1967 Ryder Cup Results

	Great Britain	U.S.
Morning		
Foursomes	1.5	2.5
Afternoon		
Foursomes	1	3
Morning		
Four-balls	0	4
Afternoon		
Four-balls	.5	3.5
Morning		
Singles	3	5
Afternoon		
Singles	2.5	5.5
TOTAL	8.5	23.5

1968

PGA Championship

PGA Championship comes to San Antonio's Pecan Valley.

When E.J. Burke, Jr., first opened his 210-acre Pecan Valley Golf Club in 1963, he felt it would become one of the best in the area and one of the best in the country. Press Maxwell, son of famed architect Perry Maxwell, had devised a tough but fair challenge.

Then a par-72 layout over 7,000 yards, the course was officially dedicated by Texas Governor John Connally and represented on the PGA Tour by Texas resident Miller Barber.

While the course was achieving acclaim from local pros and golfers, Burke went to work wooing national golf figures.

He invited state and sectional PGA events to the course and lobbied national PGA members to have a national tournament at Pecan Valley. His chance came just five years after the course opened when the PGA awarded the 50th PGA Championship to Pecan Valley in 1968.

"E.J. Burke really pulled some strings to get the PGA here," *San Antonio Express-News* sportswriter Dan Cook said.

When the field arrived, the course met the challenge as players experienced a stern test and a typical Texas summer heat wave. Jack Nicklaus missed the 36-hole cut for what would only be the second time in a 20-year span.

His triple-bogey seven on the first hole during the second round doomed his chances. Nicklaus

did, however, add to his power-driving reputation when he became the only pro to drive Salado Creek from the back tees on the 18th hole.

Marty Fleckman led after every round but the last when he shot three-over 73. Arnold Palmer felt he was going to break his career-long winless streak at the PGA when he slammed a 3-wood shot 12 feet from the cup on the 18th hole.

But it was the moose, Julius Boros, who got up and down for a par on the final hole to take a one-shot victory over Palmer and Bob Charles. His 281 total was the highest winning score in PGA history.

Pecan Valley claimed more than its share of victims, but afterwards the players praised the Alamo City layout.

"This is a great course," Chi Chi Rodriguez said. "I wish we played on one like this every week."

Pecan Valley has hosted several Texas Opens, an LPGA event along with other professional and amateur tournaments, but the 1968 PGA remains the only one of golf's four majors to be played in the San Antonio-Austin area.

1968 PGA Championship
Leaderboard
At Pecan Valley Country Club

Julius Boros		
71-71-70-69 — 281	$25,000
Bob Charles		
72-70-70-70 — 282	$12,500
Arnold Palmer		
71-69-72-70 — 282	$12,500
George Archer		
71-69-74-69 — 283	$7,500
Marty Fleckman		
66-72-72-73 — 283	$7,500
Frank Beard		
68-70-72-74 — 284	$5,750
Billy Casper		
74-70-70-70 — 284	$5,750

1969
U.S. Open

Par was in season at the 1969 U.S. Open at Champions, but Orville Moody was the only player who came close to bagging his limit.

Considering the Ryder Cup financial disaster, it was a good thing Champions already had been guaranteed as the host site for the 1969 Open or the USGA may have reconsidered holding its national championship in Houston.

Getting the Open in the South was a significant achievement in the first place, because it traditionally has been held on courses in the North or on the West Coast. Champions, with its large, Bermuda putting surfaces, was the first southern venue for the Open since 1958 at Tulsa's Southern Hills.

As with any Open layout, the players found something to complain about at Champions. But while most modern golfers have grown accustomed to complaining that U.S. Open rough is too tough, on this occasion they complained it wasn't tough enough. The USGA normally likes rough to be three-to-four inches high, but the Texas summer heat had stunted the growth at Champions.

"I hit a drive 250 yards into the rough and do you know I could still see the ball," South African Gary Player said. "I don't think I've ever played in an Open with the rough so short."

Said course superintendent Vernon Nash. "Just let a couple of 'em in there and get buried and it won't be so damn easy."

Nash, as it turned out, had the last laugh. Orville Moody, an Army sergeant who left the service a year earlier, became the first player in five years to win the Open with an over-par score.

Miller Barber held a three-shot lead on the final day, but bogeyed Nos. 2, 3, 5, 6 and 8, where Moody took the lead for the first time. He finished with a 72 and a one-over total of 281, one shot ahead of Bob Rosburg, Al Geiberger and Deane Beman.

"I was in such a daze I didn't remember everything," Moody said after a phone call from President Nixon. "He said it was a great thing – not only for the elite, but for the middle class."

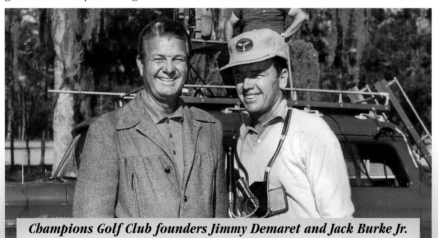

Champions Golf Club founders Jimmy Demaret and Jack Burke Jr. hosted golf's best players at the 1969. U.S. Open.

1978
Legends of Golf

In 1978, the Legends of Golf dusted off golf's best old-timers and became the foundation for the Senior PGA Tour.

Fred Raphael credits a conversation with Gene Sarazen during the 1962 Masters as planting the first seeds of the Legends of Golf and the Senior PGA Tour.

The two were talking about the old and new legends that play at August national every year in the Masters. After 16 years, the idea finally became reality with the legends of Golf at Onion Creek Country Club in Austin.

Raphael and Sarazen had already worked with Jimmy Demaret on the highly successful television series called Shell's Wonderful World of Golf.

Raphael was able to go to television producers to try and convince them people would actually watch familiar players, now over 50, play golf.

The '78 Legends of Golf at Onion Creek on a course Demaret designed was the first real test of the senior golf idea.

A total of 11 two-man teams played for $100,000, then the largest prize offered on any tour.

Sam Snead and Gardner Dickinson won the first tournament, but the 1979 event won by Julius Boros and Robert De Vincenzo was the turning point. The senior twosome faced Art Wall and Tommy Bolt in a dramatic sudden-death playoff that captured the imagination of the golfing nation.

The team of Boros and De Vincenzo birdied the last seven holes, five in sudden death, to take the Legends titles.

The television ratings swamped any regular PGA Tour event on the schedule and the idea for the Senior PGA Tour was born.

From two tournaments in 1980 to 43 in 1994, the Senior PGA has become as popular or even more so than the regular tour, all dating back to the birth in Austin at the Legends of Golf.

The tournament moved from Onion Creek to Barton Creek in 1990. It was played as a stroke play event in 1993, but reverted back to the familiar team format for 1994.

Raphael, who still produces each tournament, has proven to be a true sports visionary but admits to even a bit of surprise how big his small Central Texas creation has grown.

1991

U.S. Women's Open

Fifty years after the first U.S. Open came to Colonial, the best women in the world returned and up-start Meg Mallon outlasted veterans Pat Bradley and Amy Alcott.

It was a battle between golf's old guard and new wave, between ladies who are living legends and those who aspire to be.

Meg Mallon started the 46th U.S. Women's Open in the latter category, but finished a lot closer to the former.

By shooting a four-under 67 in the final round at Colonial Country Club, Mallon charged from two shots out of the lead to a two-stroke victory over veteran Pat Bradley and earned her second major championship in three weeks. While some of the game's best players faltered in the Texas heat, the fifth-year pro who had never finished higher than third hit 17 of 18 greens on the way to victory. She finished with a one-under total of 283.

"No one is more surprised than I am right now," said the 28-year-old Mallon, who was voted by her peers as the friendliest player on tour. "This surpasses my expectations. Once you get that winning feeling, you never want to lose it."

Bradley, who held or shared the lead all week, shot 71 on Sunday and finished second for the third consecutive week at 285. Amy Alcott, who needed only one victory to get into the Hall of Fame, bogeyed the 16th and 18th holes to shoot a 71 and finish alone in third at 286.

It was appropriate that at the end of a week highlighted by gripping and difficult pin placements to Texas' good ol' boys, that the quietest player stood alone in the spotlight.

Bradley and Alcott were tied for the lead going into the final nine holes, when Mallon got the hot hand with her putter and shot a three-under 32. She forced a three-way tie when she birdied the par-4 11th, then made her 15-foot birdie at the 14th and a 25-footer at the 15th to take the lead for good.

"Meg is a great champion to carry the flag for our national championship," Alcott said. "It's great to see some new blood. She's very popular, and she proved today that good guys do finish first."

With a growing emphasis being placed on equality in golf for women, the USGA began a concerted effort to play its championship on the same type of courses played by its men. It was the first Women's Open in Texas, and only the third national championship here since the 1941 Open at Colonial and the 1952 Open at Northwood. Mallon's 283 total (par 71, with No. 3 playing as a par 5) was one shot better than Craig Wood's winning score 50 years earlier. Ben Hogan helped celebrate the 50th anniversary by showing up on Sunday.

In spite of temperatures in the upper 90s, consistent crowds made it one of the best Women's Opens in history.

1991 U.S. Women's Open Leaderboard

Meg Mallon		
70-75-71-67 — 283	$110,000
Pat Bradley		
69-73-72-72 — 285	$55,000
Amy Alcott		
75-68-72-71 — 286	$32,882
Laurel Kean		
70-76-71-70 — 287	$23,996
Dottie Mochrie		
73-76-68-71 — 288	$17,642
Chris Johnson		
76-72-68-72 — 288	$17,642
Joan Pitcock		
70-70-72-75 — 289	$14,623
Jody Anschutz		
73-72-72-73 — 290	$12,252
Brandie Burton		
75-71-69-75 — 290	$12,252
Beth Daniel		
74-76-75-66 — 291	$9,738
Tina Barrett		
74-74-72-71 — 291	$9,738
Debbie Massey		
72-72-75-72 — 291	$9,738
JoAnne Carner		
73-72-73-73 — 291	$9,738

1993

U.S. Amateur

*John Harris let his actions –
and his tears – do his talking
at the 1993 U.S. Amateur.*

If pictures tell 1,000 words, then 1,000 tears paint a pretty picture and tell an even greater story.

John Harris tried to put his victory in the 93rd U.S. Amateur in perspective. How humble were his beginnings on the sand greens in northern Minnesota. How hard he had worked under the supervision of his father. How proud his father and his family would be.

But when words failed to capture the essence of the moment, he covered his face and cried.

It was with a teardrop — not an exclamation point — that Harris punctuated the 1993 U.S. Amateur and reminded the 25 million American amateur golfers there is more to winning and losing than the difference between first and second prize.

In amateur golf, winning is the only prize. After finishing a 5 and 3 victory over Danny Ellis on August 30, Harris left Champions Golf Club no richer or poorer than when we arrived, but with the Havermeyer Trophy in his hand, pride in his heart and his name in the history book.

"I feel like the luckiest guy in the world," said Harris, a 41-year-old insurance executive from Edina, Minn.

It was a victory for the aged, since Harris became only the fifth player over 25 to win the Amateur in the previous 21 years. He arrived in Houston coming off the psychological high of playing on the American Walker Cup team in

his hometown. Because of age, many expected Harris to falter on the final 18 during the sweltering 36-hole finale. But just when everybody was giving up on him, Harris drew on all his experience as a former pro to put his game into overdrive.

The match was even after the first 18 holes, but Harris hit every fairway and every green in the second round and won five of the last eight holes to put the match away. He finished three-under through 15 holes.

It was a dramatic turnaround. After blowing a 3-up lead on the last nine of the first 18, Harris skipped lunch and, instead, he and his son Chris went to the practice tee to regain the Midas touch. He hit 50-60 balls, then went to meet his destiny.

"I'm awfully proud of the way I played the last 18 holes," he said.

1997

Tour Championship

David Duval got the monkey off his back. "I kind of let the match get away from me in the morning and I developed a little virus in my swing. I was lucky to fix it in time."

Not less than a month before the tournament started, people were starting to wonder about David Duval.

He would walk down the fairway, and spectators would turn to each other and whisper, "He's a great player, but he doesn't seem to have what it takes to win."

It is a fine line that separates

the great players on the PGA Tour from the faces in the crowd. After several years of playing the tour with some success but no victories and seven second-place finishes, David Duval finally crossed that line with his first victory.

It felt so good, in fact, that Duval has been virtually unstoppable ever since. He won the next two tournaments, including the $4 million Tour Championship at Champions Golf Club in Houston, to become the first player in tour history to win his first three tournaments in consecutive starts.

Duval rallied from three shots behind leader Davis Love with scrambling pars at the 17th and 18th holes to finish with a three-under 68 and a one-stroke victory over Jim Furyk. Duval's 11-under 273 total earned him the $720,000 first prize, the largest in tour history.

Duval, a 25-year-old player distinguished by his blond goatee and Darth Vader sunglasses, said, "It was a fun-packed day."

At the same time, Duval's victory helped another one of the Tour's young guns – Tiger Woods – retain his spot at the top of the money list. Woods finished in only 12th place in the last official tour event of the year, but earned enough to become the first tour player to go over $2 million in a single season. Duval finished second in season earnings with $1.8 million.

"A lot of it boils down to good breaks and making some putts when you need to," Duval said. "I've been fortunate the last few weeks to get the good breaks. I've had enough patience and resolve to make the putts when I needed it.

"And that adds up to what it hadn't added up to in the past, and those are tournament wins."

Although as many as eight

players had the chance to win when the final round began, Love took control early when he birdied the first two holes to forge a three-shot lead. It was his tournament to lose.

But a few hours later, the momentum quickly changed when Duval rolled in a 40-foot eagle putt on the par-5 13th to pull into a tie with Love.

In a rare — and typically understated — display of emotion, the former Georgia Tech All-American poked his finger into the air as the ball curled into the cup.

"It got me right back in the ball game," said Duval, who had reached the par five with a three-iron that traveled 246 yards. "You know, the hole was sitting in the shade. I was putting from the sun into it. I hit it really good. As I was watching it, I had to kind of look up a little bit more than usual to see the hole because of it being in the shade. I saw, you know, six or eight feet short of the hole and I knew it was going in. Just had an exact line it needed to have. So that was nice."

David Duval conquered Champions Golf Club to win the 1997 Tour Championship.

Dave Lineman

Love came to the 551-yard 13th well aware of Duval's eagle. He knew he needed at least a birdie, but his tee shot strayed into the rough and he eventually settled for par.

Love's bogey at the 14th hole then put the ball in Duval's court down the final stretch. It was now Duval's tournament to lose, which he had done many times before, but this time he failed to collapse under the pressure.

"I felt like the way he was playing, he was going to be the guy to beat today," Love said. "You know, he just hung in there very, very well.

"But David has been close a lot of times. It's not like he just all of a sudden won twice and he doesn't have any experience at all. He's been through a lot of Sundays that he's had chances to win. It's just coming back to him now. He's been there.

"So I look at him a little differently. You know that up-and-down he made at 17 was just all world. My brother, Mark, when he made the putt, said, 'This guy's really showing me something.' He's played great for the last month.

"He's showed that — you know, a lot of people talked about he couldn't finish. He's proven that the last month that he can, and he will be able to for a long time."

Duval got one of those breaks at the 17th hole on Sunday. He made one of those putts there, too — and the one-stroke victory was all but assured.

His drive had strayed right — "a high plains drifter," he called it — and landed between two trees, a mere six feet from the fence that guards the out-of-bounds area. He punched a six-iron into the rough, short of the bunker,

and then chipped to 12 feet.

Furyk, who finished the 1997 season with 13 top 10 finishes, said he thought he might have a chance to get in a playoff.

"But it wasn't meant to be," Furyk said. "David played well — got it up and down on 17 and 18 from trouble off the tee. I mean, that's what you have to do to win golf tournaments. I congratulate him. He did it."

Tour Championship Final Results
At Champions Golf Club

David Duval		
66-69-70-68 — 273	$720,000	
Jim Furyk		
66-68-73-67 — 274	$432,000	
Davis Love III		
68-68-69-70 — 275	$276,000	
Mark Calcavecchia		
69-66-72-70 — 277	$176,000	
Bill Glasson		
68-69-68-72 — 277	$176,000	
Jesper Parnevik		
66-73-69-70 — 278	$140,000	
Brad Faxon		
67-69-69-73 — 278	$140,000	
Justin Leonard		
70-69-72-68 — 279	$124,000	
Loren Roberts		
72-68-69-70 — 279	$124,000	
Vijay Singh		
70-70-70-70 — 280	$110,800	
Scott Hoch		
68-65-74-73 — 280	$110,800	
Tiger Woods		
69-68-75-69 — 281	$97,600	
Greg Norman		
73-69-69-70 — 281	$97,600	
Scott McCarron		
69-70-71-71 — 281	$97,600	
Tom Lehman		
72-71-68-71 — 282	$86,400	
Andrew Magee		
69-70-70-73 — 282	$86,400	
Mark O'Meara		
68-74-72-70 — 284	$80,000	
Paul Stankowski		
70-69-72-73 — 284	$80,000	

History of Texas Golf: The Biggest and Best

History is our most precious national resource. Unlike most natural resources such as water, silver and gold, there is an inexhaustible supply of history.

No one person can ever hoard it up or have a monopoly on history. It is there for all to learn from and to try to make our own place in its pages.

History reminds us where we've been so we can appreciate how far we've come. It's a road map to show us where we're going and how far we have to go.

In no other sport does history play such an important role as it does in golf. The lore of the game and the triumphs and tribulations of past players shape the way we think and play the game. Just imagine how fast you could improve if you learned something each time on the golf course and didn't make the same mistakes over and over.

Therein lies the value of history. It doesn't add yardage off the tee or touch around the greens, but it gives you an appreciation for the game that drives you to achieve all of the above. Texans such as Ben Hogan, Byron Nelson and Harvey Penick each set a standard for all golfers to follow, and history is the way they passed the baton to the next generation.

"The lore of the game," the legendary Bobby Jones once wrote, "the story of its development and the stirring deeds of the great players of the past must always command the respectful attention of all who play golf regularly. To be reasonably knowledgeable in such matters comes close to being an obligation to the true golfer."

Golf in Texas celebrated its 100th anniversary in 1996. Over that century, the sport has evolved slowly from its beginnings with the creation of Dallas and Galveston Country Clubs to its current status as the golf capital of the south.

Texas has a rich golf heritage. Once a distant outpost on golf's frontier, Texas is home of some of the nation's most prestigious golf courses, and has produced some of the best players in the history of the game.

In The Beginning . . .

Texas. Few words illicit more images. Cowboys and ranchers. Oil men and real-estate brokers. Snazzy cars and glitzy bars. JFK and Lee Harvey Oswald. The Dallas Cowboys and the Super Bowl. Texas Longhorns and Texas Aggies.

Texas may be the best single example of what's good in America. On one hand, it offers the down-home, friendly, laid-back attitude of the old west. On the other, it offers enough hustle and bustle, wheeling and dealing and high society to make the staunchest Yankee feel at home.

To the rest of the world, Texas still evokes images of cowboys in white hats riding high on dusty, unpaved streets.

The taming of the west can be traced partly to the introduction of the game of golf in Texas. Golf was introduced in America in the late 1800s, long known as a game of royalty, ladies and gentlemen. It gave birth to a new fraternity of Americans who enjoyed the outdoors, enjoyed competing against themselves and each other, and settling bets at the 19th hole.

In Dallas, it all started in 1896, when Dallas Country Club was founded on Oak Lawn Avenue as the Dallas Golf and Country Club.

With an outstanding piece of rolling, wooded terrain now at their disposal on the banks of Turtle Creek and Exall Lake, Dallas CC members hired Tom Bendelow, one of the fathers of American golf course architecture who was dubbed "the Johnny Appleseed of American Golf," to design an 18-hole layout.

Bendelow said that as a natural golf course the land at Highland Park had "no superior in this country."

Bendelow was the most prolific golf course builder in America, designing 514 golf courses in the U.S. and Canada. The going rate for all designers was $25 a job, even though it took two years from start to finish.

Bendelow was often criticized by modern-day architects for his "18 stakes on a Sunday afternoon," design technique, but among his works are such classic layouts as Medinah, Dallas CC, Fort Worth's River Crest and nearby Lakewood.

The fame of the new layout, boasting grass greens, spread throughout the state. To celebrate the opening of the club and its spectacular clubhouse, the club's

In 1898, Dallas Golf & Country Club became the first course in Texas. It was a nine-hole layout with sand greens. Even today, it ranks in the top 100 courses in the state – minus the sand greens.

leading players entered a tournament on Feb. 22, 1912. Sam A. Lake won the tournament and the President's Cup.

Meanwhile in Galveston, a group of 30 members were building Galveston Country Club in 1898. It had a membership of 30, with a nine-hole course located just west of what is now the San Luis Hotel and Condominiums.

The club, however, was wiped out on Sept. 8, 1900, when North America's greatest natural disaster swept clean the southern half of Galveston island and claimed 6,000 lives. In view of the tragic loss of life and property, the destruction of the course was a minor consequence. A new clubhouse was built from the debris and nine sand greens were arranged in the same general location of the first course near

53rd Street and Avenue S.

And in Austin, an elite group was building the first Austin Country Club, a nine-hole layout with sand greens. Little did they know that a 13-year-old caddie would eventually become the head pro, one of the greatest teachers the game has known and home of such golf superstars as Ben Crenshaw and Tom Kite.

The Fever Catches On

It didn't take long for the popularity of the game to spawn the birth of other clubs. Houston Country Club was founded in 1903 and Bendelow built River Crest Country Club in Fort Worth and Dallas' Lakewood Country Club in 1912. A.W. Tillinghast, another world renowned architect, built Cedar Crest Country

Club in 1919 and Brook Hollow Golf Club in 1921.

On Oct. 22, 1912, such notable figures as Herbert Marcus, Edward Titche, W.J. Lawther and the Linz Brothers — Albert, Ben and Simon — were among a small group of men who assembled to incorporate as Lakewood Country Club with the purpose of "supporting and maintaining the ancient game of golf and other innocent sports."

They purchased land in a largely undeveloped area east of downtown, and capitalized at $15,000 with 300 shares of $50 each.

The original Lakewood layout was designed by Bendelow. As the surrounding community grew up around it, however, the club sold some of its land to developers and the layout was redesigned in 1956 by Ralph Plummer, two years after he built Dallas Athletic Club and a year after he built Columbian CC.

Lakewood was the site of the first Dallas Open, won by none other than Byron Nelson in 1944 with a total of 276. That year, Nelson was to win seven of the 22 tour events. Nelson won by 10 strokes over wartime playing pal Harold Jug McSpaden. He went on to become the AP's Athlete of the Year, an award he earned again the following year by winning a record 11 consecutive events.

At Brook Hollow, architect A.W. Tillinghast carved his layout out of 129 acres near where the Elm Fork emptied into the main part of the Trinity River a few miles from downtown. Then, and now, Brook Hollow is a timeless masterpiece with classic shot-making values that put a premium on concentrating on every shot.

Golfcrest Country Club in Houston was one of several early Texas country clubs that later moved to a new location or no longer exist.

Here, every hole is a signature hole. During his playing days, Nelson played and practiced here so much he was made an honorary member.

In 1917, banker Sol Dreyfus wanted to build a golf course near his mansion on South Boulevard. Unlike most modern courses built on cheap flood-plain land, Dreyfus selected a prime piece of real estate with rolling terrain, heavy tree coverage and panoramic views of a downtown skyline that had yet to come.

He hired A.W. Tillinghast to design the course and called it Cedar Crest Country Club. In addition to golf, Cedar Crest offered tennis, riding stables and scenic riding paths.

Like most of Tillinghast's courses, he went into painstaking detail to build a demanding course that required accuracy.

Nine years after the course opened, Dreyfus put up a purse and hosted the first Dallas Open, which was an unofficial event until 1944.

Cedar Crest received such rave reviews from the top pros of the day that Dreyfus decided to offer $12,000 to bring the 1927 PGA Championship to Dallas the following year. The PGA accepted and the best players in the world came to Dallas for the first time.

Players such as Walter Hagen, Gene Sarazen, Al Espinosa and Harry "Lighthorse Cooper" gave many Texans their first glimpse at this new game called golf.

One of the youngsters in the galleries that week was a kid named Byron Nelson, who was nipping at Hagen's heels as he walked down the fairways. It was then that Nelson decided he, too, wanted to grow up to become a pro golfer.

Finally, Courses For The People

While the roots of Texas history go back to the Alamo, pioneers of a different kind helped bring golf to the Texas public a few years later.

Up until 1916, all of the golf courses in Texas were private clubs, built for the rich and famous.

When it came to golf, it was still a case of the haves and have nots until Brackenridge Park Golf Course in San Antonio became the state's first public course.

Designed by legendary architect A.W. Tillinghast, the course opened in 1916 and brought the game of golf, which had been restricted for the wealthy for its first two decades, to the masses.

Old Brack was named after local developer George W. Brackenridge, who donated much of the land just north of downtown. Broadway, the major road in front of the golf course, was Brackenridge's private drive into his estate. He decided to donate the land to allow citizens of the growing city (200,000 in 1922) a chance to try the sport of golf, which was becoming increasingly popular across the U.S.

Although the course has undergone many changes over the years, it remains in its original location with a clubhouse that's over 70 years old.

"All the greats have played here, everybody who was anybody," head pro John Erwin said.

The course hosted the PGA's Texas Open from its inception in 1922 for 21 years, until 1959. Brackenridge has also played host to the Texas State Junior Tournament from 1927–1979 and the San Antonio Men's

City Amateur since 1922.

In 1922, the City of Houston responded by opening Hermann Park Golf Course, a golf course named after a Swiss immigrant who arrived in America in 1838 and went on to become a millionaire in the real estate and lumber business.

Hermann never forgot his humble beginnings, and he envisioned a place where wayfarers and homeless people could

The 1927 PGA Championship gave Texans their first exposure to pro golf — and players like Gene Sarazen.

come without being molested. When he died, he donated his $2.5 million and his prime real estate holdings to the city for that purpose.

In 1924, the City of Dallas responded to the growing demand for public golf with the opening of Tenison and Stevens Park golf courses.

In March of 1923, the president of the City National Bank of Dallas, Mr. and Mrs. Edward O. Tenison, donated 105 acres of land to the city for a park as a memorial to their son, Edward. The land was located on what was then the eastern edge of Dallas on heavily-wooded, greatly rolling terrain along White Rock Creek.

Taking advantage of the free land, the city hired architect John Bredemus to build what is now the West Course at Tenison Park along with a clubhouse. This course was opened to the public in 1924, and became the home of such golfing legends as Lee Trevino, who first learned to play golf there using a soda bottle.

On May 17, 1924, just a few weeks after the opening of Tenison, the city opened another course at Stevens Park. The city couldn't afford to buy enough land to build a course, so in 1922 leased land on the Cole Estate in North Dallas. Walter Stevens and his sister Annie donated 40 acres of their Oak Cliff estate to the city in memory of their parents, Dr. and Mrs. John H. Stevens, making the golf course possible.

It was a training ground for players like Don January, who led nearby Sunset High to the state championship in the 1940s before he turned pro. Frank Beard played there during his high school days, and Trevino, who spent most of his time at Tenison Park, shot an occasional round there.

Jack Burke Comes To Texas

Houston's River Oaks Country Club was developed in the early 1920s and has been the address for Houston's rich and famous ever with black gold running through their veins.

After legendary architect Donald Ross designed this classic, timeless layout on this rolling, garden-type setting on the banks of Buffalo Bayou, members hired Jack Burke Jr. to become the city's first head pro.

Burke started out as a caddie at Philadelphia Country Club, but went on to establish himself as a great player and one of the game's best teachers. He finished second at the Houston Invitational at Houston Country Club in 1920 and fourth in 1921, during which he met River Oaks member William C. Hunt.

In 1924, Hunt gave Burke a personal check to retain him as head pro, where he stayed for 18 years until he died suddenly of a heart attack in 1943. During his lifetime, the diminutive man affectionately referred to as "the little fellow" won five Texas PGA titles and the 1941 PGA Seniors Championship. He also influenced many of the players of the day, namely Jimmy Demaret and his son Jackie Jr, as well as Ben Hogan and teaching legend Harvey Penick.

Burke also authored one of the first golf instruction books ever published known as *Ten Lessons in Golf*.

Burke's Houston address helped bring many of the game's

Jack Burke Sr. was one of the game's earliest teachers. His "Ten Lessons in Golf" was one of the game's first instruction books.

Ben Hogan, Byron Nelson and Jimmy Demaret were among the first generation of pro golfers who were born and raised in Texas.

best players to Houston, and gave rise to the first generation of Texas golf legends.

Texas PGA Is Formed

Architect John Bredemus will go down in history as the Father of Texas golf since he designed and built many of the state's early courses, but he also was an accomplished player who helped start the Texas Open and the Texas PGA in 1922.

Bredemus teamed with Houston CC pro Willie Maguire in 1922 to establish the Texas PGA, with the vision of creating a series of pro golf tournaments in the Southwest. The first event was held in Shreveport, La., in 1922

and was followed by the Corpus Christi Open and the Houston Open in 1923.

Harry "Lighthorse" Cooper won the first Houston event against a field that included the best golfers of the era in an event *Golf Illustrated* called "the Southwest Invasion."

The next Houston Open was played in 1924 at Hermann Park. It was a 64-hole event instead of 72, since the old Hermann Park layout had only 16 holes.

Joe Kirkwood, who later went on to become a famous trick-shot artist, won the first prize of $500. The purse was $2,000, which was raised by $2 and $3 donations from fans, who got their names in the newspaper for amounts given.

Texas Open Is Born

San Antonio News Sports Editor Jack O'Brien covered many South Texas sporting events during his tenure at the local paper, but he had a special love for the game of golf.

O'Brien decided San Antonio's mild winter and top public course at Brackenridge Park would be a perfect combination to host a professional golf tournament.

Pro tournaments those days were a rarity, with amateurs dominating the game of golf. In fact, there were only four major pro events: the U.S. and Canadian Opens, PGA Championship and Western Open in Chicago, when

When was the last time you saw a ticker-tape parade for a golfer? Ben Hogan enjoyed that honor after winning the 1953 British Open.

Saturday and Sunday to decide the tournament.

"Some people don't realize this was the tournament which helped launch the PGA Tour," said longtime Austin Country Club pro Harvey Penick, who played in 20 early opens. The pros played in San Antonio and moved onto Los Angeles or over to Shreveport, New Orleans and Florida."

In 1928, players' association president Tommy Armour helped draw up articles of incorporation in San Antonio for the Professional Touring Golfers Association, what is now known as the PGA Tour.

Today the tournament is the fifth oldest stop on the Tour and the first in what has become more than 40 weekly PGA Tournaments.

Leonard Opens Colonial

After getting the opportunity to putt on the superior putting surfaces of bentgrass greens while on a vacation in the 1930s, Fort

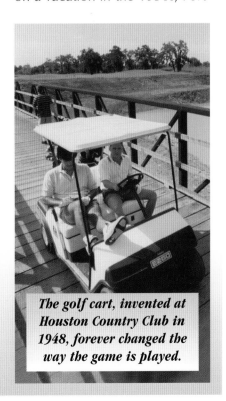

The golf cart, invented at Houston Country Club in 1948, forever changed the way the game is played.

O'Brien proposed the Texas Open in 1922.

He enlisted the help of the cities' business community along with golfer/architect John Bredemus who had recently come to San Antonio and was working at Brackenridge Park.

In late 1921, the committee sent out telegrams to the leading pro golfers of the day inviting them to San Antonio in January of 1922 to compete in the first Texas Open. The prize money was then an unheard-of $5,000, almost 10 times more than the U.S. Open was offering at that time. The mild weather and top money attracted a full field for the first event.

The course conditions were less than ideal by today's stan-dards, but Scotsman Bob MacDonald won the first tournament with a 281 total.

While more than 4,000 fans turned out for the first competition, O'Brien's financial estimates were a little overly optimistic and he passed the hat among spectators on the 18th green to help pay expenses.

The second tournament in 1923 helped cement the Texas Open's place in golf history. British Open champion Walter Hagen charged from six shots behind on the final day to capture the title, earning national headlines.

In the early years, players participated in pro-ams early in the week and played 36 holes on

Worth businessman Marvin Leonard returned home an enlightened man. No longer satisfied with the slow and bumpy Bermuda greens found in Texas, Leonard began campaigning to get existing courses to change.

Despite his clout as owner of the Leonard Brothers Department Stores, Leonard was rebuffed at every turn. Bentgrass greens won't work in Texas, he was told, because of the summer heat and humidity. If he wanted bentgrass greens so badly, they told him, why didn't he build a course all his own?

The rest, as they say, is history. In 1936, Leonard took them up on the idea. He bought some rich land in the Trinity River bottom and began sowing the seed for what has been Texas' best golf course for the past 60 years. Colonial Country Club is rated in the top 50 in the world and the top 30 in the U.S. Designed by John Bredemus with later assists from Ralph Plummer and Press Maxwell, Colonial is a monument to the golden age of American golf architecture.

Dallas Open Begins

In the inaugural 1944 Dallas Open, Byron Nelson, the man for whom this event would later be named, got off to a great start by posting a 10-stroke victory over Harold McSpadden at Lakewood Country Club.

Nelson went on to be named the Associated Press Athlete of the Year, an award he would repeat the next year with his 11 consecutive victories.

Nelson fired four sub-par rounds of 69-69-70-68 for a 276 total, and accounted for three of only five scores in the 60s all week.

Colonial NIT Is Born

The idea for the Colonial National Invitation was conceived in 1941 after the U.S. Open was held at Colonial. The Open was so well received by fans and players alike that Colonial officials resolved that the club should have an annual tournament.

Appropriately Fort Worth native Ben Hogan won the first Colonial on May 19, 1946. He did it by firing a final round 65 to post a new course record and beat Harry Todd by one stroke for the $3,000 first prize. Hogan finished with a 279 total. Todd, a Dallas native and the third-round leader, finished with a 69 for a 280 total. Fred Haas Jr. was third at 281 and Sam Snead was three back of Hogan at 282.

Colonial would eventually become known as Hogan's Alley – and probably always will. No

Jimmy Demaret and Jack Burke Jr. retired from golf to build Champions Golf Club in 1957. Architect George Fazio points out the highlights of a layout that would host the 1967 Ryder Cup and 1969 U.S. Open.

one man ever dominated a tournament the way Hogan did the Colonial NIT. Five times Hogan won the NIT and at one time or another he held practically every record on the plush carpets of Colonial. It was also appropriate that Hogan's final career PGA Tour victory was at Colonial in 1959.

Even after his golfing prime, Hogan was a consistent finisher in the Colonial top 10. After turning 50, Hogan competed in four consecutive NIT events (from 1964-67), carding finishes of fourth, 10th, fifth and third. At the time, only 13 sub-par totals over the full-route of 72 holes had been recorded in Colonial history and Hogan owned four of them.

Houston Golf Association Created

The number of golf courses and golfers in Houston didn't really take off until a group of men formed the Houston Golf Association in 1945 with the intention of bringing an annual pro tournament to town instead of those "fly by night" affairs.

The year was 1945 and Lonnie Douglass, George Ross, George O'Leary, A.A. Gharrett, Bennie Strickland and Dr. Harry Coffman were on their way back to Houston from the Texas Open in San Antonio when they decided Houston deserved to have a tournament of its own.

Knowing it would take a tremendous effort to put on such a tournament, they formed the Houston Golf Association and held their first tournament in May of 1946. The HGA has continued to promote golf the past 50 years and still operates the Houston Open.

On November 10, 1957, Charlie Sifford became the first African-American to win on the professional golf circuit. Sifford's victory came three years after Charles Washington broke the color barrier on Texas' public golf courses.

Nelson, Hogan Duel In First Houston Open

Although other tournaments by the same name were held prior to 1946, the first official Houston Open was played in 1946 at River Oaks Country Club. Sponsored by the HGA, it was called the Tournament of Champions and offered a $10,000 purse.

Lloyd Mangrum and Ben Hogan took the lead after the first round with a pair of 67s, and amateur Frank Stranahan grabbed the 36-hole lead with a 68 on Friday that gave him a seven-under total of 137. But then came Nelson, who had won a record 11 consecutive tournaments the year before, charging into the lead with a 67 on Saturday. A crowd of 10,000 watched him shoot a 68 on Sunday to hold on for a two-

shot victory over Hogan.

Attendance, however, had been disappointing and Houston Golf Association member Dr. H.N. Coffman realized the gate receipts wouldn't cover the expenses, so he went downtown to a banker and took out a loan to cover the prize money.

LPGA Comes To Dallas

While men's pro golf in Dallas was struggling to regain its pro tournament, the women's pro tour came to the metroplex for the first time in 1951 only to endure some hardships of its own.

Long before the equal-rights movement, women were starting to hone their talents in the gentleman's game. In 1951, the top women professionals made their first appearance in Dallas at Lakewood Country Club in the

Weathervane Women's Open. A field of 34 players challenged gusty winds for the $3,000 purse. Alice Bauer took the first-round lead with an even par 40-35-75, but women's golf legend Babe Zaharias claimed victory in the 36-hole event with a 149 total to beat Patty Berg for the $750 top prize.

Burke Wins Four In A Row

Jack Burke Jr. turned pro at the age of 17, but in 1952 he managed to do something nobody else has been able to do since. He won four consecutive tournaments, including the Houston Open as the second tournament in the string.

Playing under the pressure of winning in his hometown, Burke led from the second round and entered the final day with a five-shot lead at Memorial Park.

"I remember I had a good round in the rain at Memorial Park and went way ahead and stayed ahead the rest of the way," Burke recalls. "When you win in your hometown, it's not easy. My friends were betting on me. All the caddies were betting on me. My mother was in the gallery."

Burke went on to win at Baton Rouge, La., and St. Petersburg, Fla., before his string ended at the Masters, where he finished second, two shots behind Sam Snead.

Burke's streak is still the longest in modern history, since Byron Nelson was an incredible 11 in a row in 1945.

"When I was on the hot streak, my clubs didn't know I was winning everything," Burke said. "The ball didn't know it. The

course didn't know it. Listen, I didn't start playing well until I figured out that I was responsible for my own actions. Blaming it on other factors doesn't help.

"You can't start looking for excuses. You can't say I've won two in a row. I'm not destined to win a third. Athletes are the biggest bunch of complainers. They're looking for alibis and when they've reached a certain level they find them. After winning one tournament, I went to the

next stop ready and confident. I didn't look back and ponder whether I was destined to win.

"The only people who put pressure on a golfer is himself. The gallery doesn't put it on you. They want you to win. If you make four putts in a row and don't think you can make the fifth, the putter and ball don't know you made the last four.

"There's a lot of poor thinking in today's golf, but I had supreme confidence."

Jimmy Demaret helped increase golf's worldwide popularity on the 1960's primetime TV series, **Shell's Wonderful World of Golf.**

Ben Hogan played his last pro tournament in 1971 at Champions Golf Club, where he re-injured his leg in the Houston Open.

Souchak's Timeless Record

Former Duke fullback Mike Souchak's PGA career record includes 14 victories, mostly in regional events. He never won a so-called major and has been quiet on the Senior PGA tour since turning 50, but he has one bit of PGA history that endured for nearly 40 years.

On a frigid mid-February week in 1955, Souchak put together an unbelievable hot streak at the Texas Open and produced the tour's 72-hole record.

Playing at the par-71 Brackenridge Park Golf Course, Souchak flirted with a 59 in the opening round before he finished with a 60. He added rounds of 68-64-65 for a total of 257 for a 72-hole total of 27-under par.

The total gave him a seven-stroke victory over Fred Haas and a scoring mark that has stood the test of time. Donnie Hammond came within one shot of the record in the 1989 Texas Open. It was not until 1998 — 41 years later — that someone finally broke Souchak's record.

The record stood for 41 years before it was broken in 1998.

"When you talk about breaking the 257 mark, you're talking about four consecutive 64s or the equivalent of that," Souchak says. "As tough as the PGA Tour makes courses today, I don't think that will happen."

Aside from the first-round 60 that set an 18-hole record that Al Geiberger later broke, the most memorable thing about Souchak's record was the freezing temperatures during the mid-February week in 1955, which made his record even more remarkable.

Washington Breaks Color Barrier

Minorities have always had a difficult time getting into the game of golf. It is an aristocratic sport with a price tag beyond the means of many would-be minority players.

Until 1954, Houston's public courses were open only to whites but Lone Star Golf Association founder Charles Washington and a group of other black businessmen took the city to the Supreme Court until they were allowed to play. The Supreme Court turned down an appeal by the City of Houston to keep the city courses segregated. On June 3, 1954, Washington fired the first shot by a black man at Memorial Park.

Mancil Davis has made more than 50 aces in his career.

The Arthritis Special

Dick Jackson just wanted to play golf. He didn't realize he was about to forever change the way the game would be played.

The year was 1948 when Jackson developed a severe case of arthritis and doctors told him he was going to have to give up his daily golf game at Houston Country Club.

But Jackson didn't give up so easily. He purchased an industrial vehicle from Cushman and took it to his Dodge dealership, Jackson

Motor Company, and began working on it. He put a swivel seat on the driver's side, a seat in front that carried three people and a compartment in back that carried four bags and a caddie.

There were plenty of objections at the exclusive club when Jackson's gas-powered machine sputtered and spewed smoke up and down the fairways, but he had a doctor's permit. Before long, he was selling The Arthritis Special to other members.

"We never envisioned it was going to take over like it did," said Dick Forester, who was HCC's head pro at the time. "It enabled people to play much longer in life. It's a very big part of a club's income. There's no way we could go back to caddies now."

A Home For Champions

Long before Jack Burke Sr. died, Jimmy Demaret and Jack Burke Jr. had become best friends. When Burke Sr. died, Demaret took the younger Burke under his wing and they traveled the pro tour together.

They were strange bedfellows. Demaret having grown up as a caddie at Hermann Park and Burke, 13 years younger, who grew up among the bluebloods at River Oaks. But they shared the same passion for winning and for being the best.

In 1957, Demaret was 47 and at the end of a Hall of Fame career which saw him win 32 tournaments, including three Masters titles. Burke, who turned pro at the age of 17, was only 34 but already had 16 victories and two Masters titles to his credit.

So they left the tour to give something back to the game by building the ultimate golf club

and promoting the game of golf in Texas. They wanted Houston to become the mecca of golf in the southwest.

It would be called Champions Golf Club, and it would eventually host such major championships as the 1967 Ryder Cup, the 1969 U.S. Open, the 1990 and 1997 PGA Tour Championships and the 1993 U.S. Amateur.

"Just as A.J. Foyt could design a good race car, we knew what the good golfer was looking for from the minute he got out of his car," Burke said. "So that's the way we painted the canvas."

It's A 'Wonderful World'

Houston-based Shell Oil Company was one of the innovators in golf television in 1962 with its series, *Shell's Wonderful World of Golf,* which featured matches between the world's best players on the world's best courses.

Over a period of nine years, 92 matches were held featuring such greats as Sam Snead, Arnold Palmer, Ben Hogan, Byron Nelson, Lee Trevino and Jack Nicklaus in more than 50 locations worldwide. Snead and Hogan met in one of the greatest matches of all time at River Oaks.

Each program had an estimated 10–12 million viewers around the world, giving golf its widest exposure ever and helping turn it into an international game.

The series was hosted by Gene Sarazen and Houston native Jimmy Demaret, both of whom became international ambassadors for golf.

The series was produced by Fred Raphael, who later teamed up with Demaret to establish the Legends of Golf senior event in Austin.

Three Giant Shots For Mankind

Alan Shepard, on Feb. 6, 1971, put Houston on the universal golf map when he traveled 220,000 miles to become the first and only man to hit a golf shot on the surface of the moon.

Shepard hit three shots with a specially made utility tool that had a six-iron head screwed onto it. He hit three surlyn-covered balls with the name of Jack Harden, pro at River Oaks Country Club at the time, engraved on them. The club is now in the USGA Museum in Far Hills, N.J., but the balls are still on the moon.

Shepard was only able to hit the ball with one arm because of the huge backpack on his space suit. While most Americans were still asleep at 4 a.m. CST, Shepard climbed out of the Apollo 14 and told Mission Control he would be trying a "sand trap shot."

Despite the lack of gravity, the balls traveled only 600 yards before they fell back to earth — er, the moon.

In 1971, using a makeshift golf club, Houston's Alan Shepard became the only person to hit a golf shot on the moon.

Hogan's Last Stand

Champions always was one of Ben Hogan's favorite courses.

"It is a magnificent course," he said during the 1967 Ryder Cup. "It takes skill to play it."

Four years later, however, it was the site of an ugly finish to Hogan's awesome career. Hogan was competing in the first round of the 1971 Houston Champions International when he re-injured the left knee that had been shattered in a near-fatal car accident earlier in his career.

The day was May 13, 1971. Hogan was 11-over par through 11 holes, which included a nine on the par-3 fourth hole. This is a treacherous hole that is built on a sharp curve in Cypress Creek and requires players to hit a long carry to reach the green. Hogan hit three balls into the ditch and re-injured his knee while climbing down into it.

He made the turn at 44, but was limping noticeably by the time he reached the 12th. After he hit his tee shot, he sent his caddie after the ball and summoned a cart to take him back to the clubhouse.

The King Of Aces

Mancil Davis has the best aim in golf or is the luckiest man alive. He holds the world record with more than 50 aces in his lifetime.

Davis, an LSU graduate who came to Houston as an assistant pro at The Woodlands and eventually became the director of golf there, broke Art Wall's record of 41 on June 2, 1982, at the age of 38.

During a tournament being hosted by Mitchell Energy, Davis was supposed to hit a shot on the par-3 11th hole with each group as they came through. But he aced the first shot and continued playing the full 18 holes to make the ace official.

"The one thing so amazing with Mancil is his age," says John Everheart, founder of the Dallas-based National Hole-in-One Association. "It's startling to find a person that young with that kind of hole-in-one record."

He made his first ace at the age of 12 and made eight during one 12-month span. He once made three within five days in 1967.

"People ask if there's a secret to making aces," says Davis, who since has made eight more aces. "I do two things differently. I'm trying to make aces. Second, I never use a tee. And I never complain about luck."

The Father Of College Golf

"When you talk about college golf," Keith Fergus says, "the first words out of your mouth are Dave Williams and the University of Houston."

Nobody could have described any better Dave Williams, the one-time chemical engineering professor who stumbled into the golf coaching job at UH in 1952 but retired 35 years later as "the father of college golf."

Williams was a master motiva-

Current PGA Tour stars Steve Elkington and Tray Tyner (second and third from left), and Billy Ray Brown (lower right) gave Dave Williams and the University of Houston their 16th national title at Houston's Bear Creek Masters Course in 1984.

tor and recruiter. He believed he could do anything and made his players feel the same way. That's why he led the Cougars to 16 national titles, four seconds and four third-place finishes — 24 top three finishes in 35 years.

That makes Williams the most successful coach in NCAA history in any sport, with more national championships than UCLA basketball legend John Wooden.

Before he retired in 1987, Williams had produced more than 80 players who went on to a professional career, including Dave Marr, Nick Faldo, Bill Rogers, Fred Couples, Keith Fergus, Steve Elkington, Homero Blancas, Fuzzy Zoeller, Bobby Wadkins, Kermit Zarley, Blaine McCallister, Jim and Babe Hiskey and Ed Fiori.

Williams coached eight NCAA individual champions and seven

runners-up, won 342 tournaments (including an incredible streak of 21 in a row between 1957 and 1960), coached 41 All-Americans and was enshrined in the Texas Golf Hall of Fame.

"It's phenomenal that a man could dedicate his life to that," says Bruce Lietzke.

The Hole Truth

Before the first tee shot was ever fired at Tour 18, Dennis Wilkerson started hearing rumors that he could expect lawsuits to be filed after he built a course in Humble by re-creating 18 of the best holes in the United States.

He sought the legal advice of Fulbright and Jaworski before he spent $5.5 million to build the course and they advised Wilkerson that there could be no patent or copyright on a golf course.

"We certainly didn't jump into this thing half-cocked," Wilkerson said. "Anybody can file a lawsuit, but that doesn't mean they have grounds. The only thing you can't say is that we're Augusta National."

The first rumors involved Augusta, which supposedly planned to sue Tour 18 because Wilkerson re-created Amen Corner, the most widely-known three-hole stretch in all of golf.

But the rumor came and went and Augusta chairman Jack Stephens later dismissed the lawsuit idea at the Masters saying, "imitation is the sincerest form of flattery."

So Wilkerson went on his way, Tour 18 became wildly successful and paid for itself in its first year. And then on December 7 — Pearl Harbor Day — the Japanese dropped a bomb on "America's Greatest 18."

The Japanese-owned Pebble Beach Company filed a lawsuit in U.S. Southern District Court, claiming that Tour 18's re-creation of the 14th hole at Pebble Beach diluted the value of their course.

"What this person has done is take famous holes from famous name courses and tried to make money on it," Pebble Beach attorney Stephen Trattner said.

"We don't want other people like him to get the impression they could copy our course."

The issues were 1) Can you copyright golf course architecture as intellectual property, or are they in the public domain? and 2) Can you use the name of the courses you copied in your marketing material?

The case received national attention in the news media and was tried in 1995 at U.S. District Court in Houston. It lasted nearly a month, with more than 30 witnesses called to testify.

In 1996, Federal Judge David Hitner made a partial ruling against Tour 18, forcing some changes in Harbor Town's lighthouse hole and changes in its marketing and advertising material.

Jeff Maggert and Fred Couples are two of the hundreds of professional golfers who have grown up in Texas, played collegiately in Texas or make their home in Texas.

Greatness is an adjective that is not easily bestowed. Greatness is something that is achieved over time with hard work above and beyond the call of duty.

It is not achieved overnight.

Our selection of 150 Three-Star Courses include many of the state's rising stars that are still striving for recognition as one of the Lone Star State's top courses. It also includes some of the state's most historic courses that once were considered great, but over the years have been bypassed by newer, more modern courses built with bigger budgets and better technology.

With more than 800 courses in Texas, not every golf course can be considered the best. At the same time, that doesn't mean they won't stop trying.

Abilene Country Club

4039 South Treadaway Boulevard
Abilene 79602
915-692-1855
Pro: Allen Botkin
A par-71, 6,310-yard private club.
From Fort Worth, take I-20 west exit at
Buffalo Gap, turn left to Industrial, then
right to Treadaway and left to entrance.

• • •

USGA rating: 70.1
Slope rating: 125
Sand traps: 46
Water holes: 5
Doglegs: 5 left/2 right
Type greens: Bermuda
Record: 64
Designer: George Williams
    and Garrett Gill
Year opened: 1920

• • •

Hole	Par	Yards	Hole	Par	Yards
Out	36	3,230	In	35	3,080

For years, Abilene Country Club was the only game in town. Built in 1920, it has seen the likes of Texas golf legends Tommy Bolt, Charles Coody and Don Cherry cross its fairways.

Over the past seven decades, newer courses have been built in the area, but Abilene Country Club still continues to be the center of attention. In modern days, in place of Bolt, and Coody and Cherry, current PGA Tour stars Mike Standly and Bob Estes learned the game here. Their parents are still members. This club also has hosted the Texas Senior Amateur three times.

The club has undergone several renovations over the years to keep up with the changing times. In 1993, the course was redesigned by George Williams and Garrett Gill. They designed 10 new holes and kept eight of the original holes to produce the current par-71, 6,310-yard layout with open fairways but numerous bunkers coming into play.

No. 9 is the signature hole. It plays 390 yards into the wind and uphill into a green that requires a long carry over a heart-shaped water hazard in front.

No. 5 is one of the prettiest holes on the course. It is only a 360-yard, dogleg left par 4. Most players aim at the three oaks in the right corner of the fairway and try to draw the ball around the corner.

No. 14 is a 190-yard par 3 where the prevailing wind is behind the golfer, making a high soft shot difficult to hit into a green that is protected by water in front and on the left.

Carlton Gipson and J.B. "Bruce" Belin are a pair of Texas A&M graduates who came to the golf business from different paths. Gipson was superintendent at Cherry Hills in Denver and had done some work under some of the game's best architects. Belin was a budding real-estate developer who already had developments started at Hilltop Lakes and Elkins Lake.

It turned out to be a marriage made in Houston, as the two formed a partnership that would make Gipson Houston's most prolific architect and Belin one of Houston's most prolific developers.

April Sound was one of their first projects together, but it still exhibits the same characteristics for which Gipson was known at all his courses. It is a short layout that plays only 6,207 yards from the championship tees. It emphasizes accuracy and is playable for all players. The course is short by modern standards, but the abundance of doglegs and tight placement shots take your driver out of the equation on many holes.

The back nine plays approximately two shots harder than the front and features many of the layout's best holes.

The 437-yard, par-4 No. 15 is probably the hardest hole on the course. It requires good shots to reach the green in regulation, with water in play off the tee and a creek threatening any approach left of the green.

"Probably the neatest thing about the layout is that it's not so hard it beats you to death," says pro David Scott. "It allows you to have a good time."

April Sound Country Club

1000 April Sound Boulevard
Montgomery 77356
409-447-1700
Pro: Chris Lauterbach
A par-71, 6,207-yard semi-private resort. From Houston, take I-45 north past Conroe to Highway 105. Go west seven miles to entrance on right.

• • •

USGA rating: 69.5
Slope rating: 112
Sand traps: 81
Water holes: 7
Doglegs: 5 left/6 right
Type greens: Bermuda
Record: 63
Designer: Carlton Gipson
Year opened: 1972

• • •

Hole	Par	Yards	Hole	Par	Yards
Out	35	2,941	In	36	3,266

Atascocita Country Club

20114 Pinehurst Trail Drive
Atascocita 77346
281-852-8115
Pro: Scott Shelby
A 27-hole private club.
From Houston, take U.S. 59 north to FM
1960. Go east 7.5 miles to Pinehurst.
Turn left on Pinehurst to club entrance.

• • •

USGA rating: 71.7
Slope rating: 121
Sand traps: 33
Water holes: 11
Doglegs: 5 left/2 right
Type greens: Bermuda
Record: 63
Designers: Ralph Plummer
*   Don January/Billy Martindale (1985)*
Year opened: 1957

• • •

Hole	Par	Yards	Hole	Par	Yards
Out	35	3,239	In	36	3,422

Old settlers will tell you that an Indian trail used to wind through the land off the shores of Lake Houston, where Atascocita Country Club sits. The name Atascocita was derived from an old Indian word that meant "swamp land."

In 1956, two families who owned the property hired famed architect Ralph Plummer to build a golf course to enhance the value of the property and attract a buyer willing to invest in the future.

Plummer was one of the top architects of his day, having trained under original Texas golf course architect John Bredemus. Plummer built the original course at Atascocita at the same time he was working on Champions Golf Club 30 minutes away. After it opened, former University of Houston coach Dave Williams selected it as the site of the All-America Intercollegiate tournament. "The Masters of College Golf" featured the top teams in the nation.

In 1973, the development was sold to Johnson-Loggins, who had 17 subdivisions totaling nearly 15,000 acres in Houston at the time. They began a major facelift to the clubhouse and planned 18 new holes to be designed by Don January and Billy Martindale.

The second course was scheduled to be completed in 1974. January and Martindale began carving out the new course when the project was put on hold.

As it turned out, only nine new holes were built but it wasn't until 1985, when the club was purchased by Dallas-based Club Corporation of America.

Balcones Country Club has come a long way since its humble beginnings, but is now one of the largest clubs in the Austin area with two 18-hole golf courses.

The Balcones course first opened in 1956 as a small nine-hole layout. In the past four decades the club has grown into a 36-hole facility with two 18-hole courses known as Balcones and Spicewood. The Balcones Course is a par-70, 6,649-yard layout. It is the easier of the two layouts, with only two water holes.

The No. 1 handicap hole is the long, straight No. 6, a 456-yard par 4. Golfers must thread their tee shots through trees on both sides while avoiding the large oak tree in the landing area. Water comes into play on only two holes, with 26 sand traps and plenty of natural foliage.

Water comes into play on only two holes in the layout, on the 170-yard par-3 15th and the 112-yard par-3 17th. Both holes require a carry over water to reach the green.

What the course lacks in water, it makes up for with its tree-lined fairways. No. 12, for instance, is a 506-yard par 5 that doglegs to the right and has two trees in the fairway with which golfers must contend — both off the tee and on their approach to the green.

"We have two distinct courses here," says head pro Philip Miranda. "The Balcones Course is more of the rolling, friendly type of layout for those who prefer walking. The Spicewood Course is more of a championship-type layout, a little longer and steeper."

Balcones Country Club Old Course

8600 Balcones Club Drive
Austin 78750
512-249-9776
Pro: Philip Miranda
A par-70, 6,649-yard private course that is part of a 36-hole complex. From Austin, take Mopac to Highway 183, then go north to Oceanaire. Go one block to club entrance.

• • •

USGA rating: 71.6
Slope rating: 114
Sand traps: 26
Water holes: 2
Doglegs: 1 left/2 right
Type greens: Bermuda
Record: 63
Designer: Bill Cotton
Year opened: 1961

• • •

Hole	Par	Yards	Hole	Par	Yards
Out	35	3,420	In	35	3,229

Battle Lake Golf Course

Route 1
PO Box 82
Mart 76664
254-876-2837
Pros: Chuck Higgins
A par-72, 6,601-yard public course.
From Dallas, take I-35 to Highway 6
exit and course entrance.

• • •

USGA rating: 70.7
Slope rating: 116
Type greens: Bermuda
Water holes: 11
Doglegs: 2 left/3 right
Sand traps: 2
Designer: N/A
Year opened: 1970s

• • •

Hole	Par	Yards	Hole	Par	Yards
Out	36	3,356	In	36	3,245

In a day and age of golf courses operated by major corporations, Battle Lake Golf Course is a tribute to the old days when they were family operations.

Battle Lake was originally a nine-hole course with sand greens, but was expanded to 18 holes in the 1970s. It is surrounded by cotton farms, wildflowers and grazing cattle.

In 1990, Battle Lake began its last stage of evolution when brothers Chuck and Tim Higgins bought the course and made it something special. Chuck Higgins was a two-year All-America golfer at the University of California-Davis. After graduation he became a sales rep for a manufacturing company until he developed a burning desire to get back into golf. He and his brother decided owning their own golf course would be the best way to combine their golf and business experience. Just because this is a small-town golf course by no means implies it is small time.

No. 3 is a 215-yard par 3 that is one of the toughest par 3s in North Texas. It requires a carry of 190 yards into the wind. Golfers must also contend with a large oak tree that obscures the left side of the green. No. 16 is a 415-yard par 4 that opens with a blind tee shot and requires a downhill, downwind approach to a small green with a lack behind it.

No. 17 is Battle Lake's signature hole. It is a 370-yard, dogleg right par 4 that starts and finishes at the lake. The green is protected by water in the front and in back with bluebonnets everywhere in the springtime.

Deer Park is known as the birthplace of Texas, since in 1836 this is where Sam Houston led the battle for Texas' independence from Mexico against Santa Anna and his troops.

The San Jacinto Monument still stands here as a sentinel in memory of that battle.

Deer Park also is known as the home of 1995 Miss Universe Chelsi Smith.

More recently, Deer Park is known as home of the Battleground at Deer Park, a city-owned daily-fee course that takes its players on a hole-by-hole lesson in Texas history.

In November 1993, Deer Park approved an $8.25 million bond issue to construct the golf course. The course opened to the general public on April 21, the 160th anniversary of the Battle of San Jacinto. The course pays homage to the battle, which won independence for the Republic of Texas, and provides its players with a walking history lesson in Texas history.

Holes are named after Sam Houston, Santa Anna and Twin Sisters, a pair of twin cannons that helped win the battle.

The course could best be described as a links course with narrow fairways surrounded by heavy rough and lots of water.

The prevailing coastal winds from the southeast increases the difficulty because it will involve driving into the wind on five of the 18 holes, including the 175-yard par 3 No. 8, which requires a carry over a lake and a beautiful waterfall, that guards the front of the shared green.

Battleground at Deer Park

1600 Georgia
Deer Park 77536
281-478-5898
Pro: Ken Kelly
A par-72, 6,943-yard public course.
From Houston, take Highway 225 to Deer Park, exit Center Street. Turn right to Georgia and right on Georgia one mile to entrance on the right.

• • •

USGA rating: 73.6
Slope rating: 130
Sand traps: 38
Water holes: 1
Doglegs: 2 left/1 right
Type greens: Bermuda
Record: N/A
Designer: Tom Knickerbocker
Year opened: 1996

• • •

Hole	Par	Yards	Hole	Par	Yards
Out	36	3,462	In	36	3,480

Bay Forest Golf Course

201 Bay Forest Drive
La Porte 77571
281-471-4653
Pro: Alex Osmond
A par-72, 6,756-yard public course.
From Houston, take Highway 225 east to
Highway 146. Go south to Fairmont
Parkway. Turn east to South Broadway,
then turn south to course entrance.

• • •

USGA rating: 72.4
Slope rating: 126
Sand traps: 28
Water holes: 16
Doglegs: 6 left/2 right
Type greens: Bermuda
Record: 66
Designer: Jay Riviere
Year opened: 1988

• • •

Hole	Par	Yards	Hole	Par	Yards
Out	35	3,159	In	37	3,597

Municipal golf courses were popular in the early days of golf. Cities were glad to use a piece of undeveloped land to build a golf course or park for their residents to enjoy.

But those were the days before golf courses became so expensive to build and maintain. In the past 10 years, most of the new golf course development has been in the form of privately owned, daily-fee layouts.

Bay Forest is a rare exception to that trend. It opened in August 1988 and is operated by the city of La Porte. The course was designed by Houston-based architect Jay Riviere.

If you don't like to mess with water, perhaps you should find another course to play. Water channels wind their way through the heavily wooded front nine and open up into larger lakes on the more open back nine. In all, water comes into play on 16 holes. Hazards come into play off the tee on 12 holes and the last four require long carries over water.

The most difficult holes are on the back nine, where players must deal with a prevailing south wind. No. 15 plays 451 yards and many golfers may have difficulty carrying the water off the tee. Water runs down the left side and protects the front of the green.

No. 18 is a good finishing hole, a 452-yard par 4. This hole also requires another big tee shot then another long second shot over water, giving players plenty of chances to head to the 19th hole on a sour note. Only accomplished players will be able to get home in two.

Bayou Golf Club is the crown jewel of Texas City's $1.688 million parks expansion program that voters approved in 1970. The city fathers went all out on the project and hired Houston-based architect Joe Finger to convert the flat 200-acre site on the bank of Moses Bayou into a championship layout.

Finger designed somewhat of a links-style course with elevated greens and tee boxes, but the course is relatively flat and open. The course is built on Moses Bayou and water comes into play on 12 holes. There are 23 sand traps to demand accuracy, but the biggest enemy can be the winds off Galveston Bay.

There are few "gimme" birdies here. All par 5s are 500 yards or more, including the 580-yard No. 15, which is a double-dogleg and almost impossible to reach in two without a tailwind. There are four par 4s longer than 420 yards, including the 435-yard No. 10 and the 475-yard No. 17, where a lake is a threat off the tee and approach.

The 420-yard, par-4 No. 6 is the toughest hole. Players are forced to lay-up short of the bayou, then hit their approach over the bayou to a small green.

The 475-yard, dogleg left par-4 No. 17 also presents a challenge off the tee and on the approach. Off the tee, players must negotiate their drive between the bayou on the left without driving through the fairway into the lake. On the approach, players must use a long iron to an elevated green protected in front and on the right water.

Bayou Golf Club
2800 Ted Dudley Drive
Texas City 77590
409-948-8362
Pro: Tom Ashworth
A par-72, 6,835-yard public course.
From Houston, take I-45 south to FM 1764, turn east to Highway 146, turn north to 25th Avenue, turn west to Ted Dudley Drive.

• • •

USGA rating: 71
Slope rating: 114
Sand traps: 23
Water holes: 12
Doglegs: 5 left/5 right
Type greens: Bermuda
Record: 63
Designer: Joe Finger
Year opened: 1974

• • •

Hole	Par	Yards	Hole	Par	Yards
Out	36	3,331	In	36	3,425

Beaumont Country Club

5355 Pine Street
Beaumont 77703
409-898-7011
Pro: Brian White
A par-72, 6,418-yard private club.
From I-10, take Highway 69 north, turn
right on Lucas, Lucas stops at Pine
Street, turn left on Pine Street.
Club is on left.

• • •

USGA rating: 69.7
Slope rating: 111
Sand traps: 55
Water holes: 1
Doglegs: 2 left/2 right
Type greens: Bermuda
Record: 61
Designer: Alex Findlay
Year opened: 1906

• • •

Hole	Par	Yards	Hole	Par	Yards
Out	36	3,210	In	36	3,204

Beaumont will forever live in American history as the home of Spindletop. In school history classes, most of us saw the old black and white footage of black gold spewing up from the earth in one of the biggest oil finds in American history.

Talk about striking it rich.

After that discovery on January 10, 1901, major oil companies set up refineries and drilling rigs across the country side and people migrated to Beaumont from all over the nation to take part in the Texas Black Gold Rush. Many of those who came, came to stay.

Beaumont is still built on the oil industry, and the economy has historically gone up and down with the price of oil. Refineries are still the area's major employer.

But Beaumont also is home of the state's oldest existing golf course. Eight years after Galveston Country Club, which was wiped out by a hurricane in 1900, built the first club in Texas, Beaumont Country Club opened in 1906.

The course was designed by legendary architect Alex Findlay, who built the course on a rare swing through Texas during which he also built San Antonio Country Club in 1908. By its very nature, Beaumont Country Club was a club built with black gold. To this day, it is an old-line club comprised of families who trace their origins to the Spindletop days. One of those is the family of W.C. Tyrrell Jr. They were in the oil business and owned much of the land around Beaumont. The city named a golf course after W.C. Tyrrell Sr.

olf course architecture has evolved over the years into a high science, requiring a knowledge not only of golf but of landscape architecture, agronomy and engineering. It has come full circle from the days of the natural setting of St. Andrews to the contrived-style architecture of PGA West back to the traditional, more natural approach.

Architects will never go back to using mules and frescoes, mind you, but Jay Riviere and Dave Marr never got caught up in that diabolical trend in the first place. They always have been traditionalists since their days of working at the famed Winged Foot Golf Club. And now that their peers are returning to their roots, Riviere and Marr are on the front lines showing them the way.

Their latest project is a private club on an 800-acre site about 40 minutes north of downtown that opened in 1993. Riviere has built more than 20 courses in Houston, but gets giddy when he talks about Bentwood. He says it may be every bit as good as The Falls, which is in the Texas Top 100.

Don't let the term naturalist fool you. While the site is densely covered with a combination of pines and hardwoods, Riviere and Marr moved more than 500,000 yards of dirt before they finished. Naturalist doesn't mean they play the land as it lies, but make it look natural when they are finished.

"I'm really excited about this piece of property," Riviere says. "What Dave and I want to do here is return to the more natural layout. We've always been traditionalists anyway."

Bentwood Golf Club

19980 Bentwood Oaks Drive
Porter 77365
281-354-GOLF
Dir.: Phil Davis
A par-72, 6,903-yard semi-private club.
From Houston, take Highway 59 north to FM 1314, U-turn under freeway, look for tower at club entrance.

• • •

USGA rating: 71.4
Slope rating: 125
Sand traps: 58
Water holes: 5
Doglegs: 2 left, 2 right
Type greens: Bermuda
Record: 64
Designer: Jay Riviere and Dave Marr
Year opened: 1992

• • •

Hole	Par	Yards	Hole	Par	Yards
Out	36	3,446	In	36	3,457

Berry Creek Country Club

30500 Berry Creek Drive
Georgetown 78628
512-930-4615
Pro: Michael Grindle
An par-72, 6,648-yard private club.
From Austin take I-35 north to Highway
266, take first left to Berry Creek Drive
and club entrance.

• • •

USGA rating: 71.6
Slope rating: 126
Sand traps: 30
Water holes: 6
Doglegs: 6 left/6 right
Type greens: Bermuda
Record: 65
Designer: Carl Doering
Year opened: 1986

• • •

Hole	Par	Yards	Hole	Par	Yards
Out	36	3,352	In	36	3,296

Jack Haby and Ed Kitzer never did any hard labor, but they have spent some time working at a rock pile just north of Austin.

When Berry Creek first opened in 1986 in the bedroom community of Georgetown, it was named after the tributary that winds through the property. Carl Doering designed the original 18 before Haby, the club's first pro, and Kitzer decided to turn some old limestone quarries into two new holes that now rank among the best in Central Texas.

No. 8 is a 175-yard par 3. The tee box is on top of the quarry and requires golfers to hit over a large lake. The quarry wall on the other side of the green provides a dramatic backdrop.

No. 9 is a 326-yard par 4.

While some gambling big-hitters might be tempted to go for the green, the fairway tightens into a small landing area and the green is protected by a water hazard that starts 35 yards in front of the green. Most players choose to lay up over the first lake and leave themselves about 140 yards over the second lake to the green.

The back nine is tighter with trees lining both sides of the fairways. There are 30 sand traps spread out along the course with two large lakes coming into play on six different holes. The greens and fairways include different strains of Bermuda.

The par-3 12th might be one of the prettiest on the course. The golfer has to thread his ball through a narrow chute in the trees then avoid a lake on the left side of a narrow green.

Bluebonnet Hill — like its blueberry sibling — was designed with enough thrills and frills for everyone. Opened in 1991, the layout designed by architect Jeff Brauer has more than exceeded its mission. The short layout provides ample birdie opportunities if — no pun intended — you are good or you get lucky.

Brauer learned the design trade under the tutelage of Chicago-based Dick Nugent, whose claim to fame is Kemper Lakes Golf Club, which hosted the 1989 PGA Championship.

Golfers will find plenty of rolling, Hill Country landscape on this 6,500-yard, par-72 layout. To make up for the lack of trees, Brauer used grass bunkers and mounding around the greens to create a short-game challenge for golfers who miss the greens.

"The countryside, along with the few trees and artful contouring, create quite an aesthetic challenge," Brauer said. To shoot a good score, golfer smust also keep the ball in play off the tee."

The signature hole is the par-5 12th, measuring 488 yards. The gambler will be eager to go for the green in two, but there is plenty of trouble to ruin the best-laid plans. A small pond guards the landing area on the left and the green has three different levels. A second shot must find the proper tier or the golfer will be looking at a possible three-putt. In fact, the greens could be the most challenging part of the course.

All greens are tiered, meaning "you have to hit the green at the right place," pro Jeff Wilson says.

Bluebonnet Hill Golf Course

9100 Decker Lane
Austin 78724
512-272-4228
Pro: Jeff Wilson
A par-72, 6,500-yard public course
From Austin, take Highway 290 east
to Decker Lane, course is on right.

• • •

USGA rating: 70
Slope rating: 113
Sand traps: 21
Water holes: 6
Doglegs: 5 left/4 right
Type greens: Bermuda
Record: 65
Designer: Jeff Brauer
Year opened: 1991

• • •

Hole	Par	Yards	Hole	Par	Yards
Out	36	3,264	In	36	3,239

Brackenridge Park Golf Course

2315 Avenue B
San Antonio 78215
210-226-5612
Pro: Richard Hocott
A par-72, 6,182-yard public course.
From San Antonio, go north on
Broadway past Josephine, left after
ButterKrust Bakery, course is on left.

• • •

USGA rating: 67
Slope rating: 118
Sand traps: N/A
Water holes: 6
Doglegs: 3 left/4 right
Type greens: Bermuda
Record: 59
Designer: A.W. Tillinghast
Year opened: 1916

• • •

Hole	Par	Yards	Hole	Par	Yards
Out	36	3,127	In	36	3,058

San Antonio is known for its important place in Texas history. It was here the Battle of the Alamo was waged and became the rallying cry for Texas independence. Those were the days when Sam Houston, Davey Crockett and William Travis helped tamed the wilderness and gave Texas a reputation for being a maverick place that is home of the free and brave.

In the same way but to a slightly different degree, the birthright of Texas golf can also be traced to San Antonio. While the roots of Texas history go back to the Alamo, pioneers of a different kind helped bring golf to Texas a few years later.

Brackenridge Park Golf Course is the oldest 18-hole public course in the state, designed by legendary architect A.W. Tillinghast in 1916. This was where Jug McSpadden shot the first score of 59 in a PGA event in 1939 and where Mike Souchak, in 1955, set the Tour record of 27-under-par 257 in a 72-hole event. The record stood for 32 years.

In the early 1920s, there was very little professional golf in America and none outside the Eastern seaboard. John Bredemus, along with *San Antonio News* sports editor Jack O'Brien, dreamed up a professional tournament to attract the leading pros of the day to San Antonio and Brackenridge. The first Texas Open was held in 1922 and won by Bob MacDonald.

Today, despite modern advancements in equipment, Brackenridge has stood the test of time and is alive and well.

Time has a way of changing things at a country club. Members come and go, neighborhoods change, the golf course suffers from Mother Nature and the club suffers hard economic times.

To have staying power, a club must have the hindsight to remain true to its traditions and history, but the foresight to see the future and the guts to make changes to keep up with the times.

It is that combination of character traits that has enabled BraeBurn Country Club to roll with the punches for seven decades to become the fourth-oldest, not to mention one of the most elite, clubs in Houston.

BraeBurn was built in 1926 by architect John Bredemus. It was called Colonial Country Club, but like many other clubs during the Depression, the club was lost to foreclosure in 1929. In 1931, River Oaks pro Jack Burke Sr. formed a new group that bought the club and renamed it BraeBurn.

While Bredemus went on to re-use the Colonial Country Club name in 1936 at his new course in Fort Worth, the members at BraeBurn continued to fight for survival through tough economic times. In 1942, Demaret helped sell war bonds on the 18th green along with Byron Nelson, Bing Crosby, Bob Hope and Johnny Weismuller. And in 1952, the club hosted the NCAA Championships.

The course was renovated in 1992 when architect Carlton Gipson moved 300,000 yards of dirt to create elevation changes of up to 20 feet. "I'm a little bit partial," Gipson said, "but I believe this is my best work."

BraeBurn Country Club

8101 Bissonnet
Houston 77040
713-774-8788
Pro: Breene Cantwell
A par-72, 6,808-yard private club.
From Houston, take U.S. 59 south to Bissonnet, then turn left. Club is between Gessner and Fondren.

• • •

USGA rating: 72.1
Slope rating: 126
Sand traps: 47
Water holes: 12
Doglegs: 4 left/6 right
Type greens: Bermuda
Record: N/A
*Designers: John Bredemus
    and Carlton Gipson (1990)*
Year opened: 1926

• • •

Hole	Par	Yards	Hole	Par	Yards
Out	36	3,368	In	36	3,440

Brookhaven
Country Club
Champions Course

3333 Golfing Green
Dallas 75234
972-241-2761
Pro: Bill Dowling
A 54-hole private club.
From Dallas, take I-35E north to I-635.
Go east to Webb Chapel, then north to
Golfing Green and east to entrance.

• • •

USGA rating: 71.2
Slope rating: 122
Sand traps: 35
Water holes: 9
Doglegs: 4 left/3 right
Type greens: Bermuda
Record: N/A
Designer: Press Maxwell
Year opened: 1957

• • •

Hole	Par	Yards	Hole	Par	Yards
Out	36	3,236	In	36	3,299

With 54 holes of golf, Brookhaven Country Club was designed to offer a golf course for everyone, from professional to the beginning player.

Architect Press Maxwell designed three courses all at the same time in 1959. The Masters is Brookhaven's most demanding tests, and hosted the LPGA's Civitan Classic from 1972–77.

The President's Course is designed for seniors and beginning players.

That brings us to the Champions Course at Brookhaven, which fits somewhere in between. It's challenging enough for good players, but not so demanding that it discourages beginners.

To have a 54-hole facility was a trailblazing concept for 1959, and nearly four decades later it remains the largest club — public or private — in North Texas and one of the largest in the state. Joe Black, former president of the PGA of America, was the club's long-time pro and he made sure Brookhaven always set the standard for all country clubs to follow.

The 6,535-yard, par-72 Champions layout is more than 300 yards shorter and a few strokes easier than the Masters Course, and Maxwell gave players a good birdie opportunity at the 456-yard par-5 fourth hole, but the other par 5s are all over 500 yards and are more demanding.

Most of the par 3s are shorter, requiring a medium to short iron to reach the green.

No. 10 is a 446-yard par 4 that presents golfers with a tough two-shot challenge to start the back nine.

You know the place is big when, after you finish your round of golf and you sign your scorecard, you head for a drink at the 55th Hole, not the 19th.

No, you didn't make a wrong turn. You're just at Brookhaven Country Club, which in 1959 became a trailblazing pioneer. When it opened with three golf courses Brookhaven became the largest golf complex — public or private — in Texas.

Since then, a lot of big names have walked these fairways. Byron Nelson was chairman of the advisory board. Former PGA president Joe Black was the longtime head pro. It once was home of the LPGA's Civitan Golf Classic. And PGA Tour pros Scott Verplank and Andrew Magee.

As president of the PGA of America, an organization of 13,000 professionals around the nation, Black was always obligated to lead by example. And Brookhaven always set the standard for all country clubs to follow.

Long before the advent of multiple-course, golf course complexes, Brookhaven set the standard when architect Press Maxwell was hired in 1959 to build three 18-hole golf courses known as the Champions, Masters and Presidents courses.

Brookhaven was the site of the Civitan Open, the LPGA's annual stop from 1972–77. Jane Blalock won the first event at over Kathy Whitworth with a 5-under total for the $4,950 top prize.

Among the most difficult holes on the Masters course are the 591-yard, par-5 third; the 453-yard, par-4 ninth; and the 468-yard, par-4 13th.

Brookhaven Country Club Masters Course

3333 Golfing Green
Dallas 75234
972-241-2761
Pro: Bill Dowling
A 54-hole private club.
From Dallas, take I-35E north to I-635.
Go east to Webb Chapel, then north to
Golfing Green and east to entrance.

• • •

USGA rating: 72.9
Slope rating: 130
Sand traps: 62
Water holes: 6
Doglegs: 4 left/3 right
Type greens: Bentgrass
Record: 62
Designer: Press Maxwell
Year opened: 1957

• • •

Hole	Par	Yards	Hole	Par	Yards
Out	36	3,542	In	36	3,324

Canyon West Golf Club

4701 Quanah Hill Road
Weatherford 76087
817-599-4653
Pro: Joe Meador
A par-72, 6,653-yard public course.
From Fort Worth, take I-20 west to
Dennis Road (exit 403). Go to first stop
sign, turn left across freeway, go west
on service road 2.5 miles to entrance.

• • •

USGA rating: 71.0
Slope rating: 124
Type greens: Bermuda
Water holes: 10
Doglegs: 3 left/2 right
Sand traps: 34
Record: N/A
Designers: Wes and Stan Mickle
Year opened: 1997

• • •

Hole	Par	Yards	Hole	Par	Yards
Out	36	3,315	In	36	3,338

Equine enthusiasts know Wes and Stan Mickles as some of the top equine breeders in the nation. Now, they are known to North Texas golfers as golf course owner-operators.

After breeding horses for three generations at the Mickle's Valley View Ranch just outside of Weatherford, the father-son duo decided to turn part of their land into a golf course as the centerpiece for an exclusive residential homes in the $2 million price range.

So what did the Mickles know about the golf business? Only what they learned in years of playing golf courses all over the world. They built this golf course from the eyes of an amateur, with play ability the overriding factor.

What they didn't know about golf course design, Mother Nature did for them. Canyon West was hand-crafted from this rugged piece of North Texas Hill Country and offers dramatic mesas, deep canyons, eight lakes and miles of creeks. Hundreds of species of native prairie grasses and wildflowers run the length of a natural wildlife refuge and golf course. It features spectacular views from Parker County's highest summit (elevation 1,042 feet), and the fairways wind through century-old live oaks along with native pecans, red oaks, elm, Mexican plum and a few unusually large mesquite trees.

The par-72, 6,653-yard layout opened in 1997, offering a great combination of creative, play ability, elevation changes and spectacular scenery. The course allows for run-up shots to the greens and has wide fairways and large undulating greens.

One of Fort Worth's newest public golf courses is actually one of the oldest. Built over four decades ago, it was open only to military personnel until 1993.

The course has a history that is rich in Texas golf. Ben Hogan hit the first tee shot to open the course in the early 1950s. Legendary players such as Byron Nelson and Charles Coody, who holds the course record of 63, head a long list of great players who have matched their skills here.

Brooks-Baine Golf took over the facility in 1993 after government downsizing of Carswell Air Force Base. Mark Brooks is a Fort Worth native and five-time winner on the PGA Tour. Burt Baine has been golf professional at Cherry Hills in Denver as well as Ridglea Country Club and Mira Vista Golf Club in Fort Worth.

The course is in a natural setting, with many huge oak trees lining the fairways and several creeks and springs meandering through the course to give it a mystical feel. Four demanding par 3s require a variety of clubs. The par-4 closing holes on each nine test your golfing skills as well as your course management discipline.

The most memorable and one of the toughest holes is the par-4 ninth. The hole is listed at 425 yards from the back tees, but at least 225 yards of that is uphill. A creek crosses the fairway, forcing the golfer to either lay-up or try to cross it with a drive. The green is surrounded by sand traps, making accuracy on the approach a must.

No. 18 plays 421 yards from the back tees. Water crosses the fairway of this gentle dogleg left.

Carswell Golf Club

6520 White Settlement Road
Fort Worth 76114
817-738-8402
Pro: Stack Bowers
A par-71, 6,568-yard public course.
From Fort Worth, take I-30 west to Roaring Springs Road, then north about 3 miles to course entrance on the left.

• • •

USGA rating: 72.5
Slope rating: 126
Sand traps: 13
Water holes: 11
Doglegs: 4 left/3 right
Type greens: Bermuda
Record: 63
Designers: Charles Akey
Year opened: 1950

• • •

Hole	Par	Yards	Hole	Par	Yards
Out	35	2,989	In	36	3,579

Cedar Creek Golf Course

8250 Vista Colina
San Antonio 78255
210-695-5050
Pro: Steve Lennon
*A par-72, 7,150-yard public course.
From San Antonio, take I-10 west to
FM 1604, go west to Kyle Seal Parkway,
turn right to Vista Colina and
left to course entrance.*

• • •

USGA Rating: 73.4
Slope rating: 132
Sand traps: 34
Water holes: 5
Doglegs: 3 left/5 right
Type greens: Bermuda
Record: 65
Designer: Ken Dye
Year opened: 1990

• • •

Hole	Par	Yards	Hole	Par	Yards
Out	36	3,570	In	36	3,580

City golf courses are typically flat, functional and underwhelming. Pay your money and get a place in line.

Most city-owned courses in Texas were built in the 1960s and '70s, when money was easier to come by and courses cost only about $300,000 to build. Now, the price tag runs about $3 million and city governments have higher priorities.

But San Antonio's Cedar Creek is anything but stereotypical. Owned by the city of San Antonio, the layout designed in 1989 by architect Ken Dye is carved out of limestone hillsides, oak thickets and creeks.

Golfers must overcome waterfalls, large natural areas and fairways going up and down. The course is a visual treat than can play tricks on your eyes as well as your scorecard.

"I don't like to use the words, but this course has country-club quality," said Harold Henk, San Antonio's director of golf. "I don't know where you could find a nicer public course."

While that high praise is somewhat debatable, apparently the local golf community agrees. Cedar Creek was voted the top public course in South Texas in the first *San Antonio Express-News* golf survey in 1992. Again, high praise for a course that competed against resorts and daily-fee layouts.

The first hole, a 395-yard par 4, gives golfers a taste of what to expect during the round. The hole slopes down more than 100 feet with a large hill all the way down on the right and an oak thicket left of the green.

W hen it comes to Dallas golf, Cedar Crest Golf Course is like an ancient artifact like the Holy Grail or Dead Sea Scrolls. It is hallowed ground.

It was the host of the first Dallas Open in 1926. The following year, the best players in the world came to Dallas to play in the PGA Championship.

It all started back in 1917 when banker Sol Dreyfus selected a prime piece of real estate with rolling terrain, heavy tree coverage and panoramic views of a downtown Dallas skyline that had yet to come. He hired legendary architect A.W. Tillinghast, who built a demanding course that required accuracy with its tree-lined fairways and postage stamp greens.

Nine years after the course opened, Dreyfus put up a purse and hosted the first Dallas Open. The course received such rave reviews, that he offered $12,000 to bring the PGA Championship back to Dallas the following year. The PGA accepted.

Golf fans turned out in droves to see the likes of Walter Hagen. Tommy Armour, Gene Sarazen and Harry "Lighthorse" Cooper compete in the match-play competition. In the end, Hagen emerged champion and it is interesting to note that a little boy who was nipping at Hagen's heels was a kid named Byron Nelson.

Shortly afterward, however, Cedar Crest fell on hard times during the Depression and World War II. It was sold to the city in 1947 for $130,000.

The ghosts of Hagen still lingers, and the layout has stood the test of time and technology.

Cedar Crest Golf Course

1800 Southerland
Dallas 75203
214-670-7615
Pro: Leonard Jones
A par-72, 6,550-yard public course.
From Dallas, take I-35E south to Illinois Avenue, then turn east to Southerland. Go north on Southerland to entrance.

• • •

USGA rating: 71
Slope rating: 121
Sand traps: 8
Water holes: 4
Doglegs: 2 left/7 right
Type greens: Bermuda
Record: 63
Designer: A.W. Tillinghast
Year opened: 1917

• • •

Hole	Par	Yards	Hole	Par	Yards
Out	36	3,119	In	35	3,021

Chester W. Ditto Municipal

801 Brown Boulevard
Arlington 76011
817-275-5941
Pro: Michael Krsnak
A par-72, 6,661-yard public course.
From Dallas, take I-30 west to Collins
Street, then north on Collins to Brown.
Turn east on Brown to entrance.

• • •

USGA rating: 72.1
Slope rating: 117
Sand traps: 14
Water holes: 9
Doglegs: 2 left/4 right
Type greens: Bermuda
Record: 67
Designer: Ken Killian and Dick Nugent
Year opened: 1982

• • •

Hole	Par	Yards	Hole	Par	Yards
Out	36	3,354	In	36	3,307

As a Chicago native who grew up working in the caddie shack at the ultra exclusive Bob O'Link Golf Club, architect Dick Nugent had an idea what great golf courses are supposed to look like.

Nugent was a product of the environment. Having walked the fairways of a Donald Ross layout time and again, he pictured tree-lined fairways and greens with subtle undulations that places a premium on accuracy and the short game.

But when it came to Texas golf, Nugent didn't have a clue what it was all about. Nugent, who was on the board of the society of golf course architects, called Texan Joe Black, to get his advice.

"Well, there's not a whole lot of great golf courses," Black said at the time, "but there are a hellu-va lot of great golfers."

In 1982, Nugent received his first taste of Texas when he was hired to design this course for the city of Arlington.

"We tried to work within the city's parameters," Nugent said. "It's a little tighter than I like for a public golf course. God, I thought some of those parks people were going to chain themselves to some of those trees. You just don't want to be off the fairway."

Among the more memorable holes at Ditto are the 185-yard, par-3 No. 3. With a long iron in their hand, players must calculate cross winds to reach the green.

And then there's the 427-yard, par-4 13th, which is a slight double-dogleg that requires a long-iron approach to a green nestled in a grove of trees.

When Barton Creek opened in the 1980s, it set a new standard for all other resorts and private clubs to follow. Big name architects. Posh facilities. Scenic surroundings. In other words, something for everyone. Well, everyone, that is, who could afford it.

Several years later, a group of investors decided it was time to take golf in a different direction. So instead of building another country club, they decided to make that same type of country-club atmosphere available to the masses.

Circle C Ranch was born.

The layout, designed by noted architect Jay Morrish, opened in 1992 and was named one of the best new courses of 1992 in a statewide poll. It was five years in the making, however, since ground was originally broken in 1987 before funding and environmental problems slowed the project to a halt. Morrish finally got the green light to complete construction in 1991.

Unlike its posh neighbor Barton Creek, Circle C is flatter and not as difficult. There is some water and Hill Country nature areas, but most fairways have wide landing areas and the greens are fairly large. Morrish scattered 57 bunkers throughout the layout to force golfers to be focused off the tee. Most of the par 5s play downwind and reachable in 2 shots. The par-5 No. 2 and No. 11 holes are just over 500 yards, giving big hitters an eagle chance if they can avoid the pot bunkers and tree-filled thickets.

The signature hole is No. 13, a 168-yard par 3. It features the only forced carry over water.

Circle C Golf Club

11511 FM 1826
Austin 78737
512-280-5213
Pro: Mark Lewis
A par-72, 6,859-yard public course. From Austin, take Mopac South until it turns into Highway 45 then go another 1.5 miles to course on left.

• • •

USGA rating: 72.7
Slope rating: 122
Sand traps: 57
Water holes: 5
Doglegs: 6 left/5 right
Type greens: Bermuda
Record: 65
Designer: Jay Morrish
Year opened: 1992

• • •

Hole	Par	Yards	Hole	Par	Yards
Out	36	3,388	In	36	3,471

Clear Lake Golf Course

1202 Reseda Drive
Houston 77062
281-488-0252
Pro: Marc Maley
A par-72, 6,757-yard public course.
From Houston, take I-45 south to Bay
Area Boulevard, go east to Diana, turn
left to Reseda and entrance.

• • •

USGA rating: 70.5
Slope rating: 111
Sand traps: 47
Water holes: 4
Doglegs: 3 left/2 right
Type greens: Bermuda
Record: 62
Designers: Jay Riviere
*   and Milton Coggins*
Year opened: 1964

• • •

Hole	Par	Yards	Hole	Par	Yards
Out	36	3,362	In	36	3,395

Shortly after John Glenn became the first American to orbit the Earth and NASA selected Houston to be the control center of the U.S. Space Program, Friendswood Development started one of the nation's first master-planned communities at Clear Lake City.

Part of the development included the construction of an exclusive, first-class country club that would serve the needs of the professional community. Friendswood was a joint venture of Humble Oil and the late Del Webb, the Arizona developer and former co-owner of the New York Yankees.

Webb sold his interest when Clear Lake City failed to develop as quickly as first planned. The first nine opened for play in 1964 and the course was completed in 1967 on 200 acres of open prairie less than two miles from the Johnson Space Center. When they turned the first shovel, there was only a mound here and there and a few saplings.

The first nine was designed by Milton Coggins. Houston-based architect Jay Riviere was called in to design the second nine, his first solo project after an apprenticeship under George Fazio.

The club struggled in its early years as a private entity, but golf pro Johnny Maca arrived in the late 1960s to help steer it into the future. Knowing it was necessary to keep players coming to keep the club open, he did a major cosmetic job by planting hundreds of trees that have turned the once open prairie into a formidable challenge. The course, now open to the public, is owned and operated by Dallas-based GolfCorp.

Texas architect Dave Bennett has done most of his work in Texas on daily-fee and municipal golf courses, but in 1982 he got a chance to build a golf course for an exclusive private club.

The Club at Cimarron is the crown jewel as far as country clubs in the Rio Grande Valley. Even though it is not located in the big city, he built a golf course that compares favorably with any course you'll find in the state - whether it is in a big town or a small town.

The Club at Cimarron is a par-72, 6,821-yard layout where water provides much scenery, but also is the golfer's worst enemy as it comes into play on 16 holes. The fairways are plush and the greens are elevated.

The course, which plays to a slope rating of 129 from the back tees, starts off with a 532-yard par 5 that will give some players a chance to get a birdie in the bag to start the round.

The hardest hole on the layout is No. 13, a 434-yard par 4 that plays uphill directly into the prevailing wind.

Three holes later, golfers are faced with another difficult two-shot challenge at the 423-yard, par-4 16th hole.

The signature hole is No. 18, a scenic par 5 with an island tee box and water running all the way down the left side of the fairway and coming into play on all three shots into the green.

Club at Cimarron is owned and operated by Dallas-based Club Corporation of America.

Club at Cimarron

1200 Shary Road
Mission 78572
956-581-7408
Pro: Craig Woolly
A par-72, 6,821-yard private club.
Take Expressway 83 to Shary Road, turn left to course entrance.

• • •

USGA rating: 129
Slope rating: 71.9
Sand traps: 54
Water holes: 18
Doglegs: 4 left/3 right
Type greens: Bermuda
Record: 62
Designers: Dave Bennett
Year opened: 1985

• • •

Hole	Par	Yards	Hole	Par	Yards
Out	36	3,492	In	36	3,429

Club at Mission Dorado

No. 1 Mission Boulevard
Odessa 79765
915-561-8811
Pro: Blake Bingham
An par-72, 7,135-yard private club.
From Fort Worth, take I-20 to Warfield
(exit 126), right to Highway 80, turn
left to Faudree Road, right to Dorado
Drive, then right on Dorado to entrance.

• • •

USGA rating: 72.5
Slope rating: 115
Sand traps: 56
Water holes: 6
Type greens: Bentgrass
Doglegs: 3 left/3 right
Record: 62
Designer: Dick Nugent
Year opened: 1983

• • •

Hole	Par	Yards	Hole	Par	Yards
Out	36	3,580	In	36	3,555

Good golf courses are about as few and far between in West Texas as big cities, so when the Club at Mission Dorado was built by architect Dick Nugent in 1983 — it immediately became one of the best courses in West Texas if not the state.

The long 7,135-yard, par-72 layout, where winds reign supreme, has hosted the Nike Permian Basin Open since 1990, challenging some of the rising young American golf stars.

Nugent is a Chicago-based architect who grew up playing and caddying on traditional, tree-lined courses.

It was not until he conferred with longtime Texas pro Joe Black in the mid-1970s that he brought his unique architectural style to the Texas panhandle.

"There are not a lot of great golf courses," Black told Nugent, "but there are whole lot of great golfers."

With a better knowledge of Texas' supply and demand for good golf courses, Nugent produced a smooth, links-style layout where he had to move a large amount of earth just to create some movement to the otherwise flat terrain.

To help compensate for the length of the layout and the omnipresent winds, Nugent designed greens that average 8,000 square feet to give golfers a larger target to hit on their approach from the fairways.

Just getting on the greens, however, is only half the battle. The bentgrass greens are undulating and fast.

Before they changed the name to the Club at Sonterra, and to the South Course and to the Deer Canyon Course, this golf course built in 1960 was known as Canyon Creek Country Club.

Twenty-five years before gas station moguls Tom Turner Sr. decided to built his dream course and country club to entertain his friends, architect Press Maxwell had first dibs on the property when he designed a 6,535-yard layout. But it was not until Turner came along and built his dream course that anyone took notice.

Turner hired architects Robert von Hagge and Bruce Devlin to build the Club at Sonterra. What evolved was nothing short of a masterpiece, and the 7,070-yard layout still ranks among the best courses in the state. The club gained instant popularity and grew so quickly that Turner annexed the Canyon Creek Country Club on the opposite side of Loop 1604, to form the only 36-hole country club complex in the San Antonio city limits.

Although Turner eventually sold the club, he hired von Hagge and Devlin to renovate the layout, which was later named Deer Canyon. Like the name implies, it plays down in a valley through large oak trees. Rock walls come into play on several holes, including the left side of the first fairway and the right side of No. 17.

"Both courses are really nice," pro Gary Bailey says. "Deer Canyon forces you to play several different shots. Golfers go over to Deer Canyon thinking they're going to shoot a low number and it doesn't happen."

Club at Sonterra Deer Canyon Course

901 Sonterra
San Antonio 78258
210-491-9900
Pro: Gary Bailey
A 36-hole private club.
From San Antonio, take Highwa 281 north to Loop 1604, take access road to Stone Oak Parkway, left to entrance.

• • •

USGA rating: 70.7
Slope rating: 123
Sand traps: 38
Water holes: 9
Doglegs: 3 left/5 right
Type greens: Bermuda
Record: 62
Designers: Press Maxwell and Robert von Hagge and Bruce Devlin (1985)
Year opened: 1960

Hole	Par	Yards	Hole	Par	Yards
Out	36	3,284	In	36	3,251

Coronado Golf and Country Club

1044 Broadmoor Drive
El Paso 79912
915-584-3841
Pro: Danny Swain
A par-70, 6,475-yard private club.
Take I-10 to Sunland Park exit, go
towards the mountain to Thunderbird
Street, then right to Broadmoor and left
on Broadmoor to entrance.

• • •

USGA rating: 70.9
Slope rating: 120
Sand traps: 39
Water holes: None
Doglegs: 4 left/6 right
Type greens: Bermuda
Record: 60
Designer: Marvin Ferguson
Year opened: 1956

• • •

Hole	Par	Yards	Hole	Par	Yards
Out	35	3,207	In	35	3,268

As a noted agronomist and turfgrass specialist from Texas A&M, Marvin Ferguson was famous for developing quality turfgrasses with which most golf courses are built, and was instrumental in developing the standard by which the U.S. Golf Association recommends all greens and fairways are built.

But at Coronado Golf & Country Club, Ferguson was introduced to golf on the rocks.

On the western side of the Franklin Mountains, Ferguson got the opportunity to build a golf course that looks more like it's mailing address should be Arizona instead of Texas, although for most Texans El Paso is indeed halfway to Arizona.

Built in 1956 at an elevation of 3,800 feet, this par-70, 6,475-yard layout offers golfers panoramic views of Mexico, New Mexico and Texas. As could be expected of a Ferguson course, the fairways are plush and the well-maintained greens are considered by some to be the fastest in the nation. In fact, some PGA Tour players have been known to come here to prepare for the Masters and the slick greens at Augusta National. While the layout is short, it has hosted several Nike Tour events in the past.

Coronado may be one of the hardest short courses in the state with its 129 slope rating. While it measures only 6,475 yards, it features long par 4s of 453 yards (No. 6), 421 yards (No. 10), 422 yards (No. 11) and 436 yards No. 18) and a 212-yard par 3 at No. 12. The layout features only two par 5s.

Cottonwood Creek was one of the last projects Joe Finger worked on before he retired at the end of a career in which he built more than 100 courses — some private, some public and some for the military.

At Cottonwood Creek, he teamed with protege Ken Dye to combine all their experience to offer golfers the best of all worlds. A championship, country-club quality layout for the masses.

In 1985, they produced this rolling, links-style course for the city of Waco. Five par 4s are between 430–460 yards, which is a problem for anyone who doesn't average 250 off the tee.

No. 15 is a double-dogleg, 541-yard par 5. The hole turns left to right off the tee, then back to the left to a green that is protected by a large lake. Water shouldn't come into play off the tee, but protects the inside corner of the dogleg on the approach. Players going for the green in two will have a 200-yard carry over water.

The No. 1 handicap hole is the 435-yard par 4 No. 5, where a creek runs down the left side of the first half of the fairway and down the right side. It is a dogleg left with trees on both sides of the fairway, so brains and brawn are required to walk away with a par.

No. 16 is one of those long par 4s. At 453 yards, you need a big drive to set up a good approach to a heart-shaped green that is protected by water on the left. The lake on the left side the comes into play off the tee.

No. 7 is a 554-yard par 5 with one of the narrowest fairways on the course.

Cottonwood Creek Golf Course

5200 Bagby Avenue
Waco 76711
254-752-2474
Pro: Brent Springer
A par-72, 7,123-yard public course.
From Dallas, take I-35 south to New
Road (exit 331). Turn right on New
Road, then left on Bagby to entrance.

• • •

USGA rating: 73.8
Slope rating: 129
Sand traps: 33
Water holes: 11
Doglegs: 4 left/5 right
Type greens: Bermuda
Record: N/A
Designers: Ken Dye and Joe Finger
Year opened: 1985

• • •

Hole	Par	Yards	Hole	Par	Yards
Out	36	3,522	In	36	3,601

Country View Golf Club

240 West Belt Line Road
Lancaster 75146
972-227-0995
Pro: David Royer
*A par-72, 6,609-yard municipal layout
owned and operated by the city of
Lancaster. From downtown, take I-35E
south to Belt Line Road, then go east on
Belt Line to entrance on the right.*

• • •

USGA rating: 71
Slope rating: 121
Sand traps: 18
water holes: 7
Doglegs: 1 left/3 right
Type greens: Bermuda
Record: 63
Designer: Ron Garl
Year opened: 1989

• • •

Hole	Par	Yards	Hole	Par	Yards
Out	36	3,346	In	36	3,263

You probably don't get many opportunities to sit down over a cup of coffee with a golf course architect to talk about his strategy in building the course you are about to play.

By the time the first ball is struck at a golf course, in fact, the architect is usually long gone to the next project. Most players, in fact, never even know who built the courses they play.

We would like to introduce you to Ron Garl, the Florida-based designer who made a rare trip to Dallas in 1989 to build Lancaster's Country View Golf Club. We did all the work for you. The questions, answers and coffee are on us.

"Our No. 1 goal is to design a course that challenges players to excel, not to penalize them," Garl says. "The total golf experience should be equal in beauty, strategy and skill."

Lancaster residents had waited a long time for their own golf course. A first attempt was started in 1981, when architect/developer Billy Martindale partially completed the course and left many residents holding worthless $75 memberships when he filed bankruptcy.

The city eventually took over the project, which was funded by $2.4 million in certificates of obligation to buy 171 acres and build an 18-hole course on the site of the former Pecan Hollow Golf Club.

The 420-yard seventh is the hardest hole on the course because it features the best of everything that God and Garl had to offer. It is a dogleg right, with a pond off the tee to the right and a creek running across the fairway about 225 yards from the tee.

North Texas golfers are certainly familiar with the architectural work of Phelps and the outstanding 36-hole public courses he has turned out at Firewheel in Garland, Indian Creek in Carrollton and Iron Horse in North Richland Hills. Firewheel has been ranked as the top municipal course in the Dallas area and one of the tops in the state.

Creekview Golf Club in the rural town of Crandall is his newest creation.

Like many courses, Creekview was a long time in the making, but golfers should feel it was worth the wait. Phelps made great use of the native scenery along with the natural grasses and mounding. Phelps created a Pinehurst feel on the course with the use of subtle mounding around the greens

"Players really enjoy this layout and the way he routed some of the holes out here," pro Kit Thompson says. "When this course is finished maturing, it will really be very pretty."

The signature hole at Creekview comes at you early. The third hole is a par 5 that measures 584 yards from the back tees. The hole is a slight dogleg left off the tee, but the combination of length, sand and water make it nearly impossible to reach in two strokes. This is one par 5 where birdies are nice, but far from certain, and par is an acceptable score.

One of the most scenic holes is the par-3 15th. The distance is 210 yards, but the wind usually helps off the tee. The bad news is there is a water carry on the approach to a two-tiered green.

Creekview Golf Club

911 South Fourth Street
Crandall 75114
972-427-3811
Pro: Kit Thompson
A par-72, 7,100-yard, 18-hole
championship public course.
Take Highway 175 past I-635 to
Crandall. Take the first exit after FM 148
and turn right to golf course entrance.

• • •

USGA rating: 74.1
Slope rating: 119
Sand traps: 40
Water holes: 9
Doglegs: 6 left/2 right
Type greens: Bentgrass
Record: 69
Designers: Dick Phelps
Year opened: 1995

• • •

Hole	Par	Yards	Hole	Par	Yards
Out	36	3,519	In	36	3,719

Cross Timbers
Golf Course

1181 South Stewart Street
Azle 76020
817-444-4940
Pro: Carl Fisher
A par-72, 6,417-yard public course.
From Fort Worth, take Highway 199
north to Stewart Road, then turn west
to course entrance on the left.

• • •

USGA rating: 72.8
Slope rating: 128
Sand traps: 28
Water holes: 4
Doglegs: 3 left/3 right
Type greens: Bermuda
Record: 67
Designers: Jeff Brauer
Year opened: 1995

• • •

Hole	Par	Yards	Hole	Par	Yards
Out	36	3,311	In	36	3,106

Every golf course starts out as a dream for someone. Some dreams, and courses, simply take longer than others to achieve. That's the case for the Cross Timbers Golf Course in Azle. The idea for a public course in this small town outside of Fort Worth had been a dream for a long time, but the dream finally became reality in February of 1995.

The public course has been in the planning stages since late 1988. The Azle Parks and Recreation board and local golfer Robert Landers, began to do feasibility studies on the economics of building a golf course for this town of 9,000 people.

City fathers held a referendum to gauge support and received overwhelming approval for a $3.5 million project.

Landers, a pro on the Senior PGA Tour, called the opening one of the happiest days of his life.

Arlington architect Jeffrey Brauer designed the layout on 200 acres of rolling countryside. The layout resembles more of a rugged Texas Hill Country layout and is heavily wooded with numerous pot bunkers and water hazards to catch errant shots.

The signature hole at Cross Timbers is the par-3 seventh. The 175-yard hole usually plays downwind to an elevated green. The front is guarded by pot bunkers and the back is rimmed by a rock wall. The final three holes wind around and through the scenic countryside.

"Once everything grows in and greens up, the course will be a beauty," Landers said. "Some dreams are worth waiting for."

Take the dramatic Texas Hill Country landscape and a city looking to build a top-level golf facility, and the results can be spectacular.

We present Exhibit A.

Owned and operated by the city of Leander, Crystal Falls opened in 1990 and is already drawing raves as one of the best new layouts in the Austin area.

The course was designed by Charles Howard. Taking full advantage of the scenic surroundings, Howard fashioned a course that is ranked as one of the best municipal courses in South Texas in surveys of South Texas PGA pros. Water comes into play on 11 holes, but there is very little sand. The Hill Country surroundings allows plenty of great views.

Measuring 6,654 yards from the back tees, this par-72 course provides a chance for good players to shoot a low score providing they keep the ball in the fairway. Part of the Crystal Falls charm is the trees that line many of the fairways and the natural areas between the tees and fairways. In keeping with the theme, there is plenty of water to snare wayward shots.

"This is a thinking man's course," says former pro Eric Kaspar, "but it also has a lot of character to it."

One of the many highlights on the course is the par-3 11th. Golfers stand at the top of a large hill with a view of much of the back nine.

There are nature areas on both the left and right. A 200-foot drop to the green provides the golfer with a deceptive and challenging shot to the pin.

Crystal Falls Golf Club

3400 Crystal Falls Parkway
Leander 78641
512-259-5855
Pro: Archer Logan
A par-72, 6,654-yard public course.
From downtown Austin, take Highway 183 north to Leander, left at Crystal Falls Parkway, 3.5 miles to club.

• • •

USGA rating: 72.3
Slope rating: 126
Sand traps: 0
Water holes: 11
Doglegs: 6 left, 3 right
Type greens: Bermuda
Record: 66
Designer: Charles Howard
Year opened: 1990

• • •

Hole	Par	Yards	Hole	Par	Yards
Out	36	3,433	In	36	3,221

Cypress Valley
Country Club

PO Box 307
Marshall 75671
903-938-4941
Pro: Lou Dechert
A par-71, 6,953-yard semi-private club.
From Dallas, take I-20 east to exit 628,
then west to entrance.

• • •

USGA rating: N/A
Slope rating: N/A
Type greens: Bermuda
Water holes: 6
Sand traps: 0
Doglegs: 3 left/4 right
Record: N/A
Designer: Clinton Howard Mace, Sr.
Year opened: 1971

• • •

Hole	Par	Yards	Hole	Par	Yards
Out	35	3,174	In	36	3,463

If good things come in small packages, those who stumble across Cypress Valley Country Club are in for a pleasant surprise.

Located in Marshall just 30 miles from the Louisiana border, Cypress Valley is certainly off the beaten path for most Texans, but its well worth the trip into the heart of East Texas where golfers get the best of both worlds — a big city golf course at small town prices.

Golfers can still play all day here for one green fee at this family-built, and family-owned club that built in a densely-wooded area with subtle elevation changes throughout the layout.

There are only two straight holes on the course and everything is else is carved through the trees with numerous doglegs.

Dense woods surround the property on all four sides.

Clinton Howard Mace, Sr., and his two sons built the golf course, proving that you don't have to be a big-name architect to design a championship layout.

This course is a real sleeper near the Texas-Louisiana border. The plush grounds and tree-lined fairways make it worth bringing a camera. The water protected greens and elevation changes will challenge golfers of all skill levels — from beginner to pro.

The signature hole is the 375-yard, par-4 No. 7, which features a sharp dogleg to the right through a dense thicket and over a large valley to the green.

No. 15 is a unique, 376-yard dogleg left with a horseshoe-shaped lake at the green.

Jack Forester was just a kid when his father, Dick, left a comfortable head pro job at Houston Country Club to pursue a dream. While Dick worked behind the ivory walls of one of the city's most exclusive clubs, he realized there was a desperate need for public golf facilities in Houston in the late '60s.

So it was that Forester left the cozy confines of HCC to build Bear Creek Golf World, which to this day is one of the largest public facilities in the Southwest with its three 18-hole courses.

Two decades later, Rick followed in his father's footsteps. Houston once again was in need of public courses and Forester started a new trend toward high-quality, daily-fee facilities with Cypresswood Golf Club in 1987.

It was the first daily-fee facility in Houston since Bear Creek opened two decades earlier.

The Creek Course was the second of the two courses. When it opened in 1989, it was named to *Golf Digest's* Best New Courses list. It is a classic driving golf course, but accurate iron play is also a must since the large rolling greens can create some nasty pin positions.

Contrary to its name, water comes into play on only nine holes of the Creek Course, but the fairways are wider and forgiving to errant tee shots. It features back-to-back par 5s that are reachable in two and the par-4 16th plays 412 yards but requires a 230-yard carry into a prevailing wind off the tee. No. 13 is a 469-yard par 4 that is a dogleg right that requires two good shots.

Cypresswood Golf Club Creek Course

21602 Cypresswood Drive
Spring 77373
281-821-6300
Pro: Kelly Walker
A 54-hole, daily-fee facility. Take I-45 north to FM 1960, then go east 6 miles to Cypresswood Drive. Go left on Cypresswood 1 mile to course entrance.

• • •

USGA rating: 71.8
Slope rating: 123
Sand traps: 54
Water holes: 16
Doglegs: 4 left/4 right
Type greens: Bermuda
Record: 65
Designers: Rick Forester
Year opened: 1989

• • •

Hole	Par	Yards	Hole	Par	Yards
Out	36	3,409	In	36	3,528

Cypresswood Golf Club Cypress Course

21602 Cypresswood Drive

Spring 77373

281-821-6300

Pro: Kelly Walker

A 54-hole daily-fee facility.

From Houston, take I-45 north to FM 1960, then go east to Cypresswood Drive. Go left to course entrance.

• • •

USGA rating: 71.8

Slope rating: 123

Sand traps: 54

Water holes: 16

Doglegs: 4 left/4 right

Type greens: Bermuda

Record: 65

Designers: Rick Forester

Year opened: 1988

• • •

Hole	Par	Yards	Hole	Par	Yards
Out	36	3,472	In	36	3,434

The Cypress Course at Cypresswood was the first of the two layouts designed by Rick Forester on 548-acres of flood-plain land on the banks of Cypress and Spring creeks. The land was leased from the county, and it stands as a great example of public and private entities working together.

Cypresswood has become one of Houston's premier facilities, hosting numerous charity events as well as the qualifier for the Shell Houston Open.

"I think the success of the two golf courses," Forester says, "has been the way the golf courses complement each other. They are equally demanding, but present different kinds of challenges."

The Cypress Course was the first of the two courses and was voted among the best new courses in '88 by Golf Digest. It measures 6,906 yards from the back tees and usually plays 2-3 shots tougher than the Creek with its tee shots demanding accuracy more than length, rolling fairways and uneven lies. Water comes into play on 16 holes and there are 54 bunkers.

Two of the most difficult holes on the Cypress are the 427-yard par-4 No. 9 and the 586-yard, par-5 15th. No. 9 is a long dogleg left that requires a long drive to reach the corner for a clear approach to a green protected by four traps. No. 15 is long enough as it is, but a creek that runs across the fairway 50 yards from the green makes it almost impossible to reach in two. The par-4 No. 18 can vary from 413 yards to 450 depending on the pin setting.

Less is more: No, this is not another beer slogan. It is the philosophy behind the golf course at Delaware Springs.

Delaware Springs, located just northwest of Austin, is one of many new courses that breaks the old stereotype of crumbling, bland city courses that have been trampled into submission under the feet of countless hackers.

Architects Dan Proctor and Dave Axland, former members of the Ben Crenshaw-Bill Coore design team, built the course like the old days in that less is more - in other words, the more natural the course, the better.

In some parts of Texas, where the land is flat and barren, that is a difficult task. But at Delaware Springs, they had plenty of elements with which to work to pro-duce a 6,819-yard, par-72 course that features rolling hills and undulating greens. Consistent with the Crenshaw-Coore standards are the huge greens, which measure more than 5,000 square feet. Putts of more than 100 feet are common on the undulating greens.

The layout requires bump-and-run shots, long putts and the ability to avoid or hit out of fairway waste bunkers. Another common feature from Crenshaw is the descriptive names for each hole, many of them Scottish in nature. No. 4 is named "Roon the Ben" for around the bend. No. 7 is named "Spoon" after the old name for a 3-wood; and the 18th is called "Hame" for "home hole."

The course is named after a spring that comes into play on several holes. The first hole is named "Crossing the Delaware."

Delaware Springs Golf Course

127 East Jackson
Burnet 78611
512-756-8471
Pro: Al Pryor
A par-72, 6,819-yard municipal course. From Austin, take I-35 north to Highway 29, go west to Burnet and follow signs to course entrance.

• • •

USGA rating: 72.0
Slope rating: 121
Sand traps: 26
Water holes: 6
Doglegs: 6 left/2 right
Type greens: Bermuda
Record: 65 back tees
Designers: Dan Proctor and Dave Axland
Year opened: 1992

• • •

Hole	Par	Yards	Hole	Par	Yards
Out	37	3,492	In	35	3,492

Denton Country Club

PO Box 1069
Denton 76202
940-387-2812
Pro: Alan Poynor
A par-71, 6,303-yard private club.
From Dallas take I-35E north to
Highway 377. Right on 377 to Country
Club Road. Turn east on Country Club
Road to entrance on the left.

• • •

USGA rating: 71.4
Slope rating: 128
Type greens: 32
Water holes: 6
Doglegs: 2 left/3 right
Sand traps: 32
Record: N/A
Designer: Dick Nugent (1985)
Year opened: 1922

• • •

Hole	Par	Yards	Hole	Par	Yards
Out	35	3,076	In	36	3,227

Denton Country Club is modern-day evidence of Charles Darwin's theory of evolution. This was no six-day, seven-night success story. This was a 70-year metamorphosis from cow pasture to country club.

It all started back in 1922, when members turned 125 acres of pasture into a nine-hole golf course with sand greens. The club closed during the Depression, but was re-chartered in 1934 as the New Denton Country Club. It closed again during World War II and reopened when the troops returned home.

In 1960–61 members rebuilt the golf course with grass greens. In 1970–71, the club expanded to 18 holes. In the 1980s, it made its final transition to its 6,625-yard layout when member Joe Black, president of the PGA of America at the time, called on longtime friend and architect Dick Nugent to update the course.

No. 7 is the most difficult hole on the layout. It is a slight dogleg left with water coming into play in several places. Off the tee, players must cross a horseshoe-shaped lake in the fairway but also avoid a small creek that runs through the trees on the left.

No. 13 is another interesting design where players must carry water twice and a sand trap to reach the green. A winding creek crosses the fairway in front of the tee from left to right, runs down the right side and crosses the fairway 270 yards from the tee. That leaves 143 yards to the green, but golfers must carry a sand trap in the middle of the fairway about 20 yards in front of the green.

It all started in the summer of 1959 when a group of men got together in the back yard of Dick King and, as men are apt to do, had a few beers and dreamed a dream.

King and his neighbors had grown road weary of their long drives across town to play golf and their wives urged them to start their own country club. The idea snowballed, and by the next year they had sold $250,000 in memberships and broken ground on Diamond Oaks Country Club.

Charles Akey, the field engineer who did all the dirty work for architects Robert Trent Jones and Ralph Plummer a few years earlier at Shady Oaks, was hired to design 18 holes on 149 acres of what used to be the Haltom Family's Diamond H. Ranch in Haltom City.

Akey built the golf course around the beautiful but sometimes dangerous Fossil Creek and through the densely wooded hillsides. Most of the fairways at Diamond Oaks are lined with trees from tee to green, and and water comes into play on seven holes.

The back nine is 350 yards longer than the front, and you won't find a par 4 under 400 yards from the back tees. Actually, the 460-yard, par-4 ninth, the 447-yard, par-4 10th and the 440-yard, par-4 11th are the most difficult.

No. 10 is a slight dogleg left over the water and through the trees. No. 11 is a sharp dogleg left that requires a strong tee shot to reach the corner, but also has water down the right side. Those holes are followed by a 215-yard par 3, a 462-yard par 4, a 609-yard par 5 and a 447-yard par 4.

Diamond Oaks Golf Club

5821 Diamond Oaks
Fort Worth 76117
817-838-8821
Pro: Dan Gibler
A par-70, 6,941-yard private club.
Take Highway 183 to Denton Highway exit, left to Glenview, then second left to Diamond Oaks. Left to club entrance.

• • •

USGA rating: 73.4
Slope rating: 120
Sand traps: 25
Water holes: 8
Doglegs: 3 left/5 right
Type greens: Bermuda
Record: 63
Designer: Charles Akey
Year opened: 1960

• • •

Hole	Par	Yards	Hole	Par	Yards
Out	35	3,292	In	35	3,649

Eagle Mountain Golf Club

7200 Golf Club Drive
Fort Worth 75179
817-236-3400
Pro: Steve Townsend
A par-72, 6,550-yard private club.
Located 4.5 miles north of Loop 820
off Boat Club Drive (FM 1220)
off Highway 199.

• • •

USGA rating: 73.4
Slope rating: 129
Type greens: Bermuda
Water holes: 4
Sand Traps: 40
Doglegs: 4 left/3 right
Record: N/A
Designer: Don January
Year opened: 1997

• • •

Hole	Par	Yards	Hole	Par	Yards
Out	36	3,329	In	36	3,329

Don January grew up in Dallas, however the game of golf took him around the world as a professional.

In 40 years on tour, January learned a lot about what he liked and he didn't like in a golf course.

So in the late 1960s he began working as an architect, and he learned the hard way why some golf courses don't turn out as good as they should be.

Budget, and the fact that his golf courses almost always took a back seat in importance to selling homes, almost always seemed to get in the way.

"I built a bunch of courses in the 60s and 70s, but never any like I really wanted," January says.

"We were always dealing with tight budgets. I would like to have had the freedom to build a golf course without worry about selling houses.

"Golf course design later became a contest who could build the best sand traps. I hated to see golf get into that. I'm older, conservative, and people were using a lot of different ideas I never even dreamed of.

"As a player I saw a lot of mistakes that were made that I didn't want to repeat. I liked the older style architecture. Things flowed more from one hole to the next.

"There were no abrupt changes of elevation. The courses I'm talking about are courses that have stood the test of time."

Capitalizing on all his experience, January produced one of those types of layouts at Eagle Mountain Country Club, a 6,550-yard, par-72 layout on Eagle Mountain Lake in Fort Worth.

Ralph Plummer grew up in the same caddyshack at Fort Worth's Glen Garden Country Club that produced Ben Hogan and Byron Nelson. But while Hogan and Nelson made a name for themselves on the golf courses, Plummer created an equally lasting legacy for himself by building the golf courses they played.

Plummer was the protege of John Bredemus, the architect of Texas golf. Over his 40-year career, Plummer designed some of Texas' best golf courses that are void of such modern-day trickery and elements such as railroad ties, island greens or long, forced carries. When he died in 1982, his obituary summed up his work as "characterized by subtlety seldom found these days."

Perhaps nowhere was his style more on display than at Eastern Hills. Plummer designed a layout that measures only 6,431 yards, but is uncharacteristically hilly for North Texas and features sidehill and downhill lies that challenge shot-making ability.

Take, for example, the 545-yard, par-5 14th. Off the tee, you hit uphill to a landing area that slopes off to the right. On the second shot, the fairway drops down to a valley and curves sharply to the left to a green protected by a small grove of trees. It is almost impossible to get home in 2 shots.

The 219-yard, par-3 10th is one of the toughest holes in Dallas. It requires a long iron or fairway wood into the wind to a green protected by bunkers left and right and a creek further to the right. A mis-guided shot into the wind is destined for trouble.

Eastern Hills Country Club

3000 Country Club Road
Garland 75043
972-278-3051
Pro: Brad McCollum
A par-70, 6,331-yard private club.
From Dallas, take I-30 east to Belt Line Road, then left to Wynn Joyce Road. Right on Wynn Joyce to Country Club Drive, then left to club entrance.

• • •

USGA rating: 71.0
Slope rating: 128
Sand traps: 46
Water holes: 9
Doglegs: 2 left/2 right
Type greens: Bentgrass
Record: N/A
Designer: Ralph Plummer
Year opened: 1956

• • •

Hole	Par	Yards	Hole	Par	Yards
Out	35	3,184	In	35	3,147

Eldorado Country Club

2604 Country Club Drive
McKinney 75070
972-529-2770
Pro: Tim Brown
A par-72, 6,625-yard private club.
From Dallas take I-75 north to
Eldorado Parkway, head west on
Eldorado a half mile to Country Club
Drive. Turn right to club entrance.

• • •

USGA Rating: 71.8
Slope Rating: 130
Sand Traps: 33
Water Holes: 12
Doglegs: 4 left/5 right
Type greens: Bentgrass
Record: 63
Designer: Gary Roger Baird
Year Opened: 1981

• • •

Hole	Par	Yards	Hole	Par	Yards
Out	36	3,353	In	36	3,272

A t Eldorado — also known as the country side of the city — there's a history and a commitment to enhance and preserve a certain standard of living. Numerous buildings are listed in the National Register of Historic Places, reflecting the area's turn of the century heritage.

Architect Gary Roger Baird hopes his golf course at Eldorado Country Club will also one day be added to that list. Baird has built courses all over the world, but in 1981 he came to Texas to build his first and only course here and meet Eldorado's goal to offer a small-town atmosphere with a big-time golf course.

Baird designed his course on the gently rolling, tree-lined terrain so that many of the homes and home sites overlook the fairways.

Water comes into play on eight holes, most of the water comes from one large irrigation lake and a creek that feeds into it.

The 433-yard, par-4 fifth is the most difficult hole. Players must avoid out-of-bounds on the right side and a pond that crosses the fairway about 200 yards from the tee. The green is guarded by three bunkers, including one in front that requires an all-carry approach.

The back nine has two demanding par 5s, including the 529-yard 11th and the 493-yard 15th. No. 11 is a dogleg right with a narrow fairway, where a small pond on the right side of the green prevents many players from going for the green in two. At No. 15, a creek crosses the fairway off the tee and curves around the right side of the fairway all the way to the green.

Elm Grove was built in 1940. The par-71, 6,401-yard layout features bentgrass greens (billed as the "best in West Texas"), tree-lined fairways and greenside bunkers. Not to mention plenty of hot air.

As with any West Texas course, wind is an omnipresent factor at Elm Grove, where the wind can sometimes make the yardage on a hole irrelevant. When the wind isn't blowing, the course can be attacked, as evidenced by Roland Adams when he set the course record of 59 back in June of 1969.

"With our West Texas winds," says pro Jim Brisbin, "Elm Grove is a good test of golf."

The fairways are tree lined, but they afford generous landing areas, and the greens are large and well maintained. There are fourteen sand bunkers incorporated into the layout's design, and water hazards and ponds- come into play on at least three separate occasions.

At the par-4, 454-yard No. 12, however, both wind and yardage work together to make the most difficult hole on the course. Even on a calm day, the yardage alone requires two good shots to reach the green. But when you consider the hole plays into a prevailing wind, you'll understand why it takes most golfers three shots to reach the green. Bogey here feels like a par.

No. 9 and No. 15 can also be demanding at 434 yards each, while the best opportunity for birdie may come at the 475-yard, par-5 No. 4 or the 137-yard, par-3 No. 5.

Elm Grove
Golf Course
23202 Milwaukee Avenue
Lubbock 79407
806-799-7801
Pro: Mark Cunningham
A par-71, 6,401-yard public course.
Take Loop 289, exit 34th and go
1/2 mile to course entrance.

• • •

USGA rating: N/A
Slope rating: N/A
Sand traps: 11
Water holes: 3
Doglegs: 4 left/4 right
Type greens: Bentgrass
Record: 57
Designer: Billy Maxwell
Year opened: 1940

• • •

Hole	Par	Yards	Hole	Par	Yards
Out	35	2,961	In	36	6,401

Fair Oaks Ranch Golf and Country Club Blackjack Oak Course

7900 Fair Oaks Parkway
Boerne 78006
830-981-9604
Pro: Bill Keys
A 36-hole private club.
From San Antonio, take I-10 west to
Fair Oaks Parkway, go right to entrance.

• • •

USGA rating: 73.1
Slope rating: 131
Sand traps: 121
Water holes: 7
Doglegs: 7 left/7 right
Type greens: Bermuda
Record: N/A
Designers: Ron Kirby, Gary Player
*   and Dennis Griffiths*
Year opened: 1979

• • •

Hole	Par	Yards	Hole	Par	Yards
Out	36	3,398	In	36	3,486

Fair Oaks Ranch is one of the largest and most successful clubs in the San Antonio area with 36 holes built on the former 5,000-acre ranch of San Antonio oilman Ralph Fair. It is not uncommon for deer to wander free through both courses, each of which has its own special character.

Club co-developer Don Smith hired Gary Player and Ron Kirby to design the Live Oak in 1979. Player was always an excellent irons player, and his layouts demand no less of its players. Live Oak is to be considered among the most scenic with its tree-lined fairways. It takes full advantage of the Hill Country landscape with its sweeping views of the area.

The par-3 16th and par-5 17th are prime cases in point. The 16th plays uphill to a green on top of a knoll. A shot that doesn't make the green will fall into a bunker or a scrubby ditch. The 17th is a long, winding 512 yards from the back tees. The golfer must hit a blind drive over a hill to a landing area just in front of another large ditch. The big hitter might be able to reach the green in two, but most are happy to lay up in front of the ditch and then use a short iron on the uphill approach to a green protected by traps and more rough.

The Blackjack Oak 18 was designed by the team of Kirby and Dennis Griffiths and opened in 1994. This course begins with a long, downhill par 5 and ends with a par 4 that goes straight uphill. In between are plenty of scenic with water and sand coming into play. The newest nine, Nos. 6-14, are more of a links-style design with more length required from the tee.

You don't get many opportunities to sit down over a cup of coffee with a golf course architect to talk about his strategy in building the course you are about to play. By the time the first ball is struck at a golf course, in fact, the architect is usually long gone to the next project. Most players, in fact, never even know who built the courses they play.

We would like to introduce you to Ron Garl, the Florida-based designer who made a rare trip to Dallas in 1989 to build Lancaster's Country View Golf Club. We did all the work for you. The questions, answers and coffee are on us.

"Our No. 1 goal is to design a course that challenges players to excel, not to penalize them," says Garl, who teamed with Texas Golf Hall of Famer Charles Coody to build Fairway Oaks in 1979.

"The total golf experience should be equal in beauty, strategy and skill. Golf is a game played through golfer's eyes and the golf course must be appealing to the eye. The emphasis on any great design is on strategy. The golfer must have options. The greatest player of all time, Bobby Jones, once said that he hit only a few good shots each round. Golf is a game of recovery; we must give each golfer a chance to recover."

Since Fairway Oaks was Garl's first Texas project, Coody, a Texas native who won the 1971 Masters, gave him the background he needed to produce a 7,020-yard layout that is one of the best courses in the state west of Dallas-Fort Worth and has hosted PGA and Senior PGA tour events as well as top amateur events.

Fairway Oaks Golf and Country Club

32 Fairway Oaks Boulevard
Abilene 79606
915-695-1800
Pro: Doug Fair
A par-72, 7,020-yard private club.
From Abilene, take Highway 83/84 south to Antilley Road, then go west on Antilley to Fairway Oaks.

• • •

USGA rating: 73.1
Slope rating: 131
Water holes: 11
Doglegs: 11
Sand traps: 40
Record: 61
Course designer: Ron Garl and Charles Coody
Year opened: 1979

• • •

Hole	Par	Yards	Hole	Par	Yards
Out	36	3,545	In	36	3,473

Firewheel Golf Park Lakes Course

600 Blackburn Road
Garland 75040
972-205-2795
Pro: Jerry Andrews
A 36-hole public facility.
From Dallas, take Central Expressway
north to Arapaho, go east to North
Garland, go north to Blackburn,
then east to club entrance.

• • •

USGA Rating: 72.0
Slope rating: 126
Sand traps: 50
Water holes: 13
Doglegs: 5 left/2 right
Type greens: Bermuda
Record: 62
Designer: Dick Phelps
Year opened: 1987

• • •

Hole	Par	Yards	Hole	Par	Yards
Out	35	3,219	In	36	3,406

Dick Phelps rarely wears out his welcome. When he designs one golf course, he usually gets invited back to design another.

That was the case in 1984, when Phelps designed two courses in the Dallas area — the Creek Course at Indian Creek and the Old Course at Firewheel Golf Park. In 1987, he was invited back to both courses to design a second layout.

His second effort at Firewheel is known as the Lakes Course, a links-style course that lives up to its name with water coming into play throughout the course.

While Phelps had vast experience in golf course design, he had explicit instructions from the golf course steering committee:

1) Maintain the natural beauty of the land; 2) Design a golf course that would be economical to maintain; and 3) Design a course that would involve strategy, but also accommodate players of all levels.

Those were the ingredients of what has become one of DFW's most successful municipal golf operations.

Named after the red and yellow wildflower that blooms from April to July, Firewheel already has 36 holes and 18 more holes are on the drawing board.

There are also numerous water hazards such as the pond at No. 7, a 549-yard, par 5. Golfers must hit their approach shot over the body of water to have any chance at a birdie.

"We're very proud of the Firewheel project, and the type of reception it has received," Phelps says. "We can't wait to come back and do it again."

Great golf courses give rise to great golfers. The more demanding the course, the more precise the golfers who play it must become.

Forest Creek Golf Club has only been around for a few years, but it already has served as home of one of the best club professionals in South Texas. J.L. Lewis used to be the pro here, but he honed his game at Forest Creek and is now on the PGA Tour.

Lewis was the first head pro at Forest Creek when it opened in 1991 and was the top playing pro in the Southern Texas PGA Section before he earned full-time playing privileges on the PGA Tour.

Lewis offers praise for the Dick Phelps-designed layout, which measures 7,154 yards from the back tees and is owned by the city of Round Rock. It features a heavily wooded tract with gently rolling hills and a creek, befitting the course name, running through it. In fact, water comes into play on 11 holes. Combined with 22 bunkers and 11 holes that dogleg through the trees, it challenges even the best shot makers.

Lewis proved the layout wasn't too hard, however, when he set the course record of 65 in its first year. Lewis' dream of holding a pro tournament was realized last year when the Ninfa's Texas Tour made a stop at Forest Creek. The course also has hosted the $12,000 Coca-Cola Open.

No. 15 is a 472-yard par 4 that, for most golfers, will play like a par 5. There are several other long par 4s, including the 442-yard 18th, the 432-yard 10th and the 452-yard fourth hole.

Forest Creek Golf Club

99 Twin Ridge Parkway
Round Rock 78664
512-388-2874
Pro: Doug Turner
A par-72, 7,154-yard public course.
From Austin, take I-35 north to
Round Rock exit, turn right and
follow signs to entrance.

• • •

USGA rating: 73.5
Slope rating: 130
Sand traps: 22
Water holes: 11
Doglegs: 4 left/7 right
Type Greens: Bermuda
Record: 65
Designer: Dick Phelps
Year opened: 1991

• • •

Hole	Par	Yards	Hole	Par	Yards
Out	36	3,508	In	36	3,576

Four Seasons Resort at Las Colinas Cottonwood Valley Course

4200 North MacArthur Boulevard
Irving 75038
972-717-2530
Pro: Paul Earnest
A 36-hole resort and country club.
Take I-35 east to Highway 183, west to
MacArthur, then north to club entrance.

• • •

USGA Rating: 73.4
Slope rating: 133
Sand traps: 56
Water holes: 7
Doglegs: 3 left/3 right
Type greens: Bentgrass
Record: 61
Designers: Robert Trent Jones, Jr.
Year opened: 1985

• • •

Hole	Par	Yards	Hole	Par	Yards
Out	36	3,344	In	36	3,583

So many factors go into building a golf course, it is difficult to get them right from the start. From obtaining the financing to obtaining the land to obtaining the right architect to the right concept, the path from start to completion is doused with opportunity for failure.

Donald Ross constantly tinkered with Pinehurst No. 2. Augusta National has been tweaked more than Dr. Alister Mackenzie would like to know.

If following in those footsteps is any indication, then the evolutionary process as the Las Colinas Sports Club could also one day lead to greatness. Over a period of 10 years, Robert Trent Jones Jr. and Jay Morrish have had their say. So have Byron Nelson, Ben Crenshaw and Tom Watson. Contrary to the "too many cooks spoil the stew" adage, this is one that keeps getting better.

It all started in 1985, when Jones was hired to build a TPC stadium course to become the new home for the PGA Tour's Byron Nelson Classic, which draws annual crowds of 200,000.

That course, with a first green shaped like Texas and a bunker shaped like Oklahoma, was used as the tournament site until 1987, when Morrish built 18 holes to blend with the original 18 Jones built. The Cottonwood Valley Course is for members only.

The Byron Nelson Golf School shares the resort's driving range, which offers 88,000 square feet of teeing area. One of the highlights is a nine-foot tall bronze statue of Byron Nelson, which was erected in 1992 to celebrate Nelson's 80th birthday.

Galveston has the distinction of being home of the state's first golf club, although that first layout was wiped out a few years later by the storm of 1900. Galveston Golf Club was formed in 1898 as a nine-hole course with a membership of 30.

North America's greatest natural disaster destroyed that course on Sept. 8, 1900, but the loss was trivial in light of the 6,000 people who lost their lives. Storm scared, the members rebuilt the course in 1912 on a 100-acre inland tract and renamed it Oleander Country Club. By 1918, members were ready to move back to the island and reformed the new Galveston Country Club on the beach at 61st Street. They continued to operate until there until 1946 but eventually sold the course to the city and moved to their current 200-acre site in 1947.

Architects John Bredemus and Ralph Plummer designed the new layout. Like the original course, this one also is short at 6,347 yards but water on 16 holes, tight fairways and omnipresent Gulf breezes more than make up for the lack of distance.

The club, however, continued to struggle until Galveston-born oilman and developer George Mitchell worked out a deal in 1965 to trade for some land owned by the club to develop a residential area.

It was just the beginning of a relationship in which the club eventually leased the club to Mitchell in exchange for long-term improvements. The course later was updated by late architect Carlton Gipson.

Galveston Country Club

12 Mile Road at Stewart Road
Galveston 77551
409-740-6476
Pro: Bruce Rodysill
A par-72, 6,347-yard private club.
Take I-45 south to 61st Street. Go right on 61st to Seawall, then west to Twelve Mile Road. Turn right to club.

• • •

USGA rating: 70.7
Slope rating: 118
Sand traps: 59
Water holes: 16
Doglegs: 2 left/2 right
Type greens: Bermuda
Record: 65
Pro: Bruce Rodysill
Designer: John Bredemus (1948)
        and Carlton Gipson (1992)

• • •

Hole	Par	Yards	Hole	Par	Yards
Out	36	3,122	In	36	3,215

Garden Valley
Golf Resort
Hummingbird Course

22049 FM 1995

Lindale 75771

903-882-6107

Pro: Eric Eitel

A 36-hole semi-private resort.

From Dallas, go 80 miles east on I-20 to Highway 110, go south to Garden Valley Resort sign. Follow sign to entrance.

• • •

USGA rating: 71

Slope rating: N/A

Sand traps: 25

Water holes: 5

Doglegs: 4 left/2 right

Type greens: Bermuda

Record: 63

Designer: Leon Howard

Year opened: 1976

• • •

Hole	Par	Yards	Hole	Par	Yards
Out	36	3,423	In	36	3,331

Rarely has there been a golf course more appropriately named than Garden Valley.

With its maze of 100-foot pines, crepe myrtle, Carolina jasmine, hollies, cedars and dogwoods and 1,500 azaleas, rolling elevation changes and bentgrass greens, it is Texas' most reasonable facsimile of August National.

This garden setting is home to two championship golf courses. The Dogwood Course, designed in 1992 by architect John Sanford, is the highest-rated and most demanding of the two and is listed in the Texas Top 100.

The Hummingbird Course is the easier of the two, measuring only 6,441 yards and playing to a par of 71.

Garden Valley was designed as a getaway resort for big-city golfers, luring them about an hour or so off the beaten path of the Dallas-Fort Worth area. The only thing that keeps the courses from being rated even higher is that not enough golfers have made the trip.

The course features elevated greens and tees and thickly tree-lined fairways.

The Hummingbird Course is the oldest of the two, having been built in 1976 by Texas architect Leon Howard. It offers a fine day of recreational golf for the less experienced golfer as well as the low handicapper.

The signature hole on the Hummingbird Course is No. 2, a 580-yard par 5. The hole requires players to hit their first two shots up to the crest of a hill, then hit a downhill approach shot to the green. It is nearly impossible for most golfers to reach it in two.

If great golf courses breed great golfers, then Glen Garden Country Club can certainly make a case as one of the best of all time.

Three Texas Golf Hall of Famers — Ben Hogan, Byron Nelson and architect Ralph Plummer — all got their first impressions of the game here. LPGA Hall of Famer Sandra Palmer is the daughter of former club president James Warren Jr. and also grew up on these links. This was what a golf course was supposed to look like. And this was the way you were supposed to play.

Sixteen years after architect Tom Bendelow passed through town to lay out Fort Worth's first golf course, Hogan and Nelson squared off in the Glen Garden Caddie Championship. Nelson sank a long putt on the ninth hole to tie with Hogan. Par was 37, and they both shot 40. Members decided to let them go another nine, and Nelson emerged with a one-stroke victory.

That was only the beginning. Nelson went on to win 52 tournaments, including an incomprehensible streak of 11 in a row in 1945. Hogan went on to win 63 times. Between them, they pulled down 14 major championships.

One thing Nelson says will never forget is the back nine at Glen Garden. Of the final five holes, four are par 3s.

"Of the par 3s, the 17th was the only easy one," Nelson recalls. "Nos.14 and 15 were both over 200 yards long, and the 15th was a blind 213-yard shot to an uphill green. You couldn't even see the flag from the tee."

Glen Garden Country Club

2916 Glen Garden Drive
Fort Worth 76119
817-535-7582
Pro: Alan Courtney
A par-71, 6,166-yard private club.
From Fort Worth, take Highway 287 south to Berry Street, turn right to Glen Garden Drive and left to club entrance.

• • •

USGA rating: 69.3
Slope rating: 117
Sand traps: 30
Water holes: 1
Doglegs: 2
Type greens: Bermuda
Record: N/A
Designer: Tom Bendelow
Year opened: 1912

• • •

Hole	Par	Yards	Hole	Par	Yards
Out	37	3,149	In	34	2,926

Golfcrest Country Club

2509 Country Club Drive
Pearland 77581
281-485-4550
Pro: David Pilsner
A par-72, 7,051-yard private club.
From downtown Houston, take I-45
south to Dixie Farm Road, right to
FM 518, right to Country Club Drive.
Turn right to entrance.

• • •

USGA rating: 74.2
Slope rating: 131
Sand traps: 56
Water holes: 13
Doglegs: 7 left/3 right
Type greens: Bermuda
Record: 64
Designer: Joe Finger
Year opened: 1971

• • •

Hole	Par	Yards	Hole	Par	Yards
Out	36	3,542	In	36	3,512

After watching the success of River Oaks Country Club in the 1920s, Houston real-estate developer Earl Gammage Sr. designated 117 acres in southeast Houston to build a golf course of his own.

Golfcrest Country Club opened in 1927, a couple of years after River Oaks. While River Oaks' membership was dominated by old money, Golfcrest was popular among the nouveau riche of the day. In 1932, Golfcrest became one of the first clubs in the nation to experiment with night golf when it installed floodlights on the front nine holes.

When people think about Golfcrest, they think of the Golfcrest Four-ball, which was one of the city's most popular amateur events that started in 1951. It once was dominated by current Senior PGA Tour pro John Paul Cain, and other regulars included Homero Blancas, Rex Baxter, the late Jim Hiskey, Bobby Walzel, Keith Fergus and Bill Rogers.

In 1965, much like Houston Country Club a decade before, Golfcrest was choked off by industrial development and moved to a 200-acres site 12.2 miles away in Pearland. The old course, which measured only 6,000 yards, closed on Dec. 31, 1970, and the new $2.5 million club opened on Jan. 2, 1971.

The club hired architect Joe Finger to build a new 6,900-yard layout that is much tougher than the original. He moved 160,000 cubic yards of soil to create mounds on the fairways and greens and built his lakes and ponds in the shallow places.

You don't know how lucky you are to be reading this story. If it had not been for a little bit of fate, this story would be about mini-warehouses instead of a golf course.

Although it lies in the shadows of bustling tourist attractions like Six Flags over Texas and The Ballpark at Arlington, Great Southwest was struggling for survival in the mid 1980s. Dallas developer Jim Sowell was preparing to bulldoze the 160-acre course and build mini-warehouses, until he gave members one last shot at survival.

"He gave us a call as a last resort to see what we had to say," says architect Dick Nugent. "So we came down and made some modifications so they could do a little real-estate work on a few holes. All of a sudden, things turned around."

What survived is a 7,000-yard layout that was designed in 1965 by architect Ralph Plummer and features three interconnecting lakes, 69 bunkers and clusters of trees throughout. Nugent led the renovation effort in 1983.

The most memorable hole is the 223-yard, par-3 No. 3. From the back tees, the hole plays over water and is usually downwind, making it difficult to stop a long iron on the small green.

Nos. 9 and 18 are almost identical par 5s. No. 9 plays 539 yards with water left of the landing area and a creek crossing the fairway in front of the green. The 18th is guarded by water to the right of the landing area, and the same creek that crosses the fairway in front of the green.

Great Southwest Golf Club

612 Avenue J East
Grand Prairie 75050
972-647-0116
Pro: Kevin Semtner
A par-71, 6,771-yard private club.
From Dallas, take I-30 west to Great Southwest Parkway. Turn north to Avenue J, then left to entrance.

• • •

USGA rating: 72.3
Slope rating: 136
Sand traps: 63
Water holes: 10
Doglegs: 3 left/1 right
Type greens: Bentgrass
Record: 63
Designer: Ralph Plummer
Year opened: 1964

• • •

Hole	Par	Yards	Hole	Par	Yards
Out	35	3,300	In	36	3,471

Hearthstone Country Club

7615 Ameswood Drive
Houston 77095
281-463-2204
Pro: Darren Busker
A 27-hole private club.
Take Highway 290 west, turn left on
Huffmeister, right on Ameswood
and left to club entrance.

• • •

USGA rating: 71.0
Slope rating: 118
Sand traps: 67
Water holes: 13
Doglegs: 6 left/4 right
Type greens: Bermuda
Record: 63-Carl Cooper
Designers: Jay Riviere and Joe Finger
Year opened: 1977

• • •

Hole	Par	Yards	Hole	Par	Yards
Out	35	3,205	In	36	3,343

C ountry clubs have an image of being stodgy institutions where old-money families sip tea in their later years, play bridge and a little bit of golf with other well-to-do members.

Certainly there is nothing wrong with enjoying the fruits of your labor, but Hearthstone was designed in the mid-1970s to accommodate the baby boomers who were making the move out of the city and buying their first homes in west and northwest Houston. It has been home of one of the youngest and most active memberships of any club in Houston with an average age at one time as low as 36.

There were virtually no trees when architect Jay Riviere built the first 18 holes in 1977, but more than 2,000 trees have been planted to define the fairways.

In 1986, Hearthstone added a third nine designed by arch-itect Joe Finger. Out-of-bounds exists on almost every hole as the layout winds through the surrounding neighborhood.

The courses are noted for their long and difficult par-3 holes, although No. 6 on Wolf's Corner is only a precarious 106-yard shot to a green protected by water on three sides. No. 3 on Horsepen measures 232 yards, while No. 5 is 198 yards with a green protect-ed by a lake on the right side.

Jackrabbit features two 200-plus par 3s. No. 4 is 220 yards and guarded by a lake that runs the length of the fairway down to the left side of the green.

No. 8 is 202 yards and is protected by a lake that runs down the right side.

The business of building municipal golf courses went out of style in the 1980s, when golf courses became too expensive to build, land became harder to procure, environmental controls became more stringent and local governments had larger problems on their hands than building a golf course.

But the boom is back.

In the past two years, three Dallas-area suburbs have built golf courses that now rank among the best — public or private — in the state: Texas Star in Euless, TangleRidge in Grand Prairie and Hidden Creek in Burleson.

Most of the state's courses built in the 1950s to 1970s were municipal layouts were built with taxpayer money, but they were typically low-budget operations built for the masses. Now, city governments are starting to produce courses that compete with the state's best country clubs.

Hidden Creek is nestled along the banks of the creek amidst stands of mesquite and hardwoods. At 6,753 yards, architect Stephen D. Plumer designed a combination links-style/traditional course with tree-lined fairways.

Two holes have split fairways that give a player the option to play it safe or go for broke. The bentgrass greens average 7,200 square feet and are among the best in the metroplex. Water comes into play on seven holes.

The signature hole is No. 8, a 448-yard, par 4 that requires a 220-yard tee shot over a creek to a narrow landing area, then a second shot down a tight, tree-lined fairway to a two-tiered green.

Hidden Creek Golf Course

700 South Burleson Avenue
Burleson 76028
817-447-4444
Pro: Bruce Lang
A par-71, 6,753-yard municipal course.
From Fort Worth, take I-35W south to Exit No. 36, go south on the west frontage road to the main entrance.

• • •

USGA rating: 73.2
Slope rating: 139
Water holes: 7
Sand traps: 38
Doglegs: 8
Type greens: Bentgrass
Record: 64
Designer: Stephen D. Plumer
Year opened: 1996

• • •

Hole	Par	Yards	Hole	Par	Yards
Out	36	3,403	In	35	3,350

Houston Oaks Golf Club Links Course

22602 Hegar Road
Hockley 77447
281-757-4000
Pro: Todd Harbour
A 36-hole public course.
From Houston, take U.S. 290 to Hockley,
turn right on Hegar Road, then 6 miles
to Magnolia Road and right to entrance.

• • •

USGA rating: 70.8
Slope rating: 120
Sand traps: 37
Water holes: 8
Doglegs: 3 left/1 right
Type greens: Bermuda
Record: 63
Designer: Tom Fazio
Year opened: 1979

• • •

Hole	Par	Yards	Hole	Par	Yards
Out	35	2,961	In	37	3,436

Imagine a Rolls Royce Corniche that has been sitting in the garage but never driven. Or an original Picasso discovered in the attic, never before seen by public eyes. Or a vault of Beattles' songs that were recorded decades ago but never released. Or a dusty old bottle of vintage Bordeaux that somehow was lost in the wine cellar.

When it comes to Houston-area golf courses, Houston Oaks Golf Club is the "little old lady from Pasadena." It has been around for more than four decades, but has only been driven around the block but a relatively few times.

Located in the community of Hockley in northwest Harris County, these two courses were built in 1957 as a recreational facility for employees of Tenneco.

The club was recently sold to a private company and renamed Houston Oaks.

After years of being one of the most exclusive clubs in town and unknown to the large majority of Houston golfers, the courses are now open to the public.

The Links Course has the distinction of being the first solo effort of Tom Fazio, who is now one of the nation's premier architects. The layout features nine classic holes and nine links-style holes. The front is more open with subtle mounding. The back is tree-lined and tight with small greens.

No. 2 and No. 18 are the two signature holes. No. 2 is a 400-yard par 4 with water in play off the tee and down the left side. No. 18 is a 390-yard par 4 with bunkers on both sides and an approach to a two-tiered green.

At the same time Ralph Plummer was shaping Texas golf history down the road when he built the Cypress Creek Course at Champions Golf Club, he was hired by Tenneco to build a golf course that would be the centerpiece of a recreational facility for Tenneco employees.

After 40 years of being one of the most exclusive courses in the Houston area, the course was sold in 1998 to a private California-based company who opened the course to the public and renamed it Houston Oaks Golf Club.

While Houston golfers may have a hard time ever setting foot on the first tee at Champions, they can get the same feel at Houston Oaks, where Plummer designed a layout that resembles his other more famous courses.

While it is shorter than most Plummer layouts, his original course is a classic design with beautiful old oak trees lining the fairways.

No. 4 is a 400-yard dogleg left with a tight driving area. Out-of-bounds is down the right side and trees line the fairway all the way to a very small green. No. 5 is 450 yards with mounds and bunkers by the green and water down the right side.

"It's a classic design," a former pro says. "You can see Plummer's hand both here and at Champions. He originally wanted to make it longer — there's plenty of room for it to grow — but the members said no. Both courses are sneaky hard and put a premium on iron play rather than length because the greens are so small."

Houston Oaks Golf Club Old Course

22602 Hegar Road
Hockley 77447
281-757-4000
Pro: Todd Harbour
A 36-hole public course.
From Houston, take U.S. 290 to Hockley, turn right on Hegar Road, then six miles to Magnolia Road, then right to entrance.

• • •

USGA rating: 70.5
Slope rating: 121
Sand traps: 30
Water holes: 10
Doglegs: 3 left/1 right
Type greens: Bermuda
Record: 63
Designer: Ralph Plummer
Year opened: 1957

• • •

Hole	Par	Yards	Hole	Par	Yards
Out	35	3,033	In	36	3,442

Hurricane Creek Country Club

1800 Fairway Lane
Anna 75409
972-924-3247
Pro: Greg Morrison
A par-72, 7,022-yard semi-private club.
From Dallas, take Highway 75 to exit 48
west, then go north about 2 miles
on service road to entrance.

• • •

USGA rating: 73.7
Slope rating: 123
Sand traps: 14
Water holes: 10
Doglegs: 5 left/4 right
Type greens: Bermuda
Record: 52
Designer: Leon Howard
Year opened: 1968

• • •

Hole	Par	Yards	Hole	Par	Yards
Out	36	3,525	In	36	3,527

They don't call it Hurricane Creek for nothing.

Built in 1968 on a hilltop ridge between Dallas and Sherman, Hurricane Creek Country Club is named both for the creek that runs through its property but also the winds that sweeps across its fairways.

On a good day, golfers just hope to be in the eye of the storm.

There weren't many golf courses around this rurall area in 1968, when a group of golfers who had grown weary of driving to either Dallas or Sherman to play golf decided to get together and start a new country club.

They hired architect Leon Howard, who produced more Texas courses than any other architect during the 1960s, to produce a par-72, 7,022-yard layout that plays to a 123 slope rating from the back tees. Wind and water are its most dangerous natural hazard.

The signature hole at Hurricane Creek is No 18, a 430-yard dogleg right par 4 through the trees. On the approach, golfers must hit uphill and into the wind to reach the green. It's a difficult combination, considering most players use a long iron or fairway wood.

No. 5 is a 209-yard par 3 that plays uphill to the green, which is protected by a bunker on the right side.

No. 15 is a 194-yard par 4 that requires golfers to carry over the pond in front of the green but thread their tee shot between bunkers on both sides of the green.

Dick Phelps is a thinking man's architect who likes to require players to think before they pull the club out of their bag on the tee. Instead of wailing away, he forces you to pre-plan your attack or pay the consequences.

And there's nothing that will get a golfer's attention faster than water. At Indian Creek, we suggest packing a life-jacket.

Considering construction was delayed time and again by major flooding, it seems appropriate that on the 36 holes Phelps designed in the bottomlands where Indian Creek meets the Elm Fork of the Trinity River, that water comes into play on 34 of them.

Phelps produced a Creek Course that measures 7,218 yards and features water on all 18 holes; if the Trinity doesn't come into play, Indian Creek does.

"Indian Creek was a difficult project," Phelps recalls. "The best thing about it was the abundance of cedar, oak and elm trees.

"We recognized when we started that occasional flooding would be inevitable, and the idea was to build a course that would survive and be playable as quickly as possible afterward. The course officials have done a terrific job keeping the course in shape."

The 466-yard, par-4 No. 6 on the Creek Course features a split fairway around a grove of trees in the middle. Indian Creek also runs in front of the tee and down the right side of the fairway. The safest bet off the tee is the left fairway, but you still must hit a long approach to a green protected by a creek on the right and a pond on the left.

Indian Creek Golf Club Creek Course

1650 Frankford Road
Carrollton 75232
214-492-3620
Pro: Stan Roberts
A 36-hole public facility.
From Dallas, take I-35 north to Trinity Mills exit. Stay on access road one mile to Frankford Road. Go right to entrance.

• • •

USGA rating: 74.7
Slope rating: 125
Sand traps: 32
Water holes: 18
Doglegs: 3 left/5 right
Type greens: Bermuda
Record: 64
Designer: Dick Phelps
Year opened: 1984

• • •

Hole	Par	Yards	Hole	Par	Yards
Out	36	3,588	In	36	3,630

Indian Creek Golf Club Lakes Course

1650 Frankford Road
Carrollton 75232
214-492-3620
Pro: Stan Roberts
A 36-hole public facility.
From Dallas, take I-35 north to Trinity Mills exit. Stay on access road 1 mile to Frankford Road. Go right to entrance.

• • •

USGA rating: 74.7
Slope rating: 125
Sand traps: 32
Water holes: 18
Doglegs: 3 left/5 right
Type greens: Bermuda
Record: 64
Designer: Dick Phelps
Year opened: 1984

• • •

Hole	Par	Yards	Hole	Par	Yards
Out	36	3,460	In	36	3,570

The first course at Indian Creek was such a success, that the city of Carrollton invited architect Dick Phelps back three years later to build a second course known as the Lakes Course.

Built in the same flood plain below Indian Creek and the Elm Fork Trinity River, the Lakes Course has a similar feel to its older brother. It measures 7,030 yards and holes No. 5 and 6 are the only ones on the property where water doesn't come into play.

Phelps' design definitely requires players to think before they pull a club out of their bag. Instead of wailing away, he forces you to pre-plan your attack or pay the consequences.

Among the best holes at the Lakes Course is the 453-yard, par-4 ninth on the Lakes Course, which leaves absolutely no margin for error with water in play off the tee and on both sides of the approach. The hole is a slight dogleg left, with one pond protecting the left elbow of the fairway and extending all the way to the green.

If you can manage to make it to the dry landing area, players then must thread a shot between the ponds on the left and right to a green guarded by bunkers.

"Indian Creek was a difficult project," Phelps recalls. "It was a very flat, heavily wooded site in the river bottom. We recognized when we started that occasional flooding would be inevitable, and the idea was to build a golf course that would survive and be playable as quickly as possible afterward. The superintendent and the city have done a terrific job keeping the course in shape."

From the time you turn into the parking lot at Iron Horse to the time you walk into the pro shop to turn in your scorecard, you'll notice a certain theme.

Iron Horse gets its name from the railroad that cuts through the property and divides it into three parts along with Loop 820 just outside downtown Fort Worth. The clubhouse looks like an old train depot, and you'll find three cabooses throughout the course that serve as rest rooms or snack bars.

While the course was named for other reasons, this is not to forget that this is a layout that will test your mettle.

Architect Dick Phelps, designer of such notable public layouts as Firewheel and Indian Creek, rose to the occasion to build a challenging course in the bottom lands of Fossil Creek.

The course is built on 180 acres of densely wooded flood plain land previously used by motocross enthusiasts and people looking for a place to dump old refrigerators. Phelps cleaned it up, and worked around the inconveniences of the railroad and freeway to build a layout that demands concentration and strategy.

"We don't really go for the signature hole concept," Phelps says. "We would rather design a full, balanced 18 holes. We like to make a golfer tighten down the screws and concentrate."

Iron Horse has only two par 5s, so the yardage is deceiving. Eight of the 12 par 4s are over 400 yards, including the 462-yard No. 3 — the toughest hole on the course. Both par 5s (Nos. 4 and 11) are true three-shot holes.

Iron Horse Golf Club

6200 Skylark Circle
North Richland Hills 76180
817-485-6666
Pro: Jay Clements
A par-70, 6,580-yard public course.
From Fort Worth, take Loop 820 to Glenview Drive.

• • •

USGA rating: 71.8
Slope rating: 130
Sand traps: 32
Water holes: 17
Doglegs: 5 left/6 right
Type greens: Bermuda
Record: 66
Designer: Dick Phelps
Year opened: 1990

• • •

Hole	Par	Yards	Hole	Par	Yards
Out	35	3,267	In	35	3,313

Kingwood Country Club Lake Course

1700 Lake Kingwood Trail
Kingwood 77339
281-348-2217
Pro: David Preisler
A 72-hole private club. From downtown Houston, take Highway 59 north to Kingwood Drive, then right six miles on Lake Kingwood Trail to entrance.

• • •

USGA rating: 73.4
Slope rating: 125
Sand traps: 46
Water holes: 9
Doglegs: 5 left/4 right
Type greens: Bermuda
Record: N/A
Designer: Joe Finger
Year opened: 1978

• • •

Hole	Par	Yards	Hole	Par	Yards
Out	36	3,531	In	36	3,558

When Joe Finger started building the first course at Kingwood Country Club, golf course architects were still in the mindset that you would take whatever the land gave you. When it came to comparing golf courses on Houston's flat terrain to courses outside the city limits on the rolling countryside, well, there is no comparison.

That philosophy worked just fine for Finger, who has had five courses in *Golf Digest's* 100 Greatest Courses at one time or another. And, at Kingwood, he built three distinctive courses on the shore of Lake Houston and banks of the San Jacinto River.

While Kingwood's Island Course is ranked in the Texas Top 100, his Lake and Marsh courses both present a formidable chal-lenge. They are just two of five courses within a 3-mile radius.

The Lake Course is built in a heavily-wooded area with several large lakes and numerous ponds and creeks. All of these factors combine to put heavy demands on accuracy. Be ready when you reach the No. 1 tee. Water is in play on the first six holes.

No. 10 is a 546-yard par 5 with water in play on every shot. The hole doglegs left around the edge of a large lake, leaving little margin for error off the tee or on the approach. The 549-yard, par-5 fifth hole presents a similar chal-lenge, although it doglegs to the right around another large lake.

No. 17 is a 459-yard par 4 that is already long enough, but on the approach players must carry a lake that protects the front of the green.

The Marsh Course was Joe Finger's last finger print at Kingwood Country Club, having been built seven years after the original Island Course in 1974.

The Marsh Course is a challenging layout that twists and turns through the marshy backwaters of Lake Houston.

This is a golf course that, given today's stringent environmental standards, might never have been built a decade later. As the name indicates, this layout is built around the environmentally sensitive marshlands of Lake Houston.

Driving is important on the Marsh layout, as 11 of the 18 holes are doglegs and water comes into play off the tee on 12 holes.

Golfers get the message from the start that accuracy is impor-

tant. No. 1 is a 406-yard par 4 and is a sharp dogleg right, with a lake cutting in from the right side of the fairway into the middle of the landing area.

No. 9 is a 516-yard, dogleg left par 5 where a lake in the corner comes into play off the tee and on the approach.

The 443-yard, par-4 15th is a demanding driving hole. The hole requires two good shots to reach the green, but off the tee players must skirt past a long lake that cuts into the landing area from the right side.

No. 5 is a 178-yard par 3 that is all carry over water, as is the 182-yard, par-3 17th.

The par-3 14th is a stout 205 yards to a green protected by a pond on the left and a sand trap on the right.

Kingwood Country Club Marsh Course

1700 Lake Kingwood Trail
Kingwood 77339
281-348-2217
Pro: David Preisler
A 72-hole private club. From downtown Houston, take U.S. 59 north to Kingwood Drive, then right 6 miles on Lake Kingwood Trail to entrance.

• • •

USGA rating: 74.8
Slope rating: 136
Sand traps: 25
Water holes: 13
Doglegs: 7 left/4 right
Type greens: Bermuda
Record: 72.3
Designer: Ken Dye
Year opened: 1981

• • •

Hole	Par	Yards	Hole	Par	Yards
Out	36	3,381	In	36	3,554

Kingwood Cove Golf Course

805 Hamblen Road
Kingwood 77339
281-358-1155
Pro: Jerry Honza
A par-71, 6,732-yard public course.
From Houston, take Highway 59 north
to Loop 494/Townsend exit. Stay on
feeder Hamblen Road, then right one
mile to club entrance.

• • •

USGA rating: 71.9
Slope rating: 118
Sand traps: 43
Water holes: 10
Doglegs: 2 left/3 right
Type greens: Bermuda
Record: 64
Designer: John Plumbley
Year opened: 1966

• • •

Hole	Par	Yards	Hole	Par	Yards
Out	35	3,253	In	36	3,479

Long before anyone ever heard of Kingwood, long before anyone decided it would be a great place to build stately homes and an award-winning community, someone else recognized it as a great place for a golf course.

Set amidst a dense forest of hardwoods on rolling terrain on the north bank of the San Jacinto River, Kingwood Cove Golf Club was a great golf course that was ahead of its time when it first opened in 1966. It would be another decade for the community of Kingwood and other golf courses to spring up around it, but it is still recognized as one of Houston's best golfing values and challenging layouts.

The course plays 6,700 yards with a masterful combination of short par 4s, strong par 3s and a set of par 5s that range from reachable in two to hard pars. Every fairway is lined by trees.

One of the more interesting holes is the 360-yard, par-4 No. 8. While the length doesn't sound impressive, the hole doglegs right around a lake that also cuts into the fairway in front of an elevated green and curls around the back. The two-tiered green that is sloped rather severely to the right.

The 527-yard, par-5 No. 10 also requires some local knowledge. The fairway doglegs left about 220 yards off the tee, and the tendency is to take a driver over the corner to cut off enough distance to get home in two. A drive at the wrong angle, however, can wind up i the creek on the right side of the fairway that also cuts in front of the green.

The intentions were good and pure. To name a golf course after the former First Lady was admirable, especially since Lyndon and Lady Bird Johnson grew up in the area.

When George Hoffman designed the original nine holes in 1969, the course wasn't worthy of the First Lady's name or anybody else's, for that matter. While the former First Lady still lives only 40 miles away, it took more than two decades before change came and the course received a facelift that finally made it worthy of its name.

In 1992, the city of Fredericksburg decided to spend $1.7 million on the course, including a new nine holes. In short, they turned Lady Bird Johnson into a championship layout that is maintained, well, like the front lawn of the White House. Architect Jeff Brauer designed a new nine that, in contrast to the tight fairways of the original layout, is more open with extensive mounding, grass bunkers and enlarged sand traps were added.

"We were able to incorporate half of the existing holes so there isn't a stark contrast as the golfer goes from one nine to the next," Brauer said. "We kept the greens small to match the character of the existing course."

No. 5 is a 552-yard par 5 with a wide fairway. The approach shot to the green must carry a large rock wall with a creek at the bottom. The carry off the tee isn't that far, but the first sight can be frightening. The Hill Country mountains in the background make it one of the prettiest finishing holes in the area.

Lady Bird Johnson Golf Course

Highway 16 South
Fredericksburg 78624
830-997-4010
Pro: Russell Parsons
A par-72, 6,432-yard public course.
Take I-10 west to Comfort, take Highway 87 north to Fredericksburg, left at first light and left at next light to entrance.

• • •

USGA rating: 70.3
Slope rating: 125
Sand traps: 18
Water holes: 5
Doglegs: 3 left/ 3 right
Type greens: Bermuda
Record: N/A
Designer: George Hoffman and Jeff Brauer (1992)
Year opened: 1969

• • •

Hole	Par	Yards	Hole	Par	Yards
Out	36	3,228	In	36	3,204

Lago Vista Resort and Country Club Highland Lakes Course

PO Box 4500
Lago Vista 78645
512-267-1685
Pro: Jeff Thomason
A 36-hole country club and resort.
Take I-35 north to Highway 183, left on
FM 1431, go 11 miles to Bogey Drive,
and right three miles to club.

• • •

USGA rating: 71.0
Slope rating: 129
Sand traps: 41
Water holes: 4
Doglegs: 3 left/4 right
Type greens: Bentgrass
Record: N/A
Designer: Leon Howard
        and Dave Bennett (1992)
Year opened: 1972

Hole	Par	Yards	Hole	Par	Yards
Out	36	3,286	In	36	3,393

Highland Lakes is the flashier of the two Leon Howard courses at Lago Vista, with its numerous sand traps and its tricky bentgrass greens.

Howard built the Highland Lakes course shortly after he completed the original course at Lago Vista in 1967. Like the original, it is built on the rugged, hilly terrain of Texas Hill Country, 30 miles northwest of Austin.

In 1990, the golf course was given a $1.7 million facelift and architect Dave Bennett came in to add deep bunkers. The bentgrass greens can be especially tricky. Most slant in one direction or another and many are multi-tiered pin placement and club selection often mean the difference between a birdie and a bogey.

The layout measures only 6,529 yards, but looks are deceiving with the layout's many elevation changes.

The first hole sets the tone for the rest of the day. From the tee box, players start with a view of the lake but the fairway drops straight down and out of sight.

Bennett added deeper bunkers along with leaving the natural areas intact. Also unchanged is the par-4, 348-yard second hole, which once was featured in *Golf Digest* as the "tough hole of the month."

The back nine features more pretty views and ugly places to lose a ball. The 183-yard, par-3 13th has a green-side bunker in the shape of Texas. No. 16 is a 528-yard dogleg right where players must work past bunkers on both sides and through a chute of trees to the green.

Leon Howard will never forget the day John Moss walked into his office across the street from the Austin airport and dropped an 18-hole golf course in his lap.

Moss was well acquainted with Howard as a versatile land planner/golf course architect, and in 1967 he charged Howard with turning 1,000 acres of rugged Hill Country terrain into a golf course community on the shores of Lake Travis.

"That's tough country out there," Howard says. "We had a very large amount of acreage to work with and the owner basically gave me carte blanche.

"He told me to take the land that was feasible to build a golf course, then subdivide everything else. The land dictated the shape of the golf course."

Located 30 miles northwest of Austin, Lago Vista has long been a favorite in the area with four water holes and 41 sand traps and 100-foot elevation changes.

At the same time, Moss gave Howard another 800-acre site at Highland Lakes. Highland Lakes was closed in 1990 and underwent a $1.7 million facelift by architect Dave Bennett.

"Golfers now have the best of both worlds," says pro Mark Klement. "Lago Vista is an excellent members or resort course. Highland Lakes is really an excellent resort setting."

No. 10 is a 495-yard par 5 that can be easily reached in two, but a creek runs the length of the fairway on the right side. The par 3s are demanding, ranging in distance from 199 to 204 yards.

Lago Vista Resort and Country Club
Lago Vista Course

PO Box 4500
Lago Vista 78645
512-267-1685
Pro: Jeff Thomason
A 36-hole country club and resort.
Take I-35 north to Highway 183, left on
FM 1431, go 11 miles to Bogey Drive,
and right three miles to club.

• • •

USGA rating: 70.0
Slope rating: 118
Sand traps: 41
Water holes: 4
Doglegs: 3 left/4 right
Type greens: Bentgrass
Record: N/A
Designer: Leon Howard
    and Dave Bennett (1992)
Year opened: 1967

Hole	Par	Yards	Hole	Par	Yards
Out	36	3,286	In	36	3,293

Lake Arlington Golf Course

1516 Green Oaks Boulevard West
Arlington 76013
817-451-6101
Pro: Jim Sanders

A par-71, 6,637-yard public course. From downtown Dallas, take I-20 west to Green Oaks Boulevard, then north on Green Oaks 5 miles to course entrance on the left.

• • •

USGA rating: 70.7
Slope rating: 117
Sand traps: 0
Water holes: 9
Doglegs: 5 left/4 right
Type greens: Bermuda
Record: 61
Designer: Ralph Plummer
Year opened: 1963

• • •

Hole	Par	Yards	Hole	Par	Yards
Out	35	3,128	In	36	3,509

The City of Arlington has long been noted for its famous Six Flags over Texas Amusement Park, but golfers should experience at least that many thrills when they play the nearby Lake Arlington Municipal Golf Course.

Owned and operated by the city, Lake Arlington has been providing plenty of fun and challenge for golfers since it was opened in 1963. Lake Arlington was one of the first public courses to open in the city and has delighted decades of golfers.

Golfers don't have much time to rev up their games as the first hole is one of the toughest. It plays as a 419-yard par 4 where golfers must work their drive for a dogleg left off the tee. The fairway is very tight with a big pecan tree blocking your path to the green if you go too far off course. Many golfers will attempt to lay up short of the pecan tree with their drive. The second shot usually requires a strong effort against the wind to a well-guarded green.

Nos. 13 and 14 play closest to the lake and dam. The par-4 13th is 389 yards and is an uphill dog-leg right. The fairway is very tight with trees on both sides and water not too far way.

The par-3 14th measures 240 yards, but plays downhill with the wind at your back. The fairway drops dramatically from tee to green, with water on the left side.

Many golfers simply aim at the green and hit away, hoping the wind and distance don't turn their drive on this one-shooter into a watery disaster.

Bear Creek Golf World opened a whole new world to Houston golfers when it opened in 1971, relieving much of the congestion on the scarce few public golf courses in the city and giving rise to the wave of the future.

After Bear Creek met Houston's growing need for public courses on the city's west side, club owners decided to take the same concept to another scenic piece of property on the city's far northeast side north of Lake Houston in Huffman.

Jay Riviere, who built the Masters layout at Bear Creek that still ranks in the Texas Top 100, carved out a demanding layout through the thick woods of Roman Forest. The course, however, never enjoyed the same success of Bear Creek because of its remote location until it was purchased by American Golf Corporation in 1984.

The 358-yard first hole offers a quick start with its easy, wide-open fairway, but can lure a player into a false sense of security. But the course bears down immediately on No. 2 with a tight, 506-yard par 5 and No. 3, a 163-yard par 3 that requires an all-carry approach to a green protected by water.

The finishing holes can quickly turn a good round sour. The most interesting is the 520-yard, par-5 No. 17. A drive of 175-200 yards is needed to clear water off the tee, leaving a second shot requiring another carry of 175 yards over a ravine.

On No. 18, a 419-yard par 4, water comes into play off the tee and approach.

Lake Houston Golf Club

27350 Afton Way
Huffman 77336
281-324-1841
Pro: Jim Belcher

A par-72, 6,844-yard public course. From Houston, take U.S. 59 north to FM 1960, then east across Lake Houston to FM 2100. Turn north to Afton Way, then right to entrance.

• • •

USGA rating: 73.3
Slope rating: 129
Sand traps: 32
Water holes: 7
Doglegs: 4 left/6 right
Type greens: Bermuda
Record: 62
Designer: Jay Riviere
Year opened: 1971

• • •

Hole	Par	Yards	Hole	Par	Yards
Out	36	3,397	In	36	3,447

Lake Park Golf Course

6 Lake Park Road
Lewisville 75057
972-436-5332
Pro: Martin Coulson
A par-72, 6,751-yard public course.
From Dallas, take I-35E north to Lake
Park Road. Turn east on Lake
Park to club entrance.

• • •

USGA rating: 68.6
Slope rating: 108
Sand traps: 12
Water holes: 9
Doglegs: 3 left/4 right
Type greens: Bentgrass
Record: 64
Designer: Lanny Wadkins
    and Richard Watson
Year opened: 1957

• • •

Hole	Par	Yards	Hole	Par	Yards
Out	36	3,516	In	36	3,243

Lanny Wadkins is known around the world as one of the most intense competitors in the game of golf.

Hot-tempered, maybe.

Outspoken, probably.

Clutch player, definitely.

Wadkins has ridden his volatile personality and his golf game to a career that has so far seen him win more than tournaments around the world and $5 million in earnings.

But Wadkins wants to be remembered for more than trophies and dollar signs and outspoken comments. He wants to help shape the way we play the game both now and in the future.

In 1989, Wadkins teamed up with golf course construction engineer Richard Watson to form a partnership to build courses.

Lake Park was their first project.

The course located below the levee along Lake Lewisville was originally known as Oak Ridge Park since it opened in 1957 and was operated by the city. When the city decided to put the course up for sale, Team W came in to do an extensive redesign job. The new layout measures 6,759 yards.

The 465-yard, par-4 first hole is the hardest. It is a slight dogleg left, with water to the left and right off the tee. No. 8 is a 312-yard par 4 that can be reached, but at the risk of finding one of the two small ponds that protect the right side of the green. No. 10 is a 344-yard par 4 where a lake crosses the fairway in the middle of the landing area to force players to lay up or try to carry the ball 230 yards to the other side.

Clifford Moore was an eccentric oil-man who once owned a heavily-wooded 210-acre tract of land in West Houston called "Pine Lakes Farms," a retreat where he entertained his family and friends in the expansive mansion he built in 1939.

In 1951 a syndicate of 10 prominent Houstonians bought the farm to build a country club. After Lakeside Country Club received its charter on Nov. 9, 1951, members hired nationally known architect Ralph Plummer to build a championship course that four decades later has helped Lakeside grow into one of the city's most exclusive clubs.

In 1990 the club hired architect Ron Pritchard to renovate the golf course to restore Plummer's classic layout as one of the best in the state. Lakeside had become as flat as a pancake over the years, but Pritchard fluffed it up a bit by adding mounds and moguls throughout the course, planting new grass and reshaping some of the holes to give it a modern look without completely retooling Plummer's traditional style. The goal was to help the course keep up with the advancements in modern golf technology.

"Ron did a great job in transforming the course," says former pro Jerry Smith. "Not only has the property's beauty been magnified, but he has provided a just test for our golf enjoyment."

The 592-yard, par-5 No. 3 is the toughest on the course, measuring almost 600 yards and featuring an L-shaped green. Four of the par 4s on the front nine are more than 400 yards.

Lakeside Country Club

100 Wilcrest Drive
Houston 77042
281-497-2228
Pro: Gary Ray
A par-72, 6,983-yard private club.
From Houston, go west on Westheimer
to Wilcrest then north to entrance.

• • •

USGA rating: 73.7
Slope rating: 132
Sand traps: 52
Water holes: 13
Doglegs: 5 left/7 right
Type greens: Bermuda
Record: 66
Designers: Ralph Plummer
    and Ron Pritchard (1990)
Year Opened: 1952

• • •

Hole	Par	Yards	Hole	Par	Yards
Out	36	3,608	In	36	3,375

Lakeway Resort
Live Oak Course

602 Lakeway Drive
Austin 78734
512-261-7173
Pro: Joey Yadouga
A 36-hole resort.
Take Mopac south to Southwest
Parkway, right at light to Highway 71,
then right to Highway 620, then
left at Lakeway Boulevard

• • •

USGA Rating: 71.5
Slope rating: 123
Sand traps: 45
Water holes: 5
Doglegs: 5 left/3 right
Type greens: Bermuda
Record: 64
Designer: Leon Howard
Year opened: 1977

• • •

Hole	Par	Yards	Hole	Par	Yards
Out	36	3,328	In	36	3,315

Long before Jack Nicklaus came on the scene to leave his paw-prints on the Hill Country down the street at the Hills of Lakeway, the Live Oak and Yaupon courses have been serving members and guests for years at the prestigious Lakeway Resort just outside of Austin.

While the two older courses may lack the glitz and glamour of Nicklaus' course at the Hills of Lakeway or even new courses nearby at Barton Creek Resort, both are solid tests of golf that have stood the test of time.

The Lakeway Resort was opened in 1963 to give area residents a chance to combine the beauty of the Austin outskirts with the tranquillity of Lake Travis. The chance to get away from it all without having to go very far and to play golf on two courses designed by architect Leon Howard.

Live Oak was the first course at Lakeway when it opened in 1965. While it just turned 30 — which for some courses marks a mid-life crisis — it has remained faithful to Howard's plan.

Befitting its name, the layout is lined with live oak trees. Of the two layouts at Lakeway, Live Oak comes closest to Lake Travis with Nos. 5 and 6 situated just off the tip of the marina. The 10th runs alongside the air strip that transported many of the golfers who played more than 70,000 rounds at the two courses in 1993.

Of all the holes Howard built in his career, he says the par-3 No. 3 is his favorite. It plays 195 yards from the back tees over a canyon to a green just 15 feet on the other side of a 30-foot cliff.

Golf courses built on rugged, mountainous terrain make for spectacular golf, but they also create a challenge before the first shot is ever fired.

Twelve years after architect Leon Howard built the Live Oak course at Lakeway Resort, he returned to build Yaupon on an adjoining piece of property overlooking Lake Travis from the limestone hillsides outside of Austin.

While Howard had a scenic piece of property overlooking the lake, he had virtually no soil to work with on the limestone hillsides. So in 1964, after sculpting the shape of a golf course out of stone, he gained permission from the state to dredge 100,000 cubic yards of soil from the lake bottom. They spread a six-inch layer of soil over the entire property so grass could grow.

"That was the only way we could build it," Howard says. "In this day and age, with all the environmental restrictions, that course might never have been built."

Like its predecessor, it also offers more open views of Lake Travis and the surrounding area. While the Live Oak doesn't have any sand traps, the Yaupon Course has 45 bunkers and five water holes. It also features dramatic elevation changes that can make any hole play shorter or longer than the official yardage.

A case in point is the par-5 18th. It starts with a sweeping view of the area from the tee, then drops more than 50 feet to the fairway. Golfers must lay up in front of a pond on their second shot and then hit their approach over water to an elevated green.

Lakeway Resort Yaupon Course

602 Lakeway Drive
Austin 78734
512-261-7172
Dir.: Ron Miller
A 36-hole resort.
Take Mopac south to Southwest Parkway, right at light to Highway 71, then right to Highway 620, then left at Lakeway Boulevard.

• • •

USGA Rating: 71.5
Slope rating: 123
Sand traps: 45
Water holes: 5
Doglegs: 5 left/3 right
Type greens: Bermuda
Record: 64
Designer: Leon Howard
Year opened: 1977

• • •

Hole	Par	Yards	Hole	Par	Yards
Out	36	3,263	In	36	3,302

Legacy Hills Golf Club

301 Del Webb Boulevard
Georgetown 78628
512-864-1222
Pro: Suzy Davis
A par-72, 7,088-yard semi-private club.
From Austin, take I-35 north to FM 2338
(Lake Georgetown exit). Go west five
miles to course entrance.

• • •

USGA rating: 73.4
Slope rating: 127
Sand traps: 43
Water holes: 3
Doglegs: 4 left/3 right
Type greens: Bermuda
Record: 68
Designers: Billy Casper and Greg Nash
Year opened: 1996

• • •

Hole	Par	Yards	Hole	Par	Yards
Out	36	3,430	In	36	3,658

Life is better here. That's the slogan at Del Webb's Sun City Georgetown, a retirement community where golfers can live out their dream of playing golf every day for the rest of their lives.

Yes, life is better here.

The golf is, too.

Over the past four decades, the Del Webb Corporation has perfected the science of retirement communities.

With similar developments in Arizona, Florida and Southern California, they brought the concept to Texas in 1994.

Like its predecessors, golf is the center of attention at Sun City Georgetown, a complete master-planned community just north of Austin that is designed to eventually include four 18-hole golf courses.

If Legacy Hills is any indication of what is to come, this will become another Texas golf mecca.

Golf Hall of Famer Billy Casper and architect Greg Nash have teamed up to design virtually all of the Del Webb courses and they teamed up again at Legacy Hills to produce a par-72, 7,108-yard layout that will challenge players of all skill levels.

And, in this case, all ages.

Most of the Casper-Nash layouts are open with rolling fairways that keep in mind their purpose of serving a wide range of players.

At Legacy Hills, they produced a layout on just 110 acres that offers spectacular panoramic views of the surrounding Hill Country and large greens.

It is rare indeed when a public golf course outshines an elite private club. Most public courses are built with less money, and by design are meant to handle the masses instead of an elite few. Five times as many feet walk across them. Five times as many divots are hacked out of them.

But for one glorious year in 1923, the Lions Club became the underdog of Austin golf when it opened an 18-hole golf course called Austin Municipal with bermuda greens. It upstaged Austin Country Club, whose members had been putting on sand greens since it opened in 1898.

Life at the top, however, was short. Austin Country Club quickly followed suit and, after a few years, Lions Club members decided they would be better off raising money for charity than running a public golf course. In 1930 the city of Austin took over and named it Lions Municipal Golf Course to preserve the Lions' contribution to Austin golf.

Legendary pro Ben Hogan called the 403-yard, par-4 No. 16 one of the best tests of golf he had seen. Known locally as Hogan's hole, it features a tight, tree-lined fairway that slopes downhill to a large pond. It takes two well-placed shots to reach the elevated green in two.

As a boy, future PGA superstar Ben Crenshaw wore out the putting green at the Lions.

"It's not very long, but you have to be accurate," city golf director Gene Faulk says. "With the trees out here, it narrows the fairways and promotes accuracy more than distance."

Lions Municipal Golf Course

2901 Enfield Road
Austin 78703
512-477-6963
Pro: Lloyd Morrison
A par-71, 6,001-yard public course.
From Austin, go west on 15th Street past Exposition Boulevard to course entrance on the left.

• • •

USGA rating: 68.9
Slope rating: 118
Sand traps: 10
Water holes: 5
Doglegs: 3 left/5 right
Type greens: Bermuda
Record: 59
Designer: Lions Club members
Year opened: 1923

• • •

Hole	Par	Yards	Hole	Par	Yards
Out	36	3,180	In	35	2,841

Los Rios Country Club

1700 Country Club Drive
Plano 75074
972-424-8913
Pro: Joe Linnemeyer
A par-71, 6,507-yard private course.
From Dallas, take Central Expressway
(Highway 75) north to Plano Parkway,
go east 3.5 miles to Los Rios Boulevard,
then north to Country Club Drive.

• • •

USGA rating: 70.7
Slope rating: 118
Sand traps: 20
Water holes: 10
Doglegs: 1 left/ 3 right
Type greens: Bentgrass
Record: 61
Designer: Don January
Year opened: 1974

• • •

Hole	Par	Yards	Hole	Par	Yards
Out	35	3,188	In	36	3,319

As a former pro golfer and president of a company that operates public golf courses, Mark Silverstein saw the wave of the future. While the business of operating golf courses became more sophisticated in the 1970s and '80s, he saw a need for a small, boutique company that specialized in revitalizing golf courses and country clubs that were undermarketed and undervalued.

In December 1991, Silverstein started his own company and purchasing Los Rios Country Club from his former company. By 1993, Silverstein's company had purchased several other clubs in the state, which he recently sold for a handsome profit to the Cobblestone Golf Group.

Los Rios was built in 1974 by PGA Tour pros Don January and Billy Martindale. They used the lovely wooded site with a eight small ponds and a winding creek to create a picturesque layout. The course has six moderately difficult holes, six that are easy and six that are difficult.

No. 7 is the No. 1 handicap hole. At 431 yards, it requires two good shots to reach the green in regulation. The hole plays straight ahead to give players the opportunity for a big tee shot. The bigger the better, since that will shorten the approach to a shallow green on the other side of a creek.

The 14th is a 493-yard par 5 where golfers must cross water three times and a sand trap to reach the green. The serpentine creek crosses the fairway in front of the back tee and again about 100 yards out, then cuts back in front of the green.

Build it and they will come. Well, not necessarily right away.

In the increasingly competitive golf business, the members at Lost Creek Golf Club the Field of Dreams axiom doesn't always come true. Once a private club, it has changed hands four times in the past five years and is now open to the public.

Lost Creek is a relatively short layout designed in 1971 by architect Leon Howard. As the name implies, the course is built around a tree-lined creek that runs through the property. While the 13th and 17th are strong par 4s of 433 and 423 yards, respectively, most are in the 325-390 range. For big hitters, that can mean a lot of driver-wedge play and, depending on your touch, a lot of birdies. But this isn't a golf course that can just be taken for granted, primarily because out-of-bounds comes into play on every hole. For every birdie you make, there is a double-bogey awaiting.

Among the best holes at Lost Creek is the 526-yard, par-5 18th. It veers left then back to the right. A creek runs down the right side and crosses the fairway once in the landing area and again in front of the green. Even big-hitters are hard-pressed to carry the first creek (about 270 yards), so to get home in two golfers have a 270-yard carry over water to the green.

And then there's the straight-away, 433-yard 13th. A creek crosses in front of the tee and runs down the left side of the fairway, pinching the landing area about 240 yards out to put a premium on accuracy off the tee.

Lost Creek Country Club

4101 Lost Creek Boulevard
Aledo 76116
817-244-3312
Pro: Shannon Cox
A par-71, 6,388-yard semi-private club.
From Fort Worth, take I-30 west to
Lost Creek Boulevard. Go across
overpass and go east on I-30 service
road to entrance.

• • •

USGA rating: 70.6
Slope rating: 115
Sand traps: 14
Water holes: 10
Doglegs: 3 left/3 right
Type greens: Bermuda
Record: 64
Designers: Leon and Charles Howard
Year opened: 1971

• • •

Hole	Par	Yards	Hole	Par	Yards
Out	35	3,088	In	36	3,200

Magnolia Ridge Country Club

Route 3
PO Box 212B
Liberty 77575
409-336-3551
Pro: Vic Krenek
A nine-hole semi-private layout.
From Houston, take Highway 90 east to
Highway 146 Bypass, then go north to
Old Beaumont Road and right to club.

• • •

USGA rating: 71.9
Slope rating: NA
Sand traps: NA
Water holes: 7
Doglegs: 4 left/3 right
Type greens: Bentgrass
Record: NA
Designer: Ralph Plummer
Year opened: 1951

• • •

Hole	Par	Yards	Hole	Par	Yards
Out	36	3,245	In	36	3,193

Six years before Ralph Plummer made his way to Houston to build the famed Cypress Creek course at Champions, he made a little practice run in Liberty that turned out to be known as "The Best Little Golf Course" in Texas.

Plummer is more well known for producing some of Texas' most enduring layouts, but in 1951 he was still relatively young in the profession and the bulk of his business was building nine-hole courses around the state.

One of those was Magnolia Ridge, which for many years has been named the No. 1 nine-hole course in Texas by *The Dallas Morning News.*

Plummer was lured to Liberty by Milton Demaret, the brother of Texas legend Jimmy Demaret, who had been hired to become the head pro. Plummer's name wasn't yet big enough for him to turn up his nose at any job, so he made the most of the opportunity on a property with towering pines, magnificent magnolias and sturdy oaks.

Just because he built only nine holes, this is far from half a golf course. He took advantage of the abundance of trees, rolling terrain and Abbots Creek to produce a layout that twists and turns through the woods.

No. 6 is 364-yard par 4 that is typical of the demand for accuracy at Magnolia Ridge. Abbots Creek runs down the right side then cuts in front of the green. There is out-of-bounds all the way down the left side. On the approach shot, golfers must try to get the ball on the proper level of a two-tiered green.

Legend has it that Don Johnson, while filming a movie at Caddo Lake during the 1980s, showed up one day in a limo at the front door of Marshall Lakeside. His chauffeur entered the pro shop and announced that Johnson wanted to play.

The response was, "Who the hell is Don Johnson?"

When the chauffeur explained that Johnson had a TV show called Miami Vice, he was told, "Well, he ain't playing here."

Marshall, Texas, is about as far from Miami Vice as you can possibly get. Nestled in the heart of East Texas, for 70 years it has served the locals with a nine-hole layout that packs more punch than most 18-hole courses.

Besides Johnson, this tiny club has hosted players such as Mickey Mantle, Y.A. Tittle and Roy Clark.

Designed in 1920, this is a traditional course with narrow, tree-lined fairways and small undulating greens.

The signature hole is the 431-yard, par-4 second hole. It doglegs left 90 degrees, just 180 yards off the tee, leaving a long approach.

Lakeside hosted the annual Birdie Call tournament, which started in 1939 and was won by Tommy Bolt, who was notorious for his temper but later turned pro and won the U.S. Open.

A 1939 announcement that the club planned to expand to 18 holes, however, has never come to fruition. During the mid-1950s, the course was renovated by using clay models to redesign the greens and tee boxes. Dallas-based architect Lee Singletary also has helped update the course.

Marshall Lakeside Country Club

Highway 43 North
Marshall 75670
903-938-4211
Pro: Bud Gibbs
A nine-hole private course.
From Dallas, take I-20 east to Highway 59, then go north on Highway 59 to Highway 43, then east on Highway 43 to entrance.

• • •

USGA rating: 69.3
Slope rating: 116
Sand traps: 18
Water holes: 4
Doglegs: 2 left/1 right
Type greens: Bermuda
Record: 63
Designer: Gus Carter
Year opened: 1920

• • •

Hole	Par	Yards	Hole	Par	Yards
Out	36	3,126	In	36	3,131

Max Starcke Park Golf Course

PO Box 591
Seguin 78155
210-401-2490
Pro: Biff Alexander
A par-71, 6,720-yard public course.
From San Antonio, take I-10 west to
exit 603. Turn right on Highway 90A to
Guadalupe, right to Highway 123,
then right to course entrance.

• • •

USGA rating: 70.8
Slope rating: 115
Sand traps: 34
Water holes: 8
Doglegs: 3 left/5 right
Type Greens: Bermuda
Designers: John Bredemus
　　and Ralph Plummer (1979)
Year opened: 1936

• • •

Hole	Par	Yards	Hole	Par	Yards
Out	35	3,284	In	36	3,437

At about the same time John Bredemus was brushing strokes of genius on the canvas that is now Fort Worth's Colonial Country Club and Houston's Memorial Park, he ventured to Hill Country to build a nine-hole course named after the former mayor of Seguin.

While recognized as "the father of Texas golf," Bredemus was an often misunderstood man, most likely because he was a creative genius who was ahead of his time. In 1936, he earned the nickname "Barefoot" when he took his shoes off before entering the office of Houston banker Jesse Jones to plead the case for Memorial Park.

Max Starcke was a golf course designed by Bredemus in 1936 but built by the hands of Depression-era workers of the Works Progress Administration. Much of the front nine borders the Guadalupe River and the rest weaves through a grove of pecan trees. The back nine was designed by architect Ralph Plummer and Texas Golf Hall of Famer Shelly Mayfield, a native of Seguin.

Among the toughest holes on the front side is the par-4, 457-yard No. 3. It plays uphill with a gentle dogleg left. A lake on the left side spells trouble for anyone who hits a ball in that direction.

No. 11 is a long, uphill par 5. Nos. 12 and 13 are elevated with water in front of the greens. No. 13 is a 191-yard par 3. The hole plays to an elevated green with water in front. No matter the weather conditions, many golfers report the wind is always coming into the golfer's face.

Although many of his original fingerprints have now been smudged by several generations of golf course architects, John Bredemus is still known as the "Father of Texas golf course architecture."

Bredemus was a multi-talented man that would have put Deion Sanders and Bo Jackson to shame. He attended Dartmouth, then Princeton and finished second to Jim Thorpe in the Olympic all-around competition in 1912. He graduated from Princeton as a civil engineer, but became a math teacher and later took up golf and turned pro. In 1919, he moved to Texas and became a high school principal in San Antonio.

It was then he realized golf in Texas was almost non-existent, so he combined his engineering background with his love for golf to build golf courses.

Some eight years before Marvin Leonard would employ him to build Colonial Country Club, Bredemus came to Fort Worth to build an 18-hole layout for a private club that was later sold to the city and made public.

The 475-yard, par-4 No. 5 is one of the longest par 4s in the D/FW area and features a tight fairway between water down the left side and trees on the right.

No. 16 is a 435-yard par 4 where players must tee off through a chute of trees and hit a long carry over a lake on their approach shot to the green.

Players should have a chance to get some strokes back on the 313-yard No. 7 and the 324-yard No. 14, both of which can be reached off the tee by big hitters.

Meadowbrook Municipal Golf Course

1815 Jensen Road
Fort Worth 76112
817-457-4616
Pro: Gary McMillian
A par-71, 6,416-yard public course.
From Fort Worth, take I-30 east to
Woodhaven exit. Turn right one mile
to course entrance on the left.

• • •

USGA rating: 70.2
Slope rating: 126
Sand traps: 18
Water holes: 5
Doglegs: 4 left/3 right
Type greens: Bermuda
Record: N/A
Designer: John Bredemus
   and Ralph Plummer (1960)
Year opened: 1928

• • •

Hole	Par	Yards	Hole	Par	Yards
Out	33	2,062	In	33	2,062

Mission Del Lago Golf Club

1250 Mission Grande
San Antonio 78221
210-627-2522
Pro: Rubin Cedillo
A par-72, 7,208-yard public course.
Take Highway 410 south to exit 44
(Roosevelt), left on Roosevelt for two
miles to course entrance on right.

• • •

USGA rating: 72
Slope rating: 129
Sand traps: 124
Water holes: 10
Doglegs: 3 left/3 right
Type greens: Bermuda
Record: 69
Designers: Dennis Griffiths
and Ron Kirby (1989)
Year opened: 1989

• • •

Hole	Par	Yards	Hole	Par	Yards
Out	36	3,546	In	36	3,434

Ron Kirby and Dennis Griffiths got their first taste of golf in the Texas Hill Country back in the late 1970s, when they renovated a couple of holes at the famed Oak Hills Country Club in 1978 and built Fair Oaks Ranch the following year in 1979.

A decade later, they returned to San Antonio to build Mission del Lago, a municipal golf course that is one of the top courses and toughest in San Antonio.

The plan for the golf course was to make it the centerpiece of a master-planned community. Developers wanted to bring a championship course and fine homes to an area of town that didn't have much of either. Griffiths and Kirby didn't leave much in their bag of tricks on this demanding public layout. The course measures 7,208 yards and, with its 124 bunkers, 10 water holes, severe greens and constant breezes off lake Mitchell, it is well suited for a battlefield.

The hardest hole is the 435-yard, dogleg left, par-4 No. 6. The approach is uphill to a severely sloped green guarded by several bunkers.

No. 9 is a tough par 5 that measures 548 yards. It is bordered by out-of-bounds markers on both sides of the fairway.

The par-3 No. 16 is the signature hole. It plays 194 yards from the back with water in front of the green and to the right. Several large bunkers guard the green and a player may face the challenge of being in the sand and having to blast toward the water to get out. The green is slick, making a par or birdie a real feat.

While Crown Colony gets many votes as the No. 1 course in Texas, there is a little course just up the street in its shadows that just might be the No. 1 underrated course in the state.

R.C. Slocum, John David Crow, Larry Nelson, Keith Fergus and Homero Blancas have all graced the fairways at one time or another at Neches Pines Golf Course in Diboll.

This is a public daily-fee facility where green fees are still only $15, but it can be every bit as scenic and challenging as Crown Colony just nine miles up the road.

The land and construction costs (about $1.6 million) for the golf course were donated by East Texas paper magnate Arthur Temple, who wanted his employ-ees to have an affordable course on which to play.

Architect Leon Howard designed the first nine in 1967, and Dave Bennett returned to design the second nine in 1990 to complete a championship layout that winds through the tall pines of East Texas. The front nine is longer and more open than the back nine.

No. 14 is a 152-yard par 3 that maybe the hardest par 3 in Texas. It doesn't look difficult from the tee, except for the bunker at the right front edge of a sharply-sloped green. When the Lone Star Tour played here in 1996, the women's tees was used so players could hit wedges to the green just to give the ball a chance to stick. Hit right of the green and an up-and-down is nearly impossible.

Neches Pines Golf Course

900 Harris
Diboll 75941
409-829-5086
Pro: Jimmy Medlin
A par-72, 7,014-yard public course.
From Dallas, take I-20 east to Highway 59, then go south on Highway 59 to Harris Street.

• • •

USGA rating: 73.9
Slope rating: 133
Sand traps: 13
Water holes: 12
Doglegs: 4 left/3 right
Type greens: Bermuda
Record: 64
Designer: Leon Howard
Year opened: 1967

• • •

Hole	Par	Yards	Hole	Par	Yards
Out	36	3,580	In	34	3,400

NorthShore Country Club

34801 Broadway Street
Portland 78374
512-643-2798
Pro: Jeff Smelzer
A par-72, 6,805-yard private club.
From Houston, take Highway 59 south
to Highway 181, then north on Highway
181 to course entrance.

• • •

USGA rating: 73.5
Slope rating: 135
Sand traps: 63
Water holes: 16
Doglegs: 4 left/5 right
Type greens: Bermuda
Record: N/A
Designer: Robert von Hagge
and Bruce Devlin
Year opened: 1985

• • •

Hole	Par	Yards	Hole	Par	Yards
Out	36	3,527	In	36	3,278

Robert von Hagge and Bruce Devlin are famous — notorious? — for building some of the most difficult golf courses in Texas. From the back tees, most of their layouts have produced golf courses with an average slope rating of 130.

They produced Walden on Lake Conroe and Crown Colony, The Cliffs on Possum Kingdom, the King's and Queen's courses at Gleneagles, the Club at Falcon Point, all of which are not only included in the Texas Top 100, but are among the most scenic and most difficult courses in the state. NorthShore Country Club is no exception.

Built in 1985 at the height of their careers, NorthShore is a seaside links course that is one of the hardest in the Gulf Coast. It has hosted a Nike Tour event and annually hosts many pro events in the Southern Texas PGA Section.

NorthShore is more reminiscent of a Florida course or Hilton Head, South Carolina, as it plays along the Corpus Christi Bay with troublesome Gulf Breezes an ominipresent factor on every shot. The par-72, 6,805-yard layout plays to a 135 slope rating.

The bermuda grass greens are large and fast, and there are several natural water hazards coming into play on some holes.

A difficult finish awaits on No. 18, a 555-yard par 5, requiring a tee shot over water and onto a narrow fairway protected by a large bunker on the left.

The green is tucked back into another water hazard, so lay up if you want to play it safe and save a ball.

If there is one description of the courses built by the team of Robert von Hagge and Bruce Devlin, it's that they are shotmaker layouts that require thinking one shot at a time. Some players love them; others claim they are too severe.

Perhaps nowhere is that more evident than at Northgate Country Club, the centerpiece to the relatively small but upscale housing development in.

Given a limited amount of space in which to work but plenty of trees, von Hagge-Devlin proved courses do not have to be long to be difficult. In a day and age of jumbo drivers and hot balls, they put strategy back into the game.

Even though it plays to par 70 and is a deceivingly long 6,540 yards, Northgate is ranked among the toughest courses in Houston with its combination of ultra-tight fairways, small, undulating greens and water on 15 holes. Sixty-five bunkers also came into play in the fairways and around the greens.

"We feel that it is a fair test of golf, one that forces you to play lots of different types of shots and to think your way around the course," the architects wrote in a letter to developer Jack Thoner.

"We think Northgate may provide the most challenging golf for its acreage size and length compared with any course in Houston, if not the state."

Take the par-4 first hole, for instance. It is a 413-yard dogleg right that has a narrow landing area. A huge bunker protects the right corner, while a lake guards the right side of the fairway and green on the approach.

Northgate Country Club

17110 Northgate Forest
Houston 77068
281-444-5302
Pro: Dave Esch
A par-70, 6,540-yard private club.
Take I-45 north to FM 1960, go west four miles to subdivision entrance on right, go right to club entrance.

• • •

USGA rating: 71.3
Slope rating: 126
Sand traps: 65
Water holes: 15
Doglegs: 5 left/3 right
Type greens: Bermuda
Record: 65
Designers: Bob von Hagge and Bruce Devlin
Year opened: 1984

• • •

Hole	Par	Yards	Hole	Par	Yards
Out	35	3,284	In	35	3,256

Oak Cliff Country Club

2200 West Red Bird Lane
Dallas 75232
214-333-3595
Pro: Russell Orth
A par-70, 6,579-yard private club.
From Dallas, take I-35E south to
Laureland Road, then right to entrance.

• • •

USGA rating: 72.1
Slope rating: 129
Sand traps: 52
Water holes: 7
Doglegs: 4 left/2 right
Type greens: Bentgrass
Record: N/A
Designers: Press Maxwell
Year opened: 1952

• • •

Hole	Par	Yards	Hole	Par	Yards
Out	35	3,277	In	35	3,302

Notoriety is a double-edged sword. It is nice for a golf course to be recognized by the general public, but the reason members join a club in the first place is to enjoy their privacy away from the general public.

Oak Cliff has been on both sides of the fence. Shortly after it opened, it became the home of the PGA Tour's annual Dallas Open from 1958–67. Then, after the tournament moved to Preston Trail in 1968, Oak Cliff fell out of the public eye as the city's growth moved north of downtown Dallas. In 1994, the spotlight returned when Oak Cliff became host of the Senior PGA Tour's Dallas Reunion Pro-Am.

Architect Press Maxwell built the layout in 1952 on a 171-acre tract spanned by Five Mile Creek.

In the first four years of hosting the Dallas Open, the winners were Sam Snead, Julius Boros, Johnny Pott and Dallas' Earl Stewart Jr. became the Tour's first hometown winner in '61.

Two holes show up quite frequently in ballotting for the toughest holes in Dallas, including the 225-yard, par-3 13th and the 385-yard, par-4 10th.

No. 13, for most golfers, takes all they've got just to reach an angled green that is protected by bunkers right and left and leaves little margin of error.

No. 10 is a slight dogleg left, where golfers must hit an accurate tee shot to get in position for an approach to a tiny green. The second-half of the dogleg is protected by a row of trees on both sides, and a creek runs the length of the left side of the fairway.

Having grown up in Dallas, few people had their fingers more on the pulse of the Dallas golf scene during the past few decades as Don January.

As a PGA Tour professional with more than 30 career victories around the world, this golf course architect grew up on Dallas' public courses and brought a unique insight to the game.

It was with this vision that January built such area courses as Royal Oaks, Los Rios, Plano Municipal, Woodhaven, Wood Crest and Walnut Creek. Each was built with a particular purpose and budget in mind.

January temporarily retired from the architecture business during the early 1980s to join the Senior PGA Tour, but he came out of retirement in 1986 when he convinced developers to spend $4 million on a golf course/real estate development in the tiny town of Corinth.

At Oakmont, January produced what he calls "the best combination of natural beauty and challenging play that I've seen in the Southwest."

Like many other Texas real-estate projects in the mid-80s, it fell on hard times. Dallas-based Club Corporation of America purchased Oakmont in late 1992.

January gave golfers a birdie opportunity at the 320-yard No. 14, where golfers are tempted to go for the green off the tee.

But he saved two demanding par 4s for the final three holes. No. 16 measures 442 yards and the 18th is 432 yards providing a tough finish. No. 9 is also a 445-yard par 4.

Oakmont Country Club

1200 Clubhouse Drive
Corinth 76205
940-321-5599
Pro: John Ericson
A par-72, 6,908-yard semi-private club.
From Dallas, take I-35E north across
Lake Lewisville to the Shady Shores exit.
Turn left and follow signs to
the club entrance.

• • •

USGA rating: 72.7
Slope rating: 123
Sand traps: 51
Water holes: 5
Doglegs: 3 right/0 left
Type greens: Bentgrass
Record: 63
Designers: Don January
Year opened: 1986

• • •

Hole	Par	Yards	Hole	Par	Yards
Out	36	3,495	In	36	3,413

Oakridge Country Club

2800 Diamond Oaks
Garland 75044
972-530-8004
Pro: Mike Hodgins
A par-71, 6,516-yard semi-private club.
Take I-635 to Shiloh Road then turn
north to Buckingham. Turn west to
Diamond Oaks and left to entrance.

• • •

USGA rating: 125
Slope rating: 71.2
Sand traps: 50
Water holes: 13
Doglegs: 6 left/5 right
Type greens: Bermuda
Record: N/A
Designers: Jack Kidwell
*   and Michael Hurdzan*
Year opened: 1982

Hole	Par	Yards	Hole	Par	Yards
Out	36	3,319	In	35	6,516

Surprise. Surprise. That's what the members at Oakridge Country Club were in for on April 7, 1988, when the Internal Revenue Service came calling.

Unbeknownst to them, the previous owners of the club had failed to pay nearly $250,000 in employee taxes over a period of several years. Federal officials came out on the course and asked players to return their carts to the clubhouse, quickly empty their lockers and leave.

Tax liens were posted on the doors and the doors were locked.

It was not one of the highlights in the young history of this course built by architects Jack Kidwell and Michael Hurdzan in 1982 along the banks of Duck Creek.

The club was originally started by Robert Holmes Sr. and a group called Oakridge Country Club. It is now owned by Cobblestone Golf Group.

Kidwell and Hurdzan maximized the use of the winding creek, since water comes into play on 13 holes, including every hole on the back nine.

The toughest hole is the 393-yard, par-4 18th, a dogleg left with water in play off the tee and on the approach and little margin for error. A creek crosses from right to left in front of the tee, then runs down the left side of the fairway and cuts back across in front of the green. A series of bunkers on the right side further squeeze the landing area, which gets smaller the further you go.

No. 3 is a 475-yard par 5 that can be easily reached in two, but golfers must contend with water off the tee and on the approach.

Carlton Gipson was a longtime architect who was one of the most active golf course architects in the state. It is important to note, however, that he chose to live at Peach Tree.

Gipson, who died in 1998, already lived in the rural community of Bullard just outside of Tyler. When he was approached by longtime local doctor Dick Hurst to build a second course at the Peach Tree development, he built it with his own money.

After building the first course himself, the second time around Hurst hired Gipson, since he already lived on the premises, to built a golf course that would bear Hurst's own name. The new layout was called the Oak Hurst Course, and is one of the most challenging courses in East Texas.

Four years before he lost his long battle with lung cancer, Gipson designed a par-72, 6,813-yard layout that one regular says is "a young course, but it plays like an old master."

The 415-yard No. 16 is a very demanding test, with two lakes coming into play on the drive and the approach. The hole is a dogleg left, with a lake protecting the left side of the fairway and corner of the dogleg. On the approach, golfers must carry another lake that curls around the front of the green and protects it on three sides.

No. 10 is a 595-yard par 5, but presents a similar challenge. The hole veers left, with a lake that cuts into the fairway in the landing area. On the approach, a lake hugs the front and left sides of the green to discourage anyone from going for the green in two.

Peach Tree Golf Club Oak Hurst Course

6212 County Road 152 West
Bullard 75757
903-894-7079
Pro: Darrell Chase
A par-72, 6,813-yard private club.
Take Highway 69 south off Loop 323 in Tyler. Go south on Highway 69 to County Road 152. Go west to course entrance.

• • •

USGA rating: 72.3
Slope rating: 126
Water holes: 10
Type greens: Bermuda
Doglegs: 3 left/2 right
Sand traps: 15
Record: 65
Designer: Carlton Gipson
Year opened: 1993

• • •

Hole	Par	Yards	Hole	Par	Yards
Out	36	3,338	In	36	3,475

Peach Tree Golf Club
Peach Tree Course

6212 County Road 152 West
Bullard 75757
903-894-7079
Pro: Darrell Chase
A 36-hole semi-private club.
Take Highway 69 south off Loop 323 in
Tyler. Go south on Highway 69 to County
Road 152. Go west to course entrance.

• • •

USGA rating: 65.7
Slope rating: 109
Sand traps: 37
Water holes: 7
Doglegs: 1 left/2 right
Type greens: Bermuda
Reocord: N/A
Designers: C.R. Hurst and Buddy Bridges
Year opened: 1985

• • •

Hole	Par	Yards	Hole	Par	Yards
Out	35	2,699	In	36	2,864

Dick Hurst is known around the Tyler area as a sage-old doctor and humanitarian, who has made many medical missions to Iraq and southern Russia.

But his more lasting legacy might be Peach Tree Golf Club, a pristine 36-hole semi-private golf facility in East Texas just outside of Tyler.

Like many doctors, Hurst was an avid golfer. Unlike most doctors, Hurst decided in 1985 to build his own course on the site of an old peach orchard with the help of his son Don and Buddy Bridges.

In an era of golf courses owned and operated by multi-million dollar corporations, Peach Tree Golf Club is a throwback to golf's old days. When the course owner was also the operator who would greet before and after your round.

They built the clubhouse out of remnants from the World War II barracks from nearby Camp Fannin. Don oversaw most of the construction on the original course.

After building the first course himself, the second time around Hurst hired Gipson, since he already lived on the premises, to built a golf course that would bear Hurst's own name.

The new layout was called the Oak Hurst Course, and is one of the most challenging courses in East Texas.

The original course is known simply as the Peach Tree Course. The layout is short by modern standards, measuring only 5,556 yards from the back tees, but its well-maintained conditions make it a great place for beginning golfers and seniors like Hurst to enjoy the game.

The Richmond-Rosenberg area has played an important role in Texas history. Jane Long, the first woman of English descent to enter Texas and bear a child of such parentage, lived here. Mirabeau B. Lamar, the second president of Texas, lived in Mrs. Long's hotel from 1838 to 1841.

This land is still considered "in the country" by most Houstonians, with its vast undeveloped open spaces and dense stands of native oak and pecan trees. It was the perfect place, developer J.B. Belin thought, to build a community based on the traditional country living of those early Texas settlers.

In 1978, Belin began construction on the $300 million, 1,400-acre Pecan Grove Plantation on land that was rich in vegetation and dense forests of native oak and pecan trees. Architect Carlton Gipson took advantage of that when he built the original 18 holes in 1979. Gipson added a third nine in 1988 called Pecan. The layout weaves through the homes in the surrounding neighborhood. Here is a look at the best holes:

Plantation No. 2: At 456 yards, this is a dogleg right and well bunkered, with traps in both corners of the dogleg and on the left and right sides of the green.

Pecan No. 9: This 444-yard par 4 is a dogleg right to an elevated green. Take your par and skip on over to the 19th hole.

Grove No. 5: A 436-yard par 4, it is a dogleg right with bunkers in both corners. Most of the distance on the hole is after the corner, so many players try to cut the corner off the tee.

Pecan Grove Country Club

Plantation Drive
Richmond 77469
281-342-9940
Pro: Jimmy Cunningham
A 27-hole private club.
Take U.S. 59 south to Highway 90, then left for 7 miles to FM 359. Turn right one mile to club entrance on right.

• • •

USGA rating: 73.1
Slope rating: 125
Sand traps: 60
Water holes: 9
Doglegs: 3 left/5 right
Type greens: Bermuda
Record: 63
Designer: Carlton Gipson
Year opened: 1978

• • •

Hole	Par	Yards	Hole	Par	Yards
Out	36	3,425	In	36	3,556

Pecan Hollow
Golf Course

4501 East 14th Street
Plano 77074
972-423-5444
Pro: Steve Heidelberg
A par-72, 6,879-yard public course.
From Dallas, take I-75 north to Plano
Parkway, then turn east to Shiloh Road.
Go north on Shiloh to 14th Street,
then east on 14th to entrance.

• • •

USGA rating: 72.1
Slope rating: 122
Sand traps: 0
Water holes: 7
Doglegs: 4 left/3 right
Type greens: Bermuda
Record: N/A
Designers: Don January
and Billy Martindale (1973)

• • •

Hole	Par	Yards	Hole	Par	Yards
Out	36	3,348	In	36	3,531

After building the best golf course of his career at Royal Oaks, Don January and partner Billy Martindale decided it was time to pick up the pace in their golf course design business. January was a professional golfer by trade, but having grown up on the public links around Dallas he was in touch with the needs of the area golfers and also in touch with the mistakes of past architects.

January and Martindale contracted with the growing city of Plano in 1973 to build a municipal golf course for its growing population. It was one of the first courses in the area, and they were given a 30-year lease to build and operate the course. After 15 years they turned it back to the city.

Originally known as Plano Municipal Golf Course, it recently was renamed Pecan Hollow.

"As a player I saw a lot of mistakes that were made that I didn't want to repeat," January said. "I liked the older style architecture. The courses I'm talking about are courses that have stood the test of time. I built a bunch of courses in the 60s and 70s, but never any like I really wanted. I never had the freedom to build a golf course without worrying about selling houses. Golf course design later became a contest of who could build the best sand traps. I hated to see golf get into that."

January's Plano layout will test your stamina, because it closes with three demanding par 4s that make for one of the toughest finishing combinations in D/FW. The 16th, 17th and 18th holes are long par 4s over 445 yards with water in play on all three.

ranbury — despite the spelling of the city, was named after General Hiram B. Granberry. It is a historic town where tourism has supplanted agriculture, and Victorian charm has been revitalized at its popular bed-and-breakfasts. Brothers Jesse and Jacob Nutt helped found the town in the late 1800s on the banks of Lake Granbury. The town square was the first in Texas to be listed on the National Register of Historic Places. Within a 10-block radius, there are three dozen century-old buildings and houses.

Granbury's population only recently topped the 5,000 mark, but dozens of residential developments outside the city limits on the shores of the 33.5-mile long lake help bring the trade area to about 30,000. As the city of Fort Worth grows to the southwest, Granbury is becoming a popular bedroom community where residents can have the best of both worlds — a country lifestyle within driving distance of the big city.

Fort Worth's Leonard brothers were the first to develop residential communities in the area with Pecan Plantation and DeCordova Bend. Both developments were centered around a golf course, and by 1991 the area had grown enough to support the addition of the Nutcracker Course.

Built in the Brazos River bottom, Nutcracker is a par-72, 6,743-yard, semi-private layout that plays to a 132 slope rating from the back tees. The course features a good mixture of long, short and medium holes, including par 3s of 226 and 152 yards, and par 5s ranging from 530 to 482 yards.

Pecan Plantation Golf Club Nutcracker Course

9500 Orchard Drive
Granbury 76049
817-579-1811
Pro: Robbie Loving
A 36-hole private club.
From Fort Worth, take Highway 377 to Granbury to course entrance.

• • •

USGA rating: 72.1
Slope rating: 132
Sand traps: 15
Water holes: 12
Doglegs: 4 left/3 right
Type greens: Bermuda
Record: N/A
Designer: Lee Singletary
Year opened: 1991

• • •

Hole	Par	Yards	Hole	Par	Yards
Out	36	3,357	In	36	3,386

Pecan Plantation
Golf Club
Old Course

8650 Westover Drive
Granbury 76049
817-573-2641
Pro: Jacke Bechtold
A 36-hole private club.
From Fort Worth, take Highway 377 to
Granbury to course entrance.

• • •

USGA rating: 72.2
Slope rating: 124
Sand traps: 39
Water holes: 7
Doglegs: 3 left/3 right
Type greens: Bermuda
Record: N/A
Designer: Leon Howard
Year opened: 1972

• • •

Hole	Par	Yards	Hole	Par	Yards
Out	36	3,409	In	36	3,421

Bob Leonard had a dilemma. Leonard, the nephew of Fort Worth's famous Leonard Brothers, was a noted conservationist and environmentalist who was awarded time and again for his efforts.

But Leonard was also a developer who owned a large amount of land in the Lake Granbury area southwest of Fort Worth. He wanted to develop this property to lure big-city residents out into the country.

Granbury is a historic town where tourism has supplanted agriculture. Its Victorian charm has been revitalized at its popular bed-and-breakfasts.

One of Leonard's biggest properties was a 3,000-acre commercial pecan orchard in the Brazos River bottom. He wanted to build homes and he wanted to build a golf course, but he wanted to remove as few trees as possible.

The challenge was this: The trees were about 15 years old at the time and stood about 30 feet tall and were planted in rows about 40 feet apart.

"He gave me very explicit instructions," architect Leon Howard said. "He told me first to design a good hole. But if there were two ways to design it and one was more environmentally sensitive than the other, to always choose that route."

Being in the river bottom, there wasn't much terrain to work with and, because of the abundance of trees, Howard had to use his imagination to keep the holes from being redundant. He used some bunkering and mounding to make each hole a different.

Behind every famous golf course architect, there is a man who draws the lines and does the dirty work. While the architect travels from site to site around the country, someone has to stay behind to check on the day-to-day operations and make sure that what was put on paper is actually being carved out of the landscape.

In 1992, Derrell Witt decided it was time to step out of the shadows after working as the man behind architect Carlton Gipson's projects at Greatwood, Old Orchard and a dramatic renovations at BraeBurn Country Club.

"I would like to think I can account for some of those success stories," Witt said. "I just wasn't ever getting much credit for my work, so I decided it was time to break away on my own."

Witt's background is in landscape architecture, and he put that philosophy into use on his first solo project at Pine Crest Golf Club, a daily-fee course that opened in 1992 and is one of only two courses built in the Houston city limits in at least a decade. Witt moved 250,000 cubic feet of dirt to create a chain of 13 lakes and ponds on the relatively small property.

"My philosophy about the design of a golf course goes back to my background as a landscape architect," Witt says, "that being to let the land and environment dictate what you should do rather than try to force a design on the land. It should look like nature has developed a golf course and man has only planted grass and put a few holes in the ground."

Pine Crest Golf Club

3080 Gessner
Houston 77080
713-462-4914
Pro: Steve Bratcher
A par-72, 6,927-yard public course.
From Houston take I-10 west to Gessner, go north for five miles to club entrance on the right.

• • •

USGA rating: 72.1
Slope rating: 124
Sand traps: 57
Water holes: 10
Doglegs: 4 left/4 right
Type greens: Bermuda
Record: 71
Designer: Derrell Witt
Year opened: 1992

• • •

Hole	Par	Yards	Hole	Par	Yards
Out	36	3,395	In	36	3,532

Pinnacle Club

200 Pinnacle Club Drive
Mabank 75147
903-451-9797
Pro: Terry Perry
A par-71, 6,441-yard semi-private club.
From Dallas, take Highway 175 east
to Mabank.

• • •

USGA rating: 72.9
Slope rating: 135
Sand traps: 44
Water holes: 8
Doglegs: 3 left/5 right
Type greens: Bermuda
Record: N/A
Designer: Don January
Year opened: 1985

• • •

Hole	Par	Yards	Hole	Par	Yards
Out	36	3,235	In	35	3,216

Most big-time golf courses with big reputations are found in the big city. They cater to a virtual Who's Who in the local business community. They get more press to fatten their reputations. And they get more players, which means they make more money to pay for better maintenance conditions.

The Pinnacle Club never had that luxury. Nestled in a rural setting on the sleepy banks of Cedar Creek Lake, it was ahead of its time when it opened as a nine-hole course in the 1970s under the name Arrowhead Country Club. It endured some early hardships and even closed. However, new owners came in and built a new nine holes in the '80s. Now, Dallas is growing eastward and The Pinnacle Club has been rediscovered.

The tree-lined fairways are narrow with overhanging trees and water frequently comes into play, so accuracy is at a premium. The front side is tight with a lot of out-of-bounds coming into play, in some cases on both sides of the fairway. The back nine has less out-of-bounds area but more water. If you're in command of your driver, you can make a lot of birdies here since the course measures only 6,641 yards from the back tees. Only one bad shot can undo a day of hard work.

No. 15 is a short par 5 at 511 yards with high risk and low rewards. After teeing off to a wide landing area, golfers are faced with a choice. The fairway curls to the left around a large lake that protects the front of the green. To get home in two requires a 250-yard carry over water.

In the late 1980s, one of Texas' top amateur golfers, Richard Ellis, set out to design a unique golf course that would be truly user-friendly and enable players to have fun instead of being brow-beaten into another hobby.

At 6,382 yards from the back tees, the Plantation gives you the chance to shoot a good score if you are willing to gamble.

The course is now owned and operated by Dallas-based Club Corporation of America, the nation's largest owner-operator of golf courses.

For big hitters, the layout features four par 4s that are almost driveable on Nos. 6, 9, 11 and 15. All four holes, however, are protected by water and you go for the green at your own risk.

No. 6 is only 301 yards, but is guarded by a lake that runs all the way down the left side and cuts both in front of and behind the green to leave no margin of error. To get home off the tee, a player would have to carry the ball all 300 yards to the green.

No. 9 is a 326-yard straightaway with only one bunker guarding the front left of the green.

No. 11 is almost the same design as No. 6, but measures 351 yards with the water on the right side of the fairway and in front and behind the green.

No. 15 is only 308 yards, but is guarded by a pond that protects the front and left side of the green.

No. 17 is a short par 3 of 148 yards, but golfers must contend with a lake the cuts across the right side of the fairway. No. 7 is a 188-yard par 3 that requires players to carry water to reach the green.

Plantation Golf Club

4701 Plantation Lane
Frisco 75034
972-335-4653
Pro: Paul Kenney
A par-72, 6,382-yard public course.
From Dallas, take North Dallas Tollway to Highway 121. Turn right to Hillcrest one mile past Preston and right on Lebanon to club entrance.

• • •

USGA rating: 70.9
Slope rating: 122
Sand traps: 18
Water holes: 8
Doglegs: 5 left/0 right
Type greens: Bentgrass
Record: 62
Designer: Richard Ellis
Year opened: 1988

• • •

Hole	Par	Yards	Hole	Par	Yards
Out	36	3,193	In	36	3,189

Prestonwood Country Club Creek Course

15909 Preston Road
Dallas 75240
972-233-6166
Pro: Cotton Dunn
A 36-hole private club.
From Dallas, take Dallas North Tollway to Belt Line Road, then east on Belt Line two miles to club entrance.

• • •

USGA rating: 74.0
Slope rating: 130
Sand traps: 87
Water holes: 16
Doglegs: 1 left/2 right
Type greens: Bentgrass
Record: 65
Designer: Ralph Plummer
Year opened: 1965

• • •

Hole	Par	Yards	Hole	Par	Yards
Out	35	3,114	In	36	3,370

Go north, young man. Vance Miller watched closely as a group of influential Dallas businessmen began plans to develop an exclusive all-men's club in North Dallas in the mid-1960s.

While most people laughed at the idea of building such an exclusive club so far north of downtown, Miller jumped on a slightly different bandwagon. His own.

Miller was a developer who also believed Dallas would eventually grow to the north, and the move being made by such influential leaders at Preston Trail confirmed his belief.

So while Preston Trail offered an exclusive club for men only, Miller established Prestonwood Country Club to service the many families that would be moving northward.

Prestonwood opened in 1968, actually a year before Preston Trail. Miller even hired Ralph Plummer, who conspired with golf legend Byron Nelson to build Preston Trail just down the road, to design his course on rolling land covered with pecan and live oaks as well as creeks and lakes. The original course, known as the Creek Course, is a position course that requires accurate tee shots and good iron play to negotiate many forced carries over water on the approach.

The layout requires more brains than brawn with its tight fairways and water coming into play on 16 holes. Four holes were nominated among the toughest in D/FW, including the 410-yard first, the 540-yard fifth, the 570-yard 15th and the 230-yard 17th.

The 1960s and '70s proved developer Vance Miller correct in his assessment that Dallas would grow northward.

Miller had banked on that idea in the 1960s, when he built the first course at Prestonwood Country Club. Miller had watched closely as a group of influential Dallas businessmen built an exclusive all-men's club just down the road at Preston Trail.

Miller decided to jump on a slightly different bandwagon by building an exclusive country club for men and women alike.

While Preston Trail offered an exclusive club for men only, Miller established Prestonwood Country Club to service the many families that would be moving northward.

Nearly two decades after building the Creek Course in 1968, Miller had been proven right. So right, in fact, that the club decided to build a second 18-hole course and clubhouse to serve the sprawling North Dallas community.

Ralph Plummer's original course is a position course built on rolling land covered with pecan and live oaks with several creeks and lakes on the property, The second course — known as the Hills Course — was designed by Dallas-based architect Dave Bennett. It plays 6,451 yards to a par of 72 with a slope rating of 122 from the back tees.

The front nine is a links-type course with pot bunkers and grass bunkers; the back nine is scenic with lots of hills, trees and undulating greens.

The toughest hole on the Hills is the fourth, a 217-yard par 3.

Prestonwood Country Club Hills Course

15909 Preston Road
Dallas 75248
972-307-1508
Pro: Cotton Dunn
A 36-hole private club.
From Dallas, take Dallas North Tollway
to Belt Line Road, then east on Belt Line
two miles to club entrance.

• • •

USGA rating: 73.0
Slope rating: 122
Sand traps: 52
Water holes: 11
Doglegs: 0 left/2 right
Type greens: Bentgrass
Record: 63
Designer: Dave Bennett
Year opened: 1986

• • •

Hole	Par	Yards	Hole	Par	Yards
Out	36	3,251	In	36	3,200

Quail Valley
Country Club
El Dorado Course

2880 La Quinta
Missouri City 77459
281-437-8277
Pro: Pat O'Hara
A 36-hole private club.
Take U.S. 59 south to Highway 6, turn
east and go five miles to FM 1092, then
left on El Dorado. Turn right to entrance.

• • •

USGA rating: 71.0
Slope rating: 119
Sand traps: 34
Water holes: 13
Doglegs: 4 left/1 right
Type greens: Bermuda
Record: 63
Designer: Jack Miller
Year opened: 1969

• • •

Hole	Par	Yards	Hole	Par	Yards
Out	35	3,184	In	35	3,496

Throughout the 1960s, there were three attempts to build a golf course on the fringe of the Houston city limits near Missouri City. The land was considered a combination of cow pasture choked with underbrush and a natural habitat for numerous types of wildlife. Few city folk ever ventured out that way, but no trespassing signs were staked along a desolate road to keep hunters out.

Finally, developers turned Quail Valley into one of the city's largest golf course/residential developments in 1969.

Most of the land was covered with native pecan and oak trees and architect Jack Miller transplanted trees to cover other parts that were open prairie. The property had five natural lakes in addition to Oyster and Stafford Run creeks running through it.

"We believe we've got enough timber and romance and contour to build a good golf course," Miller said. "In some areas, it looks as if God created this land for a golf course. The only problem we faced was completing the courses fast enough to accommodate the membership because the sales record was furious."

Miller had the first nine ready by August of 1970. In 1973 and '74, Quail Valley hosted the PGA Tour's Houston Open.

El Dorado plays to a par of 70 with five par 3s that measure 190 or more from the back tees. No. 11 is a difficult 224-yard par 3 with water behind the green. No. 14 is 209 yards with a pond protecting the green in front.

After watching the success of Champions Golf Club in the 1950s and early '60s, developers believed it was no longer the great American dream to own just a home — but a home on a golf course.

Five years after Champions became the first country club in Houston with two golf courses, developers worked furiously at Quail Valley to construct two new courses to accommodate the fast pace of new home sales and new golfers.

The tract of land in 30 minutes southwest of downtown Houston had been studied as possible site for a golf course for several years. The Houston Golf Association was the first to consider the area's potential and hired architect Henry Ransom as a consultant and designer. Later, Ben Hogan and a development agency surveyed the land and got down to the fine print before the deal fell through.

Most of the land was covered with native pecan and oak trees and architect Jack Miller transplanted trees to cover other parts that were open prairie. The property had five natural lakes in addition to Oyster and Stafford Run creeks running through it.

After completing the first 18 holes in 1969 and Quail Valley became the host site for the 1973 and '74 Houston Open, Miller completed a second 18 in 1974 and the two courses were combined into the El Dorado and La Quinta courses. La Quinta is the newest and slightly more difficult course with water coming into play on 10 holes.

Quail Valley Country Club La Quinta Course

2880 La Quinta
Missouri City 77459
281-437-8277
Pro: Pat O'Hara
A 36-bole private club.
Take U.S. 59 south to Highway 6, turn east and go five miles to FM 1092, then left on El Dorado. Turn right to entrance.

• • •

USGA rating: 71.0
Slope rating: 119
Sand traps: 34
Water holes: 13
Doglegs: 4 left/1 right
Type greens: Bermuda
Record: 63
Designer: Jack Miller
Year opened: 1969

• • •

Hole	Par	Yards	Hole	Par	Yards
Out	36	3,353	In	36	3,463

Rancho Viejo Resort and Country Club El Angel Course

1 Rancho Viejo Drive
Rancho Viejo 78575
965-350-4000
Pro: Robert Lindsay
A 36-hole semi-private resort.
From Harlingen, take Highway 77 south.
Club is on the west side of Highway 77
just outside of Brownsville.

• • •

USGA rating: 73.7
Slope rating: 129
Sand traps: 32
Water holes: 11
Doglegs: 6 left/6 right
Type greens: Bermuda
Record: N/A
Designer: Dennis W. Arp
Year opened: 1971

• • •

Hole	Par	Yards	Hole	Par	Yards
Out	35	3,209	In	35	3,092

Rancho Viejo is located on the southern most point of Texas, just 15 minutes from the U.S.–Mexico border. It was founded in 1771 as the first settlement of the Rio Grand Valley.

While the Rancho Viejo Resort is only two decades old, not two centuries, it has its own share of history.

Rancho Viejo is a destination resort that draws players from all over the world. After Dennis Arp built the first course — known as El Angel — the club's annual Hacker's Tournament drew entertainers such as Dean Martin, Willie Nelson and Joey Bishop as well as Texas pro legends Jimmy Demaret and Jack Burke Jr.

The resort was totally renovated in 1995 and has hosted PGA Tour qualifying events and is the host site of the Tommy Jacobs Golf Instruction school. It was recently selected as one of the top 10 golf resorts in Texas.

The El Angel Course is a links-style design that measures 6,487 yards with a par of 70. It features subtle mounds and dips in the fairways, so you can expect many uneven lies. The unpredictable tropical breeze can make a proper club selection an important part of the game.

The resort offers golf villas throughout the course with lodging for up to 100 people as well as other resort amenities.

No. 16 is a 488-yard par 5 that offers a good birdie opportunity if players can avoid water on both sides of the fairway.

No. 17, on the other hand, is a 465-yard par 4 that can play like a par 5.

Seven years after the first course at Raveneaux Country Club was built and deemed a success, the demand grew for a second course at Raveneaux to keep up with the growing number of residents in the area just north of Houston.

Raveneaux was built just down the road from the world-renown Champions Golf Club, but has developed a great reputation in its own right.

Despite the construction problems architects Robert von Hagge and Bruce Devlin had on the first course when a severe flood washed away most of their work and forced them to start over, they returned to build another challenging layout.

With von Hagge and Devlin as its creator Raveneaux enjoys championship bloodlines along with other Texas Top 100 courses such as Crown Colony, Walden on Lake Conroe, The Cliffs on Possum Kingdom, the King's and Queen's Courses at Gleneagles, Hollytree Golf Club and the Club at Falcon Point.

Both courses at Raveneaux were renovated in 1986 by Ken Kavanaugh feature long, tight fairways and undulating greens.

The New Course is more of a shot-maker's course. It greets players with elevated greens and tight fairways and imposing lakes. Like most of their courses, the architects used heavy bunkering (100, to be exact) to put a premium on accuracy. At 6,515 yards, it is not long but demands precision off the tee and from the fairway with its tricky greens that are heavily guarded by bunkers.

Raveneaux Country Club New Course

9415 Cypresswood Drive
Spring 77379
281-370-3670
Pro: Matt Swanson
A 36-hole private club. From Houston, take I-45 north to Highway 249, go west to Cypresswood Drive, right to entrance.

• • •

USGA rating: 72
Slope rating: 118
Sand traps: 100
Water holes: 11
Doglegs: 1 left/3 right
Type greens: Bermuda
Record: N/A
Designers: Robert von Hagge
    and Bruce Devlin
    and Ken Kavanaugh (1989)
Year opened: 1979

Hole	Par	Yards	Hole	Par	Yards
Out	36	3,371	In	35	3,087

Raveneaux Country Club Old Course

9415 Cypresswood Drive
Spring 77379
281-370-3670
Pro: Matt Swanson
A 36-hole private club. From Houston,
take I-45 north to Highway 249, go west
to Cypresswood Drive, right to entrance.

• • •

USGA rating: 72
Slope rating: 118
Sand traps: 100
Water holes: 11
Doglegs: 1 left/3 right
Type greens: Bermuda
Record: N/A
Designers: Robert von Hagge
    and Bruce Devlin
    and Ken Kavanaugh (1986)
Year opened: 1979

Hole	Par	Yards	Hole	Par	Yards
Out	35	3,290	In	36	3,405

The idea for Raveneaux Country Club was born in the offices of architects Robert von Hagge and Bruce Devlin shortly after they moved to Houston and completed Walden on Lake Conroe in 1974.

While Walden is still ranked among the top courses in the state, it was too remote from downtown Houston for most Houstonians and the architects saw a need for an upscale, club in northwest Houston.

In keeping with the theme of the club, they decided to call it Raveneaux, a place of majestic beauty and solitude where Napoleon celebrated his victories in battle.

Von Hagge and Devlin were ready for a vacation by the time they were through. In one 36-day period during the critical part of construction when the topsoil was in place and grass was being planted, the club experienced a 100-year flood and then shortly after a 25-year flood.

Most of the newly shaped golf course washed away in the raging floodwaters of Cypress Creek, forcing them to start over.

They regrouped to get another construction loan to rebuild the course, and instead decided to build two 18-hole courses.

Carved out of 300 acres of Champions Forest, the land features tall pines and majestic oaks cloaked in Spanish moss.

The Old Course is known for its long, tight fairways and unpredictable greens. The 618-yard, par-5 No. 2 is nicknamed "Waterloo" by members in remembrance of Napoleon's last battle.

Rayburn Country is just a two-hour drive from Houston or Dallas, but is lightyears away from the hustle and bustle of the city. It is secluded in the East Texas pines on the shores of Lake Sam Rayburn and the edge of the Big Thicket.

The resort offers something for everyone, but for golfers it starts with three-nine hole courses designed by architects Robert Trent Jones Jr., Robert von Hagge, Bruce Devlin and Jay Riviere. The golf is everything you'd expect of an East Texas layout with its thickly tree-lined fairways. It also features the rolling terrain and elevation changes typically found only in Texas Hill Country.

The Gold Nine was the original layout designed by Riviere and features tree-lined fairways. It is the flatest of the trio and has water in play on only one hole. The Green Nine designed by von Hagge and Devlin features tight driving areas and tricky approaches. The Blue Nine designed by Jones usually surrenders the best scores with its wide landing areas.

The Green Nine has a collection of holes you won't find anywhere else, starting from the first tee. No. 1 is a 373-yard dogleg left par 4 with a fairway that sweeps downhill through a chute of trees then uphill to an elevated green with a blind approach.

No. 4 is a 590-yard, double-dogleg par 5. The fairway bends to the right off the tee, then back to the left and downhill to an elevated green. A ravine runs down the left side of the fairway and water protects the back right side of the green.

Rayburn Country Resort

Wingate Boulevard
Sam Rayburn 75951
409-698-2958
A 27-hole resort course.
From Houston take I-10 east to U.S. 96
Go north on U.S. 96 through Jasper, left
on Highway 255 to entrance on right.

• • •

USGA rating: 71.3
Slope rating: 116
Sand traps: 24
Water holes: 12
Doglegs: 12
Type greens: Bermuda
Records: N/A
Designers: Jay Riviere
*   and Robert Trent Jones (1969)*
*   and Robert von Hagge*
*   and Bruce Devlin (1973)*
Year opened: 1965

Hole	Par	Yards	Hole	Par	Yards
Out	36	3,104	In	36	3,140

Ridgeview Ranch
Golf Club

2701 Ridgeview Drive
Plano 75025
972-390-1039
Pro: Brett Fletcher
A par-72, 7,025-yard public course.
From Dallas, take Highway 75 to Custer,
then go north on Custer to Ridgeview
Drive and course entrance.

• • •

USGA rating: 74.1
Slope rating: 130
Sand traps: 77
Water holes: 16
Doglegs: 2 left/1 right
Type greens: Bermuda
Record: N/A
Designer: Jeff Brauer
Year opened: 1996

• • •

Hole	Par	Yards	Hole	Par	Yards
Out	36	3,413	In	36	3,612

Ridgeview Ranch is one of the newest daily-fee facilities in the Dallas-Fort Worth area, and it is also one of the most unique.

Dallas-based architect Jeff Brauer, who has designed numerous courses throughout the state over the past decade, took advantage of two creeks that run through the property.

His final product is a challenging, par-72, 7,025-yard daily-fee layout that has a slope rating of 130 from the back tees.

The layout opened in October 1996 and features rolling hills and tree-lined fairways.

To make the course user-friendly to all types of players, Brauer made all of the greens large and accessible from the front to run-up shots. Players are never forced to carry water or sand to reach the green and can opt to use old-fashioned pitch-and-run shots.

Once you are on the green, however, two-putts are no guarantee. The well-bunkeredgreens are large, fast and undulating.

The fairways are lined by 77 bunkers, but the landing areas are fairly flat and generous.

The signature hole is No. 7, a 161-yard par 3, which requires a tee shot over White Rock creek to a large, sloped green.

No. 11 is an uphill 435-yard par 4 that plays directly into the prevailing south wind.

Located adjacent to the third green is a cemetery with a historical marker of the original settlers of northeast Texas commissioned by Stephen F. Austin with grave sites dating back to 1800.

Jim Hardy has seen the golf business from all sides now. The longtime Houston-area pro has seen the boom in golf and, to his dismay, a commensurate boom in green fee prices. That's why he formed the Golf Services Group, to combine his golf expertise to provide turnkey services to government agencies who want to build a golf course but don't have the money or knowledge to do it themselves.

Welcome to Rio Colorado.

Hardy's group produced a $2.9 million clubhouse and layout that — if you could pick it up and move it to Houston — would be sure to rank among Houston's best. Hardy knew he would have to produce a special golf course to lure Houston golfers to make the 90-minute trip to Bay City.

"It's one helluva golf course," Hardy says. "There are a lot of good courses in Houston, but they're all very expensive. Our goal was to build a good golf course that offered a good price."

The course was designed by the Gary Player Design Co., although Player himself never set foot on the property. The layout features its fair share of memorable holes. The front is built on an open prairie, while the back nine winds through wooded terrain overlooking the Colorado River.

There is no mistaking the 322-yard, par-4 No. 14, Rio Colorado's signature hole that doglegs along the bluff 150 feet above the river. The hole dares you to cut the corner of the dogleg by hitting a 240-yard carry across the river and the tall oaks lining the fairway.

Rio Colorado Golf Course

FM 2668-Riverside Park Drive
Bay City 77414
409-245-9567
Pro: Nancy Bunton
A par-72, 6,834-yard public course.
From Houston, take U.S. 59 south to
Highway 60, go south to FM 2668 to
course entrance on the right.

• • •

USGA rating: 73.1
Slope rating: 127
Sand traps: 25
Water holes: 13
Doglegs: 3 left/1 right
Type greens: Bermuda
Record: N/A
Designer: Gary Player
Year opened: 1993

• • •

Hole	Par	Yards	Hole	Par	Yards
Out	36	3,361	In	36	3,463

River Crest Country Club

1501 Western Avenue
Fort Worth 76107
817-738-9221
Pro: Mac Spikes
A par-70, 6,246-yard private club.
Take I-30 west to Camp Bowie
Boulevard, then north three miles to
Western Avenue. Left to club entrance.

• • •

USGA rating: 70.8
Slope rating: 132
Sand traps: 55
Water holes: 5
Doglegs: 2 left/3 right
Type greens: Bentgrass
Record: 63
Designer: Tom Bendelow
    and George Williams (1996)
Year opened: 1911

• • •

Hole	Par	Yards	Hole	Par	Yards
Out	35	3,181	In	35	3,065

Members at River Crest have much to be proud of. Having been built in 1911, their club is the oldest in Fort Worth and second oldest in the metroplex behind only Dallas Country Club.

Then there's the history. It has been a host site for the LPGA Tour and Women's Texas Open.

There is Crestival, the club's annual invitational golf tournament.

There is the white-columnar clubhouse, which was rebuilt in 1984 and won an award from the Texas Society of Architects.

There is so much to be proud of, in fact, that *Golf Magazine* once named River Crest "one of the snootiest clubs in America."

While that may be the subject of much debate, there is no debate about the timeless River Crest layout designed by architect Tom Bendelow, who built Dallas Country Club in 1908 and the original Lakewood Country Club a few years later.

The layout is short by modern standards at 6,246 yards, but plays longer than the yardage indicates.

On the front nine, in fact, Nos. 3 and No. 5 are par 4s that measure 430 and 458 yards. No. 8, however, is a 292-yard par 4 that some can reach off the tee.

River Crest hosted the 1952 Women's Texas Open, where LPGA Hall of Famer Babe Zaharias defeated Polly Riley 7 and 6 for the first title. In 1954, LPGA Hall of Famer Betsy Rawls defeated Betty Hicks. It also has hosted the Texas Amateur, Texas Cup and other pro events.

The club celebrated its 85th birthday in 1996 with a renovation by architect George Williams.

Competition is one of the great aspects of golf. It allows man to compete with himself, nature and his opponents.

Golf is never as competitive as when it comes to building the most prestigious golf courses and country clubs.

In 1957, the prestige clubs in Houston were River Oaks, Houston Country Club, Lakeside, BraeBurn and Westwood. So when Dallas-based architect Press Maxwell was hired to build Riverbend on the southwest edge of the Houston city limits, the challenge was to produce a timeless layout that would stand up to the competition.

Riverbend was built through a pecan orchard on the north shore of Oyster Creek and surrounded on three sides by cattle grazing land. Unlike most modern courses, it was not originally part of a housing subdivision. Its fairways were not lined with houses. It wasn't built to sell real estate. Riverbend stood the test of time. Longtime Riverbend pro Art Hodde retired in 1993 after earning a place in the Texas Golf Hall of Fame.

Riverbend has enjoyed growth due to its location on the edge of Fort Bend County, one of the nation's fastest growing areas.

The original layout remained the same until 1972, when architect Joe Finger re-routed some of the holes. In 1988, late architect Carlton Gipson helped modernize the layout again to keep up with the growing competition. Gipson used the 18th hole as an experiment to show members what he wanted to do, then was hired to complete the other 17.

Riverbend Country Club

1214 Dulles Avenue
Sugar Land 77478
281-491-2552
Pro: Kevin Hood
A par-72, 6,712-yard private club.
From Houston, take U.S. 59 south to the Airport-Kirkwood exit, left on Kirkwood (it turns into Dulles) and right to the club entrance.

• • •

USGA rating: 72.5
Slope rating: 129
Sand traps: 57
Water holes: 13
Doglegs: 4 left/4 right
Type greens: Bermuda
Record: 62
Designer: Press Maxwell
Year opened: 1957

• • •

Hole	Par	Yards	Hole	Par	Yards
Out	36	3,300	In	36	3,377

Riverchase Golf Club

700 Riverchase Drive
Coppell 75019
972-462-8281
Pro: Rich Richeson
A par-71, 6,598-yard public course.
From Dallas, take I-35E north to Sandy
Lake Road, then west on Sandy Lake
four miles to club entrance on the left.

• • •

USGA rating: 72
Slope rating: 124
Sand traps: 36
Water holes: 15
Doglegs: 2 left/0 right
Type greens: Bentgrass
Record: 62
Designer: Jim Fazio
Year opened: 1988

• • •

Hole	Par	Yards	Hole	Par	Yards
Out	36	3,306	In	35	3,287

When it comes to golfing households, the name Fazio ranks right up there with the likes of Nicklaus and Palmer. And when it comes to golf course architecture, everybody is trying to keep up with the Fazios.

The Fazios are a classic golfing family. First came George, a successful touring pro who lost to Ben Hogan in a playoff in the 1950 U.S. Open and later became a top course architect. And then came nephews Jim and Tom, the latter of which became the nation's top architect with seven courses in America's top 100.

While Tom has grown up to become the biggest name in modern golf course architecture, Jim has become a strong architect in his own right. He completed one of his first solo projects at Riverchase in bottom land below the banks of the Elm Fork Trinity River. Water comes into play on every hole, but there are no forced carries. On 12 holes, in fact, water comes into play on the right side. Out-of-bounds comes into play on 14 holes.

The hardest hole is the 396-yard, par-4 No. 5. It is a slight dogleg right, with water in play off the tee and on the approach. Off the tee, golfers must avoid the small lake to the right and a fairway bunker that guards the left elbow of the dogleg. Golfers are faced with an approach to a long, narrow green with bunkers on the left side and a lake on the right.

Fazio designed an elaborate chain of interconnecting water hazards to handle heavy spring rains and an occasional surge from the Elm Fork.

Ben Crenshaw grew up in Texas. He has played most of Texas' top courses. He has played on the best golf courses all over the world. He has won 20 PGA Tour events and two Masters titles. And he has designed some of the best golf courses in the world.

Suffice it to say, he knows a good golf course when he sees one.

And Rockport Country Club is one of them.

Maybe Crenshaw is a little partial, since longtime architectural partner Bill Coore designed this layout in 1982 shortly before the two joined forces. But many others concur that this layout on the Gulf of Mexico is one of the best courses in South Texas.

Coore's design features a variety of holes that require all types of shoe-making. It is scenic from start to finish. A trip across it gives a players views of dozens of different birds, including scores of large white egrets, with their long necks, pencil-like legs and long bills, plus beautiful blue herons. There are short doglegs with slim fairways. Water comes into play on 12 holes, although none ever quite make it down to the Gulf waters. And there are long holes with wide fairways and big greens. And there are huge bunkers everywhere.

Rockport is home of the biggest bunker in Texas, stretching nearly 400 yards. A bunker stretches from just off the tee, down the left edge of the fairway for nearly 400 yards, and wraps around behind the green.

The signature hole is the 552-yard, par-5 No. 14, which forces players to hit across different bodies of water to reach the green.

Rockport Country Club

101 Champions Drive
Rockport 78382
512-729-4182
Pro: Thane Emerson
A par-71, 6,469-yard private club.
From Houston, take Highway 59 south to Victoria, then Highway 77 south to Tivoli exit, then left to Highway 35, then right to Rockport and club entrance.

• • •

USGA rating: 72.0
Slope rating: 123
Sand traps: 50
Water holes: 12
Doglegs: 10
Type greens: Bermuda
Record: 63
Designer: Bill Coore
Year opened: 1982

• • •

Hole	Par	Yards	Hole	Par	Yards
Out	35	2,788	In	36	3,145

Shady Valley Golf Club

4001 West Park Row
Arlington 76013
817-275-8771
Pro: David Hersman
A par-70, 6,554-yard private club.
From Dallas, go east take I-30 west to
Fielder Road, go south to Park Row,
right 2.5 miles to the course entrance.

• • •

USGA rating: 70.7

Slope rating: 115

Sand traps: 37

Water holes: 10

Doglegs: 1 left/3 right

Type greens: Bermuda

Record: 64

Designer: N/A

Year opened: 1960

• • •

Hole	Par	Yards	Hole	Par	Yards
Out	35	3,173	In	35	3,381

Hit it straight and celebrate.

That is the slogan at Shady Valley, a heavily-wooded golf course where the fairways wind through 120 acres of seemingly endless walls of pecan, cedar, elm, post oak, water oak, red oak, sweet gum, bald cypress and pines. Rush Creek wiggles devilishly through the tract and water comes into play on 14 holes. Sand bunkers guard each of the greens.

Shady Valley Golf Club opened on Labor Day in 1960 and golf is still the overwhelming passion here. The course has matured into a challenging test that calls for accuracy off the tee and subtle club and shot-making decisions through the greens. Do you bump and run, or do you float it onto the green below the hole?

Rush Creek comes into play most on the 394-yard, par-4 sixth and the 410-yard, par-4 eighth, both of which play parallel to the water's edge. The sixth veers slightly to the left through a chute of trees, with water all the way down the right side. At the 398-yard seventh, players must clear the creek off the tee and on the approach, with a small landing area in between. At No. 8, players must clear the creek off the tee on a dogleg left, but avoid the creek that runs down the right side of the fairway to the green.

The 437-yard No. 10 is a dogleg right with lakes on the left and right about 250 yards from the tee. No. 11 is a narrow, 437-yard hole through a chute of trees. And No. 12 is a dogleg right through the trees with a lake on the right.

You've probably heard the story about a man without a plan. This is a story about a golf course without land.

In 1972, the bustling suburb of Richardson decided it was time to build a public golf course in the northeast corner of the city limits. So the city fathers contacted architect Leon Howard to design 18 holes on 165 acres of undeveloped land.

The only problem was, the city didn't own the land.

This was the deal: Former city manager Bob Sherrill worked a deal with a local developer to obtain the land at a bargain-basement price if Howard could design the course to give the developer enough frontage on the course to help sell homesites.

There are two especially memorable holes at Sherrill Park's No. 1 course, including the 375-yard, par-4 first hole. It is a sharp dog-leg right through a chute of trees that overhang the fairway.

"I have to admit, that was a pretty tough starting hole," Howard says. "It's laid out naturally for a slicer and I wanted to get them off and going."

And then there's the 588-yard par-5 14th, which plays into the wind with a water protecting the right side of the fairway and green on the approach.

"I thought, 'Well, we've been pretty easy on them in some of these other holes, let's let them have one tough one.'

"There were enough trees and creeks on the course to create challenge and interest. We didn't need to do much extra to make it tough."

Sherrill Park Golf Course No. 1 Course

2001 Lookout Drive
Richardson 75081
214-234-1416
Pro: Ronny Glanton
A par-72, 6,800-yard public course.
From Dallas, take Central Expressway north to Campbell, go east to Jupiter, and north to entrance on the left.

• • •

USGA rating: 72
Slope rating: 126
Sand traps: 12
Water holes: 8
Doglegs: 4 left/3 right
Type greens: Bermuda
Record: N/A
Designer: Leon Howard
Year opened: 1960

• • •

Hole	Par	Yards	Hole	Par	Yards
Out	36	3,401	In	36	3,399

Sherrill Park Golf Course No. 2 Course

2001 Lookout Drive
Richardson 75081
214-234-1416
Pro: Ronny Glanton
A par-72, 6,800-yard public course.
From Dallas, take Central Expressway
north to Campbell, go east to Jupiter,
and north to entrance on the left.

• • •

USGA rating: 71.2
Slope rating: 116
Sand traps: 12
Water holes: 11
Doglegs: 5 left/2 right
Type greens: Bermuda
Record: N/A
Designer: Leon Howard
Year opened: 1960

• • •

Hole	Par	Yards	Hole	Par	Yards
Out	35	2,927	In	35	3,156

The first course was so successful and the population continued to boom in the North Dallas area, so in 1980 the city of Richardson called Howard again to build a second course.

This time, there was a new challenge. The course would have to be built on only about 120 acres, some of which was on a former landfill site.

While the No. 2 course plays only 6,083 yards, it has its share of difficult holes as it also weaves its way up and down hills and through the tall oak trees. It is much shorter, but the fairways are tighter and more water comes into play on 11 holes.

The hardest is the 440-yard No. 2, a dogleg left par 4 that requires players to carry a creek off the tee and again on the approach. It is the only par 4 over 400 yards on the No. 2 course.

No. 3 is only a 325-yard par 4 that some big hitters can reach off the tee but must thread their tee ball over water off the tee and between hazards on both sides of the fairway.

The course features back to back par 5s at Nos. 5 and 6. No. 9 is a 306-yard par 4 that also can be reached, but water crosses the fairway in front of the green to force most players to lay up and hit a short iron approach.

No. 17 is a demanding 199-yard par 3, with water in front of the tee and on the left and right of the green, living little margin for error. The 18th is a 475-yard par 5 where the only water in play is off the tee, so most players have a good chance of finishing with a birdie.

If you are a fan of Ralph Plummer, the late Texas golf architect, it would behoove you to live on the east side of Dallas. It is here you will find four of his works, each of which is unique in design but features the shot values for which he is famous.

After building two courses at Dallas Athletic Club and later Eastern Hills, in one of his last projects before he died in 1982, Plummer returned to the area to build The Shores in 1979. He capitalized on four decades of experience and a great piece of real estate on the windswept shores of Lake Ray Hubbard.

The Shores is typical Plummer, measuring 7,200 yards. The lake comes directly into play on five holes, then other lakes and tributaries come into play on

seven holes. The land is only sparsely covered with trees, so the 56 bunkers and gusting winds off the lake are the layout's biggest obstacles. The back nine rolls along the water's edge, adding to the difficulty and natural hazards.

The 452-yard, par-4 18th is without doubt one of the most difficult holes in D/FW. It is far from the lake, but water comes into play on the tee and the approach. A small lake in the middle of the course cuts into the fairway on the right side about 200 yards from the back tee. A fairway bunker guards the left corner of the slight dogleg left, which doesn't leave the golfer much of a landing area beyond 250 yards. That means you have to carry water again on an uphill approach to the green with a long iron or fairway wood in your hand.

The Shores Country Club

1600 Champion Drive
Rockwall 75087
972-771-0301
Pro: Devin Thomas
A par-72, 7,200-yard private club.
From Dallas, take I-30 north to Dalrock exit. Turn left five miles to Lakeview Parkway, then right to Lakeshore Drive and left to club entrance.

• • •

USGA rating: 73.4
Slope rating: 124
Sand traps: 60
Water holes: 7
Doglegs: 3 left/2 right
Type greens: Bentgrass
Record: 63
Designer: Ralph Plummer
Year opened: 1979

• • •

Hole	Par	Yards	Hole	Par	Yards
Out	36	3,532	In	36	3,606

Sleepy Hollow Golf and Country Club Lake Course

4745 South Loop 12
Dallas 75216
214-371-3430
Pro: Chuck Tabor
A 36-hole private club.
From downtown, take I-45 south
to Loop 12, go east to entrance.

• • •

USGA rating: 73.4
Slope rating: 108
Sand traps: 25
Water holes: 9
Doglegs: 3 left, 2 right
Type greens: Bermuda
Record: 66
Designers: Press Maxwell (1956)
and Karl Litten (1984)
Year opened: 1957

• • •

Hole	Par	Yards	Hole	Par	Yards
Out	35	3,108	In	35	2,944

In 1956, Sleepy Hollow was the place to be in Dallas golf.

This is where Dr. Cary Middlecoff, winner of 40 professional events and the 1956 U.S. Open, used to be the head pro.

This is where LPGA Hall of Famer Kathy Whitworth, the winningest golfer of all time with 88 victories, was once a dues-paying member. This is where PGA Tour star Tom Kite won his first tournament at the age of 11. And this is where NFL Hall of Famer Doak Walker was the first club president.

Architect Press Maxwell designed the first of two golf courses along the banks of the Elm Fork Trinity River in 1957 and they have stood the test of time.

Both were renovated in 1981 by Florida-based architect Karl Litten. Over three years, 23 acres of lakes and 25 new greens were built and 12 holes redesigned.

Unlike its sister course, which features some of the toughest holes in the Dallas area, the Lake Course is a kinder, gentler layout measuring only 6,052 yards from the back tees.

While it features par 5s of 529 and 576 yards, only one par 4 is over 400 yards. That is the 425-yard, par-4 seventh hole, where golfers must contend with a lake down the left side of the fairway and again on their approach to the green.

No. 2 is a 529-yard par 5 with a sharp dogleg off the tee. Golfers may be tempted to cut the corner off the tee, but a pond in the corner of the fairway will catch anything but a perfect tee shot.

This is a story about legends, but it doesn't have anything to do with Halloween or Ichabod Crane. When you cross the small bridge and enter the world of Sleepy Hollow, you don't have to worry about being decapitated like the Halloween legend but you'd better be prepared to tighten your golf cap a little.

The River Course is by far the most demanding of the two courses at Sleepy Hollow, with a course rating that makes it one of the most difficult in DFW. It is very long with lots of lateral water hazards, trees and about 60 bunkers.

It includes Dallas' longest par 5 (634 yards) and par 3 (238) back to back. The back nine not only has an island green, but gets progressively tighter in the landing areas and the greens get progressively smaller. The last five holes are about as tough a finish as you'll ever experience.

"Sure, we're prejudiced," head pro Charles Tabor says, "but we believe we've got five of the toughest 18 in town."

Let's take a couple of examples: No. 5 is a 634-yard par 5 that doglegs left around a pond that comes into play on all three shots to the green. No. 6 is a 238-yard par 3 that some people may not even be able to reach in one. No. 16 is a 586-yard par 5 that doglegs right with the Trinity running down the left side. No. 17 is a 205-yard par 3 that requires you hit a long iron into the wind through a tunnel of 80-foot tall trees. And then there's No. 14, a 435-yard, dogleg left, par 4 that 150 mini-tour pros played without making a birdie.

Sleepy Hollow Golf and Country Club River Course

4745 South Loop 12
Dallas 75216
214-371-3430
Pro: Chuck Tabor
A 36-hole private club.
From downtown, take I-45 south to Loop 12, go east to entrance.

• • •

USGA rating: 73.4
Slope rating: 128
Sand traps: 25
Water holes: 14
Doglegs: 6 left/1 right
Type greens: Bermuda
Record: 67
Designers: Press Maxwell (1961) and Karl Litten (1984)
Year opened: 1957

• • •

Hole	Par	Yards	Hole	Par	Yards
Out	36	3,676	In	35	3,355

South Shore Harbour Country Club

4300 South Shore Boulevard
League City 77573
281-334-0525
Pro: Jimmy Terry
A 27-hole, semi-private resort and club.
From Houston, take I-45 south to Exit
518, go east to South Shore Boulevard,
left on South Shore Boulevard to
club entrance.

• • •

USGA rating: 71.8
Slope rating: 124
Sand traps: 50
Water holes: 14
Doglegs: 1 left/4 right
Type greens: Bermuda
Record: 63
Designer: Jay Riviere and Dave Marr
Year opened: 1983

• • •

Hole	Par	Yards	Hole	Par	Yards
Out	35	3,323	In	36	3,340

All his life, Dave Marr was a master at making a little go a long way. From humble beginnings, he took a little talent and combined it with a lot of personality and a lot of hard work and became one of golf's greatest ambassadors.

Marr won only four tournaments in his career, highlighted by the 1965 PGA Championship, but the Houston native went on to become the most recognized voice in golf as a TV color commentator on telecasts.

When his playing days were over, he teamed with longtime friend and architect Jay Riviere to leave another lasting legacy by building golf courses. Their first project was the first 18 holes at South Shore Harbour.

Riviere and Marr needed all their experience to create a memorable course on terrain that had only a one-foot elevation change. The other constant is the prevailing wind off Galveston Bay.

They elevate greens and tee boxes and created contoured greens. They protected the greens with 62 sand traps and mounding. They incorporated 20 water hazards (a total of 23 acres) to make up for the lack of trees.

While the original links-style layout is fairly flat, late architect Carlton Gipson added a third nine holes in 1994. Gipson moved enough earth to create 25-foot elevation changes in some places and will plant as many as 400 trees on the site.

"For what Mother Nature gave them," said original South Shore pro Jim French, "what they produced was exceptional."

Glen Rose has long been known as one of Texas' real-life Jurassic Parks, an ancient playground where Tyrannosaurus Rex and Brontosaurus Bill once roamed the countryside millions of years ago.

Dinosaur tracks are still found along the banks of the Paluxy River, but now humans are making tracks of their own to Glen Rose for a different reason. Squaw Valley, designed by architect Jeff Brauer, has become one of the area's biggest tourist attractions.

Brauer took an otherwise flat piece of land added mounds and moguls to define the fairways. The layout plays alongside or across the picturesque creek eight times – including six holes on the back nine. Most of the holes around the water are densely wooded, while Nos. 3-9 are mostly open.

No. 15 is a 462-yard par 4. It is a dogleg right, where players must carry the river off the tee and then hit far enough to get past the long row of trees from the corner to the green.

No. 16 is a straight-away, short but tricky par 4 with an elevated green poised just above Squaw Creek. No more than a fairway wood is necessary off the tee for position, and a solid tee ball leaves only about 140 yards or less to the green.

No. 9 features a double-fairway, one for the brave and one for the faint-hearted. The hole measures 362 yards if you choose the safe route and take the fairway that doglegs to the left around a large lake. But some big hitters choose to go for the green by hitting over the lake.

Squaw Valley Golf Course

HCR 51-Highway 45 B
Glen Rose 76043
800-831-8259
Pro: Johnny Pilcher
A par-72, 7,062-yard public course.
From Dallas, take Highway 67 south.
Course is on right side of highway,
20 minutes southwest of Cleburn.

• • •

USGA rating: 73.6
Slope rating: 130
Sand traps: 75
Water holes: 9
Doglegs: 2
Type greens: Bentgrass
Record: N/A
Designer: Jeff Brauer
Year opened: 1992

• • •

Hole	Par	Yards	Hole	Par	Yards
Out	36	3,520	In	36	3,542

Starr Hollow
Golf Club

Route 1, PO Box 176

Tolar 76476

254-834-3464

Director: Jim Woo

A 9-hole private club.

From Fort Worth, take Highway 377 west nine miles past Granbury to Tolar. Turn right at FM 56 and go seven miles to Starr Hollow gate. Turn right to entrance.

• • •

USGA rating: 68.6

Slope rating: 115

Sand traps: 23

Water holes: 10

Doglegs: 3 left/3 right

Type greens: Bermuda

Record: 63

Designer: Ralph Plummer

Year opened: 1970

• • •

Hole	Par	Yards	Hole	Par	Yards
Out	35	2,975	In	35	2,975

The name Marvin Leonard has long had a special meaning for anyone associated with North Texas golf.

Leonard, a wealthy Fort Worth merchant, founded and helped develop the world-famous Colonial Country Club, which has hosted a men's and women's U.S. Open, along with an annual PGA tour stop. He later helped found Shady Oaks Country Club in his hometown, which was adopted as the home of golf legend Ben Hogan.

But the most unique and certainly the least-known of Leonard's courses is located just west of Granbury, some 60 miles southwest of Fort Worth. In the tiny town of Tolar, Starr Hollow Golf Course stands as a monument to the purity of golf and the rich history of the Leonard family.

Located in the middle of a 3,000-acre ranch, the course is named for the notorious Texas outlaw Belle Starr, who hid out here with her gang more than a century ago. It is a nine-hole golf course with only 60 members, primarily friends of the Leonard family and nearby ranchers.

One pro calls Starr Hollow "Little Augusta." Leonard bought the ranch in 1965, but did not complete the final holes until just before his death in 1970. Leonard's daughter now runs the course.

Each hole has a different name ranging from Catfish Cove, Bass Bait, Jack Rabbit Run and Belle's Trap. A large lake is visible from almost every hole, but it comes into play on only one hole. The green for holes nine and 18 is shaped like the state of Texas.

Stevens Park is one of the oldest courses in Dallas and is a throwback to the old days of golf. But even in today's long-game era, and age of hot era, Stevens still has enough bite to require thought and strategy.

This is by no means a golf course you can take lightly. It is tightly wooded and offers more trouble than one wild swinger can handle. The greens are about the size of a king-size bed. And the course plays much longer than the yardage indicates because of sharp doglegs where you can't hit a driver and narrow holes where you shouldn't.

No. 6 is the No. 1 handicap hole. It is a 416-yard, windswept par 4 with out-of-bounds running down the left side and trees on both sides. On the approach, players must hit across a swale and through a chute of trees to a small green.

You may be able to reach green off the tee at the 272-yard No. 8. The hole veers slightly to the right, with a creek cutting across the fairway and then turning along the right side. The fairway slopes toward the creek, and trees that overhang into the fairway leave a small landing zone.

No. 18 measures only 353 yards, but is a sharp dogleg left with 100-foot tall trees down the left side that make cutting the corner impossible. A handful of trees in the right corner, however, prevent you from playing too conservatively to the right. While the approach is short, golfer's must hit to a two-level green that makes club selection important to be on the same level as the flagstick.

Stevens Park Golf Course

1005 North Montclair
Dallas 75208
Pro: Jim Henderson
214-670-7506
A par-71, 6,005-yard public course.
From Dallas, take I-30 west to Sylvan Boulevard, then go south five miles to Colorado. Go west two miles to Montclair, then left to entrance.

• • •

USGA rating: 66
Slope rating: 98
Sand traps: 12
Water holes: 7
Doglegs: 3 left/3 right
Type greens: Bermuda
Record: 61
Designer: N/A
Year opened: 1924

• • •

Hole	Par	Yards	Hole	Par	Yards
Out	36	3,001	In	35	3,004

Sugar Creek Country Club

420 Sugar Creek Boulevard
Sugar Land 77478
281-494-9135
Pro: J.D. Murchison
A 27-hole private club.
From Houston, take U.S. 59 south to
Sugar Creek Boulevard., then left to
club entrance on right.

• • •

USGA rating: 72
Slope rating: 119
Sand traps: 60
Water holes: 11
Doglegs: 2 left/2 right
Type greens: Bermuda
Record: 63
Designer: Robert Trent Jones Sr.
Year opened: 1972

• • •

Hole	Par	Yards	Hole	Par	Yards
Out	36	3,186	In	36	3,357

Robert Trent Jones has built golf courses all over the world — more than 450, to be exact, in 42 states and 23 countries. In a career that now spans six decades, he annually logs 300,000 frequent-flier miles.

Through all his travels and all his courses, Jones finally found a golf course that he could put his name on at Sugar Creek Country Club, where each of the three nine-hole layouts are named in his honor. Robert, Trent and Jones.

Sugar Creek is one of only five courses in Texas built by the legendary architect, so to have a course designed by Jones is truly something special. But building a course on the flat Texas terrain was a challenge for even Jones, who is accustomed to building golf courses on the best land God has to offer.

At Sugar Creek, he started with a blank canvas of open prairie.

"You have to be more creative and imaginative," Jones said when he returned to Sugar Creek in 1992 for a $1.5 million renovation, "but you can build your lakes and greens to give the terrain a rolling effect. Of course, you have to have your own watershed and use trees more than you normally would."

While the terrain was flat, it offered Jones plenty of pecan, oak and elm trees on the 150-acre site to provide definition for his fairways. Oyster Creek provided a natural watershed. It is a good members' course that you don't get tired of playing because of the various hole combinations. The Trent-Jones nines comprise the original course and feature water on 11 holes. The Robert nine has only one water hazard.

Sugartree Country Club could be one of the best golf courses in the state that was built by its owner with his own hands and his own money.

Arlington businessman Phil Lumsden reaped his handiwork 40 miles west of Fort Worth in the rural town of Dennis on the site of the original Dennis estate. The old barn from the original estate still sits left of the 15th fairway.

Lumsden bought this 600-acre tract of land in 1981 specifically to build a golf course. Over a period of 30 months and at a cost of approximately $3 million, Lumsden routed and helped construct the course and now has plans for a second course on the drawing board.

The 6,726-yard, par-71 layout features tree-lined fairways and water hazards coming into play on 15 holes. The bentgrass greens are medium in size and some are elevated. Eight holes have blind or semi-blind tee shots, and five require a fairway wood or less to reach the landing area from the tee.

The first hole is a tough starting hole. It is a 402-yard par 4 with a creek down the left side then cutting across in front of the green.

No. 5 is a 547-yard par 5 with a row of trees down the right center part of the fairway, making it difficult for golfers to decide where to aim when standing on the tee.

The signature hole is the 210-yard, par-3 No. 12. It is picturesque with a green framed by an old water wheel on the left. A stream runs left of the tee and crosses the fairway to the right side of the green. The water wheel looks old but was built by Lumsden.

Sugartree Country Club

PO Box 68
Dennis 76037
817-596-0020
Pro: Joe Henshaw
A par-71, 6,726-yard private club.
From Dallas, take I-20 to Dennis
(exit 403). Left on Dennis across
Brazos River to course entrance.

• • •

USGA rating: 72.8
Slope rating: 138
Sand traps: 39
Water holes: 13
Doglegs: 7 left/3 right
Type greens: Bentgrass
Record: N/A
Designer: Phil Lumsden
Year opened: 1987

• • •

Hole	Par	Yards	Hole	Par	Yards
Out	36	3,478	In	35	3,248

Sunset Grove Country Club

2900 Sunset
Orange 77630
409-883-9454
Pro: Jeff Cooper

A par-72, 6,412-yard private club.
From Houston, take I-10 east to 16th
Street exit in Orange, then right to
Sunset, the right on Sunset to
club entrance.

• • •

USGA rating: 69.7
Slope rating: 117
Sand traps: 45
Water holes: 4
Doglegs: 7
Type greens: Bermuda
Record: N/A
Designer: Donald Ross
Year opened: 1925

• • •

Hole	Par	Yards	Hole	Par	Yards
Out	36	3,215	In	36	3,197

Donald Ross courses are to golf what Rolls Royces are to the automotive industry. Top of the line. It doesn't get any better. The only difference is there are a lot fewer Ross courses on the road than Rolls Royces.

Like the Rolls Royce owner who takes his car out for a Sunday drive, the members at Sunset Grove are justifiably proud to have one of only two Donald Ross courses in Texas.

Ross built Sunset Grove at the same time he was building the exclusive River Oaks layout in Houston. While Sunset Grove is relatively unknown, nearly 80 years later it is true to its maker.

It all started back in 1923, when timber baron H.J. "Letcher" Stark watched with envy as some of his friends built pasture-land golf courses. While Stark achieved wealth by chopping down trees for paper and lumber, he designated a 200-acre site of swampland and hardwoods for a golf course. At the same time, Stark charged Ross with uprooting as few trees as possible.

"He told Mr. Ross, 'I want as many trees as possible on this golf course,'" son Homer Stark says. "He didn't even allow anybody to trim trees unless he was here. He'd go berserk."

It originally was known as Pea Vine Country Club when it opened in 1925, and the price tag was $700,000, which was extremely high for that era. Like most Ross courses, it is full of hammocks and dunes with a premium on tee shots of 200–220 yards with greens that require difficult recovery shots.

Roger Packard won't soon forget his infrequent ventures to Texas. A native of Chicago, where he and his father have built many top courses in one of the birthplaces of American golf, Packard came to Texas in the early 1980s charged with the responsibility of putting women's golf in general and Sweetwater Country Club, in particular, on the American golf map.

Sweetwater is best known as the former home of the Ladies Professional Golf Association and LPGA Hall of Fame, which it housed from the day it opened in 1983 until 1990.

Sweetwater developer Gerald Hines put together a sweetheart deal that was supported by powerful influence of LPGA Hall of Famers Patty Berg, Betsy Rawls and Carol Mann. The LPGA could use Sweetwater as headquarters rent-free as long as it held a tournament in Houston, a deal that commissioner Ray Volpe couldn't refuse even though Houston had a track record of failing to support the seven other LPGA events that had been held there since the late '60s.

The course originally operated as three nine-hole layouts known as the Palm, Pecan and Cypress, until Packard returned to finish the final nine holes in 1990 creating two 18-hole championship layouts.

The 6,687-yard Cypress layout is comprised of the original Palm nine and Packard's newest nine. It is a perfect match, because both are short, placement layouts with tight fairways and numerous water hazards. Packard also transplanted 400 trees to put an extra emphasis on accuracy.

Sweetwater Country Club Cypress Course

4400 Palm Royale
Sugar Land 77479
281-980-4653
Pro: John Kennedy
A 36-hole private club.
From Houston, take U.S. 59 south to Sweetwater Boulevard. Turn left to Palm Royale Boulevard and right to entrance.

• • •

USGA rating: 71.9
Slope rating: 120
Sand traps: 54
Water holes: 13
Doglegs: 5 left/4 right
Type greens: Bermuda
Record: 65
Designer: Roger Packard
Year opened: 1983

• • •

Hole	Par	Yards	Hole	Par	Yards
Out	36	3,373	In	35	3,314

Sweetwater Country Club Pecan Course

4400 Palm Royale
Sugar Land 77479
281-980-4653
Pro: John Kennedy
A 36-hole private club.
From Houston, take U.S. 59 south to Sweetwater Boulevard. Turn left to Palm Royale Boulevard and right to entrance.

• • •

USGA rating: 73.7
Slope rating: 125
Sand traps: 47
Water holes: 12
Doglegs: 6 left/4 right
Type greens: Bermuda
Record: 65
Designer: Roger Packard
Year opened: 1983

• • •

Hole	Par	Yards	Hole	Par	Yards
Out	36	3,586	In	36	3,566

Roger Packard would be pleased to know the sweat of his brow is still reaping dividends long after he's been gone. While the LPGA moved greener fairways in 1990 after holding the Mazda Hall of Fame there in 1985 and 1986, Sweetwater is still one of Houston's largest clubs.

Sweetwater is an immaculate, $29 million facility that is just a small part of the 9,500-acre First Colony development in Sugar Land. Packard designed the first 18 in 1983 and added nine more in 1984. The 36-hole complex was scheduled to be completed in 1985, but the slowdown in Houston's economic growth delayed completion of the final nine until late 1991. The addition of the new nine reasserted Sweetwater as one of Houston's most prestigious clubs.

With that goal in mind, Packard's assignment was to build the first course in America designed specifically with women in mind. The course was honored by *Golf Digest's* Best New Resort Course in 1984 and Best New Private Course in 1990.

"I tried to make exciting golf here," Packard says. "I tried to make each hole individual, unique. The better the player, the more challenging

"It was so hot down there in Houston and the humidity was unbelievable. Sweat would just be rolling down our faces. We'd look at each other and think, 'When does the plane leave?'"

The Pecan is a long course with pecan and live oak trees throughout the layout and water comes into play on 12 holes.

Combine the 40 years of golf course design of Ralph Plummer and 40 years of championship golf played by Arnold Palmer and you get a great golf course called Tanglewood on Texoma Resort and Country Club.

Before he got into golf course design himself, Palmer was still learning the ins and outs of the business when he worked with Plummer as a consultant on the design of this golf course near the Texas-Oklahoma border.

Architects Ken Dye and Baxter Spann renovated the course in 1988.

Palmer and Plummer built a challenging test of golf on rolling terrain overlooking scenic Lake Texoma. The par-72 layout measures 6,993 yards with wind and water often coming into play as well as large sand and grass bunkers.

Tanglewood is a resort and country club, so the club is semi-private but you have to be a guest of the resort to get a tee time.

The layout plays to a 128 slope rating with its wide variety of short, medium and long holes to challenge all types of shot-making abilities.

No. 14 is one of the more difficult holes. It is a 230-yard par 4 with water on the right side.

No. 18 is a reachable, 496-yard par 5, but a lake on the right side comes into play on the first two shots.

The hardest hole is the 414-yard, par-4 No. 1. It is a dogleg right through the trees, with a fairway bunker pinching the landing area at the corner of the dogleg. That is followed by a 444-yard, dogleg left par 4.

Tanglewood On Texoma Resort and Country Club Resort

Highway 120 North
Pottsboro 75076
903-786-4140
A par-72, 6,993-yard semi-private resort. Take Highway 75 north to Dennison, go left on Highway 120. At last stop sign turn left to club entrance.

• • •

USGA rating: 73.5
Slope rating: 128
Sand traps: 55
Water holes: 7
Doglegs: 3 left/3 right
Type greens: Bentgrass
Record: 65
Designer: Ralph Plummer
Year opened: 1970

• • •

Hole	Par	Yards	Hole	Par	Yards
Out	36	3,515	In	36	3,488

Tenison Park Golf Course East Course

3501 Samuell Boulevard
Dallas 75223
214-670-1402
Pro: Jason Aguirre
A 36-hole, public facility.
From Dallas, take I-30 east to East
Grand Boulevard, turn left go one-half
mile to course entrance on the right.

• • •

USGA rating: 72
Slope rating: 123
Sand traps: 0
Water holes: 17
Doglegs: 8
Type Greens: Bermuda
Record: 60
Designer: Ralph Plummer
Year opened: 1960

• • •

Hole	Par	Yards	Hole	Par	Yards
Out	36	3,377	In	36	3,425

Forty years after John Bredemus designed the West Course at Tenison Park, former Bredemus assistant Ralph Plummer returned to the scene in 1960 to design the East Course.

The East Course is a flat layout, 6,762 yards long from the back tees. It is bisected by White Rock Creek and water comes into play on half the holes.

Plummer's layout is flatter, but it is also tighter and plays alongside the banks of White Rock Creek. It is rare in that it opens with a pair of par 5s that could give big hitters the opportunity to start their round under par.

No. 1 is a 524-yard par 4 where golfers hit from the top of a hill down to a sweeping fairway that makes the hole play shorter than the yardage. Trees line both sides of a wide fairway that is a slight double dogleg, but a creek comes into play on the right-hand side. It is possible to reach the green in 2 strokes, or at least get close enough to chip for an easy birdie.

While No. 1 is fairly open, No. 2 measures 519 yards through a tight, tree-lined fairway with White Rock Creek running down the right side of the fairway and then cutting across in front of the green. The hole doglegs to the right at the end, and it takes an excellent tee shot to even consider going for the green in two.

The key is to pick up strokes while you can, because you'll probably need them later. Especially on the 236-yard, par-3 11th, which in addition to its length requires a carry over a creek that also turns and runs down the right side of the hole.

Tenison is perhaps Dallas' most nostalgic public golf facility, offering two distinctive 18-hole public courses.

This is where Lee Trevino got his start as a caddy, learning to hit a golf ball with a coke bottle and hustle players out of their money.

John Bredemus, the father of Texas golf course architecture, built the West Course in 1920, making it one of the state's first public golf courses. The West is hilly and 6,872 yards long with a tight layout requiring long, straight tee shots. The abundance of large old trees provides a picturesque setting in one of Dallas' oldest parks. It is a timeless layout that has a great combination of uphill and downhill holes, all of which wind through the heavily wooded forest of one of Dallas' oldest parks.

Indeed, Tenison West is still one of those golf courses that you could enjoy playing every day. Bredemus has a great collection of holes, including a 257-yard par 4 that you can reach off the tee, back-to-back par 5s on Nos. 2 and 3 and a series of strong par 4s.

No. 15 is a 444-yard par 4 with a tight, tree-lined fairway. Players hit uphill off the tee to a fairway that slopes from right to left. If you hit into the trees, they are so thick it is almost impossible to reach the green in regulation.

No. 16 measures only 257 yards and can be reached with an accurate drive. Players tee off at the bottom of a hill to an uphill fairway that obscures the green. The biggest danger here is landing in the rocky, tree-covered hill that guards the green on the left and can produce an unplayable lie.

Tenison Park Golf Course West Course

3501 Samuell Boulevard
Dallas 75223
214-670-1402
Pro: Jason Aguirre
A 36-hole public facility.
From Dallas, take I-30 east to East Grand Boulevard, turn left go one-half mile to course entrance on the right.

• • •

USGA rating: 72.0
Slope rating: 121
Sand traps: 0
Water holes: 4
Doglegs: 4 left/2 right
Type greens: Bermuda
Record: N/A
Designer: John Bredemus
Year opened: 1924

• • •

Hole	Par	Yards	Hole	Par	Yards
Out	37	3,665	In	35	3,237

Texas National Country Club

PO Box 585
Willis 77373
713-353-2972
Pro: David Pate
A par-72, 6,700-yard public course.
From Houston, take I-45 north to Seven
Coves Road, go east two miles to Highway
75. Go north on Highway 75 two miles to
FM 2432, then east to entrance on left.

• • •

USGA rating: 72
Slope rating: 113
Sand traps: 68
Water holes: 13
Doglegs: 8 left/1 right
Type greens: Bermuda
Record: 67
Designer: Jack Miller
Year opened: 1977

• • •

Hole	Par	Yards	Hole	Par	Yards
Out	36	3,400	In	36	3,300

If imitation is indeed the most sincere form of flattery, then the members of Augusta National Golf Club should be proud.

Augusta National was the inspiration for Texas National Golf Club in Willis. Architect Jack Miller got the idea for Texas National on a return plane flight home from the Masters in 1975 for a golf course he was building on rolling terrain with elevation of 230 and 340 feet and covered with a forest of dogwood, holly, hickory and pine trees.

The countryside was reminiscent of Augusta, the most famous inland golf course in America . So Miller figured he would borrow from the Augusta National name, if not the layout of Alister MacKenzie's legendary course that was built on the former site of a nursery.

"It was potentially the best site for a golf course that I had seen," Miller said.

Miller was one of four original co-owners of the Texas National development, but the project got caught in the money crunch of the mid-1970s. Work ceased until 1977 when new owner Russell Wiggins got it off the ground.

"There were money problems from the beginning," Miller says. "If we had an adequate budget for construction, it could have been one of the outstanding golf courses in the area."

The layout is unlike any in Houston with its combination of tree-lined fairways and Hill Country elevation changes. Accuracy is at a premium here to keep the ball in play.

I f Thorntree Country Club was a stock on the New York Stock Exchange, volume would be high and the stock price would keep rising.

The operating philosophy in the investment business is to buy low and sell high. The key to making that philosophy work is to have money to invest when the time is right to buy. Thorntree has been bought and sold several times since it first opened in 1984, but each move has meant an upgrade for members golfers in the Dallas suburb of DeSoto.

In 1991, Thorntree was sold to a group of Japanese investors who purchased six D/FW-area golf courses and country clubs. They were interested in undervalued golf properties in the D/FW area in general and in Thorntree, in particular.

The course was later sold to the Dallas-based IRI Golf Group and in 1998 was sold to California-based Cobblestone Golf Group.

"People are just looking at them as investments, period," said one real estate broker. "It's just like an office building or a shopping center."

Thorntree was built in 1984 on a natural rolling piece of terrain in this growing suburb of the metroplex. The par-72, 7,050-yard layout features six lakes and three creeks. No. 10 is a 666-yard par 5 that double doglegs with out-of-bounds all the way down the left side. No. 11 is a 382-yard par 4 that winds through a row of trees on the right to a shallow green nestled in a grove of trees. No. 5 is a 414-yard par 4 through a chute of trees that doglegs to the right to a green surrounded by bunkers with a pond on the right.

Thorntree Country Club

825 West Wintergreen
DeSoto 75115
Pro: Ron King
972-296-7317
A par-72, 7,050-yard private club.
From Dallas take I-35 south to Wintergreen, go west on Wintergreen to the club entrance.

• • •

USGA rating: 70.6
Slope rating: 122
Sand traps: 75
Water holes: 8
Doglegs: 5 left/5 right
Type greens: Bentgrass
Record: N/A
Designer: N/A
Year opened: 1984

• • •

Hole	Par	Yards	Hole	Par	Yards
Out	36	3,199	In	36	3,188

Tour 18
Houston

3102 FM 1960 East
Houston 77338
281-540-1818
Dir.: Greg Saul
A par-72, 6,807-yard public course.
From Houston, take U.S. 59 north to
FM 1960, go east 3.5 miles to club
entrance on right.

• • •

USGA rating: 72.2
Slope rating: 126
Sand traps: 90
Water holes: 10
Doglegs: 4 left/5 right
Type greens: Bermuda
Record: 66
Designer: Dave Edsall
Year opened: 1992

• • •

Hole	Par	Yards	Hole	Par	Yards
Out	36	3,303	In	36	3,504

Sooner or later, it was bound to happen. Somebody comes up with a great idea and makes a lot of money, then somebody files a lawsuit to get a piece of the action.

Welcome to Tour 18, home of "America's Greatest 18 Holes."

Tour 18 is capitalism at its best. It was built in 1992 with computer technology that enabled owner Dennis Wilkerson and engineer Dave Edsall to re-create some of golf's best holes on a 200-acre site in Humble.

It was a $5.5 million gamble that paid off. It was such a huge success, that the course paid for itself in the first year and owners are now expanding to other cities.

Among the holes re-created are the infamous Amen Corner holes at Augusta National, where Nos. 11, 12 and 13 are the three most memorable holes in golf.

"This gives golfers a chance to see these holes on television on Sunday," says Tour 18 partner Barron Jacobson, "then come play them on Monday."

However, the Japanese owners at Pebble Beach filed a lawsuit in 1993 to prevent Tour 18 from duplicating its holes.

Pinehurst and Sea Pines Plantation also joined in the lawsuit. In 1996, federal Judge David Hittner ruled Tour 18 would have to make only minor changes.

"What this person has done is take famous holes from famous courses and tried to make money on it," said Pebble Beach attorney Stephen Trattner. "We don't want other people like him to get the impression they could copy our course."

Ben Hogan is one of the most revered names in golf. His flawless swing, his fierce determination and his will to win were unlike anything the golf world had seen before or since.

After learning the game as a caddie along with Byron Nelson at Fort Worth's Glen Garden Country Club, Hogan grew up to become one of the greatest players of all time.

His resume reads like this: 63 career victories, including 13 in 1945, two Masters titles, four U.S. Opens, two PGA Championships, one British Open, four-time player of the year, three-time Vardon Trophy Winner and, of course, the golf hall of fame.

It is a shame Hogan didn't leave a more lasting legacy than a trophy case filled to overflowing.

Of all the knowledge he had about the golf swing and the way the game should be played, he kept most of it to himself.

The members at the Trophy Club, then, take great pride in the fact that this is the only course that Ben Hogan helped design.

Hogan was a perceptive critic of golf course architecture throughout his playing career.

He especially admired the works of Dick Wilson and shortly before the architect's death had talked about doing a course with him. Ten years later, Hogan did collaborate with Wilson's chief assistant, Joe Lee, at the Trophy Club.

Typical of Hogan's intensity, he attacked each phase of the project with painstaking detail, even going so far as to personally hand-rake the green contours.

The Trophy Club Hills Course

500 Trophy Club Drive
Trophy Club 76262
817-430-0444
Pro: Jim Rose
A par-72 6,807-yard public course.
From Dallas, take I-35E north to Highway 183, then west on Highway 183 to Highway 114. Go north on Highway 114 to Trophy Club exit.

• • •

USGA rating: 73.0
Slope rating: 125
Sand traps: 42
Water holes: 10
Doglegs: 4 left/5 right
Type greens: Bentgrass
Record: 64
Designer: Arthur Hills
Year opened: 1984

• • •

Hole	Par	Yards	Hole	Par	Yards
Out	36	3,435	In	36	3,507

Treeline Golf Club

17505 North Eldridge Parkway
Tomball 77355
281-376-1542
Pro: Cliff Rampy
An 18-hole public course.
From Houston, take Highway 290 to
FM 1960, go north to Highway. 249, left
to Spring Cypress, left to North Eldridge
and right to club entrance on left.

• • •

USGA rating: 68.8
Slope rating: 114
Sand traps: 6
Water holes: 12
Doglegs: 2 left/2 right
Type greens: Bermuda
Record: N/A
Designers: Lester Hodges
      and Clarence Hodges
Year opened: 1952

• • •

Hole	Par	Yards	Hole	Par	Yards
Out	34	2,845	In	34	2,525

Lester and Clarence Hodges loved golf, but back in the late 1940s and early '50s there weren't many golf courses available in the rural town of Tomball in northwest Harris County. The nearest course was Conroe Country Club, a little nine-hole layout that still was more than 30 minutes away.

In 1952, they decided to build three holes on their dairy farm for recreational purposes. They invited their friends to come play. It was at their friends' request that the Hodges built six more holes to complete a nine-hole layout and start charging people to play.

The demand for golf continued to grow, so in 1955 the Hodges decided to build nine more holes to complete the 18-hole, par-72 layout.

Treeline's success has served to disprove the theory that there is no more room for small family-run operations and giving way to corporate management companies.

"This is a short but sweet layout," owner Cliff Rampy says. "We still have a family atmosphere here and we have a very loyal group of players who have a good time when they play here and they keep coming back."

In 1983 Rampy remodeled the course to its current par-68, 5,370-yard layout that includes seven par 3s. The golf course is well kept with a lot of water and trees.

The toughest hole is the 450-yard, par-4 No. 4. No. 16 is a 173-yard par 3 over water and No. 3 is a 160-yard par 3 that is mostly over water. No. 11 is a 225-yard par 3.

Dick Murphy was a career pilot at American Airlines. In 1982, he and his wife decided to move to the rural town of Muenster, where they bought 247 acres and turned it into a cattle ranch.

While Murphy continued to make the 1-hour, 15-minute commute every day until he retired in 1994, he was an avid golfer and decided to turn part of his ranch into a golf course since there were no quality public courses in the area.

With no prior experience in golf course architecture, construction or maintenance, Murphy personally designed the front nine based on his own golf experience and broke ground in 1989.

While still flying for American Airlines, Murphy would work on the construction of the golf course the days he was not flying.

Murphy spent 15,000 man hours and $1.2 million before his dream became a reality in 1993 when his first nine holes opened for public play with impeccable bentgrass greens that are hailed by many as some of the best in Texas.

Upon completion of the first nine, Murphy immediately began designing a second nine.

Murphy's masterpiece is the picturesque par-3 11th, which has a 120-foot drop from the elevated tee to the green. From the tee, golfers get a breathtaking view and can see all the way to Oklahoma seven miles away.

"This is down-home country, but it's one of the top golf courses you'll play," said Scott Brewer, general manager. "We know what we're not. But we try to be the best at what we are."

Turtle Hill Golf Course

Route 373 North
Muenster 76252
940-759-4896
Pro: Scott Brewer
A par-72, 6,510-yard public course.
From Dallas, take I-35 north to Highway 82, go west 13 miles to Muenster. Turn right at red light (Highway 373) eight miles to entrance.

• • •

USGA rating: N/A
Slope rating: N/A
Sand traps: 20
Water holes: 12
Doglegs: 6 left/5 right
Type greens: Bentgrass
Record: N/A
Designer: Dick Murphy
Year opened: 1993

• • •

Hole	Par	Yards	Hole	Par	Yards
Out	36	3,354	In	36	3,354

Valley International Country Club

FM 802 and Expressway 77
Brownsville 78520
956-548-9199
Pro: Jerry Klinger
A par-70, 6,538-yard semi-private club.
Take Highway 77 south to FM 802, turn
right on FM 802 and left on Country
Club Road to club entrance.

• • •

USGA rating: 72.3
Slope rating: 125
Sand traps: 46
Water holes: 10
Doglegs: 4 left/4right
Type greens: Bermuda
Record: 62
Designer: N/A
Year opened: 1920

• • •

Hole	Par	Yards	Hole	Par	Yards
Out	35	3,321	In	35	3,217

Valley International Country Club is one of the first golf courses built in the Rio Grande Valley. It offers both 18- and nine-hole regulation courses.

With its tall palms and tropical-like conditions near the Gulf of Mexico, it looks more like a Florida golf course than a Texas golf course.

The main course measures 6,538 yards and plays to par 70. It is built on both sides of a coastal tributary which brings water into play on 12 holes. Windy conditions is even more of a hazard.

Water is also a major factor at the 512-yard No. 17. Water runs all the way down the right side of the fairway, and players also must carry a creek that crosses the fairway about 100 yards short of the green.

No. 4 is the No. 1 handicap hole. It measures 422 yards from the back tee. Water crosses the fairway in the landing area forcing players to lay up or hit a big drive to carry across the water. Water protects the right side of the fairway and the right side of the green and out-of-bounds runs down the right side off the tee.

No. 10 is a 185-yard par 3 where the peninsula green extends out into the river and is surrounded by water on three sides, leaving small margin for error.

There is no water to be found on the 441-yard, par-4 No. 14, but that doesn't keep it from being the hardest hole on the course.

The executive course measures just 1,052 yards, but the greens are small and difficult to hit, so shot accuracy is at a premium with the short irons.

Developers Conrad Weil and Jerry Deutser enjoyed such success with Walden on Lake Conroe in the mid-70s, they called on architects Bob von Hagge and Bruce Devlin to duplicate their effort on the shores of Lake Houston in 1982.

Following in the footsteps of one of the state's best golf courses was a difficult task, but Walden on Lake Houston bears many of the same characteristics of all von Hagge-Devlin courses and has achieved success in its own right. While the land is not as rolling as its older sibling, it features 110 sand traps — by far the most of any course in the Houston area.

"The layout, with its many lakes and traps, places a premium on shot-making ability," pro J.D. Murchison says. "The length is not overwhelming, but the course is long in the right places and the wind is almost always present."

No. 1 is a 399-yard par 4 that turns slightly to the left with an intimidating lake strategically placed on the right side and bunkers on the left. The approach requires a medium iron to a well-bunkered, two-tiered green.

And then there's the 429-yard, par-4 No. 8, which gives the advantage to a long drive to the left side of the fairway. The approach requires accuracy and proper club selection to clear the channel in front of a small, well-bunkered green.

The par-4 No. 14 is 444 yards with a large lake situated between the landing area and green. The approach requires a long iron to hit a small green guarded by front and left-side sand traps.

Walden on Lake Houston Golf Club

18100 Walden Forest
Humble 77346
281-852-3467
Pro: Jimmy O'Dell
A par-72, 6,781-yard private course.
From Houston, take U.S. 59 north to FM 1960, then go east for 7.5 miles to Walden Forest Drive and entrance.

• • •

USGA rating: 71.9
Slope rating: 126
Sand traps: 110
Water holes: 12
Doglegs: 6 left/4 right
Type greens: Bermuda
Record: 62
Designer: Robert von Hagge and Bruce Devlin
Year opened: 1982

• • •

Hole	Par	Yards	Hole	Par	Yards
Out	36	3,287	In	36	3,494

Wedgewood Golf Course

5454 Highway 105 West
Conroe 77304
409-539-4653
Pro: Joe Priddy
A par-72, 6,817-yard public course.
From Houston, take I-45 north to
Highway 105, then go west on Highway
105 to course entrance on right.

• • •

USGA rating: 73.6
Slope rating: 133
Sand traps: 33
Water holes: 10
Doglegs: 7 right/5 left
Type greens: Bermuda
Record: 70
Designer: Robert von Hagge, Bruce
*   Devlin, Ron Pritchard and Bill Rogers*
Year opened: 1988

• • •

Hole	Par	Yards	Hole	Par	Yards
Out	35	3,527	In	35	3,290

Standing on the first tee at Wedgewood will bring back memories of your first-grade teacher and walking down the hallways single-file from homeroom to the lunch room. Get out of line, and it's off to the principal's office for an introduction to corporal punishment.

There was a time when the fairways at Wedgewood were as narrow as those schoolboy portals and, if you strayed off the beaten path, you'd just as soon pull your own wooden paddle out of your golf bag and beat yourself.

Wedgewood originally was designed as an exclusive club and a demanding test of golf for only the best golfers. Original developer Dale Marsh was inspired by the Masters and Augusta National, and he hired architects Robert von Hagge and Bruce Devlin to design a golf course for the best of the best. The idea caught on, with 53 investors putting money into the project before the first shovel was turned.

But timing couldn't have been worse. The bottom dropped out of the economy, and loan money was hard to come by. New owners hired former PGA Tour pro Bill Rogers and architect Ron Pritchard to finish the job. But the exclusive club concept never took off and the club has been public since BSL Golf Corporation bought it in 1989 and made it more user friendly.

No. 18 is a 451-yard par 4 that requires a demanding tee shot and a semi-blind approach. No. 10 is a 164-yard, downhill par 3 that requires a precise shot to a tiny, well-protected green.

Developer J.B. Belin has perfected the business of building master-planned communities. He has built many of them since the 1960s and each new one seems to get a little better.

After watching Houston grow westward from River Oaks to Memorial, Belin looked a little further west and designed Weston Lakes as the next address of choice for Houston's rich and famous. It was a 1,400-acre property with rolling hills and valleys and dotted with natural lakes and covered with centuries-old pecan trees. He came up with the Weston Lakes concept after returning home from a 30-day tour of England in 1984.

Belin called on architect Carlton Gipson to design the first nine holes (Nos. 1–6, 16–18) in 1985. Three-time U.S. Open champion Hale Irwin designed the second nine (Nos. 7–15) in 1986. One advantage that Gipson and Irwin had at Weston Lakes that Donald Ross didn't have at River Oaks was elbow room.

And as if the 7,033-yard layout isn't long enough, and winds sweep across the prairie and make it play even longer.

"Wind is a major factor, and the golf course shouldn't be taken lightly," says former pro Perry French. "The course plays into the wind on the first 10 holes. The ability to play in the wind is definitely an advantage."

Weston Lakes has its own version of Augusta National's Amen Corner with a rare combination that puts the three hardest holes — Nos. 8, 9 and 10 — in a row. All three play into a prevailing wind.

Weston Lakes Country Club

32611 FM 1093
Fulshear 77441
281-346-1228
Pro: Pat Fitzpatrick
A par-72, 7,083-yard private club.
From Houston, take U.S. 59 south to the Sam Houston Tollway, go west to Westheimer, go left and proceed to club entrance at FM 359.

• • •

USGA rating: 74.5
Slope rating: 131
Sand traps: 69
Water holes: 12
Doglegs: 7 left/3 right
Type greens: Bermuda
Record: 64
Designers: Carlton Gipson and Hale Irwin
Year opened: 1985

Hole	Par	Yards	Hole	Par	Yards
Out	36	3,441	In	36	3,642

Westwood Country Club

8888 Country Creek Drive
Houston 77036
713-774-3011
Dir.: Michael Longpre
A par-72, 6,989-yard private club.
From Houston, take U.S. 59 south to
Bissonnet, go right past Westwood Mall to
Country Creek Drive and right to the club.

• • •

USGA rating: 73.1
Slope rating: 122
Sand traps: 61
Water holes: 15
Doglegs: 6 left/4 right
Type greens: Bermuda
Record: 63
Designers: John Bredemus
*   and Joe Finger (1957)*
Year opened: 1929

• • •

Hole	Par	Yards	Hole	Par	Yards
Out	36	3,443	In	36	3,546

Westwood is one of Houston's oldest and most historic golf courses, having been built by legendary architect John Bredemus in 1929 shortly before he went on to build Memorial Park Golf Course and Colonial Country Club, which is still the state's No. 1 course.

Westwood was just a nine-hole course at the time, but it had some impressive founders, including a virtual Who's Who in the Houston business and social scene.

In the 1950s, a bayou was rerouted through the golf course as part of a flood control project, and the members decided to build a new 18-hole golf course and clubhouse. In 1957, they hired architect Joe Finger, whose father built Westwood's original clubhouse, to design the new layout. Finger had plenty of trees and enough water to create a timeless layout with water in play on 15 holes and wind is a constant factor. The 437-yard, par-4 13th is one of the toughest in Houston as golfer's negotiate a tight fairway through the trees.

In 1972, Westwood hosted the PGA Tour's Houston Open and the following year hosted the S&H Green Stamps Ladies Golf Classic the following March.

"It's a very fair course but it requires straight driving and accurate second shots to small greens," says former pro David Findlay.

Like many of Houston's old establishment clubs, however, Westwood was hurt by Houston's economic downturn in the 1980s, but in 1990, initiated a $1 million renovation, including new greens that are among the most undulating in Houston.

Two years after Bruce Lietzke completed the first course at White Bluff, he returned to build the second 18 simply known as the New Course.

In keeping with the resort theme at White Bluff, where golf is supposed to be fun and not some form of cruel and unusual punishment, Lietzke produced another laid-back design that keeps the local residents and conventioneers coming back for more.

From the back tees, however, the New Course measures 6,964-yards and plays to a 139 slope rating — one of the state's highest.

The 36 holes at White Bluff are the centerpiece of a residential community on the shores of Lake Whitney and were designed to attract home buyers.

There is also a resort and conference center facility to attract conventions and meetings, which also want golf to be one of the feature attractions.

The signature hole on the New Course is the par-4, 398-yard No. 12. This hole demands accuracy from start to finish.

From the tee, the green is not even visible. A straight drive about 240 yards is needed to set up the approach. A longer shot will end up in the water.

There's more trouble waiting for any drive that drifts right or left. The fairway is guarded on the left by large mounds and on the right by a large, deep bunker.

The green, almost surrounded by huge live oaks, is two-tiered and is guarded in front by water. The right side of the green is sloped, directing errant shots into double-bogey land.

White Bluff Golf Club New Course

No. 4 White Bluff Drive
Whitney 76692
254-694-3656
Pro: Brad Wells
A 36-hole semi-private resort.
From Dallas, go south on I-35 to Whitney/Corsicana exit (exit 368). Turn right on Highway 22 to FM 523, then right for six miles to entrance on the left.

• • •

USGA rating: 73.9
Slope rating: 139
Sand traps: 25
Water holes: 17
Doglegs: 3 left/3 right
Type greens: Bentgrass
Record: 69
Designer: Bruce Lietzke
Year opened: 1995

• • •

Hole	Par	Yards	Hole	Par	Yards
Out	36	3,440	In	36	3,524

White Bluff Golf Club
Old Course

No. 4 White Bluff Drive
Whitney 76692
254-694-3656
Pro: Brad Wells
A 36-hole semi-private resort.
From Dallas, go south on I-35 to
Whitney/Corsicana exit (exit 368). Turn
right on Highway 22 to FM 523, then
right for six miles to entrance on the left.

• • •

USGA rating: 73.3
Slope rating: 132
Sand traps: 12
Water holes: 10
Doglegs: 4 left/3 right
Type greens: Bentgrass
Record: 67
Designer: Bruce Lietzke
Year opened: 1993

• • •

Hole	Par	Yards	Hole	Par	Yards
Out	36	3,464	In	36	3,402

Bruce Lietzke is known as one of the most laid-back players on the PGA Tour. He plays golf whenever he finds time between fixing up old cars, fishing trips and coaching his sons' Little League games.

Yet whenever Lietzke decides to play, he still is among the best in the game. Even though he gave up the game temporarily after an All-America career at the University of Houston, he has since won 13 times and more than $6 million.

It was appropriate that Lietzke design courses at White Bluff Golf Club. After all this is a resort where laid back is the modus operandi. The 36 holes at White Bluff are the centerpiece of a residential community on the shores of Lake Whitney, and were designed to attract home buyers.

There is also a resort and conference center facility to attract conventions which also want golf to be one of the feature attractions.

Lietzke, a Texas native designed the old course first at White Bluff in 1993.

The signature hole is No. 12, a 389-yard, par 4 that goes straight uphill and has a bite much bigger than its bark. At first glance, it appears to be a potential birdie opportunity. But after a closer look, the player will notice that the tee shot requires a minimum carry of 200 yards over water to a bunker-guarded fairway.

The second shot is uphill to a green guarded in front by a bunker and a steep slope to the left. If you are lucky enough to hit the green, ball placement is still crucial. The green has an extreme slope from back to front.

Willow Creek was once considered one of Houston's best-kept secrets, but its reputation as a challenging layout is finally starting to spread after it struggled to survive some difficult economic times in its early days. This is where many Houston-area pros go to play on a rare day off.

The course was built by renowned architects Robert von Hagge and Bruce Devlin and is named after Willow Creek, a normally peaceful stream that meanders through the layout but at one time caused major flood problems before precautions were taken to protect the course. It is built rolling terrain and is filled with tall pines and dogwoods.

Typical of the von Hagge-Devlin style, it rewards thinkers and shot makers for well-planned and well-executed shots.

"You took the natural undulating terrain, trees and creeks and created one of the most beautiful golf courses in this part of the country," former treasurer Donald Harris wrote in a letter to the architects.

In 1993, members sold the club to Dallas-based Club Corporation of America.

The signature hole at Willow Creek is No. 12. Water in front of the tee and to the left is barely a factor, but the combination of length and narrow, partially concealed green make it difficult.

"The grit and determination of the membership is the main reason the course exists today," von Hagge says. "It enjoys a strong, loyal membership and I personally remain very much in love with the club's potential."

Willow Creek Golf Club

24525 Northcrest Drive
Spring 77389
281-376-4061
Pro: Brett Baske
A par-72, 6,920-yard private club.
From Houston, take I-45 north to FM 2920, west to Kuykendahl, right to Spring-Stuebner, right to Northcrest, then left to club entrance.

• • •

USGA rating: 73
Slope rating: 136
Sand traps: 63
Water holes: 13
Doglegs: 4 left/5 right
Type greens: Bermuda
Record: 65
Designer: Robert von Hagge and Bruce Devlin
Year opened: 1981

Hole	Par	Yards	Hole	Par	Yards
Out	36	3,497	In	36	3,422

Willow Fork Country Club

21055 Westheimer Parkway
Katy 77450
281-579-6262
Pro: Duane Criswell
A par-72, 6,853-yard private club.
From Houston, take I-10 west to Fry
Road, go south on Fry about three miles
to Westheimer Parkway. Go west
to entrance.

• • •

USGA rating: 71.9
Slope rating: 119
Sand traps: 53
Water holes: 9
Doglegs: 7 left/2 right
Type greens: Bermuda
Record: N/A
Designers: Jay Riviere and Dave Marr
Year opened: 1990

• • •

Hole	Par	Yards	Hole	Par	Yards
Out	36	3,420	In	36	3,433

Looks can be deceiving. When you look out across the open prairie in Katy at Willow Fork, it looks like a defenseless course that is vulnerable to attack and low scores. But don't judge a golf course from the parking lot.

"It looks a lot easier than it is," architect Jay Riviere says. "People walk up to the first tee and think they're going to eat it up, but they end up getting burned. Sooner or later it will reach out and grab them."

Willow Fork opened in 1990 on a prairie that once was a rice field and cattle ranch. The land, which originally comprised part of the old Cinco Ranch, was owned by two developers who eventually parted ways and divided the land. One development became Cinco Ranch. The other became Willow Fork Country Club.

The breakup delayed construction, and when Riviere went back to work budget cutbacks prevented him from building as many bunkers and lakes and from moving as much dirt as he wanted. The club later went back and added 30 fairway bunkers and two green-side bunkers in Riviere's original design.

The toughest hole is the par-4 No. 9, a 447-yard dogleg left with a bayou running down the left side and a lake that protects the front of the green.

Nos. 4, 5 and 6 were cut out of existing wetlands and are the most picturesque on the course. Shots hit into the lakes on these holes are best left where they lie, since the resident alligators claim all balls in the water.

To golf course architects, courses are like golf shots to a golfer. You build a lot of them, but only a few come out exactly the way you envisioned them.

The only difference, a bad golf shot is quickly forgotten. The work of a golf course architect, on the other hand, is around forever for all to see.

A number of elements have to be in place for an architect to pull off a good golf course. The right piece of land. The right amount of money. And the right idea.

At Wood Crest, architects Don January and Billy Martindale teamed with developer Kirk Waggoner to build a master-planned community and private country club that filled a void in the Grand Prairie area in the early '80s.

Waggoner owned a piece of heavily wooded property filled with creeks and old oaks, and January had the right idea for the design.

"We made a deal with the land owner like we were going to do at Royal Oaks," January said, "in that we would be part owners of the club. Unfortunately, this all happened right about the time when money in Dallas starting drying up. The sale of the real estate was going slow — we had started construction of course — they were nice enough to let us off the hook."

At Wood Crest, January produced a traditional style, tree-lined layout where water comes into play on 14 holes and out-of-bounds on seven. The toughest stretch is at Nos. 10, 11 and 12, where golfers face the three toughest holes on the course.

Wood Crest Country Club

3502 Country Club Drive
Grand Prairie 75051
972-264-2974
Pro: Michael Hicks
A par-72, 6,437-yard private club.
From Dallas, take I-30 west to Belt Line in Grand Prairie, then south to Country Club Drive and left to club entrance.

• • •

USGA rating: 70.2
Slope rating: 119
Sand traps: 6
Water holes: 14
Doglegs: 4 left/2 right
Type greens: Bermuda
Record: 62
Designers: Don January
    and Billy Martindale
Year opened: 1973

• • •

Hole	Par	Yards	Hole	Par	Yards
Out	36	3,193	In	36	3,244

Dallas businessman Mike Myers may have developed or financed more golf courses in the Dallas-Fort Worth area than any other single man.

In 1971, Myers teamed with developer Glenn Paden to build a golf course/residential community on the edge of Fort Worth near the D/FW turnpike. There wasn't much development between Dallas and Fort Worth at the time, and Woodhaven was perfectly situated on the heavily wooded hillside overlooking the Fort Worth skyline.

The driving force of the development was to sell real estate, but developers wanted to build it around a golf course. Architect Leon Howard turned that unwanted land into a layout that has hosted three LPGA tour events won by DFW native and LPGA Hall of Famer Sandra Haynie.

"I came into the golf course architecture business as an agronomist and soil specialist and my sympathies have always been with the superintendent and the average golfer," says Howard. "When I started golf course design in the 1950s, the average golfer in the United States shot about a 95. That was the target I always tried to hit."

Howard created a great back-to-back-to-back combination with Nos. 6, 7 and 8. No. 6 is a 224-yard par 3 that requires a carry of 200 yards to clear a lake that runs from the tee to about 20 yards short of the green. No. 7 is a long and lean 569-yard par 5 with out-of-bounds on both sides. No. 8 is a 426-yard par 4 that was nominated as one of the toughest in D/FW. It plays uphill and features a long, narrow fairway.

Woodlake is one of the Hill Country's most historic courses, having been the site of the PGA Tour's Texas Open from 1972–76 and the site of Ben Crenshaw's first PGA Tour victory.

Woodlake was designed by architect Desmond Muirhead, an enigmatic figure who has been called a rebel, a radical and a visionary. Muirhead was a landscape planner by trade who held a somewhat irreverent attitude about the game that originated in his homeland of Scotland.

He didn't get interested in golf-course design until he emigrated to the United States. He later returned to his homeland to make a whirlwind tour of the greatest courses. He returned to the U.S. in 1962 convinced he could do better. He went on to become one of the most controversial architects the game has known.

Before he went off the deep end, San Antonio businessmen Doug Saunders and Jack Parker lured him to San Antonio in 1972 to build Woodlake.

Ben Crenshaw captured his first PGA Tour victory in his first tournament as a professional.

At Woodlake, Muirhead's 6,652-yard layout offers plenty of risks and rewards.

Take No. 8, for example. It is a 353-yard dogleg right that gives you the chance to gamble and go for a birdie or can stick you with a double bogey.

The course is divided by Highway 78 with Nos. 13–18 located across the highway from the clubhouse. Muirhead's original nines also have been reversed from their original order.

Woodlake Country Club

6500 Woodlake Parkway
San Antonio 78244
210-661-6124
Pro: Tim Melloh
A par-72, 6,652-yard private club.
Take I-35 north to Ritteman, stay
right to FM 78, then right at
flashing light to clubhouse.

• • •

USGA rating: 72.5
Slope rating: 129
Sand traps: 38
Water holes: 11
Doglegs: 2 left/2 right
Type greens: Bermuda
Record: N/A
Designer: Desmond Muirhead
Year opened: 1972

• • •

Hole	Par	Yards	Hole	Par	Yards
Out	36	3,227	In	36	3,425

The Woodlands Country Club North Course

2301 North Millbend
The Woodlands 77380
281-367-1100
Pros: Ray Dznowski and R. Cromwell
A 72-hole resort and club.
From Houston, take I-45 north to
Woodlands Parkway, turn left to entrance.

• • •

USGA rating: 72.2
Slope rating: 126
Sand traps: 73
Water holes: 9
Doglegs: 4 left/6 right
Type greens: Bermuda
Record: 64
Designers: Joe Lee
    and Robert von Hagge
    and Bruce Devlin
Year opened: 1975

Hole	Par	Yards	Hole	Par	Yards
Out	36	3,409	In	36	3,472

The Woodlands hosted the Houston Open from the time it opened in 1975, however the original golf course designed by Florida-based architect Joe Lee was not really intended as a test for the world's best players.

So in 1982, architects Robert von Hagge and Bruce Devlin were called to design two new courses. One would become the TPC at The Woodlands, which in 1986 became the new host course for the Houston Open. The other would be combined with Lee's original 18 and become The Woodlands' North and West courses.

The North Course, like all the Woodlands courses, is tightly wooded with rolling terrain. It is just right for golfers who don't desire to put themselves through a torture chamber. At 6,881 yards, it is the shortest and easiest of all four Woodlands courses. Most of the water hazards are lateral, with only two forced carries over water.

All of the par 5s are long, ranging from 538 to 562 yards, and features two par 5s in the first four holes on the front side and back-to-back par 5s at Nos. 13 and 14. Only two par 4s are longer than 400 yards — the 426-yard, par-4 sixth and the 448-yard, par-4 15th. They are two of the most demanding on the course.

No. 6 is a dogleg right through the trees, with a pond protecting the inside corner of the dogleg and discouraging players from trying to cut the corner. No. 15 turns right to left, with a fairway bunker on the corner. Players must carry a creek that crosses the fairway in front of the green.

Long before the Psychic Readers Network, George Mitchell had a vision. And when George Mitchell dreams, they usually come true.

Mitchell is a Houston oilman/real-estate developer who dreamed about a country-living atmosphere in a heavily wooded area 27 miles north of Houston. It was once a distant outpost on Houston's northern frontier, but is now a 25,000-acre bustling city with more than 30,000 residents and a thriving business and retail center. Population is expected to exceed 60,000 by the year 2000.

And it all started with a simple golf course.

If anybody can tame the wilderness and turn it into civilization, it is Mitchell. He was a man with a vision that was so far ahead of its time that not even his most loyal employees were sure what he had in mind. But more than 25 years later, vision has become reality and The Woodlands has become Houston's golf Mecca.

Mitchell believed it was important to make golf the centerpiece of his community, and his Woodlands Corp. spent $25 million on its four golf courses — West, North, Palmer and TPC — and clubhouse facilities all within five miles of each other. The Woodlands has been home of the PGA Tour's Houston open since it opened in 1975.

Florida-based architect Joe Lee designed the first course in 1973 and golf legend Ben Hogan, a longtime friend, also frequented the site in the early stages. It featured elevated greens and tees, tall pines and 91 bunkers.

The Woodlands Country Club West Course

2301 North Millbend
The Woodlands 77380
281-367-1100
Pros: Ray Dznowski and R. Cromwell
A 72-hole resort and club.
From Houston, take I-45 north to
Woodlands Parkway, turn left to entrance.

• • •

USGA rating: 73.4
Slope rating: 130
Sand traps: 84
Water holes: 9
Doglegs: 2 left/3 right
Type greens: Bermuda
Record: 63
Designers: Joe Lee
    and Robert von Hagge
    and Bruce Devlin
Year opened: 1975

Hole	Par	Yards	Hole	Par	Yards
Out	36	3,445	In	36	3,564

World Houston Golf Course

8000 Greens Road
Houston 77032
281-449-8384
Pro: Matt Landreau
A par-72, 6,617-yard public course.
From Houston, take U.S. 59 north to
Greens Road, then turn left two miles
to course entrance on the right.

• • •

USGA rating: 71.2
Slope rating: 117
Sand traps: 48
Water holes: 14
Doglegs: 4 left/4 right
Type greens: Bermuda
Record: 65
Designer: Unknown
Year opened: 1940s

• • •

Hole	Par	Yards	Hole	Par	Yards
Out	36	3,235	In	36	3,382

I f golf courses were given awards for transformations and comeback stories, World Houston would surely be a finalist. Long before Intercontinental Airport was ever conceived, this tiny 96-acre site served as home of the H&H Guest Ranch and a rough-hewn golf course. There also was a small airport for private planes.

"When somebody mentioned H&H," recalls former pro Skip Davis, "the first thing that came to mind was cow pasture."

But the golf course began its transformation in the early 1980s when owners and land developers began injecting $1.5 million into the facility.

Davis started reshaping the course, adding 75 bunkers, eight lakes, 600 yards in length and planting 1,200 pine, cedar and sweet gums.

American Golf Corporation took over operations of the course in 1984 and, two years later, hosted a mini-tour event that featured soon-to-be big-name touring pros as Mark Calcavecchia, Keith Clearwater, Greg Twiggs and Tom and Curt Byrum.

After two days, only 11 players had broken 70.

American Golf changed the course yet again in 1990, rebuilding the greens, tees and bunkers, and adding several new lakes and 300 new trees.

The course is fairly open and short. Water comes into play on 14 holes with lots of small lakes that can grab an errant shot. Most of the holes are short, with the 436-yard, par-4 12th the only par 4 over 400 yards.

One of the casualties of World War II was Z. Boaz Golf Course. It was a popular municipal course in Fort Worth that was closed shortly before the outbreak of war.

Golf courses were a luxury at the time, and the money and manpower used to maintain them were better used in the war effort. For nearly a decade, the golf course sat vacant and overgrown, waiting for golfers and men in uniform to return home. Return to the days of innocence, and a nice relaxing round of golf.

On July 1, 1950, they did come back. The city hired architect Ralph Plummer to come in and renovate the golf course, and Texas golf legend Byron Nelson played an exhibition match as part of the opening festivities.

Green fees were 50 cents on weekdays, 75 cents on weekends.

Since Z. Boaz is not an original Plummer design, it does not boast many of his design characteristics. Plummer liked long courses and long par 4s that tested your long iron play.

But Z. Boaz measures only 6,033 yards, with three par 4s that can be reached off the tee by long hitters.

No. 3 is a 267-yard par 4. No. 16 is 274 yards and has a sharp dogleg through the trees.

No. 17 is 293 yards that can be reached off the tee by big hitters if they choose to cut the corner of the dogleg over several groves of trees.

No. 9 is a 547-yard par 5 that is the No. 1 handicap hole. The hole doglegs left, with a pond guarding the far corner of the dogleg.

Z. Boaz Golf Course

3240 Lackland Road
Fort Worth 76116
817-738-6287
Pro: Randy Lewis
A par-70, 6,033-yard public course.
From Fort Worth, take I-30 west to Lackland, go south on Lackland to course entrance on right.

• • •

USGA rating: 69.6
Slope rating: 126
Sand traps: 13
Water holes: 2
Doglegs: 1 left/6 right
Type greens: Bermuda
Record: N/A
Designer: Ralph Plummer
Year opened: 1950

• • •

Hole	Par	Yards	Hole	Par	Yards
Out	35	3,053	In	35	2,990

Our collection of Two-Star Courses includes 200 courses that are above average to average in quality. These courses may never be great, but greatness is a relative term depending on your perspective.

If you're looking for challenging golf at an affordable price, a tee time at one of these courses is just what the Golf Doctor ordered.

Unlike many of the state's top courses that are private, most of these courses are public. Many of them are municipal courses. Most of them are older and were built with smaller budgets. And many of them feature excellent golf course architecture. In many cases, the only thing that sets them apart from the state's best courses is their level of maintenance.

Alvin Country Club is a nine-hole layout that once was a haven for former Southwest Conference athletes. One of the feature attractions was chef Andy Hillhouse, an All-SWC end at Texas A&M in 1949 and 1950.

The club was founded in 1946. It's original pro shop was a converted army barracks. Alvin caters to a different generation of players now, but it still offers that same down-home feeling. It has 200 members, 50 of which are stockholders. The club also is open to public play and every Thursday in the spring hosts an evening scramble that has become a big attraction.

Alvin Golf and Country Club

PO Box 981
Alvin 77512
281-331-4541
Pro: Frank Vita
A nine-hole semi-private course.

• • •

The stockholders voted last year to undergo a much-needed renovation, one of the first since the club was built, to help the course remain competitive with other nine-hole layouts in the area like Brazoria Bend and Hillcrest Golf Club.

"Over the years the course got kind of run down," pro Frank Vita says. "But we have a new clubhouse and have made a lot of improvements. If people haven't been out here in awhile, they would be in for a pleasant surprise."

The layout isn't reminiscent of Olympic or Winged Foot or Pebble Beach, but it is fun for beginning players.

Two bunkers have been added in front of the green on the 510-yard, par-5 No. 6, forcing players trying to reach the green in two to hit a shot with a long carry.

Despite the abundance of trees, the fairways are fairly open. The course is built along the edge of Mustang Bayou and is flat, so it is an easy course to walk.

The layout isn't reminiscent of Olympic or Winged Foot or Pebble Beach, but it is fun for beginning players.

The golf business in San Antonio has been booming for the past 10 years. It has become a destination center for golfers from around the world, with some of the biggest name architects in the business building new whiz-bang golf courses that will test all of your golfing senses.

Now, even the tiny town of Castroville, about 20 minutes outside San Antonio, is getting in on the action with the creation of Alsation Golf Club, which is good enough to compete with any of its big-city competitors. Many golfers believe it is the best golfing value in Hill Country.

Architect Steve Mrak designed

Alsation Golf Club

1339 County Road 4516
Castroville 78009
830-931-3100
Pro: Richard Russell
A par-72, 6,882-yard public course.

• • •

this links-style layout on the top of a hill, so wind is a dominant factor in the way the course plays. The terrain on the front nine is flat and the fairways are lined with young trees. On the back nine, large oak trees and more mounding in the fairways put a premium on shot placement. The greens are around 5,000 square feet in size, and they are firm. Water comes into play on five holes. Nos. 2-5 play around an irrigation lake. An old creek bed comes into play on the back nine.

The signature hole is the 160-yard, par-3 No. 5. The 430-yard, par-4 second hole is rated as the most difficult. Off the tee, players must contend with a big lake in the landing area that requires players to lay up. From the water's edge, players still have 180 yards over the lake and into the wind to reach the green.

No. 13 is a 570-yard par 5 where golfers hit from an elevated tee across a creek, then an approach shot down a narrow fairway to an elevated green.

Alsation Golf Club is good enough to compete with any of its big-city competitors. Many golfers believe it is the best golfing value in Hill Country.

In the late 1920s, Arthur Rogers had a grand dream for a large piece of land between San Antonio and Austin. It would become a grand resort with a huge hotel, recreational facilities, lakes, parks and a river running through it.

Sixty-five years later, Roger's dream is now a reality known as Aquarena Springs Golf Course and Resort in San Marcos.

While Aquarena Springs is known more for its glass-bottom boats that enable riders to explore the underwater world of the San Marcos River and Ralph the swimming pig, the golf course has been a staple for 65 years for resi-

Aquarena Springs Golf Course

Aquarena Spring Drive
San Marcos 78666
512-245-7593
Pro: Kevin Brown
A nine-hole public course.

• • •

dents and visitors alike. Rogers took advantage of the many spring-fed streams on the property and the San Marcos River.

The final product was a short, nine-hole layout that measures 2,600 yards from the back tees. Golfers get an idea of the type of challenge awaiting them when stepping to the first tee, a 378-yard

par 4 with plenty of trees and traps. Like most of the holes, the variety of pecan and oak trees squeeze the fairway in the landing area. A creek comes into play on Nos. 2, 3 and 4, with water hazards cutting across the fairway in several places to create potential danger.

No. 9 is now a relatively harmless par 4, but when Rogers laid it out it was a 660-yard, par-5 monster. The main road to the hotel ran through the hole until safety concerns forced course officials to put the teeing area in front of the road. Some longtime players will still run back and play the hole from its original tee with someone standing guard to make sure no cars are coming.

Aquarena Springs is known for its glass-bottom boats and Ralph the swimming pig, but the golf course has been a staple for 65 years.

George Hoffman was a native of Hackensack, N.J., who moved to Texas at the turn of the century when his parents purchased a ranch in West Texas. He gained experience in golf construction by helping build a golf course in the Dominican Republic in 1919.

He returned to Texas in the 1920s and started his own design business. Articulate in Spanish, he landed jobs in Mexico and Central and South America.

His first solo project in Texas was the 27 holes at Ascarate Park in El Paso, where he designed a regulation 6,565-yard, par-71 layout and a nine-hole layout that

Ascarate Park Golf Course

6900 Delta Drive
El Paso 79905
915-772-7381
Pro: Ramon Valdez, Jr.
A par-71, 6,565-yard public course.

• • •

plays 2,677 yards to a par 36.

The 18-hole Ascarate Course was built on flat terrain, but there are some mounds that can cause uneven lies. There are many trees that can alter shots, and water hazards come into play on six holes throughout the back nine.

The Delta Nine Course is short, but shot accuracy is still

essential. This is a great course for beginners or for seniors who like to walk. If the more popular Ascarate Course gets too busy, there's always room on the Delta Nine. There are no slope or course ratings available for either tees on the Delta Nine Course.

The signature hole is the 407-yard, par-4 No. 18. No. 5 is a 217-yard par 3 that plays downhill from an elevated tee.

No. 4 is a 415-yard par 4 with narrow green that requires a big hit of at least 250 yards to set up the approach shot.

No. 15 is a 426-yard par 4 that requires at least a 250-yard drive off the tee. No. 11 is a 190-yard par 3 that plays over a lake.

This is a great course for beginners or seniors who like to walk. If the more popular 18-hole course gets too busy, there's always room on the Delta Nine.

At the risk of stating the obvious to those who know all about one of the greatest athletes of all time, we're going to do a quick history lesson on Mildred Didriksen Zaharias — a.k.a "Babe" — the first woman to have a golf course named in her honor.

Didriksen was born in Port Arthur in 1914 long before the equal rights and bra-burning movements. Instead of battling for respect through the constitution, she did it on the athletic fields. She became famous at the 1932 Olympics in Los Angeles, where she won two gold medals and a silver by breaking world records in the javelin and 80-meter hurdles.

She excelled in tennis, swimming, diving, roller-skating, bowling and softball. Friends named her "Babe" (as in Babe Ruth) after she hit five home runs in one game.

Didriksen didn't pick up a golf club until three years later in 1935, when she took up the game at the suggestion of legendary sportswriter Grantland Rice. She won the 1935 Rivercrest Invitational in Fort Worth her first year, but she didn't turn pro until 1947. She helped found the LPGA in 1950, and won 31 tournaments. She was stricken with cancer in 1953 and underwent surgery, but came back to win eight more times before she finally succumbed to the disease in 1956.

While the city of Beaumont has built a museum in her honor, it was not until 20 years later that Port Arthur, the city where she was born, decided to build a golf course in her honor.

"One of these days, it will be a course the Babe would be proud of," architect Warren Howard says.

At the risk of stating the obvious, this golf course was built as a tribute to one of the greatest athletes – male or female – of all time.

Balcones Country Club has come a long way since its humble beginnings, but is now one of the largest clubs in the Austin area. The Balcones course first opened in 1956 as a small nine-hole layout in what was then secluded Hill Country. In the past four decades, however, the club has grown into a 36-hole facility and Austin has grown so much that Balcones now lies within the city limits.

The newest of the two courses at Balcones is the Spicewood Course, which offers a separate clubhouse and a par-70, 6,649-yard championship layout that is longer, steeper and more chal-

lenging than its older brother.

The Spicewood course was opened in 1978 and is located a mile from the original course.

Spicewood offers more elevation changes and water. The course plays to a 71.8 rating with a slope of 116. Water comes into play on only three holes. Nos. 8–11. The No. 1 handicap hole is the 418-yard, par-4 third hole. Golfers must drive through a narrow chute between the trees and avoid the creek that runs across the middle of the fairway and down the left side.

No. 11 is a 595-yard par 5 that has no water, but sweeps to the left off the tee through a row of trees on both sides, requiring three long, accurate shots to reach the green.

While the club has active men's and women's programs, Balcones has put a special emphasis on its junior program. Former director of golf Jackson Bradley, a member of the Texas Golf Hall of Fame, built the program based on his 40 years in the golf business.

The newest of the two courses at Balcones is Spicewood, a championship layout that is longer, steeper and more challenging than its older brother.

Far from the hustle and bustle of the sprawling Houston metropolis lies the city of Bay City, a sleepy little town where people move at their own pace in their own time.

A corner drug store. A town square. In the 1990s, it is a trip back to the 1940s.

Such is life in Bay City and at Bay City Country Club, where pro Neil Arbuckle proudly says "they have never had tee times and probably never will."

The layout was built in 1936 on a scenic setting 100 feet above the Colorado River and weaves through oak trees that now date two or three centuries old, includ-

Bay City Country Club

PO Box 2318
Bay City 77414
409-245-3990
Pro: Neil Arbuckle
A nine-hole private club.

• • •

ing one old tree near the clubhouse that measures 21 feet around the base.

Every fairway is lined with trees and either water or out-of-bounds comes into play on every hole. The course is well bunkered with 42 sand traps and water comes into play on 14 holes, including one creek that winds

through the layout on nine different holes.

The most challenging hole is the 521-yard, par-5 ninth, an outstanding finishing hole that features the Colorado River down the right side, trees all the way down the left and a creek in front of the green.

The most hectic it ever gets around here is for the annual Bay City CC Invitational, which started 43 years ago and is a big stop on the barbecue circuit.

"We'd like to think it is one of the best kept secrets in Texas," longtime pro Neil Arbuckle says. "The golf course is a little different every time you play it, so you never get tired of it."

The layout was built 100 feet above the Colorado River and weaves through oak trees that now date two or three centuries old.

To those of you familiar with the English language, Bayou Din sounds like no place anybody would want to play golf. I mean, who could concentrate with all that racket going on? To those of you unfamiliar with the English language, "din" is described in Webster's as a "loud, continuous noise; a confused clamor or uproar."

But before you go looking for another course to play, you must understand that this is Cajun Country, where it helps to have at least a working knowledge of the local vernacular. When George Brown Jr. built this course in 1958 on 2,200 acres he owned between

Bayou Din Golf Club

Route 2, PO Box 2722
Labelle Road
Beaumont 77705
409-796-1327
Pro: Donnie Allen
A par-71, 6,285-yard public course.

• • •

Beaumont and Port Arthur, he decided to name it after the little bayou that comes into play on two holes. The stream was called Bayou Din, which is Cajun for "Turkey Bayou."

Contrary to either name, there is very little noise and no turkeys in sight at this course that Brown decided to build on land that been

in his family since 1914. If you're lucky, though, you might see a few birdies or even an eagle.

It is a sleepy, no-frills golf course with three distinctly different nines. The first half of the course is heavily wooded. The second nine is wide open. And a new nine, opened in 1994, is a links-type layout with lots of rolling hills and native grasses and water in play on seven holes.

The 322-yard, par-4 12th would appear drivable to some long hitters until they step to the tee to see the green is surrounded by water.

No. 7 is the hardest hole. It is a 587-yard par 5 that plays directly into the prevailing wind.

It is a sleepy, no-frills golf course with three distinctly different nines. One is wooded. One is wide open. And one is a links-style layout.

Baywood was built in 1946 by employees of the old Humble Oil Company, but most of the original employees are no longer around and Humble has changed its name to Exxon.

For a course that was built for recreational purposes by untrained architects, Baywood has become an institution in southeast Houston. Humble employees originally built the course on a shoestring budget using oil-field equipment to design the layout along Armand Bayou. The course is reasonably challenging. Like many older courses, it is short but requires accuracy to hit some of the smallest greens in Houston.

Baywood Country Club
5500 Genoa-Red Bluff
Pasadena 77505
281-487-0050
Pro: Donnie St. Germaine
A par-72, 6,574-yard private club.

• • •

"You use all the clubs in your bag on this course and you better come equipped with a good short game," says pro Donnie St. Germaine. "The course isn't very long, but if your shots aren't accurate you'll be chipping all day. Players come out here thinking they're going to shoot 61. You can shoot a good score, but you

have to keep it in the fairway."

The course plays longer than the 6,574 yards because several of the fairways are so narrow and the doglegs so sharp they require an iron off the tee.

No. 4, for instance, is a 325-yard, dogleg right par 4 that requires a precise long iron off the tee. On No. 5, a 360-yard par 4, most players again choose a long iron to thread a shot between the creek that runs down the left side and the corner of the dogleg right. No. 10 is the most difficult. It is a 404-yard par 4 that has out-of-bounds left and trees on the right. Even with a big drive, players still have a long iron to the smallest green on the course.

The course plays longer than the 6,574 yards because several of the fairways are so narrow and the doglegs so sharp they require an iron off the tee.

Bear Creek Golf World was the forerunner to the modern golf boom in the 1970s and 1980s.

It was one of the first privately owned daily-fee facilities in the state. And it was one of the first projects that involved cooperation of public and private entities to produce something for the common good.

The Houston Post first crusaded for a golf course on the property in 1963 to help alleviate the overcrowding at the city's public courses. In 1966, the city decided it would be easier to lease land to a private group instead of overseeing another municipal course.

Bear Creek Golf World Challenger Course
16001 Clay Road
Houston 77084
281-859-8188
Pro: Ron Horton
A par-66, 5,925-yard public course.

• • •

The land in question was a 397-acre tract of county land in the Addicks Reservoir, which was ideal for a golf course. But while the surrounding area grew up around it, this land sat unused because it lay in a flood plane under the jurisdiction of the Federal Corps of Engineers.

Longtime Houston Country

Club pro Dick Forester left his cushy job to oversee the project.

When architect Jay Riviere and Forester's first course (now known as the Presidents) opened on July 4, 1969, it was a great relief for the more than 500,000 golfers in the city at the time.

Bear Creek eventually grew to include three 18-hole courses, making it one of the largest public golf facilities in the southwest. Riviere's second course — known as the Masters — has been ranked among the best public courses in the nation. It hosted the 1981 U.S. Public Links Championship and 1984 NCAA Championships, which was won by the University of Houston.

Bear Creek Golf World was the forerunner to the modern golf boom. The Masters course has been ranked among the best public courses in the nation.

Dick Forester had seen the golf world from both sides of its ivy-covered walls, and in the 1960s he decided he was on the wrong side of the fence.

Dick Forester was the long-time head pro at the exclusive Houston Country Club, where he was in charge of one of the state's top clubs and dealt on a daily basis with doctors, lawyers, bankers and oil men who made more money in a year than he would make his whole life.

While there was comfort in holding one of the state's top club pro jobs, Forester saw a vision of golf's future and risked everything to make it happen.

Bear Creek Golf World Presidents Course

16001 Clay Road
Houston 77084
281-859-8188
Pro: Ron Horton
A par-72, 6,562-yard public course.

• • •

Forester believed the future in golf would not be in ultra-exclusive clubs, but instead in building high quality public golf courses with a country club atmosphere. So he left his comfy confines in 1969 to open Bear Creek Golf World, the patriarch of Houston's public golf boom.

While Bear Creek would even-tually grow to include three 18-hole courses, Forester's Presidents Course was built at a time of severe overcrowding on Houston's courses and was designed for the average golfer. Green fees were $2.50 on weekdays and $3.50 weekends.

At 6,562 yards and a slope rating of only 107, it's not too long and is much more forgiving than Bear Creek's more highly-acclaimed Masters course. Two of the par 5s are only 470 (No. 13) and 472 yards (No. 18), and most of the par 4s are about 350 yards.

"This is going to be the greatest thing that ever happened to public golfers in Houston," golf legend Jack Burke Jr. said.

Forester left the comfy confines of Houston Country Club to open Bear Creek and become the patriarch for Houston's public golf boom.

Bentwood was built in 1979 by architect Billy Martindale after longtime golf course design partner Don January dusted off his clubs and joined the Senior PGA Tour.

In one of his first solo projects, Martindale produced a par-72, 6,932-yard private club. The course starts out fairly easy with several par 4s under 400 yards and a 523-yard par 5 that some players can reach in two.

The course measures 6,932 yards from the back tees. Blaine McCallister has done a clinic here for the junior program.

No. 2 is a 396-yard par 4 that

Bentwood Golf Club

2111 Club House Lane
San Angelo 76904
915-944-8575
A par-72, 6,932-yard private club.

• • •

doglegs to the left to an undulating green.

The layout's most difficult stretch runs from Nos. 8 through 13. No. 8 is a 464-yard par 4 into a prevailing south wind with an approach into a well-bunkered, undulating green.

On windy days, it will play harder than the best par 5s at any

other course in the state. Out-of-bounds runs down the right side of the fairway.

It is followed by a 585-yard par 5 at No. 9 and a 425-yard par 4 at No. 10, a 517-yard par 5 at No. 11 and a 224-yard par 3 at No. 12 and a 420-yard par 4 at No. 13.

No. 12 is a 224-yard par 3 that will require many players to use a wood off the tee.

No. 10 is a 425-yard par 4 dogleg left with water on the right, out-of-bounds on the left and an elevated green protected by several bunkers.

No. 18 is a 428-yard par 4 that plays into the wind with out-of-bounds left and right.

On windy days, the 464-yard, par-4 No. 8 will play harder than the best par 5s at any other course in the state.

In the early 1990s, John Leach and his wife Martha saw a chance to take their golf-related experience to new territory just outside of Austin.

The growing suburb is called Pflugerville and their golf dream is known as Blackhawk Golf Club. After seven years of operation, it appears the dream has come true.

The Leaches kept it all in the family. Realizing their inexperience in golf course design, John relied on the expertise of three-time U.S. Women's Open champion Hollis Stacy, who just so happened to be his sister-in-law. After winning 18 tournaments in her career, Stacy began to concen-

Blackhawk Golf Club

225 Kelly Lane
Pflugerville 78666
512-251-9000
Pro: Janis Swisher
A par-72, 7,103-yard public course.

• • •

trate on golf course architecture in the 1990s and Leach gave her the opportunity to break into a male-dominated profession.

Stacy was still inexperienced herself, so she enlisted Austin architect Charles Howard and his design firm to help transform a piece of dairy farmland into this links-style layout. A dairy farm still

operates to left of the 16th hole.

The results have been praised. They produced the only public course in South Texas to have bentgrass greens and over-seeded rye fairways. Water comes into play on 14 holes.

The toughest hole is the 464-yard, par-4 No. 9. Off the tee, golfers must hit a straight shot to a narrow landing area. A river cuts across the fairway with a lake to the left of the green. Water is a big factor on the par-4, 430-yard 18th. The dogleg right requires golfers to thread the tee shot between water hazards on both sides of the fairway, make the dogleg turn and then keep the second shot straight.

After winning 18 tournaments in her LPGA career, Hollis Stacy began to concentrate on golf course architecture. Blackhawk was her first project.

As a golf course designer, Jack Burke, Jr.'s claim to fame will always be his storied Champions Golf Club in Houston. But Burke, who enjoyed plenty of success on the PGA Tour, also worked on other courses with his brother Jimmy.

One Burke family combination is Blue Lake Golf Club in Marble Falls.

Jimmy gets the credit for designing this nine-hole layout that opened in 1963, but Jack set the course record of 55 a year later. The course plays 4,740 yards from the back tees. There isn't much water on site, but players can get a clear view of the waters

Blue Lake Golf Club

HCP 3, Box 24
Marble Falls 78654
830-598-5524
Pro: Roger Weathers
A nine-hole, semi-private course.

• • •

of Lake LBJ from several of the elevated tees. The course also draws irrigation from the lake.

Burke designed the course around a tight layout of houses in the Blue Lake area.

"There isn't a level spot out here, which means the terrain can be pretty tough," says Blue Lake board member Joe Plemons.

The backbone of the course is five par 3s ranging from 137 to 200 yards. No. 16 is 195 yards with trees and trouble on both sides of the fairway. The eighth hole is 193 yards with another tree-lined fairway.

"On both holes, you have to thread your tee shot through the trees, plus there is a lot of trouble on both sides of the green," Plemons says. "You'll find plenty of challenge out here."

No. 3 is a 365-yard par 4 and is the most difficult test on the course. There is out-of-bounds down the left side and trees on the right.

Out-of-bounds fences also come into play on the fifth and sixth holes.

Jack and Jimmy Burke teamed up to build this nine-hole course that offers scenic views of Lake LBJ from its tree-lined fairways.

Jay Hebert had been dabbling in real estate since he quit a club job in Florida in 1971, but he came out of retirement to take the job as the golf pro at Bluebonnet Country Club, a 2,200-acre development between Houston and College Station.

Bluebonnet Country Club was so named for reasons that become obvious as you make the springtime drive through the flower-covered prairie.

The original plan also called for horse-breeding and training facilities, five lakes, tennis courts and skeet and rifle ranges, 200-room inn operated by a national

hotel chain and 1,400 home sites. The development would be closed by 25 miles of white fencing to give the rolling terrain the appearance of being in Kentucky bluegrass country.

As for the golf course, Jay Riviere produced a par-72, 6,707-yard layout through the countryside. In keeping with Riviere's style, he provided players with birdie opportunities with relatively short par 5s of 499, 481, 505 and 487 yards, while mixing in some tough par 4s (454, 423 and 429 yards) throughout the layout.

"I got my best compliment when I took Hebert up to Bluebonnet for the first time," Riviere says. "He flipped when he saw the course."

Said Hebert: "It'll be one of the greatest second-shot courses in the country."

Hebert was a former LSU golfer and native of Lafayette, La. He moved to Houston and eventually turned pro in 1956, winning seven events. He was captain of the 1971 Ryder Cup team.

Bluebonnet has the appearance of Kentucky bluegrass country as it winds through the rolling countryside and wildflowers.

Like several other Houston courses, Houston attorney Frank Cope and his sons built this layout in 1970 for the enjoyment of family and friends. But it turned out to be a pretty good course that people paid to play.

The course is built on 80 acres surrounded by rice fields and the flat, low-lying land is subject to flooding when the floodwaters from Oyster Creek are released into the old rice canals.

There are plenty of trees on the land, but most of the fairways are 40–50 yards wide and water comes into play on four holes.

The nine-hole, 3,104-yard, par-35 layout is a good course for

beginners to learn the game and is kept in better condition than most of the city of Houston public courses.

All of the par 4s are under 400 yards, including the 297-yard No. 7 which can be reached off the tee by some big hitters.

The course is a throwback to the times when golf courses weren't crowded and it didn't take more than five hours to play a round. If you don't mind the 30-45 minute drive from Houston, the peace and quiet and the ability to play all day for one price make it worthwhile.

In the mid 1990s, the club was purchased by Steve and Vicki Reiser, who continued to make improvements to the layout.

"We really cater to players who want to play all day for the same price," says pro Ron Hollowell. "We get a lot of players from Houston who would rather drive 30 minutes and back each way and play in four hours than play in Houston in six hours."

Brazoria Bend started as a course built by Frank Cope and his sons for their own enjoyment, but it turned out to be a course people paid to play.

While some golf course architects are lucky enough to put their names on more than 100 courses, get lots of publicity and big salaries, others work behind the scenes to put their stamp on every course but remain relatively unknown. Marvin Ferguson was one of the latter.

While his name may not carry the weight in most golf households of a Donald Ross or a Robert Trent Jones, Ferguson played a major role in shaping golf as we now know it. He worked with the USGA Green Section to develop the current specifications by which all modern greens are built.

Briarcrest Country Club

1929 Country Club
Bryan 77802
409-776-1490
Pro: Mike Higgins
A par-72, 6,783-yard private club.

• • •

Ferguson decided to dabble in design some 30 years after he first got into the golf business. And one of his first of 10 design projects was Briarcrest Country Club. All of his courses are characterized by strategic holes and excellent turf conditions.

Briarcrest is no exception, with a premium on accuracy off the tee and long par 3s. The signature hole is the par-4 No. 11, which measures 430 yards from the back tees with a creek down the right side. The hole is a dogleg right with an uphill approach to a perched green.

The 438-yard, par-4 No. 8, requires a long carry over a lake that cuts across the fairway from 150 yards out and protects the green in front and on the left side.

The 15th is a 595-yard par 5 double-dogleg that is all anyone can handle. Off the tee, players must avoid two bunkers on both sides of the corner. On the approach, players must contend with two lakes on the right side of the fairway.

All of Marvin Ferguson's courses are characterized by their well thought out strategic design and excellent turf conditions.

Tyler is best known as the home of Earl Campbell, the running back who rumbled into the hearts of football fans and into the NFL Hall of Fame. He is still referred to as the Tyler Rose.

Tyler is also known for its golf courses built among the tall east Texas Pines, and Briarwood Country Club is one of the best it has to offer.

Briarwood was built in 1961 and was redesigned in 1985 by Dallas-based architect Lee Singletary. The par-71, 6,487-yard layout has hosted Southwest Conference golf championships in the past, and hosted the likes of SMU's Payne Stewart and the

Briarwood Golf Club

4511 Briarwood Road
Tyler 75709
903-593-7741
Pro: Steven Bowman
A par-71, 6,487-yard public course.

• • •

University of Houston's Fred Couples, both of whom went on to become stars on the PGA Tour.

The golf course is not difficult and has very little water coming into play. The course is well known among the locals, in fact, for its good drainage. After a two-inch rainfall, the course is ready to play within two hours.

But the tree-lined fairways can punish players who try to overpower the course. The front nine has three par 3s and three par 5s. But Singletary increased the challenge on the last five holes.

No. 15 is a 162-yard par 3 over a large pond to a small green protected by sand traps on both sides and framed by a flower garden in back.

The signature hole is No. 16, a 426-yard, par-4 dogleg right with an uphill tee shot over water.

No. 1 is a 515-yard par 5 that plays straightaway, but a fairway trap on the right catches many errant tee shots that don't find the small landing area. The approach is to an elevated green.

The layout is fairly short, but the tree-lined fairways can reach out and grab players who try to overpower the course.

This little piece of property was blessed by nature but cursed by the way the city of Houston developed.

It is one of the most scenic pieces of real estate in Houston with its combination of rolling hills, dense forest and Greens Bayou that make it the perfect setting for a golf course.

The Ray brothers recognized this in the late 1940s when they built the golf course next to the old Acme Brick Co., which supplied the material for the club's rare cobblestone cart paths, just 15 miles outside of downtown. They called it Lake Forest Country Club but sold it to the Elks Lodge

Brock Park Golf Course

8201 John Ralston Road
Houston 77044
281-458-1350
Pro: Rob Olson
A par-72, 6,487-yard public course.

• • •

in the early '50s. The city acquired the course from the Elks in 1963 to help solve a shortage of public golf courses.

"It's one of the finest public layouts in Houston," said longtime Houston pro Gene "Pop" Hill, whose name is synonymous with Brock. "You just don't find these kinds of hills and trees in

Houston. It's a great little layout."

Brock Park still presents a preponderance of trouble. Greens Bayou comes into play on six holes, with many other ravines and slopes catching shots that miss their mark. Even though Nos. 11 and 12 are driveable par 4s of 321 and 298 yards, respectively, the par-3 No. 14 is 220 yards and requires players to hit an all-carry tee shot over Greens Bayou.

"The only way to make a par on the hole," Hill says, "is to either hit the green or land in one of the traps. Anything else is dead."

No. 2 is a 222-yard par 3 that requires a long, accurate tee shot through a narrow chute of trees.

This property was blessed by nature. Its rolling hills, dense forest and Greens Bayou make it the perfect setting for a golf course.

One of the catch phrases for golf course architecture in the 1990s has been building golf courses for "players of all skill levels."

After all, if you're building an 18-hole golf course that will need to accommodate players who hit the ball anywhere from 150 yards to 350 yards off the tee, it is necessary to keep all of them in mind.

More than four decades ago, Press Maxwell had the same idea when he built Brookhaven Country Club. But instead of creating one golf course for players of all skill levels, he had the luxury of building three different golf courses catering to players of dif-

Brookhaven Country Club Presidents Course

3333 Golfing Green
Dallas 75234
972-243-6151
Pro: Bill Dowling
A par-72, 5,527-yard private club.

• • •

ferent skill levels.

In 1959, Brookhaven became a trailblazing pioneer when it opened with three golf courses to become the largest golf complex — public or private — in Texas.

Maxwell designed the Masters and Champions layouts to challenge the club's best players, and those courses have hosted the

LPGA's best during the former LPGA Civitan Open from 1974–77.

He built the President's Course to accommodate women, seniors and beginning players.

It is a par-72, 5,527-yard layout. Several of the par 4s are under 300 yards, including the 253-yard first hole, the 258-yard fifth, the 232-yard sixth, the 251-yard ninth and the 268-yard 18th. The par 5s are all under 500 yards at 468 yards, 462 yards, 485 yards and 467 yards.

Big hitters might salivate at the opportunity to drive the green on several holes, but they are out of place on the President's Course. They need to go pick on a golf course their own size.

While the Masters and Champions courses at Brookhaven were built for the best players, the Presidents was designed for beginning players and women.

The nine-hole layout at Brooks Air Force Base was built in 1971 as part of the official Air Force Health, Morale and Welfare program. It is a nine-hole layout that regulars believe is the best nine-hole course in the state.

Using two sets of tees, military personnel play it twice to produce a par-72, 6,759-yard layout.

"It's not as easy as it might look," pro Willie Boykin says. "You can't just clean up on this course."

The first sign of trouble is the hilly terrain. There aren't any flat lies available in the fairways. Many

of the greens are elevated and an approach shot without enough power will simply roll back to the fairway, making club selection vital. Two bodies of water are on the course as well as a wide variety of trees.

No. 7 is a 204-yard par 3.

With an elevated green and a trap to the right, golfers can't afford to be short. The green is one of the smaller on the course with a slant back toward the fairway.

The par-4, 386-yard fourth hole is another tester. Water cuts into the fairway on the right side to make pinpoint driving a must.

The course is open to all active duty military, reservist and retired personnel. Outside tournaments can be held if one member of the group is active or retired military. Brooks doesn't take tee times, but it is rarely crowded outside of weekends or holidays.

The first sign of trouble is the hilly terrain. There aren't many flat lies in the fairways and many of the greens are elevated.

There was a time when Bryan Muni was the only game in town besides Texas A&M football. The golf course was built in the 1920s, and for years was the only layout within 90 miles.

In those days, it was known as Bryan Country Club. It was a little nine-hole course built on gently rolling terrain. In the 1940s, nine holes were added and the course later opened to the public.

"Length from the tee is always helpful, but not necessary," says manager Scott Manda. "Accuracy from the tee and especially to the green is required because of the small size of many greens. Hazards often come into play

from the tee, so course management is also necessary. Overall, the accurate ball-striker is at more of an advantage than the long-ball hitter. However, the player who can hit it long off the tee also will be rewarded by shorter and easier shots to the green."

Course officials have no record who built the original

course, but The Architects of Golf shows that I.F. "Fred" Marberry renovated 13 holes and Texas A&M turf specialist Marvin Ferguson redid six holes in 1971.

The course is fairly short and is situated on rolling terrain with trees and water coming into play. Although not entirely tree lined, the wooded areas add a nice challenge and variety to the layout.

The signature hole is No. 3. The hole features a 169-yard carry over water to a well-guarded and relatively small green. Sand traps in front and back right and left require an accurate tee shot. The side of the green, however, rewards the well-placed tee shot with a makeable putt for birdie.

"The accurate ball-striker is at more of an advantage. However, the longball hitter will be rewarded with shorter, easier shots to the green."

Cameron Country Club has given the people of Lampasas County plenty of golfing enjoyment in its six decades of history. It was built in 1931, long before the days of pomp and circumstance.

If you remember, 1931 was during the Great Depression, and this course was built on a low budget to provide low-cost fun for its patrons. Situated between Waco and Austin but not really close to either, it was too far to drive to the other nearest courses.

The Depression, of course, is long over but the club still holds true to its theme. It was designed by an unknown architect or com-

Cameron Country Club

East 21st Street
P.O. Box 768
Cameron 76520
817-697-2371
Pro: C.E. Woodum
A par-70, 5,546-yard private club.

• • •

mittee of club members. Because space was limited, the layout measures only 5,546 yards from the back tees. To make up for the lack of distance, the course features an undulating layout that offers few level lies and undulating greens. Different sets of tees allow golfers to play the same nine twice from different angles to

prevent an 18-hole round from becoming too monotonous. Three lakes also come into play.

"It's a small, tight course with tough greens, trees, water and plenty of traps as obstacles," says Les Dorton, former pro and men's club champion.

The most memorable hole is the par-3 ninth and 18th holes. Golfers must hit a 170-yard carry over water off the tee to a small green. More than one bet or tournament has been lost on this hole.

"All in all, I'd say this is a pretty good little course," says head pro C.E. Woodum. "It's pretty hilly, which can make it tough. Plus, we have four holes from three different lakes."

To make up for the lack of distance the course features undulating fairways and greens that offer few level lies and straight putts.

The 1960s was an era of turmoil in America. John F. Kennedy was assassinated. Hundreds of thousands of America's finest young men were halfway around the globe fighting a war we didn't understand. And there was a form of rebellious music called rock 'n' roll.

In Dallas, however, things were rocking. Real-estate developments were popping up all over, and developers were learning that a golf course added value to the surrounding property.

That fact was not lost on E.E. Wallace, president of Wallace Investments, who began acquiring land in 1959 and spent two years

Canyon Creek Country Club

625 Lookout Drive
Richardson 75080
972-231-3083
Pro: Alan Johnson
A par-70, 6,648-yard private club.

• • •

planning a 1,150-acre development north of Richardson called Canyon Creek. Before the first house was sold, Wallace had already hired architect Press Maxwell, one of the hottest architects in the southwest at the time, to design an 18-hole course. It opened in 1963.

While times change and the

club is now owned and operated by Club Corporation of America, the layout has remained mostly the same and Canyon Creek continues to serve its purpose.

The par-70, 6,648-yard layout features tree-lined fairways as it winds through the surrounding neighborhoods and on the banks of Canyon Creek.

It still features the mammoth greens and long tees for which he was known. A Williamsburg colonial-style clubhouse overlooks the course from the highest point on the property.

Among the most challenging holes at Canyon Creek is the 466-yard, par-4 No. 8, the No. 1 handicap hole on the layout.

The par-70, 6,648-yard layout designed by Press Maxwell features tree-lined fairways as it winds through the surrounding neighborhood.

In real estate, they tell you one thing is more important than any other when searching for a new home.

Location. Location. And location. The same rule applies to golf courses.

While Canyon Lake is not actually close to anything, it is not exactly far from anywhere either. It is 25 miles north of San Antonio, 35 miles from New Braunfels, San Marcos and Seguin and 50 miles southeast of Austin.

This little layout with a blue water backdrop is set over rolling hills and through towering oaks. Covering 150 acres, the semi-private layout provides challenge to

Canyon Lake Golf and Country Club
Route 9, PO Box 185K
New Braunfels 78133
210-899-3301
Pro: Ward Watson
A par-70, 6,132-yard semi-private club.

• • •

beginners and advanced golfers. It is much more challenging than its short yardage implies. The course is moderately hilly and offers a variety of both narrow and open fairways.

"The greens are very contoured, putting a premium on the golfer's short game," one pro says. "Accurate driving and a

steady short game are musts to score well here."

No. 1, a 455-yard par 4, is a preview of challenges to come. The tee is located near a grove of trees with the fairway bending to the left around them. Players must avoid two greenside bunkers. Nos. 6 and 7 are par 3s, followed by the par-4, 425-yard No. 9.

The signature hole is the 538-yard, par-5 No. 18. The tee shot must be long enough to reach the corner and set up a second shot to a narrow landing area over a creek. The third shot should be a simple pitch to the green, but pin placement and accuracy are key on this narrow putting surface.

This little layout with a blue water backdrop is set over rolling hills and through towering pines.

Cape Royale was built in 1972 on a scenic piece of property on Lake Livingston. While it is not too close to anything but not too far from anywhere, it has constantly battled an "out of sight, out of mind" mentality among golfers.

For those who know it, Cape Royale is worth the 70-mile trip northeast of Houston. For those who have never made that trip, it's probably because they don't even know about it.

Part of the appeal may be the deer, fox and other wildlife that can be spotted on any given day. Part of the appeal is a course that offers plenty of birdie opportuni-

Cape Royale Golf Club
28 Cape Royale
Coldspring 77331
409-653-2388
Pro: Paul Hendrix
A par-70, 6,088-yard semi-private club.

• • •

ties. And part of it may be economics — you can play all day for under $20.

Architect Bruce Littell designed the original nine-hole layout to serve as the centerpiece of a 1,100-acre community. While it is located on the lake, only on the fourth and fifth holes are actually located on the lake shore. The

hills provide numerous elevation changes, creating plenty of uneven lies.

"This is more of a position course," says pro Ron Phillips, who has been here for eight years. "The key is to just not let your ego get in the way and try to overpower it. There's not much sand, but if you miss the greens you'll have an awfully hard time getting up and down."

The most talked-about hole is the 345-yard, par-4 18th. It is uphill all the way and a slight dogleg left. Off the tee, players are faced with a blind, uphill tee shot. Many first-timers don't realize there is a pond at the top of the hill awaiting misguided shots.

Part of the appeal is the wildlife. Part of the appeal is lots of birdie opportunities. And part of the appeal is you can play all day for $20.

Cedar Creek Country Club was built in 1967 as the centerpiece for a rural retirement community, but is now one of the oldest golf courses in a fast-growing area outside of Dallas.

When the golf course was built, Cedar Creek Lake had just been constructed and was just starting to fill with water. Three decades later the lake has breathed life into the area giving rise to major-housing developments. There are now five golf courses on the lake.

Cedar Creek is a par-72, 6,723-yard layout that was ahead of its time when it was built and is still challenging despite its rural

Cedar Creek Country Club

18392 Country Club Drive

Kemp 75143

903-498-8419

Pro: Dale Folmar

A par-72, 6,723-yard private club.

• • •

setting. Featuring tree-lined fairways with Cedar Creek meandering through the property and coming into play on six holes, the layout provides players with a good mixture of long, short and medium holes.

No. 6 is a 470-yard par 4 that borders on being a par 5. The hole is straight through a chute of trees to a large green. Who needs hazards when you have to hit two 235-yard shots to hit the green in regulation? The hole is only 15 yards shorter the than the 485-yard second, where golfers should have a good birdie opportunity.

Cedar Creek giveth, then taketh away.

The back nine features another give-and-take opportunity. The 483-yard, par-5 13th is a good birdie opportunity, but players must negotiate a pond in the middle of the fairway that keeps big hitters from pulling out their driver and requires most players to clear the water on their second shot to the green. The 18th is a 520-yard par 5 through the trees.

The layout features tree-lined fairways with Cedar Creek coming into play on six holes. It offers a mixture of long, medium and short holes.

When the United States government announced in 1993 that Bergstrom Air Force Base would fall victim to a nationwide closure of military installations, there was an all-out scramble to divvy up the property.

The Air Force sold all the land inside the gates to the city of Austin to be used as a municipal airport and industrial facility. Needing another city golf course, the scramble by longtime golfers began to preserve the 18-hole Bergstrom layout that was previously used only by military personnel. The course, originally built as a nine-hole layout by Ralph Plummer in the early 1960s, was

Cedars of Bergstrom Golf Course

Bergstrom AFB

Building 3711

Austin 78743

512-385-GOLF

Pro: Troy Gann

A par-71, 6,576-yard public course.

• • •

sold to private investors and they renamed the course Cedars of Bergstrom after the many cedar trees on the property.

Since the takeover, the new owners have worked hard to get the Cedars of Bergstrom in shape to compete with other Austin-area public courses. With the Austin airport eventually moving to Bergstrom, several changes were made on the golf course. Three holes were eliminated and three new ones constructed to bring the layout that measures 6,576 yards and plays to par 71.

The course is fairly wide open with 45 sand traps and one irrigation pond in the center of the layout. The five par 3s form the backbone of the course. The holes range in length from 165 to 220 yards, all with traps and tough, tight greens. The back nine was added in the late 1960s and is longer and more difficult.

"Our play has been increasing steadily," says assistant pro Ed Perales, "and we're seeing more repeat play all the time."

It is fairly wide open with 45 sand traps and one irrigation pond in the center of the layout. The back nine is longer and more difficult.

When Anahuac residents voted in 1968 to build a golf course they figured R.T. Pinchback was the logical man to build it. Pinchback was the county engineer and an avid golfer.

They designated a 180-acre tract in an environmentally sensitive area where birds and animals of all kinds make their home in the heavily wooded wetlands on the east side of Galveston Bay.

"I've been playing golf for about 50 years but I didn't know much about building a golf course," Pinchback says, "so I went to the library to get a bunch of books to read up on it. Then we went in there and put together

Chambers County Golf Course

No. 1 Pinchback Drive
Anahuac 77514
409-267-8235
Pro: Hal Underwood
A par-72, 6,724-yard public course.

• • •

a pretty good design."

The land once belonged to J.T. White, a pioneer cattleman in Texas back in the 1800s. Given today's stringent environmental standards, the course may never have been built had it come along 20 years later.

"I went out and surveyed the land, and it was as thick and as

swampy as you could imagine with water moccasins as thick as your arm," Pinchback says.

When the course opened in 1977, the result was a 6,664-yard layout with narrow, tree-lined fairways and water hazards throughout the course.

The 438-yard, par-4 No. 6 is probably the most scenic hole, a dogleg right that requires players to hit long shots over water off the tee and on the approach.

The 430-yard, par-4 No. 18 is the most difficult, with a fairway only 25 yards wide that plays into the prevailing wind. Players must not only hit the ball straight but at least 250 yards to reach the corner and have a shot at the green.

"I didn't know much about building golf courses, so I went to the library to read up on it. Then we put together a pretty good design."

Howard Hughes was known for many things in life. His airplanes. His wealth. His women. And his hermit lifestyle. One thing he was not known for was his expertise in golf course architecture.

In the late 1940s, Hughes tried his hand at golf course design when he built an 18-hole layout near his tool and dye factory in Channelview. While the golf course still stands, it is not mentioned anywhere in Hughes' history as one of his great lifetime accomplishments.

What Channelview Golf Course is known for, however, is being a great place for beginning

Channelview Golf Course

8308 Sheldon Road
Channelview 77530
281-452-2183
Pro: Bill Stuckley
A par-72, 6,214-yard public course.

• • •

golfers to work on their game without putting themselves through the torture of a difficult layout. The course is short like most older courses, measuring only 6,267 yards from the back tees, and offers wide open, unobstructed fairways on most holes.

Perhaps the most challenging hole is the par-4, 275-yard No. 6,

a sharp dogleg left that is driveable if players are willing to take a chance. Brave individuals can reach the green by driving over a stand of trees, but a safe drive down the middle produces an easy approach to a green that is protected by a sand trap extending the entire width of the green.

Also challenging is the par-5, 477-yard No. 14. A solid drive is needed to set up a second shot that is unobstructed by trees on the left and to have a chance to hit the green in two. At the 418-yard, par-4 No. 17, water on the left awaits errant tee shots, and another hazard in front of the green forces the approach to be all carry over the water.

It is known as a great place for beginning golfers to work on their game instead of torturing themselves on a difficult layout.

Jay Schneider has always been proud to have built Chaparral Country Club in Seguin, and that pride hasn't changed much in 30 years.

"It was a great golf course — a heck of a golf course — and it still is," says Schneider, who still lives on the first hole. "It's got some of the best par 4s in the country and some great greens."

Seguin businessman Kellis Dribell owned the land and called on Schneider, who had helped design the back nine of the public Max Starcke Golf Course across the river, to build a golf course on it in 1964. The fairways are lined

Chaparral Country Club

300 Chaparral Drive

Seguin 78155

210-379-6313

Pro: Ken Holubec

A par-72, 7,008-yard semi-private club.

• • •

with more than 700 ash trees along with numerous pecan, oak, cottonwood and mesquite trees. The terrain is gently rolling with four different lakes coming into play along with a small creek that cuts through the property.

The most distinguishing characteristic of the course may be the four par 3s, which are at least

175 yards. No. 7 is 220 yards and No. 11 is 250 yards with a small lake just left of the green. No. 6 is a 450-yard par 4. Players must negotiate a slight dogleg left off the tee, only to turn the corner and face a long, uphill approach to the green.

No. 5 has a large lake in the fairway just in front of the green. Water comes into play twice on No. 18, a 590-yard par 5. It is an appropriate way to wrap up a memorable golfing experience on Schneider's masterpiece.

"I still get out there most days," Schneider says, "but there's not much of a chance of me hitting them long and straight anymore."

"It was a great golf course – it still is. It's got some of the best par 4s in the country and some great greens."

When architect Marvin Ferguson built this typical West Texas course in 1977, it was known as Del Norde Country Club. The short layout featured flat, wide-open fairways and very little water. It was built around four small ponds that come into play on just three holes.

The club members eventually defaulted on loan payments, however, and the land was given back to the city. Eventually, officials of the El Paso airport were given control of the course and renovated it into a public facility.

The course still features large bentgrass greens, and course officials have maintained a commit-

Cielo Vista Golf Course

1510 Hawkins Boulevard

El Paso 79925

A par-71, 6,411-yard public course.

• • •

ment to add 20-30 trees to the property each year to add some character and strategy to the layout. Many of the fairways are doglegs, and there are seven blind approaches into the greens.

The signature hole is No. 2, a 435-yard par 4 that requires a long approach into a narrow, two-tiered green. It is the hardest

hole on the course.

The 575-yard, par-5 11th is the second-most difficult hole at Cielo Vista. It is a long dogleg left with out-of-bounds running down the left-hand side of the airway. The fairway doesn't turn until about 150 yards from the green, meaning golfers going for the green in two must cut the dogleg to reach the green.

No. 18 is a 380-yard, dogleg left par 4 where golfers must negotiate their way around one of the four water hazards on the course. The lake in the corner of the dogleg comes into play both off the tee and on the approach and protects the left side of the green.

Officials have added 20-30 trees each year to add character and strategy. Many of the fairways are doglegs, and there are seven blind approach shots.

Houston's growth patterns have been erratic over the years.

However, the city's growth never reached the Highway 288 corridor leaving land located only 10 minutes from the Astrodome as undeveloped farmland with gently rolling hills and open prairie. That corridor is Houston's last frontier for development.

This is where you'll find Clear Creek Golf Course, a links-style layout built by the Houston based firm of Joe Finger, Ken Dye and Baxter Spann in 1988.

The links-style layout features deep valleys and undulating

Clear Creek Golf Course

3902 Fellows Road
Houston 77047
713-738-8000
Pro: Carey Swanson
A par-72, 6,758-yard public course.

• • •

greens. The only hazards are two lakes and Clear Creek. There aren't many trees, but there are 50 bunkers to encourage you to keep the ball in play.

"That course was a challenge because it took a lot of cooperation with the flood-control people," Spann says.

"We had to incorporate a flood-control channel into the layout without making it an eyesore.

"We never intended it to be a links course, but it has a links feel to it because there aren't many trees and wind is always a factor.

One of the layout's hallmark holes is the 584-yard, par-5 No. 4, a double-dogleg that starts to the right then turns back to the left to the green.

It features a tight-driving area and then requires most players to lay up at the second dogleg to set up their final approach to a narrow green protected by traps on the left side and in the back.

"We never intended it to be a links course, but it has a links feel to it because there aren't many trees and the wind is always a factor."

The Club at Runaway Bay is a masterpiece still in progress.

The resort was originally developed in 1963 by Roy Hastings as a nine-hole course. It was later developed into an 18-hole course in 1972. In 1995, it was purchased by James and Shirley Wood, who dedicated themselves to help the resort and golf course reach its potential.

Runaway Bay is a hilly community built around the shores of Lake Bridgeport, and the golf course architects have taken full advantage of the terrain.

The view in many places along the undulating fairways and

Club at Runaway Bay

400 Halfmoon Way
Runaway Bay 76120
940-575-2255
A par-72 semi-private resort and club.

• • •

from the greens is breathtaking.

Over the years, it has hosted celebrities such as CBS sports anchor Pat Summerall and NFL Hall of Famer Bob Lilly. In 1997 it hosted more than 100 mini-tour pros on the Lone Star Tour.

The signature hole is the par-5 No. 8. Players are forced to carry over a lake on their final approach

to a severely sloped green that is protected by two bunkers on the right side and is encased in trees around the back.

In 1996, all the back-nine greens and the fifth green were redesigned by Tripp Davis and associates and bentgrass greens installed. Also, three holes were changed to make the course a challenging par 72. The front nine greens were rebuilt in 1997.

The 18th hole overlooks Lake Bridgeport, with the lake in full view as players make their way from tee to green.

The club also features a 20,000-square foot clubhouse and condo accommodations for a great valued golf package.

Runaway Bay is a hilly community built around the shores of Lake Bridgeport, and the architects have taken full advantage of the terrain.

Ralph Plummer made a tremendous impact on the Dallas golf scene in the 1950s through 1970s. His layouts were known for their attractiveness and subtlety, and he was known for his ability to visualize a golf hole without detailed plans.

Plummer learned his profession as an assistant to John Bredemus, who was known as the father of Texas golf because he designed many of the state's early layouts. If Bredemus was the father, then Plummer was the son of Texas golf course architecture.

It is interesting to note that Plummer was the designer of all three Texas courses that have

Columbian Country Club

2525 Country Club Drive
Carrollton 75006
972-416-6496
Pro: Tom Struber
A par-71, 6,760-yard private club.

• • •

hosted a U.S. Open — Colonial, Northwood and Champions.

In one of his first solo projects after Bredemus died, Plummer built the first nine holes at Columbian, an ultra-exclusive Jewish club in North Dallas that was established in 1881.

Plummer built the first nine in 1956. Five years later, the mem-

bers called on architect Leon Howard to return to build a second nine to blend in with Plummer's first nine.

"I can't remember how or why they picked me to do it. But I was told they were interested, so I went to visit with them and they liked what I had to say and decided to hire me," said Howard, who did most of his work on municipal layouts. "I tried to make the two nines compatible. I didn't want to do anything that would make it obvious two different architects had done two different nines.

"They liked the nine holes they had, and they just wanted another good nine to go along with it."

Plummer's layouts were known for their attractiveness and subtlety, and he was known for his ability to visualize a golf hole without detailed plans.

Charles Howard had two major design elements to consider when he built Comanche Trail Golf Club in 1990. Most importantly were the infamous West Texas winds. Second was a drainage ditch that runs through the property, carrying drainage from Interstate 40 on its way to Southeast Lake.

Like any good architect, Howard put both elements to full use when he produced this par-72, 7,180-yard municipal layout for the city of Amarillo. He produced a links-style course with absolutely no trees, but water comes into play on 14 holes and the wind is a always a factor —

Comanche Trail Municipal Golf Course

4200 South Grand Street
Amarillo
806-387-4281
Pro: George Priolo
An 18-hole public golf course.

• • •

even on the greens.

The golf course was designed to co-exist with the constant wind that is a part of life in the panhandle. The wind blows an average of 14 miles an hour out of the south in the summer, and spring and fall can see gusts of 30 or more. In the winter, the wind blows directly from the north, but the course

accommodates all four winds with wide fairways and large greens. The drainage ditch is one of the course's key hazards, affecting play on Nos. 2-7.

The signature hole is the par-4 No. 5, a classic risk-reward hole with a slight dogleg left. A ditch runs the length of the left side of the fairway, which gently bends left at approximately 180 yards. Players can play safely to the right, leaving a long-iron approach. Those who challenge the left side are rewarded with a wedge approach — if they clear the creek.

No. 9 is a 445-yard par 4, that requires a straight tee shot up a narrow fairway, then a lengthy approach shot to the green.

Howard produced a links-style course with absolutely no trees, but water is in play on 14 holes and the wind is a always a factor – even on the greens.

In 1930, Conroe was crawling with people who were moving in from all over the nation. People who had come to search for black gold in the Conroe oil fields. The population of Montgomery County was still only 14,588, but even they needed something to do in their spare time without making the long trip into Houston for entertainment.

So in 1935, 50 different Conroe residents, all of whom were in the oil business, built this nine-hole golf course to serve the nouveau riche. It opened as San Jacinto Country Club and hosted the annual Conroe Invitational, which attracted some of the

Conroe Country Club
3051 North Loop 336 West
Conroe 77305
409-756-5222
A nine-hole private course.

• • •

state's top amateurs. Regulars included Bobby Nichols, Babe Hiskey, Miller Barber and Homero Blancas, all of whom eventually went on to turn pro.

The club later was renamed Conroe Country Club, but it still has only nine holes. The original, two-story frame clubhouse, including the upstairs ballroom with the

rustic chandeliers and ceiling fans, still stands. The club, however, has gotten lost in the shuffle of the rapid growth of Montgomery County into an affluent, golfing mecca. It now is dwarfed by bigger, more modern golf communities.

The 3,246-yard, par-36 layout regularly has some of the best greens in the area. Two of the best holes on the course are par 3s. The 179-yard No. 3 requires a medium iron approach through a tricky cross-wind, over water to an elevated green. On the 196-yard No. 8, swirling winds in the trees make it difficult to select the proper club off the tee to clear the water hazard and bunker that protect a tiny green.

Regulars included Bobby Nichols, Babe Hiskey, Miller Barber and Homero Blancas, all of whom eventually went on to turn pro.

As a noted agronomist and turfgrass specialist from Texas A&M, Marvin Ferguson was famous for developing quality turfgrasses with which most golf courses are built. He was also instrumental in developing the standards set by the United States Golf Association for all greens and fairways.

At Coronado Golf & Country Club, however, Ferguson was introduced to golf on the rocks.

On the western side of the Franklin Mountains, Ferguson got the opportunity to build a golf course that looks more like it's mailing address should be Arizona instead of Texas, although for

Coronado Golf and Country Club
1044 Broadmoor Drive
El Paso 79912
915-584-3841
A par-70, 6,475-yard private club.

• • •

most Texans, El Paso is indeed halfway to Arizona.

Built in 1956 at an elevation of 3,800 feet, this par-70, 6,475-yard layout offers panoramic views of Mexico, New Mexico and Texas.

As could be expected of a Ferguson course, the fairways are plush and the well-maintained

greens are considered by some to be the fastest in the nation. In fact, some PGA Tour players have been known to come here to prepare for the Masters and the slick greens at Augusta National.

While the layout is short, it is challenging enough to have hosted several Nike Tour events and challenge the game's rising stars.

Coronado may be one of the hardest short courses in the state with its 129 slope rating.

While it measures only 6,475 yards, it features long par 4s of 453 yards (No. 6), 421 yards (No. 10), 422 yards (No. 11) and 436 yards (No. 18) and a 212-yard par 3 at No. 12. The layout features only two par 5s.

While the layout is short, it is demanding enough to have hosted several Nike Tour events and challenge the game's rising stars.

obert Trent Jones was here. Some of the best architects the game has known have built Corpus Christi Country Club. First came Tom Bendelow around 1910 to build the first course. Along came John Bredemus in 1926 to redesign nine holes.

And then came Jones, the father of modern golf architecture.

Like Houston Country Club nearly 10 years earlier, in 1965 Corpus Christi eventually outgrew its original course.

The club members decided to start over with a clean slate, so they called on Robert Trent Jones to produce a golf course that

would last a lifetime.

It was a rare trip to Texas for Jones, who 10 years later would return to build three courses at Horseshoe Bay — all three of which are ranked among the top 100 courses in Texas.

While it may not go down in the history books as one of Jones' more famous works such as

Spyglass Hill, at Corpus Christi Jones produced a par-72, 6,494-yard links-style layout with wide open fairways and undulating Bermuda grass greens.

Jones designed a relatively short layout knowing full well the wind would be a major factor on the Gulf of Mexico.

Gulf breezes play a major role in all club selection decisions and may require players to make a variety of shots to beat the omnipresent wind. The wind can make a several club difference over the club a golf would normally select based on the yardage.

Water hazards come into play on at least nine holes. The slope rating is 129 from the back tees.

It may not go down in history as one of Robert Trent Jones' most famous works, but he produced a layout where wind is always a factor.

A. W. Tillinghast is one of the most colorful characters in the history of golf. As a the only child of a wealthy Philadelphia couple, he grew up pampered and spoiled and ran in a gang that seemd bent on engaging in the most scandolous behavior that could be attempted in the late 1880s. He was known in his day as "Tillie the Terror."

It was not until he turned 20 that he grew up and began working to develop an aristocratic image. He became a collector of fine antiquities and wrote self-published novels. He lived the life of a sportsman, dabbling in cricket, billiards, polo and bridge

before discovering golf. Tillinghast learned to play under the tutelage of Old Tom Morris and competed in the U.S. Amateur on several occasions from 1905 to 1915.

It was not until he turned 32 that he laid out his first golf course, but he eventually went on to produce some of the nation's greatest courses — including

Winged Foot and Baltusrol.

Shortly after he gave up competitive golf, he also made a swing through Texas to build Corsicana Country Club in 1914.

Tillinghast designed a links-style course with tree-lined fairways that were built around a pond and a large lake.

It features rolling hills and oak trees, offering few level lies. A lake borders Nos. 3, 4, 5 and 6, and comes into play on the back 9 on Nos. 16 and 17. No. 2 is a 225-yard par 3 that requires golfers to carry a pond in front of a green that is protected by three bunkers. The green on No.18 is the only green not surrounded by sand bunkers.

A.W. Tillinghast learned to play under the tutelage of Old Tom Morris and eventually went on to produce some of the nation's best courses.

ike Hoelzer was one of the original staff members when Lochinvar Golf Club opened in 1980. He watched Jack Nicklaus build what is still the only Nicklaus-designed course in Houston and worked at one of the nation's most exlusive clubs.

Hoelzer is in a much different atmosphere now as the head pro at Country Place, a golf course that was built as part of a U.S. Home development geared mostly for senior citizens. It is the only golf course community in Houston with seniors in mind — deed restrictions require one resident of each home must be at least 55 years old.

Country Place
Golf Club
3123 Flower Field
Pearland 77584
713-436-1533
Pro: Mike Hoelzer
A par-71, 6,247-yard semi-private club.

• • •

The course was built in 1982 by Houston architect Jay Riviere on wide open prairie just 20 minutes from downtown and seven miles outside Loop 610. Riviere built the course with seniors in mind, keeping it relatively short and open to provide a fun but challenging test of golf.

Hoelzer has continued to tweak the layout over the years, adding lakes throughout the course and lengthening some of the holes. Hoelzer has been providing the fill dirt by creating new lakes on almost every hole, and trees have been transplanted to give the course more definition.

"The course just keeps getting better and better," Hoelzer says. "There are going to be a lot of changes in the next three years. We want to extend the course to around 6,600 yards, but accuracy is important because of the lakes.

"We've come a long way and we're working hard to get the course in top condition. It's a great golf course to play no matter how old you are."

Country Place is the only golf course in Houston built with seniors in mind. At least one resident of each home must be 55 or over.

ross Creek celebrated its 70th anniversary in 1995. It was one of the state's earliest courses, but has been surpassed somewhat by time and modern technology.

The layout plays to a par 70 and measures only 6,004 yards, which is relatively short in a day and age of hard balls and hot jumbo drivers.

While the architect is unknown, the layout is definitely interesting with its narrow tree-lined fairways that wind through tall oaks in the heart of East Texas.

Cross Creek
Golf Club
800 Bellwood Golf Club Road
Tyler 75709
903-597-4871
A par-70, 6,004-yard public course.

• • •

It was built at the same time John Bredemus was building Tenison Park Golf Course in Dallas (1924) and was one of the first courses in East Texas.

No hole is the same at Cross Creek. It is a hilly golf course where each shot is different. One hole is flat, the next is uphill, the next downhill, the next sidehill and the next wide open.

It won't be hard to recap your round once you reach the 19th hole, where you should have some birdies to brag about.

A pond and some creeks come into play throughout the course, and the Bermuda greens are always maintained in excellent condition.

The signature holes are No. 11 and No. 17. No. 11 is the hardest hole, with a very tight fairway.

The layout is interesting with its narrow, tree-lined fairways that wind through the tall oaks and pines in the heart of East Texas.

When you talk about best-kept secrets, there are few golf courses in Houston that are lesser known than this little nine-hole layout that was built in the 1960s as a recreational facility for employees of the Panhandle Eastern Gas Company.

While the club is still a employee benefit for Panhandle Eastern employees, it also opened its doors to the public in 1993.

It started as a makeshift three-hole layout built around the company's compressor station. It eventually became so popular that it was expanded to nine holes. Like many of the courses on Houston's northwest side, the course is built

Cypress Golf Club

14914 Spring-Cypress
Cypress 77429
713-373-1878
Pro: Martin Stroman
A nine-hole semi-private course.

• • •

on the banks of Cypress Creek, which provides a challenging layout and nice scenery.

The layout is short and flat but the abundance of pine trees and tight, tree-lined fairways help compensate and make the course very challenging.

The tight fairways and sharp doglegs take the driver out of

your hand on most holes and make the course play longer than 6,000 yards. For example, the fairway on the 388-yard, par-4 No. 9 is only 17 yards wide.

"For a golf course not to have been designed by a real architect," pro Bobby Westfall says, "I think they did a helluva job. This is a real cute golf course."

There are two sets of tees to give players a different look when they play the course for the second time around.

For instance, on the second time around the third hole changes from a 183-yard par 3 to a 252-yard par 4 that some players can reach off the tee.

The tight fairways and sharp doglegs take the driver out of your hand on most holes and make the course play longer than it appears.

Success breeds success.

Bob Leonard grew up in a successful environment. His father Obie Leonard and his uncle Marvin established Fort Worth's legendary Leonard's Department Store chain to become some of the city's early movers and shakers.

All of the Leonards were civic minded, always remembering where they came from and always wanting to give something back to the community. It was Marvin Leonard who eventually developed two of Fort Worth's most exclusive country clubs — Colonial and Shady Oaks country clubs as well as the lesser-known Starr

DeCordova Bend Golf Club

5301 Country Club Drive
Granary 76049
817-326-4505
Pro: Bill Richards
A par-70, 6,423-yard private course.

• • •

Hollow, a nine-hole course known as "Little Augusta."

Bob Leonard chose not to rest on his family's laurels, but instead worked hard to continue the family traditions of civic and commercial involvement while also establishing himself as a conservationist and environmentalist. He worked with the Boy Scouts and expand-

ed his business interests to encompass real estate, farming and ranching and banking. In 1987 and '89, he was named Wildlife Conservationist of the Year for Johnson County. He was also a sportsman and hunter who took trips to Africa, Mexico, Alaska and China.

Leonard also was responsible for developing the Leonard family's large real estate holdings in the Lake Granbury area, including DeCordova Bend.

"It was gently rolling, basically mesquite country," architect Leon Howard says. "All they wanted was a user-friendly course that wasn't too difficult for the residents in the subdivision."

Bob Leonard had a dilemma. He was a recognized environmentalist, but he wanted to build a golf course on Lake Granbury.

Less is more: No, this is not another beer slogan. It is the philosophy behind the golf course design at Delaware Springs.

Delaware Springs, located just northwest of Austin, is one of many new courses that breaks the old stereotype of crumbling, bland city courses that have been trampled into submission under the feet of countless hackers.

Architects Dan Proctor and Dave Axland, former members of the Ben Crenshaw-Bill Coore design team, built the course like the old days in that less is more — in other words, the more natural the course, the better.

Delaware Springs Golf Course

127 East Jackson
Burnet 78611
512-756-8471
Pro: Al Pryor
A par-72, 6,819-yard public course.

• • •

In some parts of Texas, where the land is flat and barren, that is a difficult task. But at Delaware Springs, they had plenty of elements with which to work to produce a 6,819-yard, par-72 course that features rolling hills and undulating greens. Consistent with Crenshaw-Coore standards are the huge greens, which measure more than 5,000 square feet. With the greens sloping differently on almost every turn, putts of more than 100 feet are not uncommon. The layout requires bump-and-run shots, long putts and the ability to avoid or hit out of fairway waste bunkers.

Another common feature from golf historian Crenshaw is the descriptive names for each hole, many of them Scottish in nature. No. 4 is named "Roon the Ben" for around the bend. No. 7 is named "Spoon" after the old name for a 3-wood; and the 18th is called "Hame" for "home hole." The course is named after a spring that cuts through the property on several holes.

This is a golf course with an old-style feel, allowing for bump-and-run shots through its rolling fairways to its large greens.

The Galveston Bay area is a flurry of activity, with NASA Space Center, Clear Lake City and South Shore Harbour combining to make it one of the fastest growing areas in the 1970s and 1980s.

Dickinson Country Club is one of those old, established clubs that has gotten somewhat lost in the shuffle. In a modern era of space-age golf courses built by dirt-movers and mound-builders who try to bring players to their knees, Dickinson is a throwback to the days before "golf course architecture" was even considered a profession.

Jim Ed Robbins, who never

Dickinson Country Club

PO Box 432
Dickinson 77539
281-337-3031
Pro: Bob Tillison
A nine-hole private club.

• • •

became famous for building golf courses, designed the nine-hole layout in a selected wooded area along the banks of Dickinson Bayou on land that once belonged to the Del Papo estate. Throughout the club's history, much of the work on the course has been done by either the pro or the members.

It is a nine-hole course that the 200 members play twice from two different sets of tees to create a par-72, 6,425-yard layout. It is a good beginner's course with one of the easiest course ratings in the area (three strokes below the actual par). The layout is very flat and mostly open, although water comes into play on five holes.

Nos. 6 and 7 are both par 5s. The sixth is 504 yards and requires players to carry a small lake off the tee and lay up short of the two lakes that cut across the fairway in the landing area. The seventh measures 520 yards and requires players to carry a lake that protects the front and left sides of the green.

In an era of space-age golf courses, Dickinson is a throwback to the days before golf course architecture was even considered a profession.

The University of North Texas has a rich golf history. While it is not as well known as Wake Forest, Oklahoma State or the University of Texas or University of Houston, it won four consecutive NCAA tittles from 1949 through 1952 under coach Fred Cobb.

Back then — it was called North Texas State at the time — Cobb fielded a powerhouse team that included Billy Maxwell, Don January, all of whom went on to successful pro careers and are in the Texas Golf Hall of Fame.

And Eagle Point Golf Club — although it too has changed names — was their home course.

Eagle Point Golf Club

2211 North Interstate 35

Denton 76205

817-387-5180

A par-72, 6,547-yard public course.

• • •

Eagle Point was built in 1940 on a windswept hillside and valley across the interstate from the University. Typical of many Texas courses, it proved to be a great learning ground to teach players how to hit all types of shots in all types of conditions — including windy conditions.

The par-72, 6,547-yard layout is now affiliated with the Radisson Hotel and has been renovated to include more water hazards and sand bunkers.

The layout is wide open and appears to offer an all-you-can-eat birdie buffet, but all to often golfers find that's not the case.

No. 2 is a 235-yard par 3 that is one of the longest in the Dallas/Fort Worth area, but Nos. 10 and 11 are almost driveable par 4s that big hitters can reach off the tee. No. 1 plays 328 yards, and only a creek running in front of the green serves as a deterrent from going for the green. No. 11, players go for the green at the risk of finding water on either side of the fairway.

The layout is wide open and appears to offer an all-you-can-eat birdie buffet, but all too often golfers find that is not the case.

While this golf course is named after Echo Creek, all too frequently the golfers who play here become well acquainted with many other lakes and tributaries that meander through the fairways and around the greens.

Rusty Lambert is the architect, owner and operator of this scenic, par-71, 6,175-yard golf course that features rolling hills, abundant trees and water.

It used to be an old farm owned by the Smith Family since 1917 before Lambert bought the property in 1984 with the sole purpose of building a golf course.

It took five years to finish, but Lambert believes it was well

Echo Creek Country Club

FM 317

Murchison 75778

903-852-7094

A par-71, 6,175-yard private club.

• • •

worth the wait.

No. 1 is a 425-yard par 4 that is a sweeping dogleg left with a creek crossing the fairway and coming into play on the approach shot to the green.

No. 6 is a 503-yard par 5 that plays through a narrow tree-lined fairway. If players keep the ball in play, this hole can offer a good birdie opportunity.

The signature hole is No. 7, a 150-yard par 3 where golfers must carry a lake in front of the green.

No. 8 is a 469-yard, par-4 dog-leg right where a creek crosses the fairway in the landing area, leaving most players with a long approach over water to the green.

No. 12 is a 475-yard par 5 that doglegs right on the final approach, forcing players going for the green in two to cut the corner of the dogleg. A pond protects the green on the left front.

No. 14 is a 380-yard par 4 where golfers must negotiate a very narrow fairway, with a small green that is hard to hold.

It was an old farm before Rusty Lambert bought it in 1984 to build a golf course. It took five years to finish, but was worth the wait.

El Dorado was built on the estate of Noble Ginther Sr., the former president of Houston-based Associated Oil & Gas Co., just 15 miles north of downtown Houston. It is located 15 miles north of downtown Houston.

The Ginthers first built a house on the 2,000 acres they owned in that area in 1914.

When Ginther first decided to build a golf course in 1964, he hired architects George Fazio, who was building the Jackrabbit Course at Champions at the same time, and Jay Riviere to survey the flat, densely-wooded property. El Dorado is known for its long, tight fairways and small greens.

El Dorado Country Club
7900 North Belt Drive
Humble 77396
281-458-1010
Pro: Terry Tyler
A par-72, 7,118-yard private club.

• • •

Riviere did most of the design, and laid out a circular course with parallel fairways. The front nine is played clockwise, and the back nine is played counter-clockwise. It measures 7,118 yards from the back tees, with five stocked lakes also coming into play.

"Like a lot of the early courses that were built in Houston, it's amazing how little money we spent on building that golf course," Riviere says.

"There are a lot of good holes out there, but we didn't have the luxury of moving a lot of dirt around like we can today. Even if we had the chance to do it all over again with more money, I don't think I would change that much of what we did."

The front nine features three par 4s longer than 422 yards, with the longest being the 474-yard No. 9.

The toughest hole is the 443-yard No. 5, a slight dogleg left that leaves players with a long approach over a bunker in front of the green.

"It's amazing how little money we spent building that course. Even if we had the chance to do it over again, I wouldn't change much."

El Paso Country Club is historic for several reasons, not the least of which is its classic, traditional layout that is everything that you wouldn't expect of a golf course in El Paso.

El Paso Country Club was originally built in 1910 by Tom Bendelow, the man who built most of Texas' earliest courses.

Bendelow was a deeply religious man who never laid out a course or played golf on Sunday, so strict was his personal doctrine. He never drank alcohol, never swore and never told off-color jokes. His only apparent weakness was for the huge cigars he constantly smoked.

El Paso Country Club
5000 Country Club Place
El Paso 79922
915-584-0511
Pro: Cameron Doan
A par-71, 6,781-yard private club.

• • •

Ten years later, Jack Harden built a new course in 1910, producing a par-71, 6,781-yard layout. It still measures out to a 130 slope rating to keep up with its modern-day competition.

Harden would later become more famous for something other than El Paso Country Club. Harden was the pro at River Oaks Country Club and was a friend of astronaut Alan Shepard. On February 6, 1971, when Shepard hit three shots on the moon with a utility tool, Shepard hit three surlyn-covered balls off into the distance with Harden's name engraved on them. The balls are still on the moon.

The classic, old-style layout isn't long, but does require demanding approach shots. The signature hole is No. 15, a 336-yard par 4 that requires a tee shot that must avoid fairway bunkers and trees. More bunkers and an Augusta-style green await your approach shot.

Ron Fream remodeled the course in 1984.

Harden later became more famous when astronaut Alan Shepard hit three golf balls on the moon with "Jack Harden" engraved on them.

When Champions Golf Club opened in 1957, it started a new trend in leisurely, subdivision living. It was based on the same principle on which River Oaks was built in 1924: the concept of the good life was living on a golf course. Many similar clubs followed that same formula for success throughout the next 10 years, including Elkins Lake 69 miles north of Houston.

The project was the brainchild of Houston developer J.B. Belin, T.A. Robinson and Richard Allen. Belin based his philosophy on some interesting golf statistics of the day. He came across a survey that showed 17 to 20 percent of

Elkins Lake Country Club

282 Elkins Lake
Huntsville 77340
409-295-4312
Pro: Ray Sarno
A par-72, 6,640-yard private course.

• • •

the home buyers in residential developments played golf and others became addicted to it because of the easy access to the course. So in 1971, he decided this was an idea whose time had come and he allocated 350 acres for the golf course and recreational facility on the 1,000-acre development bordered by Sam

Houston National Forest on the west side of the property and Huntsville State Park on the north.

Belin discovered the Elkins Lake property by accident three years earlier. He frequently explored the back roads between Houston and College Station in search of property. That's when he stumbled across the retreat owned by Houston financier an attorney James Elkins. Elkins began acquiring the property in 1927 and used an old manor house to entertain friends.

The original homestead, a caretaker's home, bathhouse and equipment barns all were renovated and integrated into the golf course when it opened.

Bruce Belin decided the time had come for golf-course communities, and one of his first projects was Elkins Lake Country Club.

Emerald Bay sounds like a mystic place somewhere over the rainbow next to the emerald city. Emerald Bay Country Club, in fact, is serenely located in the heart of East Texas on the shores of Lake Palestine.

For the many golfers and residents who live here, Emerald Bay is a dream come true where golfers who have retired after a career of hard work can spend the rest of their life playing golf.

And if you were going to play golf every day for the rest of your life, this is a good place to be.

This par-71, 6,610-yard layout is extremely scenic as it overlooks Lake Palestine. With its narrow

Emerald Bay Country Club

208 South Emerald Bay Drive
Bullard 75757
903-825-3444
Pro: Scott Warner
A par-71, 6,610-yard private club.

• • •

tree-lined fairways and elevated greens, it plays to a moderate slope rating of 121.

This course is very scenic because it overlooks Lake Palestine. The front nine features only one par 5 — a 562-yard monster at No. 6 — and plays to par of 35. The back nine plays to par 36.

Despite its close proximity to

the lake, not much water actually comes into play. Only three holes require a carry over water to reach the green. The bermuda greens are large and undulating.

The signature hole is No. 14, a 563-yard par 5 that requires a tee shot up a very narrow (20-yards wide) and tree-lined fairway, then an approach over some oak and pecan trees to the green. It is the hardest hole on the course.

Nos. 15 and 17 are the only par 4s that are over 400 yards in length from the back tees. Most of the par 4s are just under 400 yards, so big hitters will have a lot of short-iron approach shots to the greens.

If you were going to play golf every day for the rest of your life, Emerald Bay is a good place to be.

This is where it all began for Lee Trevino. Long before Trevino ever stormed his way onto the PGA Tour and into the hearts of the golfing public by winning the 1968 U.S. Open, his rags to riches story began at Emerald Springs.

Trevino used to work here as a caddie and in the pro shop helping out members. In his spare time, he would practice and he learned how to play under pressure by playing members for more money than he had in his pocket. Ray Floyd used to play here too.

It was on this high-desert golf course with wide fairways and large greens that Trevino learned

Emerald Springs Golf and Conference Center
16000 Ashford Street
El Paso 79927
915-852-3180
Pro: Ignacio Villa
A par-71, 7,000-yard semi-private club.
• • •

his remarkable shot-making ability that enabled him to play virtually all types of golf courses in all types of conditions.

The 6,927-yard, par-71 layout, winds through a residential subdivision, and plays to a slope rating of 128. It features some of the best-maintained greens in town.

This high desert course has

wide fairways and large greens. The signature hole is No. 13, a 463-yard par 4 that requires a tee shot past water on the right. Another difficult hole is No. 2, a 453-yard par 4, with water running down the right side of the dogleg right fairway and a green that slopes toward the water. There are two ponds that come into play on five holes altogether.

No. 2 is a 450-yard par 4 with water in front of the green and out-of-bounds running down the left side of the fairway and trees on the right.

No. 14 is a 470-yard par 4 that is a big challenge where golfers are typically left with a 200-yard approach.

Lee Trevino used to caddie here and this is where he learned his great shot-making ability that made him one of the game's legends.

The Cisco Kid was here. And, not to forget, Pancho.

The Flying L Guest Ranch, located 38 miles north of San Antonio in Bandera, is where the original Cisco Kid movies were filmed in the 1940s. Instead of good guys and bad guys chasing each other, people now chase birdies and pars.

The resort first opened in the early 1960s when Col. Jack Lapham, a retired officer from San Antonio, decided the scenic Medina Valley would be an ideal setting for a guest ranch.

Bandera bills itself as the Cowboy Capitol, so the Flying L took on a strong western flavor,

Flying L Ranch
PO Box 1959
Bandera 78003
210-796-8466
Pro: Carl Worley
A par-72, 6,635-yard public course.
• • •

but Lapham also built a nine-hole golf course. The back nine was added in 1972.

"People think they will eat this course up, but it's tough to get close to the pins," former head pro and current general manager John Junker said.

"We've added a lake to the 15th hole along with some rock

work to the pond on the fourth hole. We've added a bunch of sand traps to toughen things up with more water hazards planned for the future."

The par-4 fourth hole is just 318 yards from the back tees, but most of it is over water. The par-4 fifth isn't much easier. The hole takes a big dogleg left with out-of-bounds on the right and a lake on the left of the green.

The par-4 ninth is the No. 1 handicap hole. It measures 435 yards from the back tees and plays as much or more with the fairway sloping uphill to an elevated green. The tee at the par-5 13th offers a sweeping view of the entire Medina Valley.

Flying L Ranch is where the Cisco Kid series was filmed. Instead of good guys chasing bad guys, people are now chasing birdies and pars.

In 1951, Houston's Southwest Freeway was just a figment of someone's imagination at the Texas Highway Department. The cities of Richmond and Rosenberg were still known mostly for their farming and grazing land.

With no golf courses within reasonable driving distance, a group of golf-oriented families founded Fort Bend Country Club that year. Longtime Houston pro Frank Hughes built the first nine holes on 120 acres on the high side of the Brazos River bottom.

It was a nine-hole course until 1966, when Leon Roberts, who became pro two years earlier, built the second nine based on draw-

Fort Bend Country Club

2627 FM 762
Richmond 77469
281-342-8368
Pro: Eddie Carter
A par-71, 6,346-yard private club.

• • •

ings designed by late architect John Plumbley. The course is short but has a tight layout with fairways that wind through the native pecan trees to small greens and around and across Rabbs Bayou.

Rabbs Bayou comes into play on all three of the closing holes. No. 16 is a 393-yard par-4 with a very narrow fairway. The bayou

runs alongside the fairway on the left and trees are on the right. No. 17 is a 363-yard, dogleg right par 4 that requires a 220-yard carry to clear the bayou or a 190-yard lay-up that still leaves you a long iron approach over the bayou. No. 18 is a 394-yard, dogleg right par 4 that requires a 180-yard carry.

"We feel like we have a golf course with good variety," says pro Eddie Carter, who replaced Roberts. "The front nine is longer and more open and the back nine is shorter and tighter because it winds through an old pecan grove. It's more of a placement course, but I think our finishing holes are some of the best in the Houston area."

The course is short but has a tight layout with fairways windin through pecan trees to small greens around and across Rabbs Bayou.

From famous architects to PGA stars, from enlisted men to five-star generals, Fort Sam Houston has seen it all the first five decades of its history.

Fort Sam Houston is one of the few military installations in the state with 36 holes, and it is the only military facility anywhere known to have hosted a PGA Tour event.

A.W. Tillinghast, who lists on his resume such famous layouts as Winged Foot, San Francisco Golf Club and San Antonio's own Oak Hills, designed the first of the two courses in 1937 while doing some renovation work across the way at the exclusive San Antonio

Fort Sam Houston Golf Course La Loma Grande Course

Fort Sam Houston, Building 2901
San Antonio 78234
210-222-9386
Pro: Dick Bartel
A par-72, 6,750-yard military course.

• • •

Country Club.

The first course, called La Loma, was laid out inside the still-growing army post near the national cemetery and several hundred feet from the more established San Antonio Country Club.

At 6,750 yards from the back tees, La Loma is considered the tougher of the two layouts. In fact,

it has been tough enough to withstand any attack by America's finest.

The Texas Open, which is the fifth-oldest stop on the PGA Tour, has been played on La Loma four different times. The first time was in 1950 when superstar Sam Snead took the tournament title with a 265.

Ten years later, Arnold Palmer won the first of his three consecutive San Antonio titles at Fort Sam. Palmer's 72-hole total of 276 gave him a two-shot victory over Doug Ford and Frank Stranahan.

That was the last year Fort Sam Houston hosted the event before it moved across town to Oaks Hills Country Club.

Fort Sam Houston is one of the few military bases in the state with 36 holes, and the only one anywhere to have hosted a PGA Tour event.

The second course at Fort Sam Houston, Salado Del Rio, was started in 1963 with the back nine being completed in 1965. As the name implies, the course winds its way around Salado Creek.

The layout measures 6,680 yards from the back tees and plays to a par of 71. The course, however, is being caught in a space crunch between San Antonio Country Club and the expanding national cemetery.

While its big brother La Loma Grande has had the rich history of hosting the Texas Open — the state's oldest pro golf event — Salado El Rio has earned respect

Fort Sam Houston Golf Course
Salado El Rio Course

Fort Sam Houston, Building 2901
San Antonio 78234
210-222-9386
Pro: Dick Bartel
A par-72, 6,750-yard military course.

• • •

in its own right.

With the exception of the 611-yard, par-5 No. 11, the layout at Salado El Rio is a little more even keeled with holes that are not too long or too short.

It is just a consistent challenge from one hole to the next. The front nine has one par 5 and one par 3, while the back nine has

three par 5s, three par 3s and three par 4s.

The longest par 4 is 419 yards (No. 16), and they are as short as 345 yards at No. 1. The par 3s on the back nine are 190, 203 and 205 yards and will definitely put your long irons to the test.

No. 11 stands out from the crowd, just by its pure length. At 611 yards, few golfers have ever been able to reach the green in two. Most players will be satisfied to reach the green in three and walk to the 12th tee with a par and a smile on their face.

There are some elevated tee shots along with plenty of trees and brush.

While its big brother has had the rich history of hosting the Texas Open, Salado El Rio has earned respect in its own right.

Once upon a time, Friendswood Country Club was an exclusive, members-only club. It was built as part of the Sun Meadows residential development in 1967 to help attract home buyers to the area.

The course was the brainchild of investors Bob Holcomb, Tom Wright and L.E. Bradbury and was designed by architect Jay Riviere.

Out-of-bounds comes into play on all but one hole, forcing players to keep the ball in play and out of people's backyards. This is not the place to play if you are having trouble keeping the ball in play.

Chigger Creek runs through

Friendswood Country Club

No. 3 Country Club Drive
Friendswood 77546
281-482-4725
Pro: Bob Kirkpatrick
A par-72, 6,721-yard semi-private club.

• • •

the property, and there are also six lakes scattered throughout the par-72, 6,721-yard layout.

The front nine is wooded and tight, while the back is more open but still has plenty of out-of-bounds that comes into play.

One of the toughest holes is the 400-yard, par-4 No. 3, which features a lake on the right side

that is a threat to snare an errant tee shot or approach. The lake curls around the right side and back of the green, forcing players who find the fairway off the tee to still hit an accurate approach.

Another good hole is the 204-yard, par-3 No. 15, where the green is surrounded by water on three sides. Players are forced to hit a wood or long iron to reach the green, but hitting too much club could put you in the water behind the green.

The only par 4 over 400 yards is the 443-yard No. 18. The hole is straight and has an open fairway, but requires two solid shots to reach the green in regulation.

Out-of-bounds comes into play on all but one hole, forcing players to keep the ball in play and out of people's back yards.

Baytown's first country club was organized in 1923. It was called Baytown Country Club and was open only to employees of the Humble Oil Company. Dave Marr Sr. was the head pro. Humble later sold that land to real estate developers, but a new group organized in 1956 to form Goose Creek Country Club.

They purchased a 33-acre rice field in Baytown, with Goose Creek meandering through the property, and hand-planted numerous trees throughout the property. It wasn't until five years later that they finally completed the first nine holes.

The course is moderately diffi-

cult and is known for its unusual combination of five par 3s and five par 5s. Out-of-bounds comes into play on nine holes and Goose Creek either crosses or borders seven others, and the last five of the front nine. The front nine is narrow, has many wooded areas and tends to play a stroke or two tougher than the back nine,

which is more open but features more water.

"The course tends to favor a person who draws the ball because the majority of the holes turn from right to left," says pro Glenn Von Bieberstein. "The long ball hitter will have an advantage, but length is not needed to play the course well."

Two of the more challenging holes are the 457-yard, par-4 No. 2 and the 365-yard, par-4 No. 17. No. 2 is rated as the toughest on the course as it requires players to carry water off the tee. No. 17 is short, but it's a great driving hole with water extending from the front of the tee down the left side of the fairway to the green.

Out-of-bounds comes into play on nine holes and Goose Creek crosses or borders seven others, including the last five on the front nine.

Let's get one thing straight before we go any futher. This golf course was named after Gabe Lozano Sr., who owned the golf course before the City of Corpus Christi took it over and turned it into a municipal course for tourists and residents.

It is not, as the name might imply, a golf course for seniors.

This 6,953-yard, par-72 layout is all most players can handle, whether they are young or old.

In addition to the course length, omnipresent breezes off the Gulf of Mexico and water hazards on most holes and bunkers on the fairways and around the

greens put a premium on accurate shot placement.

The course is wide open, so wind is always a factor. It has a slope rating of 128.

Architect Leon Howard built this course in 1965, and three decades later it can still bring good players to their knees.

Roger Salazar, a pro on the PGA Nike Tour, set the course record of 64.

The course underwent a needed renovation in 1983 to help keep up with the 70,000 rounds it hosts every year as Corpus Christi's most popular public golf course.

The hardest hole is No. 10, a dogleg left with water on both sides of the fairway and green.

The golf course also features a state-of-the art driving range, putting green and a nine-hole executive course which is, after all, the preferred course of senior golfers.

The omnipresent breezes off the Gulf of Mexico and water hazards on most holes put a premium on accurate shot placement.

Some people laugh at nine-hole golf courses. Nobody ever laughed at Gaines County Golf Course.

For 33 years, Gaines County operated as a nine-hole golf course since it was designed by Jim Terry in 1958.

It was even good enough for Jack Nicklaus and Arnold Palmer to play an exhibition match here in 1963, the same year they dueled it out in Dallas for the PGA Championship at Dallas Athletic Club.

Located outside of Lubbock in the tiny town of Seminole, Gaines County Golf Course is a hidden gem. It expanded to 18 holes in

Gaines County Golf Course

Seagrades Highway 385
Seminole 79360
915-758-3808
Pro: Shawn McDonald
A par-72, 6,685-yard semi-private club.

• • •

1991 to complete a par-72, 6,685-yard layout that is one of the most refreshing golf experiences the state has to offer. In an era of $50 and $100 green fees, non-members can still play 18 holes for $12.50. You can't beat the price for what you get.

The Texas Golf Association rated this course as one of the top 75 courses in Texas. The bent-grass greens are large and fast, and the fairways are tree lined. The par 4s are punishing and the par 3s are no slouches, so you'd better pick up your strokes on the easy par 5s.

The course is built on slightly rolling terrain with the front nine accented by trees and numerous fairway and greenside bunkers.

The hardest hole is No. 5, a 435-yard, par-4 dogleg right that is long and requires an approach to an elevated green that makes club selection deceiving.

The signature hole is No. 8, a 384-yard par 4 that requires an approach shot over a pond to a well-bunkered green.

This is a hidden gem that the Texas Golf Association ranks as one of the best in Texas with its rolling, tree-lined fairways.

Golf courses are supposed to be built to serve as a source of recreation, but every once in a while they turn out to be more of a headache than they're worth.

This saga has a happy ending, but it took 30 years to get there. It all started on March 11, 1962, when Galveston residents first approved a plan to sell the city's golf course at 61st Street and Seawall to residential and commercial developers. The profits would be used to build a new 27-hole facility, including a lighted nine-hole course.

It was a good idea, but neither city officials nor voters had any

Galveston Municipal Golf Course

1700 Sydnor Lane
Galveston 77553
409-744-2366
Pro: Joe Russo
A par-72, 6,739-yard public course.

• • •

idea of the kind of headache, heartache and embarrassment they were in for. It took 15 years of red tape, legal battles and cost overruns before the new course finally opened in 1974. A later study by an engineering firm hired by the city showed the city actually got a $360,000 golf course for a whopping $1.8 million.

Architect Carlton Gipson said that was quite evident when the city decided to give the golf course another try and hired him in 1991 to revamp it. It's still not St. Andrews, but Gipson designed a links-style layout that has few trees, but has the same kind of rolling terrain and ocean breezes characteristic of golf's original courses. Water comes into play on all 18 holes.

"They had done a terrible job when they built the golf course in the first place," Gipson says. "So they wanted me to create some roll to the course. It's a good course now, but there are still a lot of people who don't know about it."

It took 15 years of red tape and cost overruns before the course opened in 1974. In the end, the city got a $360,000 course for $1.8 million.

From its beginnings as a small nine-hole military course, Gateway Hills has grown to become one of the finest private courses in San Antonio. The layout is part of the Lackland Air Force Base and serves the huge military community in San Antonio. It was opened as a nine-hole layout in 1946 as part of an effort by the U.S. Air Force to boost morale after World War II. Nine more holes were added in the early 1950s and, after years of molding and shaping, it has become a stern test for any general or airman basic.

Gateway Hills is full of hills that result in blind or hidden shots

Gateway Hills Golf Club

Lackland AFB, Building 2901
Lackland AFB 78236
210-671-2517
Manager: Judy Stillman
A par-72, 6,883-yard, layout on the
site of Lackland Air Force Base.

• • •

as you make your way over the hills and through the woods, and its tight fairways put a premium on driving accuracy.

"I think it's one of the best courses you'll find anywhere," former manager Bud Gentle says. "The greens are some of the best in San Antonio. It's got rolling hills and tight fairways, which puts a

premium on driving. Some of the holes require precise shot placement, but the yardage can be deceiving because of the hills and gradual elevation."

The hardest hole is the par-4 sixth. Measuring 454 yards from the back tees, the hole appears to be simply straight-away, but looks can be deceiving. The golfer must hit a good drive off the tee and is still faced with a long iron to the green. There are traps around the green, which is heavily contoured with drop-offs on the sides and back. The par-4 ninth hole is one of only two where water comes into play. Golfers must hit a tee ball over a ditch before their second shot to an elevated green.

"The greens are some of the best in San Antonio. It's got rolling hills and tight fairways, which puts a premium on driving."

The town of Georgetown, located north of Austin, has two of the oldest operating golf courses in this part of the state to go along with the oldest university in Texas.

Southwestern University is the oldest college in the state dating back to the 1830s. The nine-hole course on campus dates back to the 1940s.

But it seems virtually modern in comparison to Georgetown Country Club, which opened in 1924 as a nine-hole layout but has grown into an 18-hole course.

The golf course and area around it was once plowed farmland, but now has blossomed into

Georgetown Country Club

1500 Country Club Drive
Georgetown 78626
512-930-4577
Pro: Dave Preston
A par-70, 5,471-yard private club.

• • •

a fun golf layout for many of its regular members.

Despite the advent of metal drivers and graphite shafts, the front nine plays to the same par and yardage as it did when it opened 70 years ago.

A back nine was added in the late 1970s, giving the 500 members and their guests more room

to play their favorite sport.

"It's a fun, little course," head pro Dave Treston says. "It's a pretty layout, but you have to hit the ball straight and keep it in the fairway or you'll be in trouble."

Typical of the style of early Texas golf course architecture, the front nine is simple and takes advantage of the natural hazards.

The mid-San Gabriel River comes into play on 11 of the 18 holes, forcing players to be accurate with their shot placement or reach in their bag for another ball.

The signature hole is the 538-yard, par-4 No. 13. It crosses the San Gabriel twice to a tight green with trees in the background.

Despite the advent of metal drivers and graphite shafts, the front nine plays to the same par and yardage as it did 70 years ago.

When history is lost or golfers are not well versed in it, the natural tendency is to think what they see is the way it has always been. Few golf courses in Houston are more historic than Glenbrook, but most golfers are unaware of its legacy and the course no longer resembles the original layout along Sims Bayou.

Glenbrook is the third-oldest course in Houston, predated only by Houston Country Club. When it was first built in 1924, it was a nine-hole course with sand greens. Jimmy Demaret recalled that it started out as Glenbrook, but the name was changed to Rio Rita Country Club. Al Espinosa

Glenbrook Golf Course

8205 North Bayou
Houston 77017
713-649-8089
Pro: Paul Donnelly
A par-71, 6,427-yard public course.

• • •

won the Houston Open when it was played here in 1929.

In the 1980s, the city completed an eight-year project during which the flood control district turned Sims Bayou into a 250-foot wide waterway to provide flood relief for the area.

More than 421,000 cubic yards of dirt were moved on the project which destroyed a large part of the Glenbrook forest, but most of the damaged areas were reforested.

The only problem was that the new channel went through the old layout instead of meandering around it like before.

Architect Robert McKinney redesigned the layout, incorporating the bayou into seven of the new holes. The result is a layout that is 300 yards longer than before, as many as 6–8 shots harder, and requires carries of up to 200 yards off the tee.

"We routed the course so that you won't be just slugging your driver," McKinney said. "You're going to have to play every shot."

A flood control project through the course forced the rerouting of some holes, so now golfers must hit across the bayou on several holes.

Leon Howard grew up in the small West Texas town of Graham. While he went on to college and became a golf course architect that traveled throughout the United States building golf courses in major cities, he wanted to take the game into the highways and byways.

In the 1960s, Howard was instrumental in pushing the Farm and Home Administration to launch an innovative program helped fund the creation of golf courses for rural communities. For every member the club signed up at $100 each, FHA would loan $1,500 at 5 percent interest over a 40-year period. If the club

Granbury Country Club

Highway 377 East
Granbury 76048
817-573-9912
Pro: Mac McKinney
A nine-hole semi-private course.

• • •

signed up 500 members, it was given a budget of $750,000 to build the golf course.

Howard ended up designing 21 of the 69 courses that received such funding. Of those 69 courses, however, only 19 ended up being financially successful. Of those 19, 17 were designed by Howard.

Granbury Country Club is one of the survivors. Like most of the FHA courses, Howard built a short nine-hole layout that would be user friendly to most of the men and women who worked hard on the farm during the week. The layout measures only 2,990 yards from the back tees, and water comes into play on only three holes, but it features a lot of tree-lined fairways.

No. 8 is a 498-yard par 5 where trees on both sides of the fairway create a very narrow chute that golfers must negotiate all the way to the green. No. 5 is a 360-yard par 4 that doglegs to the left with a creek running down the left side of the fairway and crossing in the landing area.

Granbury Country Club is one of the few survivors of an FHA program designed to build recreational facilities in rural communities.

Golf architect Ralph Plummer has been credited, and rightfully so, with building some of the top golf courses in Texas, including Preston Trail Golf Club in Dallas. But at the same time Plummer was building Preston Trail in 1965, he also designed and built the Grand Prairie Municipal golf course.

The City of Grand Prairie purchased the land on the shores of Mountain Creek Lake from Dallas Power and Light, which uses the lake to provide electricity for much of the area. Plummer agreed to help design and build the course. While the layout was built for the masses and hasn't

Grand Prairie Municipal Golf Course

3203 Southeast 14th Street
Grand Prairie
972-263-0661
Pro: Jan Smith
A 27-hole municipal course.

• • •

received the type of care that a private country club gets, it remains a classic Plummer gem.

"This is one of the nicest and most enjoyable municipal golf courses you will find," says Jan Smith, who has been pro since the course opened.

The course is divided into red, white and blue nines. The Red

and Blue nines produce the longest and most challenging 18-hole layout. Mountain Creek Lake provides a pleasing backdrop to several of the holes.

The course is set on a gently rolling piece of land, which means a well-struck shot can get a good roll on the downward side and increase the length of the drive. Another Plummer trademark is the undulation of the greens.

Players hitting the bermuda greens in regulation aren't guaranteed any easy putts. The key to success on any of the 27 holes is to keep the ball in the fairway. Trees provide some measure of difficulty should you stray too far off the beaten path.

The Red and Blue nines produce the most challenging 18-hole layout. Mountain Creek Lake provides a pleasing backdrop on several holes.

When Byron Nelson and Joe Finger wiped the dirt off their hands and looked out over their brand new golf course in 1974 and saw that it was good, Nelson said this:

"You know, Joe, this is a heckuva golf course,'" Finger recalls. "I think we could build a U.S. Open golf course without using a single sand trap and using mounding and swales instead."

Finger replied: "Sure, but nobody would appreciate it."

Appreciation never has been a problem at Grapevine Municipal, where in 1978 Nelson and Finger combined all their knowledge and experience on a shoestring budg-

Grapevine Municipal Golf Course

3800 Fairway Drive
Grapevine 76051
817-481-0421
Pro: Sid McCleskey
A par-72, 6,953-yard municipal course.

• • •

et to build what has been ranked as one of the best public golf courses in America. And there are only, count 'em, 18 bunkers.

"Byron never liked to use a lot of bunkers," Finger said. "These days, good players can get out of a bunker a lot easier than hit a trick chip shot off a slope. Sand traps may look good on TV, but

they cost a lot of money and cost a lot to maintain. And the golfer ends up paying for it."

In 1978, Grapevine was on the cutting edge of America's new upscale, daily-fee movement. Keeping in mind the city of Grapevine's desire to keep maintenance costs down, they designed a straightforward, but subtly difficult golf course below the dam of Lake Grapevine. It was ranked on *Golf Digest's* list of America's Top 50 Public Courses for several years. No. 9 is the most difficult hole. It is a 447-yard par 4 where on the approach golfers must hit to a green protected by a small pond on the right and a bunker on the left.

Finger and Nelson combined their experience and a small budget to build what has been ranked as one of the nation's best public courses.

Ward Stanberry and M.L. Scott are brothers-in-law who fell in love with golf in the 1940s. But they happened to grow up in Katy, which at the time was 20 miles from the nearest golf course. So they decided to turn the 97-acre cow pasture behind their homes into a golf course. They also planted more than 2,000 pines, maples, elms and oaks that now have grown up and turned the pasture land into a veritable forest. The first nine opened for business in 1968. Three years later, after the revenues started coming in, they reinvested it and completed the second nine.

Green Meadows Golf Club

6138 Franz Road

Katy 77450

281-391-3670

Pro: Mike McRoberts

A par-70, 5,440-yard public course.

• • •

"This is our pride and joy," says Stanberry. "You couldn't do now what we did back then. We were never more than $200,000 in debt. We've had some attractive offers to buy the land, but it's our backyard. Our families still own it and will continue as long as I have any say-so."

There was a time when you could see across the entire golf course, but the tree growth has made the layout a formidable test even though it measures only 5,440 yards. Eight par 4s are under 350 yards, many of which can be driven if you are willing to take a chance. But beware of the narrow fairways, overhanging limbs and sharp doglegs.

"Several of the holes are driveable but you don't see many of them driven very often because of the trees and narrow fairways," McRoberts says. "It would take an almost perfect shot and you're risking an awful lot of trouble. It doesn't lend itself to being overaggressive, because many times it's a losing gamble."

Eight par 4s are under 350 yards, but beware of the narrow fairways, overhanging limbs and sharp doglegs.

Green Tree Country Club is unique to Texas golf for several reasons. PGA Tour star Tom Kite represented the course on tour for five years after it opened in 1980. And Texas Golf Hall of Famer Judy Rankin is a member.

Rankin, who turned pro at the age of 17 and won 26 times on the LPGA Tour and fell just short of a berth in the LPGA Hall of Fame, made her home in West Texas since marrying former Texas Tech football star Yippy Rankin.

She is now an on-course commentator for ABC's golf coverage. She won those titles over a 12-year span, including her best year when she won seven events in

Green Tree Country Club

4900 Green Tree Boulevard

Midland 79707

915-694-7726

Pro: Chris Carpenter

A 27-hole private club.

• • •

1976 to become the first woman to pass $100,000 in a single season. In 1977, she set a record of 25 top 10 finishes that still stands.

Not to forget the golf course at green tree, which features three nine-hole layouts.

The North and East combination is the toughest, creating a par-72, 6,811-yard layout with a

slope rating of 121.

There are more than 6,000 trees on this layout to define the fairways. Wind is still a major factor here. Five lakes also come into play throughout the three courses.

The East/West Course was the original course and has homes lining the fairways. The West/North Course has water that comes into play several times.

No. 9 on the West Course is a 557-yard par 5 with a narrow fairway only about 25 yards wide. Also, there is a prevailing wind in your face.

No. 16 is a 165-yard par 3 that requires a carry over water to a narrow green that is protected by bunkers left and right.

Green Tree is unique because Tom Kite represented the club for several years and Texas Golf Hall of Famer Judy Rankin is still a member here.

Greenbrier Golf Club is like a family heirloom passed on from one owner to the next for three decades.

Greenbrier got started as part of the Farm and Home Administration's program to help rural communities build recreational facilities. Texas architect Leon Howard was instrumental in ushing the FHA to help fund the creation of golf courses. For every member the club signed up at $100 each, FHA would loan $1,500 at five percent interest over a 40-year period.

Howard ended up designing 21 of the 69 courses that received such funding. Of those courses,

Greenbrier Golf and Country Club
7810 South Lone Star Parkway
Highway 317
Moody 76557
254-853-2927
Pro: Jim Budziszewski
A par-70, 6,457-yard public course.

• • •

however, only 19 ended up being financially successful. Of those 19 courses, 17 were designed by Howard.

Greenbrier was built in 1968 but was eventually foreclosed on in 1980. Morris Ellis purchased the course at auction in 1980 and initiated some improvements, then pro Jim Budziszewski bought

it in 1990.

The course is built on 205 acres of rolling terrain, so you can expect some uneven lies. The fairways afford generous landing areas, and water hazards come into play on fourteen holes.

The signature hole is No. 14, a 375-yard par 4 that is difficult because a creek runs across the fairway and a gully on the right. Trees in the middle of the fairway, players have to fly over the trees to get the green, about 170 yards out from the hole.

No. 12 is a 520-yard par 5 with a creek running across the fairway into a bigger pond. Players have about a 20-yard window in the landing area.

Greenbrier is like a family heirloom passed from one owner to the next for three decades.

The marines say they do more before 8 a.m. than other people do all day. Well, the military personnel at the Gulf Winds Naval Air Station in Corpus Christi might have something to argue about.

In the same way military personnel start out in boot camp and work their way up through the officer ranks, the Gulf Winds Golf Course has undergone its own evolutionary process from a one-star goat ranch to a five-star military public golf course. And it has been a total team effort.

It all started out in 1955 as a six-hole golf course that was built by off-duty navy personnel. The

Gulf Winds Golf Course
Building 1272, US Naval Air Station
Corpus Christi 78419
512-939-3250
Pro: Greg Yourkinas
A par-71, 6,316-yard, military course.

• • •

course was expanded by three holes to complete a nine-hole layout. In 1961, former pro Butch O'Hara used a $60,000 grant to build three additional holes, and the course operated as a 12-hole golf course for the next 24 years. Six of the holes were played twice to make an 18-hole layout.

In 1985, thanks to the support

of commanding officers, Fred Blackmar (father of PGA Tour star Phil Blackmar) received a $150,000 grant to finish the 18-hole layout. The final product is a diverse course that is only 6,316 yards but is well maintained and cared for. Many military personnel work on the course for free in exchange for free green fees.

Because of the wind, the course plays much longer than the yardage would suggest. Water comes into play on Nos. 4, 7, 11, 12, 15 and 16.

No. 18 is the signature hole. It is a 420-yard par 4 that plays 40 yards longer because of a prevailing head-wind. Out-of-bounds runs down the left side.

A total team effort by Navy personnel has turned Gulf Winds from a six-hole course to a five-star, 18-hole military golf course.

Rarely do public golfers get a chance to play the most prestigious country club in the city, but that's exactly the opportunity players get at Gus Wortham. The course is the site of the old Houston Country Club, which was built in 1908 when the Houston Golf Club moved from its original site near downtown.

When Houston Country Club decided to move to a new site in the 1950s, American General Insurance President Gus Wortham bought the club.

Wortham bought the club and turned it into a public course and park. The name was changed to

Gus Wortham Golf Course

7000 Capital
Houston 77017
713-921-3227
Pro: Paul Reed
A par-72, 6,314-yard public course.

• • •

Executive Country Club and Houston Golf Course. In contrast to the exorbitant initiation fees of the past, he charged only a $60 annual membership in a concept that lasted for another 20 years.

Wortham eventually sold it to the city in 1973 for $3.6 million — more than twice the original asking price — and renamed it after Wortham.

While the course has not received the pampering from the city that it once did from its members, it still features some interesting holes in the 6,314-yard layout. For years, the course was the site of one of the nation's top amateur tournaments, the Houston Invitational.

No. 16 is a 249-yard par 3 that rates as one of the longest in the Houston area.

No. 9, on the other hand, is a 294-yard par 4 that many long hitters can drive. It also features the rare combination of three consecutive par 5s on Nos. 2, 3 and 4.

Gus Wortham is the original site of Houston Country Club built in 1908, but is now owned by the city of Houston and open to the public.

Hancock Park is the original Austin Country Club, which became the state's second oldest club when it was founded in 1898.

Legendary golf instructor Harvey Penick got his start in golf here as a caddy in 1913 for 20 cents a day.

It is named for Lewis Hancock who, along with other Austin Country Club members, helped build the nine-hole course that served the club for more than three decades until members decided to move to a new location in 1950.

The club sold Hancock Park to the city, which still operates it

Hancock Park Golf Course

811 East 41st Street
Austin 78751
512-453-0276
Pro: Stephen Darby
A par-35, 2,633-yard nine-hole course.

• • •

as one of five city courses.

While some of the original holes Hancock and his friends designed still remain, much has changed about the layout. It plays at 2,633 yards on the banks of Waller Creek, which comes into play on five holes.

When the new layout first opened, the course had finely smoothed sand greens until 1924, when members installing Bermuda greens. Among the players who have graced the fairways here is former president William Howard Taft.

No. 9 is a fitting end to a still challenging layout. The hole is a par 4, just 264 yards, but one with the creek in front of the green and more water along the putting surface.

"It's either feast or famine out here," head pro Stephen Darby says. "With the greens so small, you can just as easily make birdie or double bogey. People may think it's easy, but you can easily mess up."

Hancock Park is the original site of Austin Country Club, where Texas legend Harvey Penick started out as a caddie for 20 cents a day.

Every true golfer knows practice makes perfect and you can improve your game a lot more on the practice range than the golf course. But give the golfer a chance to practice at an extensive golf learning center, then apply those lessons at a neighboring Pete Dye course and the result is total golf satisfaction.

That's the premise behind Hank Haney's Golf Ranch and it has been highly successful for the golf complex that opened in 1991. This is where Haney teaches everyone from the top pros on the PGA and LPGA tours to everyday amateurs looking to shave a few strokes from their game.

Hank Haney Golf Ranch

4101 Custer Road
McKinney 75070
972-542-8800
Pro: Hank Haney
A par-33, 3,000-yard public course.

• • •

Haney has long been recognized as one of the top teachers in the nation. A member of Golf Digest's National Teaching Staff, Haney has taught some of the best players in North Texas and professionals from around the country. In 1988, Haney was named Director of Golf at the exclusive Stonebridge Country Club in McKinney.

Once he arrived, Haney bought a ranch nearby and began to develop a state-of-the art indoor/outdoor learning center, including a full-scale, nine-hole course designed by Pete Dye.

He turned the barn and stables into his learning center, while the par-33 layout measures 3,000 yards. The course offers several different kinds of holes through the rolling countryside and dense brush.

"Hank has brought national recognition to this area with his teaching abilities," said a member of his instructional staff. "I think he created the new wave in upscale practice facilities."

Hank Haney is one of the game's most respected teachers, and his golf ranch started the new wave of upscale, high-tech practice facilities.

Many golfers love to fish. In fact, at most PGA Tour events, as soon as the round is over and the galleries have gone home and the cheers have become a faint whisper, many of the pros sneak back out to the golf course with their rods and tackle box to enjoy golf's golden hour just before sunset.

At Heather Run Golf & Fish Club, golfers have the best of both worlds. Some good golf holes. Some great fishing holes.

Heather Run was built in 1968 as Western Oaks Country Club and was renamed Heather Run in 1997. The par-70, 6,377-yard layout is built around numer-

Heather Run Golf and Fish Club

1600 Western Oaks Drive
Waco, 76712
254-772-8100
Pro: Jerry Swain
A par-70, 6,377-yard public course.

• • •

ous small lakes that come into play throughout the course.

The signature hole is No. 13, a 382-yard par 4 that is a narrow dogleg right that plays uphill through a tree-lined, sloping fairway.

No. 12 is a 567-yard uphill par 5 to an undulating green.

No. 6 is a 193-yard par 3 that plays downhill to a green that

slopes from right to left, with heavy rough lining the left side of the green.

The course is not overly long. It is a placement course. The front nine is open and short; the back nine is more hilly and tree-lined with oaks and mesquite trees.

The No. 1 handicap hole is the 402-yard, par-4 13th, a dogleg right with a narrow fairway and out-of-bounds along the left side.

No. 14 is a 375-yard dogleg right par 4 where golfers must clear a small lake in front of the green. No. 15 is a 194-yard par 3 that requires golfers to carry their tee shots over the corner of Lake Juster, named after club operator Greg Juster.

At Heather Run Golf and Fish Club, golfers have the best of both worlds. Some good golf holes. And some great fishing holes.

This golf course is almost as much of a Beaumont institution as the men for which it has been named.

The course was originally built as a nine-hole layout by the Corps of Engineers and the Works Progress Administration in the 1930s. It originally was named after W.C. Tyrrell, one of the patriarchs of Beaumont whose family donated the land to the city of Beaumont.

Next came Henry Homberg, for whom the golf course is now named. Homberg worked as a caddy at the old Beaumont Municipal and eventually became head pro in 1941. PGA champion

Henry Homberg Golf Course

5940 Babe Zaharias
Beaumont 77720
409-866-9484
Pro: Andy Hebert
A par-72, 6,846-yard public course.

• • •

Dave Marr, touring pro Bert Weaver, NCAA Division II champion Mike Nugent, LSU golf coach Britt Harrison and Texas Golf Hall of Famer Bruce Lietzke are among the thousands of junior players who were influenced by Homberg, who eventually earned a place in the Texas Golf Hall of Fame. Homberg died on

October 24, 1990, but city officials ensured his name would live on by naming the f course in his honor 1983.

The two nines provide different challenges. The front nine is fairly long and open, while the back nine is shorter and tighter.

The par-4 No. 4 is 445 yards from the back and plays into a strong southeasterly wind. No. 9 is another long par 4 at 435 yards. It is a dogleg right that is lined with trees on both sides of the fairway, creating a tight driving area off the tee.

No. 9 is another long par 4 at 435 yards. It is a dogleg right that is lined with trees on both sides of the fairway.

Henry Homberg influenced thousands of junior players, including Texas Golf Hall of Famers Dave Marr and Bruce Lietzke.

George Hermann was the fourth son of a Swiss immigrant who arrived in Houston in 1838. His parents died at an early age and he quit school about the same time, but that didn't prevent him from going on to make a fortune in cattle, real estate and lumber. When he died in 1914, Hermann left behind a fortune of $2.5 million and a lot of real estate. One of the stipulations of his estate was to donate one of the city's most scenic sites to be used as a much-needed park that would later be home to a zoo and Hermann Park Golf Course.

City fathers hired famed Texas architect John Bredemus to build

Hermann Park Golf Course

6201 Golf Course Drive
Houston 77031
713-526-0077
Pro: David Henning
A par-71, 5,965-yard public course.

• • •

a public golf course and make good use of the wooded terrain. It was a short but sweet 6,300-yard layout, with tight fairways that forced players to be exacting with their shots.

This was where Jimmy Demaret, Tommy Bolt, Jack Burke Jr. and late Memorial Park pro Robie Williams learned the game

as caddies and later learned to play the game.

After a National Golf Foundation report in 1985 showed Houston's municipal courses were being poorly managed, the city began an initiative to lease its courses to private management companies. BSL Golf Corporation won the lease at Hermann Park and has since put numerous improvements in place.

The combination of time and neglect took their toll on Hermann and it was closed in 1997 to undergo an extensive renovation and reforestation program to help bring the golf course back to its proper place in the history books.

Hermann Park was Houston's first public course built in 1918, and is where Jimmy Demaret, Tommy Bolt and Jack Burke Jr. got their start.

Pampa is home of one of the state's oldest clubs. In 1990 architect Ray Hardy built Hidden Hills Golf Club to serve the growing golf population.

The par-71, 6,463-yard course was built in two deep valleys, and Hardy designed a layout that goes up and down the many hills, producing good elevation changes from tee to green and very few level lies.

Out-of-bounds comes into play on Nos. 1, 2, 3, 4 and 5 on the front nine and 10, 11, 14 and 18 on the back. Water comes into play on seven holes.

The course features only three par 5s, but two of them are under

Hidden Hills Golf Course

North Highway 70
Pampa 79065
806-669-5866
Pro: David Teichmann
A par-71, 6,463-yard public course.

• • •

500 yards and present good birdie opportunities.

The 496-yard, par-5 No. 13 is a dogleg right, where water crosses the fairway about 150 yards from the green and forces players to carry water on their approach to the green.

No. 4 is a 487-yard par 5 that is relatively short, but is guarded by out-of-bounds down the entire left side of the fairway.

No. 12 is a 203-yard par 3 that is all carry over a creek.

The hardest hole on the course is the 420-yard No. 9, which is a dogleg left.

All of the other par 4s are under 400 yards, so big hitters will spend a lot of time with their short irons during the day setting up birdie opportunities.

No. 7 is a 335-yard par 4 that some golfers may be able to reach with a big drive.

The fairway is a slight dogleg right and there is no water in play to detract golfers who want to go for the green.

Hidden Hills was built in two deep valleys, providing elevation changes from tee to green and few level lies.

Lindale is home to two of Texas' most under-rated golf facilities. One is Garden Valley Golf Resort, which has one course in the Texas Top 100. The other is Hide-A-Way Lake Club.

Hide-A-Way Lake has three nine-hole courses that can be played in any of three 18-hole combinations.

The designs feature small, elevated greens, scenic woods and a lake that comes into play on a couple of holes.

The West Nine is the shortest of the three nine-hole layouts. It plays 2,993 yards from the back tees with a par of 35. It features three par 3s and two par 5s.

Hide-A-Way Lake Club

302 Hide-A-Way-Lake
Lindale 75771
903-882-8511
A 27-hole private club.

• • •

The nine starts with a 489-yard par 5, offering many players a good chance to start the round with a birdie. The most difficult hole on the West is the 547-yard, par-5 fifth hole.

All of the par 4s are under 400 yards, and the par 3s are 185, 167 and 186 yards, respectively.

The Central Nine is the longest nine at 3,305 yards and a par of 36. It opens with the most difficult hole, a 561-yard par 5, and then comes back with its shortest hole at No. 2, a 140-yard par 3. No. 7 is a 422-yard par 4 that requires two long shots to reach the green.

The East Nine plays 3,274 yards and also starts out with its hardest hole, a 571-yard par 5, and comes back with another short par 3 at 130 yards. No. 4 is a 430-yard par 4, and then side finishes with four short par 4s.

The hardest combination at Hide-A-Way is the Central/East nines, which play to a 124 slope rating from the back tees.

Hide-A-Way Lake has three nine-hole courses that feature small, elevated greens, scenic woods and a lake that comes into play.

I f the skies above the Alvin countryside become aglow sometime during the next year, don't be alarmed.

It's not a UFO. It's Hillcrest Golf Club.

The new owners of this nine-hole executive course in Alvin have big plans for the next 12 months that include the installation of lights on the 65-acre site for night play.

Charles Wilson, who began operating the course in 1972 before buying it in 1991, opened the driving range in 1993 and has spent the past two years studying the logistics of becoming one of Houston's only night golf courses.

Wilson said the most difficult part of the planning is determining where to position the lights to provide the fullest coverage. They also want to prevent cluttering the course with light poles.

The 2,448-yard layout was built in the late 1960s by the late Shorty Plaster. Shorty was a sand man who realized his pit was

about to fill up with water and wanted to make use of the land. The sand pit is now a 15-acre lake that serves as the centerpiece of the golf course.

"This is one of the best courses in the state for beginners," says pro Dean Wilson. "The course doesn't defeat you. Most beginners and average players just want to go out and have a good time.

"Out here, they can enjoy themselves without being defeated. That's why a lot of courses that aren't tough get so much play, because the average golfer can't handle Greatwood or Old Orchard. They want to enjoy a round of golf."

"This is one of the best courses in the state for beginners. The course doesn't defeat you. Most players want to go out and have a good time."

B etween Ralph Plummer and Leon Howard, they designed nearly 50 percent of the golf courses in Texas between the 1950s and 1970s.

After criss-crossing the state from El Paso to Nacogdoches and from Brownsville to Amarillo, their paths finally crossed at Hilltop Lakes Resort.

Built in 1963 as the centerpiece of a residential community between Houston and Bryan-College Station, this extremely scenic course has homes and trees lining all its fairways. In addition, the fairways are all bordered

by a standard cut of rough.

This is a private club for members only. Only homeowners of Hilltop Lakes are allowed to be members of this private club.

Plummer designed the first nine holes in 1963, several years after he built the famed Cypress

Creek Course at Houston's Champions Golf Club.

As the development continued to grow, developers hired Howard in 1970 to design the last nine holes.

When they were through, they produced a relatively easy layout (111 slope rating) with water hazards coming into play on a number of holes and bunkers strategically placed throughout the course.

The most difficult hole is No. 14, a 396-yard par 4 that requires a tee shot over a creek, then an approach shot over a small pond to the green.

After criss-crossing the state designing courses, architects Ralph Plummer and Leon Howard finally crossed paths at Hilltop Lakes.

Hogan Park golf course has been serving Midland residents since 1959. First there were 18 holes. Then there were 27. Soon there will be 36 holes of championship golf.

The original 18-hole course at Hogan Park, which was named after the man who donated the land it is build one, ranks No. 23 in the Texas among municipal courses in an annual poll by *The Dallas Morning News*.

It is a traditional layout that measures 6,615 yards and plays to a par of 70 as it winds through the mesquite trees on the West Texas prairie. Both golf courses are flat and easy to walk. A lake

Hogan Park
Golf Course

3600 North Fairgrounds Road
Midland 79705
915-683-3621
Pro: Terry Lester
A 27-hole public course.

• • •

comes into play on several holes, and the course features small greens and wide fairways.

No. 4 on the original course is a nasty 445-yard par 4 that plays uphill through a tree-lined chute then doglegs right to a two-tiered green that is protected by water on the front right. Proper club selection is paramount since there

is a four-foot difference between the top and bottom tier.

In 1983, architect Ron Kirby came back to the scene to build another nine holes to produce a 27-hole facility. In 1998, Kirby is returning to complete the second 18 to give Midland residents two championship 18-hole golf courses.

Kirby's first nine was a links-style design with narrow fairways and large, undulating bentgrass greens. The layout measures 3,410 yards and, when played twice, has a slope rating of 111.

Kirby's new nine is under construction and is expected to be completed in the fall of 1998.

Hogan Park is a traditional layout with fairways that wind through the mesquite trees on the West Texas prairie.

Big Sandy may be best known as the home of David Overstreet, one of the best high school running backs in the history of Texas high school football, who went on to play at the University of Oklahoma.

But for two and a half decades, Big Sandy also has been known as home of Holly Lake Ranch, a rural golf-course residential community. When the course opened in the 1970s, the development offered free weekend getaways to families that were interested in buying real estate there.

The biggest selling point for the real estate, besides its rural setting amidst the tall oaks and

Holly Lake Ranch
Golf Course

Farm Market 2869
Big Sandy 75765
903-769-2397
Pro: Jeff Davis
A par-72, 6,705-yard private club.

• • •

pines, was a par-72, 6,705-yard golf course designed by architect Leon Howard.

This layout is far from the D/FW metroplex, but its narrow, tree-lined fairways and well-manicured greens make it worth the drive. Out-of-bounds comes into play throughout the course, but errant shots will usually be deflect-

ed by the trees before they get that far off track.

No. 12 is a 425-yard par 4 that takes a sharp dogleg to the left off the tee and a water hazard that players must carry. The combination of long carry and the tight fairway and well-bunkered green make this a hard par.

No. 16 is another demanding par 4. The 423-yard hole is the No. 1 handicap hole on the course as it veers slightly to the left through a row of trees. No. 13 is the No. 3 handicap hole. It is a 560-yard par 5 that doglegs left.

The par 3s are manageable — ranging from 148 to 188 yards — and give golfers a good chance at birdie or at least an easy par.

This layout is far from the D/FW metroplex, but its narrow, tree-lined fairways and well-manicured greens make it worth the drive.

Chuck Berson started playing golf when he was 8 and grew up to enjoy marginal success as a professional on various pro tours. He eventually became a PGA Club professional and spent four years as an assistant at the Houston Country Club. It was there, in the ultra-exclusive confines along Buffalo Bayou, that Berson saw the future.

He saw the golf industry was about to explode and there was not enough public golf facilities in Houston to accommodate the masses of new golfers. So he decided to leave the security of his club job to open a driving range, a fly-by-night business that comes and goes as fast as people at a bus stop. But Berson got lucky. The range was a success, and in 1988 he took a chance and a loan to buy a 150-acres to build an affordable golf course.

"There is a huge market for my kind of course," Berson says. "The golf industry needs more access to courses that offer a quality product with a friendly atmosphere and affordable rates. There's going to be a rude awakening in golf one of these days when people get tired of paying $50 or more to play golf.

"I've got so much time and money and work invested in this place, that if they offered me the job at Augusta I'd have to turn them down."

Berson built the 3,200-yard layout around one three-acre irrigation lake that comes into play on three holes. No. 9 is the signature hole. Off the tee, players use anywhere from a driver to two-iron to lay up short of the lake. That leaves them about 150 yards over the water to an island green.

Houston Hills Golf Course
9720 Ruffino Road
Houston 77031
281-933-2300
Pro: Chuck Berson
A nine-hole public course.
• • •

"There is a huge market for my kind of course. There's going to be a rude awakening when people get tired of paying $50 to play golf."

Credence Clearwater sang about being born on the bayou. He wasn't talking about Idylwild Golf Club, but his song could definitely serve as the club's anthem.

In 1962, Texas golf legend Henry Ransom slipped into his rubber boots and waded off into the wilderness to stake out a championship layout on the edge of the Big Thicket.

Ransom was a childhood pal of Jimmy Demaret, who while growing up in a single-parent household, helped pay the bills as a dancer in a comedy act and also as a professional boxer under the name "Hammerin' Henry."

Ransom was known more for his exploits as a pro golfer, where he won 12 events, including the Texas PGA and Texas Open in 1941 and 1961, as well as the golf coach at Texas A&M.

He knew enough about the game to design a championship golf course, even if he had to risk life and limb.

While designing this par-72, 6,727-yard layout, Ransom had to battle alligators, snakes, wild boar and other wildlife that called the area around this old mineral lake their home.

Ransom survived his experience with the wild kingdom and produced a golf course known for its tight, tree-lined fairways with numerous bayous. Every hole has either trees, water hazards and many have both.

The signature hole is No. 7, a 390-yard par 4 dogleg right over a bayou to the green.

No. 10 is a 410-yard par 4 dogleg left that requires an approach through a narrow fairway into the green.

Idylwild Golf Club
1100 Pine Shadows Drive
Sour Lake 77659
409-753-2521
Pro: Michael Smith
A par-72, 6,727-yard private club.
• • •

Ransom knew enough about the game to design a championship golf course, even if he had to risk life and limb to do it.

Inwood Forest was the brainchild of a handful of members at several of Houston's prestigious clubs, all of whom wanted to incorporate an existing golf course into their subdivision in West Houston.

The club was an immediate success, reaching a membership of 425 in its first year. Noted golf course architect Jay Riviere designed the first nine holes at Inwood and Jackson Bradley, a former pro at River Oaks, designed the second nine. The third nine was built in 1970 by Don Collett, one of the nation's best teaching pros at the time.

"It was a very low budget golf

Inwood Forest Country Club
7603 Antoine
Houston 77292
281-448-0239
Pro: Mike Baker
A 27-hole private country club.
• • •

course designed to sell housing and lots," Bradley remembers. "Jay started the project and when I came into the picture I was asked to complete the job as soon as possible.

"I was introduced to a construction crew chief named 'Bitching Mitch,' who didn't have much regard for golf or golf pros.

Strangely enough, we got along because I let him do most of the talking. But the most difficult task was communicating to equipment operators what greens and bunkers looked like."

The three nine-hole layouts are built around 11 lakes, White Oak Bayou and Vogel Creek and feature 90 bunkers. Water comes into play on 19 of the 27 holes.

No. 9 is a great challenge. A 454-yard par 4, it is a dogleg right with water in play on the left side of the fairway, and again just to the left of the green. No. 11 is a 447-yard par 4 with water running down the left side of the fairway and a creek crossing in front of the tee box.

The three nine-hole layouts are built around 11 lakes, White Oak Bayou and Vogel Creek. Water comes into play on 19 of the 27 holes.

Most of Ralph Plummer's golf courses turned out to be private country clubs with exclusive memberships.

In the heart of Central Texas, however, he left behind a great municipal layout that still ranks as one of the best city-owned courses in the state.

James Connally Golf Course is a par-72, 6,975-yard layout that Plummer built in 1955.

Four decades later, it is still the most popular course in Central Texas. Longtime Texas pro Jack Barger is the head pro.

Plummer liked to build long layouts with lots of long par 4s and there are plenty of those at

James Connally Golf Course
7900 Concord Road
Waco 76715
254-799-6561
Pro: Jack Barger
A par-72, 6,975 yard municipal course.
• • •

Connally that require golfers to hit two good shots to have a chance at a birdie.

Instead of tree-lined fairways where golfers are threatened by disaster every turn, Connally features wide-open fairways that give golfers the opportunity to "let the big dog eat" on almost every hole with its generous landing areas.

Water, however, does come into play on 11 holes.

The signature hole is No. 16, a 575-yard par 5 that requires a series of uphill shots to the green. It is the No. 1 handicap hole.

No. 8 is 213-yard par 3 that is one of the most difficult on the course. Players must hit their tee shots to an elevated green protected by a bunker on the left side.

And typical of Plummer's style, he challenges anyone who sets foot on the back tees.

No. 2 is a long par 4 that measures 459 yards. No. 6 is a 445-yard par 4 and Nos. 11 and 12 measure 426 and 423 yards, respectively.

Ralph Plummer liked to build long layouts with lots of long par 4s, and there are plenty of those at James Connally.

Like many of Houston's early courses Jersey Meadow has a storied history and has changed names and owners several times over the years before being eventually transformed into one of the best public facilities in northwest Houston.

The golf course once was known as Long Meadows Golf Course in the 1960s before Texas Golf Hall of Famer Vic Cameron was instrumental in Cameron Iron Works purchasing the 122-acre facility in 1974 for $500,000.

The course was purchased by BSL Golf Corporation in 1991. BSL pumped $3 million into renovations, the construction of nine

Jersey Meadow Golf Course

8502 Rio Grande
Houston 77040
713-896-0900
Pro: Darryl Henning
A 27-hole public course.

• • •

additional holes by architect Carlton Gipson, a new driving range and a miniature golf course.

The original 18-hole layout is fairly short, but the tree-lined fairways put a premium on accuracy off the tee. The three nines give players an option to play a different 18 each time out.

On a good driving day, play-

ers will be rewarded with lots of medium to short-iron approach shots and birdie opportunities.

As with most of his new courses, Gipson built the new nine with the growing number of women and seniors in mind.

It is more of a links-style course with a lot of new trees that don't yet come into play, but three new irrigation lakes come into play on six holes.

No. 1 is a 464-yard par 5 from the tips that will give many players a birdie opportunity to start their round.

No. 2 is a 300-yard par 4 with a 40-yard wide lake in front of the green to prevent most players from going for the green.

On a good driving day, golfers will be rewarded with medium to short iron approach shots and birdie opportunities.

Austin has long been home to some of the best golfers in America.

First came Harvey Penick, then George Hannon, Ben Crenshaw and Tom Kite and now, most recently, 1992 U.S. Amateur champion Justin Leonard. All of them played or coached at the University of Texas.

From future college stars to local hackers, Jimmy Clay Golf Course in Austin has played host to all kinds of golfers in its 20-year history. Considering Austin is the state capital, it's only appropriate that Jimmy Clay is an equal opportunity golf course.

Since Jimmy Clay opened, it

Jimmy Clay Golf Course

3400 Jimmy Clay Drive
Austin 78744
512-292-4523
Pro: Janna Benton
A par-72, 6,857-yard municipal course.

• • •

has hosted the Texas state high school boys championships on an annual basis, several national Pan Am championships, Texas State Amateurs and men's city championships. Not overly long, it remains a timeless layout for thousands of golfers.

"It's a fine golf course, one of the best the city has," Finger says.

"Every architect would love to have a piece of ground with unlimited funds to turn out the prettiest course ever. I think we did a good job. It's a fun course to play."

No. 1 is a par 4 that requires a blind second shot over a hill to a narrow green. A small creek comes into play on Nos. 3-6. No. 9 is a short dogleg par 4 and the 18th is a longer dogleg with large bunkers protecting the green.

In 1994, Jimmy Clay celebrated its 20th birthday, and also the birth of a baby brother.

The Roy Kizer Golf Course opened in '94 to make Jimmy Clay Hill Country's only 36-hole municipal golf facility.

Golfers from Harvey Penick to Ben Crenshaw to Tom Kite and Justin Leonard have graced the fairways at Austin's Jimmy Clay Golf Course.

Some five decades after John Bredemus laid out the city of Dallas' first public golf course at Tenison Park in 1924, the city fathers commissioned its last course in 1979 in the bottom lands of the Elm Fork Trinity River.

In future years, the process of building a golf course would become too complicated and too expensive for a major municipality. But with land and a little money to spare, the city of Dallas decided to build one more golf course to help meet the growing demand for tee times.

The layout measures 6,511 yards, and puts more of a premium on accuracy because of its

Keeton Park Golf Course

2323 Jim Miller Road
Dallas 75217
214-670-8784
Pro: Kim Brown
A par-72, 6,520-yard municipal layout.

• • •

tree-lined fairways and numerous lakes and ponds. Architect Dave Bennett incorporated several existing lakes and channels with 12 small ponds, bringing water into play on all but three holes. On many of those holes, water comes into play both off the tee and on the approach.

One of the most difficult

holes at Keeton is the 538-yard, par-5 third hole with an anorexic, double-dogleg fairway that is lined by trees and water. The hole veers slightly to the left off the tee through a chute of trees, with a pond protecting the right side of the fairway. The hole veers back to the left on the second shot, and the fairway funnels back to a green nestled in the middle of a thick grove of trees.

Water comes into play three times on the 522-yard, par-5 sixth hole, a sweeping dogleg left with two ponds guarding the right side of the fairway. The elevated green is situated on a peninsula, with water directly behind and on the sides.

Dave Bennett incorporated several existing lakes and channels with 12 ponds, bringing water into play on all but three holes.

The hills of southern San Antonio serve as an ideal setting for the Kelly Air Force base golf course.

The course opened on March 11, 1969. It was originally a nine-hole facility, but became so popular that a second nine was quickly approved and added.

The layout was designed by a base committee with much of the on-course work done by volunteers. What stands today is a par-72 test that plays 6,935 yards from the back tees.

"You have a lot of different shots on this course," former head pro John Mochrie says. "You can be hitting the ball up, down or

Kelly Air Force Base Golf Course

Kelly Air Force Base
San Antonio
210-977-5100
Pro: Frank Hurt
A par-72, 6,857-yard military course.

• • •

sideways. We have some great finishing holes and great par 3s."

The most noticeable feature at Kelly is the large hill upon which the ninth and 18th tee boxes sit. From the tee, you can see the entire base and downtown San Antonio in the distance.

The second hole, measuring 200 yards, is almost all carry over

what becomes a watery grave for many short-knockers. There are traps behind the green and still more water behind them.

No. 16 is only 190 yards, but features one of the smallest greens on the course. It is protected by traps on both sides.

No. 8 is the longest par 3 at 215 yards. No. 17 is a 275-yard par 4. The fairway goes straight uphill with the green sloping back toward the fairway.

Mochrie recently retired after 17 years as head pro at Kelly, but golfers have another reason other than his vast experience to listen to him. His niece is LPGA superstar Dottie Mochrie, but he doesn't take credit for her success.

"You have a lot of different shots on this course. You can be hitting the ball up, down or sideways. And we have some great finishing holes."

You can't help but notice that the character in the King's Creek logo bears a striking resemblance to the popular Saturday morning cartoon character Yosemite Sam. But make no mistake: This ain't no joke, you silly rabbit.

King's Creek was built by private owners in 1981 on the northwestern shore of Cedar Creek Lake to service the many golfers who have second homes in the country or live in bedroom communities and commute to work during the week.

It just goes to show that you don't need to be a big-name architect to produce a fun and

challenging layout. The course plays 6,700 yards and plays mostly into the prevailing south wind. Water located throughout make an errant shot a major mistake.

In 1988, Rick May purchased the facility and has since has made various improvements. He has added bunkers and renovated existing ones.

While the front nine plays only 3,099 yards from the back tees, it does feature one of the hardest holes on the course. The par-3 third is a 200-yard carry over water into a steady southerly breeze. It requires an accurate long iron or wood to a well-bunkered green.

The 442-yard 13th, the 443-yard 10th and the 576-yard 14th will test the mettle of any player. All play into the prevailing wind.

The 443-yard No. 10 is guarded by out-of-bounds to the left and water to the right. The par-5 14th has water down both sides from tee to green. Any wayward shot here will get soaked.

King's Creek just goes to show that you don't need to be a big-name architect to produce a fun and challenging layout.

They say the grass is always greener on the other side of the fence.

Well, sometimes it's true.

The King Ranch is known around the world as the largest ranch in Texas, spanning 825,000 acres and four counties.

But just on the other side of the cattle guard is King's Crossing Golf & Country Club, and 18-hole championship golf course designed in 1986 by architect Bill Coore.

Coore, who over the past decade has teamed with PGA Tour star Ben Crenshaw to build some of the best courses in the United States such as the

Plantation Course at Maui's Kapalua Resort, produced a links-style layout where wind, sand and water is a major factor.

Coore moved more than 300,000 yards of dirt to create roll and movement to the otherwise flat piece of land with moguls and swales in the fairways and mounding around the greens.

In the absence of trees, Coore used 50 bunkers throughout the course to keep players honest. Many of the fairways are doglegs, with bunkers and mounding protecting the corners. The par-71 layout is 6,762 yards.

The signature hole is No. 12, a 393-yard par 4 with water bordering the entire left side of the fairway.

No. 10 is a 633-yard monster par 5 with water on both sides of the fairway.

No. 18 is a 406-yard par 4 that requires a long carry over water off the tee. Golfers must beware, because most of the fairway slopes toward the water.

Coore moved more than 300,000 yards of dirt to create roll and movement to the otherwise flat piece of land with moguls and swales.

Leon Howard learned early in his career as a golf course architect to go where the money was.

We're talking the early '50s here, and the immediate future in golf was in building municipal golf courses.

Every year, Howard would attend the annual meeting of the National Recreation and Parks Association to schmooze with park directors from a five-state area. He talked golf. He talked economics. And, more often than not, he talked business.

Howard made a strong

enough impression on former Dallas parks director L.B. Houston to earn a phone call when the City of Dallas decided to turn nearly 200 acres in the bottom land of the Elm Fork Trinity River into a golf course.

The land was in the 100-year

flood plain and there was no way to raise the entire level of the golf course out of harm's way from potential flood waters. So Howard moved 300,000 cubic yards of dirt by creating 11 lakes and ponds and using the fill to elevate greens and tees.

All four par 3s require a carry over water, and the 16th, 17th and 18th holes are a strong finishing combination.

The 16th is a 425-yard par 4; the 17th is a 525-yard par 5 with trees down both sides of the fairway and out-of-bounds running lengthwise down the left. The 18th is a 436-yard, par 4.

The land was in a 100-year flood plain, so Howard moved 300,000 yards of dirt to create 11 lakes and ponds and elevate the greens and tees.

Two Texas golf legends, Don January and Ralph Plummer, came together to design a fine layout at Lake Country Country Club in Fort Worth.

Between them, January and Plummer designed some of the best courses in Texas. They each crafted nine holes at Lake Country before it opened in 1973.

Plummer produced both high volume and high quality courses from the 1940s to 1970s. Among his best works were Northwood, Columbian and Champions' Cypress Creek Course — all of which have hosted a U.S. Open or other major championship.

January's best work was at

Royal Oaks Country Club in 1969, and it still ranks in the Texas Top 100.

The result was a hilly and tight course that can challenge the best golfers, but still be fun for the average hacker. Located just 15 minutes northwest of downtown Fort Worth, Lake Country operates as a semi-private course.

What draws players here is the architectural excellence of January and Plummer and the enduring challenge of the course.

The greens on the front nine were redesigned in 1991, but it did nothing to damage the overall character of the course.

Lake Country has 23 traps scattered across its layout along with seven water holes, befitting its namesake, and several sloping and undulating greens.

January and Plummer combined to build more than 100 courses in Texas, but this is the only course where both of their unique design character traits are on display.

Two legends of Texas golf course architecture — Don January and Ralph Plummer, came together to design a fine layout at Lake Country.

L ake Kiowa Country Club was built in 1969 on the site of an old campsite of the Kiowa Indian tribe. When the lake was being dredged in the late 1960s, construction crews turned up hundreds of arrowheads and artifacts that are still on display at this exclusive club.

The course is the centerpiece for the lovely gated residential community. While the layout creates a picturesque back window view for the homeowners as it winds through the fairways, which intertwine with the neighborhood, for golfers it means there are out-of-bounds fences on both sides of every hole. In addition to the

Lake Kiowa Country Club

903 Kiowa Drive West
Lake Kiowa 76240
940-668-7394
Pro: Brown McCrory
A par-72, 6,605-yard private club.

• • •

threat of out-of-bounds, Lake Kiowa and two small ponds bring water into play on 13 holes. The course is only 6,605 yards, but is well-manicured with bentgrass greens and plush fairways.

Architect Leon Howard designed a challenging layout that is a shot-makers course that puts more emphasis on accuracy than

length. Big hitters have no advantage here.

No. 9 is by far the most unique hole at Lake Kiowa. It is a 318-yard par 4, with the green built on an island.

The 349-yard, par-4 No. 4 starts from the island, but requires golfers to tee off over the lake to reach the green on the other side.

No. 16 is a 420-yard par 4. It is the hardest hole on the course as it doglegs around a lake with the approach requiring a long carry over water.

No. 8 is a 180-yard par 3 with a green nestled along the banks of the lake and guarded by water in front, back and on the right side.

Lake Kiowa is a challenging shot-makers course that puts more emphasis on accuracy than length. Big hitters have no advantage here.

T erry Dear, a pro who has had varying degrees of success playing on the PGA Tour, Senior PGA Tour and a couple of U.S. Opens, is the former director of golf at Lake Ridge Country Club.

For members of this par-72, 6,762-yard private club, every day is like the U.S. Open as they battle high winds, water hazards and out-of-bounds that can make this layout every bit as difficult as a host site of the national championship.

Lake Ridge opened in 1979 and meanders through an exclusive neighborhood in Lubbock. The combination of strong winds,

Lake Ridge Country Club

8802 Vicksburg Avenue
Lubbock 79424
806-794-4445
Pro: Mark Cunningham
A par-72, 6,762-yard private club.

• • •

especially during the months of February through April, and the abundance of out-of-bounds stakes make this a very demanding layout even though there are very few trees. The layout features large heavily bunkered greens. The course is built around two large lakes that serve as the centerpiece of the front and

back nines.

All total, Lake Ridge demands pinpoint accuracy from tee to green. It plays to a slope rating of 124 from the back tees.

These are just a sample of what Lake Ridge has to offer:

No. 4 is a 178-yard par 3 with water around the green in front and on the left, and lots of slope.

No. 17 is a 453-yard, dogleg left par 4 with an undulating fairway and a bunker protecting the green on the front right. Trees line both sides of the fairway.

No. 6 is a 520-yard par 5 with a road on the right side, a lake on the left and a creek that cuts across the fairway about 260 yards off the tee.

High winds, water hazards and out-of-bounds can make this layout as difficult as a host site of a national championship.

There have been many stories in Texas golf history where golf courses start out as private country clubs, but later open to the public. It happened in Houston, when Houston Country Club moved from it's original site and sold the old course to the city. It happened in Austin. It happened in Galveston.

But rare have been the times when a golf course started out as a public course and later became a country club.

Such is the case at Lake Waco Country Club, where actually golfers have the best of all words with an 18-hole private course open to members only and an 18-hole exec-

Lake Waco Country Club

5608 Flat Rock Road
Waco 76708
254-756-2161
Pro: Larry Salter
A par-72, 6,640-yard private course.

• • •

utive course open to the public.

Lake Waco started out as a public course when it was built in 1964, but it underwent three ownership changes and became private in 1969. It is built on rolling terrain with trees and lakes coming into play on both courses. Every year, it hosts a qualifying tournament for the Texas State Open.

The private course is a par-72, 6,640-yard layout plays to a 122 slope rating from the back tees.

The No. 1 handicap hole is the 385-yard No. 15, followed by the monstrous 603-yard par 5 No. 7. No. 4 is a 566-yard par 5. No. 14 is a 410-yard dogleg left with a tight driving area.

The signature hole is No. 8, a 196-yard par 3 with lakes and trees surrounding a sloping green.

The par-3 course measures 2,705 yards and features four holes of 200 yards or more while four other holes are under 120 yards. With small greens, it provides golfers with a great opportunity to work on their short iron play.

Many courses have started out as private clubs and later turned public, but Lake Waco is a rare country club that started out as a public golf course.

From the first day a group of Galveston County golfers envisioned building a country club, improvisation has been their forte. It was opened in Nov. 5, 1949, but only after much teamwork from founding members and local businesses.

Members purchased 200 acres of land just off Main Street in La Marque. It was dotted with trees and had an old Army barracks on it that was one of the last remnants of what once was Camp Wallace during World War II.

They called the club Galco (short for Galveston County) Country Club, and converted an old army barracks into the club-

Lakeview Country Club

1291 Palm
La Marque 77568
409-935-6811
Manager: Greg Mazzantini
A par-72, 6,227-yard semi-private club.

• • •

house and ballroom. The old barracks still stands and still serves as the clubhouse. Materials for the golf course were donated, and the layout was built on a shoe-string budget.

The course is very flat and mostly open, with the gulf breeze whipping across it and 25 acres of lakes coming into play. One of

four lakes comes into play on most holes and out-of-bounds on four holes.

The toughest hole is the 410-yard, par-4 No. 8, where two lakes come into play off the tee and on the approach. Players must first negotiate a tee shot down a fairway that is protected on the left and right by water.

Architect Jay Riviere was one of several architects who have expressed interest in buying the club and renovating it, especially now that the Gulf Greyhound Park has brought growth and tourism to the area. The deal, however, never went through because of a lack of agreement of the membership.

The course is very flat and mostly open, with the Gulf breeze whipping across it and 25 acres of lakes coming into play.

A millionaire's dream has become a test of skill for South Texas golfers over the last several decades.

Joseph Landa was New Braunfels' first millionaire. To celebrate his success and share his wealth, he donated a prime piece of land near downtown to the city in the early 1900s. At the time, New Braunfels was largely a community of German families and Landa stipulated that the land was to be used for the citizens to relax, enjoy themselves and practice their favorite sports.

Mark Fuchanot built Landa Park Golf Course in 1939. Fuchanot built nine holes, and

Landa Park Golf Course
1445 Argarita Trail
New Braunfels 78132
Pro: Chris Acker
830-608-2174
A par-72, 6,103-yard public course.

• • •

Dave Bennett and Leon Howard added nine more in 1969. The layout is short and in many ways outdated by modern technology that enables golfers to hit the ball farther and straighter. It measures only 6,103 yards, but where it lacks in length, it makes up for with water and tree-lined fairways that require accurate shot place-

ment. The Comal River comes into play on six holes.

"The positioning of the tee shot is more important than length," head pro Bill Halbert says. "It's a very scenic course. The Comal River makes for some very pretty holes."

The No. 1 handicap hole is also is the longest on the course. The par-5 fourth hole measures 553 yards from the back tees. It requires golfers to hit two good shots to be able to hit a short-iron approach to the green

Landa died long ago, but he would be proud to see that the city has been a good custodian of his gift. It was the gift of a lifetime — and beyond.

Joseph Landa was New Braunfels' first millionaire. To celebrate his success and share his wealth, he donated a prime piece of real estate to the city.

When you get Joe Finger's answering machine at home, you are greeted by a message not in English, but in Spanish.

Finger designed more than 100 golf courses in his career, most in Texas but many in Mexico. At the end of his career in 1983, it was only appropriate that he would build a golf course on the Texas-Mexico border.

It's called Laredo Country Club.

Near the banks of the Rio Grande River, Finger produced one of the best courses in Texas. The par-72, 7,125-yard layout plays to a slope rating of 133 with its tree-lined fairways, demanding rough and Bermuda greens. Water

Laredo Country Club
1450 Country Club Drive
Laredo 78041
956-727-0183
Pro: Todd Zunker
A par-72, 7,125-yard private club.

• • •

hazards come into play on at least eight holes, and numerous sand bunkers are spread throughout the course.

Finger was an engineering graduate from MIT who got into the golf course design business by accident, but proved to be innovative. He liked long courses and hard courses and is known best

for the Blue Monster at Kiamesha Lake, N.Y., and the Island Course at Kingwood Country Club. At one time or another, Finger had five courses on *Golf Digest's* list of top 100 courses in America.

The signature hole is No. 18, a 430-yard par 4, requiring a tee shot up a dogleg left that has a water hazard protecting the entire length of the hole, then an approach shot to a peninsula green. All the greens are severely undulating and fast.

Another notable hole is No. 3, a 455-yard par 4, requiring a tee shot between the water on the left and the out-of-bounds stakes on the right.

Near the banks of the Rio Grande River, Finger produced one of the best courses in Texas with tree-lined fairways and demanding rough.

This public layout is located in the country with enough problem areas to keep city slickers honest. The course was originally owned and designed by golf architect Dick Norman.

He sold the course to five local individuals in 1983. Carlie Tice, one of the owners, is also the head pro and said golfers enjoy the relaxing change of pace at Leon Valley.

"It's a country golf course, with plenty of room to roll," Tice said. "We only have two sand traps and water comes into play on one hole (the par-3, No. 6)."

The greens are small, but

smooth with a 328 Bermuda surface which is often over-seeded. Tee times are taken on Saturday, Sunday and holidays.

If your game needs a lesson more than just 18 holes of continued frustration, Tice is the right man to see. He has given more than 52,000 lessons in his outstanding career and charges $50

per hour to work on your swing.

The course features an interesting combination of holes, including a 272-yard par 4 at No. 7 and a 266-yard par 4 at No. 10, both of which will catch the attention of big-hitter with dream of hitting the green off the tee.

Leon Valley also features a 224-yard par 3, and several challenging par 4s that include the 446-yard No. 2 and the 457-yard ninth hole and the 428-yard No. 11. All three holes will put your long irons to the test.

The par 5s range in difficulty and in length from the 497-yard 18th hole to the long and demanding 541-yard No. 3 and the 589-yard No. 16.

Carlie Tice is the course owner and the head pro. He has given more than 52,000 lessons in his outstanding career.

Like an old, trusted friend or a favorite traditional meeting place, Live Oak Country Club has stood the test of time for more than 60 years in Weatherford.

The course was opened in the early 1930s in what was once lonely, wide-open pasture land outside of Fort Worth.

The city of Weatherford has grown considerably over the years and Live Oak Country Club has changed from a rough-hewn layout with sand greens to a well-kept course with bentgrass greens.

Live Oak currently plays as a nine-hole course with a par 35, but don't go thinking this course

is a pushover.

The trees, consisting of live oaks and other varieties, have grown up over the last 60 years and the native brush can grab any shot that strays too far off the fairway.

While newer and more modern courses have been built around the Weatherford area,

Live Oak still draws a steady stream of customers.

As a semi-private operation, the course has members but also offers public play and tournaments.

The best holes at Live Oak include the 165-yard, par-3 No. 5, which has water around the green and trees right and left and two greenside bunkers.

No. 7 is a 204-yard par 3 with trees lining the fairway and water in front. A ditch down the left side catches any shots that wander 20 feet left of the green.

No. 9 is a 518-yard par 5 with trees on both sides of the fairway and a green protected by two sand traps.

The trees, consisting of live oaks and other varieties, have grown up over the last 60 years and native brush can grab any shot that strays off the fairway.

At most municipal golf courses around the state, you hear nothing but grumbling in the locker rooms about slow play, poor course conditions and how the golf course is not being run at maximum efficiency.

Most city governments have realized there is much truth to those complaints and have leased out their course operations to private management companies who can operate them more efficiently.

That makes Lockhart State Park Golf Course somewhat of an iconoclast.

Carved out of a 263-acre park in 1938, it is still the only golf course in the state that is owned

Lockhart State Park Golf Course
Route 3, PO Box 69
Lockhart 78644
512-398-3479
A nine-hole public course.

• • •

and operated by the State of Texas. You'll hear few complaints from the regulars here who take advantage of the $7 all-day weekday green fees.

They enjoy a well-maintained nine-hole layout that is user friendly with a 110 slope rating and no sand traps. The layout is generally open, but strategically

placed trees do require a certain degree of accuracy.

There are only two water holes on the course, with players crossing Clear Fork Creek on the first and ninth holes.

The toughest hole is the 430-yard, par-4 No. 3, which plays downhill off the tee and then back uphill to a green nestled in a grove of trees.

One of the easiest holes is the 295-yard, par-4 No. 5 that can be easily reached by big-hitters, and the other par 4s are of the driver-wedge variety — 350, 330, 325 — giving golfers plenty of opportunities to make birdies and shoot a good score.

Carved out of a 263-acre park in 1938, Lockhart State Park is still the only golf course in the state that is owned and operated by the state of Texas.

Terry Dill has had a full life. He grew up in Fort Worth and went on to get his bachelor's degree from the University of Texas in 1962. After graduation, he lived the vagabond existence of the pro golf tours for almost 13 years. After he was no longer effective against the younger players, Dill went back to school.

He enrolled at the University of Texas Law School, got his degree in 1979 and then became a law professor for three years at Texas A&M. But after another decade away from pro golf, Dill started to get the itch again. He dusted off the clubs, worked the kinks out of his body and joined

Lost Creek Country Club
2612 Lost Creek Boulevard
Austin 78746
Pro: Jim Beard
512-892-2032
A par-72, 6,861-yard private club.

• • •

the Senior PGA Tour in 1991.

Somewhere in between — 1973 to be exact — Dill got the opportunity to work as a golf course architect when he teamed up with Dave Bennett to design Lost Creek Country Club.

At Lost Creek, Dill and Bennett took advantage of the same stretch of Texas Hill Country

real estate that has produced Texas Top 100 Courses such as Barton Creek, Austin Country Club Lakeway Resort and the Hills of Lakeway. They took advantage of the natural elevation changes and tree-lined fairways, and added water on every hole. With the trees and hills lining the course, there is little room to stray.

"We have water and other hazards on each and every hole," pro Pat O'Hara says. "It will test the patience of any golfer."

Like the name implies, Lost Creek is not easy to get to for those unfamiliar with Texas Hill Country. But once they find it, most golfers agree their search is well rewarded.

Terry Dill and Dave Bennett took advantage of the same Hill Country terrain that produced courses such as Hills of Lakeway and Barton Creek Resort.

Contrary to its name, all the pines appear to be presented and accounted for here.

In fact, a more appropriate name for this little nine-hole course is "Lost in the Pines."

Lost Pines was built in the Depression era with the sweat and manual labor of hundreds of members of the Civilian Conservation Corps.

Under the direction of architect T.P. Haney, Jr., they produced a 3,223-yard, par-35 layout that is one of the most interesting courses in the state and has been ranked by *The Dallas Morning News* as the top nine-hole course in the state.

Lost Pines Golf Course

1011 Akaloa Drive
Bastrop 78602
512-321-2327
Pro: Rudy Belmares
A nine-hole public course.

• • •

The National Park Service recently approved a $500,000 grant to build nine more holes.

While the course is short, the tree-lined fairways demand accuracy to keep out of trouble.

At No. 4, bunkers in the fairway demand accuracy off the tee, and a large pond protects the front of the green.

No. 6 is a 149-yard par 3 where golfers must hit their tee shots to an elevated, kidney-shaped shaped green.

No. 7 is a long dogleg right that measures 557 yards with three great shots required to reach the green.

No. 9 is a 387-yard par 4 that requires golfers to clear two ditches en route to the green on this dogleg left hole.

"The holes have very tight, very straight fairways," pro Kevin Adare says.

"In the summer, we cut the grass short and the fairways play very narrow.

"This course may start easy, but it gets a lot tougher."

Contrary to its name, all the pines appear to be present and accounted for.
In fact, a more appropriate name for this course is "Lost in the Pines."

All golf courses start out as a vision. Eventually, the vision gets put down on paper at a drafting table. Finally, it is permanently carved into the earth for all to see. This particular vision belonged to Fred Morgan Sr., a local businessman who dreamed up Lost Valley Ranch Resort in the 1940s. The second nine was added in 1976, completing a layout that now measures 6,210 yards.

The dream, however, was in jeopardy of dying. Although the nearby race track has lured more and more out-of-town business, Morgan ran into financial trouble in the 1990s and sold the club.

Lost Valley Ranch Resort

PO Box 1509
Bandera 78003
210-460-7958
Pro: Robbie Goodwin
A par-72, 6,210-yard public course.

• • •

The course has two lakes that come into play on the front and back nines. The two nines have different styles. The front nine is shaded by several large oak trees. The back is more of a links-style layout with greens that are more undulating. When the greens were first installed on the front nine, they were intended to be temporary greens that could easily be overhauled, but they haven't been changed in more than 40 years.

No. 3 is a 360-yard par 4 with a lake guarding the green. The par-3 No. 14 is only 200 yards, but has a lake guarding the green to prevent many players from going for home off the tee.

No. 17 is a 615-yard par 5 that takes three huge shots to find the green for birdie or par. No. 18 is a 310-yard par 4 with trees in the background of the green.

"It's a fun course," greens superintendent Lionel Lopez says. "My dad was here for 20 years and and now it's my turn. We just need somebody to come in here and spend a little money."

"It's a fun course. May dad was here for 20 years and now it's my turn.
We just need somebody to come in here and spend a little money."

Lubbock Country Club was originally built by architect Warren Cantrell as the centerpiece for a golf, hunting and fishing club. The old farm house was redesigned to serve as the clubhouse when the course was built in the 1950s.

Cantrell was a multi-talented man who was good at everything he did, including golf. So he eventually left his firm due to ill health, and instead became a club pro in Lubbock, and eventually was elected president of the PGA of America from 1964–65 and served as golf coach at Texas Tech University from 1953–58.

Atypical of West Texas,

Lubbock Country Club
PO Box 1477
Lubbock 79408
806-763-1871
Pro: Mark Vinson
A par-72, 6,911-yard private club.
• • •

Cantrell designed a rolling course that features more than 5,000 trees on the 6,911-yard layout, producing a course that demands both brawn and brains.

The layout starts out with a 534-yard par 5 with out-of-bounds down the right side. No. 4 is the No. 1 handicap hole. It is a 456-yard, par 4 dogleg left with out-of-

bounds down the right side. It is followed by two more demanding par 4s at the 424-yard No. 8 and the 430-yard No. 9.

No. 9 is a 430-yard par 4 that plays along an old creek bed with a tight driving area past a large cottonwood tree that juts into the fairway. The approach is to a well-bunkered green;

The 395-yard, par-4 15th doglegs to the left around a lake that comes into play in the landing area on the left-hand side of the fairway, but should not be a factor on the approach to the green.

No. 11 is a 543-yard par 5 that doglegs to the right with out-of-bounds running down the left-hand side of the fairway.

Atypical of West Texas, William Cantrell designed a rolling course that features more than 5,000 trees and requires both brains and brawn.

More than five decades before Robert von Hagge and Bruce Devlin came along to build one of the state's best golf courses just up the road at Crown Colony, Lufkin Country Club was the center of activity for the Lufkin golf and social scene.

The club was built in 1920 on hilly, heavily-wooded terrain and the 6,347-yard layout may be short by modern standards, but still provides a stiff challenge to even the most accomplished golfer. The layout is built around a large lake that comes into play on several holes.

The front nine plays to par of 37 with three par 5s and two par

Lufkin Country Club
1624 Sayers
Lufkin 75901
409-639-3664
A par-72, 6,347-yard private club.
• • •

3s. The back nine plays to par 35 with two par 3s and one par 5.

No. 6 should be an easy birdie hole for even an average golfer. It is a 448-yard par 5 where the only obstacle is a creek that crosses the fairway about 100 yards from the green and out-of-bounds down the left-hand side. No. 8 is another very reachable

par 5 at 486 yards, but golfers again must cross a creek twice on the way to the green. Some golfers might have to lay up twice short of the creeks that cross the fairway at 225 yards from the tee and again about 100 yards short of the green. Bigger hitters can carry the first creek and put themselves in position to reach the green in two.

No. 18 is a 298-yard par 4 that is driveable for some golfers and provides an exciting finish. Two bunkers on the left and right of the green leave an opening in front, but golfers going for the green must be careful not to go out-of-bounds on the right side of the fairway.

The layout may be short by modern standards, but still provides a stiff challenge to even the most accomplished golfers.

Everyone likes a home-course advantage. Everyone feels at home at Luling Golf Club, especially those golfers who play a fade.

The opposite is true, then, if you play a hook or a draw. A fence runs down the left side of the first five holes, with out-of-bounds waiting on every shot that has the urge to take a 45-degree left turn.

"I guess that would make us a fader's paradise," manager W.H. Weeks says. "If you play a fade here, you can't get into trouble."

Accuracy is the biggest pre-requisite here, since the 5,937-yard layout will not challenge

long-ball hitters. But that out-of-bounds fence and the San Marcos River, which comes into play on five consecutive holes from Nos. 3-7, lie in wait for errant shots.

This is a nine-hole course that golfers play twice from a second set of tees. Some of the holes play as much as 40 yards longer the second time around. It is owned by the City of Luling.

The hardest hole is No. 7. It measures only 332 yards on the scorecard, but the San Marcos River runs down the left side and cuts out into the fairway between the tee and green. Players are required to carry the corner of the river about 175 yards to set up a short approach to the green.

The second time around, golfers use a second set of tees that make some of the holes play up to 40 yards longer.

That should pose no problem for big hitters, who can occasionally reach the green, "but we don't have many John Dalys out here," says Weeks. "It's a short course, but a tough little course."

A fence runs down the left side of the first five holes, out-of-bounds waiting on every shot that has the urge to take a 45-degree left turn.

Long before the North American Free Trade Agreement, people have been making a run for the border to play McAllen Country Club.

McAllen is located on the U.S.-Mexico border along the Rio Grande River, and in 1947 golf was brought to the area when McAllen Country Club started out as a nine-hole golf course.

Houston-based architect Jay Riviere came back in 1968 to build the second nine and create a championship layout.

The fairways are plush, and the greens are elevated and undulating on this layout. The course is short and flat but its narrow fair-

ways are lined with large oak trees. McAllen's combination of tight fairways and small undulating greens put a premium on accuracy.

On many holes, in fact, golfers are better off using an iron off the tee instead of a driver.

The course is actually located seven miles from Mexico and is close to the Rio Grande River.

The area continues to be one of the faster-growing areas of the state and the club continues to undergo renovations to keep it up to 21st century standards.

The greens were rebuilt in 1993, the clubhouse was remodeled in 1996 and a new irrigation system is being installed in 1998 to make sure the greens and fairways remain lush in the summer.

The signature hole is No. 7, a 410-yard par 4 that leads up to the clubhouse with a long narrow fairway and an approach shot that requires players to hit over a lake to reach the green.

No. 17 is a hard 225-yard par 3 over water.

The combination of tight fairways and small greens put a premium on accuracy. On many holes, golfers are better off using an iron off the tee.

Although many of his original finger-prints have now been smudged by several generations of golf course architects, John Bredemus was one of the pioneers of Texas golf and is still known as the Father of Texas golf course architecture.

Some eight years before Marvin Leonard would employ him to build his famed Colonial Country Club, Bredemus came to Fort Worth to build an 18-hole layout for a private club that was later sold to the city and made public. In 1957, there were discussions about selling Meadowbrook to a private group for development, but city officials decided against it.

Meadowbrook Municipal Golf Course

1815 Jensen Road

Fort Worth 76112

817-457-4616

Pro: Gary McMillian

A par-71, 6,416-yard public course.

• • •

"I'm sure the board will do all it can to keep this public golf course open on the east side — it's the only one in that part of town," former parks director Harry Taylor said.

Once the city made a commitment to keep Meadowbrook public, in 1962 architect Ralph Plummer came in to do a $100,000 renovation that included the building of several dams on a creek that winds through the course to form five lakes creating new hazards and providing irrigation. He constructed a long lake between the 12th and 13th fairways, one in front of the No. 1 green and another along the left-hand side of the 16th fairway.

The 475-yard, par-4 fifth is perhaps one of the longest par 4s in the D/FW area. It features water down the left side and trees on the right. The hole turns slightly to the right and players must cross a creek off the tee and avoid one of the four interconnecting lakes Plummer built on the inside corner of the dogleg.

Eight years before John Bredemus built his famed Colonial Country Club, he came to Fort Worth to build an 18-hole private club that later became public.

While Houston's Champions Golf Club can claim one championship golf course designed by legendary architect Ralph Plummer, Meadowbrook Golf Complex in Lubbock is the only course in the state that can claim being the home of two original Plummer designs.

Plummer built Meadowbrook in the late 1940s for the City of Lubbock — they were originally known as the No. 1 and No. 2 courses, but were renamed as the Canyon and Creek Courses.

While Plummer built some of the state's best courses — including those that have hosted national championships like Champions,

Meadowbrook Golf Complex Canyon Course

601 Municipal Drive

Lubbock 79403

806-765-6679

A 36-hole public course.

• • •

Northwood and Columbian, he designed Meadowbrook for the average golfer — not the game's greatest players.

The Canyon Course is the most challenging of the two courses. It is a par-71, 6,445-yard layout that plays to a 120-slope rating. The Creek Course is a par-71, 6,276-yard layout.

The most demanding hole on the Creek layout may be the 230-yard, par-3 sixth hole.

The Canyon Course has wide open fairways and very few hazards. It starts out with a 585-yard par 5 on No. 1 with a straight, narrow fairway that requires players to just "grip it and rip it."

Warren Cantrell renovated the courses in 1955. He was an engineering and architecture graduate from Texas A&M who became the golf coach at Texas Tech from 1953–58 and president of the PGA of America in 1964–65.

In 1988, architect Bob Lohmann gave both golf courses a facelift to help them keep up with the growing competition.

Meadowbrook Golf Complex is the only course in the state that can claim being the home of not one, but two original Ralph Plummer designs.

Meadowlakes Golf and Country Club in Marble Falls was able to blend Lake LBJ and the beautiful Hill Country into a scenic and challenging golf layout.

It opened as a nine-hole country club in October 1974 at about the same time Robert Trent Jones was building the first course at nearby Horseshoe Bay.

Meadowlakes was designed by architect Leon Howard. The par-72 course plays 6,343 yards through trees, private homes and several water hazards. It is set on 138 acres with the front nine cutting through a large pecan orchard.

Most of the Bermuda greens

Meadowlakes Golf and Country Club
220 Meadowlakes Drive
Marble Falls 78654
830-693-7826
Pro: Johnny Zavala
A par-72, 6,343 yard semi-private club.
• • •

are very large but angled and can produce many a three-putt to the unwary golfer.

It operated as a medium-sized country club until 1994, when owner Ralph Riley sold it to a Louisiana-based company who announced plans to turn it into a semi-private club and major upgrades to the property.

While the front and back nines are different in makeup, both have proven to be a fun challenge to members and guests alike. The back nine is somewhat different with more water and less elevation. Four of the back nine holes have water coming into play.

The 375-yard, par-4 No. 4 is guarded by a lake with a lay-up shot required to have an open look to the green. Out-of-bounds stakes run down both sides of the fairway.

The 175-yard, par-3 17th is guarded by a huge trap on the right side of an undulating green.

"The front nine is very scenic," pro John Steed says. "Golfers play right through the pecan orchard and Hill Country scenery."

It is set on 138 acres with the frone nine cutting through a large pecan orchard. The back nine has more water and fewer elevation changes.

Long before the days when golf course architecture was actually considered a profession, Leon Howard was busy becoming the most prolific architect in the state of Texas.

Howard never received much credit for his work like big-name Texas architects such as John Bredemus and Ralph Plummer, but Howard designed more than 100 courses around the state.

He specialized in building many low-budget golf courses for municipalities and the Farmers Home Association.

Howard realized the importance of the bottom line, and the ability to build golf courses that

Mesquite Golf Course
825 North Highway 67
Mesquite 75150
972-270-7457
Pro: Rusty Locke
A par-71, 6,280-yard municipal course.
• • •

could be easily maintained by city staff. While many of his layouts were strong, they never received the tender-loving care that is required to maintain a top-notch golf course. It was golf for the masses.

And once Howard finished a project, he never had much control over the way they were main-

tained after he left.

That was exactly the case in 1965 when the city of Mesquite hired Howard to build a golf course on a wooded, hilly-piece of property in the flood plain of Duck Creek.

Over the next 20 years, course officials found out the hard way. While Howard designed a challenging layout that took advantage of the hilly and wooded terrain and provided excellent shot-making decisions, the course was haunted by flooding on a regular basis. The layout has been re-routed a number of times to get the holes out of danger's path, but many of the original holes remain intact.

Leon Howard designed a challenging layout that took advantage of the hilly and wooded terrain and provided excellent shot-making decisions.

There are military bases throughout Texas.

Whether it is a training ground for the Army, Air Force, Navy or Marines, these are usually in out of the way places, far off the beaten path with not many recreational opportunities for off-duty military personnel.

Welcome to Dyess Air Force Base, home of Mesquite Grove Golf Course.

In the 1950s and 1960s, most of these military bases were given grants to build golf courses to provide personnel with an on-base recreational facility.

They were built from Corpus

Mesquite Grove Golf Course

766 Mesquite Trail
Dyess AFB 79607
Pro: Paul Carlisle
915-696-4384
A par-72, 7,005-yard military course.

• • •

Christi to El Paso, San Antonio to Fort Hood. Mesquite Grove is one of the best of the bunch.

The par-72, 7,005-yard layout was built in 1960 and is a challenge for players of all skill levels.

The elevated greens are bent-grass, and the bermuda fairways remain plush throughout the year.

As if the golf course wasn't long enough as it is, wind is also a major factor here.

Selecting the proper club and compensating for wind direction and velocity is a major part of the playing strategy at Mesquite Grove, which was named after the grove of mesquite trees from which it was carved on the flat West Texas prairie.

The signature hole is No. 6, a 397-yard par 4 with a water hazard in front of the green.

The most difficult hole is No. 9, a 432-yard par 4 that is already long but also plays into a prevailing head wind.

Wind is a major factor here, so selecting the proper club and compensating for wind direction and velocity is a major part of the playing strategy.

Three years before Ralph Plummer built the famed Cypress Creek Course at Champions Golf Club he came to Midland to build Midland Country Club in 1954.

While golf isn't considered to be a form of exercise, Plummer produced a golf course that will wear out even the most physically fit golfer.

Midland is one of the longest courses in the state at 7,354 yards, requiring players to hit lots of drivers, long irons and fairway woods before they earn their trip to the 19th hole. When you factor in the West Texas winds, it can be one of the most difficult courses

---

Midland Country Club

6101 North Highway 349
Midland 79705
Pro: Terry Lester
915-683-3621
A par-72, 7,354-yard private club.

• • •

---

in the state.

In addition to length, golfers must also negotiate their way through narrow fairways lined by oak and mesquite trees. The bent-grass greens are large and fast and water comes into play on seven holes.

Midland Country Club originally was organized in 1927, but

---

moved to its current location in 1954. A year after it opened in 1955, members of the U.S. Ryder Cup team — including Ben Hogan, Jimmy Demaret, Byron Nelson, Jackie Burke Jr. and Bob Rosburg — played an exhibition match here. It also the 1997 Texas State Amateur championship.

Ron Kirby redesigned the course in 1979, followed by Dick Nugent in 1985.

The signature hole is No. 15, a 601-yard par 5 that double doglegs to the left and then back to the right to the green.

No. 4 is a 411-yard par 4 that is one of the toughest on the course with its tight fairway from tee to green.

Midland Country Club is one of the longest courses in the state at 7,354 yards, requiring players to hit lots of drivers, long irons and fairway woods.

Mill Ridge Golf Club is located in the rolling hills of East Texas, near Lake Livingston. It is less than one hour north of Houston's Bush Intercontinental Airport on U.S. Highway 59.

Moderate winter weather has made the area a growing "Winter Texan" site for many retirees.

This scenic nine-hole course winds around the historic Ogletree sawmill.

The Ogletrees have been producing lumber since 1902 and the sawmill is in daily production.

Much of the sawmill's operation can be viewed while playing the course. A limited number of mill tours are available year-round.

Mill Ridge Golf Club

1501 Platt Street

Livingston 77351

409-327-3535

Pro: Bobby Brame

A nine-hole public course.

• • •

Mill Ridge offers a full-service golf facility in a small-town setting. The course was built on a hill that offers panoramic views of the countryside near Lake Livingston.

The fairways are tree-lined, with either water or out-of-bounds or both and bunkers coming into play on almost every hole. It is a short, tight course surrounded by tall pines and oaks.

The signature hole is No. 4, a 500-yard par 5 that is a slight dog-leg right that is lined by tall pines down the right side of the hole.

The tee shot requires a 200-yard carry over a lake. On the approach, golfers must clear an eight-foot bunker in front of the green.

No. 3 is a 425-yard par 4 that plays into the picnic pavilion. Off the tee, golfers are faced with a narrow driving area with a difficult long iron to a green that is protected by a lake on the left.

No. 8 is a 518-yard par 5 that doglegs right just before the green between a grove of trees on both sides of the fairway.

The course was built on a hill that offers panoramic views of the country side. The fairways are tree-lined, with either water or out-of-bounds.

Leon Howard can laugh about it now. He was just getting started in the golf course design business back in the 1950s. A former Austin parks director commissioned Howard to build what would be the first of many municipal golf courses in his career.

How ironic. A Texas Aggie was building a golf course in the shadow of the University of Texas. A golf course that would one day become home to the Texas Longhorns golf team and would be named after a former All-America player at UT who joined the air force after college and died in a training jet crash.

Morris Williams Golf Course

4305 Manor Road

Austin 73723

512-926-1298

Pro: Gib Kizer

A par-72, 6,636-yard municipal course.

• • •

Williams is an Austin native who became the city's youngest junior champion at age 13 and dominated the local junior scene for many years.

Another Austin golfer, George Hannon, served as head pro until he retired in 1994. Hannon also coached the Longhorns to 12 SWC and two NCAA titles.

Knowing the outcome of the project could make or break his future in the business, he and his wife moved into an apartment near the course to oversee every stage of construction. He wanted to make sure everything was done right. He even rigged up a tractor so his 7-year-old son Warren could help.

The course starts out simply enough with a straight 373-yard par 4. The challenge gets greater with a par-5 second hole, which measures 540 yards with woods right and a slight dogleg to the left. The back nine features heavy woods and water on Nos. 11-14. The golfer must hit over water to the green on Nos. 11 and 12.

It's ironic that an Aggie built a golf course that has been home to the University of Texas golf team and would be named after a former UT player.

The scenic Mountain Valley Country Club was built in 1965 on a piece of prime real estate alongside a large lake.

Mountain Valley is located in Joshua, a growing bedroom community just about 30 minutes south of Fort Worth.

It was built before the Fort Worth area's golf course boom in the 1990s and has continued to meet with increased competition from nearby courses such as Walnut Creek in Mansfield and Hidden Creek in Burleson.

Mountain Valley's par-71, 6,541-yard layout is open on the front nine but narrow on the back. It was designed around two

Mountain Valley Country Club

PO Box 726
Joshua 76058
817-295-7126
A par-71, 6,541-yard private club.

• • •

big lakes and a creek that runs through the middle of the golf course. The course plays to a moderate 118 slope rating.

A creek that flows into the lake comes into play on several holes. The fairways, bordered by a standard cut of rough, are narrow and lined by a variety of trees that can affect your shots.

There are no sand bunkers on the course, but there are a number of grass bunkers. The average-sized greens are well sloped and fast. Three of the tee boxes are elevated, and many of the fairways dogleg left and right.

This course's signature hole is No. 18, a 183-yard par 3 that requires a tee shot over a lake to the green. There is also water on both sides of the fairway and the green, leaving golfers with little margin of error on their long-iron approach.

No. 3 is the most difficult hole on the course. It is a 523-yard par 5. No. 11 is another par 5, measuring 535 yards. Both are difficult to reach in two.

A creek comes into play on several holes. The fairways are narrow and lined by a variety of trees that can affect your shots.

Unlike many of the fancy or exclusive courses that dot the Austin area, Mustang Creek exists solely for those golfers who want a bargain and a fun, fast round of golf.

The course was opened in early 1915 as Taylor Country Club. By the 1980s, there were not enough members or money to support the club as a private enterprise so the decision was made to go public. Since the takeover in 1989, course conditions and play have greatly improved.

"Every year, we hold the city championship in July and people show up thinking they're going to

Mustang Creek Golf Club

PO Box 1385
Taylor 76574
512-365-1332
Manager: Mike McCown
A nine-hole semi-private course.

• • •

murder this little course," pro Mike McCown says. "The wind blows and the greens are small and it just doesn't happen. The hardest thing here is to keep your shot on the green. Your short game is key."

Last year, more than 9,000 rounds were recorded and a new pond was added to the two

already on the course. At 2,600 yards from the back tees, the course has a par of only 34. There are separate tees that allow the course to be played twice with a slightly different look for a full 18-hole round.

The course lies on an open plain without a windbreak from trees. The wind, blowing mainly from the south, is a major factor. That can make it extremely difficult to hit the small Bermuda greens.

No matter where you are hitting from, No. 1 is a par 4 and has water on both sides. The new pond is just to the front of the first tee and another water hazard is directly in front of the green.

"People show up thinking they're going to murder this little course but the wind blows and the greens are small and it just doesn't happen."

New Jersey developer William H. Maurer visited Houston one day in the 1970s to look at some land on the west side of Lake Houston. He was looking for a place to build his dream of a lakeside town.

Maurer, however, didn't like what he saw and was on his way back to the airport when a headstrong Realtor tried to save the day. On the way back, Realtor Les Appelt suggested a detour to the opposite side of the lake.

"There's another piece of property on the east side," Appelt told Maurer, "but I don't think you can afford it."

The rest is history. Shortly

Newport on Lake Houston

16401 Golf Club Drive

Crosby 77532

281-328-2541

Pro: Scott Cannon

A par-72, 6,496-yard semi-private club.

• • •

thereafter, Maurer announced the development of a $700 million, 6,000-acre residential and recreational complex with 1.5 miles of shoreline on Lake Houston and one-half mile frontage on the San Jacinto River.

Maurer was a former golf pro who envisioned a 54-hole facility as the centerpiece for his community. Later, Maurer faced opposition from environmental groups when he applied to the Corps of Engineers for permission to dredge five areas along the river to transport prefabricated houses by barge to the development.

The first course, designed by architect Gary Darling, opened in 1972 and hosted an LPGA event in 1977–78. It is a test of accuracy and course management. It is not long, but features lots of out-of-bounds as it winds through the housing development and challenges shot-making with small, well-trapped greens.

The 18th is the toughest hole, with water in play both off the tee and on the approach.

It is a test of accuracy and course management. It is not long, but it challenges shot-making with small, well-trapped greens.

Long before the Field of Dreams, there was Northcliffe Country Club. Only this time, when it was built, the golfers and home buyers didn't come. Northcliffe Country Club has undergone many changes in its 20-year history, but has bounced back from every setback to remain a fine test of golf.

The course opened in 1979 and was designed by Kerrville-based architect Joe Finger as the centerpiece of a grand housing development by U.S. Homes. The plan included a retirement village called Scenic Hills, with a huge flagpole constructed to mark the entrance. But the community

Northcliffe Country Club

5301 Country Club Boulevard

Cibolo 78108

830-606-7351

Pro: John Clay

A par-72, 6,080-yard semi-private club.

• • •

never quite got off the ground. Tax-law changes prevented the retirement community from growing, leaving only the flagpole, the course and some hard financial times. In 1992, longtime pro John Clay and a group of members bought the course.

One of Finger's characteristics at Northcliffe is the prominent use of water and several dry creek beds that run through the course. Probably the most unique hole is the par-4 14th. This downhill 365-yard hole sits directly alongside Interstate 35. A shot sliced too far right could be headed to Dallas on the next 18-wheeler.

One unique aspect of the course is that it actually has 19 holes. As part of the contract with U.S. Homes, Finger agreed to build an additional nine holes when 100 homes were sold. As part of a good-faith effort, one hole, a par 4, was built with tees, fairway and a green. Today, the hole sits alone, slightly overgrown and serving as a reminder of the second course that never came.

One of Finger's characteristics at Northcliffe is the prominent use of water and several dry creek beds that run through the course.

San Antonio's Joe Behlau came out of the Army to work as a golf pro and course architect. He got off to humble beginnings, starting with a driving range on some vacant land behind his house, then adding a putting green and some practice holes. One thing led to another and, in the late 1960s, Behlau was asked to build a golf course in north San Antonio.

Behlau started construction on Northern Hills Country Club in the summer of 1968 during San Antonio's Hemisfair celebration. The first nine was opened in August of 1969 and the second nine in 1970. While Behlau had

Northern Hills Country Club

13202 Scarsdale
San Antonio 78217
Pro: Billy Newlin
210-655-8026
A par-71, 6,472-yard private club.

• • •

no experience designing a full golf course, he had read the writings of all famous architects and had definite ideas of his own. Both sides end with a par 3, an idea he picked up from none other than golf legend Gene Sarazen.

"I once read Sarazen said the fairest hole in golf was a par 3. Everybody starts from the same

place, using the same angle, from the same distance," Behlau said.

The par-5, 503-yard 10th is a dogleg right over water, downwind, with houses on the right. Another feature of the course is the long par 3s. The shortest of the four is 185 yards.

"We didn't have a lot of room to work with," Behlau says, "If you'll notice, almost every hole has its opposite.

"I designed the course clockwise on the front side so the hooker would go out-of-bounds and the slicer would come back into the course.

"On the back, the slicer goes out-of-bounds and the hooker can play down the fairway."

Gene Sarazen said the fairest hole in golf was a par 3. Everybody is starting from the same place, using the same angle, from the same distance.

As a military brat, Bill Rogers lived in Germany, North Africa and Alabama, which is where he first began to play golf.

By the age of 13, Rogers was playing competitively, but it was not until his family moved to Texarkana that he developed the game that made him a star on the PGA Tour.

In Texarkana, Rogers developed a close relationship with Northridge Country Club pro Jerry Robinson.

Under Robinson's tutelage, Roger's game progressed to earn a scholarship at the University of Houston, where he roomed with Bruce Lietzke, who also went on

Northridge Country Club

120 Bill Rogers Drive
Texarkana 75507
903-792-9331
Pro: Richard O. Rogers
A par-71, 6,471-yard private club.

• • •

to PGA Tour stardom.

Rogers was nicknamed "Panther," because he seemed like a caged cat as he paced back and forth while waiting to hit his next shot.

Rogers was a collegiate All-American in 1973 and earned his PGA Tour card the following year. Between 1975 and 1983, Rogers

won five PGA Tour events. In 1981, he put his name among golf's immortals when he won the British Open.

Northridge was a great golf course to prepare Rogers for some of the best golf courses around the world.

Built in a heavily-forested area on the Texas-Arkansas border, the par-71, 6,471-yard layout was built in 1962 and features tree-lined fairways and very undulating Bermuda greens.

Numerous creeks and lakes come into play throughout the layout, putting a premium more on length than accuracy.

The No. 1 handicap hole is the 581-yard, par-5 No. 5.

Northridge is where Texas Golf Hall of Famer Bill Rogers developed his game before going on to become a star in college and on the PGA Tour.

Billy Martindale and Don January worked as a team to build many golf courses across the state, but when the Senior PGA Tour was formed in the late 1970s January dusted off his clubs and went back out on tour.

That left Martindale to his own devices, and one of his first solo projects was Oak Forest Country Club in Longview. He built this 6,701-yard, par-72 layout on predominantly flat terrain in a valley, and scattered 30 bunkers on the course. The course is a combination of the links courses of Scotland and the traditional courses of the United States.

The front nine is more of a

Oak Forest Country Club

601 Tomlinson Parkway
Longview 75604
903-297-3448
Pro: Don Prigmore
A par-72, 6,701-yard private club.

• • •

links design with few trees and somewhat narrow fairways that are lined by either a creek or out-of-bounds stakes. There is some subtle mounding that can create uneven lies, and water comes into play on every hole on the front side. The Bermuda greens on both sides are undulating and fast. The back nine features more tree-

lined fairways through the tall oaks.

No. 8 is the signature hole. It is a 173-yard par 3 with a creek on the left and bunkers left and right. Tee shots that fall short of the intended target will likely wind up in a grass bunker in front of the green.

No. 18 is a 576-yard par 5 that features two large trees standing in the center of the fairway and come into play on the second shot.

A creek runs down the right side of the fairway, then crosses the fairway about 20 yards from the green, discouraging any long hitters who may be thinking about going for the green in two.

The front nine is a links-style design with few trees and fairways lined by a creek or out-of-bounds. The back nine features tree-lined fairways.

The logo for Odessa Country Club is an oil derrick inside a big O. It's appropriate, since the discovery of oil in the Permian Basin is the main reason people ever moved here in the first place.

It's also appropriate since it was with Black Gold that Odessa Country Club was built in 1939 by architect John Bredemus.

Just shy of its 60th birthday, Odessa is a tradition-laden club that annually hosts the Odessa Pro-Am, which over the years has attracted players such as Lee Trevino and entertainers like Steve Martin.

Bredemus' design is a typical

Odesssa Country Club

7184 Club Drive
Odessa 79760
915-366-4445
Pro: Clay Kinnaird
A par-72, 6,829-yard private club.

• • •

old-style golf course, measuring 6,829 yards with flat, tree-lined fairways, fast and undulating bentgrass greens.

The West Texas winds can make it difficult to keep the ball in the fairway.

The signature hole is No. 9, a 215-yard par 3 where golfers must hit a long iron or wood to a shal-

low green protected by a large swale in front that usually has an adverse affect on any shot that doesn't carry all the way to the green.

No. 7 is a 560-yard par 5 that plays into the prevailing wind. It's a scary sight from the tee, with water right and out-of-bounds left and a narrow fairway in between. It is the No. 1 handicap hole on the course.

No. 14 is a 430-yard par 4 with a tight, tree-lined landing area to an elevated green that is a tough target from 200 yards out. If you miss the green, most golfers are unsuccessful in their attempt to salvage par by getting up and down from around the green.

Just shy of its 60th birthday, Odessa Country Club is a tradition-laden club built with Black Gold from the Permian Basin.

O lmos Basin opened in the early 1960s and remains one of San Antonio's most popular public courses.

The course is located just minutes north of downtown and was built by the city to serve a growing population. George Hoffman, a native Yankee who moved to Big Spring with his parents at an early age, was hired to build the course after he had done several courses in Mexico and Central and South America.

When it opened Sept. 15, 1963, it became San Antonio's first municipal course in 30 years. In a press release issued when the

course opened, officials said they hoped Olmos would be used for pro tournaments, city championships and public play.

Before Cedar Creek and Mission Del Lago opened in 1989, Olmos ranked as the most popular municipal course in San Antonio with nearly 80,000 rounds a year.

"The course was easy for older men to walk and always drew a big crowd," Olmos pro Jerry Hill says. "That's one of the reasons they liked it here."

Of course, certain problems go along with being built in a flood plain, and Olmos has not been immune to flood problems during heavy rains. The course was briefly closed in May of 1993 when rains brought water almost to the front door.

The City of San Antonio began renovations to the course in 1994 including the planting of new trees and restoring cart paths. Among the improvements will be the planting of 60–70 new trees and restored cart paths.

Before Cedar Creek and Mission Del Lago opened, Olmos Basin ranked as the most popular city course in San Antonio with nearly 80,000 rounds a year.

B efore there was Horseshoe Bay, there was Packsaddle Country Club.

Six years before Robert Trent Jones Sr. put Hill Country on the map with his first of three courses at Horseshoe Bay, Texas-based architect Leon Howard also saw the beauty of this Hill Country land on the scenic shores of Lake LBJ.

Howard came here in 1968 to design a golf course to accommodate the growing number of Texas residents who were buying real estate and weekend homes in the Hill Country.

Almost three decades later, Packsaddle is still in business and

the people are still coming in record numbers.

While not as glamorous as its neighor across the lake, Packsaddle is a challenging par-72, 7,157-yard layout over rolling Hill Country terrain.

No. 7 is the prettiest hole at Packsaddle. It plays slightly uphill with the green situated between

natural granite outcroppings and a heavily-wooded area.

No. 9 and No. 11 are both 548-yard par 5s. No. 9 has a creek that runs across the fairway about 300 yards out.

The creek also crosses the 11th about 200 yards out, forcing golfers to make a decision to go for it or lay up.

No. 15 is the longest par 4. It is a 429-yard hole that requires two solid shots to reach the green in regulation.

The par-5, 532-yard No. 17 is the longest hole on the course.

Packsaddle is a semi-private club, offering daily-fee play to guests as well as resident and non-resident memberships.

Six years before Robert Trent Jones Sr. built Horseshoe Bay, Leon Howard designed Packsaddle on the Hill Country terrain overlooking Lake LBJ.

Every once in a while, Senior PGA Tour pro Joe Jimenez stops by at Palo Duro Creek Golfing Club to tune up his game before he heads back out on tour to play for big money.

Here, he doesn't have to worry about TV cameras or large galleries. The only prize money at stake might be whatever gambling game he and his playing partners come up with.

Locals figure if this layout is good enough for Jimenez, it's good enough for them.

The par-72, 6,865-yard layout features wide-open fairways and fast, undulating bentgrass greens.

Palo Duro Creek Golfing Club
50 Country Club Drive
Canyon 79015
806-655-1106
Pro: Emil Hale
A par-72, 6,865-yard semi-private club.

• • •

The layout is narrow on the front nine as it winds between houses and out-of-bounds comes into play. Water also comes into play on 12 holes.

The signature hole is No. 12, a 585-yard par 5 that requires players to hit two shots over water to reach the green.

Players start off with a drive through a chute of trees and must cross water off the tee and again on the approach.

The green is surrounded by water hazards in front and back of the green. The hole's length, coupled with the potential danger involved on every shot, make this a hard par.

No. 14 is a demanding 225-yard par 3. While most players have a difficult time hitting the ball that far, there's nothing but water between the tee and green.

No. 5 is a 549-yard par 5 that is long enough for the average golfer, but also plays uphill into a prevailing wind.

Locals figure if this layout is good enough for Senior PGA Tour pro Joe Jimenez, it's good enough for them.

Texas has produced some of the best players in golf history, from Ben Hogan to Byron Nelson, from Jack Burke to Jimmy Demaret, from Tommy Bolt to Lee Trevino, from Don January to Charles Coody and from Ben Crenshaw to Tom Kite.

The list goes on and on.

But one thing most of these players have in common is the annual Top of Texas amateur tournament, which for the past 50 years has been a tradition at Pampa Country Club.

Some of the game's greatest players at one time or another have graced the fairways of this

Pampa Country Club
1701 E Harvester Avenue
Pampa 79066
806-665-8431
Pro: Mickey Piersall
A par-71, 6,295-yard semi-private club.

• • •

par-71, 6,295-yard layout that was built in 1928.

The traditional layout with tree-lined fairways and immaculate greens provide a strong challenge to the game's top amateurs.

The historic course is hilly and tree-lined but not much water comes into play.

Texas teaching legend Chuck Cook also hosts a golf school here and longtime Texas pro Mickey Pearsall is the head pro.

No. 4 is the hardest hole. It plays to a 422-yard par 4 that doglegs left off the tee. Tall trees line the left side of the fairway. On the approach, golfers hit down into a valley to an elevated green.

No. 11 is a 420-yard par 4 down a tight fairway and which again drops down into a valley.

No. 18 is a 441-yard dogleg right down a real tight fairway. You can cut the corner of the dogleg, but at the risk of getting caught in the trees.

Texas has produced some of the best players in golf history, and one thing most of them have in common is Pampa's annual Top of Texas tournament.

There are some things about a golf course an architect has no control. It's too expensive to try to outdo Mother Nature by putting a forest in an open prairie, rolling hills in a rice field or railroad ties around the bank of every water hazard.

That was one thing architects Jay Riviere and Jack Miller didn't have to worry about at Panorama. They came along in an era before dirt-moving machines became fashionable, but in this case they just tried to stand back and not get in nature's way.

But like many early golf courses, the course was constructed on a limited budget and the archi-

Panorama Country Club
73 Greenbriar
Conroe 77304
409-856-5533
Pro: Jim Davis
A 27-hole private club.

• • •

tects left feeling like they had missed an opportunity. Riviere designed the first 18. During construction, Miller made alterations to five holes on the second nine and eventually designed and completed the third nine in his first solo project.

Panorama was built in 1965 and was the patriarch of a golf

boom in Montgomery County that saw The Woodlands, Walden on Lake Conroe, April Sound, Wedgewood, Bentwater and Texas National spring up in the next 20 years. It features some of the most drastic elevation changes of any course in the area, and its fairways are lined with hardwood trees.

The course now features 27 holes. Winged Foot is the toughest of the three nine-hole layouts, featuring tighter fairways and more undulations.

Rolling Hills is the newest of the three nine-hole layouts and was built around a large man-made lake. The signature hole features an island green.

Panorama was the patriarch of a golf boom in Mountgomery County. It features some of the most dramatic elevation changes in the area.

Paris, France, is known for its history and architectural marvels such as the Eiffel Tower and the cathedral at Notre Dame. It is known for its art, with Le Louvre containing such priceless pieces of art as the Mona Lisa.

Paris, Texas, is a long way from Paris, France, but in some ways it has a museum all of its own.

Paris Golf and Country Club is a museum in its own right with a golf course that was built in 1918 and was one of the earliest in the state, especially in a rural area.

Greatness is an equal-opportunity adjective, no matter what the latitude and longitude. That's what's so special about golf in

Paris Golf and Country Club
Route 6
Paris 75462
903-785-6512
A par-70, 6,443-yard private club.

• • •

Paris, Texas, where this little private club celebrates its 80th birthday in 1998. Its traditional design, tree-lined fairways, tiny greens and great shot values have stood the test of time.

This is a target style golf course that features narrow fairways that twist and turn through the tall pines and oaks of East Texas. There

are many creeks and ponds that come into play throughout the course, putting a premium on shot placement from tee to green. The small bentgrass greens are fast and well-manicured and put a premium on accuracy.

No. 14 is the hardest hole. It is a 423-yard par 4 with out-of-bounds down the fairway and water to the left and behind the green.

No. 18 is a 355-yard par 4 with water before the fairway and trees right and water left. The green is surrounded by five bunkers.

No. 15 is a 404-yard par 4 with a very long but narrow green. There is out-of-bounds to the right and water to the left.

Paris, Texas, is a long way from Paris, France, but Paris Golf and Country Club is a museum in its own right with a golf course that was built in 1918.

In 1976, the City of Pasadena received a rare opportunity when the defense department decided to close Ellington Air Force Base as part of sweeping military cutbacks.

Even though it was a setback for the city economy, the base facilities went up for grabs to Pasadena and the City of Houston. Included in those facilities was a nine-hole golf course that had been built for recreational purposes for off-duty servicemen.

Both cities lobbied for the rights to the air field, but while everyone awaited a decision, the course grew up with weeds and

Pasadena Municipal Golf Course

1000 Duffer Lane
Houston 77034
281-481-0834
Pro: Jon Cutshall
A par-72, 6,750-yard public course.

• • •

brush and barely resembled a golf course when Pasadena finally won the rights to it along with 100 additional acres to complete an 18-hole facility.

The original course was called Pasadena Ellington when it reopened in August 1978. The second nine, designed by architect Jay Riviere, opened in 1981.

It is a good driving course. On seven holes, players step to the tee and are confronted by water on both sides of the fairway and water comes into play in some form or fashion on all 18 holes.

The 437-yard, par-4 No. 7 is rated as the toughest. It requires players to hit a long approach over the water that cuts across 75 percent of the fairway.

The head pro is Jon Cutshall, a Houston native who grew up at Glenbrook Park and played at the University of Houston. He went on to play the PGA Tour before his career was shortened when he caught a three-iron in a palm tree and ripped all the ligaments in his shoulders.

Even though the closure of Ellington Air Force Base was a setback, the base facilities went up for grabs — including a nine-hole golf course.

The business of dusting for architectural fingerprints can get quite messy. When Pebble Creek opened in 1992, it already had a controversial heritage. Trying to figure out exactly who gets credit for the design is as difficult as its last four holes.

Legendary architect Leon Howard was hired on a contract basis to do the job one piece at a time, but when it came time to complete the job he parted company over a monetary disagreement. In came Mike Sheridan to help finish the job. Then came Houston architect Ken Dye, who designed the greens and bunkers, only to have them redesigned by

Pebble Creek Country Club

4500 Pebble Creek Parkway
College Station 77845
409-690-0990
Pro: Jim Baetge
A par-72, 6,870-yard semi-private club.

• • •

the course superintendent.

"They only changed about 10 percent of what we did," Dye says, "but it was an important 10 percent."

The final product — no matter how many fingers were in the stew — is a golf course that wanders up and down hills and through the trees. The most

scenic holes are along the rocky bottom of Pebble Creek, which winds through the course.

The 15th is a 425-yard, par-4 dogleg right. Players have the option to play a straight drive about 240 yards to the corner or try to cut the corner of the dogleg at the risk of going out-of-bounds. The 16th is a 600-yard par 5 that plays downwind with a lake in front of the green.

The 17th is a 230-yard par 3 where golfers must avoid a lake on the left. The 18th is a 450-yard par 4 that plays into the wind. A creek cuts across the fairway about 250 yards off the back tees, forcing most players to lay up and face a long approach.

The final product — no matter how many fingers were in the stew — is a challenging course that wanders up and down hills and through the trees.

City, state and the federal government are often criticized for their slow-moving bureaucracy, long paper trails and waste, but every once in a while they surprise us. They work together quickly and efficiently and — most importantly — for the betterment of society.

Pecan Valley is one of those success stories.

It was a complicated task that took about two years to pull off and required cooperation from the Army Corps of Engineers, the Fort Worth Parks and Recreation Department and the Tarrant County Water Control District.

The sale of Worth Hills Golf

Pecan Valley Golf Course Hills Course

6400 Pecan Valley Drive
Fort Worth 76126
817-249-1548
Pro: Joe Traban
A 36-hole public facility.

• • •

Course to Texas Christian University helped fund the new golf course.

In 1962, the city reached an agreement to use a 665-acre tract below the dam at Lake Benbrook for 50 years at no cost as long as all profits would go back into the development of the area.

Formerly known as Benbrook Municipal, it originally featured an 18-hole layout known as the River Course and a nine-hole layout called the Hills Course.

In 1981, architect Dave Bennett added nine more holes to complete the 36-hole facility — one known as the Hills Course and the second known as the River Course. The Hills Course is slightly shorter, but water comes into play often on the nine holes.

While the par-4 second hole is only 375 yards from the back tees, it gives many players with poor directional guidance fits. It is a dogleg left, with a pond protecting the inside corner of the fairway.

Pecan Valley is a success story of what can happen when various government entities work together quickly and efficiently.

Pecan Valley is a 36-hole golf facility in Benbrook that was built in 1962 and expanded in 1981. It is a prime example, if not rare, of the good things that can happen when government entities work together quickly and efficiently.

Pecan Valley, originally known as Benbrook Golf Course, is Fort Worth's only 36-hole golf facility. Cooperation between the Army Corps of Engineers, the Fort Worth Parks and Recreation Department and the Tarrant County Water Control District made the course below the dam at Lake Benbrook a reality.

"The Communists will have no

Pecan Valley Golf Course River Course

6800 Lakeside Drive
Fort Worth 76126
817-249-1845
Pro: Joe Traban
A 36-hole municipal course complex.

• • •

mention of what we do here today," Congressman Jim Wright said. "They won't tell about Benbrook and the thousands of similar examples of governments working together for the benefit of all people."

Architect Ralph Plummer designed the first 18-hole layout known as the River Course and

another nine-hole layout known as the Hills Course. In 1981, architect Dave Bennett returned to the scene to add nine more holes and complete a 36-hole facility.

Like most Plummer courses, the par-72, 6,579-yard River layout features some demanding one and two-shot holes.

But unlike many of his championship layouts, Plummer kept in mind the average golfer when he designed three par 5s at less than 480 yards. No. 2 is 452 yards, No. 7 is 481 yards and No. 15 is 451 yards, which give golfers birdie opportunities.

Two of the hardest holes are the par-3 sixth and 17th holes, at 234 and 218 yards, respectively.

The River layout features demanding one and two-shot holes, but Plummer kept in mind the average golfer when he made three par 5s under 500 yards.

The course Willie Nelson bought for a song in the 1970s, has been playing sweet golf music in the Austin-area for nearly two decades.

The famed country singer is also an avid golf nut and jumped at the chance to buy his own course at a bankruptcy auction nearly two decades ago.

Nelson, who also lives in the area, first used the course as his personal playground before opening it to the public in the late 1970s.

While Nelson never wrote the song, "Momma, let your babies grow up to be golfers," he still does his research on the links

whenever he's in town.

"Willie plays here more than anybody else," head pro Randy Severs said.

The course is located just off Highway 71 and Highway 2322 near Lake Travis. The surrounding Hill Country scenery is a great attraction, and Nelson isn't the only famous golfer who is a regu-

lar on the fairways at Pedernales.

The nine-hole layout plays to par 36 and measures 3,330 yards, featuring a good mixture of holes with a varying level of difficulty from 350-yard par 4s to a 525-yard par 5 to medium-length par 3s.

PGA touring pro J.L. Lewis represents the course on the pro circuit, helping Severs when not on the road. Nelson has also been known to closely check on the condition of his prized property.

"See that hole over there," Nelson reportedly once said to a playing partner at Pedernales.

"It's actually a par 34 and I almost eagled that thing the other day."

Country music legend Willie Nelson is an avid golf nut and jumped at the chance to buy his own course at a bankruptcy auction two decades ago.

With its scenic location alongside the Colorado River, Bastrop was a growing bedroom community outside of Austin that was clearly in need of a top 18-hole golf course.

That's exactly the thought that crossed the mind of architect Billy Martindale when Pine Forest Country Cub was still just an idea.

The course was originally designed in 1979 to be the centerpiece of a master-planned residential community.

Martindale did his part with a championship golf course, but the housing development was slow to get off the ground.

The golf course, then, was left

to make it on its own. Martindale's layout and the natural beauty has never failed to attract its share of golfers to this bedroom community 30 minutes east of Austin.

Before you leave the first tee at Pine Forest, make sure to strap yourself in and hold on tight for an 18-hole roller coaster ride.

The course is listed at 6,613 yards from the back tees, but it plays much longer because of the changes in elevation.

Martindale needed only 14 sand traps on the layout, but brought water into play on six holes and used seven doglegs to put a premium on accuracy.

On the 180-yard 12th, the fairway drops 60 feet from tee to green. The par-3 16th features a 70-foot drop with traps guarding the green and water nearby.

"We have tremendous undulation out here," one pro says.

"There isn't a flat hole here. The par 3s are very dramatic. I'll put our par 3s up against any in the state."

Before you leave the first tee at Pine Forest, make sure to strap yourself in and hold on tight for an 18-hole roller coaster ride.

Jack Goetz comes from a classic Texas golfing family. The Goetz brothers — Bob and Dick and Jack — grew up on the golf course and never left.

Bob Goetz was the longtime golf pro at Dallas' ultra-exclusive Preston Trail Golf Club, the former site of the Byron Nelson Classic. Dick Goetz went on to play on the Senior PGA Tour. And since 1976, Jack Goetz has been the head pro at Longview's Pinecrest Country Club, one of the oldest clubs in the state.

PineCrest was originally built in 1921 as a nine-hole course with sand greens, typical of most

PineCrest Country Club
North Cotton Road
Longview 75606
903-758-8000
Pro: Jack Goetz
A par-70, 6,500-yard private club.

• • •

of the courses of the day. It was carved out of the tall East Texas pines, with a creek winding its way through the property.

Architect Press Maxwell came along in 1959 to redesign the existing nine-hole course and add nine new holes, bringing PinecCest to its current par-70, 6,400-yard layout.

"Press Maxwell really should get all the credit for the course as it is today," Goetz says. "He did most of the things you see on the course like all the mounding around the greens and the routing of the holes as they are today."

Three of the hardest holes are on the front nine. No. 2 is a 515-yard par 5 with a creek running down the right side and crossing the fairway about 220 yards off the tee, forcing players to either lay up or try to clear the creek off the tee.

No. 5 is an excellent 437-yard, dogleg left par 4 with a creek running across the fairway about 200 yards from the tee with a long approach to a green down a narrow, tree-lined fairway.

The Goetz brothers — Bob, Dick and Jack — grew up on the golf course and never left. Since 1976, Jack Goetz has been the head pro at Pinecrest.

Around 1971, it was as if God spoke and carved an 11th commandment on the limestone countryside of Texas Hill Country.

There shalt be golf courses on Lake Travis.

And so it was. And he saw that it was good.

The surroundings of Lake Travis are some of the most scenic in God's creation and mortal men have picked up where he left off.

Jimmy Demaret was one of those men. Shortly after the popular *Shell's Wonderful World of Golf* series came to an end after introducing the game of golf to a worldwide television

Point Venture Golf Club
422 Venture Boulevard
Leander 78645
512-267-1151
Pro: Michael Pederson
A nine-hole public course.

• • •

audience, Demaret returned to his native Texas to dabble in golf course architecture.

About the same time Robert Trent Jones was building the first course at Horseshoe Bay and Leon Howard was building the Live Oak course at Lakeway, Demaret, a three-time Masters champion, tested his talents on

this nine-hole layout. He built the course around a sprawling private home and townhouse development. Since developers used all of the lakefront property for home sites, the nine holes Demaret designed don't feature any on-site water or sand, but have plenty of trees with some strong par 5s.

The par-4, 390-yard seventh hole rates high on scenery. Players start out on an elevated tee with a fairway that gradually slopes downhill. The green is framed by a breathtaking view of Lake Travis.

"The course is a lot tighter than it looks," pro Mike Pederson says. "You have to keep the ball in the fairway or you can find yourself behind a tree in a hurry."

At the same time Robert Trent Jones was building the first course at Horseshoe Bay, Jimmy Demaret tested his talents on this nine-hole layout.

Two decades before Spindletop brought black gold to the Golden Triangle, T.E. Broussard was the local postmaster who was charged with getting the mail through rain, sleet, hail or snow. Well, a lot of the former but not very much of the latter.

Anyway, Broussard operated out of a little post office that he named La Belle in honor of his fiancee Mary Belle Bordages. That was in 1886.

Fast forward to 1955 and another man came to work the land. Broussard and his post office were long gone, but architect Ralph Plummer built in its place a golf course and country club

Port Arthur Country Club

PO Box 486
Port Arthur 77640
409-796-1311
Pro: Tommy Eller
A par-71, 6,755-yard semi-private club.

• • •

that is still the talk of the town and one of the most meticulously maintained courses in the Gulf Coast area.

Three years after he designed Houston's Lakeside Country Club and two years before he built Champions, Plummer did his handiwork at Port Arthur.

He designed a par-71, 6755-yard layout that is extremely wooded and well bunkered with relatively small greens.

His signature hole is the 18th, with a bayou running along the left side of the fairway and trees running down the right side.

There's a pond about 260 yards off the tee, and leaves a precarious approach over water to the green.

No. 3 is a 203-yard par 3 with a pond just off the tee and another pond protecting the green on the front right side. No. 12 is a 236-yard par 3 where par feels like a birdie.

While the club is private, it is open to the public on Mondays with a $10 greens fee.

Plummer's signature hole at Port Arthur is No. 18, with a bayou running along the left side of the fairway and trees running down the right side.

Byron Nelson was one of the greatest golfers of all time. His streak of 11 consecutive victories in 1945 is one of the most astounding accomplishments in all of sport, and should stand from here to eternity.

While Nelson was known for his outstanding playing ability on the golf course, he was known perhaps even more as being a gentle and kind human being.

Nelson, a native Texan, used to travel the state to play all of the old courses in one professional tournament or another.

On one occasion he came to Port Groves, which was built in 1932 and is the second oldest-

Port Groves Golf Course

5721 Monroe
Groves 77619
409-962-4030
Pro: Gary Freedman
A nine-hole public course.

• • •

club in Jefferson County after Beaumont Country Club.

It should come as no surprise that Nelson shot lights out on this short course with few trees and no sand traps. He came into the final hole needing only a par to break the course record of 60. Nelson reached the green in regulation, then intentionally

three-putted so a local player would retain the record.

Nelson isn't the only famous golfer who has graced these fairways. The legendary Babe Zaharias, one of the greatest athletes of all time, grew up in Port Arthur and Beaumont and played here often.

Like most old courses, the layout is short and has succumbed a little to technological advances in equipment that enable golfers to hit the ball further.

It is a links-type layout, with lots of moguls and small undulating greens. It is a challenge to your shot-making abilities, with a premium on punch shots and bump and run.

Byron Nelson had an opportunity to shoot 59 here once, but intentionally three-putted the last hole to ensure that a local player retained the record.

Hunters and bird dogs once stalked this old dairy pasture land in search of dozens of quail in the early mornings and late afternoons.

Now, instead of being some unnamed piece of property on the other side of a barbed-wire fence, the place has a name — Quail Creek Country Club — and hunters still come in search of a different kind of birdie.

A committee of members led by Bugs Harder closely looked over the shoulder of an unnamed Oklahoma architect as he built the first nine in 1969 and the back nine in 1970. The course is also lined by many different kinds

Quail Creek Country Club

PO Drawer 2329
San Marcos 78666
512-353-1664
Pro: John Ferguson Jr.
A par-72, 6,489-yard private club.

• • •

of trees with out-of-bounds present on several holes. Water comes into play on seven of the holes with a large lake on Nos. 3, 4, 9 and 18.

"There are no easy two-putts, but quite a few three-putt greens," pro John Ferguson says. "It puts a lot of pressure on your chipping and short game. The ability to

position the ball in the fairway is really key here."

Three par 3s help form the backbone of the course. All three holes are over 190 yards with water in play.

The other par 3, No. 3, measures just 167 yards but is dominated by a huge pecan tree on the left side that almost makes the hole play like a dogleg left.

No. 13, a 435-yard par 4, is the No. 1 handicap hole. On the approach, players must fire their second shots onto one of the layout's smallest greens.

The 312-yard, par-4 No. 7 is easily the most scenic. Players must hit their second shots on this dogleg left over a canyon.

"There are no easy two putts, but quite a few three-putt greens. It puts a lot of pressure on your chipping and short game."

The job requirements for an Air Force golf architect aren't often spelled out in back and white. There isn't an official test to pass, a uniform to wear or a need to spit and shine your boots for morning roll call. You don't even have to go through boot camp. In fact, Kerrville's Joe Finger became known as Mr. Air Force Golf simply because a friend grew tired of government paperwork.

Ralph Plummer was one of the leading architects of the day in the 1940s and 1950s. He had built dozens of courses, both public and private, and had been hired by commanders at San

Randolph Oaks Golf Course

PO Box 188, Building 1300
Randolph AFB 78148
210-652-4570
Pro: Ed Schieber
A par-72, 7,172-yard military course.

• • •

Antonio's Randolph Air Force Base to renovate the existing nine-hole course and add an additional nine.

Plummer quickly grew tired of the Air Force's complicated rules and regulations and one day he was complaining about the red tape to Finger, who gladly took the work off his hands.

Finger got the Randolph job in 1957 and went on to design and build eight more Air Force courses.

In addition to the length, the other dilemma golfers face are the elevated greens that require an accurate approach.

All four par 3s are more than 180 yards with two over 200.

The four par 5s are at least 550 yards, with the longest being the 589-yard monster No. 12. It is a sweeping dogleg left that turns sharply off the tee and leaves two long shots to the green.

No. 5 is a 552-yard approach that is surrounded by water that prevents most players from going for the green in two.

In addition to length, the other dilemmas golfers face at Randolph Oaks are the elevated greens that require an accurate approach.

Jeff Brauer was a protégé of architect Dick Nugent. Together, they built numerous great golf courses throughout the United States.

Like any good protégé, Brauer finally learned enough to set out on his own in 1988.

Ten years later, you see Brauer's name scattered throughout this book as the architect of record for numerous courses. But after years of assisting Nugent and working with PGA Tour pros Larry Nelson and Jim Colbert on several other projects, his first solo project was Ratliff Ranch Golf Course in Odessa.

Brauer sculpted the flat West

Ratliff Ranch Golf Links
7500 North Grandview
Odessa 79768
915-368-4653
Pro: Christopher deKeratry
A par-72, 6,797-yard public course.

• • •

Texas ranch land into a 6,797-yard links-style layout with large, undulating greens. Golfers are required to keep the ball in the center of the fairways or lose shots in the tall rough.

As with any West Texas course, the wind is an omnipresent factor and Brauer kept that in mind when he

designed the course. He also kept in mind that this is a public golf course that serves a wide variety of players.

The course plays to a 122 slope rating from the back tees and out-of-bounds comes into play on several holes.

Among the hardest holes on the course are the par 4s, most of which require two consecutive well-planned shots to have a chance at birdie or par.

No. 5 measures 460 yards, No. 8 is 444 yards and No. 18 is the No. 1 handicap hole, even though it measures only 412 yards. No. 14, however, measures only 285 yards, so the green is driveable for some players.

Jeff Brauer sculpted the flat Texas ranch land into a 6,797-yard links-style layout with large, undulating greens.

Since the 1960s, four different groups of investors have attempted to turn a piece of uncharted territory north of San Antonio into a golf course. One by one, they fell victim to money trouble, water worries or both.

Then came former pro Kurt Cox, who accepted the challenge, and worked for the last three years to breathe life into the uncompleted 18-hole golf course now known as Rebecca Creek.

Cox, who won the men's city championship twice in the 1970s, started working on the Rebecca Creek project in early 1991. A successful local golf merchandiser at the time, Cox eventually

Rebecca Creek Golf Course
10101 Rebecca Creek Road
Spring Branch 78070
210-497-7100
Pro: Jeff Brown
A par-72, 6,470-yard public course.

• • •

hooked up with co-owner Don Glenk to build a golf course and driving range where others failed.

The layout is a testament to patience. It's only appropriate that the layout requires nothing less.

Not a golf course architect by trade, Cox consulted with other members of the George Hoffman design team and studied old lay-

out maps on building a challenging and scenic course. Hoffman, who died in 1977, is credited with eight courses in the area, all of which made use of the Hill Country scenery, water and sand.

Both the 140-yard No. 12 and the 108-yard No. 17 hit off elevated tees to scenic greens.

No. 5 is a lengthy par 5, which requires a blind drive to a landing area with a water hazard in front of the green. The par-4 18th is a fitting finish with water, trees and four traps behind the green.

"We want to stay public and serve golfers in the area," course manager Charles Walthall says. "You can never have too many golf courses."

Rebecca Creek is a testament to patience. It's only appropriate that this 6,470-yard layout requires nothing less from the golfers who play it.

Randy Metzger may not yet be a household name in the golf community, but you can be sure most everybody at Red Oak Valley knows who he is and what he did back in December 1990.

Metzger had recently quit his job at the Borden Milk Company to pursue a pro career.

He had failed on his first attempt to qualify for the PGA Tour, but was hopeful to earn a spot on the PGA's Nike Tour, a mini-tour of sorts for players waiting for a chance at the big leagues.

So Metzger was working on his game at the par-70, 5,911-yard

Red Oak course on a rare calm day.

Metzger had already set the course record of 61 the previous year. On this particular day, he was 10 under with two holes left to play.

On the 291-yard 17th, Metzger hit his blind tee shot to about five yards from the green

and chipped in for an eagle to go 12 under.

On the par-4 18th, he hit a driver down the middle, then wedged to within six inches to walk away with a 13-under 57.

He can only hope to be so lucky one day on the PGA Tour.

While every golfer may not get quite as hot as Metzger did on that one fateful day, Red Oak Valley can surrender some low numbers to any player.

Many of the layout's par 4s are reachable or nearly reachable off the tee for big hitters. For most players, they may require little more than average drive and a short-iron to get within range of a makeable birdie putt.

Red Oak Valley is a course where golfers can shoot a low score if they get a hot hand. Randy Metzger did just that when he shot a 13-under 57.

Ridglea Country Club is one of the state's largest country clubs, with a membership of 2,100 and 115,000 square feet of clubhouse that was built with stones from old Indian fences found in nehghboring counties and bricks reclaimed from buildings in Tennessee.

When you walk into the clubhouse, you walk through a rain forest atrium where tropical plants and a rare collection of birds thrive.

Ridglea is a tribute to three different eras of golf course architecture. It feaures the North Course, which was designed in 1928 by John Bredemus, and it features the South Course, which

was built in 1955 by Bredemus protege Ralph Plummer. Both courses were updated in 1988 by Jay Morrish, one of the top architects of the modern era.

Bredemus built the North Course nearly four decades before Fort Worth businessman and other community leaders formed Ridglea Country Club in

1955, but it has continued to serve its players for 70 years.

The bentgrass greens and lush fairways have been legendary examples of design and playable beauty. In 1988, Morrish lent his skills to rebuilding the greens, tees and natural streams while preserving the masterworks of yesteryear.

The North Course is a par-71, 6,467-yard layout that features tree-lined fairways and streams running throughout.

Two of the hardest holes come in the first five holes, starting with the 440-yard, par-4 second and the 430-yard, par-4 fifth. No. 4 is a slight dogleg left with water protecting the green on the back and left side.

Ridglea is a tribute to three different eras of golf architecture with John Bredemus, Ralph Plummer and Jay Morrish all contributing to the design.

Ridgewood Country Club is the old stomping grounds for Dave Eichelberger, a Waco native who learned how to play golf on this scenic course overlooking Lake Waco and then went on to a successful pro career on the PGA and Senior PGA tours.

Ridgewood Country Club was originally built in 1947 on a scenic ridge that overlooks Lake Waco and offers beautiful panoramic views of the Central Texas countryside.

Legendary architect Ralph Plummer renovated the layout in 1962 and turned it into a challenging, 6,419-yard, par-70 layout that in 1994 was good enough to

Ridgewood Country Club

7300 Fish Pond Road
Waco 76710
254-772-2050
Pro: Bruce Etter
A par-70, 6,419-yard private club.

• • •

host the Southwest Conference men's championships.

The course claims to have the best bentgrass greens in Texas, and plays through rolling hills, scenic mature oak trees and challenging greens that more than make up for the lack of length on the course.

The signature hole is No. 10, a

419-yard par 4, which was built on the side of a large hill and offers a beautiful view of the lake.

No. 6 is the most scenic hole at Ridgewood. It is a straightaway 406-yard par 4 that winds down toward the lake, which provides a beautiful but dangerous backdrop on a downhill approach to a large, deep green.

No. 8 is a 416-yard dogleg right with a fairway that slopes severely toward the right with trees running all the way down the right side of the fairway.

No. 18 is a 558-yard dogleg left par 5 that plays downhill to a very small elevated green that makes it difficult to hit in three shots, much less two.

The course boasts the best bentgrass greens in Texas, and plays through rolling hills, scenic mature oak trees and challenging greens.

Truth in advertising is alive and well at River Bend Resort and Country Club, which is built on the Rio Grande River.

Built in 1987 by John Ingram, seven holes on this par-72, 6,828-yard layout play along a bend in the Rio Grande River and overlook the U.S. Mexico border. The second nine was built in 1992.

The beautiful resort is extremely scenic, offering spectacular views and a challenge to all of your golf skills.

The course is considered to be sneaky long, since some holes play into the wind. Water comes into play on all but one hole, and the greens are small and hard to

River Bend Resort and Country Club

Route 8, PO Box 649
Brownsville 78520
956-548-0192
Pro: Jarrod Mark Flanagan
A par-72, 6,828-yard semi-private club.

• • •

hit, so accurate shotmaking is a must from tee to green.

Nos. 5 through 13 play along a scenic bend in the Rio Grande, with the river running down the entire left side of each hole.

The Rio Grande also comes into play behind the No. 4 green. No. 14 is the only hole that doesn't have water play.

The course is noted for its demanding par 3s. Nos. 15 and 18 are extremely long with out-of-bounds to the right and water left and very small greens.

The signature hole is the 157-yard par 3 17th, which although it is short requires a precise iron shot to an island green surrounded by water.

No. 18 is a 434-yard par 4 that plays into the wind with water and out-of-bounds on the left and right, respectively.

Ed Weeks set the course record of 2-under 70 in 1997.

River Bend also offers resort accommodations and conference facilities for company meetings and corporate golf outings.

The beautiful resort is extremely scenic, offering spectacular views across the U.S.-Mexico border and a challenge to all your golf skills.

The Texas-Oklahoma football rivalry plays out only once a year on the football field, but it plays out everyday at River Creek Park Golf Course.

River Creek was built by Richard Boyd and Buddy Pierson in 1968 on the Texas banks of the Red River, which serves as the boundary line for between Texas and Oklahoma.

Six greens at River Creek are actually on the north side of the Texas-Oklahoma border and many of the holes offer a spectacular view of the Red River.

While they are not mentioned anywhere in the annals of golf

course architecture, Boyd and Pierson produced a par-71, 6,727-yard layout that is definitely user friendly — no matter which side of the border you grew up on.

The course has mature trees lining most of its fairways, but the landing areas are typically wide open and the bentgrass greens well manicured.

The course plays to a slope rating of only 104 from the back tees.

The signature hole is No. 2, a 178-yard par 3 with a water hazard on the front left of the green.

This is where golfers find a large sculpture that was made out of a large oak tree that died. A team of sculptors turned the tree into a very detailed sculpture of two golfers on the left side of the green.

No. 17 is a 440-yard par 4 that goes south toward River Creek's barbecue pavillion and into the wind.

No. 12 is a 425-yard par 4 with a water hazard in front and on the right.

The Texas-Oklahoma football rivalry plays out only once a year on the football field, but it plays out everyday at River Creek Park Golf Course.

River Plantation is just a chip shot away from Interstate 45 North near Conroe, but it takes its members and guests back to a bygone era of days in the Old South when life was much simpler.

From the moment you turn off the interstate and cross the old-fashioned covered bridge to the time you drive up to the Southern Colonial clubhouse, River Plantation offers a laidback escape from the rat race and the concrete canyons of downtown.

That was the goal of investors who built the 800-acre development in 1968. Jay Riviere designed the original 18 holes,

and former River Oaks pro Jackson Bradley came in to build the final nine that serves as the centerpiece of the community just east of the San Jacinto River.

The club is built around Stewart Creek, which runs through the three nine-hole layouts nicknamed Augusta, Biloxi and Charleston.

"I got into the design business completely by accident," co-founder Jackson Bradley said. "The curious thing about my three years there was how totally fouled up we were. We were all learning by the seats of our pants."

In 1968 and '69, the club hosted the LPGA's River Plantation Women's Open.

"While you might wish to attack the course," pro Bruce Springer says, "it calls for a more conservative approach. The fairways are very tightly lined with a broad range of trees strategically placed along creeks and ponds. As many golfers say, 'You can bite off as much as you want but it might bite back.'"

"The curious thing about my three years at River Plantation was how totally fouled up we were. We were all learning by the seats of our pants."

To walk onto the premises of Riverside Country Club is like stepping onto the set of "Gone With the Wind."

The scenic golf course was designed in 1957 by architect Ralph Plummer at the same time he was building the famed Cypress Creek Course at Champions Golf Club in Houston.

The layout is built on the banks of both Brazoria Lake and Brazos River. The fairways are lined with trees covered in spanish moss.

Brazoria Lake divides the golf course in two, with many of the greens and tees on opposite sides and golfers using one of three

Riverside Country Club

PO Box 158, Highway 332
Lake Jackson 77566
409-798-9141
Pro: James Brisbin
A par-72, 6,556-yard private club
• • •

bridges to cross. Brazoria Lake comes into play on 10 holes.

Players must cross the lake on the 308-yard, par-4 second hole, then hit their approach on the 353-yard, par-4 third hole to a green protected by the lake on the right side.

The lake doesn't come back into play until the 373-yard, par-4

eighth hole, where golfers must clear a corner of the lake off the tee. On the 354-yard, par-4 ninth, players must lay up off the tee and then carry across the lake on their approach.

Players also are required to carry the lake on the tee on the 172-yard, par-3 13th and on their final approach to the 18th green. It also runs along the right side of the 12th and 14th fairways.

No. 16 is one of the more demanding holes. It is a 432-yard, dogleg left par 4. Although no water comes into play, the tree-lined fairways and the length of the hole require two long, well-placed shots to reach the green in regulation.

The course is short, but there is enough water and sand to put a premium on accuracy. The fairways are lined with trees covered in spanish moss.

Riverside Golf Course is one of two Austin-area courses that was once the former home of Austin Country Club. The course served Austin's rich and famous for 34 years until the club moved to its current location near the Colorado River.

The club already had moved once from its original site at what is now Hancock Park, and decided to move again when the sprawling Austin community continued to infringe on the country club atmosphere.

This layout, designed by Perry Maxwell, was home to teaching legend Harvey Penick and was where pros Ben Crenshaw and

Riverside Golf Course

5712 East Riverside Drive
Austin 78741
512-389-1070
Pro: Michael Hicks
A par-71, 6,500-yard public course.
• • •

Tom Kite got their introduction to the game.

Kite, the all-time money leader on the PGA Tour, and Crenshaw, a past Masters champion, both learned how to play the game under Penick's tutelage.

Penick took Crenshaw out on the putting green and taught him some short-game magic. And Kite

would spend countless hours on the driving range, practicing under Penick's watchful eye.

Penick, Kite and Crenshaw have all moved on to greener fairways, but the character and the history of the course remains.

"It's a very challenging track with towering oak and pecan trees lining the fairways," pro Tom Krause says. "It's deceivingly long for a course that's only 6,500 yards."

Some players may be able to reach the green on the first hole, a 305-yard par 4. No. 14 also is reachable at 307 yards, but it is preceded by back-to-back par 5s of 528 and 514 yards.

Riverside Golf Course is one of two Austin-area courses that can claim they once were the home of the exclusive Austin Country Club.

While the birth of Texas golf came in 1898 with the creation of Austin and Galveston country clubs, Teddy Roosevelt was looking for a few good men.

That same year, Roosevelt had bigger things on his mind than a leisurely round on the links.

Roosevelt stationed himself at a downtown San Antonio hotel to sign up men at the bar for one of the most famous battles in American history.

As soon as they became a member of Roosevelt's Roughriders, he sent them to an army campground located on what is now Riverside Golf Course — the sixth fairway to be

Riverside Golf Course
203 McDonald
San Antonio 78210
210-533-8371
Pro: Roy Truesdell
A par-72, 6,602-yard public course.

• • •

exact — to prepare for their famous charge up San Juan Hill.

It was not until 20 years after the Spanish American War that local residents returned to the old army campground to build a nine-hole golf course designed by George Hoffman on the banks of the San Antonio River.

Riverside now features a full 18-hole layout and nine-hole par-3 course.

The back nine also features some spectacular views of San Antonio's downtown skyline.

Among the troubles it presents is the 600-yard, par-5 16th and the par-3 17th. From the back tees, the hole plays 230 yards usually straight into the prevailing north wind. The 17th tee sits in a valley and leaves golfers with a full iron or wood into a small green.

"It's not a beastly layout, but it can be very challenging," pro Roy Truesdell says. "The front nine plays through the pecan trees, and seven holes on the back nine play across the river."

Teddy Roosevelt gathered his troops for the Spanish American War on what is now the sixth fairway at Riverside Golf Course.

If it was good enough for Ben Hogan, it should be good enough for everyone.

Riverview was formerly known as Nolan River Country Club before the club was moved up the road from the Nolan River in the early 1960s. At one time, Ben Hogan was the head pro.

This par-72, 6,605-yard layout is surrounded by beautiful countryside, with Buffalo Creek winding its way through the course and coming into play on 10 holes. Strategically-placed trees and nine elevated greens provide golfers with a good shot-making challenge.

The course recently changed

Riverview Golf Club
2501 South Nolan River Road
Cleburne 76031
817-641-2580
Pro: Les Oakes
A par-72, 6,605-yard semi-private club.

• • •

its name to Riverview Golf Club, and has begun placing more emphasis golf instead of social country-club atmosphere. It is now open to the public.

A small body of water along the right side of the fairway is hidden from the tee on the fourth hole, a 513-yard par 5. Those going for the green must then carry Buffalo Creek which runs in front of the green, while threading their approach between two large trees.

The eighth hole is a 157-yard par 3 that requires a shot over Buffalo Creek.

The signature hole at Riverview is a short par 3 of 146 yards. Trouble lurks in front of and behind the green.

The 14th hole is a demanding dogleg right par 4 of 418 yards that is rated as the second most difficult hole. Trees along the right side of the fairway come into play on any kind of fade or slice, and the prudent shot from there is usually a layup behind Buffalo Creek.

The layout is surrounded by beautiful countryside, with Buffalo Creek winding its way through the course and coming into play on 10 holes.

Rockdale is a nine-hole layout that golfers play twice from a separate set of tee boxes.

It is user friendly, with wide fairways, one sand trap and only two water holes, all of which make it a great course for beginning to average players.

While this course located northeast of Austin near Georgetown has been around for more than two decades, locals are saying the course is better than it has ever been under the direction of greens superintendent Terry Erhardt.

Golfers have an option here. You can pay the $9 weekday green fee or you can join the club

Rockdale Country Club

PO Box 166
Rockdale 76567
512-446-4013
Manager: Jim Barton
A nine-hole semi-private club.

• • •

with a $50 initiation fee and play all the golf your heart desires for only $55 a month.

Either way, it's a great deal.

And it's a great place for beginning players, because unlike many of the golf courses in the Hill Country area — there is not much trouble to be found — and good scores are for the taking for

players of all levels.

The layout starts with a 162-yard par 3, then gives players another birdie opportunity at the 490-yard, par-5 second.

The two hardest holes are Nos. 6 and 7.

No. 6 is a 398-yard par 4 that requires two long, straight shots.

On No. 7, a 387-yard par 4, the only sand trap on the course is strategically placed to limit the entrance to the green.

Both par 5s are reachable in two. No. 2 is 490 yards and No. 8 is 484, giving most players a good opportunity to make birdie.

All of the par 4s are under 400 yards, and the par 3s range in yardage from 145 to 162.

Rockdale is a nine-hole layout that offers wide fairways and features only one sand trap and two water holes — making it a great place for beginners.

If you want to set a record or get your name in the Guiness Book of World Records, you might try Rockwood Park Golf Course. The place seems to be conducive to that sort of thing.

In 1986, 25-year-old Mark Matthews played 724 holes in 24 hours at Rockwood to set a new world record. The previous record was 702 set by Charles Stock of Ohio.

In 1989, Rockwood regular J.J. Johnston Jr. set a record for most consecutive days playing golf. His string started in 1984. At the age of 72, he was working on 1,929 and counting. Johnston started breaking records in 1956,

Rockwood Golf Course

1851 Jacksboro Highway
Fort Worth 76114
817-624-1771
Pro: Ray Lopez
A 27-hole public course.

• • •

when he played 198 holes in a daylight-to-dark marathon. The old record had been 127. Immediately after passing the old record, Johnston told his partners he would make it to 135 holes.

Johnston broke his own record five times. He played as many as 363 holes in 24 hours at the Abilene Country Club. That

record has since been broken by other golfers.

Undaunted, Johnston kept breaking records until 1984 when he decided to begin his current streak. Johnston plans to submit his streak to the Guiness book for consideration when he stops playing — although he's not sure when that might be.

Legendary Texas golf course architect John Bredemus built Rockwood's original 18 in 1933, then Plummer renovated and added an additional nine in 1964.

No. 5 on the Blue Course is a 667-yard par 5 with water. No. 2 is a 220-yard par 3 that requires a long carry with a crossing wind to reach the green.

John Bredemus built Rockwood's original 18 holes in 1933, then Ralph Plummer added an additional nine in 1964.

Teachers are among the most under-rated people in the golf community.

You don't see them much on television, and you don't see their names in the daily sports pages.

But behind every good pro, there is a good teacher somewhere behind the scenes.

George Alexander was one of those guys, the unsung heroes of the golf business.

For many years, Alexander was the teaching professional at Rolling Hills Country Club.

It was here that he gave many players — some famous and others not so famous — their start in the game. Among his many pupils

have been PGA Tour legend Don January and LPGA Hall of Famer Sandra Haynie and former LPGA tour star Kathy Ahern.

Alexander helped bring some attention to a golf course that might be otherwise overlooked.

The course measures only 6,115 yards from the back tees and plays to a par of 71, but it is a

good place to work on your game — especially your driver and wedge.

The golf course, built by C.M. Mimms, is short in a day and age of metal woods and hot balls.

All of the par 5s, for instance, are under 485 yards and can be reached in two by most players, giving ample birdie opportunities. Two of the par 5s are back-to-back at Nos. 12 and 13 and measure only 484 and 465 yards to give a great birdie opportunity.

The toughest hole on the course is the 428-yard, par-4 16th. It is a dogleg left around a lake with two fairway bunkers guarding the approach. No. 2 is another stout par 4 measuring 453 yards.

George Alexander was a teaching pro who gave many players — including Don January and LPGA Hall of Famer Sandra Haynie — their start in the game.

Need to build a municipal golf course?

Who ya gonna call?

Leon Howard.

Probably no architect has had a bigger hand in building public golf courses in Texas than Leon Howard. He was master of the municipal layout, and he spent most of his career courting parks and recreation diretors throughout the state in a bid to build a golf course for their fair city.

While his golf courses aren't famous, Howard brought golf to the masses with his high volume of designs throughout the state. The goal was to offer good golf courses at a good price.

Howard built the East Course at Ross Rogers Golf Course in 1968, and it still ranks as one of the top municipal layouts in the state. He designed the East Course with generous fairways and medium sized, fairly flat greens with some trees along the fairways. It started out as a nine-hole layout, but was expanded to

18 holes in 1981.

Only three small lakes come into play. Players must carry a lake on the par-3 No. 6, and a lake cuts across the fairway on the 383-yard, par-4 12, requiring players to lay up or try to clear it with a drive of 225 yards or more. One lake comes into play on the par-3 second and 17th holes. And a lake on the 510-yard par 5 makes for a dangerous approach.

The East Course also has four great finishing holes starting at No. 15, a 424-yard par 4. No. 16 is a 451-yard par 4, No. 17 a 172-yard par 3 over water and No. 18 is a 483-yard, dogleg right par 5 that gives players a good chance to finish the round with a birdie.

Leon Howard specialized in building municipal golf courses, and at Ross Rogers he gave golfers high volume by building two 36-hole courses.

Nearly 10 years after Leon Howard produced the East Course at Ross Rogers, the course had become so popular that the city of Amarillo had him return in 1977 to build the West Course to accommodate the growing demand from the golfing public.

The West Course is a par-72, 6,602-yard layout that is shorter than the East but features the same playing characteristics with generous fairways and medium-sized bentgrass greens.

Head pro Sherwin Cox has been the recipient of both the PGA National junior Golf Leader Award and the PGA National Merchandiser of the Year Award.

The golf shop at Ross Rogers has been chosen by Golf Shop Operations as one of the Top 100 in the nation on numerous occasions.

Ross Rogers is the site of the original two-man Low Ball-Low Total Match Play Partnership. The tournament is held each year in July and attracts players from as far away as California and Arizona. In 1998, the tournament will mark its 47th anniversary.

Among the best holes on the West Course are No. 11, a 201-yard par 3, and No. 14, which for most golfers is a difficult 425-yard par 4.

No. 16 is a 505-yard, dogleg right par 5. No. 12 is a 537-yard dogleg left.

The city of Amarillo gave Leonard a very small tract of land on which to build two 18-hole courses, so he had to make a little land go a long way.

Most of the holes feature parallel fairways with not much space in between. There is also very little water in play on the course.

The West Course at Ross Rogers is shorter than the East Course, but features the same characteristics with generous fairways and medium-sized greens.

Roy H. Laird Country Club was built in 1935, and it is rated as one of the top 10 nine-hole courses in Texas by The Dallas Morning News.

After you are finished playing, you can stop by and meet your insurance needs at the Roy H. Laird Insurance Agency.

This nine-hole layout measures 6,367 yards and plays to a slope rating of 123 as members use two different sets of tees on each hole to create an 18-hole round.

This is a sneaky course with extremely undulating bermuda greens that are difficult to read.

Small water hazards come into play on five holes and out of

bounds comes into play on three holes, any of which can be potential disasters to golfers who are not on their "A" game.

The layout features one par 5 and one par 3. No. 4 is the longest hole on the course at 520 yards. It is a dogleg right par 5 through a narrow chute of trees off the tee.

No. 6 is the only par 3, measuring 150 yards but with out-of-bounds coming into play behind the green.

No. 7 is a driveable par 4 at 265 yards, but players going for the green off the tee must be wary of the out-of-bounds (parking lot) behind the green.

Even if players hit the green but roll over and out-of-bounds, they must re-tee from the tee box hitting three.

All of the par 4s are under 400 yards, so big hitters can spend most of the day with a driver, wedge and putter in their hands and a few birdies on their scorecard.

Small water hazards come into play on five holes and out-of-bounds on three, any of which can be potential disasters to golfers not on their "A" game.

Since opening in 1974, Jimmy Clay Municipal Golf Course in Austin has proven to be one of the most popular playgrounds for residents, visitors and politicians just passing through.

Jimmy Clay Golf Course celebrated its 20th birthday in 1994, and also celebrated the birth of a baby brother named Roy Kizer Golf Course.

While the two courses have different names, they share the same clubhouse and parking lot and combine to make the only 36-hole municipal golf facility in the Austin area.

The golf course, named after a longtime Austin golf superintend-

Roy Kizer Golf Club

5300 Jimmy Clay Drive
Austin 78744
512-444-0999
Pro: Kevin Gomillion
A par-71, 6,749 yard municipal course.

• • •

ent, was designed by former city golf director Randy Russell at a cost of $5 million. The 200-acre site contains 57 acres of lakes, including 24 acres of marshlands.

The course uses a bird as its logo because of the extensive wetlands built into the project, which provides a habitat for birds that used the old treatment plant

for shelter.

Because no Austin tax dollars were used for the project, the course must be self-sustaining. Greens fees are higher than the other four city courses, but the conditions and course will also be at a higher level.

"It's going to be good for the golfers," pro Joe Balander says. "It should have the level of maintenance of a country club for a few dollars more."

Kizer became a beloved figure in Austin as the superintendent at Lions Municipal golf course during his 36-year career. It is believed to be the only public course in the nation named after a course superintendent.

The 200-acre site contains 57 acres of lakes, including 24 acres of marshlands. Extensive wetlands were left to provide a habitat for birds.

This is the original Temple Country Club, opened in 1915 in the heart of Temple Central Park.

Now known as Sammons Park Golf Course, it has emerged from some tough financial times to become an outstanding 18-hole public layout.

The renovated course is named for John Sammons, a former mayor and longtime businessman in the city who helped save the course from extinction.

The club was built on land owned by the Sante Fe Railroad and held a lease for the property.

In 1985, a financial disagreement with the railroad forced the

Sammons Park Golf Course

2220 West Avenue D
Temple 76504
254-778-8282
Pro: Bob Bruns
A par-70, 6,100-yard public course.

• • •

club to shutdown.

That's where Sammons came to the rescue. He helped organize a city bond package and put together enough money for the city to buy the land and reopen the course in '87 with course renovations by Sammons himself. When all was said and done, it was only appropriate that they

named the course in John Sammons' honor.

Today, the par-70, 6,100-yard layout still offers plenty of challenge. There is water on 15 holes which provides plenty of business for the reclaimed-ball bins in the pro shop.

"It's a fun course, but some people don't want play it because of all the water," former pro Jeff Thomasson says.

Two of the three par 5s on the layout are reachable in two by most golfers, but the 580-yard, par-5 11th is the longest hole on the Sammons Park layout.

The layout features five par 3s, including back-to-back par 3s on the front at Nos. 5 and 6.

The club was built on land owned by the Santa Fe Railroad, but a disagreement forced the club to close until John Sammons stepped in.

You might call John Bredemus the Johnny Appleseed of Texas golf. When he first arrived on the scene in Texas, there were only a handful of golf courses in the entire state. When he was done, he had built 28 courses throughout the state to earn the title Father of Texas Golf.

Bredemus was a multi-talented man that would have put Deion Sanders and Bo Jackson to shame. He attended Dartmouth, then Princeton and won AAU national all-around competition. He graduated Princeton as a civil engineer, but became a math teacher and took up golf. He eventually turned pro. In 1919, he moved to Texas

and became a high school principal in San Antonio. It was then he realized golf in Texas was almost non-existent, so he combined his engineering background with his love for golf to build courses.

After building the state's first public golf course at San Antonio's Brackenridge Park in 1916, Bredemus introduced golf

to the heart of West Texas in 1921 when he designed San Angelo Country Club. It became the first course in the state to have bentgrass greens.

Not typical of a West Texas course, Bredemus designed a traditional-style layout known for its narrow fairways lined by mature trees, numerous lakes, excellent greens, unusually hilly terrain and the Conco River running alongside it.

The signature hole is the par-3 10th. The tee sits atop a hill and stretches some 169 yards over water to a green below. The tee overlooks the Concho River and a line of trees.

Bredemus designed a traditional-style layout known for its narrow fairways lined by mature trees, numerous lakes and for its unusually hilly terrain.

What do Tommy Lee Jones and Famous Amos cookies have in common?

San Saba Golf Club.

Go figure.

In the heart of West Texas, San Saba is home to a scenic 18-hole course that is just down the road from the ranch owned by the famous actor.

The course also produces a large number of pecans, 30,000 pounds each year, purchased by Famous Amos cookies.

Overlooking the San Saba River, architect Sorrell Smith built this par-72, 6,904-yard layout (first nine in 1972, second nine in 1987) for a total of $180,000,

which would barely buy you one hole in modern times.

Contrary to what you probably imagine a West Texas course looks like, Smith carved the first nine (now the back nine) out of a pecan orchard.

Playing through 1,200 pecan trees requires accurate shot placement and strategy. The second

nine is more open than the front nine but has more water hazards in play.

No. 9 is a par 5 that plays 600 yards from the blue tees. The 18th is a 538-yard par 5 that doglegs down a narrow, tree-line fairway and demands of approach shot over water.

Jones, by the way, doesn't play golf. But when he's not in Hollywood or on location filming his next movie, he does drop by the golf shop occasionally to buy golf gloves. He uses them when he plays polo.

Chris Goodspeed of Dallas and Ray Schwertner of Austin share the course record of 8-under 64.

Tommy Lee Jones and Famous Amos both come to San Saba Golf Club for different reasons. Golfers come here to enjoy a great golf course.

Scott Schreiner may be one of the least famous people a golf course was ever named after, but when you love golf and you grow up in a wealthy family, anything is possible.

The Schreiners, a wealthy family who helped found a college and established stores in this city northwest of San Antonio, donated land to the city with the strict stipulation that if the club ever became private again the land would immediately revert back to the Schreiner family.

So the course was named for Scott, a Schreiner family member who loved to play golf and was very instrumental in getting the

Scott Schreiner Golf Course
One Country Club Drive
Kerrville 78028
210-257-4982
Pro: Guy Cullins
A par-72, 6,500-yard municipal course.
• • •

public facility started.

The course is owned by the city of Kerrville, which has leased the course to pro/manager Guy Cullins to operate as a public facility. It is one of the few public courses available in scenic Hill Country area where many Texans choose to retire.

No. 5 is a 592-yard par 5 and

a John Bredemus classic. Water crosses the fairway twice with more water and a cliff on the right side. The green is elevated and difficult to hit with a less-than-excellent third shot.

"The course has stood the test of time with people still coming out there and enjoying themselves," pro Guy Cullins says.

The back nine was finally opened in 1977 after being designed by architect R.D. Kizer. The back side is more open than Bredemus' front nine.

Kizer also initiated a change on the par-4 No. 7. It was originally straight, but was turned into a dogleg left with trees coming into play down the left side.

The Schreiners donated land to the city of Kerrville to build a public golf course. Scott Schreiner was instrumental in getting the course started.

Shadow Hills Golf Course in Lubbock was built in 1981 by Ray Kilgore.

It is a links-style design featuring mounded fairways that stand out from the otherwise flat West Texas terrain.

Water hazards in the form of streams and ponds come into play on a number of holes.

The par-72, 6,777-yard course is wide open with little trouble to speak of.

Most of the holes are generic but the sixth is fun to play. It is a tiny 123-yard par 3 with water in front of the green that can be a lot more trouble than the yardage would indicate.

Shadow Hills Golf Course
6002 3rd Street
Lubbock 79499
806-793-9700
A par-72, 6,777-yard public course.
• • •

In west Texas the wind tends to blow — and blow hard. On this hole it is usually straight in your face. If your first shot falls short of the target and into the water, a drop area is provided about 30 yards from the green but you still have to go over the water. This time — if you're counting penalty strokes — you'll be hitting three.

Another good hole is the 404-yard, par-4 No. 10. It generally plays downwind and is wide open left and right. A solid rip here, with the help of the wind, could see a drive on the green.

The green at No. 4 is elevated with a lot of slope that makes putting extremely difficult.

No. 7 is a 439-yard par 4 that may be the most difficult on the course. It plays uphill with water all the way down the right side of the fairway.

No. 11 is a 489-yard par 5 with water down the right side and water in front protecting the green and deterring some players from going for the green in two.

No. 6 is a 123-yard par 3 that is more trouble than its yardage indicates. The wind blows straight in your face, making club selection difficult.

Sharpstown Country Club was part of a dream for Houston developer Frank Sharp. It opened on Labor Day in 1955 and memberships were included with the purchase of real estate in Sharp's booming Sharpstown development.

Unlike many country clubs, Sharp wanted his to appeal to young people, so he hired popular touring pro Doug Sanders to be the club's spokesman. The course was designed by original pro Morgan Baker, who operated out of a tiny clubhouse and charged only $1 green fees for residents to play.

Sharp was a great promoter

and, even though his golf course was never compared with Augusta National, helped bring the Houston Open here in 1964–65. Mike Souchak and Bobby Nichols were the winners and Lee Trevino won the Texas State Open there in 1965–66.

"If we had a choice of all the playing pros," Sharp said at the time, "Doug Sanders would be our man. If we had an old, sedate, mossback operation, he wouldn't fit. But we have young, vibrant members and we're going places."

Sharp's financial empire began to crumble in the late 1960s and creditors closed the club on Dec. 31, 1976.

The course was closed for three years until the city of Houston bought it in 1978 and the city hired architect Jay Riviere to come in and clean up the three years of growth and revamp the layout. He rebuilt nine greens and eight tee boxes and was forced to reroute several holes. Continued vandalism delayed the club's reopening until August 2, 1980.

Sharpstown Golf Course was once an exclusive country club where Mike Souchak beat Jack Nicklaus by one shot in the 1964 Houston Open.

Southwest Golf Course turned 35 in 1997, but it's not having a mid-life crisis.

In fact, it seems to be getting better with age.

The par-72, 7,018-yard layout was designed in 1962 by architect Joe Finger for the city of Amarillo. Like most West Texas courses, you can expect a lot of wind — so strap your hat or your hair on extra tight before leaving the locker room for the first tee.

While over the years Southwest has been given a bad wrap for poor conditioning, course officials have taken steps over the past year to update the course for the 21st century.

Southwest's bentgrass greens are developing a reputation among the locals for being the softest and most well maintained in the city.

That's a lot of bang for your buck, since this public course also offers the lowest green fees in Amarillo.

No. 5 is the most difficult hole on the course. It is a 420-yard par 5 that doglegs to the right around a pond. Any player trying to cut the corner will do so at the risk of hitting it in the water.

No. 9 is 450-yard par 4 that is another dogleg right around a water hazard.

No. 18 is a 540-yard par 5 that plays straight away, but golfers must contend with out-of-bounds down the right side and the green is protected in front and on the left by a water hazard.

Because of the wind, most golfers prefer to keep the ball low here, so shots will be affected less by the omnipresent winds. Hit the ball high, and there's no telling when or where it will come down.

Golfers prefer to keep the ball low here so shots will be affected less by the wind. Hit it high and there's no telling when or where it will come down.

Every company
has some form of
benefits for their
employees. Some have a medical
or dental plan, some offer
employee assistance programs,
some a company softball team.

But how many have a golf
course designed by a famed
Texas architect?

At Squaw Creek, that's
the case for the employees of
the Lockheed-Martin plant in
Fort Worth.

The course, actually located in
the Fort Worth suburb of Willow
Park, was opened in 1971 after
being designed by renowned
architect Ralph Plummer, who has
been credited with such gems as

Preston Trail Golf Club in Dallas.

Lockheed employees can
become members and many play
on a regular basis. But over the
past few years it has opened up
to public play, so golfers eager to
play a Plummer design can now
play with reservations.

Plummer opened the first nine
holes before a large crowd of

Lockheed employees and friends.

The second nine was added a
few years later. It is set among
some highly scenic rolling hillsides
and has some water — yes —
Squaw Creek runs through a
great deal of the layout.

When Plummer was finished,
the par-71, 6,749-yard layout
played to a challenging 126 slope
rating from the back tees.

The layout features bentgrass
greens and is built on hilly terrain,
making it strenuous to walk. Water
hazards and creeks come into
play throughout the course, so be
sure to bring extra balls.

"It's a fun and fair place to
play," pro Lynn Vaughan says.

Every company has some form of benefits for their employees. At Lockheed-Martin, one of the benefits is having their own championship golf course.

In 1951, a group of
golfers from Sealy,
Brookshire and
Katy joined together with the
objective of building a golf course
near San Felipe on a scenic bend
in the Brazos River. It was a simple idea, but in the past four
decades the members have
become experts at dealing with
natural disasters.

The land was covered by
heavy underbrush and large native
pecan trees and was part of a
larger tract donated to the State
of Texas in 1936 by the town of
San Felipe for use as a state park.

The course was opened in
1955 with all the design and construction done by the members.

During the first two years of operation, a major flood in which the
Brazos spilled out of its banks and
covered several greens for six
weeks. The members rebounded
and in 1968 sought more land to
build nine additional holes that
were completed in 1972.

Tragedy struck again in 1981
when the Brazos washed away

the scenic green on the par-3
No. 13.

The layout teems with wildlife
and features the natural contours
of the land and several small
streams, and the fairways are
tightly weaved with several thou-
sand native pecan trees. Accuracy
is a must, because the fairways
are so tight that not even a drive
in the fairway guarantees a clear
shot to the green.

"This golf course has been
through a lot of hard times over
the years," says pro Bobby
Browne. "But each time tragedy
has struck, the course has survived and come back better than
before. It seems to make us more
determined than ever."

"This golf course has been through a lot of hard times over the years. But each time tragedy has struck, the course has come back better than before."

I t is located on the outer limits of the D/FW metroplex on one of the last hills you see leaving Dallas on the long drive down I-45 toward Houston.

The Summit is aptly named because it is built on a hillside. It was the brainchild of Bill Schober, who built the golf course in 1989 but ran into financial trouble and ABK enterprises bought the golf course at auction in December 1991.

Longtime North Texas PGA member Benny Pasons is the head pro.

The 6,715-yard layout gives golfers an interesting mix of open and tree-lined holes, taking

The Summit Golf Club

102 Crescent View Drive
Ennis 75119
972-878-4653
Pro: Benny Passons
A par-72, 6,715-yard public course.

• • •

advantage of whatever the land had to offer.

While the course is built on the side of a hill as its name implies, for the most part, this is a links-style course with large greens and water comes into play on 10 holes.

Because most of the holes are on the hill and unprotected by

trees, the prevailing south winds always playing an important factor in club selection.

Five fairways are lined by trees, and course operators say they will match their greens against any in North Texas.

The layout starts with five consecutive par 4s, and the back nine is more than 200 yards longer than the front, featuring two 200-plus par 3s and a 602-yard par 5 at No. 12. The 17th is a 234-yard par 3 and the 18th is a 445-yard par 4.

Many Dallas-area golfers would prefer driving to the outskirts of town to play an uninterrupted round instead of playing a six-hour round in the city.

While the course is built on the side of a hill, this is a links-style course with large greens and water that comes into play on 10 holes.

S ycamore Creek sits almost forgotten in the shadow of downtown Fort Worth.

Many golfers pass over the nine-hole on their way to golf models in the city.

But if only these fairways and greens could talk, Sycamore Creek could bear testimony to some of the rich Texas golfing history that has passed over its landscape.

The course was originally opened in 1932 as a public golf course. It was one of the first public courses to open in Fort Worth. Located near downtown, it drew some of the best golfers in the city.

Sycamore Creek Golf Course

401 Martin Luther King
Fort Worth 76104
817-535-7241
Pro: Ira Meachem
A nine-hole municipal course.

• • •

With nine holes and 18 tees, the par-35 course plays 3,070 yards on the front nine and 3,046 yards on the second trip around.

The course was originally set on just 36 acres, so every inch was used to make this a tidy, but functional course.

The course's second life began in 1977 when the City of

Fort Worth purchased Sycamore Creek and added it to its rotation of city golf courses.

In 1992, the city managed to obtain an additional 56 acres for the layout, nearly doubling its size and closed the course for remodeling. After 18 months of hard work, the city reopened Sycamore Creek and the results have been impressive.

The Bermuda greens have been greatly enlarged, the fairways widened and new trees and sand traps added.

The layout features only one par 5 at the 532-yard No. 8, and two par 3s — the 159-yard No 3 and the 143-yard No. 7.

The course was originally set on just 36 acres, so every inch was used to make this a tidy but functional course.

While Warren Cantrell was still serving as the head golf coach at Lubbock Country Club, he continued to dabble in the golf course architecture to supplement his income.

Cantrell was a multi-talented man who was good at everything he did, including golf. When he graduated from Texas A&M with degrees in engineering and architecutre, he formed a large contractng business that would later grow to handle such major projects as the roof of the Houston Astrodome.

Long before the Astrodome was ever built, Cantrell left the firm in ill health and instead

Tascosa Country Club

2300 Northwestern Street
Amarillo 79106
806-374-2351
Pro: Alan Coe
A par-72, 6,492-yard private club.

• • •

turned pro and became a club pro in Lubbock.

He eventually became the golf coach at Texas Tech from 1953–58 and later became president of the PGA of America from 1964–65.

During all this, Cantrell combined his knowledge of engineering and architecture with his love of golf to design more than 30 courses. One of those was Tascosa Country Club in Amarillo.

Cantrell designed a par-72, 6,492-yard layout with high berms in the fairways and numerous sand bunkers.

There are few hazards on the course, but they are strategically placed. Out-of-bounds comes into play on many holes, which wind through a neighborhood.

Two of the Tascosa's hardest holes come back to back at Nos. 15 and 16.

No. 15 is a 232-yard par 3 that wears out many players, and is followed by the toughest hole, the 416-yard 16th, a dogleg left and the longest par 4 on the course.

There are few hazards on the course, but they are strategically placed. Out-of-bounds comes into play on many holes, which wind through a neighborhood.

The term family-owned, family-operated definitely applies at Tawakoni Golf Club.

In 1971, John Lively Sr. and his sons Bill and John Jr. built this golf course along the shore of Lake Tawakoni. John was a long-time golf pro and his sons followed in his footsteps, and between them they figured they knew enough about the game to build a successful golf course.

And they were right.

They produced a 6,691-yard, par-72 layout that is extremely flat, but nonetheless challenging with its difficult green-site locations and constant breezes off the lake. Even though it is located in the

Tawakoni Golf Club

2104 East Highway 276
Quinlan 75474
903-447-2981
Pro: John Lively Jr./Bill Lively
A par-72, 6,691-yard semi-private club.

• • •

rural community of Quinlan about an hour northeast of Dallas, most of its play comes from Dallas-area residents who would rather drive an hour to play a four-hour round of golf instead of playing a six-hour round at a golf course down the street.

This course features several large oak trees and out-of-bounds

stakes lining its narrow fairways. Most of the greens are tucked back into hard-to-reach places where they are surrounded or protected by large trees, which make accuracy important both off the tee and on the approach.

No. 7 is a par 5 where golfers tee off near the water's edge and must hit uphill through a chute of trees. The hole turns right at the top of the hill, and the landing area is protected by a pond on the right and a lake on the left. At the top of the hill, players must decide whether to go for the green in two, which requires a carry over more than 200 yards to reach a green tucked in a pocket of trees that is on the other side of a small creek.

The term family-owned, family operated definitely applies at Tawakoni Golf Club. The Lively family built this course in 1971 and still operates it.

Amos Beaty, as president of the Texas Company, wanted to give something back to his hard-working employees in the booming oil business. He envisioned a place where co-workers could also play together on weekends and days off to create a good camaraderie.

So it was on August 10, 1924, that Camp Beaty was born. It was a 140-acre park that featured a nine-hole golf course designed by Texas Co. employees. It was predated only by Houston Country Club and Hermann Park, and is now the oldest existing private course in Houston that is still in its original location.

Texaco Country Club
12800 Texaco Road.
Houston 77013
713-453-7501
A par-72, 6,300-yard private club.
• • •

The club was renamed Texaco Country Club in 1938 and nine more holes were built to accommodate the expanding membership.

There is a roll to the land and a variety of trees, including cypress trees that have been growing out of Cypress Pond for ages. The pond, blanketed with lilies, is a freak of nature for this part of the country and an awesome sight.

Longtime members insist the course was built by Texaco's own engineering crews, with the chief engineer consulting with the company's best players on the finer points of course design. Max Kreumcke was one of the employees who helped design the second nine.

Probably the best hole on the course is the 563-yard, par-5 No. 11. It is a double-dogleg that is loaded with trouble with heavy woods and Greens Bayou on the right, and once was considered one of the 18 best holes in the Houston area.

Texaco Country Club is the former site of Camp Beaty and was named after the former president of Texas Company — now known as Texaco.

Considering that Texas A&M produces more landscape architects and more agronomists than almost any other university and is of one of the world's best turf-grass research centers, you would expect the golf course that lies in the shadow of the sprawling university to be nothing less than state of the art.

It's a logical conclusion. You get an A in Deduction and Reasoning 101.

The course, however, is a case study in mid-20th century Texas golf course architecture and building golf courses that are playable for everyone. It was only the second course built by Ralph

Texas A&M Golf Course
Bizella Street
College Station 77843
409-845-1723
Pro: Johnny Andrews
A par-70, 6,513-yard public course.
• • •

Plummer, who later became a legend for his designs of the Cypress Creek course at Champions Golf Club and Dallas' Preston Trail.

The site with which Ferguson was given to work on the southeast corner of the A&M campus, however, wasn't necessarily the stuff of which great golf courses are made but he made it work.

Typical of many early Texas courses, it wasn't a big-budget operation and not a whole lot of dirt was moved. When the golf course opened in 1950, a student green fee was only 50 cents.

Plummer made the most of the rolling terrain with relatively wide fairways, water in play on eight holes, and well-trapped greens with deceptive contours.

The hardest hole is No. 9, a 212-yard par 3 from the back tees. Players must hit a long-iron or fairway wood to a long, narrow green that is protected by large traps in front and on the right. It is difficult to hit the green, much less get in range of a makeable birdie.

Texas A&M Golf Course was only the second course built by Ralph Plummer. Typical of many early courses, it wasn't a big-budget operation.

Golf has become a multi-billion dollar a year business in Texas. It now takes a multi-millionaire, a major corporation or a group of "thousand-aires" to underwrite the design and construction of a golf course.

Timber-View, then, is a monument to the entrepreneurial spirit and the free enterprise system. Even in this day and age, the little man still can.

Timber-View has been owned and operated by the Fouts family since it first opened for play in 1963.

It started with a 30-acre field of dreams that Thomas Fouts turned into a nine-hole golf

course, and as golfers and the money kept coming in, Fouts continued to purchase additional land and reconfigure the course as land and money permitted until it evolved into its current, 6,395-yard layout.

No. 4 is a 560-yard par 5 called Dead Man's Curve. The hole is a slight dogleg to the right

with trees lining the right side of the fairway from tee to green and two ponds protecting the left-hand side. The two-tiered, kidney-shaped green is nestled in a grove of trees.

No. 5 is only 296 yards and is named Easy Pickings. A small group of trees in the left-hand side of the fairway forces most players to the right side, but many players may choose to go for broke and try to hit the small, elevated green from the tee.

No. 8 is a 517-yard par 5 known as The Tunnel with out-of-bounds all the way down the right side of the fairway. There are very few trees, so players who hit out-of-bounds get what they deserve.

Timber-View has been a work in progress since 1963. It started out with nine holes, then 12, then 15 before finally turning into a full 18-hole layout.

Humble Oil Company once had several golf courses for its employees.

The company owned plenty of land, and it made a practice of turning dry oil fields into useful property by building golf courses for recreational purposes for its employees.

It owned one in Baytown, one in Pasadena and another in Tomball that eventually became known as Tomball Country Club.

The Tomball club was built in a heavily wooded, secluded piece of property in 1948 to accommodate the large number of oil field workers who moved to the remote area to work.

Tomball is still considered fairly remote, but back in 1948 there was little to do that far outside the city limits.

Like the other Humble courses, members later took over the club and it continues to operate as a private club today with 250 stock-holding members. While the Tomball area has grown up

and there is considerable competition for golfers with nearby Treeline and Cypress golf clubs, the members take pride in their privacy. Set amidst the tall pines and oaks, the layout features two sets of tees for an 18-hole round, with some holes playing up to 40 yards longer.

"The course has been popular over the years," says former pro Skip Theiss. "It's a fun course that is kept in great shape and is fun and challenging for everyone."

No. 6 is one of the longest holes in the Houston area. It is a 601-yard, dogleg left par 5. No. 9 is a 534-yard par 5, where golfers have to clear water in front of the green.

Tomball Country Club turns 50 in 1998. It was once owned by Humble Oil Company, but was later sold to members as a private club.

There is something for everyone at Tony Butler Golf Course. A challenging 18-hole course. A nine-hole regulation course that dates back to 1929. And a little history.

John Bredemus built the first nine holes here back in 1929. It was formerly known as Harlingen Country Club. Dennis W. Arp, who also built the two courses at Rancho Viejo Resort in Brownsville, built the 18-hole course some years later.

They combine to create a 27-hole facility that serves the public — from beginner to pro.

The 18-hole course is a par-71, 6,320-yard layout that is short and

Tony Butler Municipal Golf Course
2640 South M Street
Harlingen 78550
956-423-9913
Pro: Skip Cisneros
A 27-hole public course.
• • •

tight, with fairways lined by mesquite trees and some water. Playing conditions are almost always windy, which makes it even more difficult to negotiate the tight driving areas.

Almost all of the greens feature green-side bunkers. In 1997, the city of Harlingen added a new irrigation system to keep

the fairways in good shape. A lake winds through both layouts and comes into play several times, while the terrain is generally flat with some mounding.

Both courses feature tree-lined fairways, but the front nine on the 18-hole course has more water in play and plays longer than the back nine. The greens are fast and large.

One of the most difficult holes is No. 4, a 390-yard par 4. The signature hole is the 170-yard par 3 No. 15.

Bredemus' original nine holes is a par-35, 2,881-yard layout that will challenge your shot placement ability and your touch with the short irons.

Conditions are always windy, which makes it even more difficult to negotiate the tight driving areas. Almost all of the greens are guarded by bunkers.

As the son of the most prolific golf architect in the history of Baltimore-Washington D.C., Brian Ault may have a tougher time filling his father's legacy than to shoot par at one of his father's courses.

After growing up watching first hand as Edmund Ault built more than 200 courses in the northeast, the younger Ault followed in his father's footsteps.

Ault and design partner Tom Clark ventured far from home when they accepted this project in Irving at the fork of the Trinity River.

They produced a golf course that re-defines the term "Scottish

Twin Wells Golf Course
2000 East Shady Grove
Irving 75060
972-438-4340
Pro: Joe Worley
A par-72, 6,606-yard public course.
• • •

layout." It presents a high level of challenge through its rolling fairways with sand and grass bunkers.

Unlike most of his father's courses — which were typically over 7,000 yards and put a premium on long-iron play, Ault produced a par-72, 6,606-yard layout that is more user friendly.

The 437-yard, par-4 No. 3 is

the hardest hole at Twin Wells. The hole is a slight dogleg left, with the corner of the dogleg protected by bunkers.

No. 1 is a 387-yard dogleg left that requires a carry of about 200 yards off the tee to clear a creek that crosses the fairway.

The par-5 No. 15 is only 498 yards, but is guarded by a lake all the way down the right-hand side and features the smallest green on the course.

No. 11 is the hardest par 4 on the course at 451 yards. It is a dogleg left with a bunker protecting the left corner of the fairway and discouraging players from trying to cut the corner.

Brian Ault and Tom Clark re-defined the term "Scottish layout." Twin Wells presents a challenge with its rolling fairways and sand and grass bunkers.

The Sunrise Course was built in 1994 and reflects more characteristics of a modern-style golf course that was built with a bigger budget.

Houston-based architect Ken Dye — who also designed El Paso's Painted Dunes, which is in the Texas Top 100 — ventured far from home to design a par-72, 6,942-yard Scottish-links style design with numerous water hazards scattered throughout.

Much dirt was moved on the generally flat terrain to create rolling fairways.

A protégé of Joe Finger, who built many of the state's military courses, Dye learned how to

Underwood Golf Course Sunrise Course

3200 Coe Avenue
El Paso 79904
915-562-1273
Pro: Bobby Kaerwer
A par-72, 6,942-yard military course.

• • •

provide players with a great mixture of holes to challenge all facets of the golf game.

That's why it's the more demanding of the two courses at Underwood, which is El Paso's only 36-hole complex.

The Sunrise course has a slope rating of 126 and more trouble lurking for golfers who

hit errant shots.

No. 9 is the No. 1 handicap hole on the Sunrise Course, primarily because of its length. It is a 587-yard par 5 that will take three good shots for most players to reach the green.

The front nine also features a short 157-yard par 3 at No. 3. The 465-yard No. 5 is the most difficult par 4 on the layout and for most players will play like a par 5.

The back nine features another short par 4 — the 302-yard No. 11 — then comes back with a brutal 452-yard par 4 at No. 13.

No. 18 is a good finishing hole, a 441-yard, dogleg right par 4 that will make you glad to reach the 19th hole.

Ken Dye produced a Scottish-links style design with numerous water hazards. Much dirt was moved to create rolling fairways out of the flat terrain.

With all of the military golf courses in Texas, one might think learning to play golf is part of the basic training for today's army.

The way some people play golf, after all, golf can be considered a lethal weapon.

The Sunset Course at Underwood Golf Course at Fort Hood in El Paso was the first of two golf courses built for the base's off-duty army personnel. It was built in 1957.

The layout was built on flat terrain with a limited budget. The flat fairways make it an easy course to walk, and no water comes into play.

Underwood Golf Course Sunset Course

3200 Coe Avenue
El Paso 79904
915-562-1273
Pro: Bobby Kaerwer
A par-72, 6,942-yard military course.

• • •

Locals believe the Sunset Course is an excellent place for people who are just taking up the game. The par-72, 6,942-yard layout plays to a moderate slope rating of 116.

The front nine plays to a par 37 with three par 5s, including the 574-yard No. 9 (where out-of-bounds comes into play), the 513-

yard No. 3 and the 507-yard No. 5.

The par 3s are also challenging at 197 and 205 yards. While the front nine plays 3,556 yards, the back nine plays more than 500 yards shorter to a par of 35.

In contrast to the front side, the back nine features three par 3s and two par 5s.

With the exception of the 452-yard par-4 first hole, a sweeping dogleg right, most of the par 4s on this layout are under 400 yards.

On a day when the winds are calm, you can break out the driver and your short irons. The par 5s range in length from under 500 yards to 572 yards at No. 17.

The Sunset Course was the first of two courses at Underwood Golf Course. It was built on flat terrain, which makes it easier to walk.

Life on the Brazos River made Valley Lodge a peaceful getaway from big city life, but in December 1990 the same river that give it life nearly drowned it to death.

The little jewel of a course hidden away in the tiny town of Simonton, some 40 minutes from downtown, was wiped out by flooding when the Brazos River spilled over its banks and covered the entire course for several days.

When the floodwaters had subsided, owner Mellisa Fletcher faced a muddy mess, not to mention a financial disaster.

When the floodwaters subsided, the greens had been lost

Valley Lodge Golf Club

614 Horseshoe
Simonton 77476
281-346-1426
Manager: Mike White
A nine-hole public course.

• • •

when floodwaters from the river backed up through the drainage system and came up through the greens. Silt was everywhere and even settled into the drainage system. The course was closed for six months while Fletcher sought federal disaster assistance to rebuild the course.

The flooding came at an inop-

portune time. The club was originally built in the 1950s by a group of equity members, most of whom lived local community.

There were only 16 equity members left when Fletcher bought the course in 1989, then she poured $250,000 into improvements. She was in the process of seeking funding to build an additional nine holes when the floodwaters hit.

Valley Lodge eventually recovered and reopened. Now, they're just keeping their fingers crossed and watching the skies.

The quaint layout features some good holes, including the 211-yard, par-3 No. 8 and the 411-yard, par-4 No. 6.

This little jewel is hidden away in the tiny town of Simonton, and has overcome numerous floods from the nearby Brazos River.

Kristi Albers grew up playing golf at Vista Hills Country Club. Locals knew her back then as Kristi Arrington, before she went off to college and became an All-American at the University of New Mexcio, married sportscaster Fred Albers and became a star on the LPGA Tour.

Butch Henry, a major league pitcher, also is a member here.

Vista Hills was built in 1973 by architects Robert von Hagge and Bruce Devlin, who are known for producing some of the state's most challenging courses.

Vista Hills certainly holds its own with a par-72, 7,032-yard layout that plays to a 129 slope rating from the back tees.

Vista Hills Golf Course

2210 Trawood Drive
El Paso 79935
915-592-6565
Pro: Terry Jennings
A par-72, 7,032-yard private club.

• • •

The desert-style course tends to be somewhat hilly, so you can expect some uneven lies. The fairways are narrow, as they wind through a residential subdivision with out-of-bounds coming into play on many holes.

No. 4 is a 384-yard par 4. Trees line the left side of a narrow

fairway, which offers a panoramic view of El Paso and Mexico.

No. 17 is a demanding 450-yard par 4 with a long hole and may trees on the right and out-of-bounds left and right. A water hzard 100 yards out from the green forces players to carry a long approach shot over water to the green.

No. 13 is a 307-yard, dogleg right par 4, as the fairway curves around a lake and some apartment buildings. Some big hitters try to cut the corner and go over the top of the apartments and the lake, but doing so requires a drive with a 250-yard carry off the tee.

The desert-style course tends to be somewhat hilly, so expect some uneven lies. The fairways are narrow, as they wind through a residential subdivision.

W alnut Creek Country Club has been called a hidden gem in metroplex golf, but that's okay with the members who have already discovered this private club in Mansfield.

First opened as an 18-hole layout in 1968, Walnut Creek has a membership of 900 people, most of them very eager golfers.

The Walnut Creek membership got some additional room to roam in the fall of 1995 when a new nine holes were opened, giving the club a 36-hole facility.

"The main reason for the new nine was just to allow additional play," one pro said. "Mansfield is growing very fast

Walnut Creek Country Club Oak Course

1151 Country Club Drive
Mansfield 76063
817-473-6114
Pro: Junior Salinas
A 36-hole private club.

• • •

and we have a lot of people who like to play here."

The first 18-hole layout was designed by Texas residents and PGA stars Don January and Billy Martindale. The expansion to 27 holes came in 1985 and was done by Don Prigmore.

The latest nine was in the planning stages for more than a

year and was designed by the Fort Worth team of Mark Brooks and Burt Baine.

Brooks is another PGA star and Fort Worth native. He has done some other courses in the area, including managing the former Carswell Air Force Base golf course.

The Oak Course is a par 71 and plays 6,700 yards from the back tees.

Length is not as important here as accuracy. The trees, which crowd many of the fairways, penalize anyone who leaves the driving areas with regularity.

Walnut Creek has hosted *The Dallas Morning News* Tournament of Champions for several years.

Length is not as important here as accuracy. The trees, which crowd many of the fairways, penalize anyone who leaves the driving areas with regularity.

F ive years after Don January and Billy Martindale designed Royal Oaks Country Club in Dallas — which is still one of the state's top courses — they built an 18-hole layout in what was then the sleepy little town of Mansfield.

The year was 1974, and the place was Walnut Creek Country Club. And January and Martindale produced a challenging layout that is similar to many of their other Texas courses, such as Woodhaven, Woodcrest, Los Rios, Pecan Hollow and Oakmont.

Walnut Creek later added 18 additional holes to produce a booming 36-hole club with more

Walnut Creek Country Club Pecan Course

1151 Country Club Drive
Mansfield 76063
817-473-6114
Pro: Junior Salinas
A 36-hole private club.

• • •

than 1,000 members. The club is now owned an operated by Dallas-based Club Corporation of America.

The original January-Martindale course is known as the Pecan Course. It is a more traditional layout of the two, with long, tight fairways. It is also more difficult than the newer Oak Course.

Among the best holes on the Pecan Course are the 378-yard, par-4 No. 1. Players tee off from an elevated tee with a creek running along the left-hand side of the fairway.

The hole doglegs left with an approach to an elevated green and trees on the left and right side of the fairway.

No. 6 is a 440-yard par 4 that doglegs right with out-of-bounds down the left side. Golfers must clear a water hazard on the approach shot to a slightly elevated green.

No. 11 is a 438-yard, dogleg left par 4 down a treelined fairway. The hole plays downhill to a small green.

The Pecan Course at Walnut Creek is a more traditional layout with lots of long, tight fairways that twist and turn through the trees.

LPGA Hall of Famer Kathy Whitworth has won more professional tour victories than any other golfer in the United States. was the first female player to break the $1 million barrier.

And it all started right here in Monahans, at Ward County Golf Course.

Whitworth was born in Monahans before her family moved to New Mexico, so her first golf experience came at Ward County Golf Course. Little did anyone know what great things she would go on to accomplish.

She was the LPGA's leading money winner eight times and the Player of the Year seven times.

Ward County Golf Course

PO Box 1693, North Highway 18
Monahans 79756
915-943-5044
A par-72, 6,669-yard public course.

• • •

Whitworth's last LPGA victory came in 1985 at the United Virginia Bank Classic. That win brought to 88 her total number of career victories, an all-time record for both the men's and women's U.S. tours. Whitworth is the most decorated player in LPGA history. She was the leading money winner eight times (1965–68, and

70–73) and the Player of the Year seven times (1968–69 and 71-73). Her most successful financial season was 1983 when she won $190,000.

Tutored by Harvey Penick and Hardy Loudermilk, she was Associated Press Athlete of the Year in 1965 and '67. She was named Golfer of the Decade by *Golf Magazine* for the years 1968-77. She is in the Texas and World Golf halls of fame.

This nice and easy course offers a little bit of everything. The greens vary in size and undulation, and the wind frequently comes into play, making proper club selection an important part of the game.

LPGA Hall of Famer Kathy Whitworth got her first golf experience at Ward County and went on to become the winningest player in golf history.

Wolfe City funeral home director Bobby Owens, on behalf of the town, applied for a $500,000 FHA grant to construct Webb Hill Country Club in 1969.

The loans were designed to help rural towns build recreational facilities for their residents. While most of the courses built under that program went defunct, Webb Hill has long outlived its contemporaries.

While many of those courses turned out to be financial flops, Webb Hill is a beautiful 18-hole golf course that has long outlived its contemporaries and has continued to serve not only local residents but golfers from through-

Webb Hill Country Club

Route 1, PO Box 190-A
Wolfe City 75496
903-496-2221
Pro: Charles Ranley
A 18-hole private club.

• • •

out the state who come here to play this interesting layout.

Leon Howard designed the first nine holes on hilly, wooded terrain and produced a layout with narrow fairways and large undulating greens. Numerous lakes and ponds come into play on about half the holes.

The signature hole is No. 8, a

590-yard par 5 that requires a pair of shots onto a fairway that bends around a lake and an approach to a narrow, tree-lined green. It requires a downhill fade off the tee through a grove of cedars, pecans and other native trees. Even long hitters must fade a fairway wood on the approach and find the narrow landing area with woods left and a pond right.

There are eight blind tee shots and eight downhill tee shots, which force players to use a variety of clubs off the tee.

On a few holes, golfers must use a giant periscope constructed on the tee box to determine if the group in front has moved out of the landing area.

Webb Hill has long outlived many of its contemporaries and has continued to be one of the most interesting layouts in the state.

Some of the state's legendary players have walked the fairways at Weeks Park, which was built in 1923 and has proven to be up to the challenge for the past 75 years.

The course is highlighted by creeks coming into play on 16 holes. However, the fairways are fairly open. The greens are rolling and sloped, but putt true.

The Dallas Morning News ranked Weeks Park as the 14th best municipal golf course in Texas in 1994.

The first hole is only a 279-yard par 4 that some golfers can reach off the tee. Water runs down the left side of the fairway.

Weeks Park Golf Course

4400 Lake Park Drive
Wichita Falls 76302
940-767-6107
Pro: Dick Weston
A par-72, 6,416-yard public course.

• • •

The par-3, 212-yard No. 8 is the toughest hole on the course. A winding creek cuts into the fairway and then around the left side and behind the green, leaving golfers little margin for error on the approach.

No. 10 is a 150-yard par 3 that requires a drive over water. The green runs back toward the

water. Golfers tend to overhit here to make sure they clear the water, but they are left with a tricky downhill putt back to the hole.

No. 18 is a 396-yard par 4 with a creek crossing the fairway in the landing area. Golfers must choose either to lay up off the tee and clear the water on their second shot, or try to clear the creek off the tee to set up a short-iron approach.

Players are faced with back-to-back par 5s at Nos. 15 and 16.

No. 15 is a dogleg right with a creek crossing in front of the tee box and No. 16 is a 559-yard par 5 with a row of trees down both sides of the fairway.

The course is highlighted by creeks that come into play on 16 holes. The fairways are open, and the greens are undulating and fast.

Temple's Wildflower Country Club has more than lived up to its name in its brief life-span. It opened in 1987 with Texas architect Leon Howard as the designer.

The club has most of the members from the old Temple Country Club which was forced to shut down in 1985 due to financial problems.

Howard crafted a challenging course which plays just over 7,000 yards from the championship markers with some stunning views of the Hill Country landscape.

There is water on 10 holes and 29 sand traps scattered throughout the course.

Wildflower Golf Club

4902 Wildflower Lane
Temple 76502
254-771-1477
Pro: Bill Euler
A par-72, 7,010-yard private club.

• • •

Bill Euler is the PGA head professional. He oversees a course with a full pro shop, driving range and more than 800 members with uncounted numbers of wildflowers each spring.

One measure of a courses' reputation is the number of state tournaments it is asked to host. Already in its 10-year history,

Wildflower has played host to both the boys' and girls' Texas State Championship and the Texas Golf Association Father-Son Championship.

The par-72, 7,010-yard layout features many strong par 4s over 400 yards. No. 3, for instance, is the hardest hole on the course. It is a 446-yard par 4 where golfers must clear a creek that crosses the fairway about 100 yards off the tee.

No. 17 is a 367-yard par 4 where the green and tee are surrounded by water. On the approach, golfers must hit a peninsula green guarded by water in front, back and on the left.

Leon Howard crafted a challenging course that plays just over 7,000 yards with stunning views of the surrounding Hill Country landscape.

Wildwood is the perfect name for this 18-hole course located about 40 miles north of Beaumont near the Big Thicket National Preserve. There is plenty of wood around, and the land definitely qualifies as wilderness country.

Wildwood Resort city was developed in 1966 and architect Leon Howard designed a layout to be the centerpiece of this resort community.

It was started by a few private investors, and later sold to Recreation World. That company went bankrupt in 1986, and the course was taken over by the property owners.

Howard designed a par-72,

Wildwood Golf Club

2200 Button Willow Drive
Village Mills 77663
Pro: Louisa Bergsma
409-834-2940
A par-72, 6,696-yard public course.

• • •

6,696-yard layout with fairways lined by tall pines and oak trees and water in play on 10 holes. The course plays to a 121-slope rating from the back tees.

While the fairways are tree-lined, Howard carved out generous fairways to give golfers plenty of landing areas off the tee — it takes a really errant tee shot to

get in trouble. The hilly terrain can cause some uneven lies, and the large greens are also mounded.

No. 18 is the signature hole. It is a 477-yard par 4 with water crossing the fairway about 220 yards off the tee, forcing players to go for broke or lay up and face a nearly impossible shot to reach the green in two.

No. 9 is a similar par 4 at 455 yards and water crossing the fairway again. But this time, the water is about 270 yards off the tee, so most players must lay up and clear the water on their second shot.

No. 12 is a 221-yard par 3 that is long enough as it is, but also requires a carry over a creek in front of the green.

Wildwood is appropriately named, with tree-lined fairways carving through the tall hardwoods of the Big Thicket and creating a scenic layout.

Willow Springs has undergone many changes in its 71-year history from a private country club to PGA tournament site to a city golf facility. Located along Salado Creek in eastern San Antonio, it is now one of six San Antonio municipal golf courses and gives golfers the opportunity to walk the same fairways where Sam Snead, Ben Hogan and other top professionals once played.

The course opened in 1923, making it one of the oldest in the city. It started out as a nine-hole layout built by architect Emil Loeffler on a rare swing through Texas. Architect John Bredemus returned two years later in 1925

Willow Springs Golf Course

202 Coliseum Road
San Antonio 78219
210-226-6721
Pro: John Erwin
A par-72, 7,218-yard municipal course.

• • •

to renovate the first nine and add nine holes. Bredemus, who helped found the Texas PGA, used his influence to bring the Texas Open to Willow Springs with Bobby Cruikshank and Billy Mehlhorn capturing the title in 1927 and '28, respectively. The 1940s saw the course host the Texas Open eight times with the

likes of Hogan, Snead and Byron Nelson mastering the course.

The club was eventually sold to the city after a shortage of members during World War II and became the city's third municipal layout. It boasts one of the longest holes in the state. The par-5 second hole is listed at 663 yards from the back tees and requires three huge shots to reach the green.

"Most low handicap players will tell you the two things that make this course tough," former pro Ken Sealey says, "are the size of the greens and the length of the course. For the length of the course, the greens are small, very small."

Willow Springs is a public course where golfers have the chance to walk the same fairways that Sam Snead, Ben Hogan and other top pros once played.

In 1958, a pair of Dallas promoters built an elegant, ultra-modern clubhouse off the 14000 block of South Main and hired architect Joe Finger to convert a cow pasture into a low-budget golf course.

They called it Glenhaven Country Club and sold lifetime memberships for $1,000 out of a makeshift real-estate office.

Much to the dismay of those members, it turned out to be a get-rich-quick scam. After making their money, the developers skipped town and left the members and the country club to go bankrupt.

Investors Bob Simmer and

Willowisp Country Club

14502 Fondren Road
Missouri City 77459
713-437-8210
Pro: Randy Lewis
A par-71, 6,705-yard private club.

• • •

Bob Curtis purchased the club in 1964 and reopened Willowisp Country Club in 1964. When they took over, their first order of business was to transplant 800 pines and live oaks.

They then purchased more than 12,000 small plants and seedlings. It was so successful, they bought 30,000 additional

plants. All totaled, they planted 80,000 seedlings, installed 42 sand traps and a dual line irrigation system since taking over.

Nos. 6-11 could be one of the most difficult stretch of holes in the city. No. 6 is a 538-yard par 5 that ranks as the most difficult on the course, No. 8 is a 231-yard par 3, No. 9 is a 457-yard par 4, No. 10 is a 474-yard par 4 and No. 11 is a 538-yard par 5.

"The course has come a long way since those days," says head pro Randy Lewis, who has been at the club almost since it reopened as Willowisp. "It's a true-blue country club now. The trees have grown up to make the course very challenging."

"The course has come a long way since those days. It's a true-blue country club now. The trees have grown up to make the course very challenging."

When businessman Murrey Winn first developed the town of Windcrest, he was looking for a place of comfort, safety and recreation outside the hustle and bustle of the big city. A peaceful place where residents would be out of crime's way and traffic jams.

If it sounds too good to be true, get in line.

That's exactly what he found in Windcrest Country Club, a nine-hole course that remains popular with citizens of this North San Antonio suburb. It celebrated its 30th anniversary in 1994.

Winn's nine-hole golf course is only 2,780 yards with a par of 34,

Windcrest Golf Club

8600 Midcrown
San Antonio 78239
210-655-1421
A nine-hole private club.

• • •

but there is a two-year waiting list to join. The layout has three par 3s and one par 5, the closing hole. Different tees allow it to be played twice for 18 holes in three hours or less.

Of course, don't mistake Windcrest for your everyday, run-of-the mill pitch and putt. Wendy Ward, a 1994 Curtis Cup team

member and U.S. Amateur champion who now plays at Arizona State, played at Windcrest during her public school days.

Hazards lie along the third, fourth, sixth, seventh and ninth fairways. Water also comes into play from three ponds. Par 3s are guarded by water on Nos. 5 and 7 along with the par 4 No. 8 and the par 5 No. 9, measuring 491 yards down a narrow fairway.

"It's a very friendly, pleasant environment," club manager Dick Hickenbottom says. "It's short enough to score well and it doesn't take five hours to play. Many of the holes have narrow, tree-lined fairways. There is plenty of out-of-bounds here."

While Windcrest Golf Club is only a 2,780-yard nine-hole course in northern San Antonio, there is a two-year waiting list to join.

Lawrence Smith was a prominent developer in the Hill Country who first built Woodcreek in 1971 in the sleepy community of Wimberley, 50 miles north of San Antonio and 35 miles southeast of Austin. It was designed to lure city-slickers out into the Hill Country.

Architect Bruce Littell designed a course over oak-covered hills and around fresh streams and creeks. The first course was so successful, in fact, that Smith hired architect Leon Howard to build a second layout at the course called Cypress Creek in the mid-1970s.

The 6,805-yard course

Woodcreek Country Club

No. 1 Pro Lane
Wimberley 78676
512-847-9700
Pro: Michael Bertagna
A par-72, 6,470-yard semi-private club.

• • •

Howard built at Woodcreek was open for only a year before it was closed for financial reasons. During a period of the next eight years, the club and resort were operated on a survival budget under the guidance of the FDIC. Course workers converted the irrigation system from Howard's course to keep the one on the

original course up and running.

Woodcreek has endured and Smith's dream lives on in the eyes of new owners who bought the course in May of 1993. They immediately began to restore the course and plan to reopen Howard's course to complete a 36-hole facility. Littell's original par-72, 6,470-yard layout is still as challenging as ever with its tree-lined fairways.

Woodcreek management advertises Woodcreek Resort as golf in the Heart of Hill Country. Since Wimberley was voted one of the friendliest towns in Texas by *Texas Monthly* in 1992, They could never be accused of false advertising.

Architect Bruce Littell designed this course over oak-covered hills and around fresh streams and creeks.

Miller Barber Jr. is commonly known on PGA and Senior PGA tours as "Mr. X."

His dark-shaded glasses on the golf course were distinctive, but if you saw him anywhere else you might have thought he worked for the CIA, FBI or some government operative.

Back on the golf course, Barber was distinctive for other reasons. He was only the third player in history to win more than $4 million in combined career money on both tours.

It all started in his hometown of Sherman, where he learned to play the game at Woodlawn Country Club. He went on to play

Woodlawn Country Club

PO Box 1303, Miller Barber Road
Sherman 75090
903-893-3240
Pro: Sale Omohundro
A par-71, 6,405-yard private club.

• • •

at the University of Arkansas and eventually turned pro in 1959.

As a pro, he won a total of 35 tournaments on the regular and senior tours and represented the United States in the Ryder Cup Matches in 1969 and 1971.

He won at least one event a year from 1967 to 1974, a feat matched only by Jack Nicklaus

during that period.

Barber also is the only three-time winner of the U.S. Senior Open, and is a member of both the Texas Golf Hall of Fame and the Arkansas Hall of Fame.

Woodlawn proved to be a great proving ground for Barber. The layout was built in 1920.

The par-71, 6,405-yard layout is a traditional old-style course built on rolling terrain with tree-lined fairways.

The 140-yard, par-3 No. 5 is Woodlawn's signature hole. While the hole is short, it requires a precise tee shot into a peninsula green protected by water on three sides.

Miller Barber's career started at Woodlawn Country Club, where he learned to play the game and went on to win 35 pro tournaments.

Abernathy Country Club
PO Box 337
Abernathy 79311
806-328-5261
9 holes, semi-private

Alamo Country Club
9214 Sailfish
Boerne 78006
830-981-4276
Pro: Mac Wylie

Alamo Country Club
9700 Rochelle
San Antonio 78240
210-696-4000
Pro: Victor Yannuzzi
9 holes, semi-private

Alamo Country Club
North Tower Road
Alamo 78516
956-787-0907
Pro: Malline Green
9 holes, private

Albany Golf Club
PO Box 157
Albany 76430
915-762-3746
9 holes, public

Alice Country Club
PO Box 1428
Alice 78333
512-664-3723
Pro: Tim Miller
9 holes, private

Alice Municipal Golf Course
PO Box 646
Alice 78331
512-664-7033
Pro: Ricky Monsevias
18 holes, public

Alpine Golf Club
PO Box 610
Longview 75605
903-753-4515
Pro: Mike Williams
18 holes, public

Alsatian Golf Course
Quihi Road
Castroville 78009
210-931-3100
Pro: Tommy Real
18 holes, public

Ambassador College Golf Course
Highway 80
Big Sandy 75755
903-636-2000
9 holes, private

Andrews County Golf Course
PO Box 348
Andrews 79714
915-524-1462
Pro: Alan Pursley
18 holes, private

Anson Golf Club
Route 1, PO Box 1
Anson 79502
915-823-9822
9 holes, public

Archer City Country Club
1005 South Ash Street
Archer City 76351
817-574-4322
9 holes, semi-private

Aspermount City Golf Course
PO Box 419
Aspermount 79502
940-989-3381
9 holes, semi-private

Athens Country Club
PO Box 749
Athens 75751
903-677-3844
Pro: Gaylord Walden
18 holes, private

Ballinger Country Club
PO Box 641
Ballinger 76821
915-365-3214
9 holes, private

Baycel Golf Club
Celanese Road
Bay City 77414
409-245-4871
9 holes, private

Beacon Lakes Golf Club
I-45 and Holland Road
Dickinson 77539
281-337-1459
Pro: Dean Wilson
9 holes, private

Beaver Brook Country Club
Route 1, PO Box 306G
Daingerfield 75638
903-645-2976
9 holes, private

Beeville Country Club
Highway 181 North
Beeville 78104-0396
512-358-1216
Pro: Bobby Schauer
9 holes, private

Bellville Golf and Recreation Club
Highway 36
Bellville 77418
409-865-9058
Pro: Tim Mewis
9 holes, private

Bellwood Golf Course
800 Bellwood Golf Road
Tyler 75709
903-597-4871
18 holes, public

Better Golf, Inc.
Route 1 PO Box 715
Waco 76711
254-848-4831
Pro: Ray Lamb

Big Cedar Country Club
Route 2 PO Box 224
Teague 75860
254-739-5600
Pro: Ken Moss
9 holes, semi-private

Big Lake Golf Course
Highway 67
Big Lake 76932
915-884-2633
9 holes, private

Big Spring Country Club
East Driver Road
Big Spring 79721-3686
915-267-5354
Pro: Larry Bryan
18 holes, private

Birmingham Golf Club
Highway 69 South
Rusk 75785
903-683-9518
9 holes, semi-private

Bluebonnet Country Club
Fairy Road
Hico 76457
817-796-4122
9 holes, private

Bonham Golf Club
 501 West Russell Street
 Bonham 75418
 903-583-8815
 9 holes, private

Booker Country Club
 Highway 15
 Booker 79005-0122
 806-658-9663
 9 holes, public

Bosque Valley Golf Club
 Old Clifton Highway/FM 1991
 Meridian 76665
 817-435-2692
 Pro: Harvey Welch
 9 holes, semi-private

Brady Municipal Golf Club
 Highway 87 West
 Brady 76825
 915-597-6010
 9 holes, public

Breckenridge Country Club
 Route 3, PO Box 53
 Breckenridge 76424
 817-559-3466
 Pro: Paul Blackerly
 9 holes, public

Brenham Country Club
 Highway 105 East
 Brenham 77834-0223
 409-836-1733
 Pro: Mark R Gray
 9 holes, private

Brentwood Country Club
 4201 South Major Drive
 Beaumont 77707
 409-840-9010

Bridgeport Country Club
 Highway 2123
 Bridgeport 76426
 817-683-9438
 9 holes, semi-private

Brownfield Country Club
 Tahoka Highway
 Brownfield 79316
 806-637-3656
 9 holes, private

Brownsville Country Club
 McFadden Hut Drive No. 6
 Brownsville 78520-8905
 956-541-2582
 Pro: Scott Blundell
 18 holes, semi-private

Brownwood Country Club
 Highway 377
 Brownwood 76804
 915-646-1086
 Pro: Steven McNabb
 18 holes, private

Calvert Country Club
 PO Box 244
 Calvert 77837-0244
 409-364-2803
 9 holes, private

Canadian Golf Club
 Highway 83
 Canadian 79014
 806-323-5512
 Pro: Kirk Marrow
 9 holes, semi-private

Canyon Country Club
 Route 1, PO Box 213
 Canyon 79015
 806-499-3397
 Pro: Larry Squier
 9 holes, semi-private

Canyon Springs Golf Club
 150 Evans Road
 San Antonio 78232
 Pro: Terry Olivarri
 18 holes, semi-private

Caprock Golf Course
 PO Box 220
 Post 79356
 806-495-3029
 9 holes, public

Carmack Lake Golf Course
 Route 1, PO Box 228
 Converse 78109
 210-658-3806
 Pro: Don Carmack
 18 holes, public

Carrizo Springs Municipal
Golf Course
 Route 2, PO Box 44
 Carrizo Springs 78834
 512-876-2596
 9 holes, public

Carthage Country Club
 Highway 59
 Carthage 75633
 903-693-3313
 9 holes, private

Casablanca Municipal Golf Course
 Highway 59
 Laredo 78041
 956-727-9218
 Pro: Baltazar Ramos
 18 holes, public

Center Country Club
 Highway 96
 Center 75935
 409-598-5513
 9 holes, semi-private

Chemcel Golf Club
 Business Highway 77
 Bishop 78343
 512-584-6468
 9 holes, private

Chemlake Golf Course
 9502 Bayport Road
 Pasadena 77507
 281-474-6402
 9 holes, private

Cherokee Country Club
 Highway 79 East
 Jacksonville 75766
 903-586-2141
 Pro: Tom Campbell
 18 holes, semi-private

Childress Country Club
 Highway 83
 Childress 79201
 817-937-8552
 9 holes, private

Clarendon Country Club
 Country Club Drive
 Clarendon 79226
 806-874-2166
 Pro: Nobel Watson
 18 holes, semi-private

Clarksville Country Club
 Highway 37 North
 Clarksville 75426
 903-427-3450
 9 holes, private

Classic-3 Golf Course
 6224 Theall Road
 Houston 77066
 713-440-1308
 Pro: Randall Amason
 9 holes, public

Clay County Country Club
PO Box 494
Henrietta 76365
817-538-4339
9 holes, semi-private

Cleburne Municipal Golf Course
22000 Country Club Road
Cleburne 76033
817-641-4501
Pro: Ronnie Humphrey
18 holes, public

Coleman Country Club
206 San Angelo Hwy
Coleman 76834
915-625-2922
9 holes, semi-private

Colony Creek Country Club
301 Colony Creek Drive
Victoria 77904
512-576-0020
Pro: David Bre Turrentine
18 holes, private

Columbus Golf Course
1617 Walnut
Columbus 78934
409-732-5575
9 holes, semi-private

Comanche Creek Golf Club
PO Box 397
Mason 76856
915-347-5798
9 holes, public

Comanche Trail Golf Course
800 Comanche Trail Rd
Big Spring 79720
915-263-7271
18 holes, public

Copperas Cove Municipal
Golf Course
Golf Course Road
Copperas Cove 76522
817-547-2606
Pro: David Kasesheimer
9 holes, public

Copperas Hollow Country Club
Highway 36
Caldwell 77836
409-567-4422
Pro: David McNeely
9 holes, semi-private

Corsicana Golf Academy
PO Box 85
Corsicana 75151
903-872-1801

Cottonwood Creek Golf Course
1001 South Ed Carey Drive
Harlingen 78552
956-428-7758
9 holes, public

Country Campus Golf Course
Route 3, PO Box 558
Huntsville 77340
409-291-0008
9 holes, public

Country Place Golf Course
2727 Country Place
Carrollton 75006
972-416-0660
9 holes, private

Crane County Country Club
300 East 20th
Crane 79731
915-558-2651
9 holes, semi-private

Crepe Myrtle Creek Golf Course
514 W. Fordall
Henderson 75652
903-657-3325
Pro: Larry Sims
9 holes, public

Crooked Creek Golf Course
Highway 240
Electra 76360
817-495-3832
9 holes, public

Cuero Park Municipal GC
Route 4, PO Box 122
Cuero 77954
512-275-3233
Pro: Keith S Krueger
9 holes, public

Cypress Creek Country Club
Route 1, PO Box 95
Scroggins 75480
903-860-2155
9 holes, semi-private

Dalhart Country Club
PO Box 130
Dalhart 79021
806-249-5596
18 holes, semi-private

Decatur Golf Club
Route 3, PO Box 208
Decatur 76234
817-627-3789
9 holes, semi-private

Delta Country Club
FM 1529
Cooper 75432
903-395-4712
9 holes, semi-private

Denison Country Club
PO Box 96
Denison 75020
903-465-4485
18 holes, private

Devine Golf Course
116 Malone Drive
Devine 78016
830-663-9943
Pro: Kevin Yanity
18 holes, public

Dimmitt Country Club
PO Box 967
Dimmit 79027
806-647-4502
Pro: Kevin Gwyn
9 holes, private

Dogwood Hills Country Club
150 Highway 190 West
Woodville 75979
409-283-8725
9 holes, public

DuPont Employees
Recreation Association
2601 Irving
Orange 77630
409-886-1779
18 holes, private

Eagle Lake Recreation Center
PO Box 845
Eagle Lake 77434
409-234-5981
9 holes, public

Eagle Pass Golf Course
Fort Duncan Park
Eagle Pass 78852
210-773-9761
9 holes, public

Ebony Golf Course
300 West Palms
Edinburg 78539
210-381-1244
9 holes, public

Edna Country Club
Country Road
Edna 77957
512-782-3010
9 holes, semi-private

El Campo Country Club
PO Box 167
El Campo 77437
409-543-6592
9 holes, private

Eldorado Golf Club
PO Box 1116
Eldorado 76936
915-853-2036
9 holes, public

Elk Hollow Golf Course
2200 Elk Hollow Drive
Paris 75460
903-785-6585
Pro: Mike Bezley
9 holes, public

Elkhart Golf Club
FM 1817
Elkhart 75839
903-764-2461
18 holes, public

Fairway Farm Golf Course
PO Box 575
San Augustine 75972
Pro: Andy Stephens
18 holes, semi-private

Falfurrias Golf Course
400 East Travis
Falfurrias 78355
512-325-5348
9 holes, public

Farwell Country Club
Route 2
Farwell 79325
806-481-9210
Pro: Chris Fontanilla
9 holes, public

Flatonia Golf Course
PO Box 391
Flatonia 78941
512-865-2922
Pro: Ed Husley
9 holes, public

Floydada Country Club
Route 3, PO Box 157
Floydada 79235
806-983-2769
9 holes, semi-private

Fort Brown Municipal Golf Course
5048 Pinto Court
Brownsville 78521
956-541-9556
Pro: Scott Lucio
18 holes, public

Fort Clark Springs Golf Course
PO Box 345
Brackettville 78832
830-563-9204
Pro: Bob Delarosa
18 holes, public

Fort Hood/Anderson Golf Course
Fort Hood Golf Facility
Building 5794
Fort Hood 76544
254-287-6921
18 holes, private/military

Fort Hood/Clear Creek Golf Course
Fort Hood Golf Facility
Building 52381
Fort Hood 76544
254-287-4130
Pro: Frank Jacobson
18 holes, private/military

Fox Creek Golf Course
Route 3, PO Box 128F
Hempstead 77445
281-826-2131
Pro: Steve Green
18 holes, public

Freeport Community Golf Course
830 Slaughter Road
Freeport 77541
409-233-8311
18 holes, public

Friona Country Club
1505 West Fifth Street
Friona 79035
806-247-3125
9 holes, private

Frisch Auf Valley Country Club
575 Country Club Drive
La Grange 78945
409-968-6113
9 holes, semi-private

Gainesville Municipal Golf Course
200 South Rusk
Gainesville 76240
817-665-2161
18 holes, public

Ganado Golf and Country Club
PO Box 1218
Ganado 77962
512-771-2424
9 holes, semi-private

Gatesville Country Club
Straws Mill Road
Gatesville 76528
817-865-6917
18 holes, semi-private

Giddings Country Club
Highway 290
Giddings 7894
409-542-3777
9 holes, semi-private

Gilmer Country Club
Highway 155
Gilmer 75644
903-734-4125
9 holes, private

Gladewater Country Club
PO Box 66
Gladewater 75647
903-845-4566
9 holes, public

Goliad Country Recreation Assn.
West Fannin Street
Goliad 77963
512-645-8478
9 holes, private

Graham Country Club
Fort Belknap Road
Graham 76450
817-549-7721
Pro: JR Bohn
9 holes, semi-private

Grayson College Golf Course
7109 Dinn
Denison 75020
903-786-9719
Pro: Mike Hurley
18 holes, public

Hallettsville Golf Course
PO Box 433
Hallettsville 77964
512-798-7190
9 holes, public

Hamlin Golf Course/Joe E. Ford
130 Southwest Avenue J
Hamlin 79520-4512
915-576-3926

Hancock Park
  Highway 281 South
  Lampasses 76550
  830-556-3202
  Pro: Van Berry
  18 holes, public

Hansford Golf Club
  PO Box 335
  Spearman 79081
  806-659-2233
  9 holes, semi-private

Harlingen Country Club
  5500 El Camino Real
  Harlingen 78552
  956-412-4110
  Pro: Buddy Kalencki
  18 holes, private

Haskell County Country Club
  Route 1, PO Box 190
  Haskell 79521
  817-864-3400
  9 holes, semi-private

Hatch Bend Country Club
  PO Box 141
  Port Lavaca 77979
  512-552-3037
  9 holes, semi-private

Hearne Municipal Golf Course
  405 Norwood
  Hearne 77889
  409-279-3112
  9 holes, public

Hempstead Golf Course
  PO Box 186
  Hempstead 77445
  281-826-3212
  9 holes, public

Henderson Country Club
  1095 Highway 43 East
  Henderson 75652
  903-657-6443
  9 holes, private

Herron Lakes Golf Club
  Sam Houston Tollway
  Houston 77084
  281-894-0621
  Pro: Wayne McNary
  18-holes, public

Hillcrest Country Club
  North University Road
  Lubbock 79408
  806-765-5208
  Pro: Tommy Darland
  18 holes, private

Hillcrest Country Club
  PO Box 1433
  Vernon 76384
  940-552-5406
  9 holes, private

Hillsboro Country Club
  PO Box 455
  Hillsboro 76645
  817-582-8211
  9 holes, private

Hillside Acres Country Club
  Cotton Center Highway
  Hale Center 79041
  806-839-2188
  9 holes, public

Hilltop Country Club
  PO Box 455
  Troup 75789
  903-842-3516
  9 holes, private

Holiday Hills Country Club
  PO Box 68
  Mineral Wells 76068
  940-325-8403
  Pro: Bill McGaha
  18 holes, semi-private

Hondo Golf Course
  PO Box 2
  Hondo 78861
  512-426-8825
  9 holes, public

Horseshoe Bend Country Club
  305 Lipan Trail
  Weatherford 76086-9670
  817-594-6454
  9 holes, semi-private

Huber Golf Club
  PO Box 2831
  Borger 79007-2831
  806-273-2231
  Pro: Richard M Hale
  18 holes, semi-private

Independence Golf Course
  PO Box 198
  Gonzales 78629
  210-672-9926
  9 holes, public

Indian Hills Country Club
  PO Box 507
  Atlanta 75551
  903-796-4146
  9 holes, semi-private

Indian Oaks Golf Course
  Route 2, County Road 4067
  Peeltown 75143
  903-498-3564
  30 holes, public

Indian Oaks Golf Course
  West Highway 82
  Nocona 76255
  940-825-4213
  Pro: Bob Crowley
  18 holes, public

Indian Shores Golf Course
  2141 White Feather Trail
  Crosby 77531
  281-324-2592
  Pro: Bruce Motal
  9 holes, semi-private

Iraan Country Club
  PO Box 356
  Iraan 79744
  915-639-8892
  9 holes, public

Island Oaks Golf Course
  County Road 33
  Idalou 79329
  806-892-2839
  9 holes, public

Jacksboro Country Club
  309 North Eighth
  Jacksboro 76458
  817-567-3031
  Pros: Henry/Karen Strickland
  9 holes, semi-private

Jasper Country Club
  PO Box 477
  Jasper 75951
  409-384-4342
  9 holes, private

John C. Beasley Golf Course
  Highway 59
  Beeville 78102
  512-358-4295
  9 holes, public

Junction Golf Club
  FM 2169
  Junction 76849
  915-446-2968
  9 holes, public

Karnes County Country Club
Highway 181 South
Kenedy 78119
830-583-3200
9 holes, public

Killeen Municipal Golf Club
406 Roy Reynolds Drive
Killeen 76543
254-699-6034
Pro: Greg Antunes
18 holes, public

Knox City Country Club
PO Box 734
Knox City 79529
817-658-3313
9 holes, private

Kurth-Landrum Golf Course
Southwestern University
PO Box 6081
Georgetown 78626
512-863-1333
9 holes, public

LE Ramey Golf Course
FM 3320
Kingsville 78363
512-592-1101
Pro: Frank Monsevain
18 holes, public

La Paloma Golf Club
4302 Fairway Drive
Amarillo 79124
806-342-9915
Pro: Paul Roberson
9 holes, semi-private

Lajitas Resort Golf Course
HC70, PO Box 400
Terlingua 79852
915-424-3211
9 holes, public

Lake Arlington Golf Course
1516 Green Oaks
Boulevard West
Arlington 76013
817-451-6101
Pro: Jim Sanders
18 holes, public

Lake Cisco Country Club
Highway 6
Cisco 76437
254-442-2725
9 holes, semi-private

Lake Creek Golf Course
340 West Main Street
Munday 76371
817-422-4458
9 holes, semi-private

Lake Sweetwater Municipal
Golf Course
Route 3
Sweetwater 79556
915-235-8816
18 holes, public

Lake Whitney Country Club
Route 1, PO Box 2075
Whitney 76692
254-694-2313
Pro: Scotty Bissing
18 holes, semi-private

Lakeside Country Club
PO Box 238
Ennis 75119
972-875-3641
9 holes, private

Lakeview Golf and Country Club
1901 Valley Oaks Drive
Harker Heights 76548
817-698-4554
9 holes, private

Lakewood Recreation Center
Route 1
Rising Star 76471
254-643-7792
9 holes, public

Lamesa Country Club
PO Box 380
Lamesa 79331
806-872-2608
9 holes, private

Las Palomas Country Club
Route 1, PO Box 126D
LaVernia 78121
830-217-4348
Pro: Bart Buehler
18 holes, semi-private

Laughlin AFB/Leaning Pine
Golf Course
Laughlin AFB 78843
210-298-5451
Pro: Roy Goodwin
9 holes, private/military

Lavista Country Club
2000 Northeast Loop 11
Wichita Falls 76305-1506
940-855-0771
Pro: Ron Miller
18 holes, public

Legends Golf Club
137 Ben Hogan
Stephenville 76401
254-968-2200
Pro: Liz Albracht
18 holes, semi-private

Levelland Country Club
PO Box 40
Levelland 79336
806-894-3288
Pro: Chad Davis
9 holes, private

Littlefield Country Club
PO Box 489
Littlefield 79339
806-385-3309
9 holes, semi-private

Live Oak Country Club
PO Box 1464
Rockport 78382
512-729-8551
9 holes, private

Livingston Municipal Golf Course
PO Box 488
Livingston 77351
409-327-4901
9 holes, public

Llano Golf Club
FM 152, Robinson City Park
Llano 78643
915-247-5100
9 holes, public

Llano Grande Golf Course
PO Box 1002
Mercedes 78570
210-565-3351
9 holes, semi-private

Lone Cedar Country Club
Route 2, PO Box 152
Eastland 76448
817-647-3613
Pro: Rod Straw
9 holes, private

One-Star Courses

Longview Country Club
2300 Highway 42
Longview 75604
903-759-9251
18 holes, semi-private

Lorenzo Country Club
Route 1, PO Box 230
Lorenzo 79343
806-634-5787
9 holes, semi-private

Los Ebanos Golf Course
710 Lincoln Street
Zapata 78076
210-765-8103
9 holes, public

Marfa Municipal Golf Course
PO Box 308
Marfa 79843
915-729-4043
Pro: Ernest Villarreal
9 holes, public

Marlin Country Club
Route 1 PO Box 34
Marlin 76661
254-803-6101
Pro: Michael Stanfield
9 holes, private

Martin County Country Club
PO Box 651
Stanton 79782
915-756-2556
9 holes, private

Martin's Valley Ranch
and Country Club
PO Box 1469
Mission 78572
956-585-6330
Pros: Oscar Trevino/
Lori Gaffney
18 holes, public

Maxwell Municipal Golf Course
1002 South 32nd
Abilene 79602
915-692-2737
Pro: Dave Hand
18 holes, public

McCamey Country Club
PO Box 838
McCamey 79752
915-652-8904
Pro: Buddy Seilhant
9 holes, private

McKinney Country Club
1099 Country Club Road
McKinney 75069
972-562-7731
Pro: Dudley Wysong
9 holes, private

McKinney Municipal Golf Course
Highway 5
McKinney 75069
972-542-4523
Pro: Steve Johnson
9 holes, public

McLean Country Club
217 North Main
McLean 79057
806-779-8809
9 holes, private

Meadowbrook Country Club
2130 Country Club Road
Palestine 75802
903-723-7530
Pro: Terry Brown
9 holes, semi-private

Meadowbrook Park Golf Course
1300 East Dugan
Arlington 76010
817-275-0221
Pro: Gary Dennis
9 holes, public

Memorial Park Golf Course
329 East Garden Street
Uvalde 78801
830-278-6155
Pro: David Bessier
9 holes, public

Memphis Country Club
517 South 10th
Memphis 79245
806-259-3237
Pro: Donnie Bridges
9 holes, private

Merkel Golf Course
200 Country Club Road
Merkel 79536
915-928-3193
Pro: George DiJulio
9 holes, semi-private

Mexia Country Club
PO Box 88
Mexia 76667
817-562-2391
Pro: Paul Luna
9 holes, semi-pirvate

Mid Valley Golf Course
PO Box 236
Mercedes 78570
956-565-3211
Pro: Joe Powell
18 holes, public

Mills County Golf Association
Route 1, PO Box 66
Goldthwaite 75647
903-845-4566
9 holes, public

Mineola Country Club
225 Country Club Drive
Mineola 75773
903-569-2472
Pro: Donnie Duboise
9 holes, semi-private

Monte Cristo Golf Course
FM 1925
Edinburg 78539
210-381-0965
18 holes, public

Morton Country Club
Route 2, PO Box 53
Morton 79346
806-266-5941
9 holes, semi-private

Mount Pleasant Golf Course
1000 Country Club Drive
Mount Pleasant 75455
903-572-1804
Pro: Roy Stinson
9 holes, semi-private

Mountain Creek Golf Club
PO Box 700
Robert Lee 76945
915-453-2317
Pro: Steve Ebenstein
9 holes, public

Muleshoe Country Club
900 Country Club Road
Muleshoe 79347
806-272-4250
Pro: Jeff Baker
9 holes, semi-private

Navasota Municipal Golf Course
West Washington
Navasota 77868
409-825-7284
9 holes, public

Newgulf Golf Club
PO Box 488
Newgulf 77462
409-657-4639
9 holes, private

Nocona Hills Country Club
179 Country Club Drive
Nocona 76255
817-825-3444
18 holes, semi-private

Nocona Municipal Golf Course
West Highway 82
Nocona 76255
817-825-7250
18 holes, public

North Plains Country Club
Sunray Highway
Dumas 79029
806-935-7375
18 holes, private

Oak Creek Country Club
FM 1570, Majors Field Road
Greenville 75403
903-455-3971
Pro: Andy Holder
9 holes, private

Oak Grove Country Club
Franklin 77857
409-828-9907
9 holes, private

Oak Grove Golf Course
2000 Colquitt Road
Terrell 75160
972-563-8553
9 holes, public

Oak Lawn Country Club
4307 Victory Drive
Marshall 75670
903-935-7555
Pro: Bob Collins
9 holes, semi-private

Oakridge Country Club
PO Box 460, FM 1452 South
Madisonville 77864
409-348-5466
Pro: Neil Berry
9 holes, private

Oakridge Country Club
2800 Diamond Oaks Drive
Garland 75044
972-530-8004
Pro: Michael Hodgins
18 holes, private

Old Ocean Recreation Club
PO Box 390
Old Ocean 77463
409-647-9902
18 holes, semi-private

Oldham County Country Club
PO Box 465
Vega 79092
806-267-2595
Pro: James Basford
9 holes, semi-private

Olney Golf Course
Country Club Road
Olney 76374
817-564-2424
9 holes, public

Olton Golf Course
Highway 168
Olton 79064
806-285-2595
9 holes, public

Oso Beach Municipal Golf Course
5601 South Alameda
Corpus Christi 78411
512-991-5351
Pro: Jimmie E Taylor
18 holes, public

Overton Municipal Golf Course
South Lakeshore Drive
Overton 75684
903-834-6414
9 holes, public

Ozona Country Club
PO Box 1247
Ozona 76943
915-392-2520
9 holes, private

Padre Isles Country Club
143553 Commodore Drive
Corpus Christi 78418
512-949-8006
Pro: Patrick Kelliher
18 holes, private

Paducah Golf Club, Inc
PO Box 914
Paducah 79248
806-492-2245
9 holes, private

Palacios Golf Course
Highway 35
Palacios 77465
512-972-2666
Pro: Gerald Taylor
9 holes, public

Palm View Golf Course
Route 3, PO Box 1035
McAllen 78503
956-687-9591
Pro: Erasmo Hernandez
27 holes, public

Pamcel Golf Course
PO Box 937
Pampa 79066
806-665-1801
9 holes, private

Panhandle Country Club
PO Box 717
Panhandle 79068
806-537-3300
Pro: David Mooring
9 holes, semi-private

Par Country Club
FM 2861
Comanche 76442
817-879-2296
18 holes, semi-private

Par Tee Haus
11890 O'Connor
San Antonio 78233
210-655-3131
9 holes, public

Pecan Trails
434 Edgefield
Midlothian 76065
972-723-1376
Pro: Mark Wells
18 holes, public

Pecos County Golf Course
Highway 285
Fort Stockton 79735
915-336-7110
18 holes, public

Perry Country Club
PO Box 711
Hamilton 76531
817-386-3383
Pro: Randy Gardner
9 holes, private

Perryton Municipal Golf Course
402 Southeast 24th
Perryton 79070
806-435-5381
Pro: Tim Schiffelbein
18 holes, public

Pharaohs Golf Club
7111 Pharaoh's Drive
Corpus Christi 78411
512-991-2477
Pro: Randy Walker
18 holes, private

Pheasant Trails Golf Course
Highway 119 North
Dumas 79029
806-935-7375
Pro: Charlie Nelson
18 holes, public

Phillips Country Club
1609 North Sterling
Borger 79007
806-274-6812
Pro: Larry J Reed
18 holes, private

Pine Hill Lake and Golf Course
PO Box 157
Frankston 75763
903-876-3777
9 holes, semi-private

Pine Ridge Golf Course
PO Box 1309
Paris 75460
903-785-8076
Pro: Mike Larseingue
18 holes, public

Pine Valley Golf Club
11010 Indiana Avenue
Lubbock 79423
806-748-1448
Pro: Walter Denzer
18 holes, public

Pinecrest Country Club
Drawer 991
Longview 75606
903-758-8000
Pro: Jack Goetz
18 holes, private

Piney Woods Country Club
Highway 59
Nacogdoches 75961
409-569-6505
Pro: Dean Cole
18 holes, private

Pitman Municipal Golf Course
PO Box 512
Hereford 79045
806-364-2782
Pro: David Kaesheimer
18 holes, public

Plains Fairway Inc.
201 South Avenue South
Lamesa 79331
806-872-8100
9 holes, public

Plainview Country Club
2900 West Fourth Street
Plainview 79072
806-296-6148
Pro: Pete Petersen
18 holes, public

Plantation Country Club
2503 Palmer Drive
Pharr 78577
210-781-6613
Pro: Gabe Cabrera
18 holes, semi-private

Plantation Resort Golf Club
4701 Plantation Lane
Frisco 75034
972-335-4653
Pro: Paul Kenney
18 holes, public

Pleasanton Golf Course
1801 McGuffin Drive
Pleasanton 78064
210-569-3486
9 holes, semi-private

Practice Tee Golf Course
2950 Waterview
Richardson 75080
972-235-6540
Pro: Rhett Gideon
9 hole, public

Preston West Golf Course
9101 South Coulter
Amarillo 79119
806-353-7003
Pro: Johnny Smith
18 holes, public

Princedale Golf Club
Daingerfield Highway
Pittsburg 75686
903-856-3737
9 holes, private

Quanah Country Club
PO Box 86
Quanah 79252
817-663-2069
9 holes, private

Ranchland Hills Country Club
1600 East Wadley
Midland 79705
915-683-2041
Pro: Ken Livingston
18 holes, private

Rancho Carribe
664 Highway 87
Crystal Beach 77650
409-684-1108
Pro: Robby Sharpless
9 holes, public

Rankin Country Club
Route 1 PO Box 12580
Rankin 79778
915-693-2834
9 holes, semi-private

Raymondville Municipal
Golf Course
Hwy 77
Raymondville 78580
956-689-9904
9 holes, public

Oak Grove Golf Club
Building T-79
Red River Army Depot
Texarkana 75507-5000
903-334-2141
Pro: Tonya Dillard
9 holes, private

Reese AFB Golf Course
Reese AFB 79489
806-885-3819
9 holes, private

Reeves County Golf Course
88 Stanley Drive
Pecos 79772
915-447-2858
11 holes, public

Refugio Country Club
Woodsboro Highway
PO 689
Refugio 78377
512-526-5554
9 holes, semi-private

Rising Star Golf Club
County Road 266 South
Rising Star 76471
254-643-4653
Pro: Pat McManus
18 holes, public

River Hills Country Club
PO Box 260006
Corpus Christi 78426
512-387-3563
Pro: Tom Inman
18 holes, private

Riverside Golf Club
900 West 29th
San Angelo 76901
915-653-6130
18 holes, semi-private

Riverside Golf Course
302 McCright
PO Box 2234
Victoria 77901
512-573-4521
27 holes, public

Riverwood Golf Course
PO Box 657
Vidor 77662
409-768-1710
18 holes, semi-private

Roaring Springs Ranch Golf Club
Highway 70
Roaring Springs 79256
806-348-7267
9 holes, private

Rocksprings Country Club
PO Box 175
Rocksprings 78880
210-683-4224
9 holes, private

Rotan Golf Club
201 West Snyder
Rotan 79546
915-735-2242
Pro: Rodney Tankersley
9 holes, public

Rusty Rail Country Club
Prospect Road
Jefferson 75657
903-665-7245
Pro: Frank Kresch
9 holes, semi-private

San Felipe Country Club
PO Box 1228
Del Rio 78840
830-774-2511
Pro: Clinton Baack
9 holes, semi-private

San Jacinto College Golf Course
8060 Spencer Highway
Pasadena 77505
713-476-1880
9 holes, public

Sand Hills Golf and Country Club
Route 2, Maloy Road
Commerce 75429
903-886-4455
Pro: Mel Fox
9 holes, semi-private

Santa Fe Park Golf Course
111 River Drive
San Angelo 76901
915-657-4485
Pro: Mike Terrazas
9 holes, public

Seven Oaks Resort
1300 Circle Drive
Mission 78572
956-581-6262
Pro: Mike Fernuik
18 holes, semi-private

Seymour Golf and Country Club
1009 Mimosa
Seymour 76380
817-888-2833
9 holes, private

Shadow Hills Golf Course
6002 Third Street
Lubbock 79499
806-793-9700
18 holes, public

Shadow Lake Golf Course
Route 3, PO Box 135
Mount Pleasant 75455
903-572-1288
Pro: Coy Sevier
9 holes, public

Shady Oaks Golf Course
3542 County Road
Baird 79504
915-854-1757
Pro: Christopher Howe
18 holes, semi-private

Shallow Creek Country Club
Route 3, PO Box 212B
Gladewater 75647
903-984-5335
18 holes, semi-private

Shallow Creek Country Club
204 Wilkins Road
Gladewater 75647
903-984-5335
18 holes, semi-private

Shamrock Country Club
900 South Wall
Shamrock 79079
806-256-5151
9 holes, semi-private

Shary Municipal Golf Course
2201 Mayberry Street
Mission 78572
956-580-8770
Pro: Chencho Ramirez
18 holes, public

Silsbee Country Club
PO Box 982
Silsbee 77656
409-385-4372
9 holes, private

Singing Winds Golf Course
PO Box 525
Bronte 76933
915-473-2013
9 holes, public

Sinton Municipal Golf Course
PO Box 216
Sinton 78387
512-364-9013
18 holes, public

Slaton Golf Course
Route 2, PO Box 158B
Slaton 79364
806-828-3269
9 holes, public

Snyder Country Club
PO Box 498
Snyder 79550
915-573-7101
Pro: Rick Mammolite
9 holes, private

Sonora Golf Course
1612 Golf Course Road
Sonora 76950
915-387-3680
Pro: Steve Alexander
9 holes, public

Spring Creek Country Club
   FM 2160
   Crockett 75835
   409-544-7848
   9 holes, private

Spur Golf Course
   PO Box 1083
   Spur 79370
   806-271-4355
   9 holes, public

Stamford Golf and Country Club
   PO Box 289
   Stamford 79553
   915-773-5001
   9 holes, private

Star Harbor Municipal Golf Course
   Drawer 949
   Malakoff 75148
   903-489-0091
   9 holes, public

Stewart Peninsula Golf Course
   100 Cottonwood Springs Drive
   The Colony 78027
   972-625-8700
   Pro: Luke Anderson
   18 holes, public

Stratford Country Club
   PO Box 709
   Stratford 79084
   806-396-2259
   9 holes, semi-private

Sulphur Springs Country Club
   Route 1, PO Box 340
   Sulphur Springs 75482
   903-885-4861
   Pro: Judd Whiteman
   18 holes, semi-private

Sundance Golf Course
   2294 Common Street
   New Braunfels 78130
   830-629-3817
   Pro: Bill Halbert
   18 holes, public

Sundown Municipal Golf Club
   600 West Richardson
   Sundown, 79372
   806-229-6186
   Pro: Scott Nichols
   9 holes, public

Sunset Country Club
   9301 Andrews Highway
   Odessa 79760
   915-366-1061
   27 holes, semi-private

Sunset Golf Club
   4906 East Main
   Grand Prairie 75050
   214-331-8057
   Pro: Bobby Mims
   9 holes, public

Sunshine Country Club Estates
   7000 Michigan Drive
   Harlingen 78550
   956-425-1420
   9-holes, private

Sweetwater Country Club
   1900 Country Club Lane
   Sweetwater 79556
   915-235-8093
   Pro: Leonard Perry
   18 holes, private

T-Bar Country Club
   PO Box 415
   Tahoka 79373
   806-998-5305
   9 holes, private

Tejas Golf Course
   PO Box 326
   Stephenville 76401
   254-965-3904
   9 holes, semi-private

Temple Junior College Golf Course
   South First Street
   Temple 76501
   254-778-9549
   9 holes, public

Texas Woman's University
Golf Course
   PO Box 3926
   Denton 76202
   817-381-8613
   18 holes, public

Throckmorton Country Club
   PO Box 335
   Throckmorton 76083
   940-849-3131
   9 holes, private

Top-O-The Lake Country Club
   PO Box 829
   Bowie 76230
   817-872-5401
   Pro: Ken Rhoades
   9 holes, semi-private

Total Golf at Kingwood
   22601 Highway 59 North
   Kingwood 77339
   281-359-3995
   Pro: Tim Loiodice
   9 holes, public

Tour Play Golf Center
   920 Gus Thomasson
   Mesquite 75150
   972-270-4800
   9 holes, public

Town East Golf Course
   3134 Belt Line Road
   Sunnyvalle 75182
   Pro: Larry Billingsly
   9 holes, public

Treasure Hills Country Club
   3009 North Augusta
   National Drive
   Harlingen 78550
   956-428-0351
   Pro: KC Lauber
   18 holes, semi-private

Treasure Island Golf Center
   501 Frankford Road
   Lubbock 79416
   806-795-9311
   18 holes, public

Trinity Plantation Country Club
   Highway 19 South
   Trinity 75862
   409-594-2583
   Pro: Russell Lee
   9 holes, semi-private

Tropic Star Park
   1401 South Cage Boulevard
   Pharr 78577
   210-787-5957
   9 holes, private

Tule Lake Golf Course
   PO Box 843
   Tulia 79088
   806-995-3400
   9 holes, public

Van Horn Golf Course
　Golf Course Road
　Van Horn 79855
　915-283-2628
　Pro: Jim Hart
　9 holes, public

Van Zandt Country Club
　I-20
　Canton 75103
　903-567-2336
　Pro: Ed Gatlin
　18 holes, private

Victoria Country Club
　14 Spring Creek Road
　Victoria 77904
　512-573-3712
　Pro: Alan Wooley
　18 holes, private

Waller Country Club
　15357 Pennick
　Waller 77484
　409-931-3335
　9 holes, semi-private

Waxahachie Country Club
　1920 West 287 Business
　Waxahachie 75165
　972-937-3521
　Pro: Chance Blythe
　18 holes, private

Weimar Golf Club
　Route 3, PO Box 202
　Weimar 78962
　409-725-8624
　9 holes, public

Wellington Country Club
　PO Box 904
　Wellington 79095
　806-447-5050
　9 holes, public

Western Oaks Country Club
　1600 Western Oaks Drive
　Waco 76711
　254-772-8100
　Pro: Gregg Juster
　18 holes, semi-private

Western Texas College
Golf Course
　South College Avenue
　Snyder 79549
　915-573-9291
　9 holes, public

Westwood Shores Country Club
　Route 4, PO Box 3650,
　Highway 356
　Trinity 75862
　409-594-9172
　Pro: Jess Bonneau
　18 holes, private

Wharton Country Club
　1149 Country Club Drive
　Wharton 77488
　409-532-5940
　9 holes, private

Wichita Falls Country Club
　701 Hamilton Boulevard
　Wichita Falls 76308
　940-767-1486
　Pro: Bruce Cotton
　18 holes, private

Willow Creek Country Club
　4201 South Major
　Beaumont 77720
　409-842-9097
　Pro: Tom Brown
　18 holes, private

Willow Creek Golf Center
　1166 Ben Richey Drive
　Abilene 79602
　915-691-0909
　9 holes, public

Willow Springs Golf Course
　1714 Havondale-Haslet Road
　Haslet 76052
　817-439-3169
　18 holes, public

Willowbrook Country Club
　PO Box 4160
　Tyler 75703
　903-592-8229
　Pro: Jim Wise
　18 holes, private

Wind Creek Golf Course
　900 First Avenue
　Sheppard AFB
　Wichita Falls 76311
　940-676-6369
　Pro: Randy Stephens
　18 holes, private

Winkler County Golf Course
　1010 East Tascosa
　Kermit 79745
　915-586-9243
　9 holes, semi-private

Winters Country Club
　Route 3, PO Box 13
　Winters 75967
　915-754-4679
　Pro: Rich King
　9 holes, semi-private

Wolfe Creek Golf Course
　Route 3, PO Box 445
　Colorado City 79512
　915-728-5514
　9 holes, semi-private

Wood Hollow Golf Course
　5200 North McCann Road
　Longview 75605
　903-663-4653
　Pro: Hayden Havens
　18 holes, public

Woodland Hills Golf Club
　319 Woodland Hills Drive
　Nacogdoches 75961
　409-564-2762
　Pro: Jeff Willenberg
　18 holes, public

Yoakum County Golf Course
　PO Box 1259
　Denver City 79323
　806-592-2947
　Pro: Wiley Osborne
　9 holes, semi-private

Yoakum Municipal Golf Course
　703 Southwell
　Yoakum 77995
　512-293-5682
　9 holes, public

Yorktown Country Club
　Country Club Road
　Yorktown 78164
　512-564-9191
　9 holes, semi-private

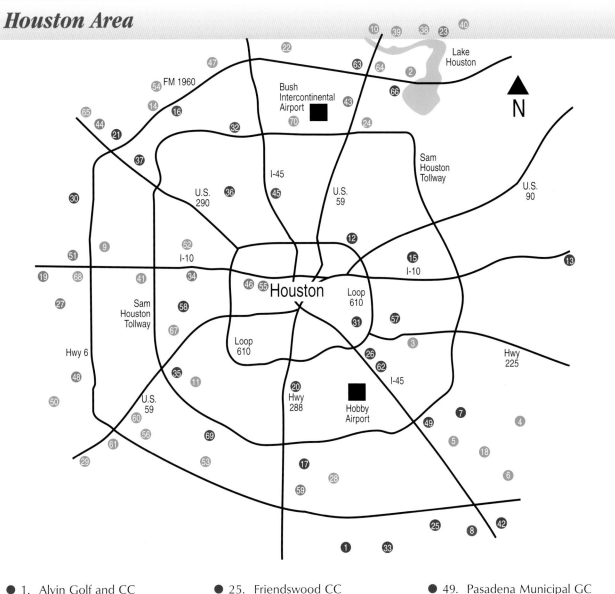

- 1. Alvin Golf and CC
- 2. Atascocita CC
- 3. Battleground at Deer Park
- 4. Bay Forest GC
- 5. Bay Oaks GC
- 6. Bayou GC
- 7. Baywood CC
- 8. Beacon Lakes GC
- 9. Bear Creek Golf World
- 10. Bentwood GC
- 11. BraeBurn CC
- 12. Brock Park GC
- 13. Chambers County GC
- 14. Champions GC
- 15. Channelview GC
- 16. Classic 3 Par 3
- 17. Clear Creek GC
- 18. Clear Lake GC
- 19. Club at Falcon Point
- 20. Country Place GC
- 21. Cypress GC
- 22. Cypresswood GC
- 23. Deerwood
- 24. El Dorado CC

- 25. Friendswood CC
- 26. Glenbrook GC
- 27. Golf Club at Cinco Ranch
- 28. Golfcrest CC
- 29. Greatwood GC
- 30. Green Meadows
- 31. Gus Wortham GC
- 32. Herron Lakes GC
- 33. Hillcrest CC
- 34. Houston CC
- 35. Houston Hills CC
- 36. Inwood Forest CC
- 37. Jersey Meadow GC
- 38. Kingwood CC
- 39. Kingwood Cove GC
- 40. Lake Houston GC
- 41. Lakeside CC
- 42. Lakeview GC
- 43. Lochinvar
- 44. Longwood GC
- 45. Melrose GC
- 46. Memorial Park GC
- 47. Northgate CC
- 48. Old Orchard GC

- 49. Pasadena Municipal GC
- 50. Pecan Grove CC
- 51. Pine Forest CC
- 52. Pinecrest GC
- 53. Quail Valley CC
- 54. Raveneaux CC
- 55. River Oaks CC
- 56. Riverbend CC
- 57. San Jacinto GC
- 58. Sharpstown GC
- 59. Southwyck GC
- 60. Sugar Creek CC
- 61. Sweetwater CC
- 62. Texaco CC
- 63. Total Golf Kingwood
- 64. Tour 18
- 65. Treeline GC
- 66. Walden on Lake Houston
- 67. Westwood CC
- 68. Willow Fork CC
- 69. Willowisp CC
- 70. World Houston CC

● Top 100 Courses   ● 3-Star Courses   ● 2-Star Courses   ● 1-Star Courses

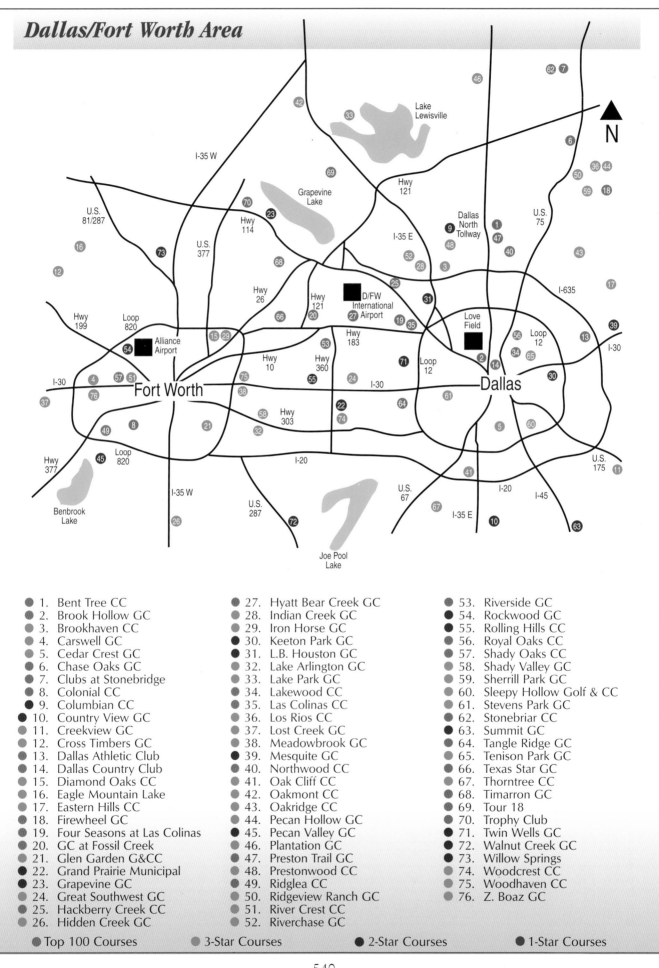

1. Bent Tree CC	27. Hyatt Bear Creek GC	53. Riverside GC
2. Brook Hollow GC	28. Indian Creek GC	54. Rockwood GC
3. Brookhaven CC	29. Iron Horse GC	55. Rolling Hills CC
4. Carswell GC	30. Keeton Park GC	56. Royal Oaks CC
5. Cedar Crest GC	31. L.B. Houston GC	57. Shady Oaks CC
6. Chase Oaks GC	32. Lake Arlington GC	58. Shady Valley GC
7. Clubs at Stonebridge	33. Lake Park GC	59. Sherrill Park GC
8. Colonial CC	34. Lakewood CC	60. Sleepy Hollow Golf & CC
9. Columbian CC	35. Las Colinas CC	61. Stevens Park GC
10. Country View GC	36. Los Rios CC	62. Stonebriar CC
11. Creekview GC	37. Lost Creek GC	63. Summit GC
12. Cross Timbers GC	38. Meadowbrook GC	64. Tangle Ridge GC
13. Dallas Athletic Club	39. Mesquite GC	65. Tenison Park GC
14. Dallas Country Club	40. Northwood CC	66. Texas Star GC
15. Diamond Oaks CC	41. Oak Cliff CC	67. Thorntree CC
16. Eagle Mountain Lake	42. Oakmont CC	68. Timarron GC
17. Eastern Hills CC	43. Oakridge CC	69. Tour 18
18. Firewheel GC	44. Pecan Hollow GC	70. Trophy Club
19. Four Seasons at Las Colinas	45. Pecan Valley GC	71. Twin Wells GC
20. GC at Fossil Creek	46. Plantation GC	72. Walnut Creek GC
21. Glen Garden G&CC	47. Preston Trail GC	73. Willow Springs
22. Grand Prairie Municipal	48. Prestonwood CC	74. Woodcrest CC
23. Grapevine GC	49. Ridglea CC	75. Woodhaven CC
24. Great Southwest GC	50. Ridgeview Ranch GC	76. Z. Boaz GC
25. Hackberry Creek CC	51. River Crest CC	
26. Hidden Creek GC	52. Riverchase GC	

● Top 100 Courses   ● 3-Star Courses   ● 2-Star Courses   ● 1-Star Courses

Austin and San Antonio Areas

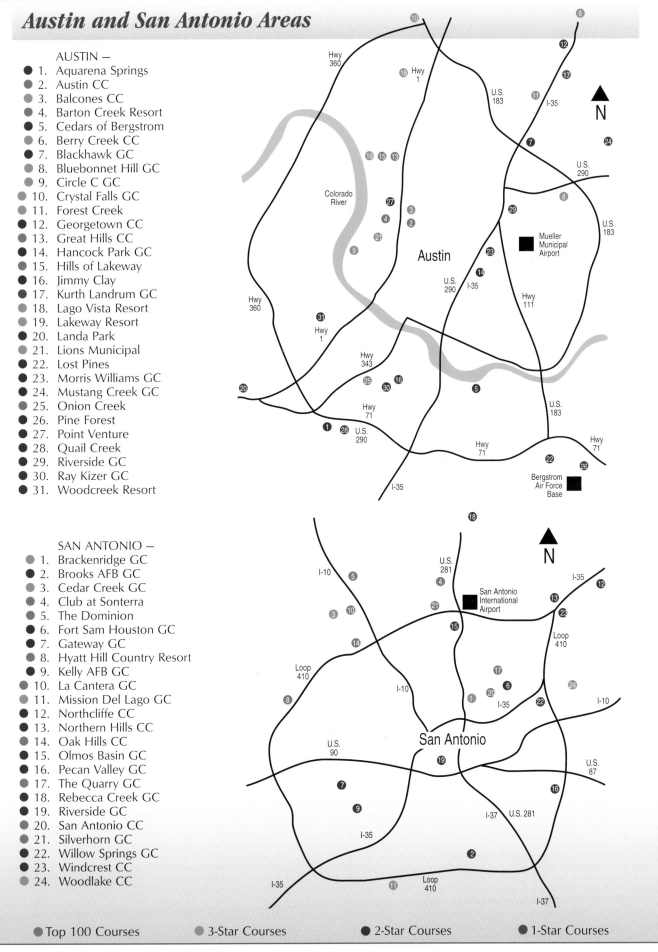

AUSTIN —
- 1. Aquarena Springs
- 2. Austin CC
- 3. Balcones CC
- 4. Barton Creek Resort
- 5. Cedars of Bergstrom
- 6. Berry Creek CC
- 7. Blackhawk GC
- 8. Bluebonnet Hill GC
- 9. Circle C GC
- 10. Crystal Falls GC
- 11. Forest Creek
- 12. Georgetown CC
- 13. Great Hills CC
- 14. Hancock Park GC
- 15. Hills of Lakeway
- 16. Jimmy Clay
- 17. Kurth Landrum GC
- 18. Lago Vista Resort
- 19. Lakeway Resort
- 20. Landa Park
- 21. Lions Municipal
- 22. Lost Pines
- 23. Morris Williams GC
- 24. Mustang Creek GC
- 25. Onion Creek
- 26. Pine Forest
- 27. Point Venture
- 28. Quail Creek
- 29. Riverside GC
- 30. Ray Kizer GC
- 31. Woodcreek Resort

SAN ANTONIO —
- 1. Brackenridge GC
- 2. Brooks AFB GC
- 3. Cedar Creek GC
- 4. Club at Sonterra
- 5. The Dominion
- 6. Fort Sam Houston GC
- 7. Gateway GC
- 8. Hyatt Hill Country Resort
- 9. Kelly AFB GC
- 10. La Cantera GC
- 11. Mission Del Lago GC
- 12. Northcliffe CC
- 13. Northern Hills CC
- 14. Oak Hills CC
- 15. Olmos Basin GC
- 16. Pecan Valley GC
- 17. The Quarry GC
- 18. Rebecca Creek GC
- 19. Riverside GC
- 20. San Antonio CC
- 21. Silverhorn GC
- 22. Willow Springs GC
- 23. Windcrest CC
- 24. Woodlake CC

● Top 100 Courses   ● 3-Star Courses   ● 2-Star Courses   ● 1-Star Courses

Index